POCKET ENCYCLOPEDIA

NEEDLE CRAFT

Contributing editor

Judy Brittain

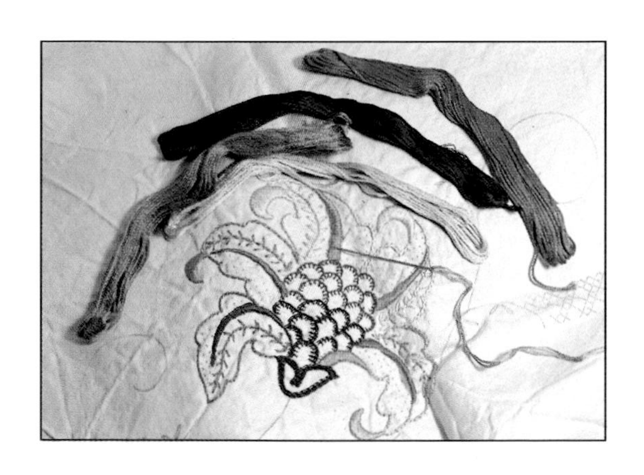

DORLING KINDERSLEY • LONDON

First published in Great Britain in 1989
by Dorling Kindersley Limited.
9 Henrietta Street, London WC2E 8PS

reprinted 1989, 1991, 1992, 1993

Designed and edited by Swallow Books,
260 Pentonville Road, London N1 9JY

British Library Cataloguing in Publication Data

DK pocket encyclopedia, needlecraft
1. Brittain, Judy
1. Needlework – Manuals
746/4

ISBN 0-86318-302-6

Printed by Kyodo Printing Co (S'pore) Pte Ltd

CONTENTS

INTRODUCTION

Since earliest times, needles and yarns have been used to make a whole range of articles from everyday clothing to beautiful works of art. Sewing or embroidery was regarded as a recreation, though for some it was often a necessary one to be enjoyed after the day's chores were finished. Grander folk, with more time on their hands, could pass the hours pleasantly making beautiful and intricate scenes or patterns with needles and thread.

With the advent of machines, life became easier for people generally. Fabrics could now be bought rather than woven at home and there was no longer any need to hand-decorate them as it became possible for designs to be printed on a range of fabrics. Many old techniques were forgotten and fewer people looked to needlecraft for either enjoyment or utilitarian purposes.

Happily, with increased leisure, people are finding they have more time for relaxation and are again turning to needles and yarn to produce unique and decorative clothes or household articles.

This book describes the basic needlecraft techniques, using step-by-step methods, for those people who have little or no knowledge of their chosen craft, or who wish to refresh their memories.

Beautiful needlework is not a thing of the past; once techniques have been mastered it is not difficult to produce very attractive contemporary designs that future generations will look at with as much admiration as we now regard needlecraft work from former years.

What you will find in this book

This book deals with many different types of needlecraft. There are six major chapters, which encompass the eight separate crafts of embroidery, needlepoint, patchwork, quilting, appliqué, knitting, crochet and basic sewing. Each section starts with the implements required and describes the basic steps in a logical sequence.

Materials and equipment

The range of materials necessary to work each craft covered by this book is fully described and illustrated. This includes not only yarns and threads or needles, hooks and pins, but, where applicable, frames, canvases, yarns and fabrics.

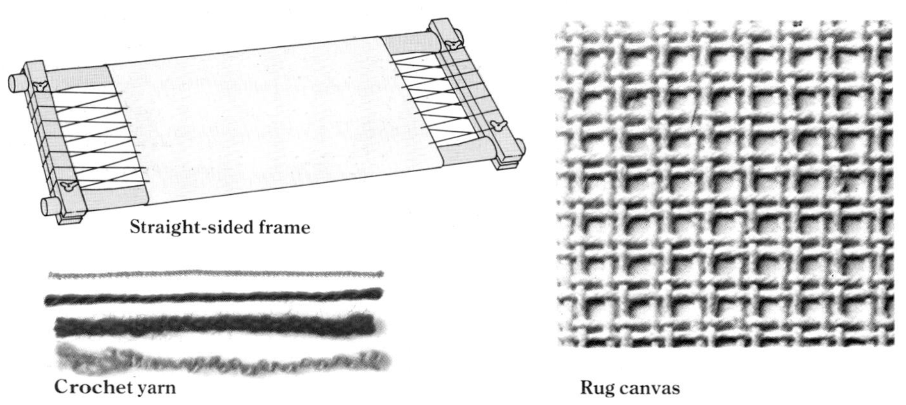

Straight-sided frame

Crochet yarn

Rug canvas

Techniques

The necessary steps involved in beginning, working, diversifying and finishing each craft forms the core matter of this book. All the techniques described in the book are clearly illustrated, usually by step-by-step drawings of work in progress.

Tracing designs using artificial light

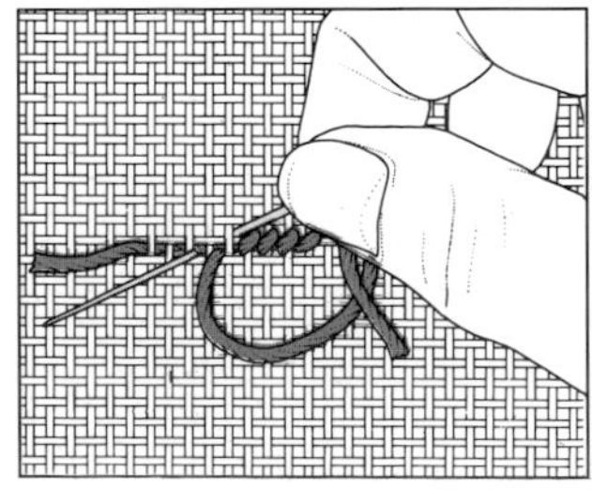

Starting a thread

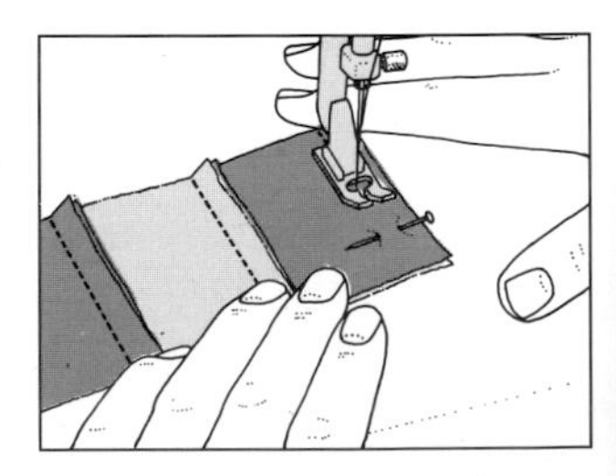

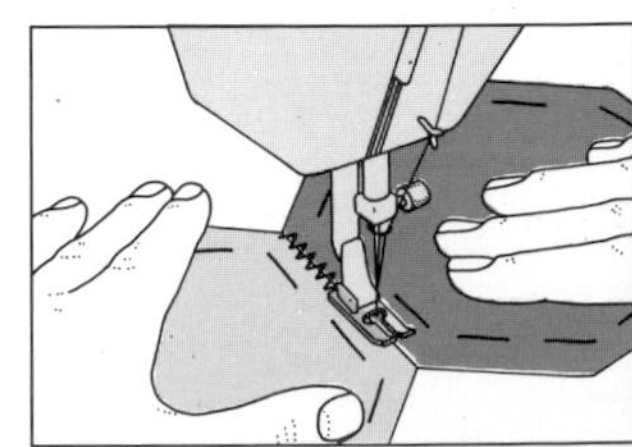

Top right **Joining squares**
Right **Joining hexagons**

Stitch glossaries

These vary in form depending on the craft to which apply. They appear in the form of written instructions in knitting and crochet, as stepped working diagrams in needlepoint and embroidery, as illustrations only and in patchwork, showing possible designs.

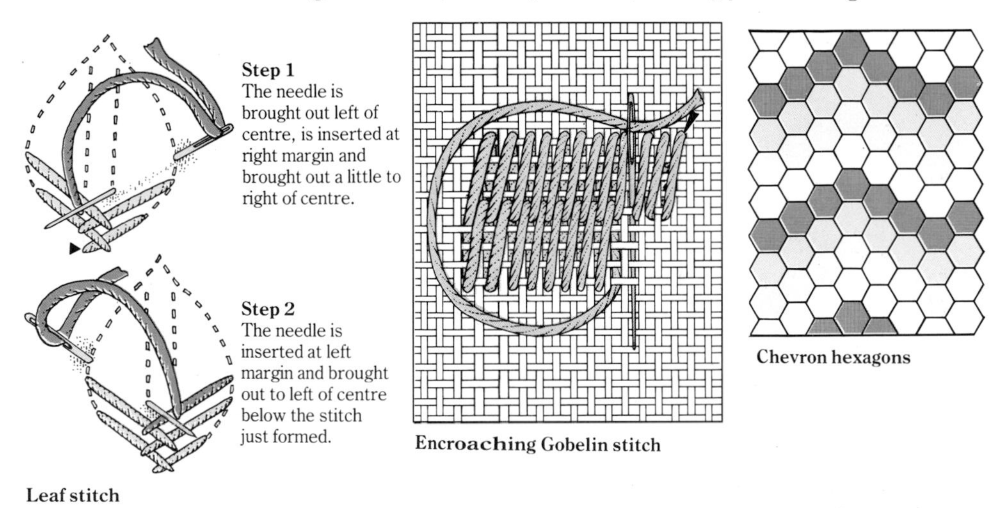

Leaf stitch

Encroaching Gobelin stitch

Chevron hexagons

Garment and household sewing

While actual patterns for garments and household items are not given, the techniques described in this section will help you to follow bought patterns more easily. You should also be able to make simple household articles like bed covers, curtains and cushions by using the methods that are described in the chapter called *Basic Sewing*.

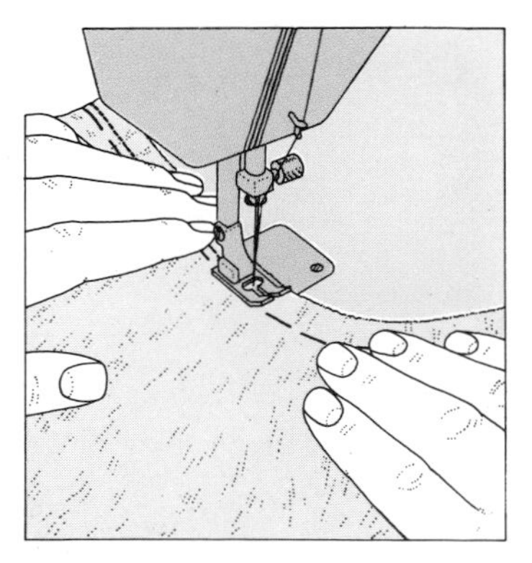

Stitching round a curve

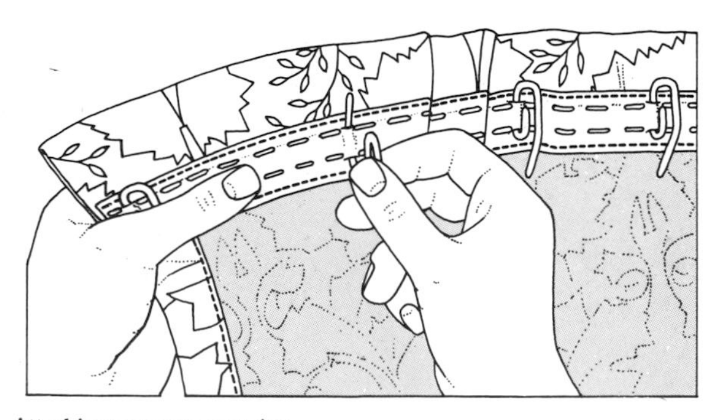

Attaching tape to curtains

1

EMBROIDERY

Including Smocking

Embroidery frames and mounting

Embroidery is the art of decorating a ground fabric with stitches to enrich it and add to its beauty. It can be worked on any pliable material from leather to gauze, in threads ranging from ordinary wool to the finest gold.

Frames

Embroidery frames are used to support the ground fabric while it is being worked. Though not always essential, their main advantage is that they keep the ground fabric stretched, enabling the embroiderer to work even stitches. Those frames which can be fitted to a stand will also leave both hands free to work the stitches more easily.

Straight-sided frames

These are available in different sizes, measured across the roller tape. The standard straight-sided frame consists of two rollers (top and bottom), to which strips of tape or webbing are nailed, and two flat sides, which fit into slots on each roller and are held with pegs or screws. Travel frames are portable versions of these.

Ring frames

These are sometimes known as tambour frames. They come in various sizes and are composed of two hoops placed one inside the other and tightened by a screw at the side.

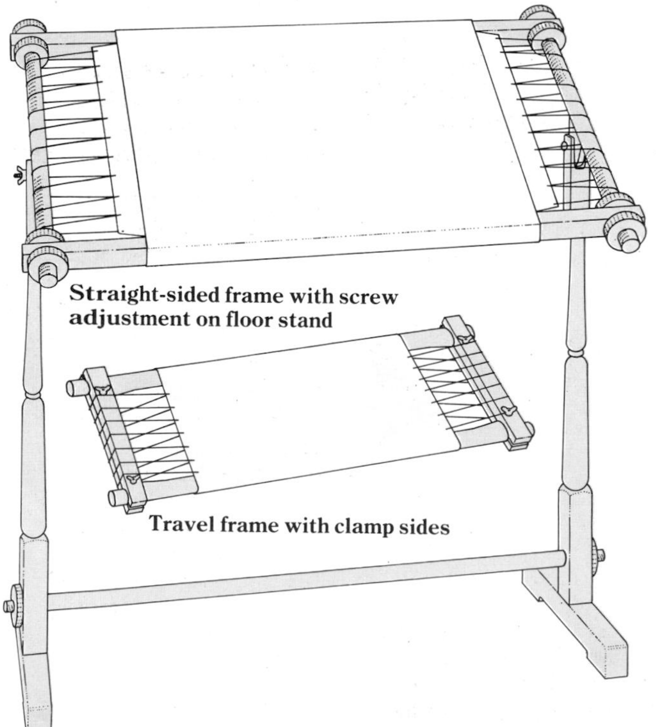

Straight-sided frame with screw adjustment on floor stand

Travel frame with clamp sides

Attaching fabric to frame

Stitch a 1.5 cm hem all round the fabric. Mark the centre of both rollers and top and bottom edges of fabric. Matching centre points, stitch fabric to webbing, working outwards from centre. Slot sides into rollers. Adjust pegs or screws.

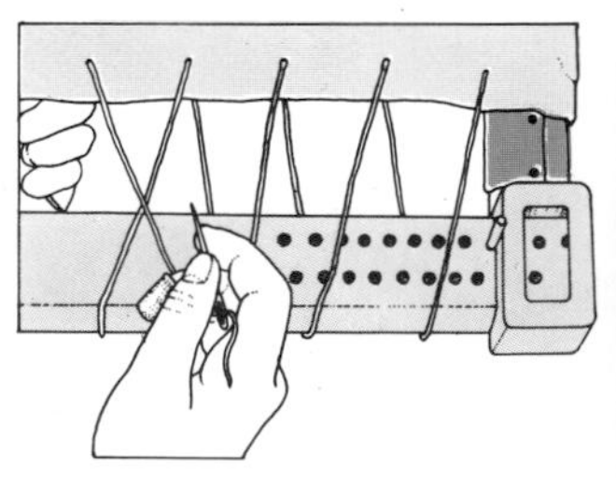

Use linen thread to lace fabric evenly to side pieces. Tighten each side alternately and then knot firmly.

Mounting ring frames

The ring frame is the most popular frame for working small areas of embroidery. Rings can be made of wood, plastic or metal and are obtainable attached to clamps or stands.

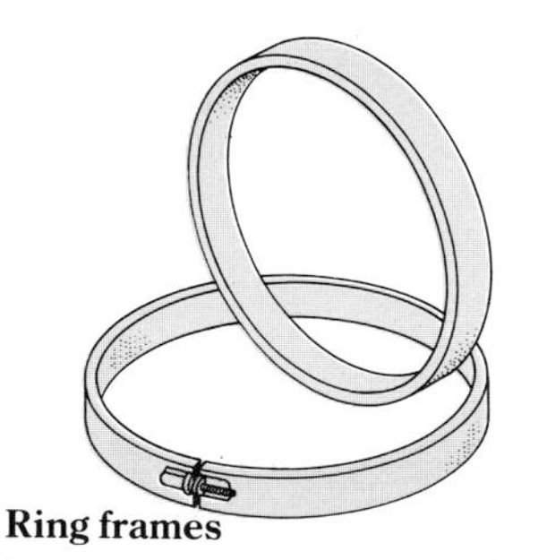

Ring frames

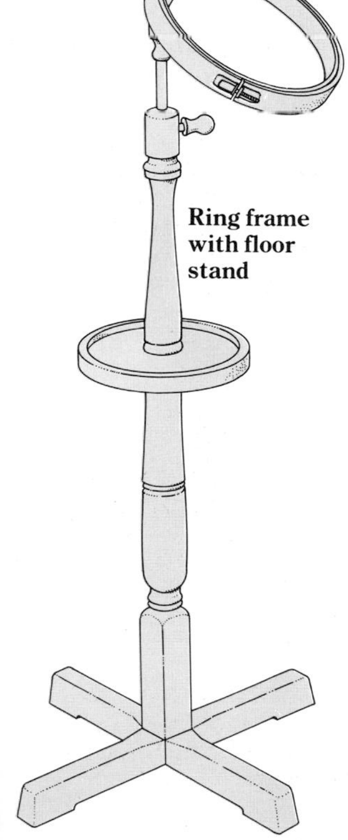

Ring frame with floor stand

Binding the ring

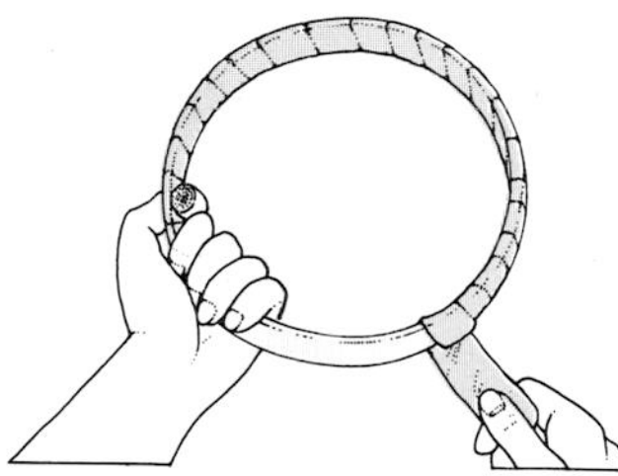

To prevent the ground fabric from marking or slipping, you can bind the inner ring with 1 in (2.5 cm) woven tape (or bandage) and fasten with a few stitches.

Mounting

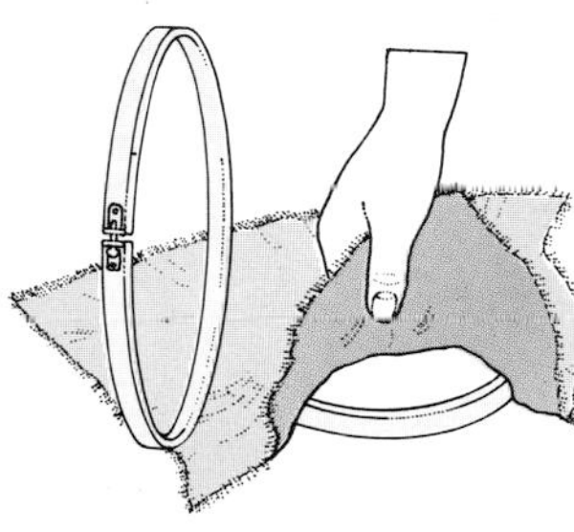

1 Lay the area to be embroidered over inner ring and press outer ring over it.

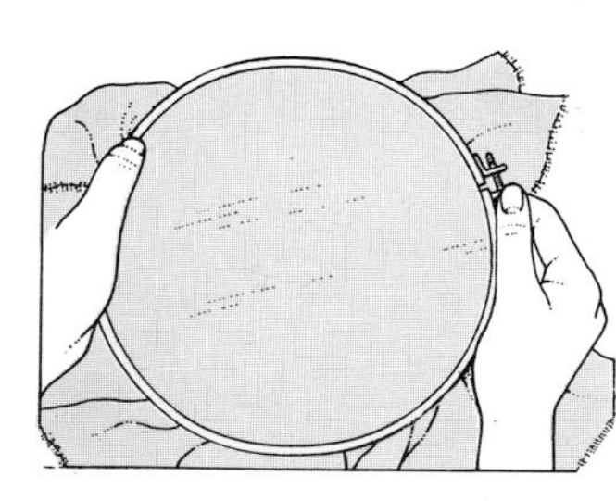

2 Tighten the outer ring by turning the screw until the fabric is both secure and evenly stretched. Do not pull the fabric once the outer ring is secure as this may snag or form stretch marks on it.

Remounting embroidery

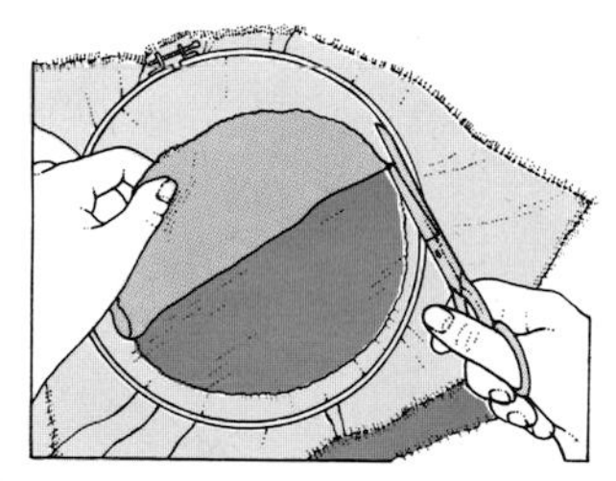

When working long border patterns, move the fabric along as each area is completed, taking care not to damage existing stitches.

Place the fabric on the inner ring and then cover it with a spare piece of fabric such as muslin. Secure the outer ring and then cut away the muslin to expose the area being worked.

Mounting odd shapes

In order to frame small cut shapes, the pieces have to be attached to a supporting fabric.

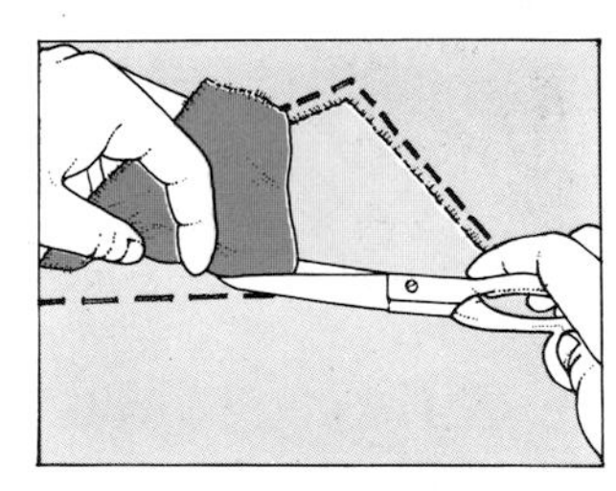

Sew the piece onto a larger supporting fabric and then mount in the usual way. With the fabric firmly in place and working from the wrong side, cut away the supporting fabric from inside the shape, leaving it secured and ready for embroidering.

Threads, fabrics and needles

Much of the beauty of embroidery depends on a harmonious working partnership between ground fabric and threads, with the stitches being worked by a needle of the correct gauge and type for the job in hand as shown on the opposite page.

The thread, fabric and needle samples illustrated here are those most commonly used for embroidery.

Threads

The important point to remember when buying thread is its weight and thickness. It should never be so heavy as to distort the ground nor so light as to be invisible.

Your choice of thread should, generally speaking, be governed by your choice of fabric and the purpose of your finished work. An important point to consider is whether or not your embroidery will be home-laundered, dry-cleaned or displayed behind glass.

Fabrics

Any surface can be embroidered as long as it is firm enough to retain the stitches, supple enough to allow the thread to pass in and out and strong enough to sustain the constant working of the stitching. The most suitable embroidery fabrics are given here ranging from fine silks to wools.

Needles

With the exception of pulled work, choose an embroidery needle with an eye large enough to hold the thread and small enough to pass easily through the fabric without distorting.

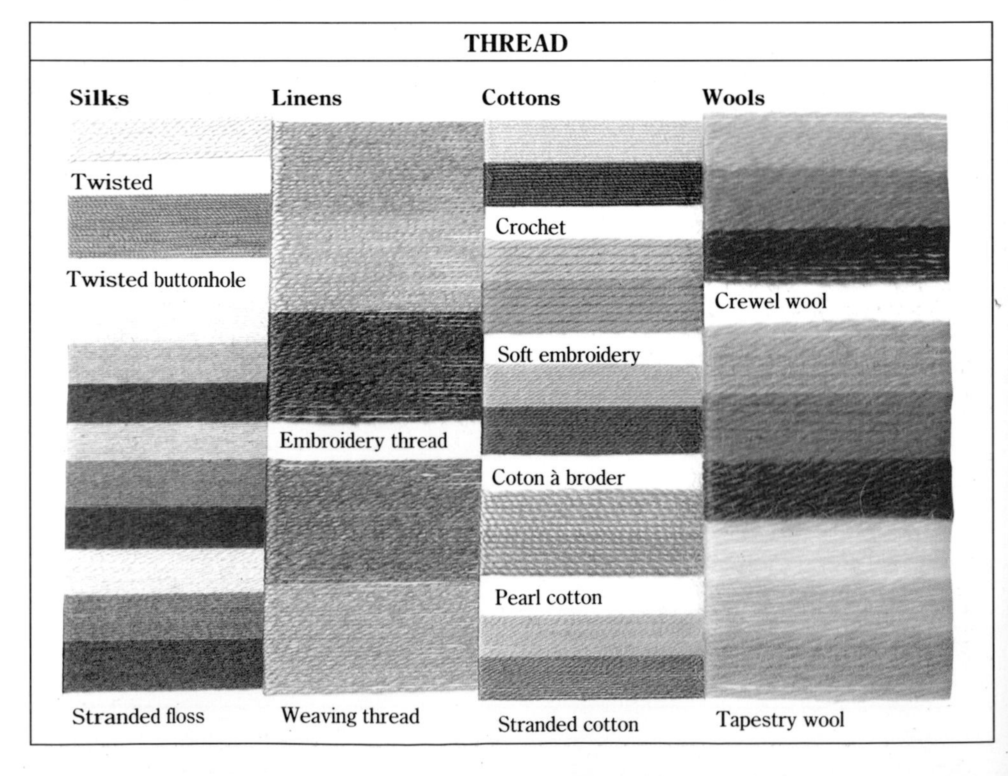

FABRIC AND NEEDLES

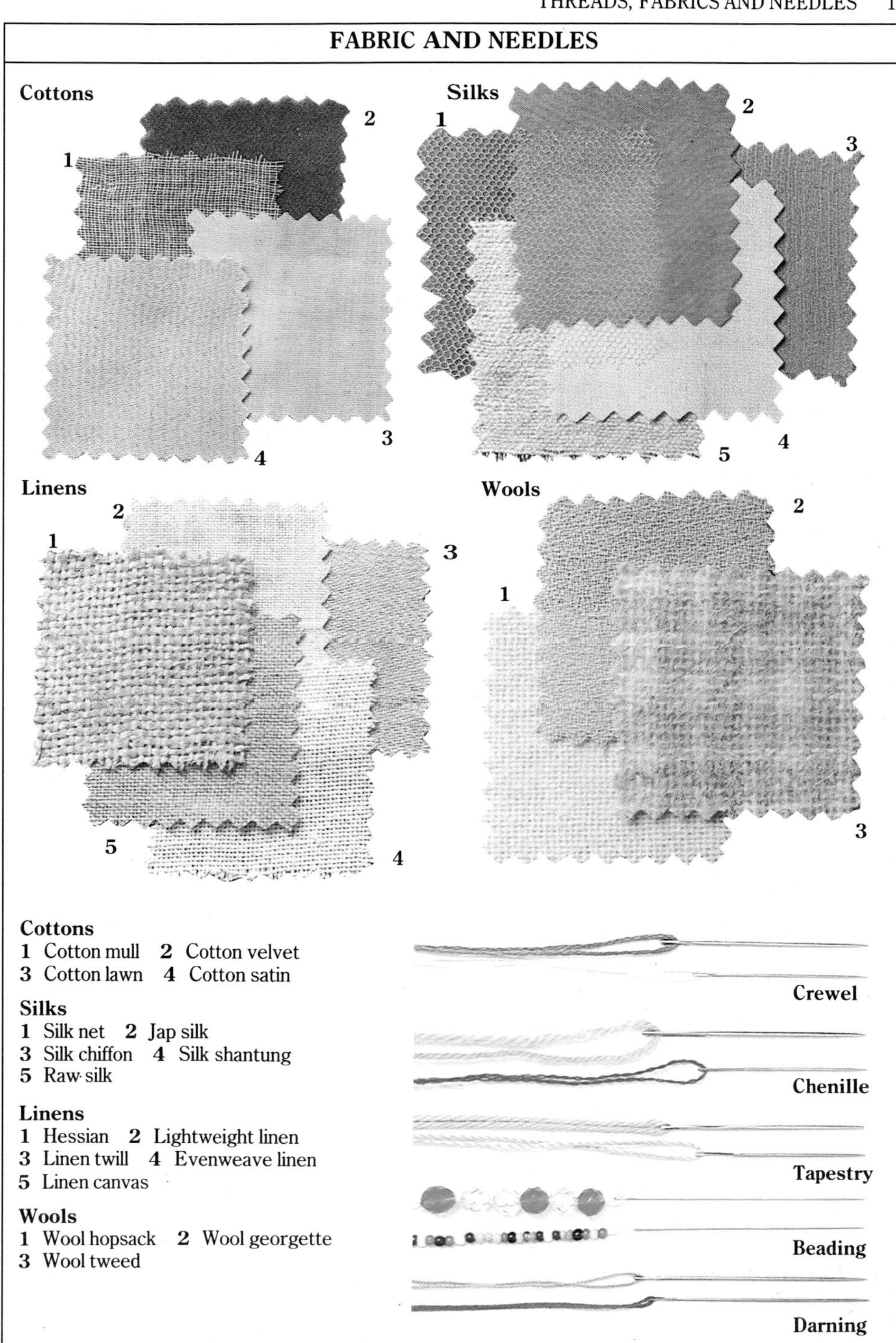

Cottons
1 Cotton mull **2** Cotton velvet
3 Cotton lawn **4** Cotton satin

Silks
1 Silk net **2** Jap silk
3 Silk chiffon **4** Silk shantung
5 Raw silk

Linens
1 Hessian **2** Lightweight linen
3 Linen twill **4** Evenweave linen
5 Linen canvas

Wools
1 Wool hopsack **2** Wool georgette
3 Wool tweed

Transferring designs

Before starting work on your embroidery you will have to determine the kind of design, type of ground fabric and the yarn or threads you wish to use. If you have not embroidered before you would do well to start with a bought pattern or ready printed design. Then, as confidence grows, gradually begin to work on your own ideas.

If you are using an original drawing or wish to copy a design you must first decide how best to transfer the design onto your chosen fabric. Here are five methods of doing this: 1 Tracing with carbon paper. 2 Tracing direct. 3 Tacking the design through tissue paper. 4 Pricking and pouncing. 5 Using light.

If you have the ability you can, of course, draw directly onto the fabric with a pencil.

Reproducing original designs

Tracing with carbon paper

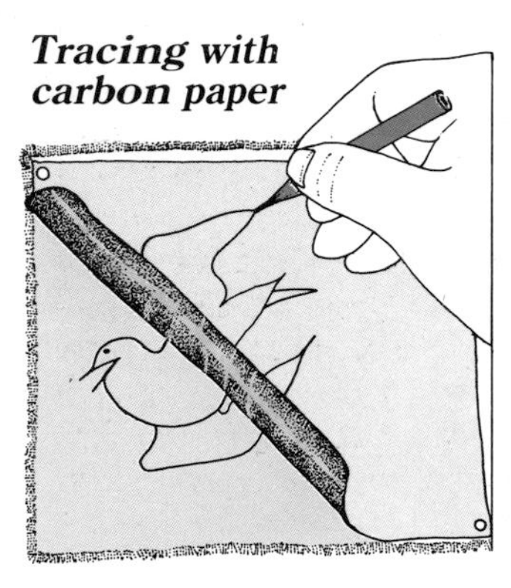

Place dressmaker's carbon paper between drawing and fabric. Draw over the outlines.

Tracing direct

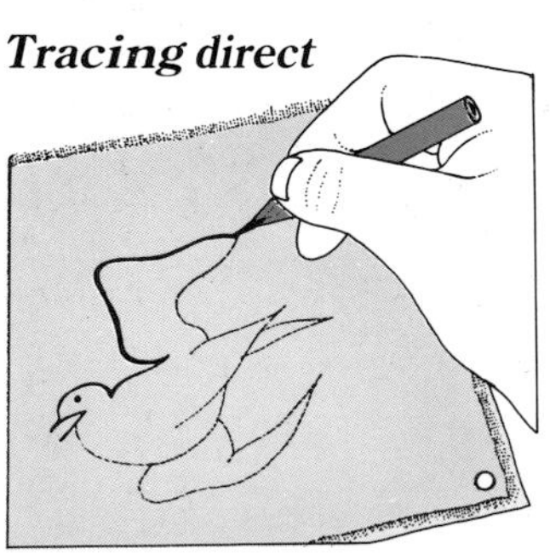

Lay fabric over design and draw design directly onto it. This is a particularly suitable method for fine fabrics.

Tacking through tissue paper

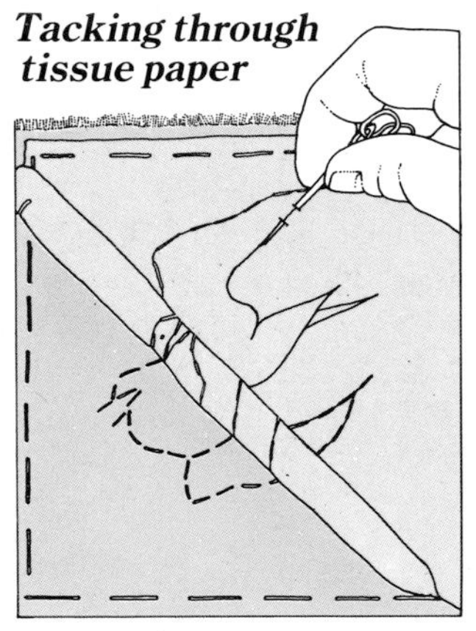

After tracing the design onto tissue paper, pin the paper to the fabric and tack over the traced lines, using small stitches so as to retain the details. Pull the tissue paper away, leaving the design outlined in stitches. If the finished embroidery completely covers the stitches, leave them in; otherwise pull them out, using tweezers.

This is the best method to use on coarse or uneven ground fabrics or pile fabric like velvet and towelling.

Pricking and pouncing

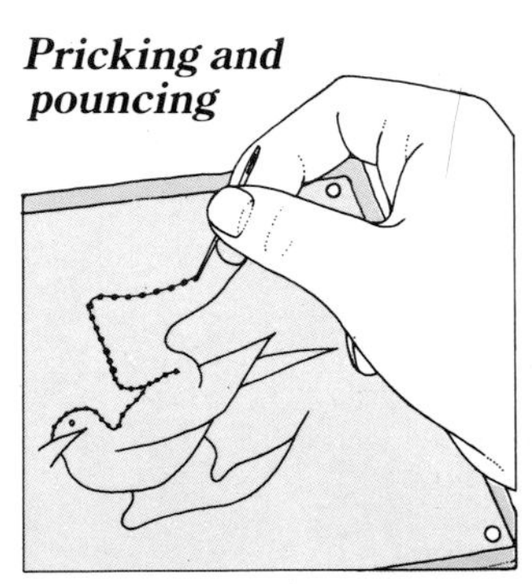

1 Use a needle to prick around traced design.

2 Pin design to fabric. Dip rolled felt pad into powdered chalk (charcoal for light fabrics); dab over holes. Lift paper and spray with fixative. Transfer large designs to smooth fabrics in this way.

Using light

Designs can be reproduced most effectively by using light, both artificial and natural, for tracing.

Artificial light

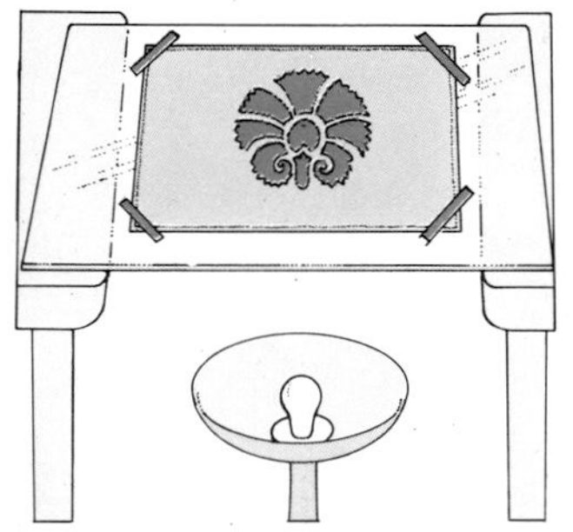

To make a simple light-box, place a strong light under a supported sheet of glass. Lay the design on top of the glass and cover it with tracing paper or the ground fabric if it is fine enough. The lines can then be traced accurately.

Natural light

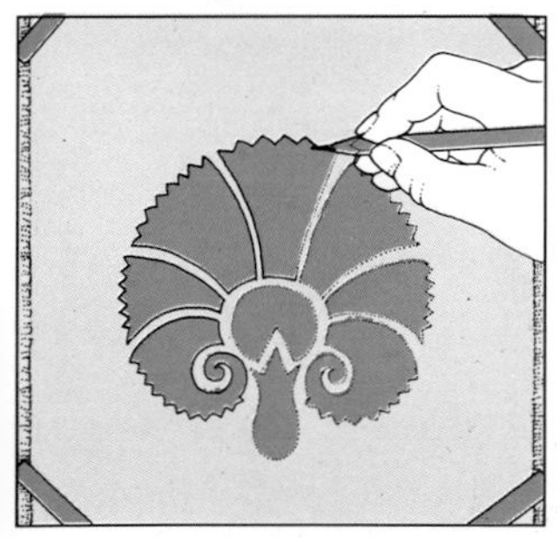

Attach the picture to be copied to the inside of a window with adhesive tape. Secure the tracing paper or fine fabric over the picture. Then, with a pencil, make the tracing over the lines of the design.

Enlarging and reducing

Existing designs can be enlarged or reduced and used in embroidery as all-over repeat patterns, borders or as single motifs. To do this, accurate measuring and correct positioning is vital. The enlarging procedure is shown below; for reducing, work in reverse order.

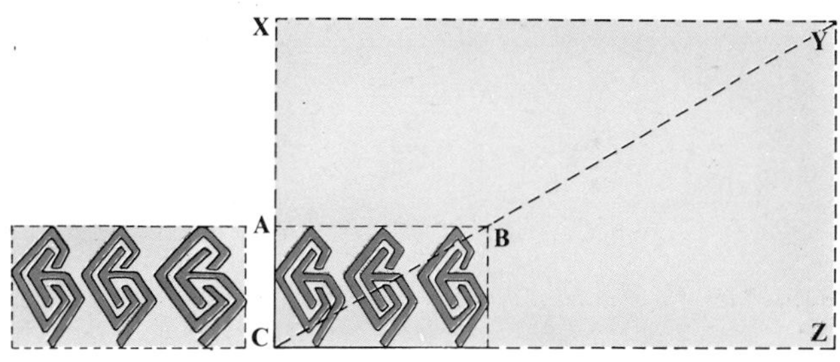

First enclose the design in a square or rectangle (above). Then take a large piece of paper and lay the original picture at the corner of it. Next draw a diagonal line from C, through B to Y. This line can be extended to any length, but to get the required height for a particular enlargement extend the line CA and measure off on this the desired height at the point called X. From here a line is drawn from X to Y and must be parallel to the base of the original design and meet the diagonal line CBY. This gives the correct position for the final line YZ and will give the required new proportion.

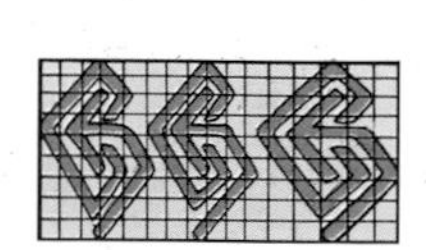

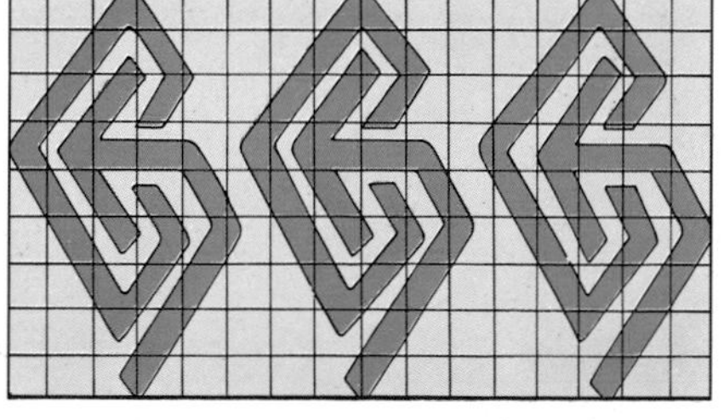

The next step is to divide the original design into equal squares. Then make the same number of squares on the enlargement paper making them proportionately larger (above right). The design is then drawn freehand over the enlargement, square by square.

Designing motifs

In the past, ideas for embroidery were often taken from nature. This still remains one of the best sources for inspiration for both colour and line. In the example below, a Peruvian lily was studied and the outline drawn, transferred to fabric and worked in cross stitch.

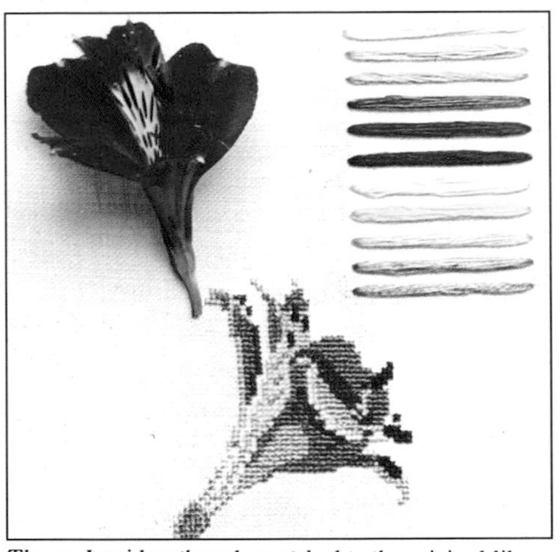

The embroidery threads matched to the original lily

Motif worked in Vandyke stitch

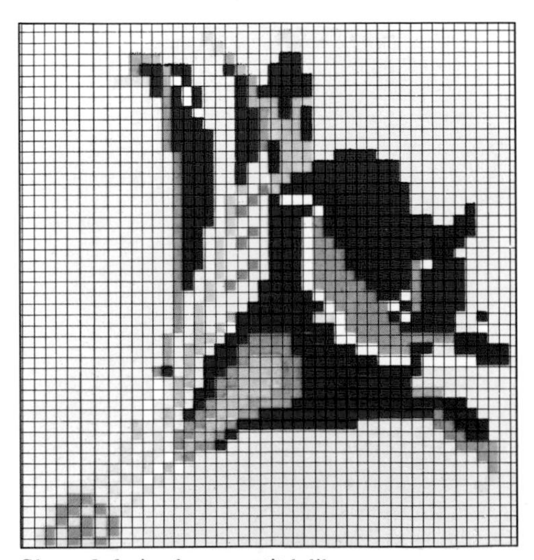

Charted design for cross stitch lily

Embroidery used as a decoration on jeans

Embroidered waistcoat

Motif worked around blouse yoke

Silk motif in chain, ermine and satin stitch

Positioning motifs

Embroidered motifs can be placed anywhere on a garment to make something plain into something special. Take care to use appropriate threads for the ground fabric, working on it, whenever possible, before the garment is made up.

Embroidery styles

Styles of embroidery can be used as inspiration for new designs. The waistcoat above left, embroidered in stranded silk floss, is reminiscent of old Chinese work. A tambour hook (see page 32) has been used to work the tiny chain stitches.

Couching and laid work

Couching and laid work are two similar techniques which have been developed to show off threads that are too delicate to be worked in and out of the fabric in the usual way. Both are used almost exclusively when working with gold and metal threads.

In couching one or more threads are laid down on the surface of the fabric and stitched into position with another less precious, more supple thread.

Method

Couching should always be worked on a supported frame, as both hands need to be free to manipulate the laid and couching threads. Couched lines and outlines are easy to work, but make sure that the laid threads lie neatly under the couching stitches, which must secure them firmly and at regular intervals. In simple couching the laid threads are brought to the surface and worked along the design line. As work progresses the laid threads are guided along loosely with the left hand while the right hand makes small overcast stitches with the couching thread. When the line of stitches is complete the laid threads are brought to the back of the work and secured. When making a curve the couching stitches are placed closer together, so that the threads lie flat; when making an angle, a couching stitch is placed at the point of the angle.

A bunching effect can be achieved by couching several thick threads with a tight overcast stitch (see below). This effect is used for pronounced decorative outlines.

Threads

Although any threads can be couched, the glossy texture of silk and the glitter of metal threads will be shown off best by this technique. Invisible couching stitches can be achieved by using threads of a matching colour, but if a contrasting colour is used the couching stitches form an additional pattern over the laid threads.

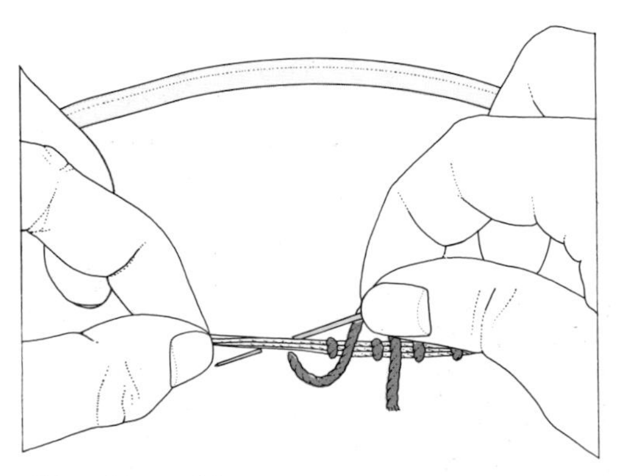

Simple couching
Bring both the laid threads and the couching thread to the surface. Then secure the laid threads at regular intervals with couching stitches. Finish by taking threads to back of work and securing.

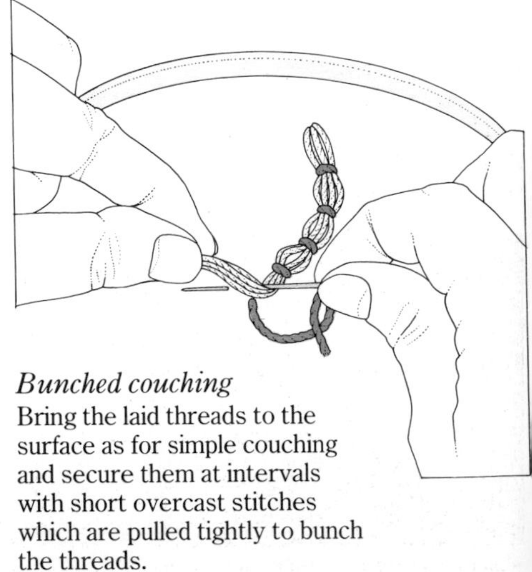

Bunched couching
Bring the laid threads to the surface as for simple couching and secure them at intervals with short overcast stitches which are pulled tightly to bunch the threads.

Couching with embroidery stitches

Make simple couching more decorative by using embroidery stitches to couch the laid threads. These stitches are used to secure the laid threads and must be worked in and out of the ground fabric.

Feather stitch

1 Lay 2 groups of threads, with a gap between them. Then work feather stitch over both lines of threads, beginning over the top group.

2 Make a second stitch over the bottom group and continue in this way alternately.

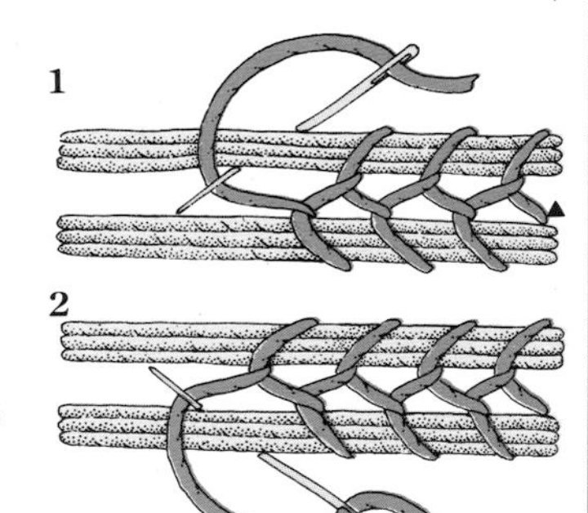

Satin stitch

Secure the laid threads by working regular groups of satin stitch over them and through the fabric.

Varied stitch groupings can be used to make different patterns over the laid threads.

Buttonhole stitch

Keeping purled side to outer edge work regularly spaced buttonhole stitches over a group of laid threads.

-This stitch can be used to give a firm decorative edge to outlines and borders.

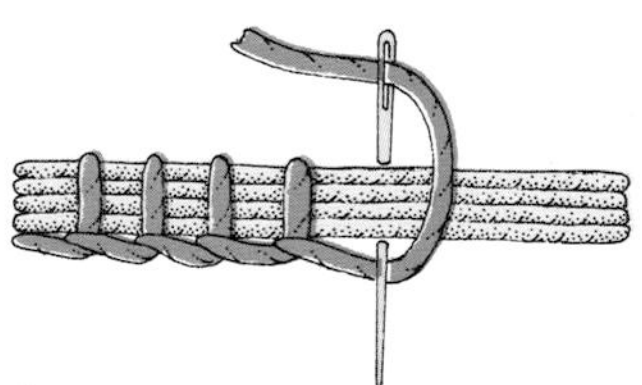

Embroidery stitches used to couch down laid threads on a border

SIMPLE LAID WORK

Laid work is an extension of couching and is a quick and effective way of filling motifs and backgrounds with long, loose satin stitches. These are then secured with couching stitches. To ensure that the satin stitches lie evenly they are best worked in two journeys.

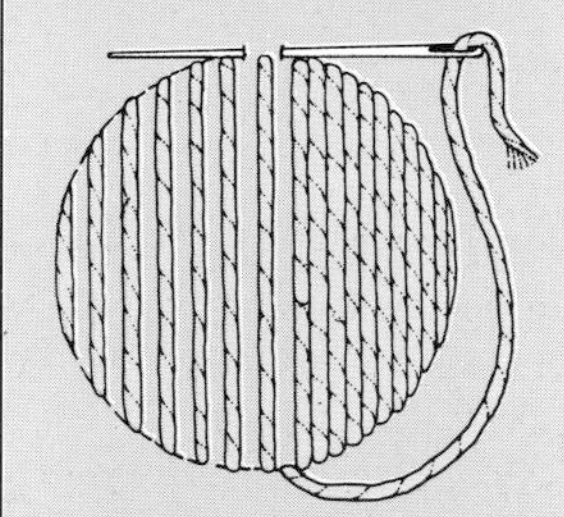

1 *Work the first journey of satin stitches to and fro across the area to be filled, picking up only a small piece of fabric at each edge. Then work the needle back, filling in the spaces left.*

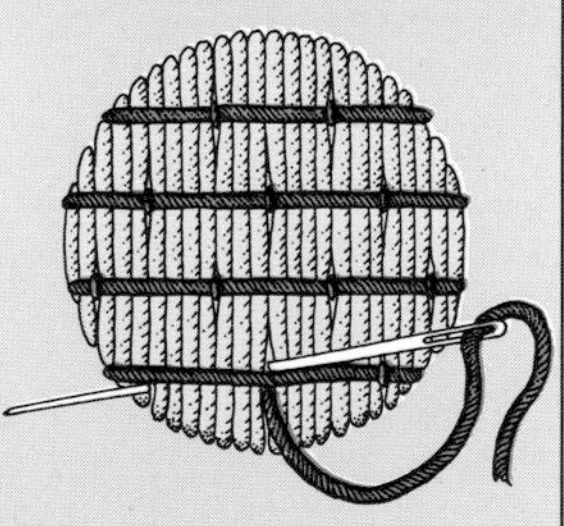

2 *Secure the laid threads by working the couched threads at right angles to the satin stitches one at a time. Lay the thread across and then couch it at regular intervals on the return journey.*

Alphabets and monograms

The use of embroidered initials and monograms on clothes and gifts turns the most mundane article into a personal and prized possession. The designs shown on these two pages are all made by a contemporary artist, and can be traced and used as illustrated in the sizes shown or they can be reduced or enlarged with a chart, and put to further uses. Very large initials can be worked across the back of kimonos, robes and jackets whilst tiny ones look good on shirts. Lettering can also be used on fabric coverings for household articles such as boxes, wastepaper baskets and writing-paper folders. Elaborate initials and monograms, together with the relative date, can be used to sign a piece of embroidery, adding an extra ornament in the process.

Valentine, Christmas, birthday and anniversary cards become very special when their messages are worked in embroidered letters thus making them into presents as well as greeting cards.

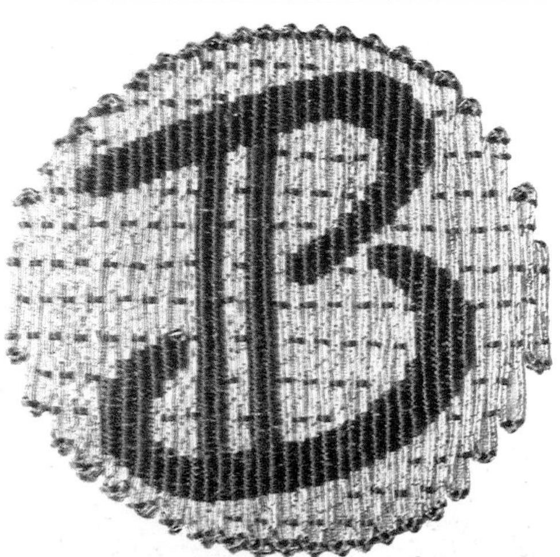

Above left *Worked detail of the alphabet shown in chart on page 25.*
Left *Couching is used here for both the background and monogram, with the couching stitches worked close together to form the letter.*
Above *Satin stitch is used for the K and encroaching satin stitch is worked for the flowers which are finished with bead details at the centres.*

The letter S is worked in padded satin stitch outlined in back stitch. Chain stitch is used for the scroll pattern.

The padded satin stitch P is worked on a pulled thread work ground within a frame of long cross stitch.

CROSS STITCH LETTERING

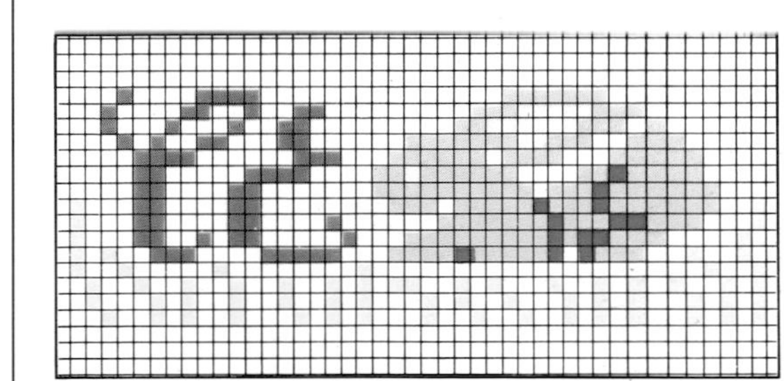

Lettering with cross stitch design

Both the stylized lettering and the rabbit design are worked in cross stitch in different coloured threads on an even-weave linen ground. The chart for working this design is shown left.

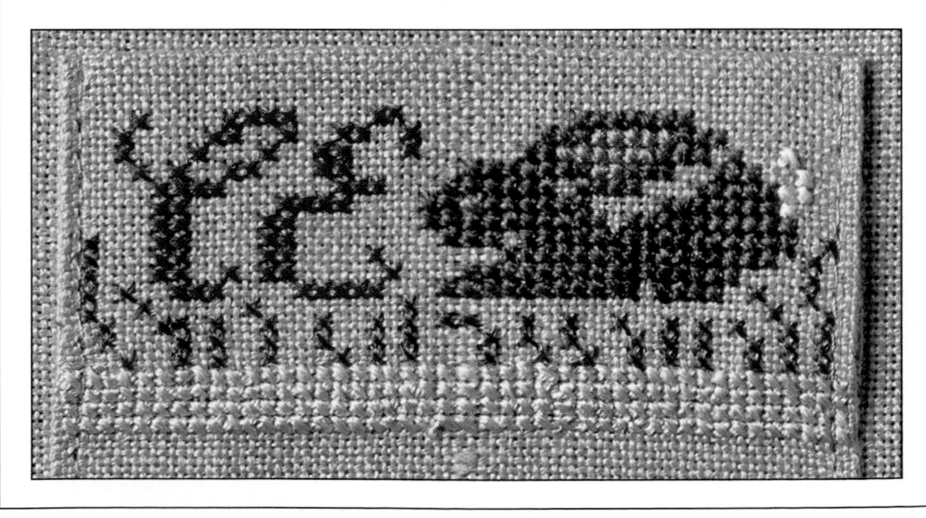

STITCH TECHNIQUES FOR LETTERING

To be effective lettering must be legible, with all the letters stitched evenly in clearly defined lines. It should ideally be worked on a frame, to prevent the fabric from puckering. Trace the letters first and then mark them onto the ground. The quickest way to work over the marked letters is to use cross, chain or satin stitch. The initials or monograms can be set in isolation upon the ground or framed with further stitching. Many stitches can be used: below are four examples, each worked in different ways.

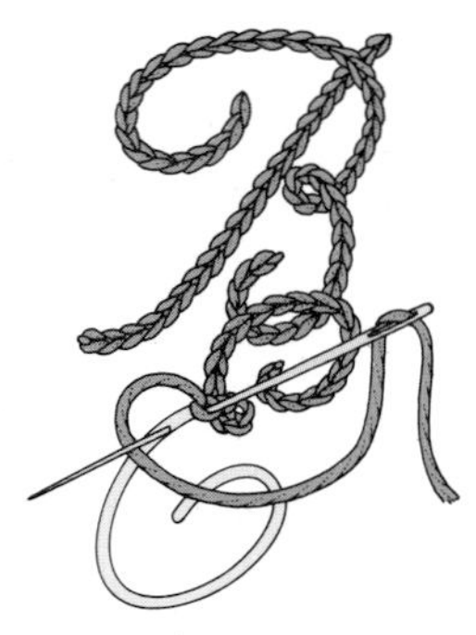

Chain stitch
This is the easiest stitch for free-style lettering. The edges of the lettering can be neatened and finished off with an outline of stem stitch.

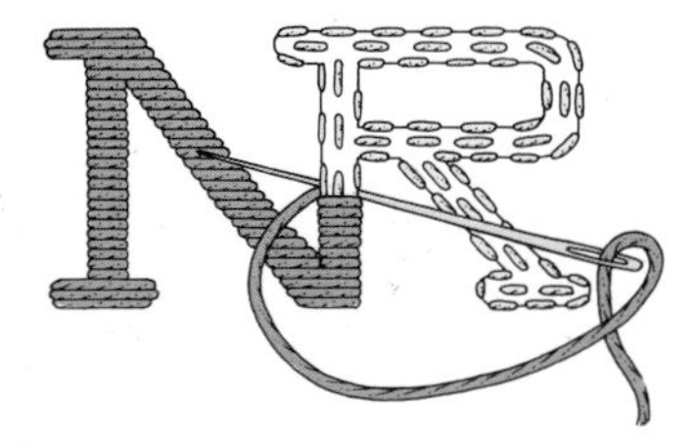

Padded lettering
Padding is used to emphasize lettering by raising it. This is achieved by working a padding of running or chain stitches first and covering these with satin stitch.

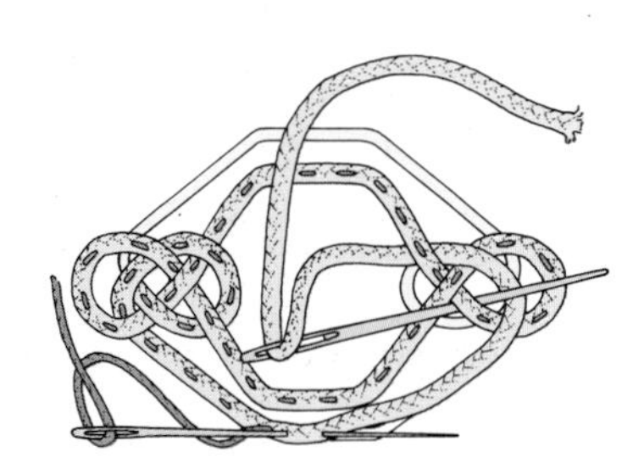

Couched braid
Attach the braid with small, invisible running stitches starting at a place where the join will be least noticeable and completing the design without a break. Leave a gap in running stitches at intersections so that the braid can be threaded through on returning to this point. Cord or ribbon may also be used.

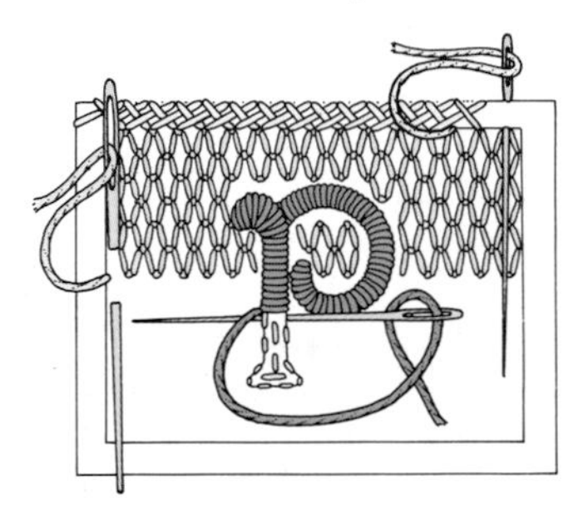

Openwork lettering
Openwork can be used on fine, even-weave fabrics either for lettering or the background, but in both cases always work the letter first.

Letter D with encroaching foliage

Cross and satin stitch alphabets

The two alphabets shown here are designed to be worked in cross stitch and satin stitch respectively. The cross stitch alphabet is one of the quickest and easiest to do and can be worked directly from the chart but the satin stitch alphabet will need to be traced and then transferred to the ground fabric as described on page 16.

Any decorative lettering can be traced and used as long as the outline is defined enough to be easily legible with embroidery stitches.

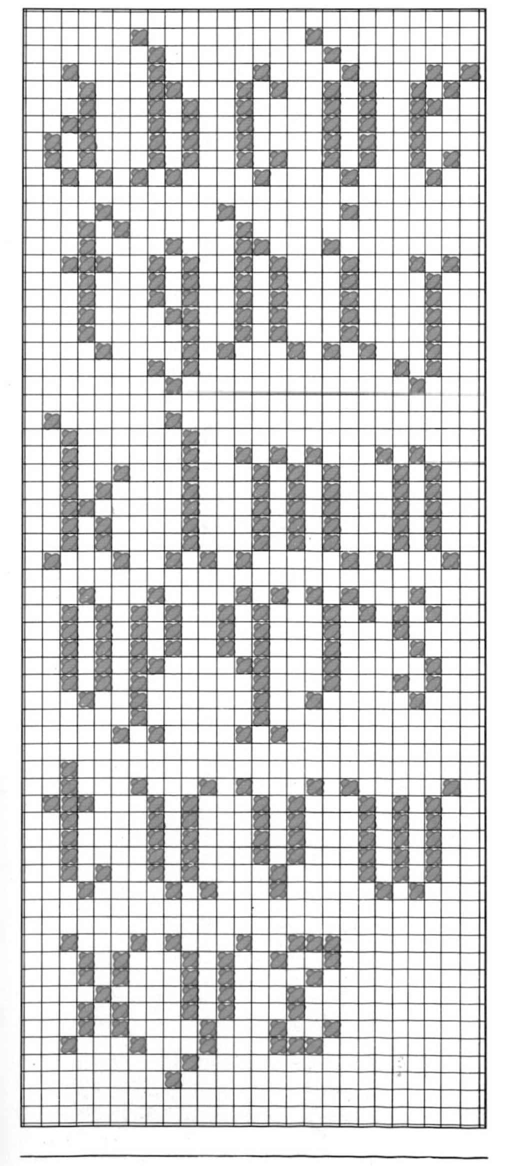

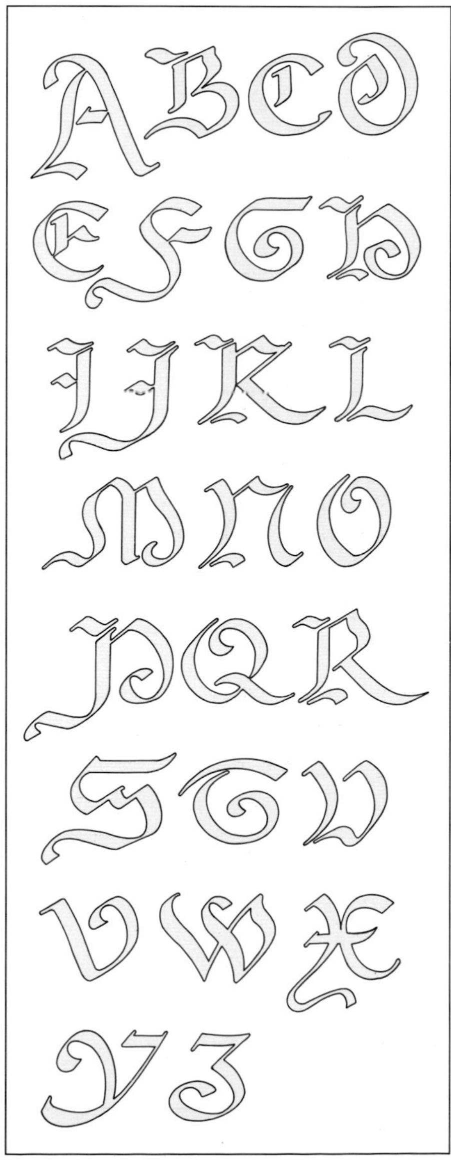

Openwork

Openwork embroidery is the collective name for all forms of embroidery which have the appearance of lace and yet are worked on fabric.

There are three distinct techniques for making openwork embroidery: pulled thread work, withdrawn thread work and cutwork – also known as eyelet lace.

In pulled thread work the threads of the ground fabric are pulled back tautly with special embroidery stitches to make decorative holes, whereas in withdrawn thread work threads are drawn out from the ground fabric and embroidery stitches used to group the loose strands into patterns.

Cutwork is well known as broderie anglaise. Here the embroidery designs are worked first and the fabric is then cut away from around the stitches.

Pulled thread work

Honeycomb darning stitch

Bring needle out at arrow; insert it 3 horizontal threads down and bring out 3 vertical threads to left. Insert up over 3 horizontal threads and bring out 3 vertical threads to left. Continue to end of row. Work subsequent groups into the base of the previous ones.

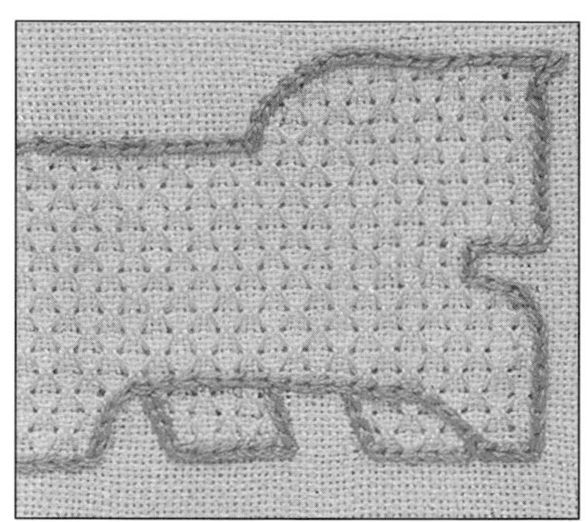

This stitch forms a lattice pattern with regular perforations.

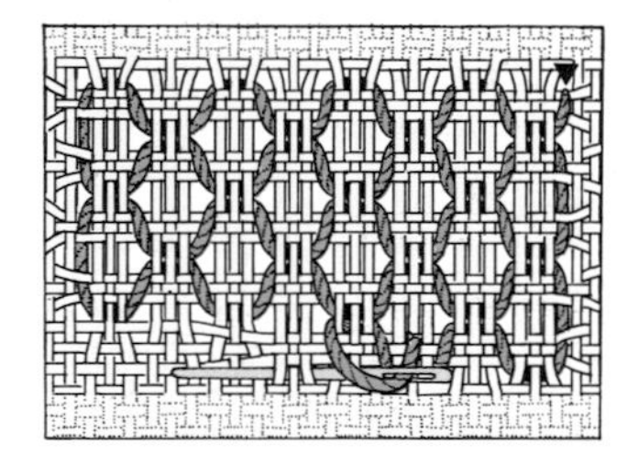

Algerian eye stitch

Begin at arrow and work 8 straight pulling stitches, each over 2 threads or any even number worked from the outer edge into the same central hole, as shown.

When using as a filling stitch, work in 2 journeys, making the 1st side of the star on the downward journey and the 2nd on the upward one.

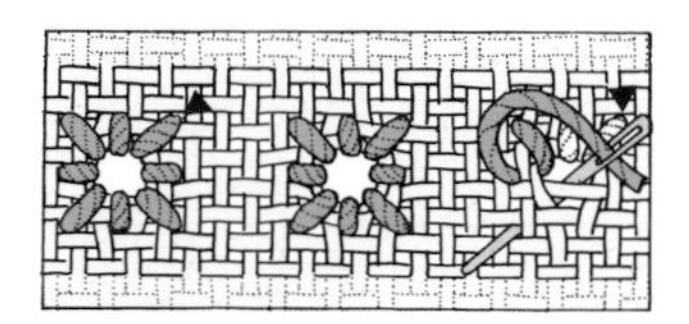

Withdrawn thread work

Withdrawn thread work is often used for borders on tablecloths, napkins, sheets and skirts. It is worked by withdrawing threads from the ground fabric and then securing the remaining ones into clusters and grouping them with embroidery stitches to make regular patterns. Where a single border only is required, as on sheets or towels, threads can be withdrawn to the limit of the fabric. The edges of the borders are mostly hem-stitched while the depth can vary from a single withdrawn thread to really decorative borders several centimetres deep.

Single borders

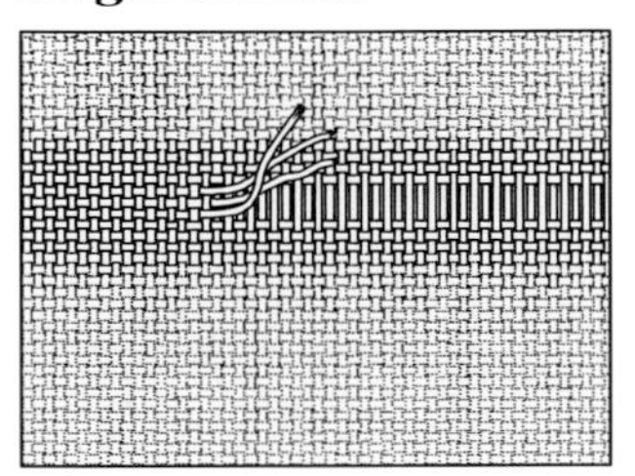

Measure the hem allowance across the width of the fabric and slip a pin under thread marking hemstitching line. Withdraw this thread right across the fabric and any further threads as required. Fold the hem over to drawn thread line and tack, ready for hemstitching.

Single hemstitch

Front **Back**

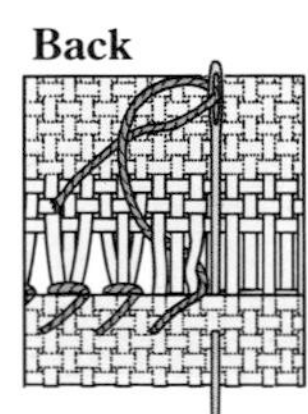

Withdraw about 4 or 5 threads. Fold hem down and work from left to right on wrong side of fabric. Insert needle under 2 or more of the loose strands, then pick up 2 threads of the ground fabric on the folded edge. Pull the working thread through fairly tightly so as to cluster the loose strands. Repeat to end.

Trellis hemstitch

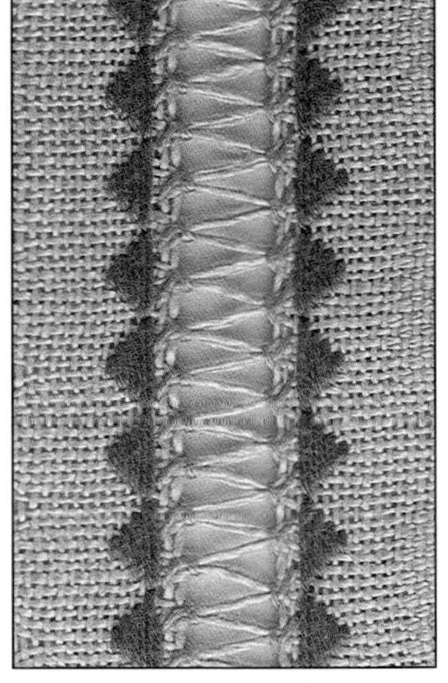

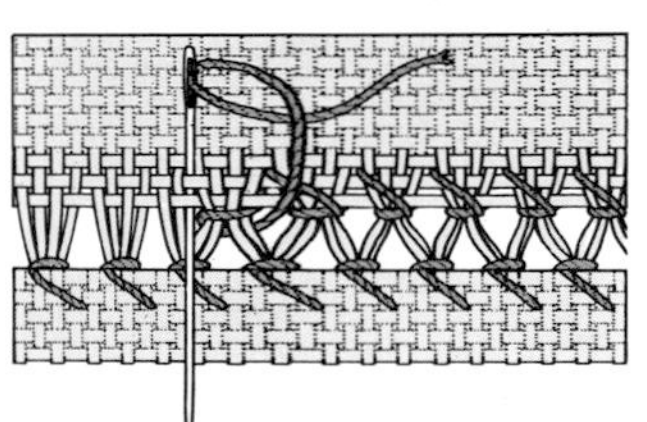

Withdraw several border threads. Hemstitch along top line in 4-thread clusters; the needle encircles 4 vertical threads before passing behind 2 threads of main fabric. Hemstitch along bottom line, starting with 2 threads, thus dividing upper clusters into pattern.

Single crossing clusters

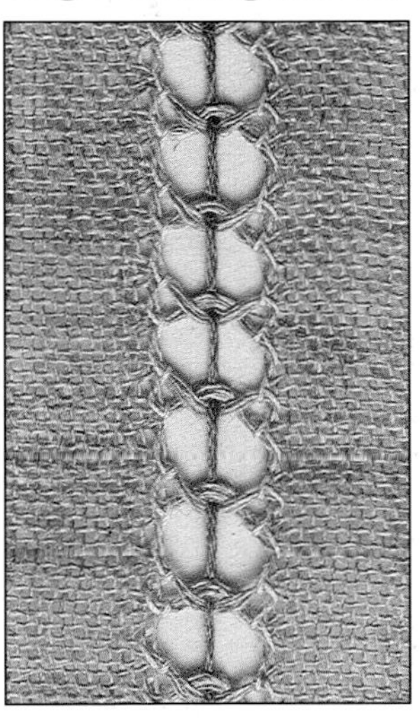

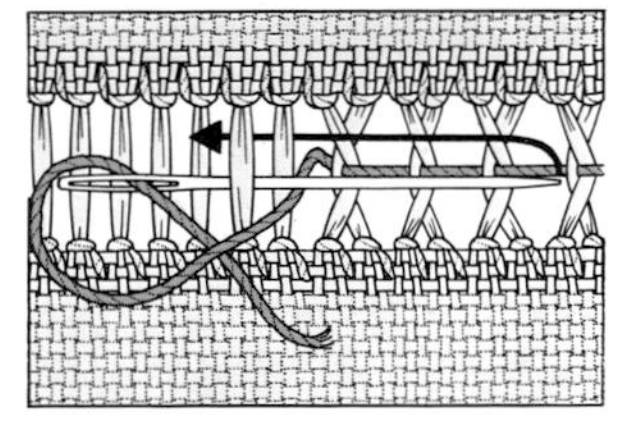

Withdraw required number of threads and hemstitch border with even clusters on both sides. Secure working thread centrally to fold line at right. Pass thread over 2 clusters and insert needle from left to right behind 2nd cluster, twist it back, inserting needle behind 1st cluster from right to left. Bring thread through, pulling firmly, ready to cross following 2 clusters.

Withdrawing threads for grounds

So far we have only dealt with borders of various depths but complete grounds (see below), backgrounds and individual motifs can also be worked over withdrawn threads. All the techniques are the same but are used differently in order to cover the open fabric. The preparation of the ground fabric is more involved as the threads are withdrawn in both directions over the surface of the fabric.

The threads can be withdrawn in regular grid formations as shown or in certain areas only to form patches, panels or frames with intervening solid fabric.

Preparing fabric for withdrawn grounds

1 To withdraw threads in both directions mark the limits to which the threads may be withdrawn and then withdraw all border threads. The ground threads are then ready to be withdrawn.

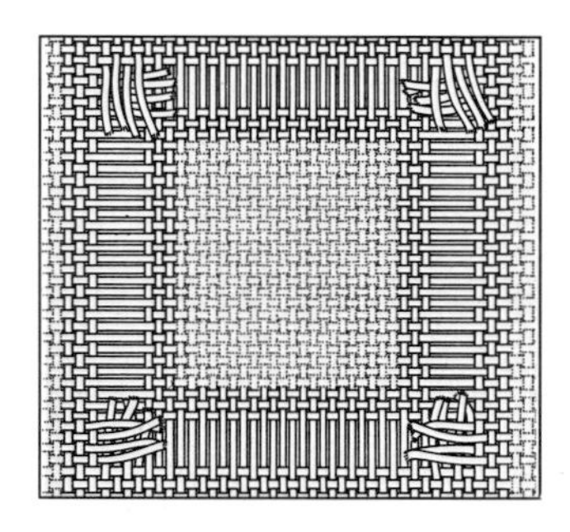

2 Start with vertical (warp) threads, withdrawing 4 threads and leaving 4 threads. Cut threads 3 in. (7.5 cm) away from limits and withdraw these central threads the whole way up fabric. Cut back, trim and secure loose 3 in. (7.5 cm) ends.

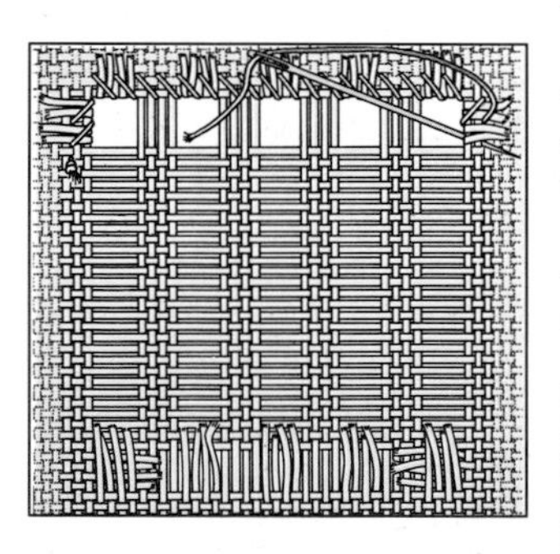

3 Then withdraw 4 and leave 4 horizontal (weft) threads in the same way. Use overcast stitch or buttonhole stitch around the perimeter of the fabric. Two ways of grouping the remaining stitches are by knotting and cording.

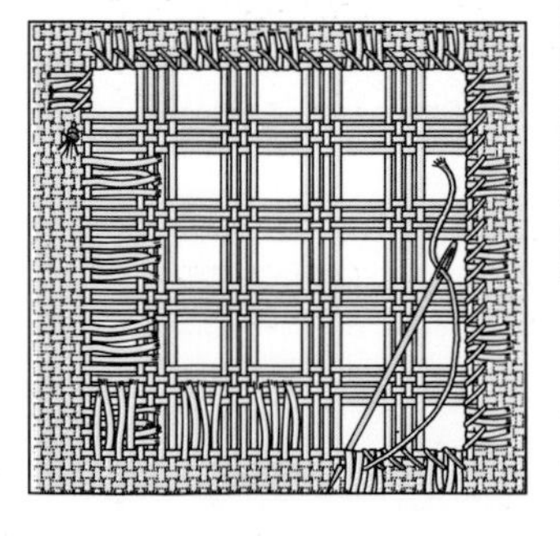

Lace pattern with knotting

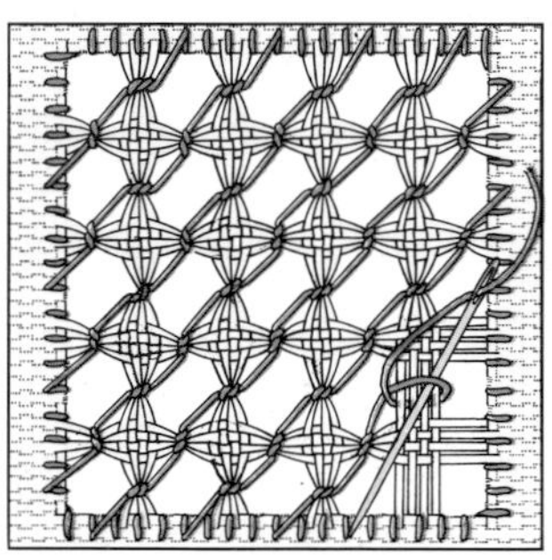

Withdraw 4 and leave 4 threads in each direction. Then work single knot stitch diagonally connecting clusters.

Lace pattern with cording

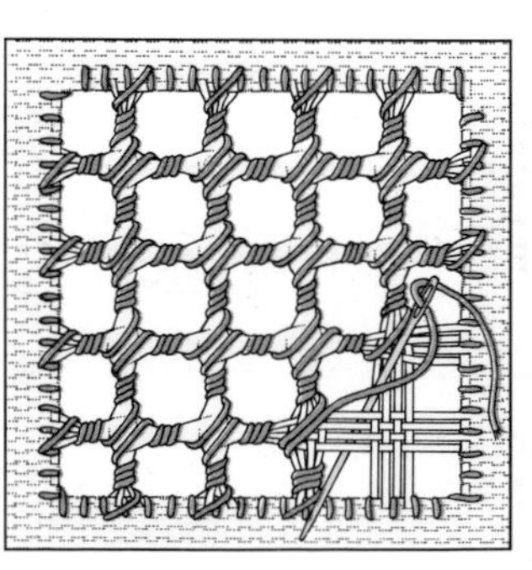

Withdraw 4 and leave 4 threads in each direction. Then work cording diagonally making a slanting stitch at intersections.

Cutwork

Cutwork is made by cutting holes in the ground fabric in pattern formation. It is used for all types of decorative table and bed linens as well as for the borders, hems, collars and cuffs of clothing.

Materials and implements

Firm, tightly woven fabrics which do not fray easily are essential for cutwork. For whitework use cambric, lawn and fine linen. For coloured work, flannels and crêpes de chine are also suitable. All cutwork should be mounted on a frame to ease the stitching and sharp embroidery scissors should be used to form neatly cut shapes and edges.

Cutwork edges

Scalloped edges are very often used in broderie anglaise and make beautiful finishes for all types of linen and clothing.

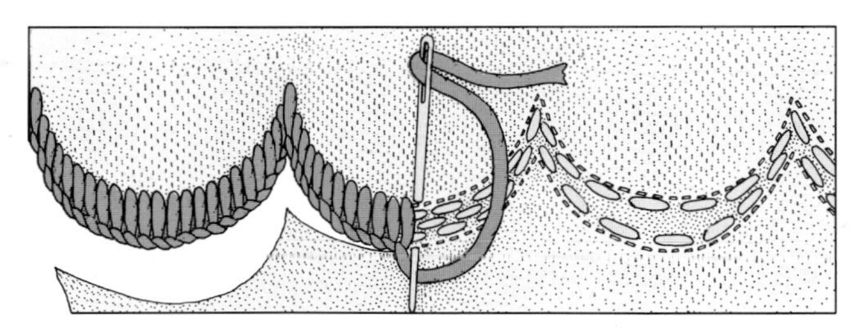

Scalloped edgings

Mark pattern onto fabric, then outline inner and outer edges and fill with running stitches. Work buttonhole stitch over outlines. Finally, cut away outer fabric.

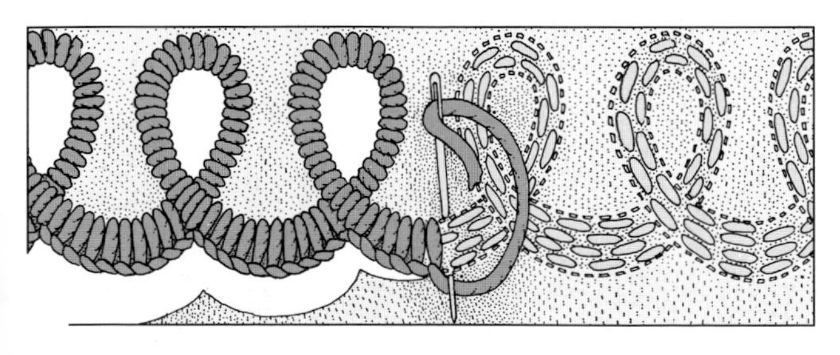

Oval eyelet scallops

Mark pattern onto fabric, then outline and fill with running stitches. Work overcast stitch over the inner pattern and buttonhole stitch along the edge. Cut away outer fabric and then cut out the eyelet centres.

Eyelet holes

The holes in cutwork motifs are known as eyelets and can be made in various different shapes. The raw edges around the motifs are covered with overcasting or buttonhole stitches.

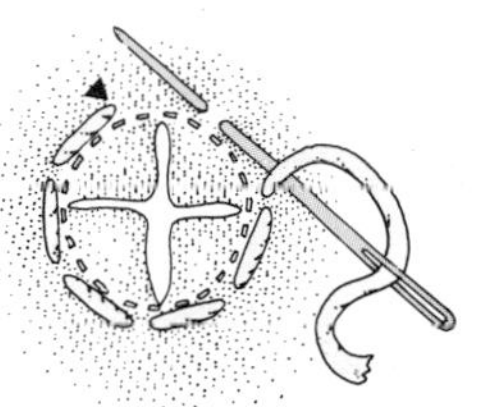

1 Work running stitch around the outline, then snip centre twice (as shown).

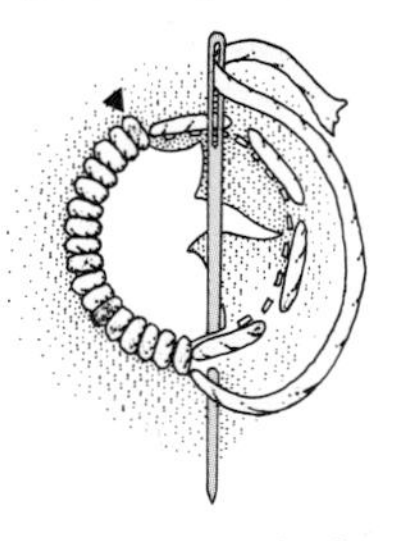

2 Turn corners to back and overcast around edge.

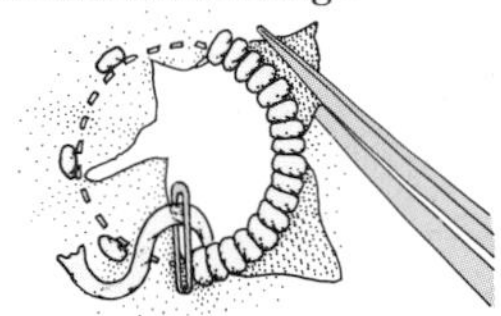

3 Complete overcasting and cut away corners at back.

Designing embroidery

In the past, embroidery was rated as a high art form and designs were produced by specialist embroidery designers. For those people not rich enough to have their own designers, inspiration came from a range of different sources, such as biblical stories, book illustrations and the natural world. These old embroideries are worth studying for their brilliant use of stitch, thread and subject matter.

Embroideries made for pictures, screens or fire screens should be mounted on a hardboard backing before framing. A margin of unworked ground all around the embroidery will be needed so that it can be folded to the back of the hardboard.

Children's drawings can be an excellent source for original designs. The embroidery (left) was copied from this drawing which was done by a child of six. The simplicity of the drawing has been retained in the embroidery by the fresh colours and the clever use of outlines and exposed ground. Stitches worked in chain, satin and French knots.

DESIGNING AN EMBROIDERED PICTURE

Jonathon Langley is both an embroiderer and a painter and the step-by-step construction of one of his designs is shown here. First of all stretch the material to be embroidered in a ring frame and mark out the design in pencil. Then proceed as shown. Although it is more satisfying to work from one of your own designs, a tracing of a drawing or painting could easily be used instead.

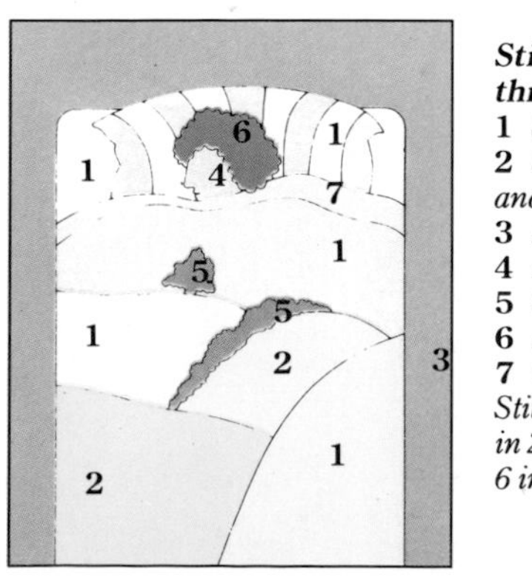

Stitches and threads

1 *Satin stitch*
2 *Satin with long and short stitch.*
3 *Brick stitch*
4 *Brick stitch*
5 *Speckling*
6 *French knots*
7 *Chain stitch*
Stitches 1, 2, 3 and 7 in 2-strand; 4, 5 and 6 in 1-strand

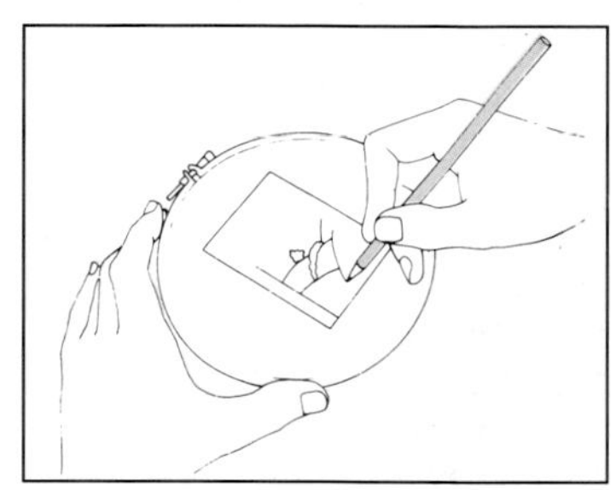

1 Using a pencil, mark out the design.

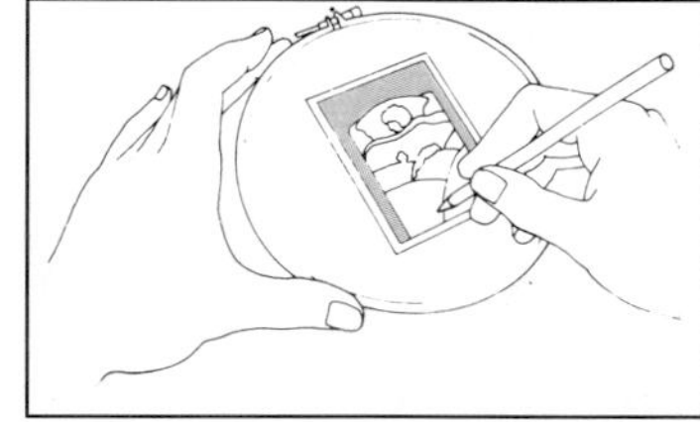

2 Then, with coloured pencils, block in the areas of colour.

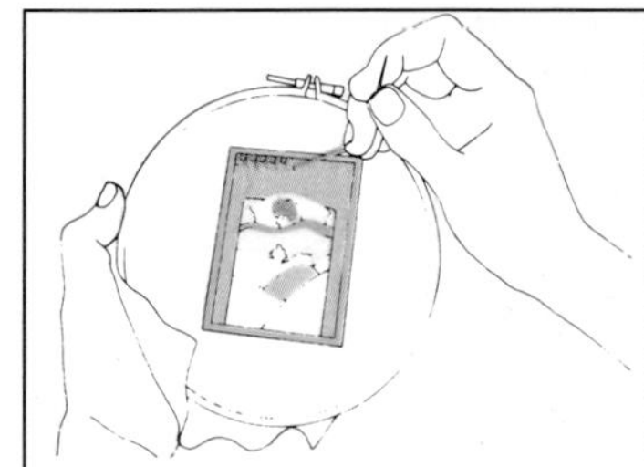

3 Start to work the main areas of the background.

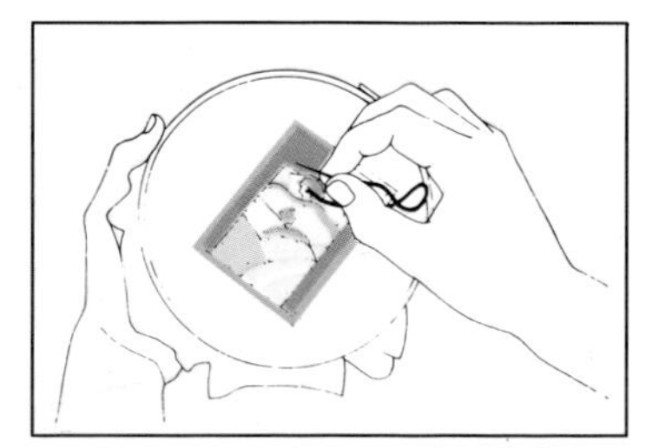

4 Then work the more detailed parts of the design, using the appropriate stitches for each part. Finally, stitch the border.

Designing in embroidery

When choosing or originating a design, also keep in mind the fabric, thread and stitches to be used. Different methods of working and combinations of stitches can produce many and varied effects.

Preparing the designs

When the design has been planned it is transferred to the ground fabric by any of the methods described on page 16. The ground fabric is then mounted onto an embroidery frame, where it is stretched firmly into position ready for working.

Type of ground fabric

As alternatives to working a plain ground fabric, prints and brocades can be used to form the design if their motifs are worked over with embroidery stitches. The motifs can be raised by using matching coloured thread or filled with contrasting coloured threads to give multicoloured effects.

Voiding

The ground fabric itself can be used as part of the design by working stitches over the background and around the outlines of the motif but leaving the ground within the motif exposed. This is known as voiding.

Outlines

Outlines used to define the pattern shapes can be made almost invisible by using a thread which is only slightly different in colour to the ground, or they can be emphasized by using a sharply contrasting thread or even couched metal threads.

Backgrounds

Backgrounds can be left exposed or covered with quick filling stitches, such as chain or darning stitch. They can be shaded from dark to light or made richer by darning with gold and metal threads.

EMBROIDERING LARGE AREAS

The quickest way to cover large areas of fabric with embroidery is by tambouring. In this method of embroidery, a tambour hook – which is small, metal and slightly pointed at the tip – is used instead of a needle to work chain stitches through the ground fabric. It should be worked on a frame, as the surface of the fabric needs to be tautly stretched in order to work the hook easily in and out of the fabric.

1 Knot the end of the working thread and hold it in the left hand underneath the ground fabric. Insert the hook downwards, from front to back of fabric, and draw through a loop of working thread and pull it up through fabric.

2 Then, with loop still on hook, insert hook a little further along design line and draw through another loop of the thread. Draw this 2nd loop through first, forming a chain stitch and continue in this way.

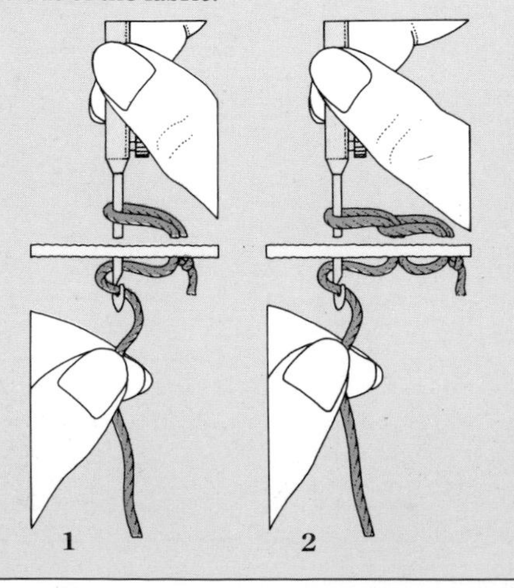

Detail of a Chinese sleeve ribbon showing how laid and couched threads can create textures

Detail of a Kutch Indian wall hanging worked in chain stitch

Pictorial embroidery

Certain subjects, such as animals and birds, lend themselves well to pictorial embroidery, as fur and feathers can easily be translated into stitches, whereas other subjects are more difficult to capture, such as features and skin tones in human faces.

Feathers

These can be worked in satin stitches of different lengths and directions to follow the line of the feather.

Fur

Work straight-haired fur in satin stitch, wavy fur in chain stitch, ridged fur in buttonhole stitch and wool in bullion or French knots.

Sky and water

Use flat stitches or laid threads for calm effects, and coiling, swirling stitch arrangements for storms. Clouds can be introduced, emphatically shaped and filled with white chain stitches.

Wind and rain

Gusts of wind can be interpreted by a sudden change of stitch direction on the subject matter. Rain can be shown by top stitching in light-coloured glossy threads, using irregular-sized stroke stitches.

Landscapes

When portraying landscapes the stitches can be changed and graded so that those in the foreground are longer than those in the background, giving a sense of distance.

Beads and sequins

Beads and sequins are probably the most effective way of transforming quite simple patterns into rich, exotic designs. When working with them, the main point to bear in mind is that they should lie neatly together in prearranged order. Not only beads and sequins but buttons, shells and pebbles can be used in embroidery provided they have holes of a convenient size to secure them to the fabric. Make sure the fabric is strong enough to support the weight of heavy beads. A small selection of beads and sequins is shown below.

Because the beads and sequins are fragile, it is best to keep them in separate containers and handle as little as possible. They should be stored away from direct light. Instructions for applying beads, sequins and shisha glass (mirrorwork) are given on pages 36 and 37.

Above *Seventeenth-century English bead-work picture* **Right** *Detail of brightly beaded motif*

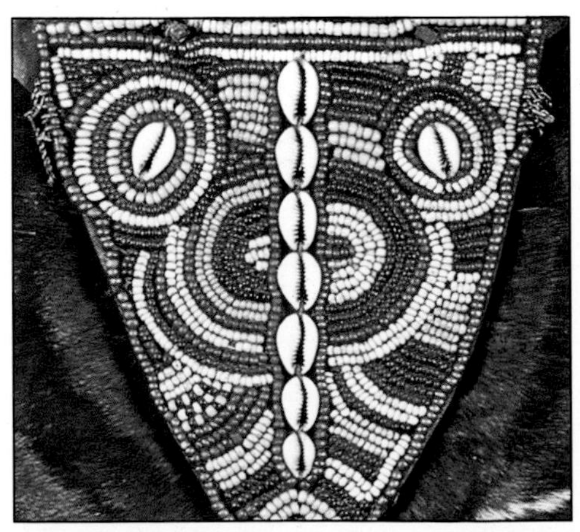

Shells and beads have been used for this traditional Masai warrior's apron.

The sequins in this ceremonial Hungarian head-dress are stitched with gold thread on applied silk and velvet.

Beads

Beads can be applied singly or in rows, as here, by couching the laid rows of beads to the fabric. The pattern for this modern bead work belt has been taken from a Sioux chief's headband.

Sequins

Sequins are almost always made to glitter and catch the light and therefore are usually of gold or metal.

Sequinned motifs, like this spray of flowers, are often used to decorate formal dresses, belts and evening bags with stunning effect.

Mirrorwork

Mirrorwork is a particularly effective way of decorating a linen dress or waistcoat as the shisha glass used catches the light with the movement of the garment.

Applying sequins and beads

Sequins can be attached to the ground fabric so that the stitching is either visible or invisible. The choice of method depends on whether a contrasting yarn is used for special effect, such as gold or metal threads, or whether the patterns are built up with the sequins overlapping each other and thus hiding the stitches.

Beads are used to decorate fabrics in a wide variety of ways, either as braids or to form blocks of coloured patterns, or as tassels and fringes.

Applying sequins with stitches on one side only

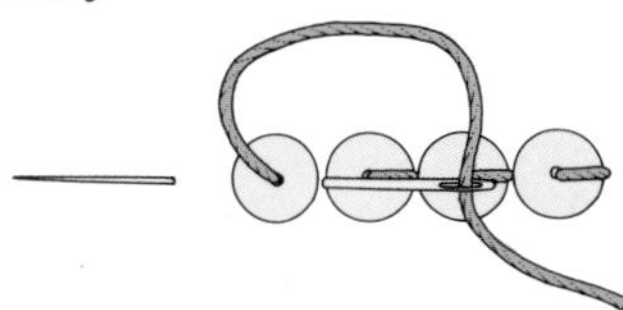

This method gives a slightly raised effect. Bring the needle with the thread to the surface from the back of the fabric and insert it through the eye of the sequin. Work a back stitch over the right side of the sequin and bring needle out to left, ready to thread through eye of next sequin which is placed edge to edge with the previous one.

Applying sequins with stitches on both sides

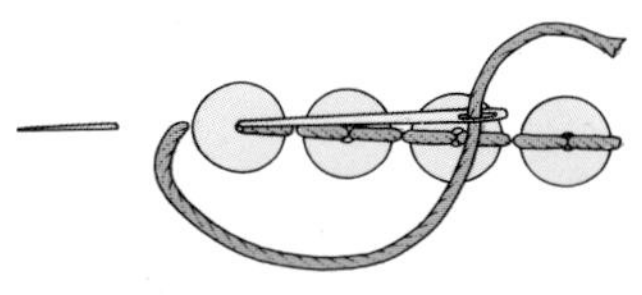

This method gives a more flattened effect. Work back stitch over right side of sequin and then bring needle out at left edge of sequin and work another back stitch through the eye of the sequin, bringing needle out to left to be threaded through eye of next sequin, which is placed edge to edge with the previous one.

Applying sequins with invisible stitches

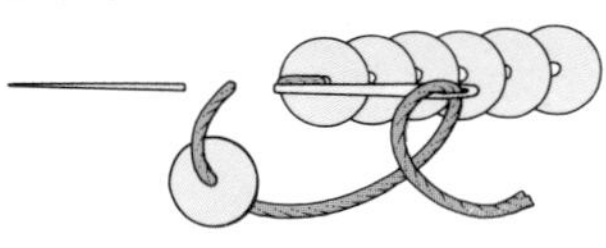

In this method the sequins overlap thus covering the stitches. Work a back stitch into the left side of the first sequin and place next sequin so that the right edge covers the eye of the previous one. Bring the needle out exactly at the left edge of it and work back stitch through the eye, inserting needle into hole of previous back stitch.

Securing sequins with a small bead

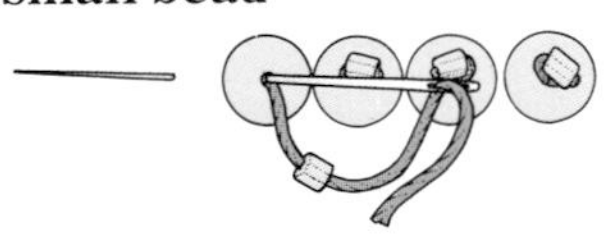

As a decorative feature the sequins can be stitched down with a bead. This also means that the thread is invisible.

Bring the needle out through the eye of the sequin and thread a small bead onto it, then insert the needle through the eye of the sequin again and pull tight so that the bead rests firmly over the eye, securing the sequin.

Applying beads individually

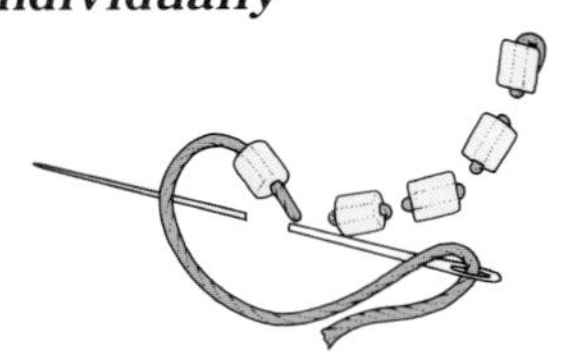

Bring needle to surface and thread bead onto it. Then insert needle back through the same hole and make a stitch slightly longer than the length of the bead. Alternatively make a stitch the length of the bead so that next bead can be secured edge to edge with the previous one.

Couching beads

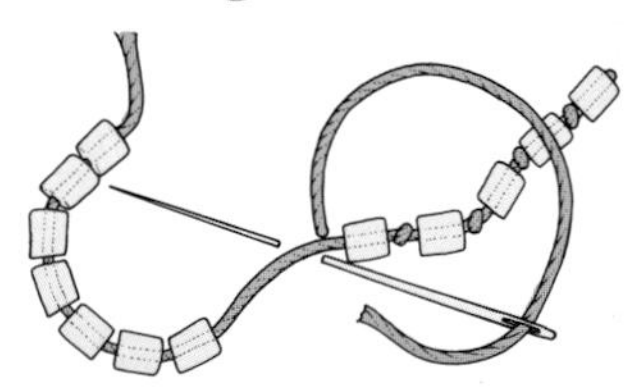

Cut 2 lengths of thread and bring one thread to surface and thread beads onto it. Slide first bead into position. With a separate needle and thread make an overcast stitch as close as possible to edge of bead. Slide 2nd bead up to first. Continue in this way until all beads have been couched into position.

APPLYING BEADS WITH A TAMBOUR HOOK

In this technique the beads are applied onto a tightly stretched fabric from the underneath.

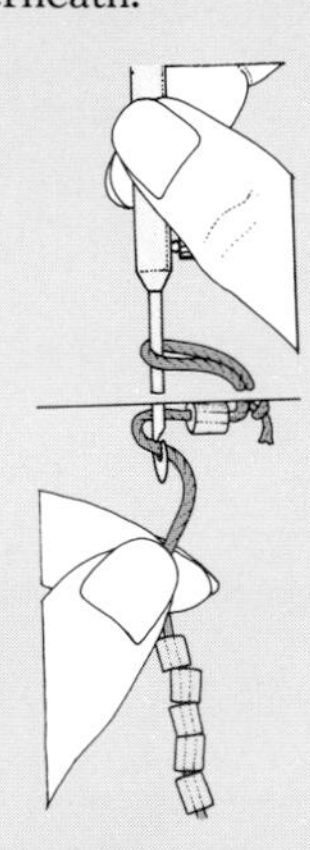

1 Thread beads and secure thread to fabric. Insert hook downwards through fabric and wrap thread around it. With hook draw loop through to surface. Push first bead up to fabric below work. Insert hook back through fabric and again draw loop through.

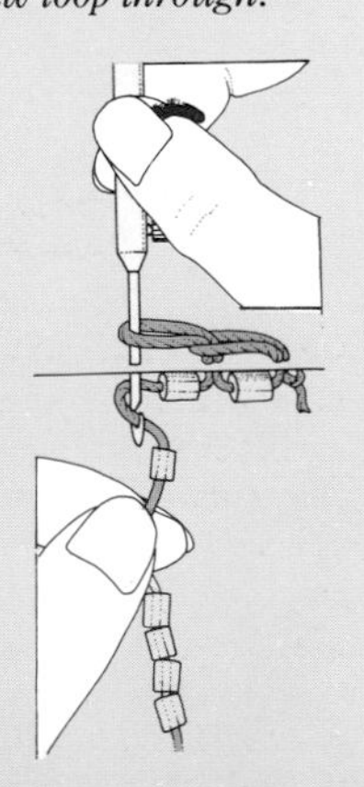

2 Continue in this way along the design line.

MIRRORWORK

This type of work is seen in the traditional embroideries of Afghanistan and in Baluchistan and Sind in India. It is worked with little discs of mirror or tin which are secured around their circumference on the surface of the fabric with a special embroidery stitch known as shisha stitch.

1 Lay disc on surface of fabric and hold it secure with left thumb. Bring needle out at A. Carry thread across from left to right over disc and insert needle at B, bringing it out at point C.

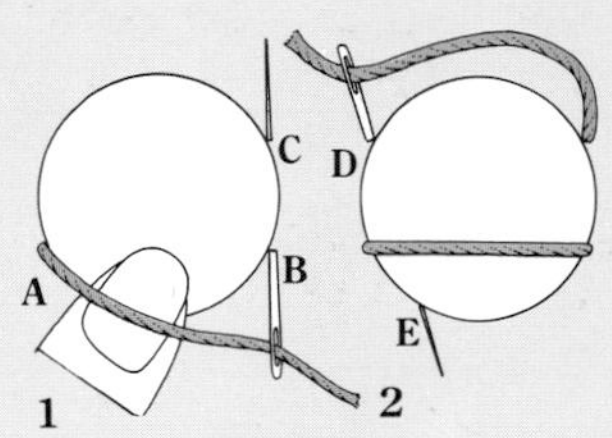

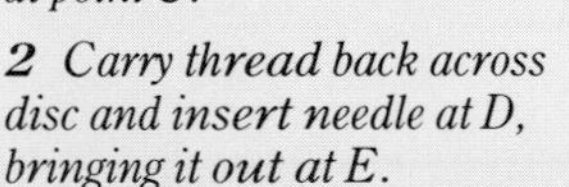

2 Carry thread back across disc and insert needle at D, bringing it out at E.

3 Pass needle over and under the first horizontal thread. Draw it through and take it up and pass it over and under 2nd horizontal thread in same way. Then insert needle at F and bring it out at G.

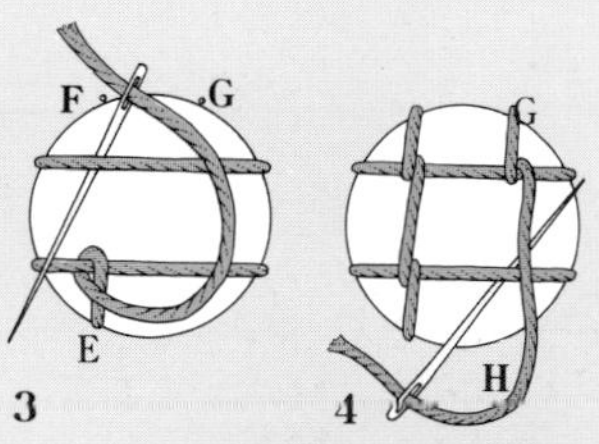

4 Again pass needle over and under both horizontal threads.

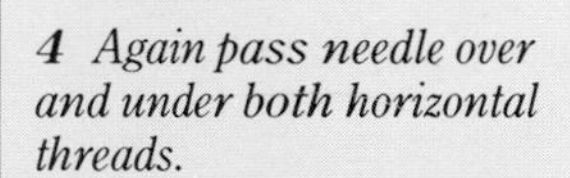

5 Insert needle at H and bring it out at I.

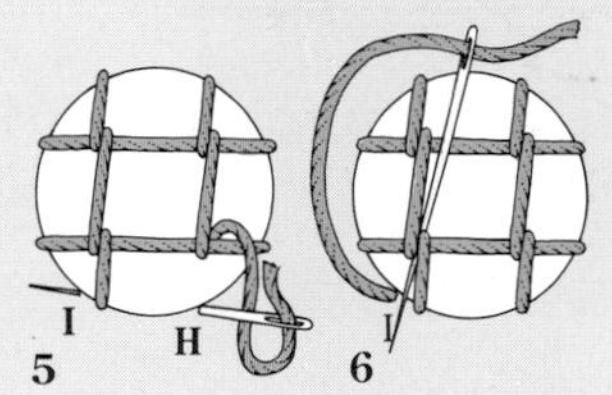

6 Pass needle under intersection on first horizontal thread and bring it out to right of working thread.

7 Insert needle at I and bring it out at J over working thread.

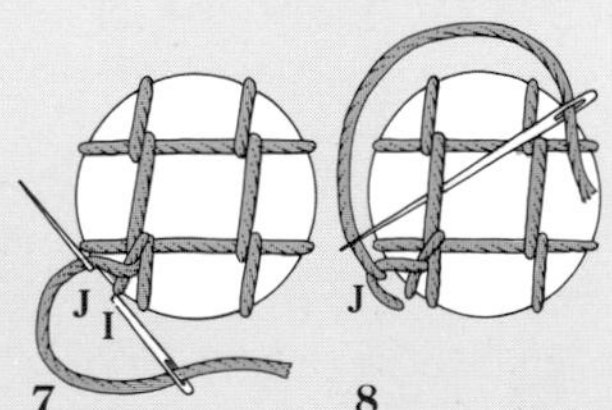

8 Pass needle under vertical thread and bring out over working thread.

9 Insert needle at J and bring it out at K over working thread.

10 Repeat steps 8 and 9 all the way round the disc.

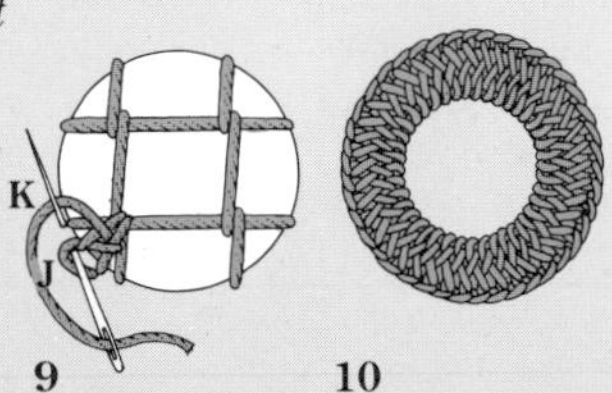

Smocking

Smocking is the only form of embroidery which has a practical as well as a decorative function, with the smocking stitches being used to gather in the fullness at the same time as decorating the surface of the folds. For traditional smocks (which were really work overalls), special motifs and stitches were used as symbols of the wearer's trade. These were worked along the borders of the smocked panels and on the shoulders, collars and cuffs.

In the example of modern smocking shown below different colours are used for each of the smocking stitches and the panels are outlined with embroidered motifs in subdued colours. A thin line of contrasting coloured stem stitch frames the honeycombing. The instructions for working honeycomb stitch are on page 41.

MODERN SMOCKING

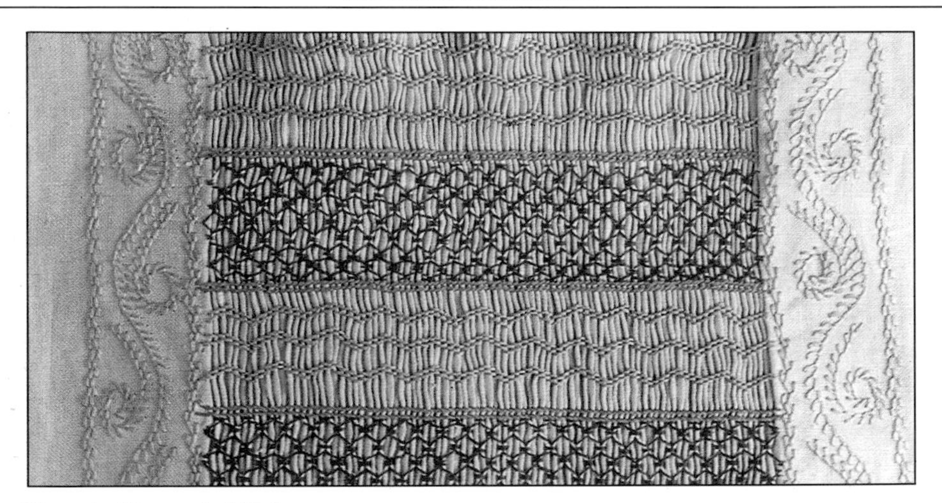

Close up of the smocked fabric

Feather stitch flower panel

SMOCKING STITCHES

Smocking can be worked on many different types of patterned fabrics with the patterns, such as dotted and checked designs, acting as the guides for the gathering. When making a garment always work the smocked areas first before you stitch the seams.

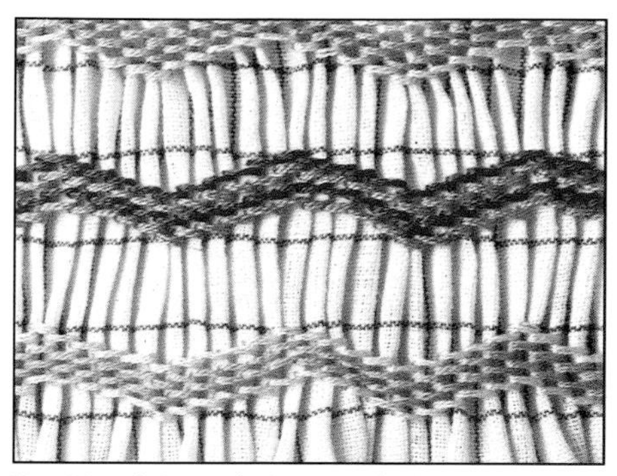

Vandyke stitch on windowpane checks

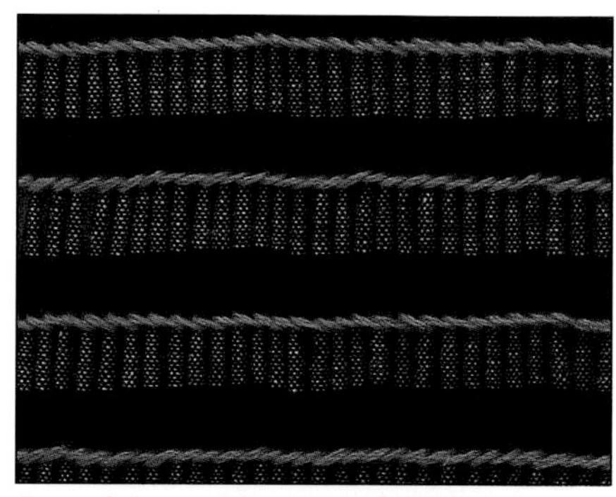

Rope stitch on stripes

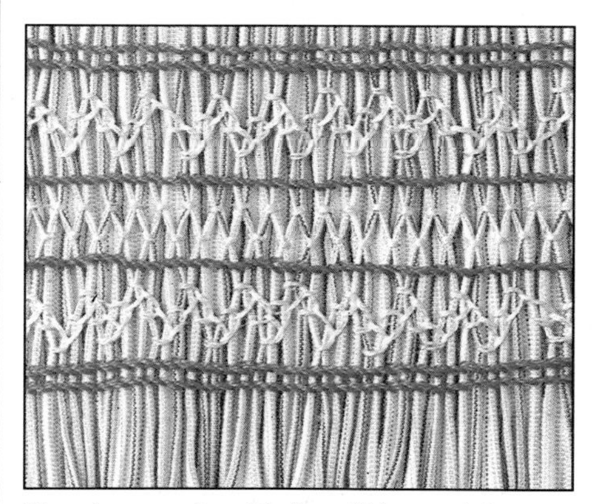

Stem, honeycomb and feather stitches on stripes

Diamond stitch on a coarse fabric

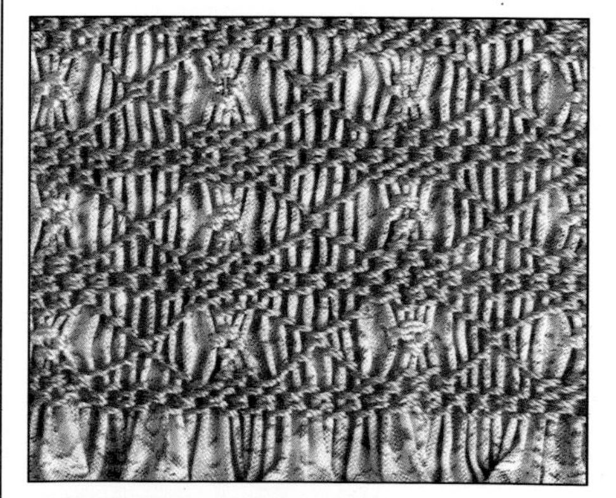

Cable stitching on a floral print

Surface honeycomb stitch on a plain ground

Method of working

Preparing to smock

Smocking is worked by gathering the fabric into even-sized folds. It is always worked before the garment is assembled. The amount of fabric needed is usually about three times the actual finished width of the smocking, but less material may be necessary if a thicker fabric such as a soft, woollen weave is used.

Traditionally the position of the folds was calculated by counting the horizontal and vertical threads in the ground fabric and marking them with ruled chalk lines. The gathering was done with a waxed thread worked over the chalk marks, with small pieces of ground fabric being picked up at regularly spaced intervals. This still remains the best method as it ensures that the gathers are on the same straight-weave lines.

Nowadays, printed transfers are readily available in the shops. They consist of a piece of transfer paper marked with equally spaced dots which are transferred onto the back of the fabric. Make sure that each dot falls on the weave line of the fabric, because if not the fabric will be strained and wrinkled when gathered.

Smocking template

If printed transfers are not available, you could make your own on a piece of card by marking evenly-spaced dots in rows along the card, and piercing each dot. This template is then placed on the ground fabric to be smocked, and each dot is marked in pencil through the holes.

Materials

Any fabric, from plain linen to cottons and printed silks, can be smocked provided it is supple enough to be gathered. Gingham and patterned fabric such as stripes and polka-dot prints, are particularly easy to smock as the pattern acts as a guide for making the gathers.

GATHERING THE FABRIC

Using a knotted thread, bring the needle through the fabric from back to front and pick up a small piece of ground fabric at each dot. Then at the end of each row, leave the surplus thread hanging loose. Rethread the needle with new thread and complete all the rows. Then pull the loose ends up a row at a time, gathering the fabric until the required width has been achieved. Tie the thread ends in pairs and stroke the gathers gently with a pin to even them out.

1 Gather the back of fabric in rows, picking up a small piece of fabric at each dot.

2 When all the rows are worked, tie the thread ends together in pairs. The gathering threads are removed when the smocking has been completed.

Smocking stitches

A wide variety of patterns can be formed from any of the basic stitches below.

Honeycomb stitch

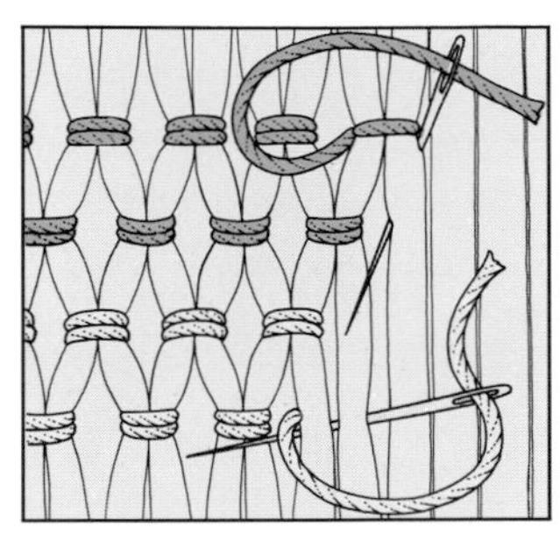

Work from left to right. Bring needle out on 1st line and backstitch 2nd and 1st folds together twice. Slip needle behind fold to emerge at 2nd fold on line below. Backstitch 3rd and 2nd folds together twice. Return needle to 1st line at 3rd fold and draw 4th and 3rd folds together as before. Continue working alternately up and down to end of row. Work next and following rows in same way.

Surface honeycomb stitch

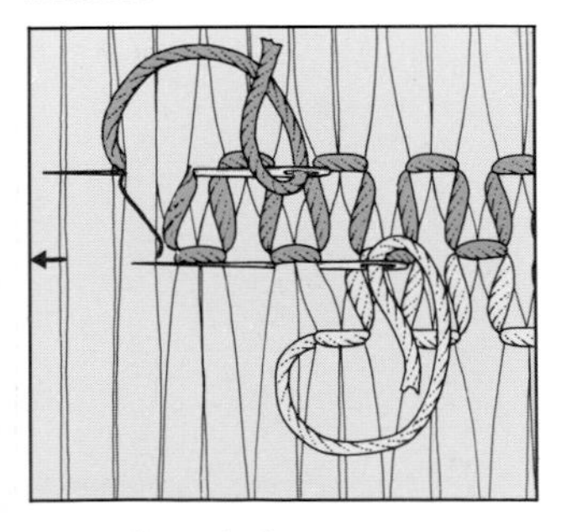

Work in a similar way to honeycomb stitch, but keep working thread on the surface of the fold.

Chevron honeycomb stitch

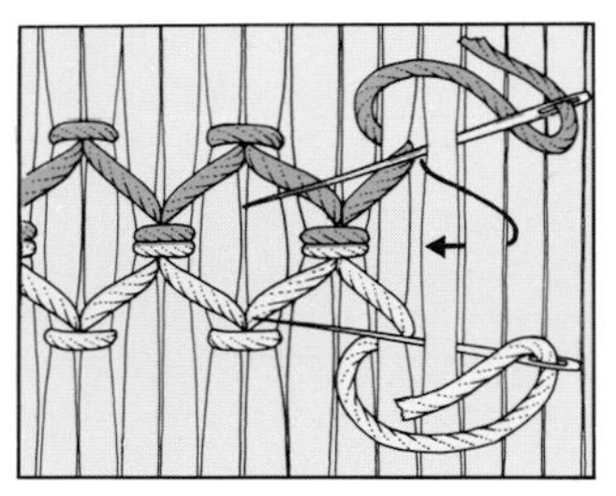

Work from left to right. Bring needle out on 2nd line then take it up to 1st line over two folds and insert it under 2nd fold. Make a back stitch over 2nd and 3rd folds emerging between the two. Take needle down over two folds and insert in 2nd line between 4th and 5th folds and bring out between 3rd and 4th. Make a back stitch over 4th and 5th folds. Continue to end of row. On next row make first stitch beneath 1st stitch of previous row and work next stitch downwards to 3rd line and so on. Repeat these two rows to form pattern.

Cable stitch

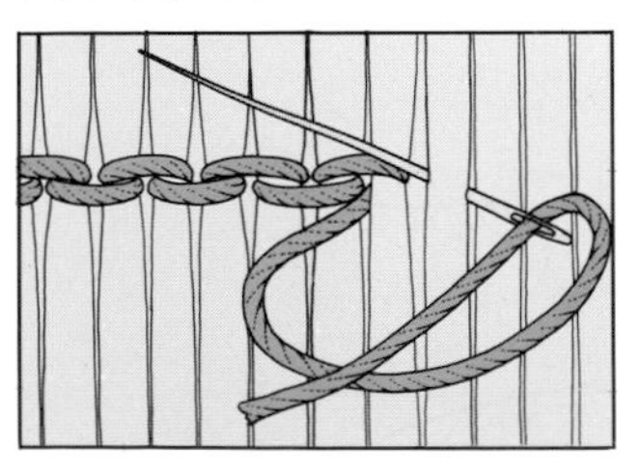

Bring needle to surface through first fold on left. Insert needle horizontally and work in stem stitch into each fold with thread positioned alternately above and below the needle.

Vandyke stitch

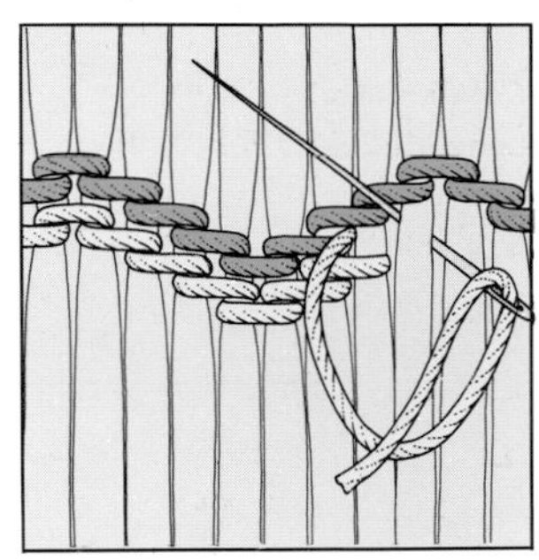

Work in 2 rows of stem stitch in chevron pattern. Keep thread below needle when working upwards and above needle when working downwards.

Feather stitch

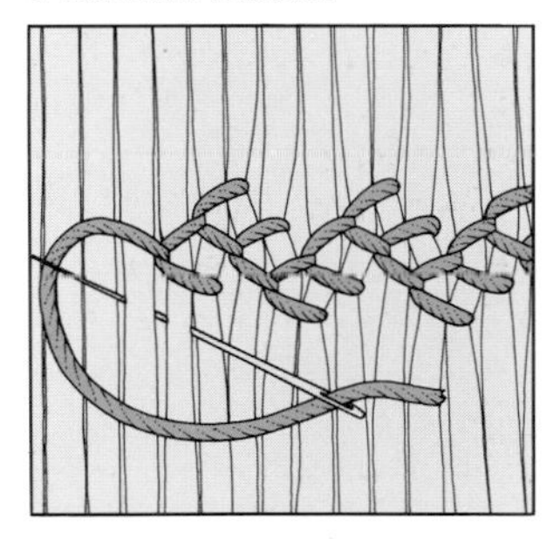

Work from right to left. Bring needle out at 1st fold and insert lower down on same fold. Take needle through 1st and 2nd folds bringing it out over working thread. Make two more stitches in the same way working down to left, make the first over 2nd and 3rd folds and next over 3rd and 4th folds. Then work two feather stitches upwards to left over next two folds. Continue in this way working two feather stitches upwards and two downwards drawing in one more fold with each stitch.

Embroidery stitch glossary

Flat stitches

These are the easiest of all sewing and embroidery stitches to work. They are formed by making straight, flat stitches, worked in a number of different sizes and directions. When used as filling stitches, they can be arranged in different ways to catch the light and make subtle shaded and patterned effects.

Running stitch

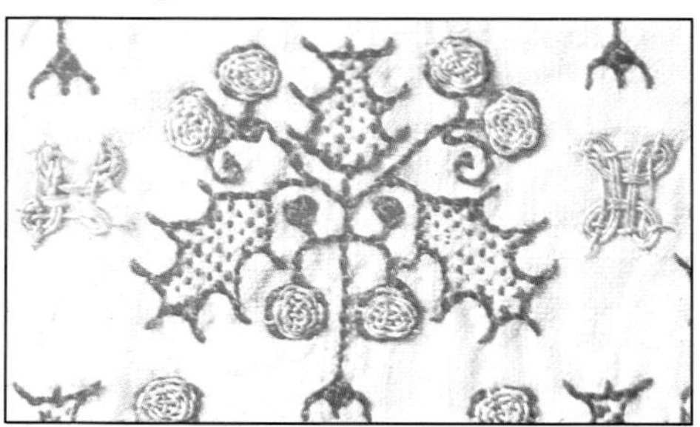

The simplest of all the stitches, running stitch is the basic stitch for hand sewing. It is used in embroidery for making lines, outlining, and as a foundation for other stitches. It is also used for hand quilting.

It is worked in and out of the ground fabric at regular intervals.

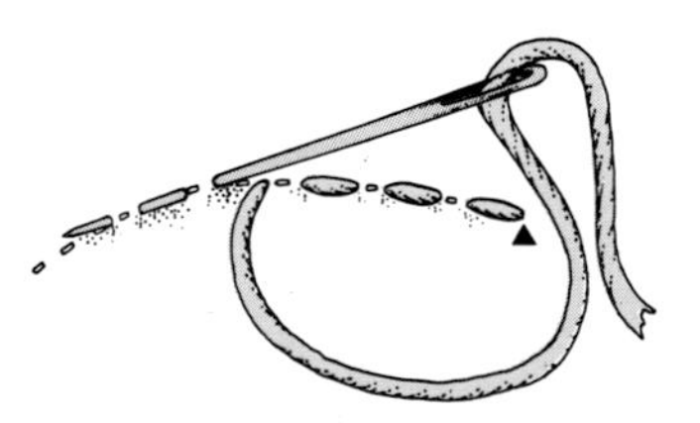

Stem stitch

This can be used for both backgrounds and outlines. It is worked with the thread kept on the same side of the needle. Place the rows close together for fillings and backgrounds. For wider effects the needle enters the ground fabric at a slight angle.

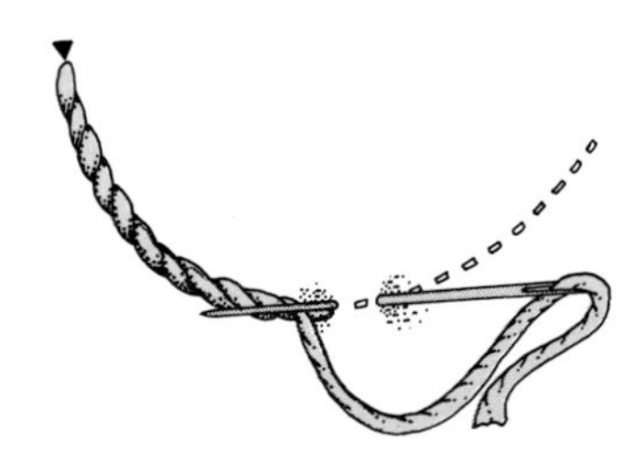

Back stitch

Used for lines and outlines, this is worked by first making a stitch forwards and then a stitch backwards.

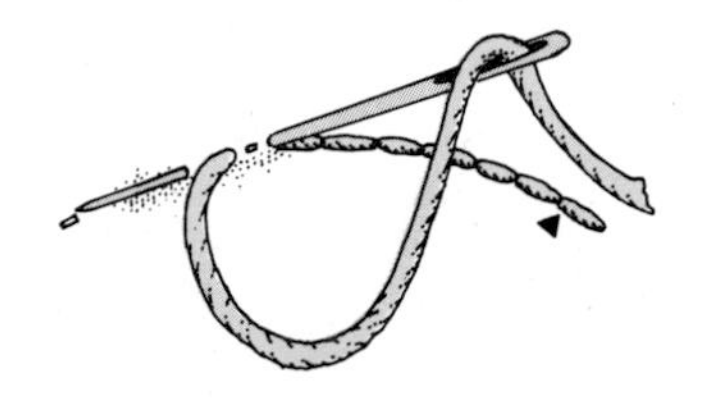

Split stitch

This is worked in the same way as stem stitch, but the thread is split by the needle as it emerges from the short back stitch.

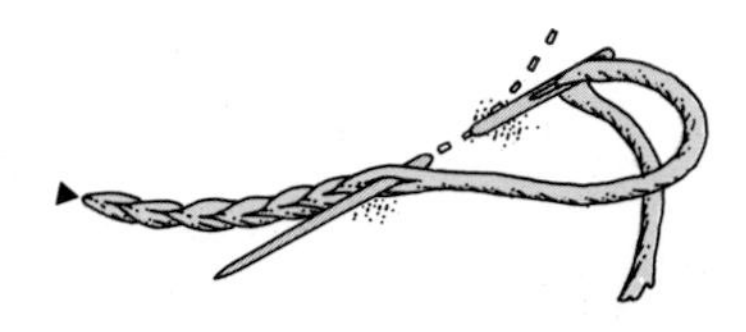

Satin stitch

This is a major embroidery stitch and, although it appears simple, it is difficult to get the stitches to lie evenly and close together to give a neat edge. It is used for outlining, filling, geometric patterns and shaded effects.

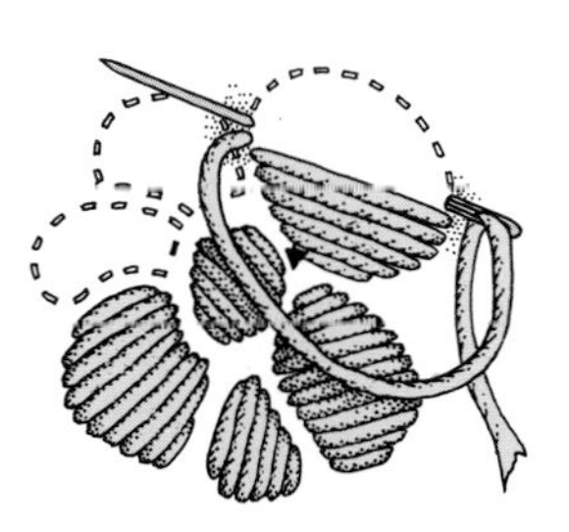

The stitch can be worked in varying lengths, but very long stitches can become loose and untidy.

Long and short stitch

This is also known as embroidery stitch, plumage stitch, shading stitch and brick stitch when used in filling patterns.

The first row is worked in long and short satin stitches. When used as a filling stitch the subsequent rows are worked in satin stitches of equal length.

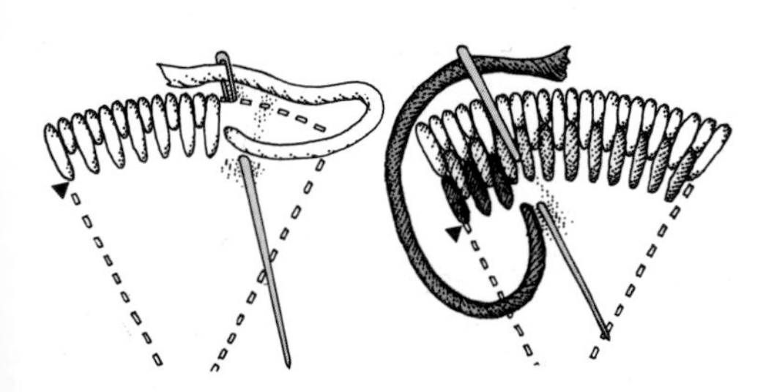

Encroaching satin stitch

This is used to produce soft tonal effects. The first row is worked as for satin stitch, but subsequent rows are worked so that the head of the new stitch is placed between the bases of the stitches above.

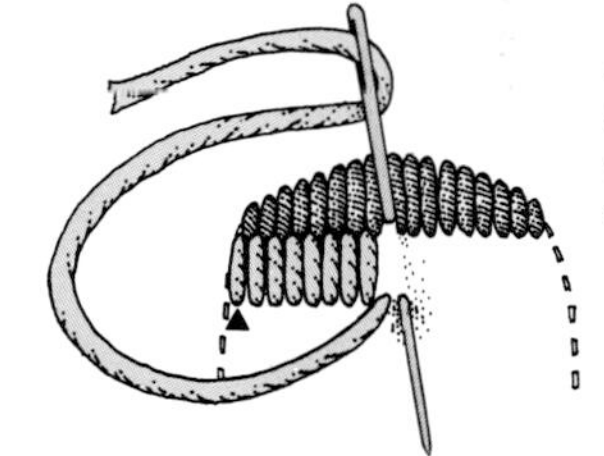

For really subtle effects, the tones can be changed in every row.

Fishbone stitch

This is worked with a small central stitch at the tip of the motif and then sloping stitches worked alternately on the right and left sides under the base of the previous stitches.

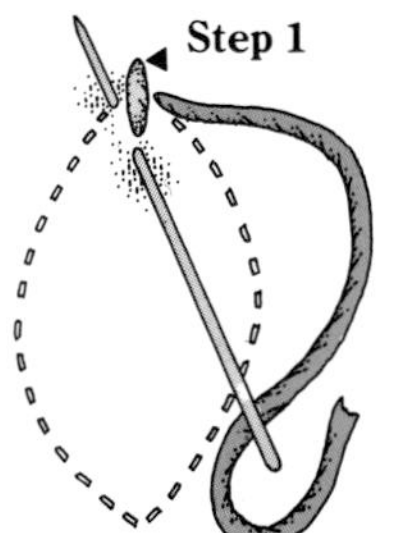

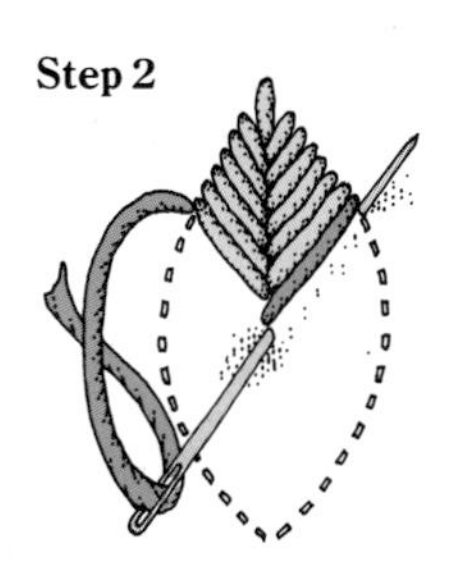

Darning stitch

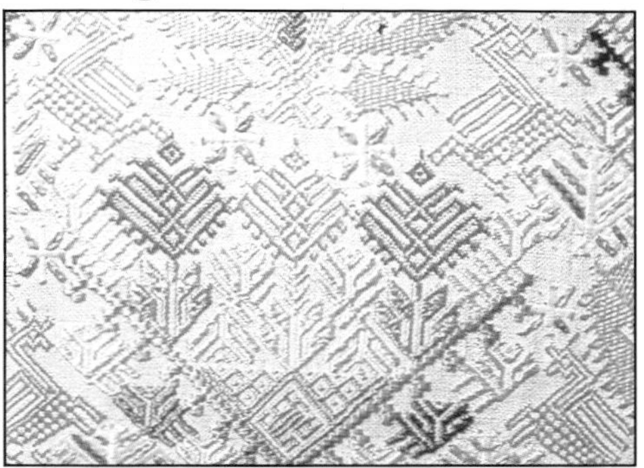

This is also known as tacking stitch. It is a long running stitch and can be used as a filling stitch by working lines of the stitches close together, or as a decorative stitch (known as damask stitch) to form geometric patterns by altering the length of the stitches.

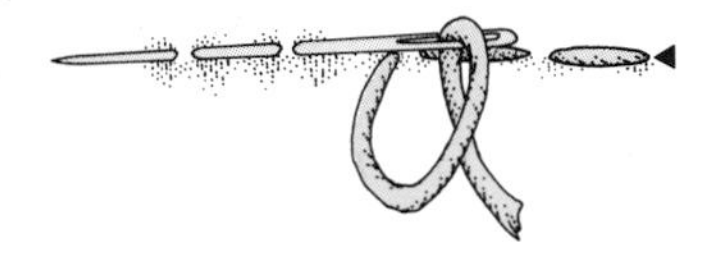

Double running stitch

This is also known as Holbein stitch and Romanian stitch. When used as a filling stitch, it is known as double darning stitch or pessante stitch. It is worked with stitches and spaces of equal length.

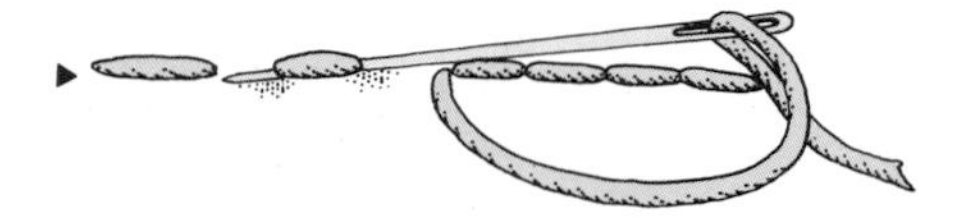

Arrowhead stitch

This is used as a light filling stitch and for lines of stitching. It is also worked in pairs for powdering effects. It can be worked either vertically or horizontally and is composed of two straight stitches at right angles to each other. Work subsequent rows touching the previous ones.

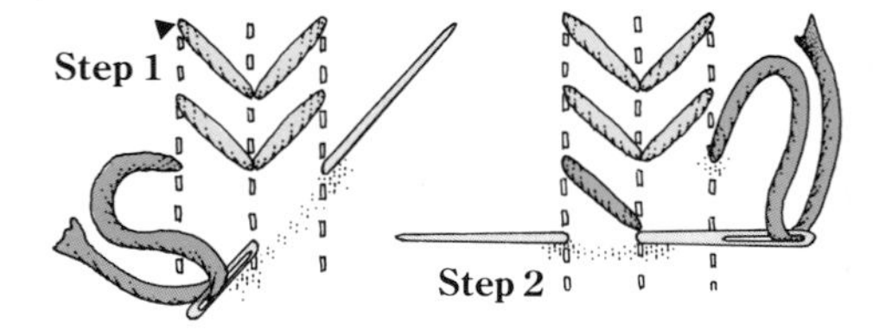

Fern stitch

This is used for feathery fillings and fern-like sprays and outlines.

Three equal length stitches are worked at angles to each other, followed by a similar group. All three stitches in each group are worked into the same base hole. If the outside stitches are worked closer together, the central stitch is shortened.

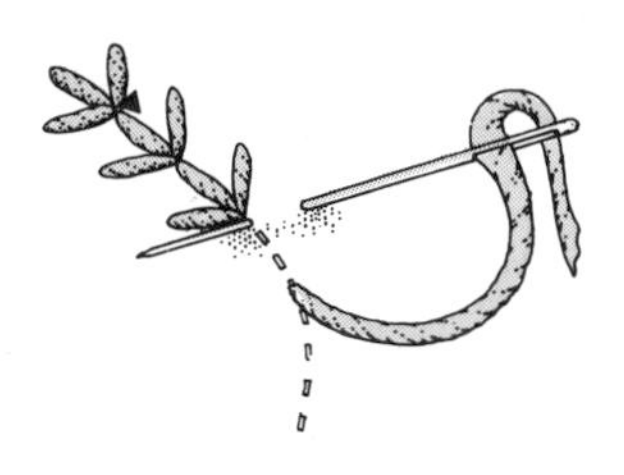

Crossed stitches

Crossed stitches are formed by two or more stitches crossing each other. The angle of crossing can vary from the simple right angles of cross stitch to the oblique angles of the herringbone and fishbone groups, all producing interesting textures.

Cross stitch

Also known as sample stitch this is the best known of all embroidery stitches and is used for outlines, fillings and borders. Unless light and shade effects are required the top stitches should always pass in the same direction.

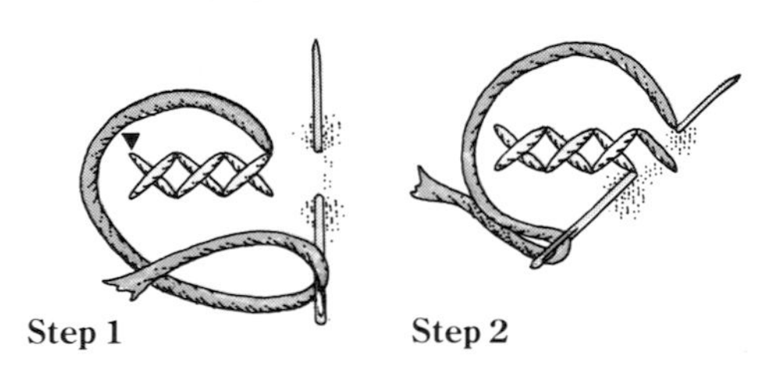

St George cross stitch

This stitch has the same uses as cross stitch and is worked by making horizontal stitches which are then covered by vertical stitches of the same length.

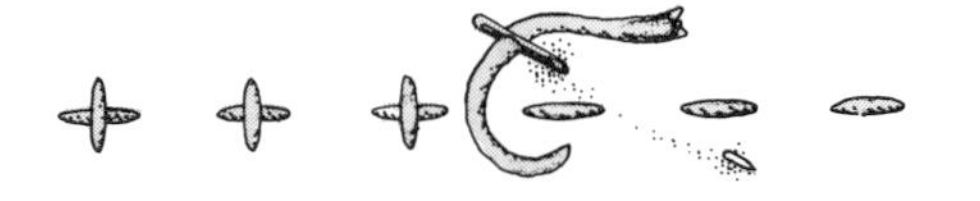

Long-armed cross stitch

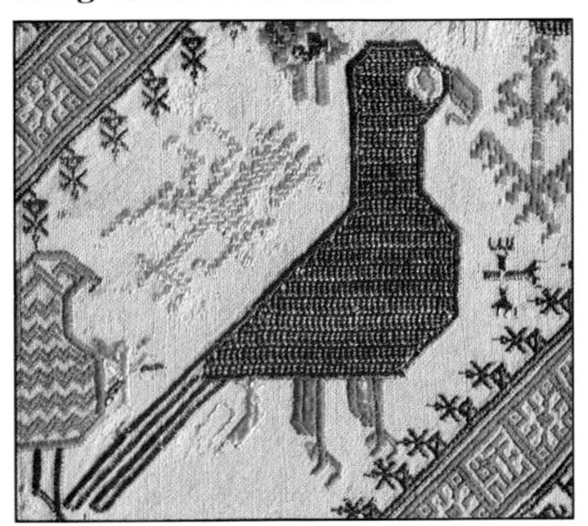

This is used for borders and fillings and is worked in long and short diagonal stitches whose subsequent crosses overlap.

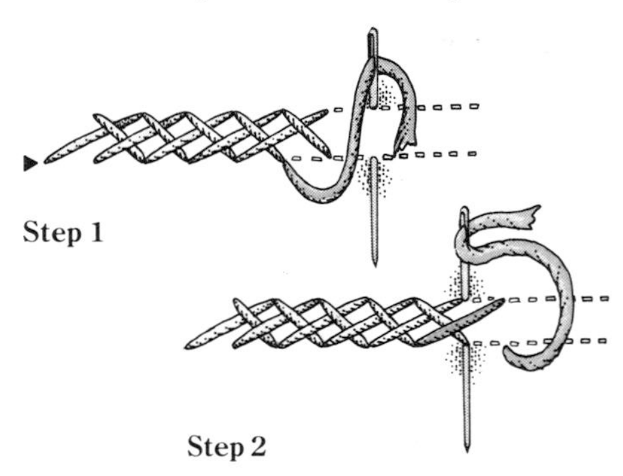

Herringbone stitch

This is also known as Russian cross stitch. It is used for edgings and fillings and is also the foundation for many other stitches. It is worked from left to right.

Star filling stitch

This stitch is used as a light filling stitch and is worked by making a St George cross which is covered by an equal sized cross stitch and topped with a tiny central cross.

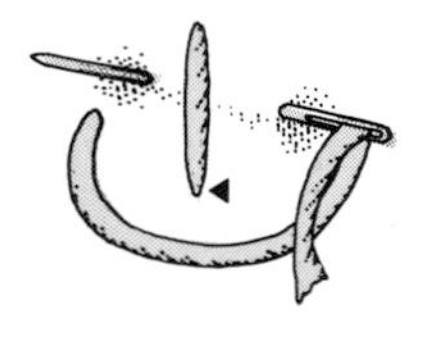

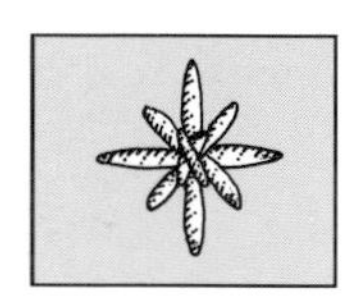

The tiny central cross is worked to a third the size of the base cross.

Ermine stitch

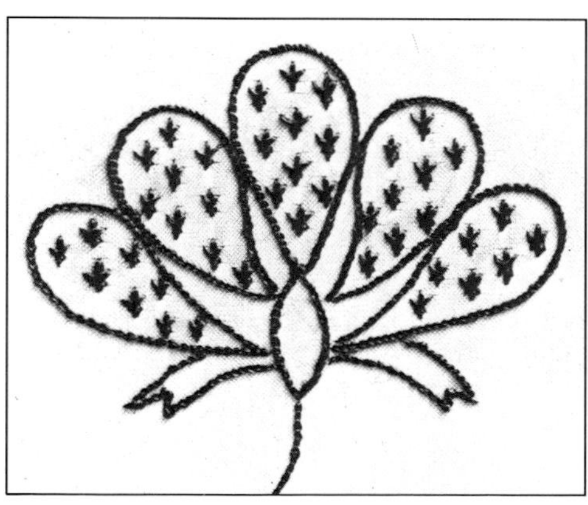

This stitch is used for fillings and borders and is worked by making a straight stitch which is then covered by an elongated cross stitch that is about one-third shorter.

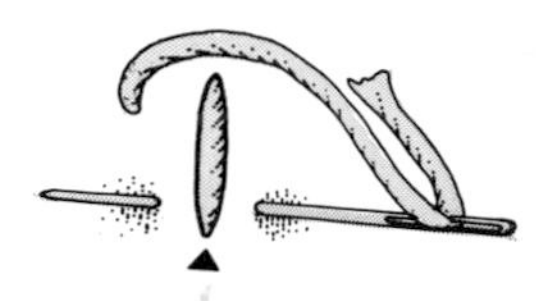

The elongated cross stitch is worked a fraction up from the base of the straight stitch.

Zigzag stitch

This stitch is used for edgings and fillings. It is worked in two journeys of alternate upright and diagonal stitches. On the return journey the upright stitches are made into the same holes as the previous journey and the diagonals cross each other.

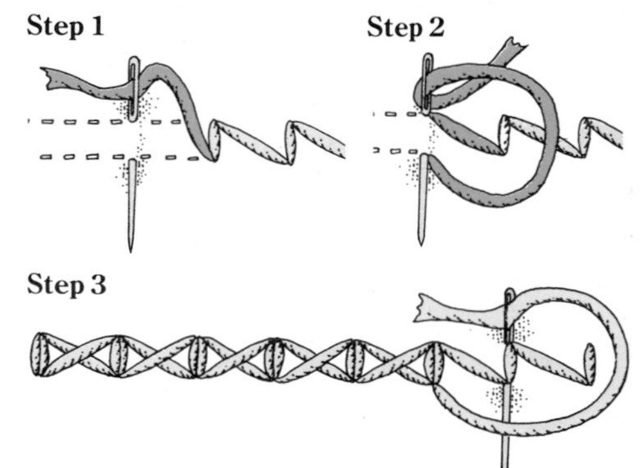

Leaf stitch

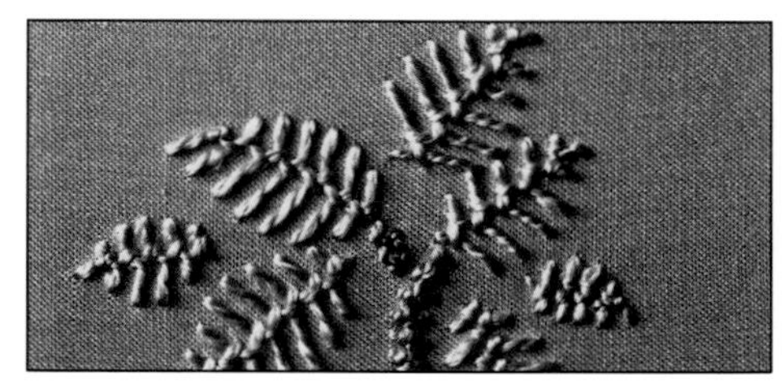

This is a light, open stitch ideal for filling leaves. It is worked upwards from side to side.

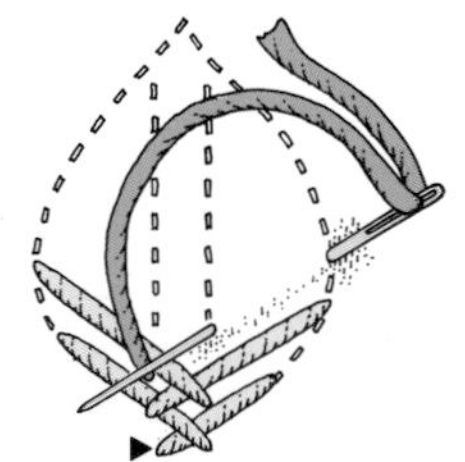

Step 1
The needle is brought out left of centre, is inserted at right margin and brought out a little to right of centre.

Step 2
The needle is inserted at left margin and brought out to left of centre below stitch just formed.

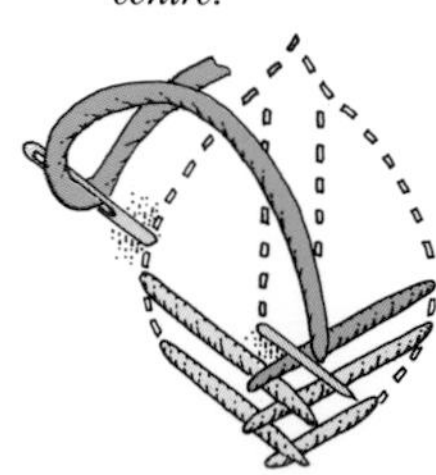

Raised fishbone stitch

This is also known as overlapping herringbone stitch. It is used for padded and raised effects and for filling such shapes as petals, leaves and lozenges.

It is worked by making a straight central stitch and then building up interlacing diagonal stitches worked from side to side. These should be placed as close together as possible to give a smooth surface.

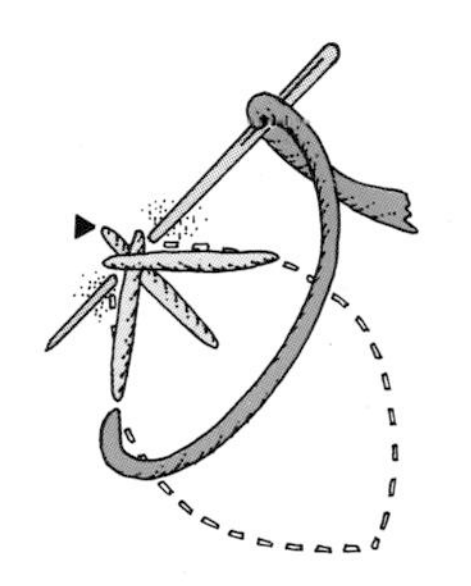

Step 1
A central stitch is made first, and then crossed with the diagonal stitches.

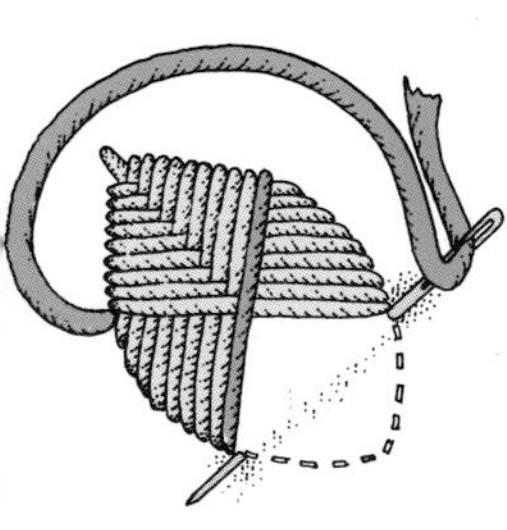

Step 2
Subsequent diagonal stitches are worked close together and cross over each other at the centre.

Flat stitch

This stitch is used in the same way as leaf stitch, but it is worked closer giving a denser effect. When worked in rows as a filling the outer edges interlock slightly, giving more substance.

It is made in a similar way to leaf stitch except that it is worked from the inner margin to the outer margin.

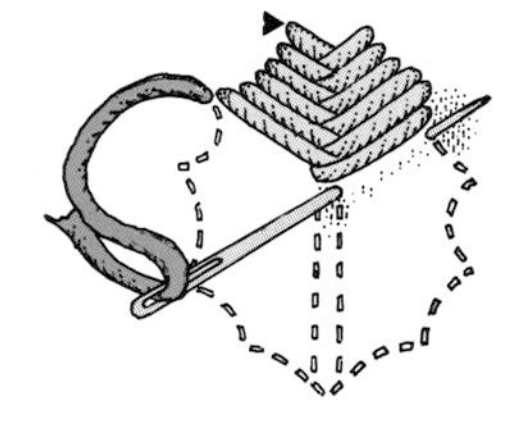

Step 1
The needle is brought out at left margin, inserted to right of centre and brought out at right margin.

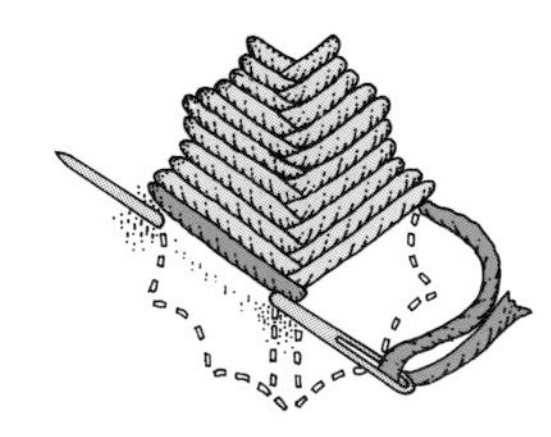

Step 2
The needle is inserted to left of centre and brought out at left margin.

Looped stitches

In looped stitches the thread is looped on the surface of the fabric and held in place with a stitch. Chain stitch and buttonhole stitch are the most well-known members of this group. Both are equally effective as line, outline and filling stitches.

Chain stitch

This is the fundamental stitch of this group and is used for fillings, edgings and outlines.

It is made with the working thread looped under the tip of the needle and held down with the left thumb, the needle picking up the same-sized piece of ground fabric for each stitch.

The needle is inserted into the same hole from which it has emerged to make the next stitch.

Detached chain stitch

This is also known as lazy daisy stitch. It is commonly used to make leaf and flower shapes, and is also a good filling stitch.

It is worked in the same way as chain stitch, except that each loop is fastened with a small tying stitch.

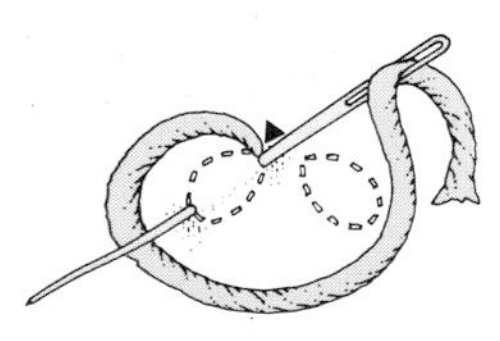

Step 1
The needle is brought out at arrow, inserted back into same hole and brought out with loop under needle.

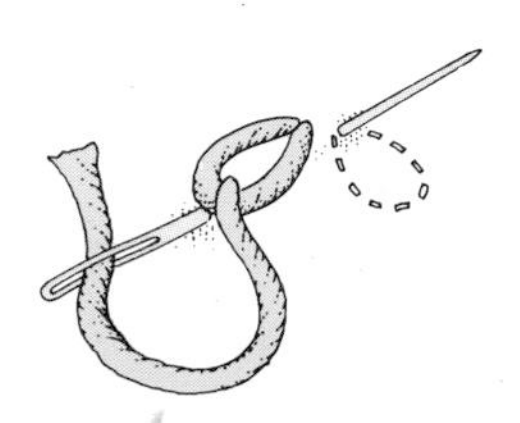

Step 2
The needle is taken over loop and inserted under it, making a small tying stitch.

Open chain stitch

This is also known as square chain stitch and ladder stitch. Used for bandings, this stitch can also be formed in varying widths to fill graduating motifs.

It is worked from top to bottom.

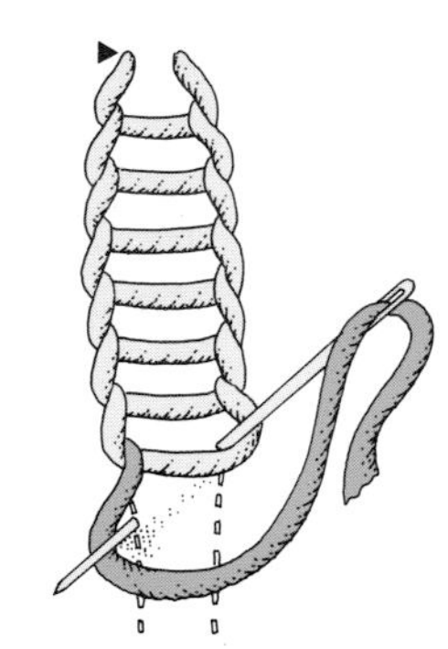

The needle is brought out at left margin, inserted at right margin and then brought out at left margin again with thread under needle.

Zigzag chain stitch

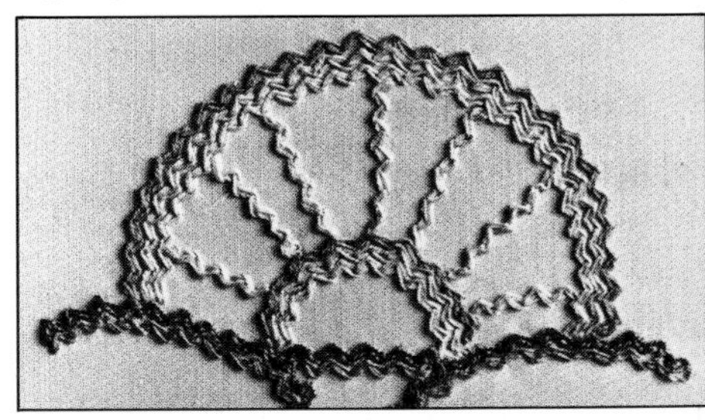

This is also known as Vandyke chain. It is used for borders, lines and outlines.

It is worked in the same way as chain stitch, except that each stitch is made at an angle to the previous one.

In order to keep the chain flat the needle pierces the previous loop whilst forming the next.

Buttonhole stitch

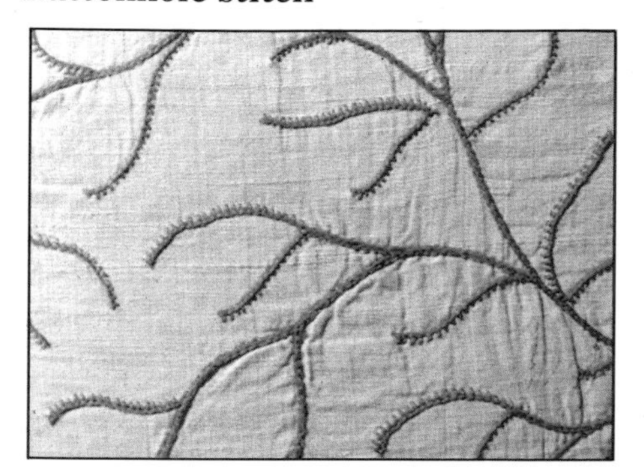

This is known as blanket stitch when the stitches are further apart. It is widely used for the practical purposes of edging hems and buttonholes and is also an important stitch for decorative embroidery. It is worked from left to right.

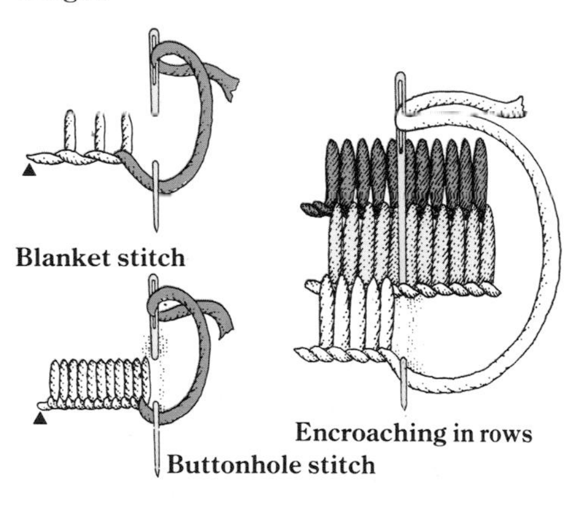

Up and down buttonhole stitch

This is a simple buttonhole variation and is worked by first pulling the needle through downwards and then inserting it upwards to make a second buttonhole stitch into the same hole. Often used for decorative edgings.

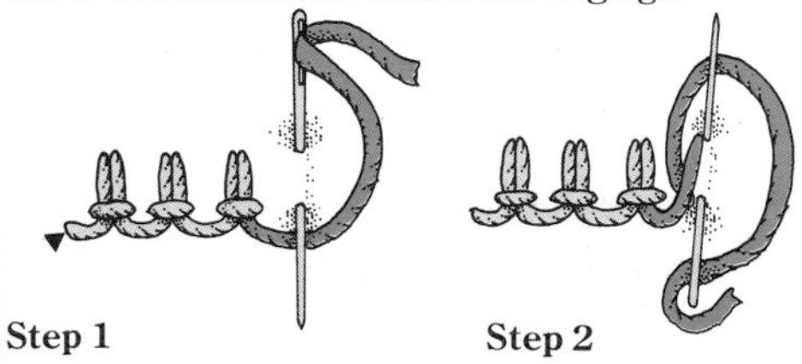

Feather stitch

This is also known as single coral stitch. It is a light, delicate filling stitch which is useful for feather effects. It can also be used for backgrounds and outlines. Feather stitch is often used for smocking.

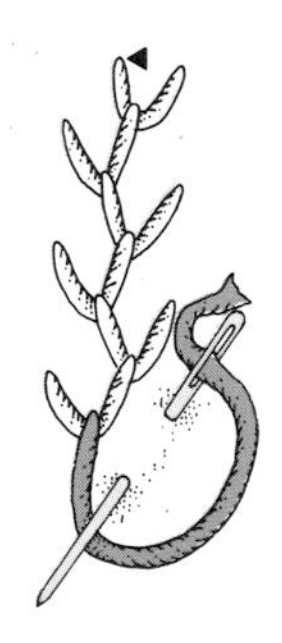

A loop stitch is made alternately to the left and the right.

Feathered chain stitch

This is a neat border stitch which is worked by making slanting chain stitches to the left and right alternately, and joining them with diagonal stitches.

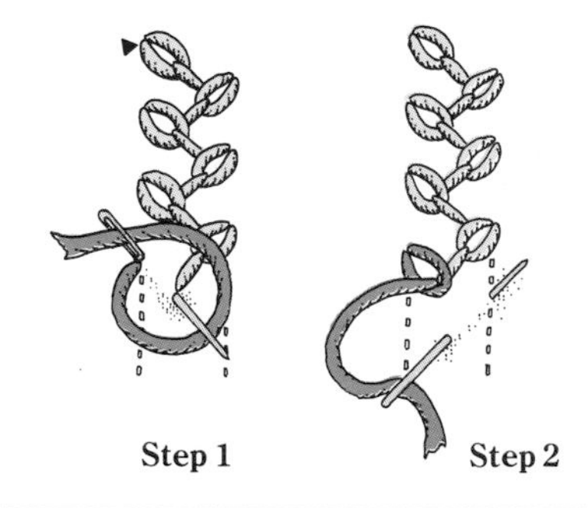

Fly stitch

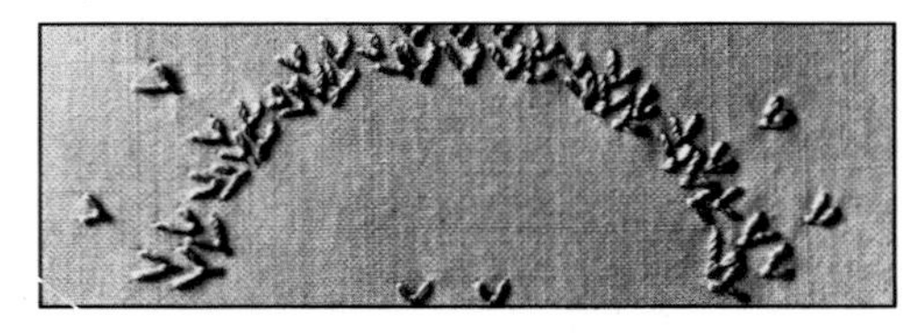

This is also known as open loop or Y stitch. It is an excellent stitch for babies' clothes and can be worked vertically or horizontally.

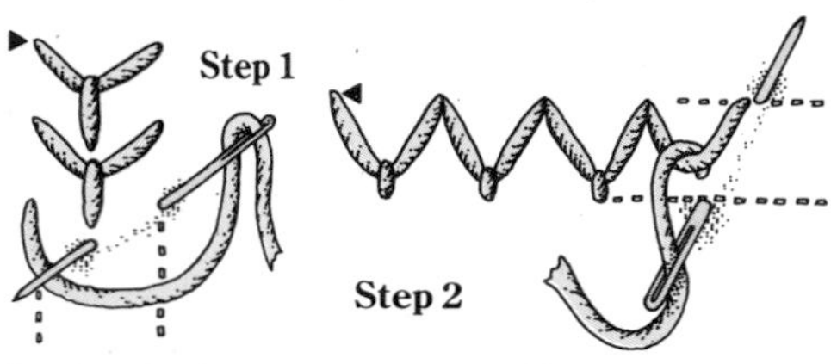

Vandyke stitch

This stitch is worked from top to bottom and is started at the left hand margin. After picking up a small amount of fabric at the centre, the needle is inserted to the right emerging just below the starting point. The thread is then passed behind the preceding stitches at the centre without piercing the material so producing a plait effect.

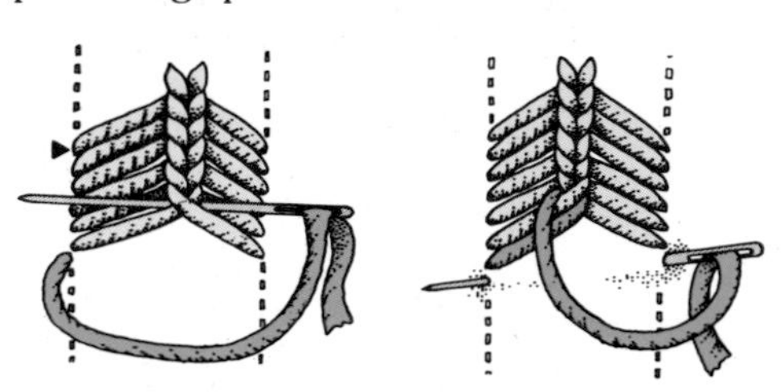

Wave stitch

This is also known as looped shading stitch. It is an effective filling stitch and is also excellent for shading and colour effects.

After beginning with a row of satin stitches the second and subsequent rows are looped into the base of the previous rows. The diagram below shows the stitches worked far apart for clarity, but they can be placed close together.

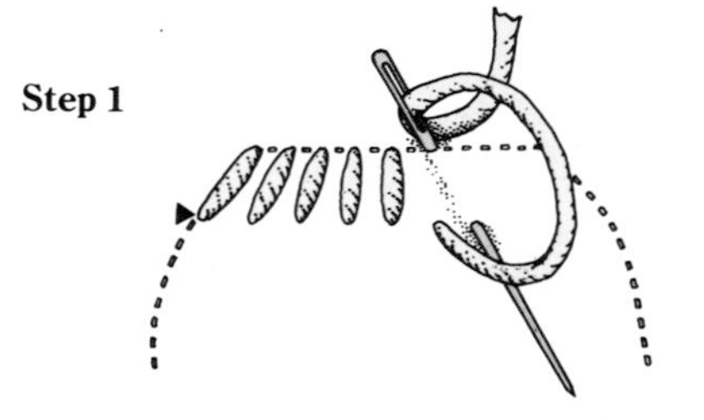

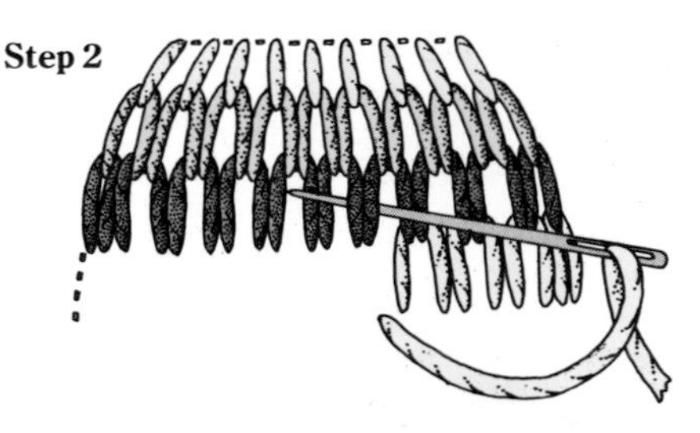

Knotted stitches

These are formed by knotting or twisting the working thread on the surface of the fabric and securing the twist or knot with a stitch. They can be used in single motifs or massed over larger areas. The principal stitches are French knot and coral stitch.

French knot

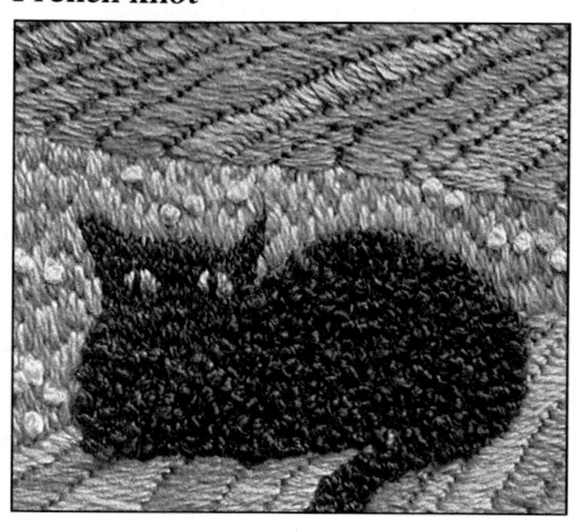

This is also known as French, dot and knotted stitch. It is commonly used for powdering and sprinkling effects or as a solid filling for motifs.

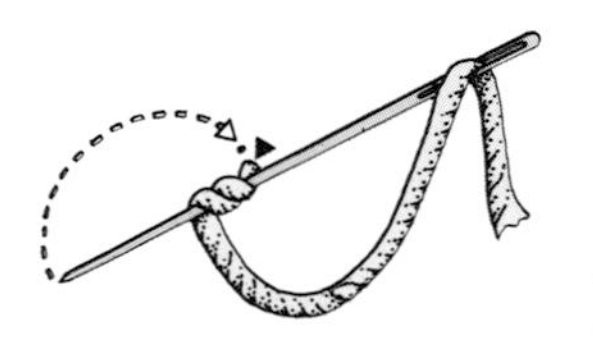

The needle is twisted several times around thread, turned and inserted into hole from which it emerged.

Coral stitch

This is also known as beaded stitch, German knot, snail trail and knotted stitch. It is used for irregular lines, outlines and borders. It can also be used for open fillings.

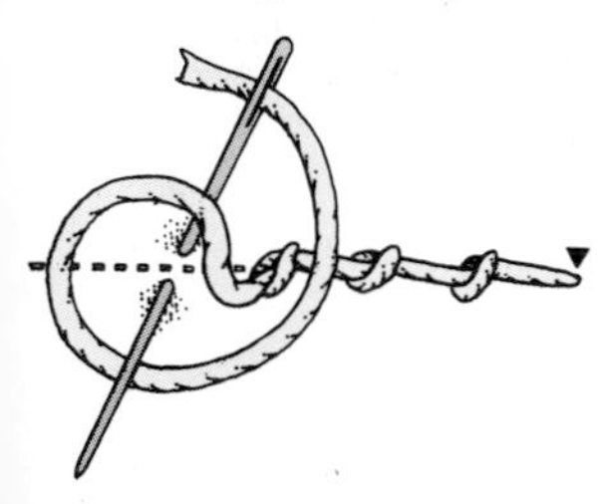

The needle is inserted under the working thread and is brought out over it.

Bullion knot stitch

This is also known as knot, caterpillar, worm, coil, and post stitch.

This large, long knot is used in much the same way as the French knot but gives greater emphasis. It is worked using a thick needle.

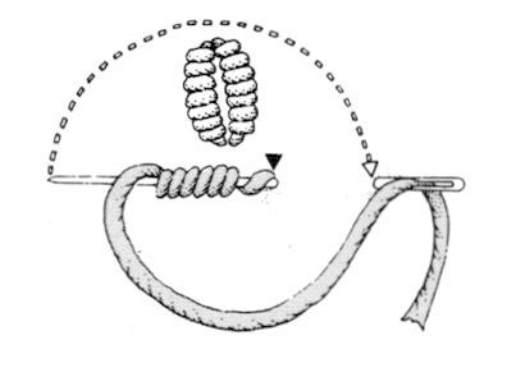

The needle is pulled through the twists, inverted and inserted at arrow.

Scroll stitch

This stitch is used where flowing lines are required and also for borders or banding.

After making the loop around to the right, the needle is inserted inside the loop and brought out (still inside the loop) over the working thread, making sure that the thread is not pulled too tightly.

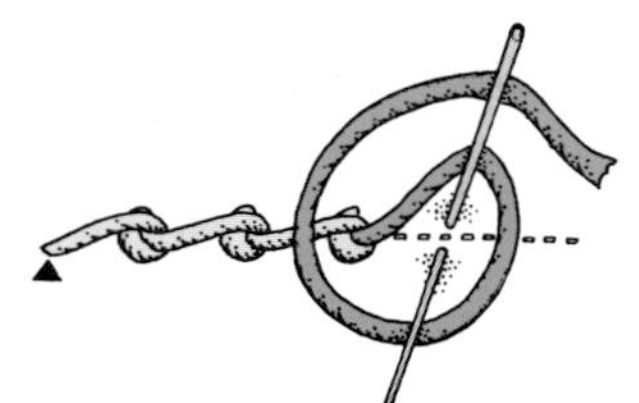

This stitch is worked form left to right, or right to left for a flatter effect.

Zigzag coral stitch

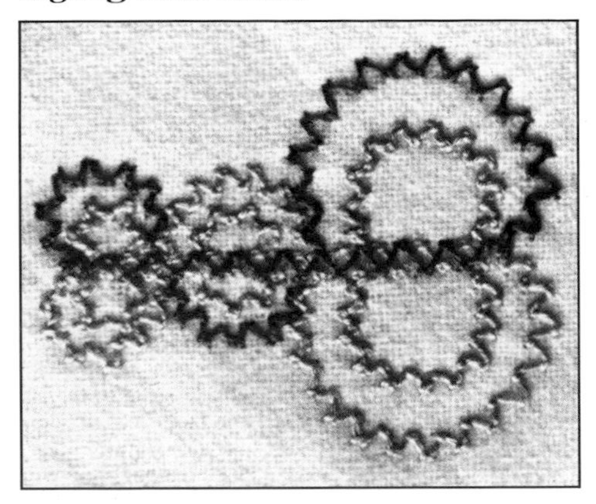

This stitch is used for decorative bands and wide borders.

It is worked in the same way as coral stitch, but making a zigzag trail.

The needle is inserted at the top and brought out in the centre of the loop. A similar stitch is then made at the bottom and so on.

Cable chain stitch

This is a fancy chain stitch with intervening links, used for outlines and edgings.

The first loop is made by a twist of the needle around the thread. The needle is then inserted downwards under this loop and is brought out ready to make the next stitch in the same way.

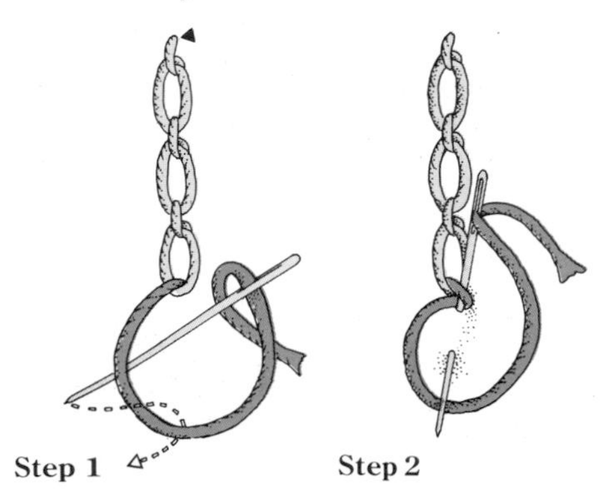

Four-legged knot stitch

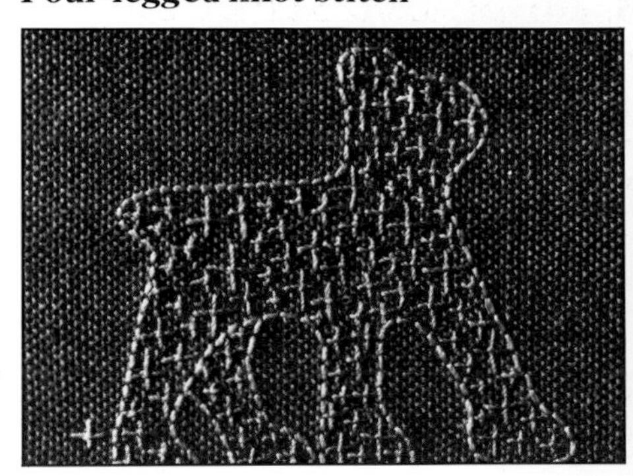

This stitch is used for fillings and borders.

Make a vertical stitch, then pass the needle under that stitch and over the working thread. Finish by working the last arm of the cross.

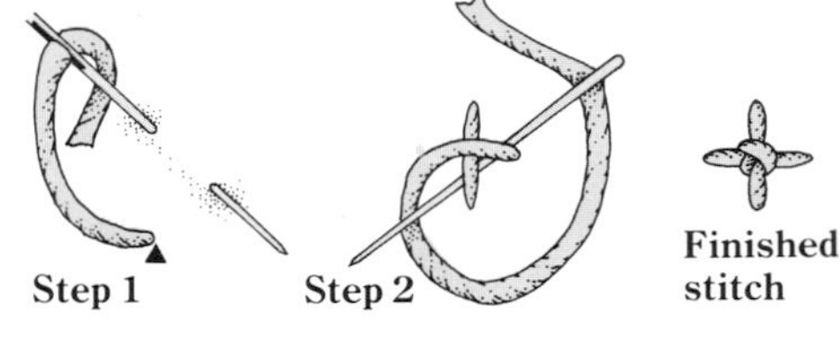

Rope stitch

This is used for spirals and curves, giving a rope-like effect.

Slanting stitches are placed close together with the needle coming through over the working thread to form small knots on the base line.

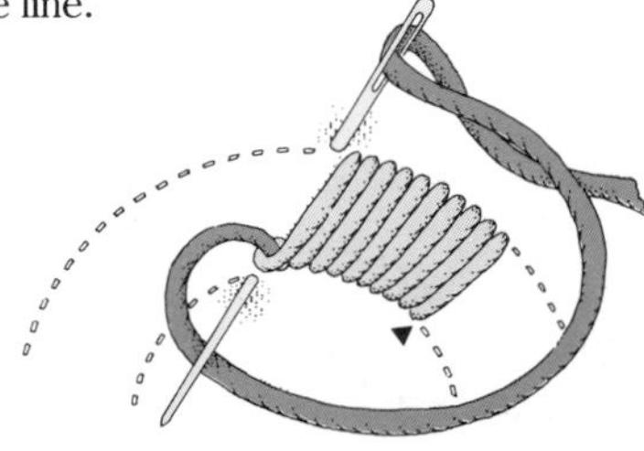

Composite stitches

These are combinations of stitches used together to create a raised, bolder and more decorative effect. They are made either by whipping one stitch over another or by threading one stitch through another. Certain stitches are worked with the second one merely going around the first without picking up any fabric.

Threaded back stitch

This stitch is used for decorative lines and edges in the same or a contrasting thread.

It is worked by making a foundation row of back stitches which are then threaded through in two separate journeys.

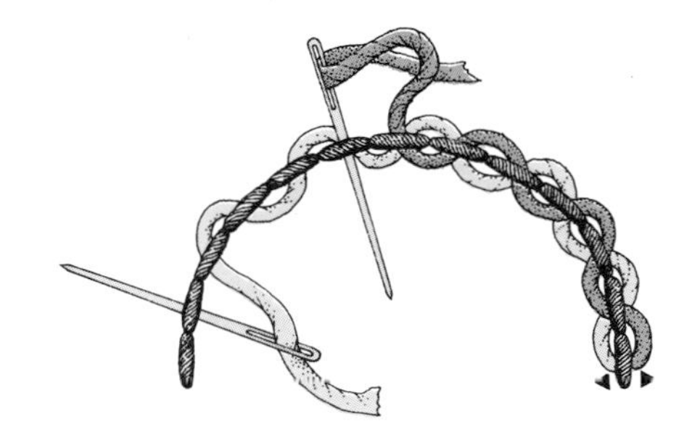

Cloud filling stitch

This is a quick and useful filling stitch. It is worked by making a foundation row of equal-sized and regularly placed vertical darning stitches (see page 44) and then threading through these to form a trellis.

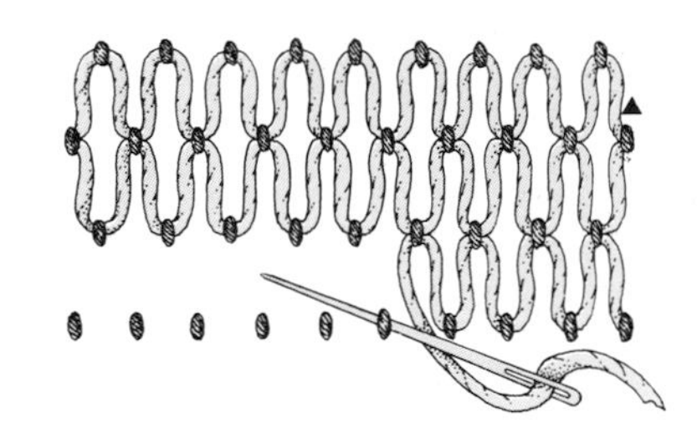

Overcast stitch

This stitch is particularly useful for making letters, monograms and figurative designs.

It is worked by making a foundation row of running stitches which are then whipped over with the overcast stitches.

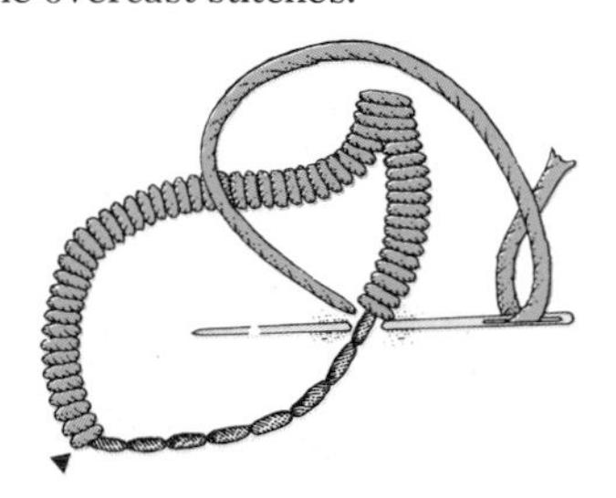

Whipped stem stitch

This stitch is used for bold lines and can be made more decorative using a contrasting thread for the whipping.

It is worked by making a foundation row of stem stitches which are covered with regularly placed whipping stitches.

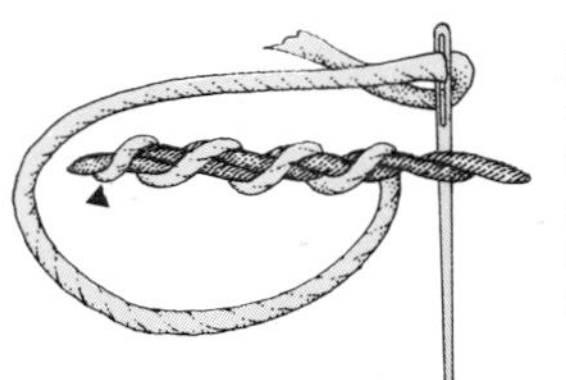

Whipping stitches are worked over and under the stem stitches without picking up any ground fabric.

2

NEEDLEPOINT

Including Florentine Work

Needlepoint materials

The basic materials for working needlepoint tapestry are canvas, threads and a blunt-pointed needle.

Canvas

There are three different types of canvas readily available: single canvas, double canvas and rug canvas. They are all available in different mesh gauges, measured by the number of threads to the inch. Straight stitches must always be worked on single canvas while double canvas is ideal for crossed stitches.

Threads

Any single thread, or any combination of threads in one needle, can be used for needlepoint. The most important thing to remember is that the thread you choose must cover the canvas ground completely.

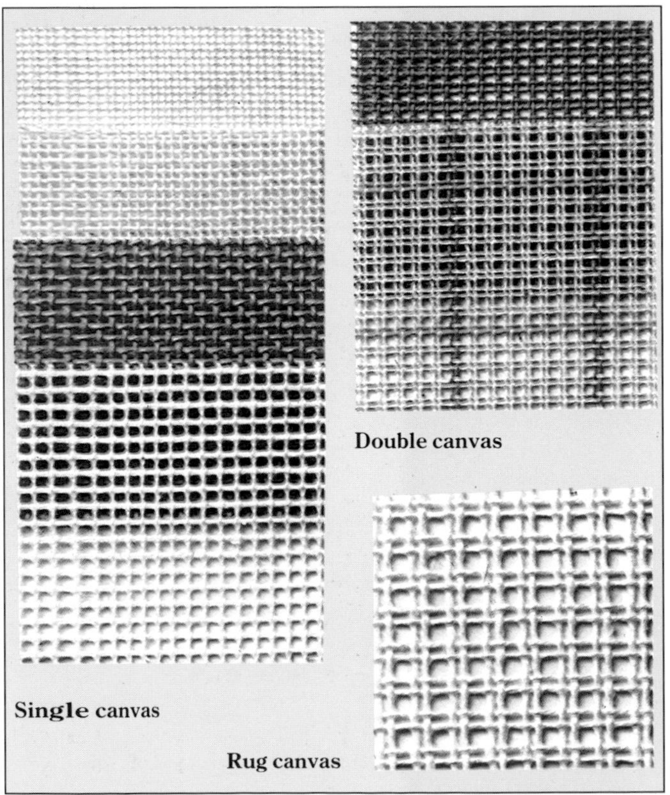

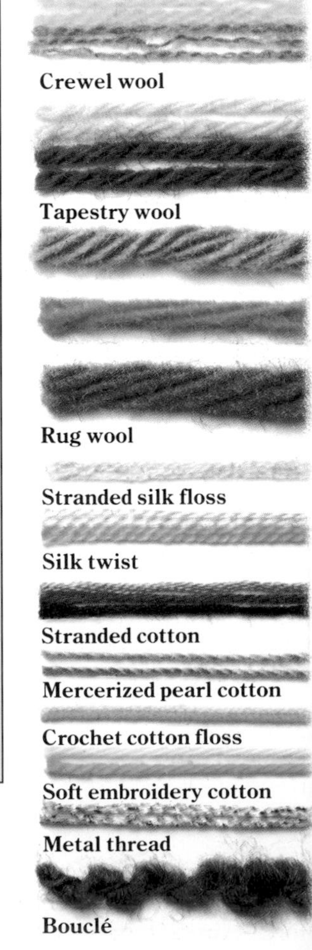

Right Crewel wool is used for very fine work or coarser work if several strands are threaded together. Tapestry wool is usually worked on medium gauge canvas, single or double. Rug wool is very thick and easily covers rug canvases. Other threads can be used alone or mixed and matched.

THREADING NEEDLES

There are two methods of threading a needle quickly and easily. Whichever method you use, do not wet or twist the end of the thread.

Thin thread method

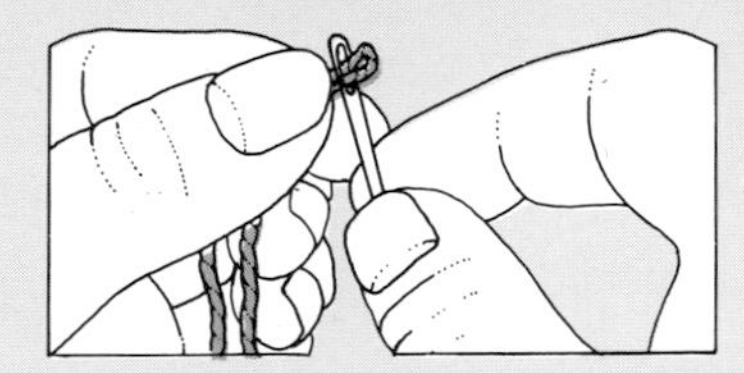

Loop the thread over the needle, pull it tight to form a fold and push the fold through the eye of the needle.

Thick thread method

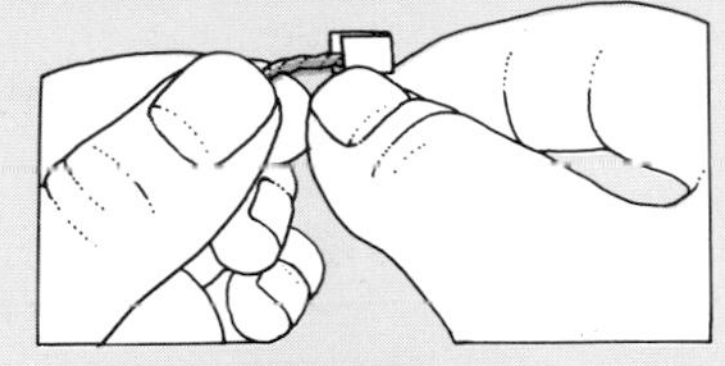

1 Cut and fold a piece of paper small enough to go through the eye of the needle. Place the end of the thread in the fold.

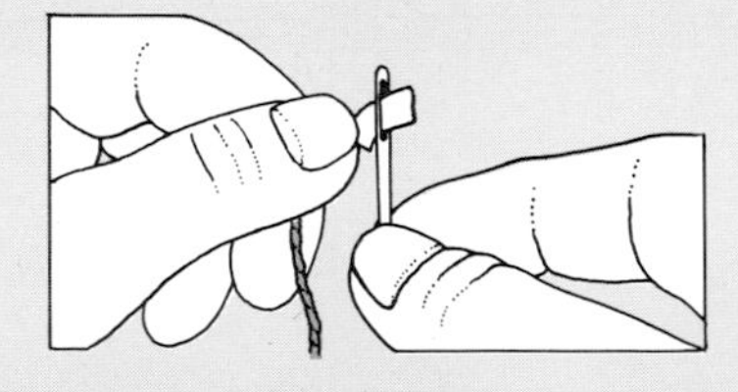

2 Pull the paper containing the thread through the eye of the needle.

10 double threads per inch (20 per 5 cm)

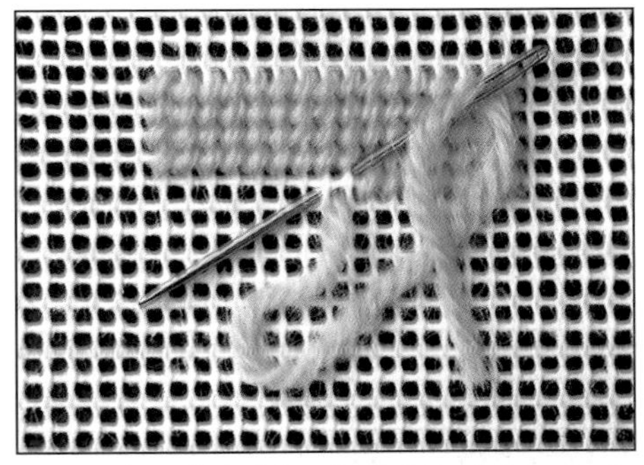

12 threads per inch (24 per 5 cm)

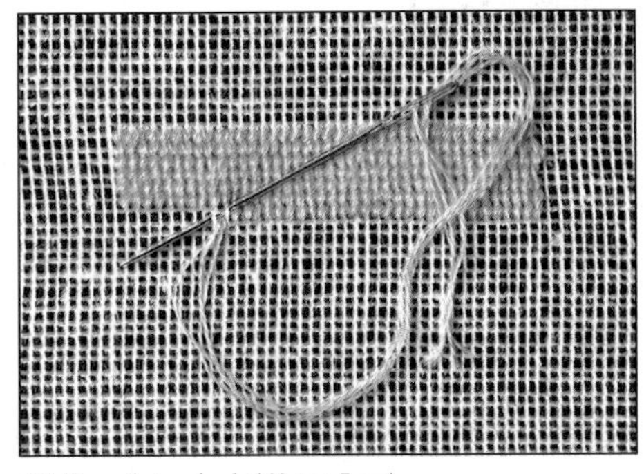

24 threads per inch (48 per 5 cm)

Needles

The right kind of needle to use in needlepoint work is a tapestry needle with a rounded point which protects both the working thread and the canvas from being split during the stitching. Choose a needle that is neither so large that it has to be forced through the canvas threads, nor so small that it frays the working threads which have to be forced through the eye.

Frames

The information given on frames for embroidery on page 12 is equally relevant for needlepoint although their use is not so essential here.

Needlepoint ideas

The items illustrated on these two pages have been chosen to represent some of the many articles that can be made using the needlepoint technique. It is also frequently used for stool covers, table tops (under glass), slippers, bags, pictures and carpets. If, like the sofa (below) or many of the articles shown here, your work will be subject to heavy wear, take care to use canvas and threads of a suitable quality and strength.

Sofa cushions worked in simple needlepoint designs

Simple figurative designs

It is possible to transfer fairly complex figurative designs into needlepoint by simplifying them into broad areas of similar colour and tone. The examples shown here have all been worked in tent stitch. The designs can either be made into pictures or used for such things as cushion covers or chair seats.

This series of twelve needlepoint panels shows landscapes at various times of the day and in different weathers.

Rainbow

Twilight

Early twentieth-century evening bag

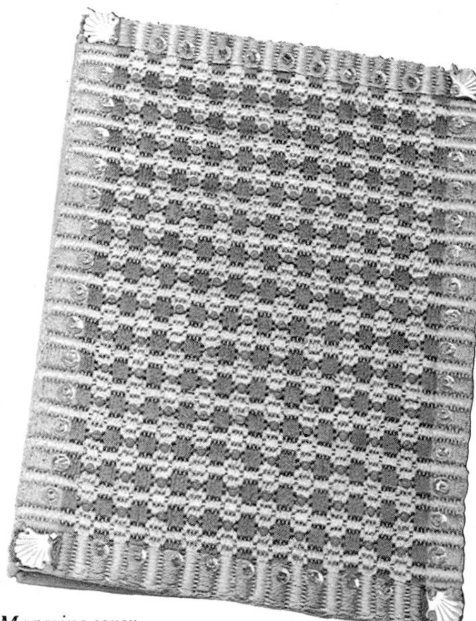

Magazine cover

Traditional cushion cover

Pin cushion

Purse

Designs on canvas

Bought patterns

When starting to work needlepoint tapestry it is often best to buy a ready-made design in order to become familiar with the needlepoint techniques. Canvases can be bought with the designs already painted on them, blank with accompanying charts or trammed. With trammed canvas the design is worked in coloured horizontal threads, over which the needlepoint is worked in corresponding colours.

Creating designs

By creating an original design you have far greater control over the colours you use and can therefore fit them in with a colour scheme in a room. Make sure the threads are suitable for the canvas mesh.

Making charts

Abstract designs can be charted on graph paper with each square representing a square of the canvas mesh.

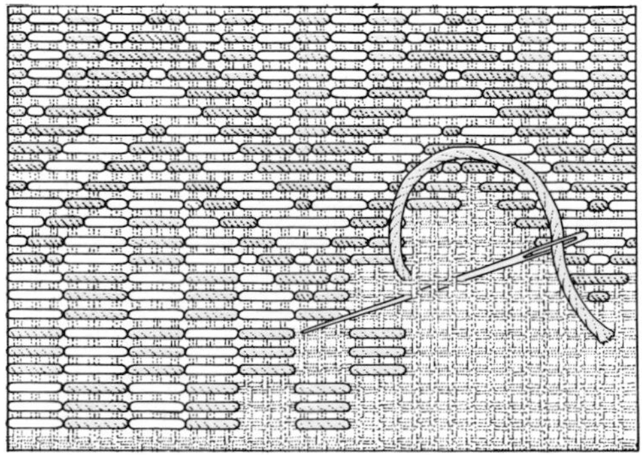

Making trammed designs

Tramming stitches are horizontal stitches of various lengths worked between the horizontal double threads to indicate the design. Begin by covering your design with tramming stitches in the relevant colours.

Stitching direct

A simple design can be either stitched directly onto the canvas or marked on using oil paints thinned with turpentine.

Using a light-box

If you want to use an existing picture as a pattern, the easiest method of transferring it is to use a light-box, as described on page 17.

Using carbon paper

This method only works successfully on a smooth, fine-gauge canvas. Trace the original drawing, place a sheet of dressmaker's carbon between it and the canvas and retrace the outline.

Blocking and setting

Blocking is the term given to smoothing the finished needlepoint or stretching it into shape. It is essential to take care over this since the final look of the work will depend on it being the correct shape and having an even finish. If a cardboard template is cut out using the original pattern or design, then the shape of the work can be checked against the template as it is stretched. Needlepoint is blocked face downwards unless it has been worked in looped stitches, in which case it is blocked face upwards to prevent the stitches from being squashed.

If the blocking is done correctly the needlepoint should not need ironing. However, should it be necessary, use a cool iron pressed lightly down on the work ensuring that the stitches are not flattened during the process.

Preparing the work

The first thing to do is to make sure that there are no stitches missing from the finished needlepoint. This is done by holding the work up to the light. If daylight shows through, there is a missing stitch and it should be inserted at this stage. Now block the work following the step-by-step instructions on the right.

Setting

After blocking, the needlepoint is given its permanent shape by setting. To do this, lightly sponge the back of the embroidery with water and leave it to dry at room temperature away from strong sunlight (the water releases the gum coating on the canvas threads and re-sets as the needlepoint dries). Where the canvas has been badly distorted, it may require repeated settings, and perhaps a final coating of a mild solution of starch. The drying process can take up to a week and it is important not to remove the work from the board until it is bone dry or you may find that it will become distorted again.

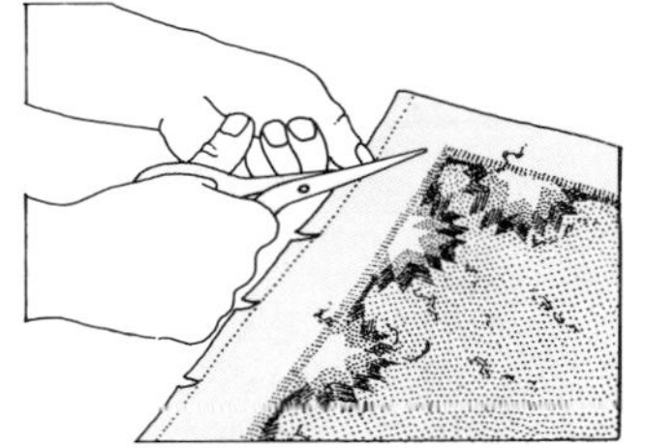

1 Place the needlepoint face downwards on a soft board which has been covered with polythene. If the canvas edge has a selvedge, cut a few nicks in it so it will stretch evenly.

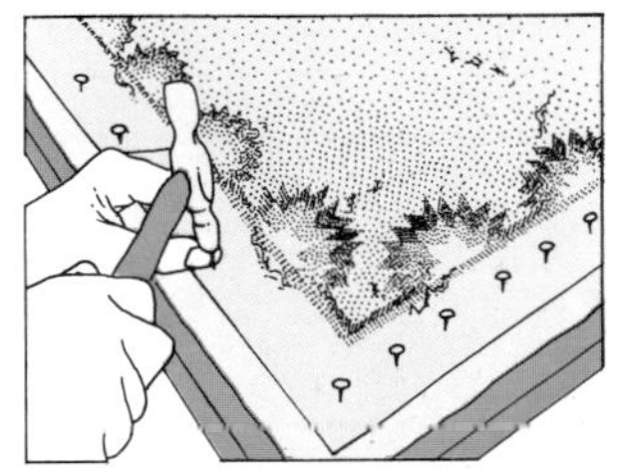

3 Ease work into the correct shape and insert more tacks lightly at 1 in. (2.5 cm) intervals around the edges, working from the centre towards the corners .

2 Hammer a single tack lightly into the board at the top in the centre of the unworked area of canvas. Stretch the work gently, ensure that all the canvas threads are at right angles to each other, and tack at the centre bottom. Place 2 more tacks at the centre of the other 2 sides so that the needlepoint is firmly stretched.

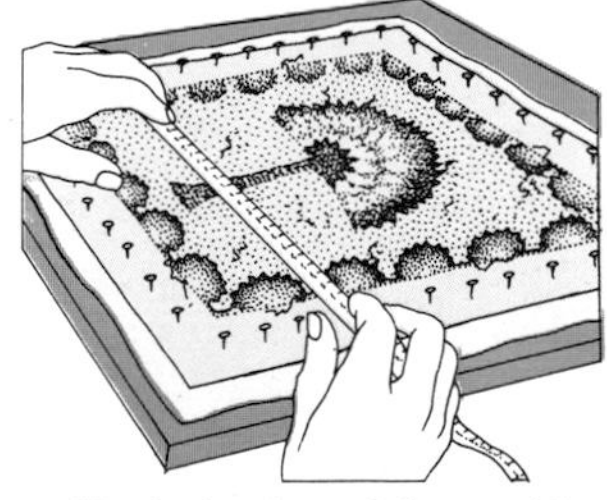

4 Work slowly and thoroughly, either measuring the needlepoint or checking its shape with the template, and adjusting the position of the tacks where necessary. Sponge lightly with cold water over areas which need a lot of stretching. When the correct shape is achieved, hammer in the tacks securely.

Needlepoint samplers

The five samplers illustrated here have been worked to show the different categories into which needlepoint stitches fall: crossed, diagonal, straight, looped and star. They have all been worked in stranded silk yarns on single canvas. Instructions for needlepoint stitches can be found in the glossary on pages 76-87.

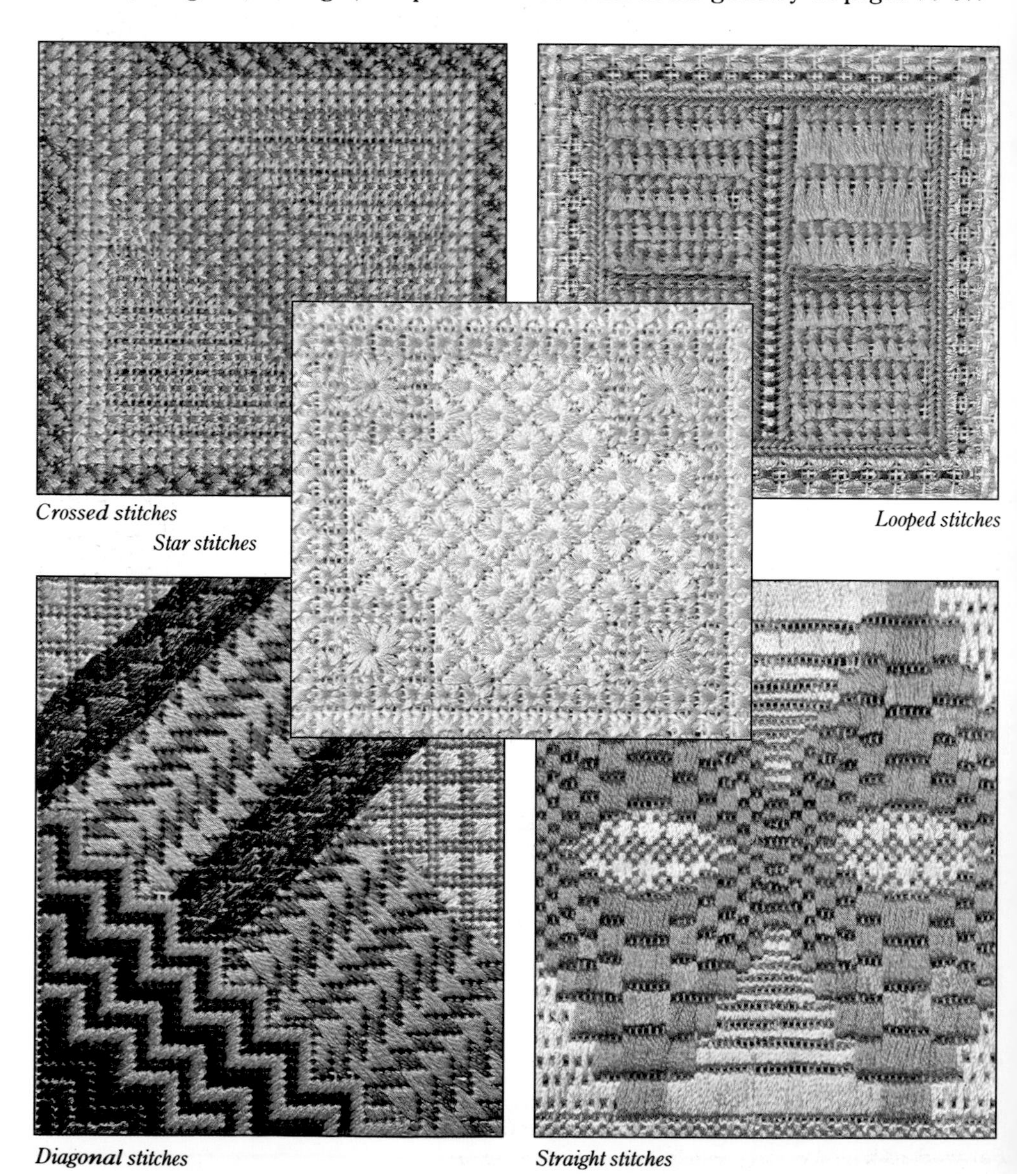

Crossed stitches

Star stitches

Looped stitches

Diagonal stitches

Straight stitches

Patchwork stitch sampler using stranded cottons on single canvas

Florentine work

This is also known as Bargello work and fiamma or flame stitch. A very popular type of needlepoint, it forms irregular patterns and is always worked in many different colours. The straight stitches are placed in graduating zigzags and once the first line is worked the following lines of stitches are used to fill in the canvas above and below it, following its contours.

A single-thread canvas should be used for best results and worked in wools or silks thick enough to cover the canvas. Though the method of working the stitches is always the same, the stitch itself can be made longer or shorter, but it is always best to use the same size throughout a pattern, so that each row can be worked in the same way.

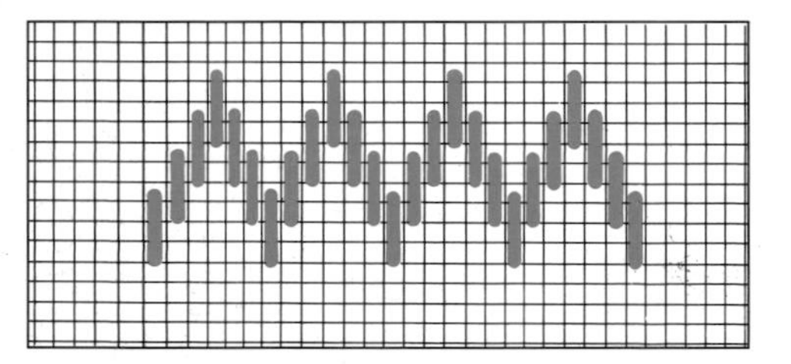

Average stitch size
Up over 4 horizontal canvas threads and back down under 2

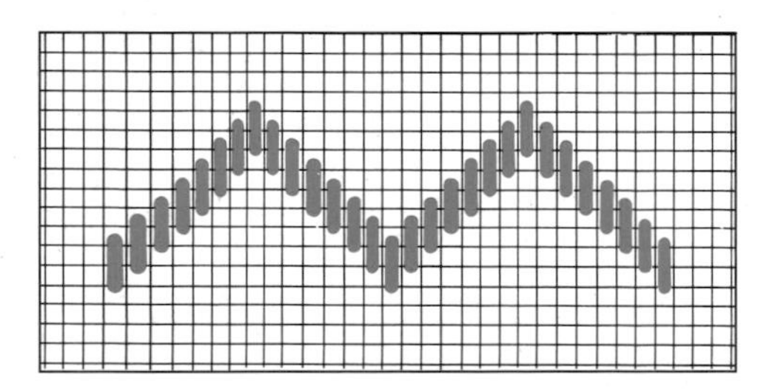

Shortest stitch size
Up over 3 horizontal canvas threads and back down under 2

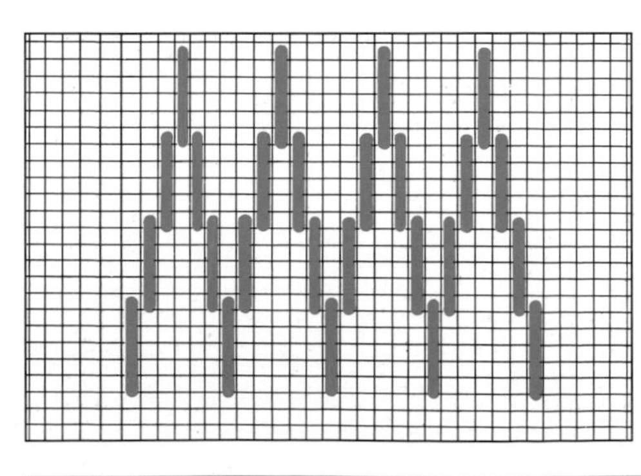

Longest stitch size
Up over 6 horizontal canvas threads and back down under 1

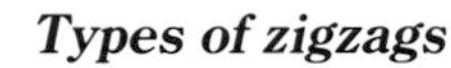

Types of zigzags

Stepped zigzags are made by working several stitches along the same horizontal threads.

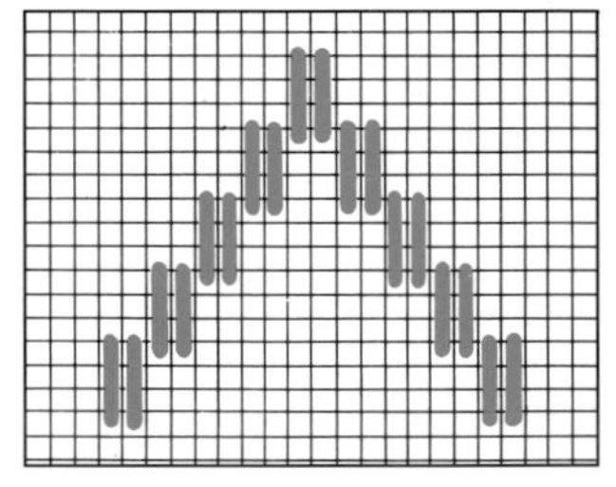

Pinnacle formation

The illustration above shows a pinnacle made in two stitch steps, but sharper effects are produced by using a longer stitch throughout, finishing the pinnacle with a single stitch at the peak (below).

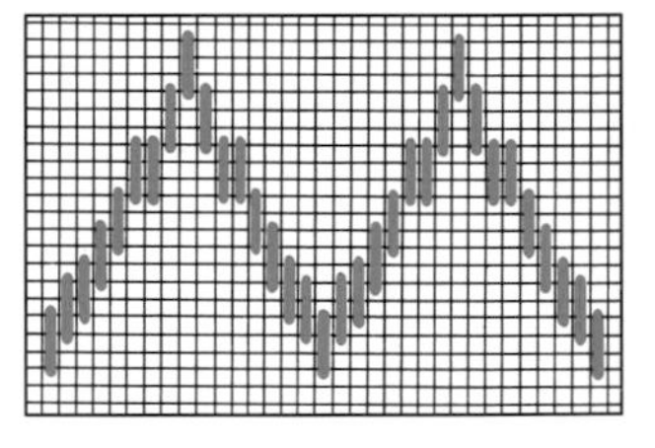

Curved formation

Pinnacles can be converted into curves by doubling and tripling the number of stitches at the peak. Curves can also be worked in step formation as shown below.

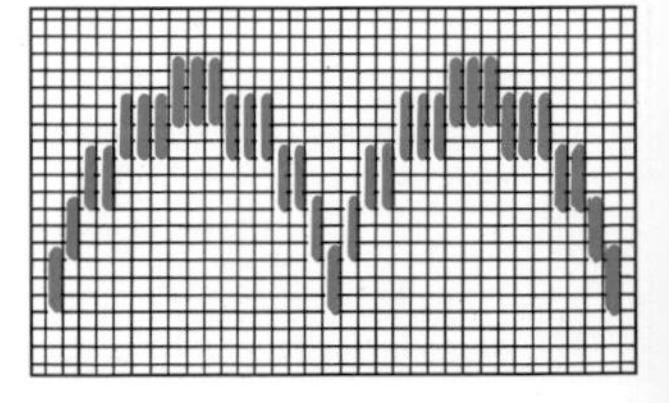

Combinations of patterns

Part of the pleasure of Florentine work comes from devising patterns using combinations of pinnacles and curves.

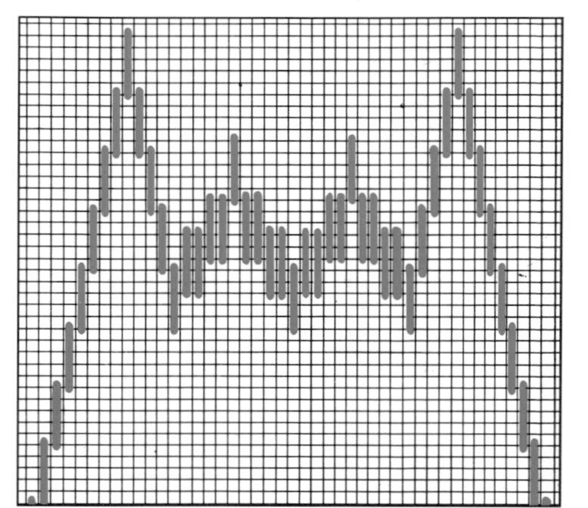

Irregular pinnacles

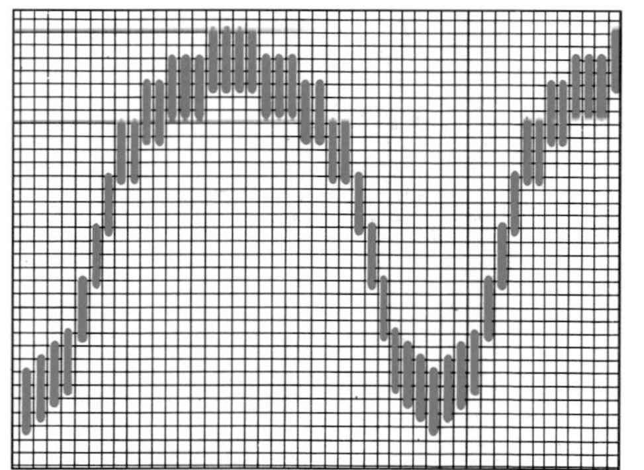

Curves and wells

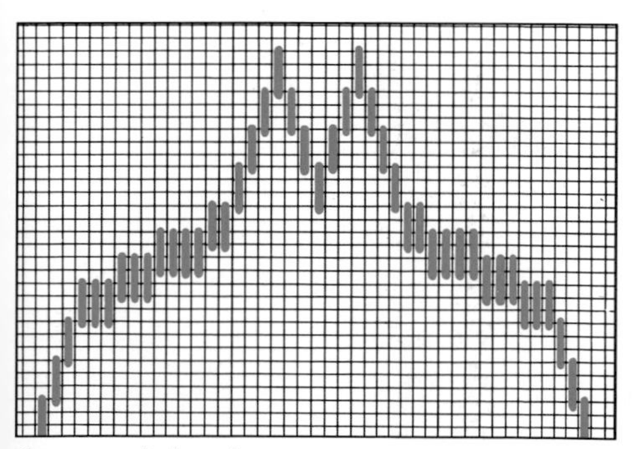

Curves and pinnacles

Making Florentine patterns

The first zigzag or skeleton line can be worked in different directions to give a variety of effects.

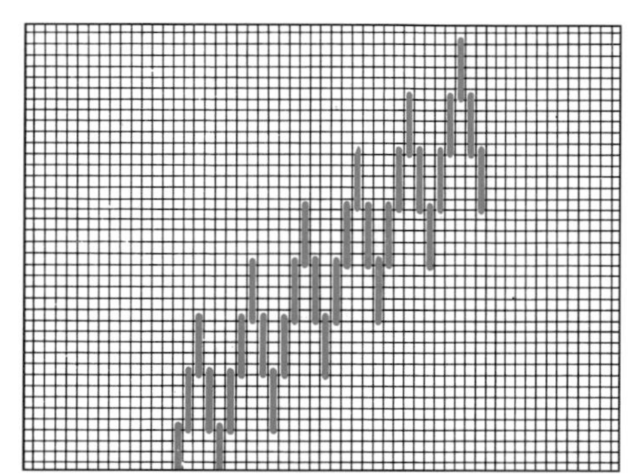

Working diagonally across the canvas

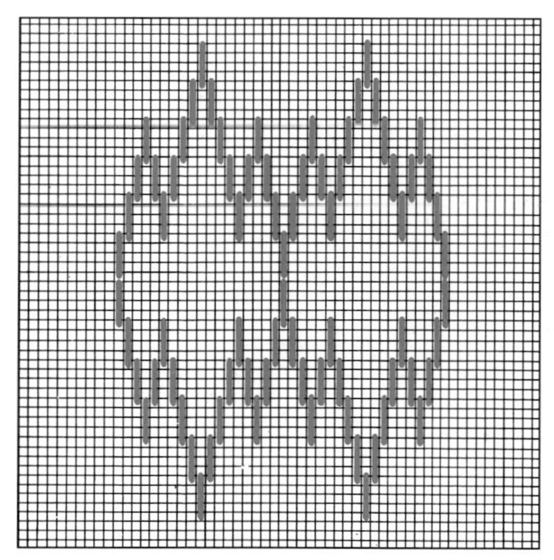

Working pinnacles in mirror image

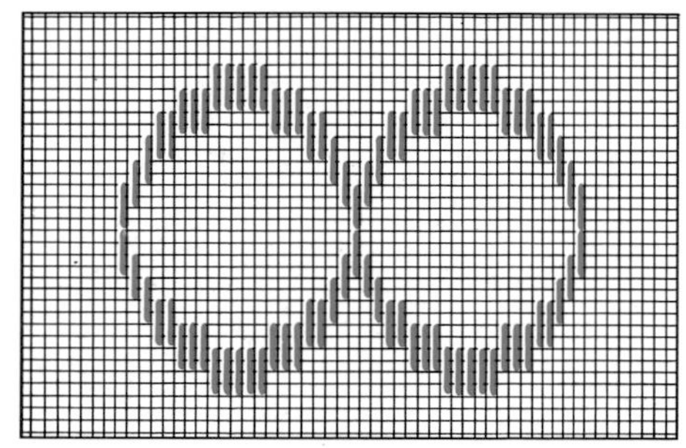

Working curves in mirror image

Florentine patterns

The patterns here (charts on pages 68-69) can be worked in the colours shown or in new colourways as long as the same number of colours is used. The choice of colour is yours but remember that the line of the zigzag looks more marked if it is started with the darkest colour and then graduated to lighter shades.

Four-way Florentine

Undulating pinnacles

Gothic pinnacles

Mirror-image pinnacles

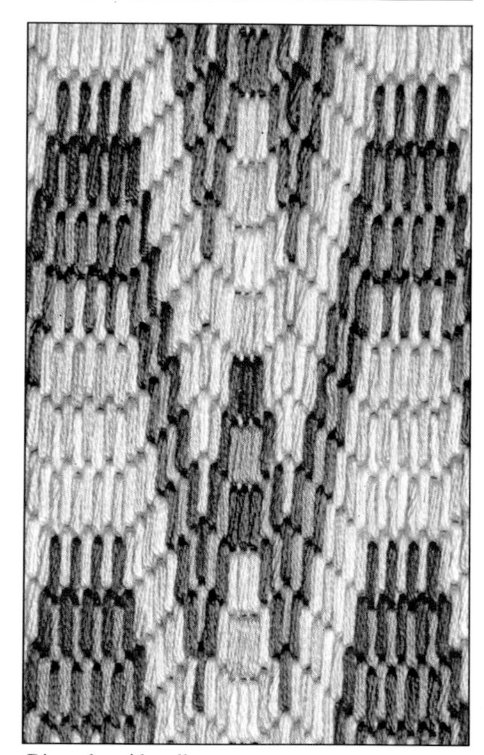

Pinnacles with wells

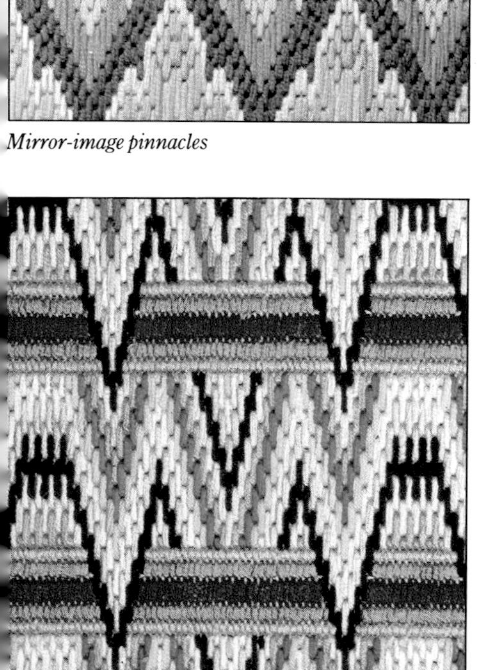

Pinnacles with stripes

Diagonal pinnacles

Florentine pattern charts

These charts are for the patterns on pages 66-67. The graph paper represents the canvas threads and the stitches are marked accordingly.

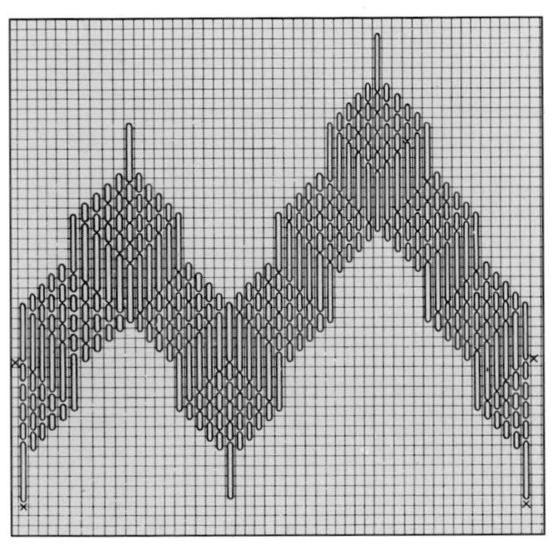

Gothic pinnacles worked over 6 and 2 threads using 8 colours

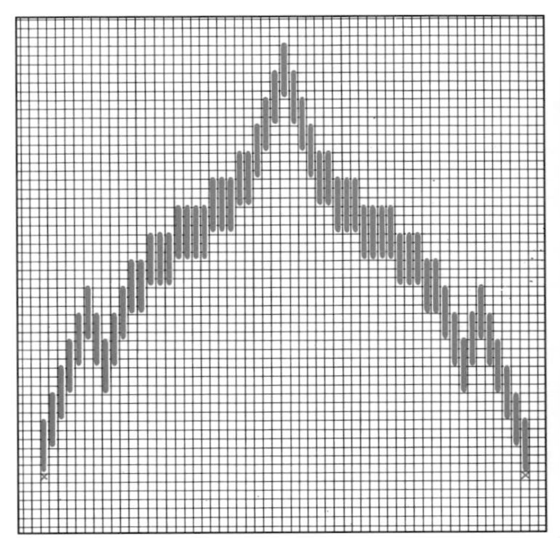

Undulating pinnacles worked over 6 threads in steps of 3 threads using 8 colours

WORKING IN FOUR DIRECTIONS

In four-way Florentine the pattern is worked in four directions either from or towards the centre of the canvas. In both cases the canvas is divided into four equal triangles. The sections can be worked separately or in rounds, the direction of the stitches changing when the diagonal line is reached.

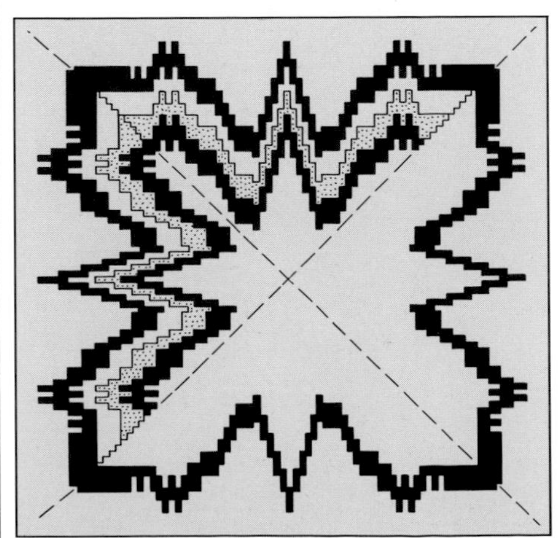

When working towards the centre, first work the skeleton pattern along all four sides.

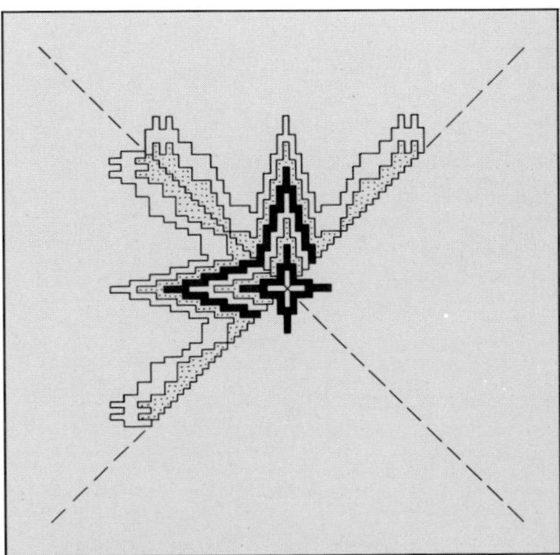

When working from the centre, start with 4 stitches made into the centre hole.

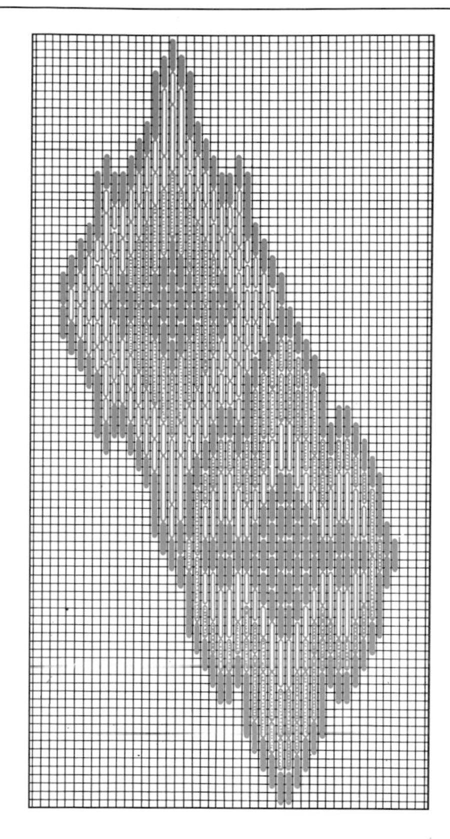

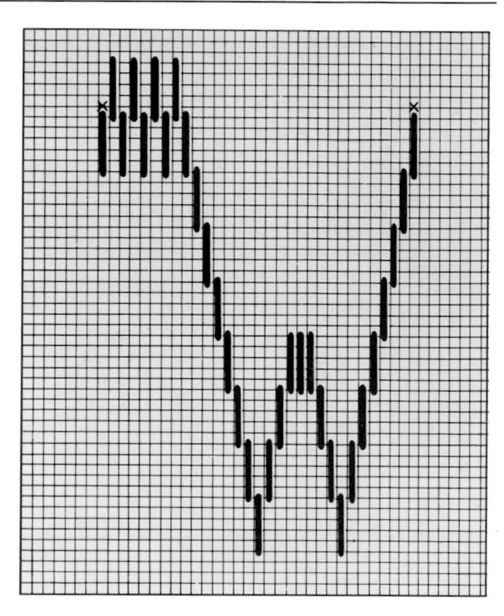

Above *Pinnacles and wells worked over 6 threads in steps of 5 threads using 7 colours*

Left *Mirror-image pinnacles worked over 3, 4, 6 and 8 threads using 7 colours*

Below *Diagonal pinnacles worked over 6 threads in varying steps using 8 colours*

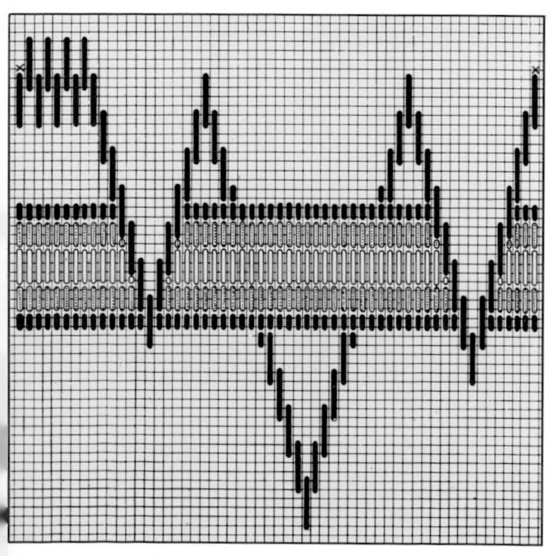

Above *Pinnacles worked over 6 threads in steps of 4 threads using 7 colours and stripes worked over 2, 3 and 4 threads using 3 colours*

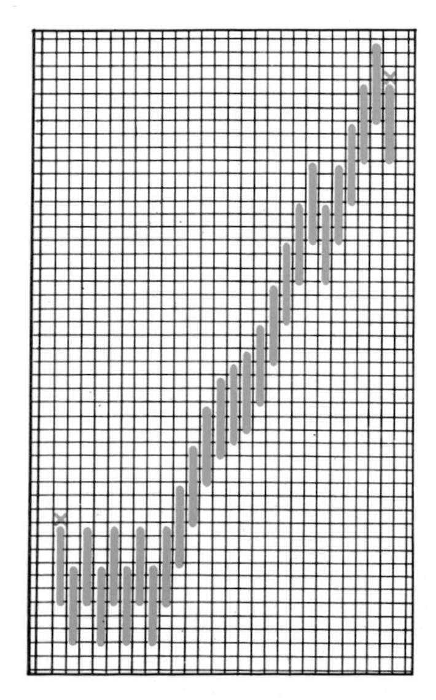

Backgrounds

Needlepoint designs often need a plain background to show up the main figurative part of the work. This large area can be dull to work unless it is treated imaginatively. Tent and cross stitch are often used but there are many other stitches that will break the monotony of a plain background.

Encroaching gobelin stitch and pre-shaded silks produce the effect of clouds and sky and give a retreating skyline to the picture

Soft diagonal stripes set off the flowers in the foreground

The same stitch gives the grass a 'realistic' texture

Use pale shades and subtle blends to achieve delicate, irregular patterning

TONED BACKGROUNDS

Subtly blended tones can be introduced into plain backgrounds to give them added interest without distracting attention from the design. This can be done either by buying special threads which are already shaded or by mixing the strands of different coloured threads. Divide the strands of varying shades or colours and then twist them into different combinations.

Twisting the strands

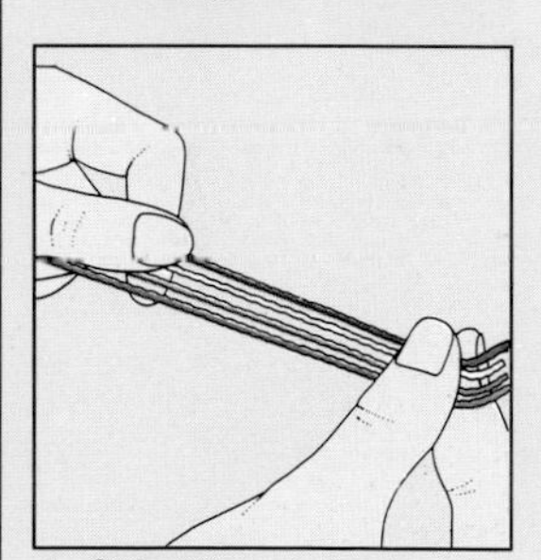

1 *Select 3 or 4 closely toning threads of stranded cotton or tapestry wool.*

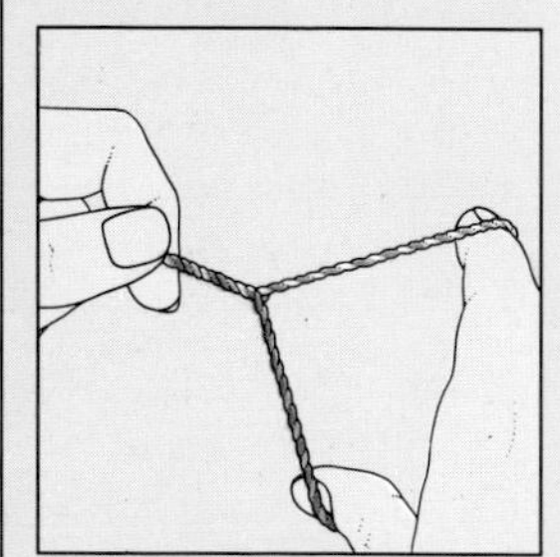

2 *Untwist the threads and then twist the different strands together to make a new thread.*

Textures

The combination of canvas, stitch and thread makes up the many different textural effects which can be achieved with needlepoint tapestry. The different stitches worked separately or in combination with each other form patterns on the surface of the canvas with more pronounced effects being made by a careful choice of colours. When designing needlepoint pictures particular attention should be paid to the various stitches so that they are used to give exactly the right textures in the different parts of the work. This can be seen in the illustration below where diagonal, brick and satin stitches have been used in opposite directions on the garden and house walls.

Textures can be depicted with a clever use of colour. The background is lighter behind the lace curtains and darker on the window panes

Raised effects

The surface of the needlepoint can also be changed by using raised or relief effects. This can be done either by using tramming stitches beneath the needlepoint stitching or by using special stitches which form relief effects themselves.

The best stitches to use for making relief effects are velvet and single knotted stitch (see page 86). In the needlepoint panel opposite, both techniques have been used in different areas. The leaves of the plant have been trammed first before being worked over in satin stitch to give them a raised appearance.

The tablecloth has been worked in velvet stitch and the loops of the stitch cut to give a similar effect to carpet pile. Velvet stitch can also be left uncut to form a looped pile.

Single knotted stitch can be used to give tassel or fringe effects as shown on the tablecloth edging.

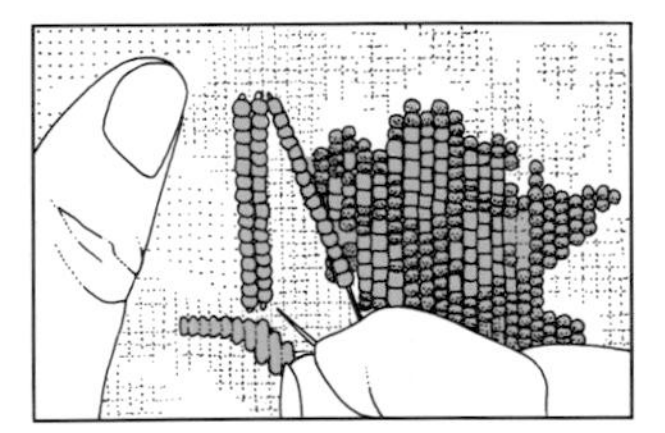

Couched beads are often used in needlepoint to form backgrounds as in the picture (right). Lay the threaded beads on the surface and secure with couching stitches (see page 36).

Needlepoint picture with relief work

Borders

Borders are used to edge the main design and can be made in many different sizes, shapes and styles so that they become either discreet frames, decorative surrounds or an important part of the central theme. Therefore, when planning the area to be worked, the choice of border should be taken into account and carefully organized so that it works in harmony with the whole design.

Border effects

By altering the depth of a border from the average 3in. (7.5cm) to a narrow 1in. (2.5cm), or to a deep band which almost engulfs the main design, quite dramatic changes can be made to the appearance of the whole needlepoint. Borders which are lighter or darker in tone than the main design can also be used to reduce or enhance the importance of the central area of the design.

Formal borders

These can be worked in one colour throughout or in many different colours to complement the main design. The stitching can be simple or textured, using any of the stitches in the glossary (pages 76-87). Formal borders can be designed using either geometric patterns or motifs, which can be worked at regular intervals.

The deep border on the needlepoint (left) gives a sense of distance to the main design. The same design, this time with a very narrow border (above), appears stronger.

Borders, when used as frames, can be made in many different shapes, from classic squares, rectangles, circles and ovals to the figurative shapes of stars, flowers, windows and doors. Windows and doors, in fact, make excellent borders for designing needlepoint pictures.

Above *A border corner decorated with a flower motif.* **Right** *The border overflows to become part of the main design.*

Needlepoint stitch glossary

The stitches in needlepoint tapestry can be made either vertically, diagonally or horizontally. They vary in size and shape according to the number of canvas threads over which they are worked.

When working needlepoint tapestry make sure that the stitches cover the canvas threads. When in doubt, make a test sample. If the stitch does not cover the canvas properly either use a thicker thread or add more strands to the needle. Alternatively, the canvas can be worked over with trammed stitches (see page 60).

If the stitch instructions do not state the type of canvas to be used, either double or single is suitable. The small arrows on the following diagrams point to the place where the work was started.

HINTS ON WORKING NEEDLEPOINT CANVAS

Never work with too long a thread as it will not only be difficult to handle but will get frayed in the process of being worked.

Secure the end of the yarn as shown here; knots create bumps and should not be used. Start and end threads in a different place each time, otherwise a ridge may appear in the work.

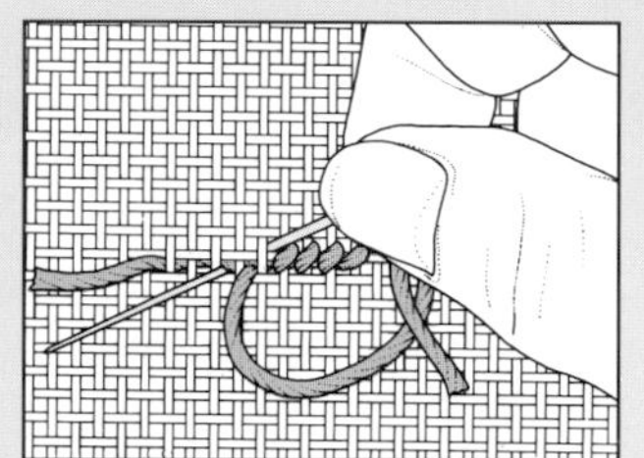

Hold end of thread at back of canvas. Secure with a few stitches.

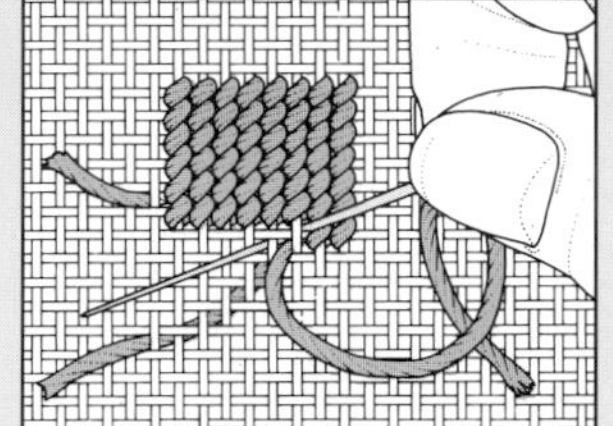

Finish off by holding end of thread at back of canvas and securing with a few stitches.

Straight stitches

These stitches, which are in general quick and easy to work, look best when worked on single canvas, building up into patterns without distorting the fabric.

Upright Gobelin stitch

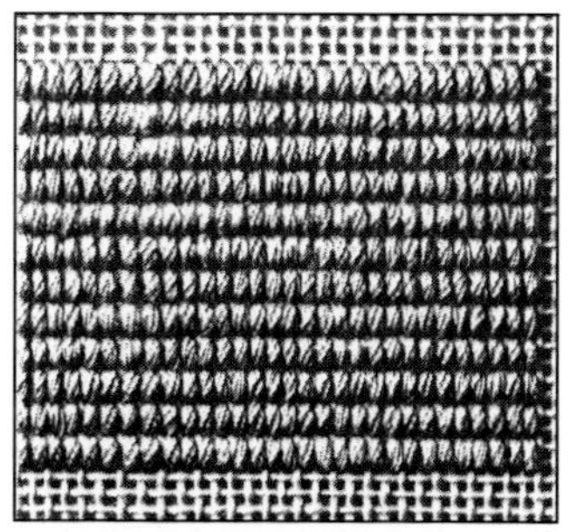

This gives a close, ridged surface, which can be worked over a trammed stitch.

Bring needle out at top left and take it up over 2 horizontal threads. Insert down to right under 1 vertical and 2 horizontal threads and bring needle out ready to form the next stitch.

Work all subsequent rows into the bottom of those above.

When working over a trammed stitch, make a horizontal stitch along the length of the row. On the return journey work straight Gobelin stitches over it.

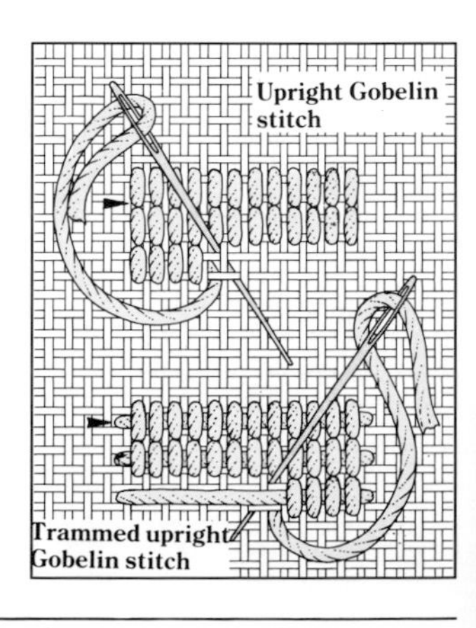

Gobelin filling stitch

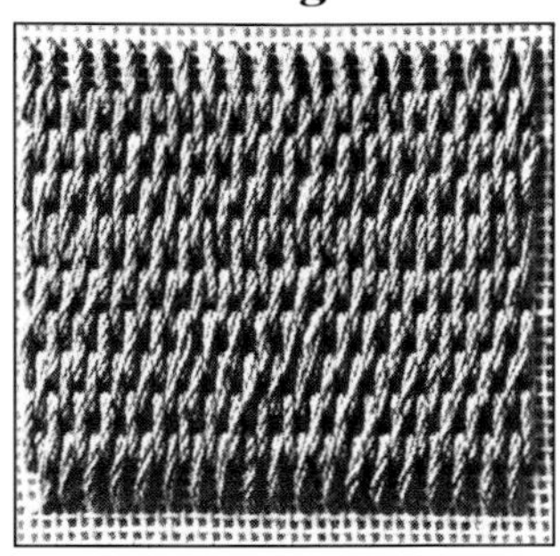

This is a very quick stitch to work and, when using more than one colour, is very good for shading and blending effects.

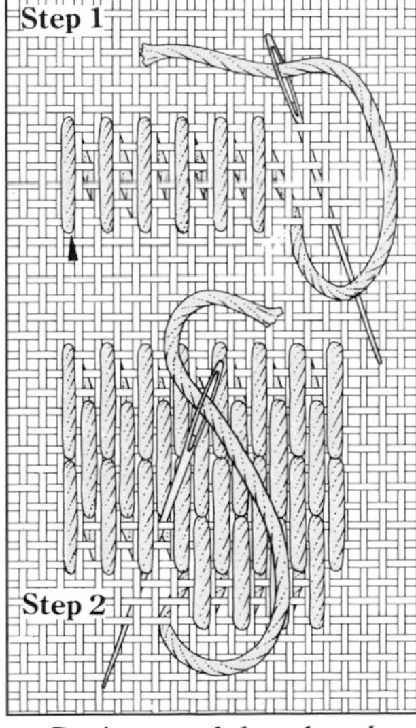

1 Begin at top left and work a row of straight stitches upwards over 6 threads leaving 2 threads between each one.

2 Work second row from right to left fitting stitches evenly into previous row. Continue working each successive row in the same way.

Long stitch

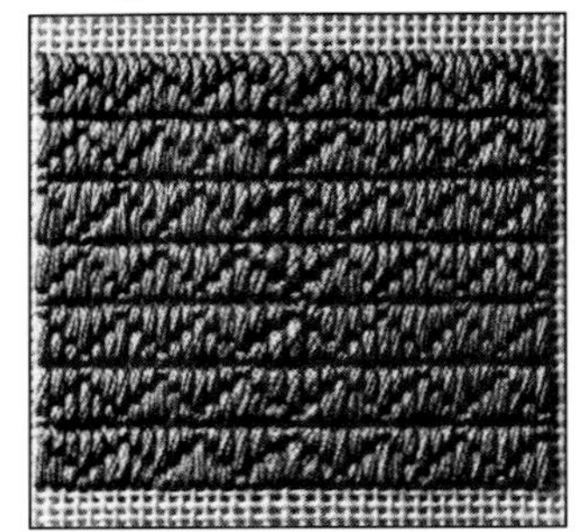

This stitch gives a brocade pattern and is formed by working graduated straight stitches in a series of triangles and reverse triangles over the two rows.

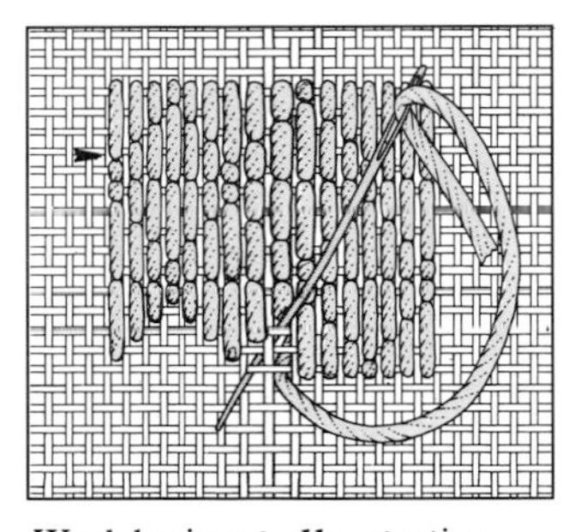

Work horizontally, starting at top left. Continue along row, working groups of 6 straight stitches in a repeated sequence over 4, 3, 2, 1, 2 and 3 horizontal threads.

Work the return row from right to left in the same sequence but so that the longest stitches fall beneath the shortest ones in the previous row. In this way the stitches will fill the spaces left by the first row and will thus complete the pattern of interlocking triangles.

On subsequent rows work into the base of the stitches in the previous row.

Florentine stitch

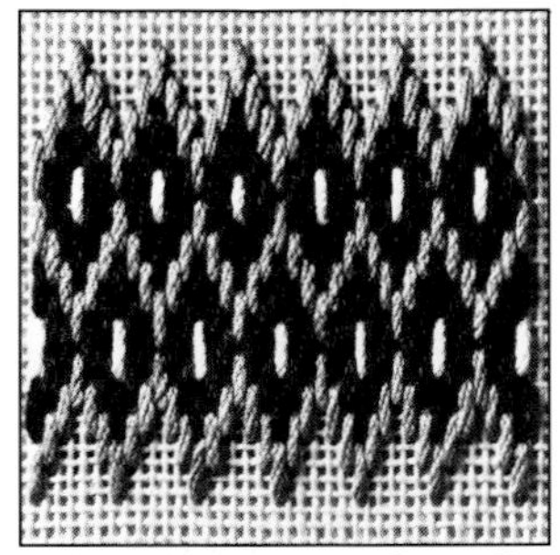

This is also known as Bargello stitch and flame stitch. It is worked in zigzag rows of stitches to form multicoloured bands of diamond shapes.

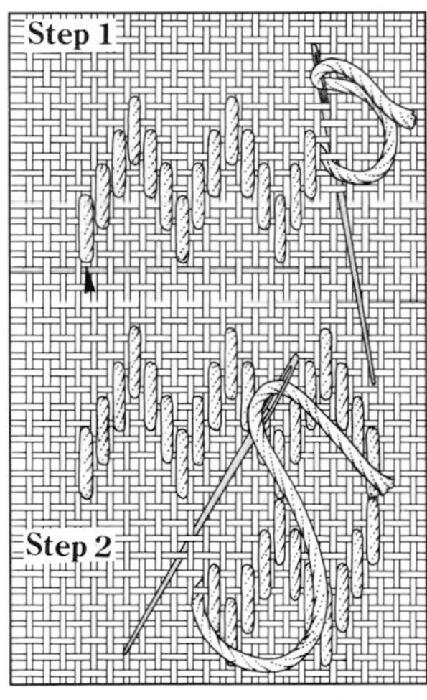

1 Work horizontally, bringing yarn out at left. Insert needle 4 threads up and bring out 2 threads down and 1 to right. Continue in this way to work 3 more stitches, each one 4 threads up and 2 back; then work 3 stitches, 4 threads down and 2 up, to end of row.

2 Working downwards first on the second row, use a different colour to make the inner diamond and a third colour for the final central stitch.

Diagonal stitches

All these stitches cover the canvas well. Whereas the smallest are often used for backgrounds, the longer sloping stitch textures show direction and shading.

Tent stitch

This is also known as petit point and is used for backgrounds, fillings and outlines. It is usually worked on a single canvas diagonally rather than horizontally across the mesh, as this gives the work extra strength.

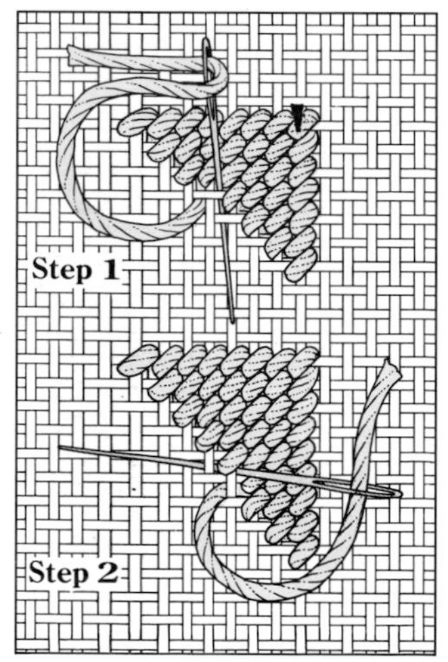

1 Work diagonally, starting at top right. Bring needle out and take it up to right over 1 canvas intersection. Insert downwards under 2 horizontal threads and bring needle out ready to form the next stitch. Continue to end of row.

2 Work back up the line of stitches filling in the spaces left on the previous journey. Take needle up to right over 1 canvas intersection and insert it horizontally under 2 vertical threads bringing it out again ready to form the next stitch.

Half cross stitch

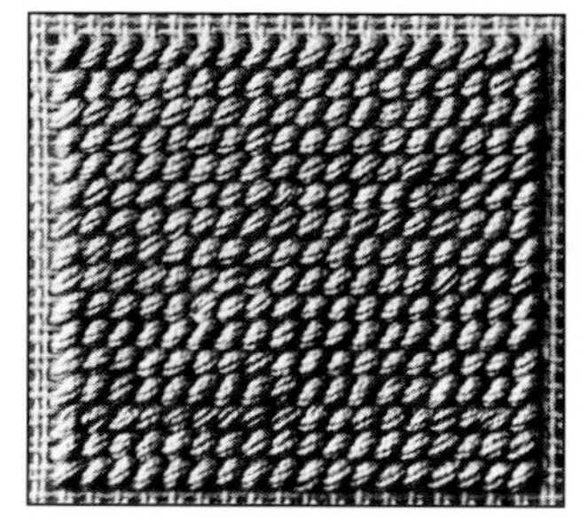

This has the appearance of tent stitch but is worked differently. The two stitches should not be used together as the different textures on the back of the work will make the surface uneven. It is worked on double canvas.

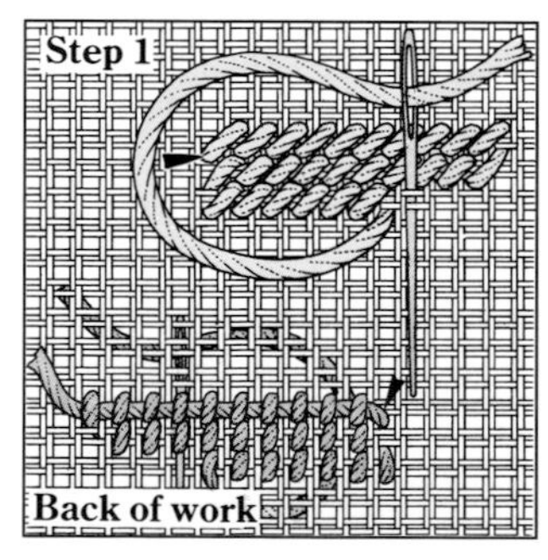

Work horizontally, starting at top left. Bring needle out and take it up to right over 1 canvas intersection. Insert downwards under 1 horizontal double thread and bring needle out ready to form next stitch.

Continue in the same way for all subsequent rows.

The back of the work is made up of short vertical stitches.

Rep stitch

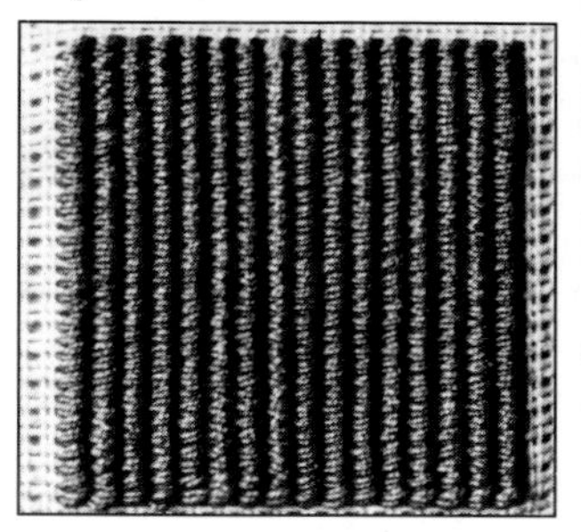

This stitch is also known as Aubusson stitch. It is a very small tent stitch, worked on double canvas and used for fine detail work. It consists of stitches that are worked diagonally over the canvas intersections and which use even the spaces between the horizontal double threads as well as the wider meshes. As the rep stitches are less slanted than half cross and tent stitches, the final texture will produce a ridged effect.

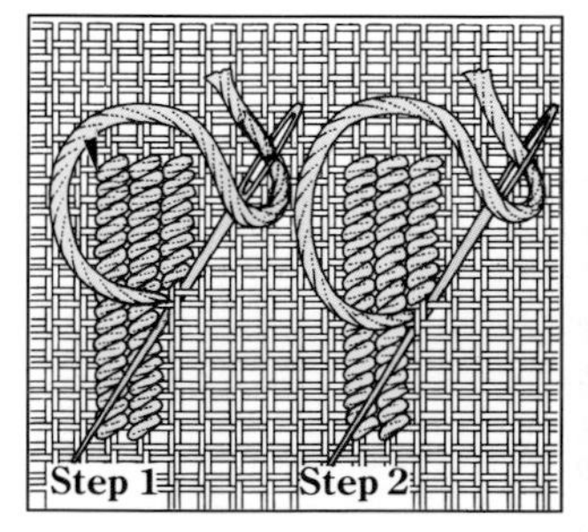

Work as shown, taking the needle in between the horizontal double threads but always over the complete vertical double threads each time a stitch is made.

Gobelin stitch

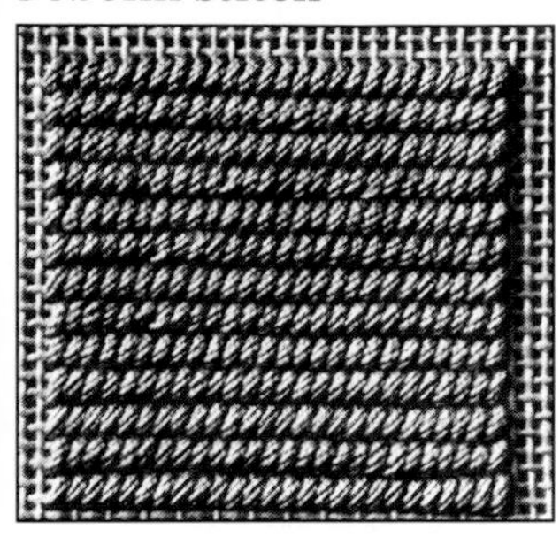

Also known as gros point this stitch is worked on single canvas.

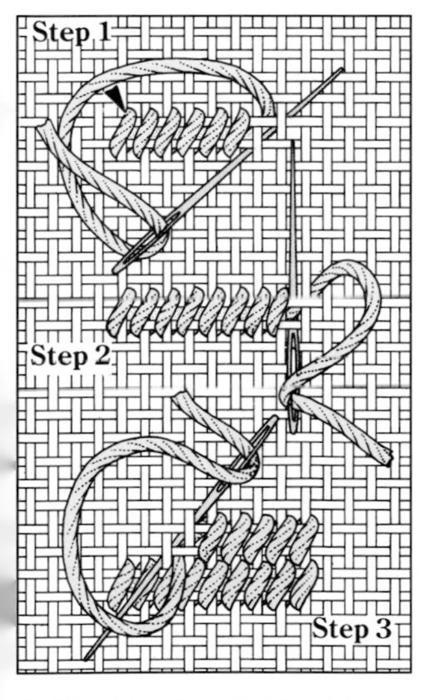

1 Working from left to right, bring yarn out at bottom left and make a diagonal stitch over 2 threads down and 1 thread to left. Pass needle diagonally behind and bring out 2 threads up and 1 thread to right. Repeat to end of row.

2 For second row, insert needle vertically upwards under 2 threads.

3 Work from right to left passing needle diagonally downwards from above.

Encroaching Gobelin stitch

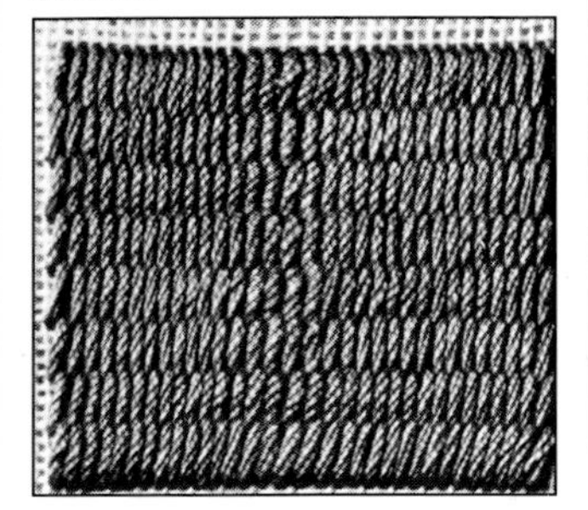

This is a good stitch for filling large areas and for shading and blending colours. The stitches are much bigger than those used in Gobelin stitch since they are usually worked over five horizontal threads and one vertical thread. It is worked on a single canvas with the subsequent rows overlapping the stitches in the previous rows by one horizontal thread.

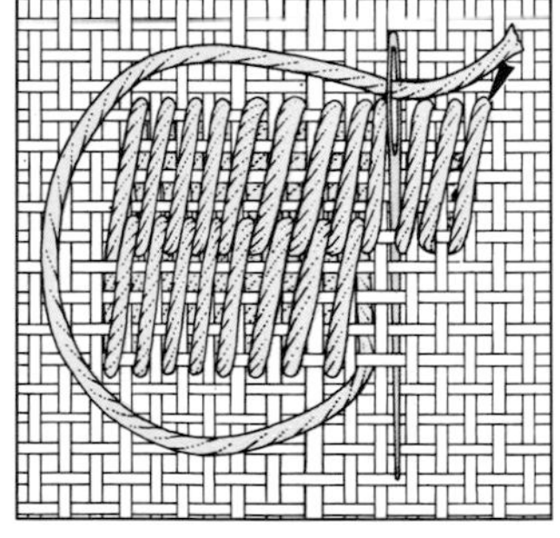

Work horizontally, starting at left or right. Bring needle out and then take it up to right over 5 horizontal threads and 1 vertical one. Insert needle downwards under 5 horizontal threads and bring it out again ready to form the next stitch.

On all subsequent rows overlap by working the stitches over the same horizontal canvas thread used at the bottom of the previous row of stitches.

Diagonal stitch

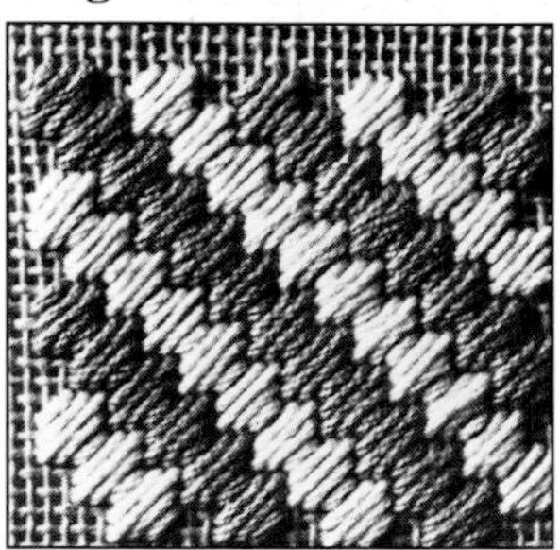

This stitch can be used to give a patterned surface when it is worked in one colour or a striped and patterned surface when worked in two or more different colours.

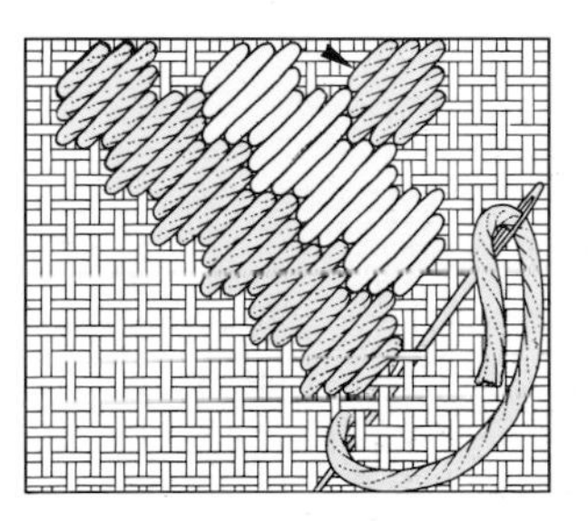

Work diagonally, starting at top right of canvas. Begin at arrow by bringing needle out and forming diagonal stitches in groups of 4. These vary in length and should be worked in a repeated sequence over 2, 3, 4 and 3 canvas intersections.

On the next and subsequent rows work back so that the shortest stitches meet the longest stitches of the previous row as shown above.

Mosaic stitch

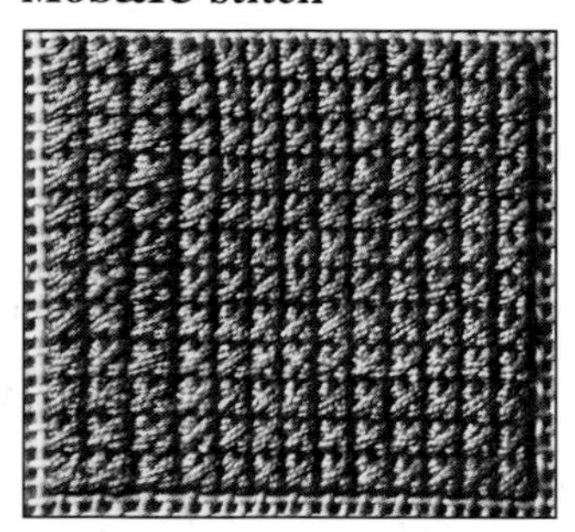

This is a quick and effective stitch composed of short and long diagonal stitches over two rows. When worked upright it is known as Hungarian stitch. The stitch gets its name because intricate patterns can be built up by using different colours for the little squares – much like mosaic work.

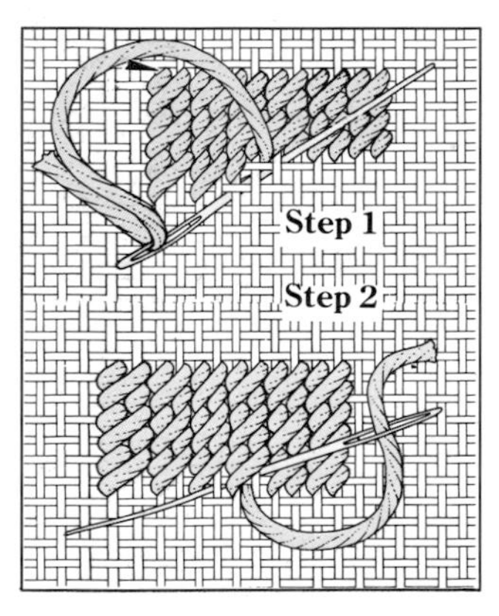

1 Work horizontally, starting with a short diagonal stitch down over 1 canvas intersection followed by a long diagonal stitch down over 2 intersections.

2 Work second row as a line of short stitches filling in the spaces left on the previous row.

Continue in the same way for all subsequent rows.

Byzantine stitch

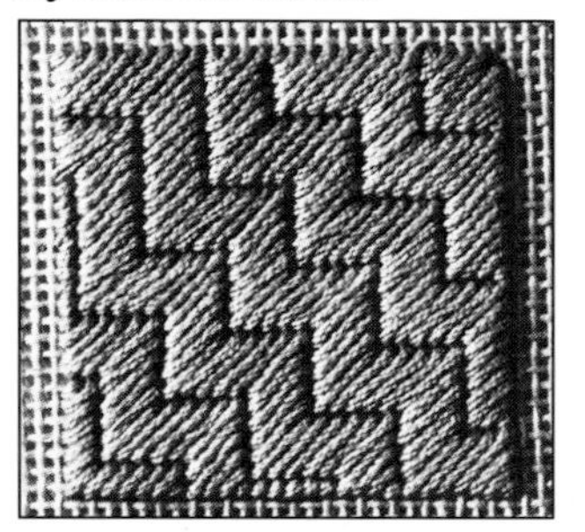

This is a quick filling stitch which is particularly useful for large areas of background. It gives a regular zigzag pattern of equal-sized steps and consists of diagonal stitches over four vertical and four horizontal threads.

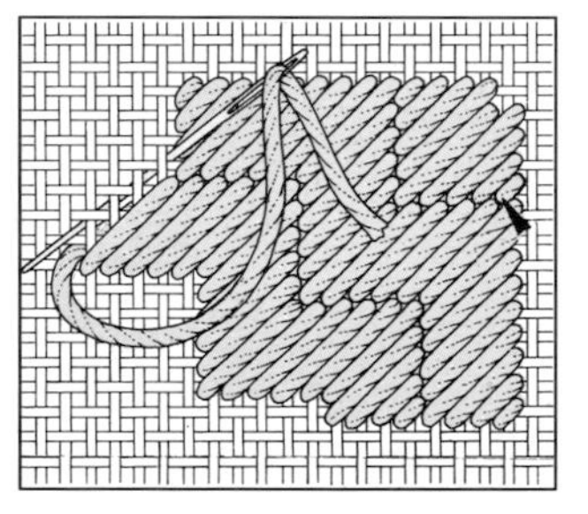

Work diagonally, starting at arrow and moving up to top left. Form the zigzags or steps by working 5 diagonal stitches to the left followed by 5 diagonal stitches upwards.

Continue in this way, working subsequent rows beside the previous ones. Fill in the corners and the edges with graduated diagonal stitches.

Canvas stem stitch

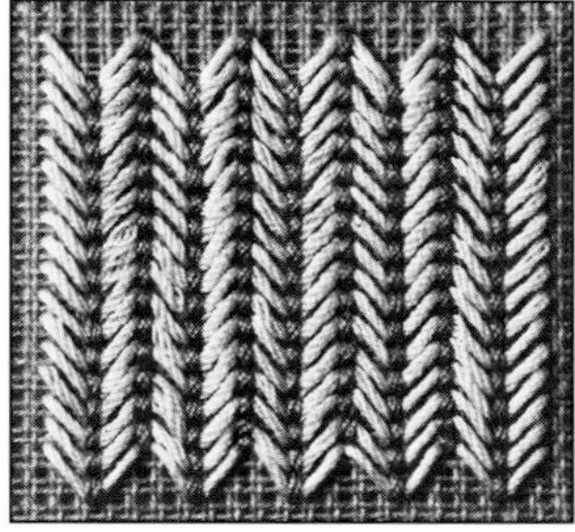

This stitch gets its name from its stem-like appearance. It is formed by two vertical lines of diagonal stitches set at right angles to each other and divided by a row of back stitches. It should be worked on double canvas.

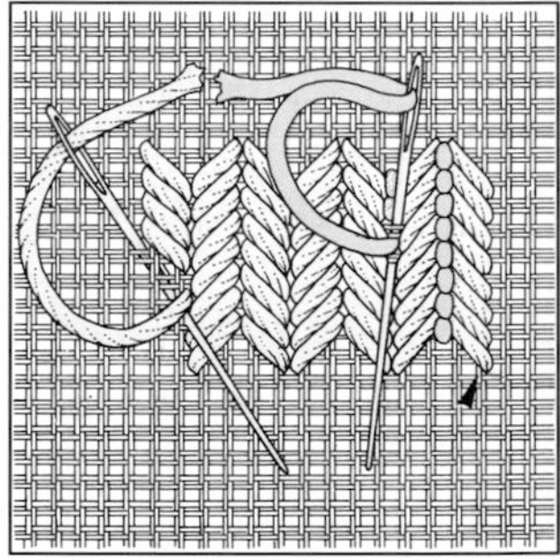

Work vertically, starting at bottom right. Work the first row in diagonal stitches slanted to the left over 2 canvas intersections. At the top work downwards, forming the same stitches but slanted the other way and placed at right angles to the previous row.

When completed, work a row of back stitches over the horizontal canvas threads between the rows.

Crossed stitches

In this category there are, in addition to the popular cross stitch, many other very attractive and distinctive variations, producing a variety of effects.

Cross stitch

This, along with tent stitch, is one of the two principal stitches in needlepoint tapestry. It is worked on double canvas for both fine or coarse work.

Horizontal method

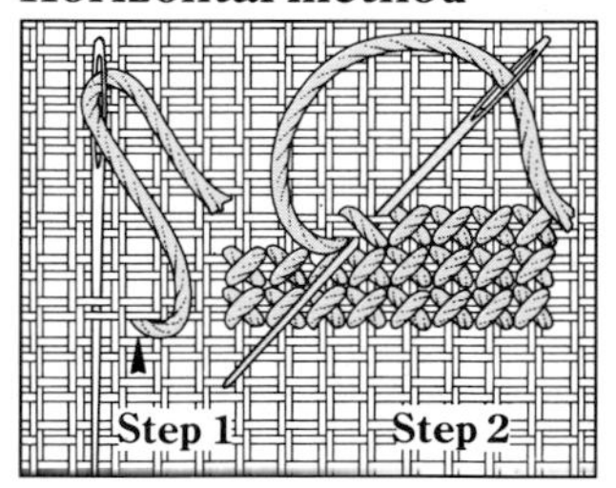

1 Bring needle out at arrow and take it up to left over 1 canvas intersection. Insert downwards under 1 horizontal double thread.

2 Take needle up to right, over the stitch that has just been formed, and insert down to left under the canvas intersection. Bring needle out again in the same spot ready to make the next cross stitch.

Diagonal method

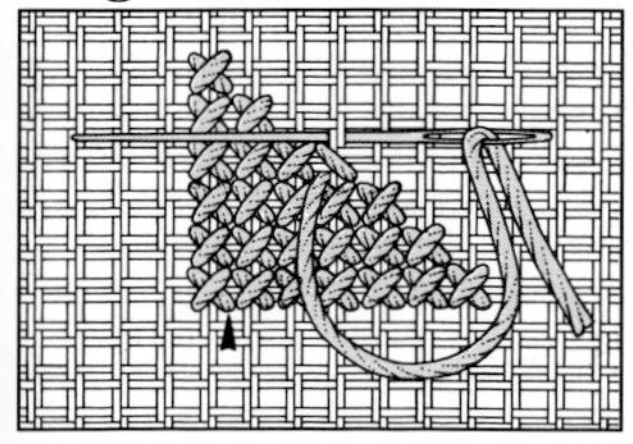

You can also work cross stitch diagonally, as shown above.

Upright cross stitch

This stitch is worked in two diagonal journeys, the first in vertical stitches and the second in horizontal stitches which cover the previous ones. It should be worked on double rather than single canvas.

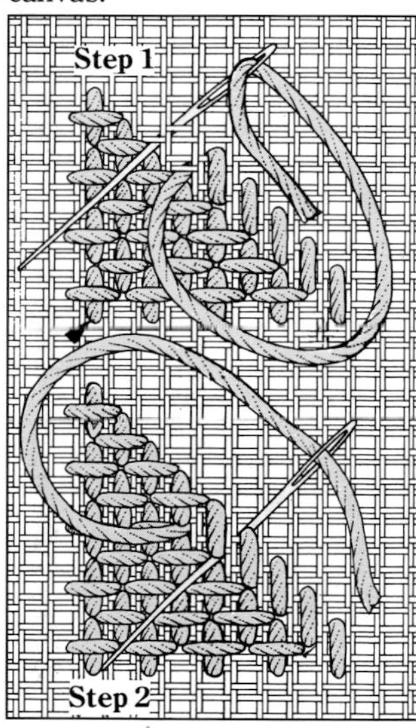

1 Work diagonally from bottom right to top left. Bring yarn out and make a row of stepped vertical stitches. Insert needle over 2 horizontal double threads and bring out 1 double thread intersection down to left.

2 On return journey, make a row of stepped horizontal stitches. With yarn at left, insert needle over 2 vertical double threads, crossing the previous stitch, and bring it out 1 double thread intersection down to left.

Oblong cross stitch

This stitch can be worked on either single or double canvas.

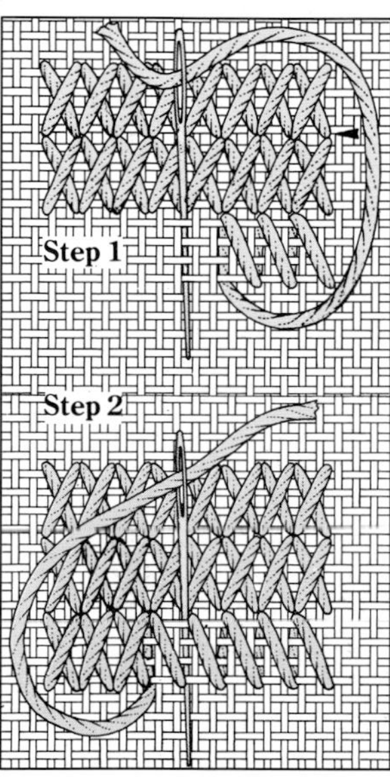

1 Work the first journey of diagonal stitches horizontally, starting at top right. Bring needle out and take it up to left over 4 horizontal and 2 vertical threads. Insert downwards under 4 horizontal threads and bring needle out ready to form the next stitch.

2 At end of row bring needle out as if to make next diagonal, but take it back up to right over 4 horizontal and 2 vertical threads. Insert downwards under 4 horizontal threads and bring needle out ready to form the next stitch.

Work all subsequent rows into the bases of the stitches in the previous rows.

Diagonal cross stitch

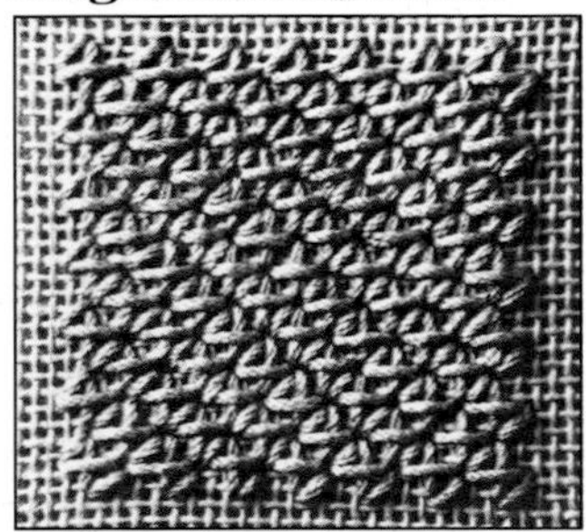

This consists of a series of upright cross stitches separated by diagonal stitches.

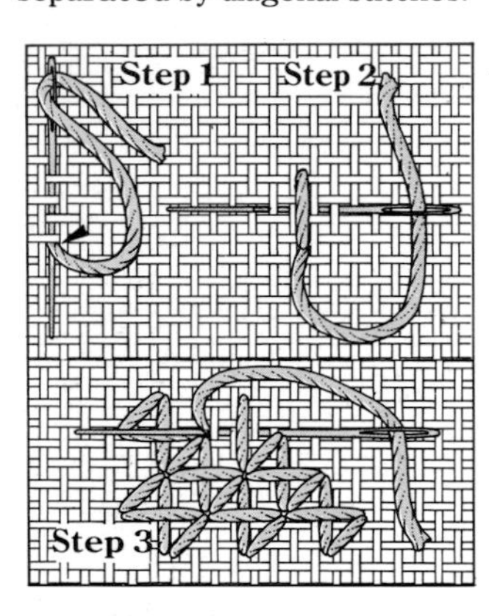

1 Work diagonally, starting at bottom left of canvas. Bring needle out at arrow and make a vertical stitch up over 4 horizontal threads. Insert needle downwards and bring it out again at arrow.

2 Make a diagonal stitch up to right over 2 canvas intersections. Bring needle out 4 vertical threads to left ready to form the next step.

3 Make a back stitch over 4 vertical threads, crossing the vertical stitch that has just been formed and bringing the needle out again in the same spot ready to form the next stitch.

Plait stitch

This is also known as Spanish stitch and is very quick and easy to work. It is useful both for backgrounds and outlines and looks best worked on double canvas in a fairly thick thread.

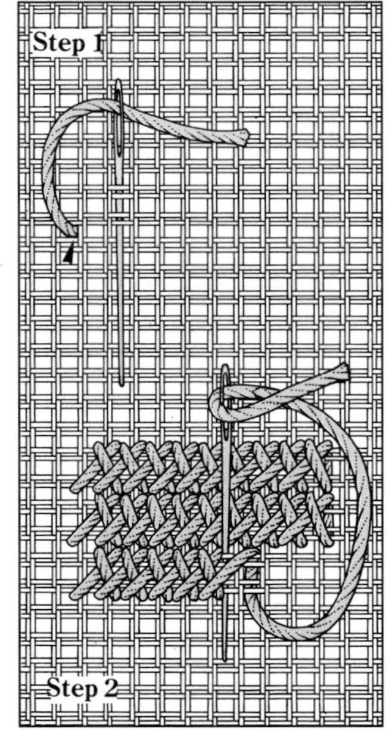

1 Work from left to right. Bring yarn out at top left and make a diagonal stitch up to right over 2 double thread intersections; bring needle out 2 double threads down.

2 Make a second diagonal stitch up to left over 2 double threads, one double thread to left, and bring out 2 double threads down. Continue to end of row. Work next and subsequent rows directly below, fitting the top of the stitch into the bottom of the stitch of previous row.

Alternating cross stitch

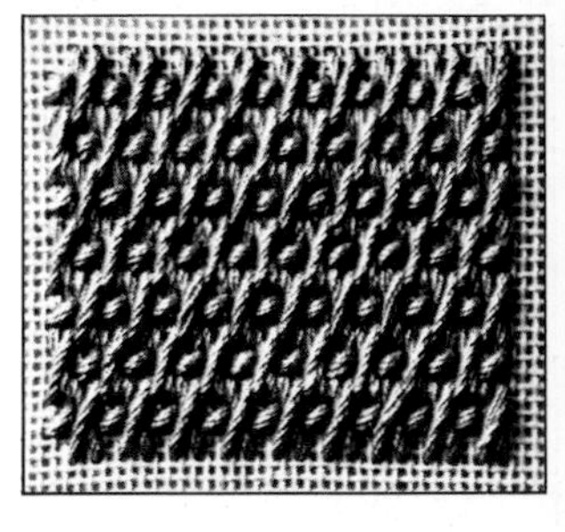

This is a combination of cross stitch and oblong cross stitch.

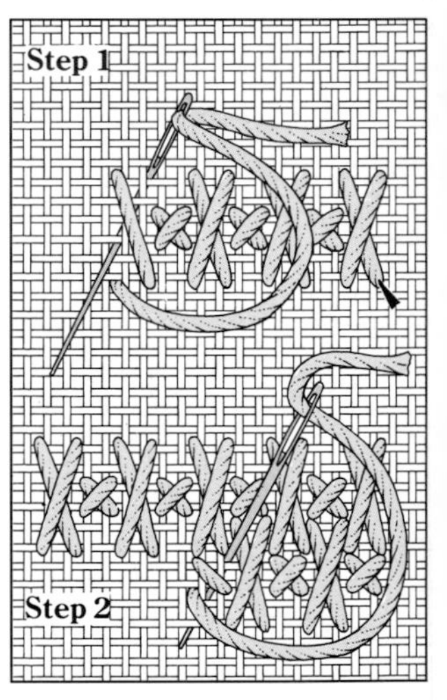

1 Begin at top right and work horizontally. Bring yarn out and make an oblong cross stitch over 6 threads up and 2 threads to right; then bring needle out 4 threads down and 2 threads to left.

2 Make a cross stitch over 2 intersections; bring needle out 4 threads down and 2 to left, ready for next oblong cross stitch. Continue in this way to end of row. Work next and subsequent rows below, fitting the oblong cross stitch directly under the cross stitch of the previous row.

Long-armed cross stitch

This is also known as long-legged stitch and plaited Slav stitch.

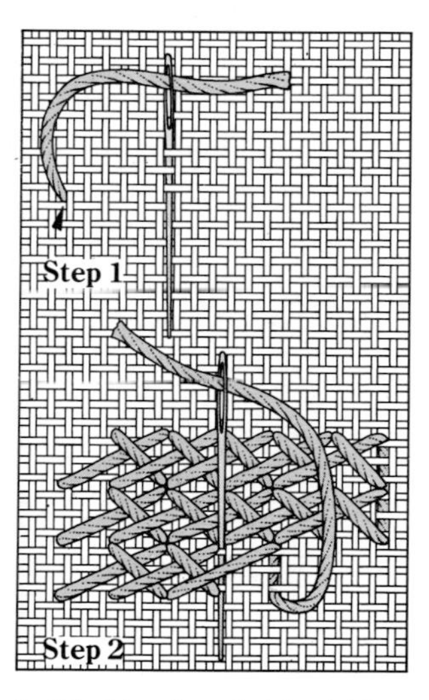

1 Working from left to right, bring needle out at arrow and make a long diagonal stitch up to right over 6 vertical and 3 horizontal threads. Insert downwards under 3 horizontal threads and bring needle out ready to form next stitch.

2 Make a diagonal stitch up to left over 3 intersections. Insert downwards under 3 horizontal threads and bring needle out ready to form next stitch.

On all subsequent rows work into the bases of the stitches in the previous row as shown.

Reversed cross stitch

This stitch is excellent for colourwork and grounds.

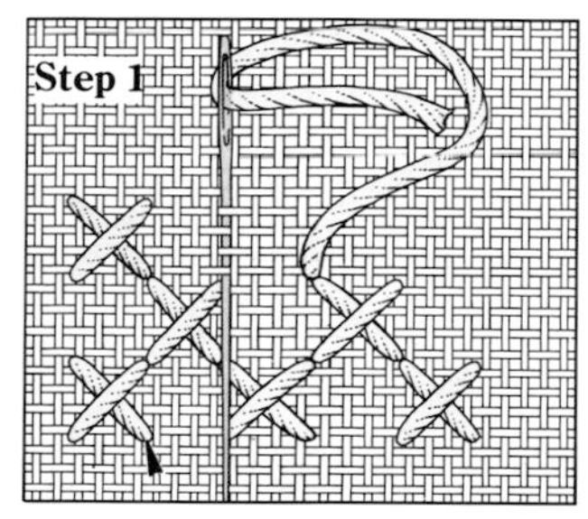

1 Begin at bottom left and work diagonal cross stitch over 4 intersections of thread, leaving 4 threads between each row.

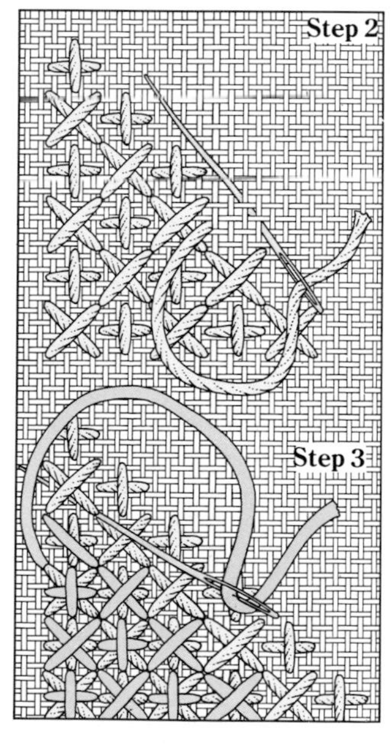

2 Work upright cross stitch over 4 threads between the rows already worked.

3 With the same, or contrast yarn, work crosses over the basic stitches in reverse sequence.

Rice stitch

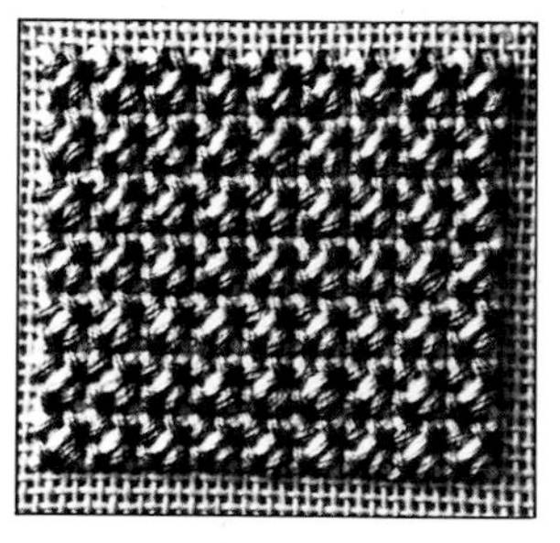

This is also known as crossed corners cross stitch. It is an excellent stitch for colourwork or for dense background textures.

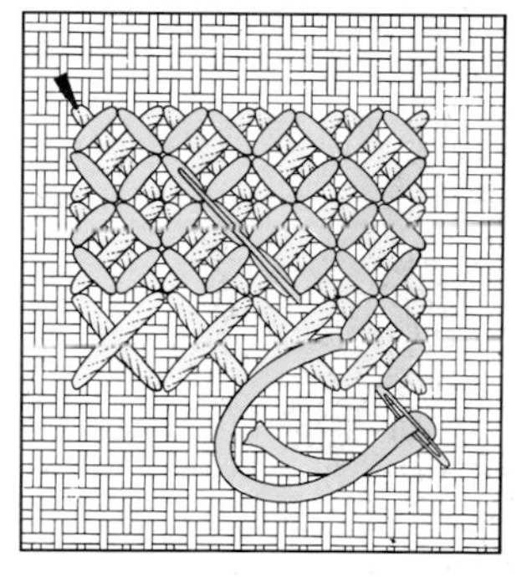

Work horizontally in 2 journeys. Start the first journey at top left and work a row of large cross stitches over 4 canvas intersections as shown, completing each cross stitch before going on to the next.

When the crosses are complete, work a return journey of back stitches at right angles over the corners of the cross stitches. Each back stitch covers 2 canvas intersections.

Work all subsequent rows into the bases of the stitches in the previous rows.

Greek stitch

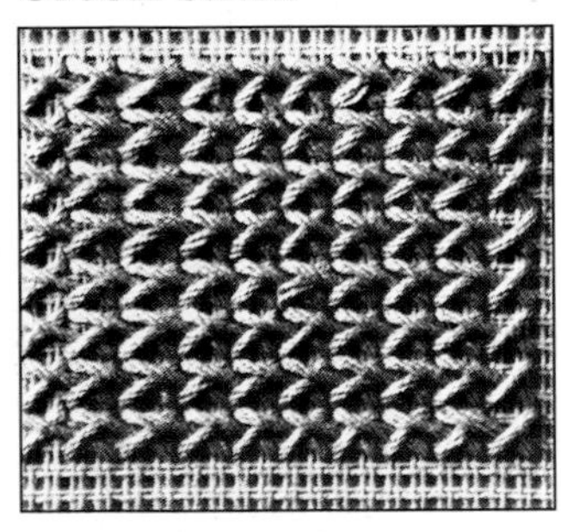

This stitch should be worked in a coarse thread on double canvas. It is worked like herringbone stitch and forms channels of back stitches on the back of the work.

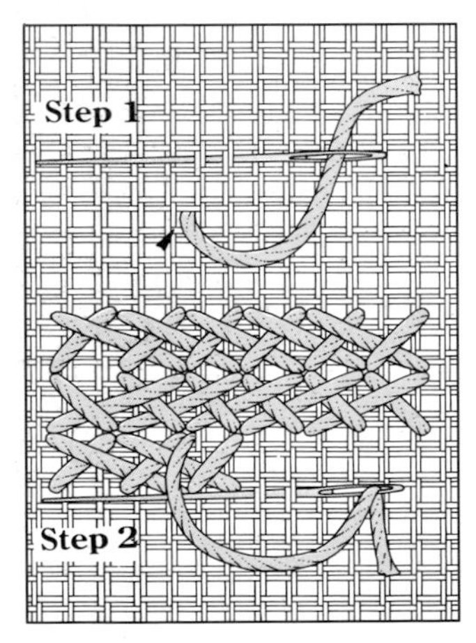

1 Work from left to right. Bring yarn out and make a diagonal stitch up to right over 2 double thread intersections. Bring needle out 2 double threads to left.

2 Make a diagonal stitch down to right over 4 vertical and 2 horizontal double threads. Bring needle out 2 double threads to left. Continue to end of row. Turn canvas upside-down to work second and every alternate row.

Plaited Gobelin stitch

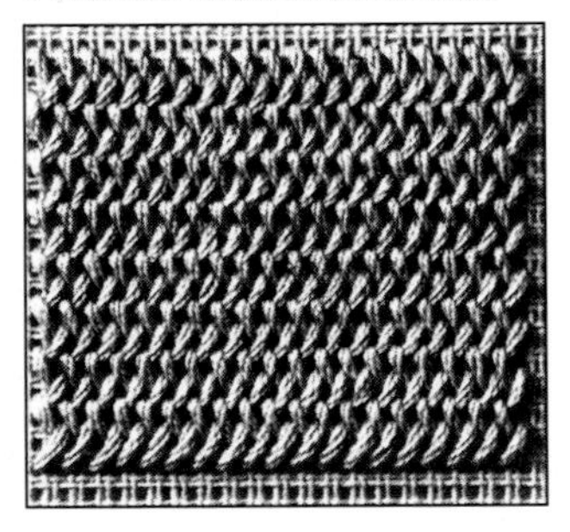

This stitch is worked in a coarse thread and looks best on double canvas.

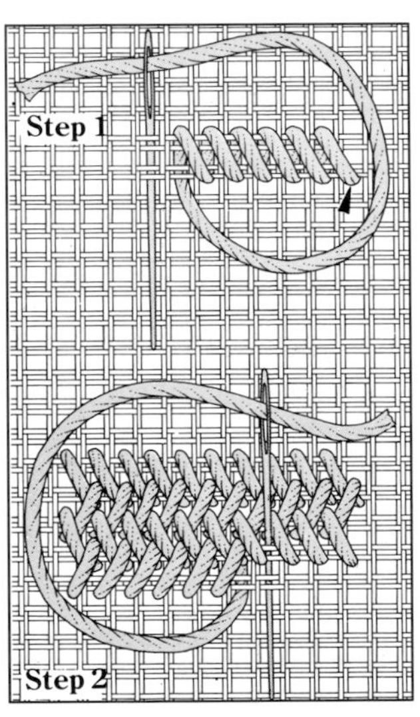

1 Bring yarn out at top right and make a diagonal stitch up over 2 double threads, one double thread to left and bring needle out 2 double threads down. Continue to end of row.

2 On last stitch of first row, bring needle out 3 double threads down. Insert needle diagonally up over 2 double threads, one double thread to right and bring out 2 double threads down. Continue in this way to end of row, overlapping the stitches of the previous row.

Fishbone stitch

For the best result, work this stitch on double canvas.

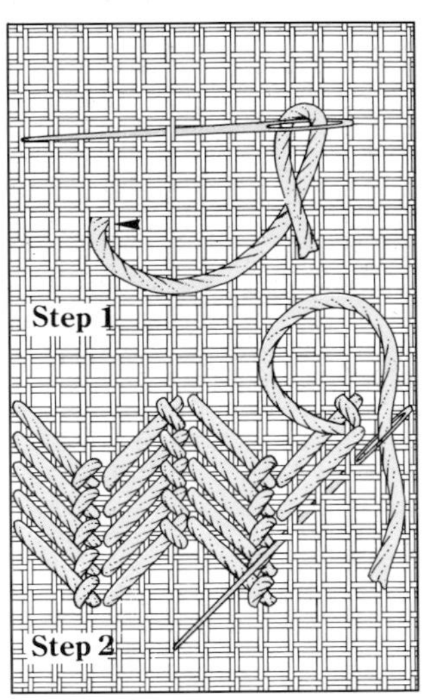

1 Working vertically downwards, bring needle out at arrow and make a diagonal stitch up to right over 3 intersections. Bring needle out 1 vertical double thread to left.

2 Make a short diagonal stitch down to right over 1 intersection so that it crosses the top of the long diagonal stitch. Then bring needle out again 3 intersections down to left, just underneath the previous long diagonal. Continue to bottom of row.

On all subsequent rows work long diagonal stitches into the heads of those in the previous row and slant them in the opposite direction.

Fern stitch

This stitch gives a decorative ridged effect and is worked down the canvas in overlapping diagonal stitches set at right angles to each other. Double canvas should be used.

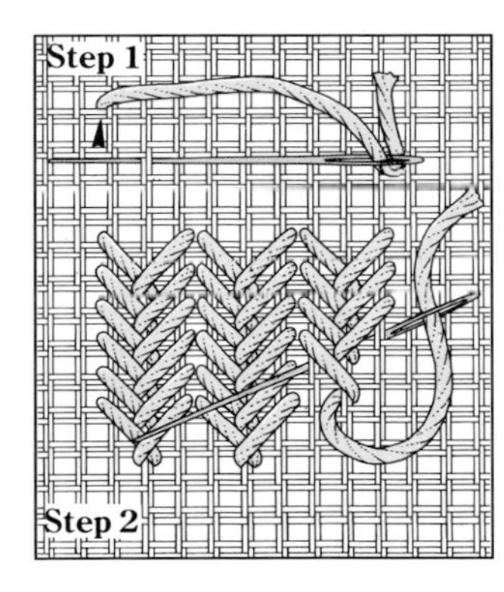

1 Work vertically downwards. Bring needle out at arrow and make a diagonal stitch down to right over 2 canvas intersections. Bring needle out again 1 vertical double thread over to the left as shown.

2 Make a diagonal stitch up to right over 2 canvas intersections. Bring needle out again 1 horizontal and 3 vertical double threads down to left ready to form the next stitch in the same way as the one above it. Work all subsequent rows into the sides of the stitches in the previous row.

Web stitch

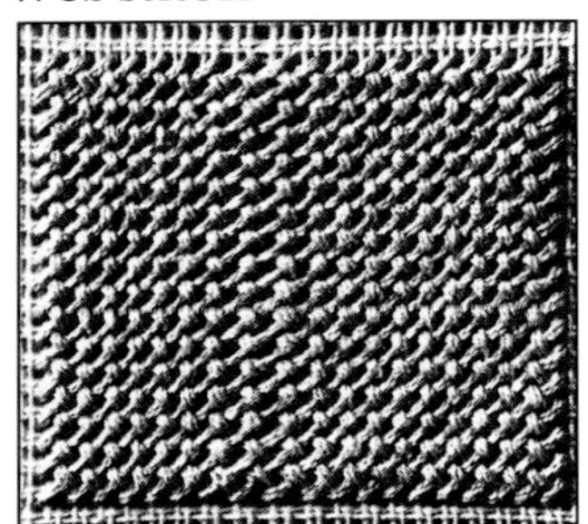

This filling stitch needs to be worked on double canvas.

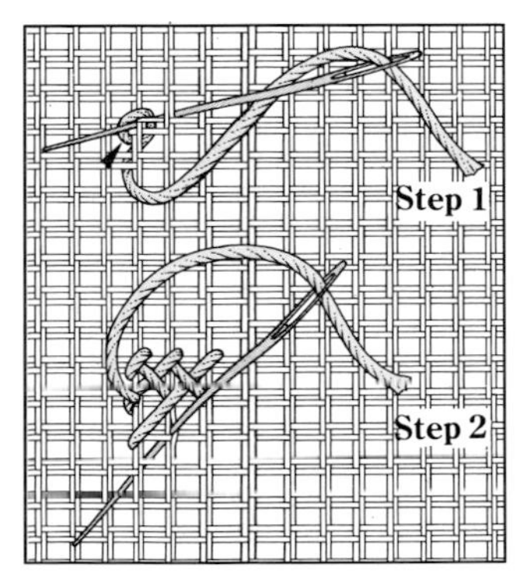

1 Work diagonally from top left to bottom right. Bring yarn out and make a diagonal stitch up to right over 1 double thread intersection. Bring needle out 1 double thread below starting point. Make a stitch up over 2 double thread intersections, pass needle behind and bring out in between double mesh of first intersection.

2 Make a short stitch over the diagonal stitch, inserting the needle in between the double mesh 1 double thread intersection down to right and bring out 1 double thread intersection down to left.

Continue to increase length of diagonal stitches. Arrange crossed stitches to alternate with those in previous row.

Knotted stitch

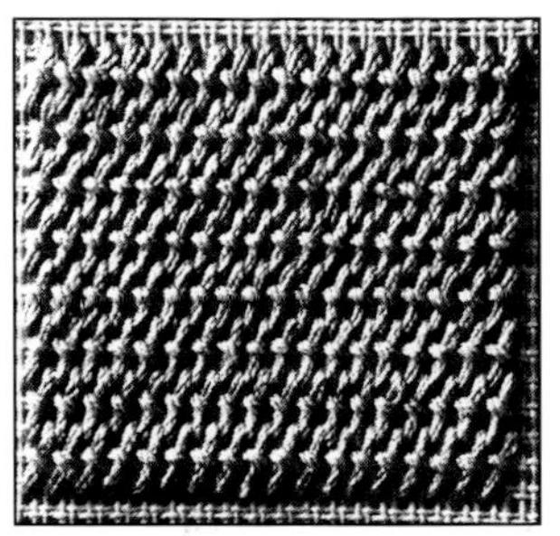

This stitch gives a "railroad" texture and is best worked on double canvas.

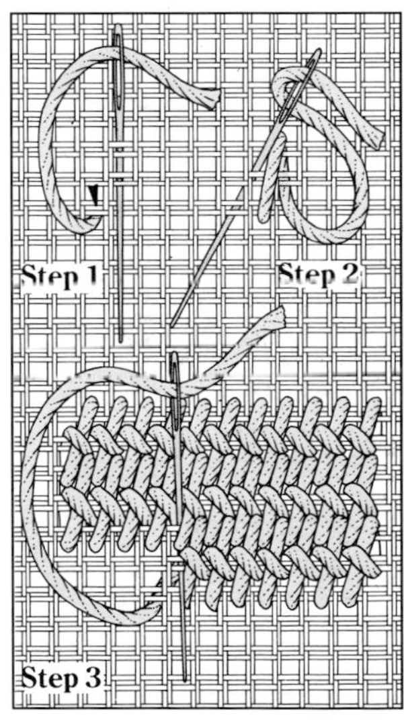

1 Work horizontally, starting at top right. Bring yarn out and make a diagonal stitch up over 3 double threads and 1 double thread to right. Bring needle out 2 double threads down.

2 Insert needle diagonally up over 1 double thread and bring out 2 double threads down and 1 double thread to left.

3 Continue to end of row, and repeat below, fitting the long diagonal stitch into the space left in the previous row.

Looped stitches

These stitches offer some of the most interesting textures, from loops, cutpile and fringing to the "knitted" look of chain stitch. They make ideal fillers for motifs.

Chain stitch

This stitch is worked on canvas in exactly the same way as when it is used as an embroidery stitch on fabric. It is worked vertically so that each successive looped stitch ties down the one preceding it. It forms a texture rather like knitting and is used as a filling stitch.

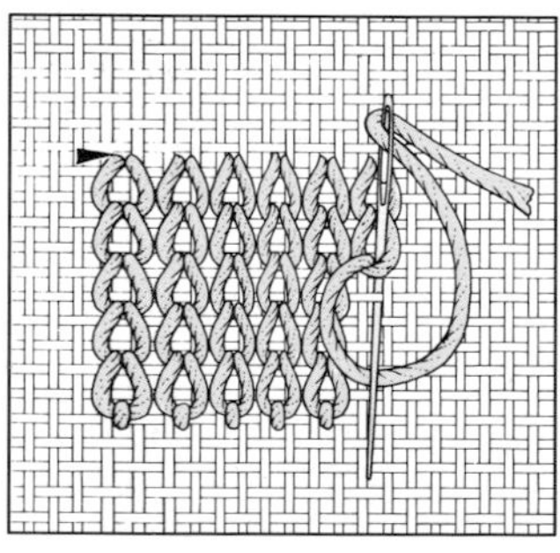

Start at top left and work in vertical rows. Bring yarn out and hold under left thumb. Insert needle into same hole and bring out 2 threads down, draw through loop. Continue in this way to end of row, finishing with a small straight stitch over the last loop.

Velvet stitch

This stitch resembles the pile of carpets and must be worked on a double canvas.

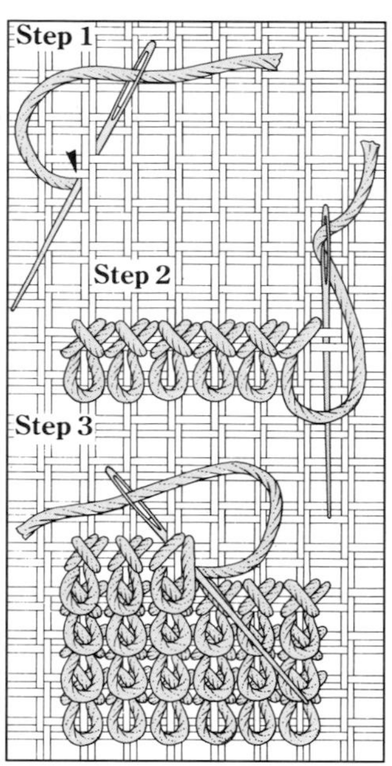

1 Work horizontally beginning at bottom left. Bring yarn out at arrow, insert needle up to right over 1 double thread intersection and bring out again at arrow.

2 Re-insert needle into same hole as before, leaving a loop of yarn at the bottom. Bring needle out 1 double thread down.

3 Take needle up to left over 1 double thread intersection and bring out in same place, ready to make the next stitch. When the work is finished, cut and trim the loops evenly.

Single knotted stitch

This stitch is best worked on single canvas.

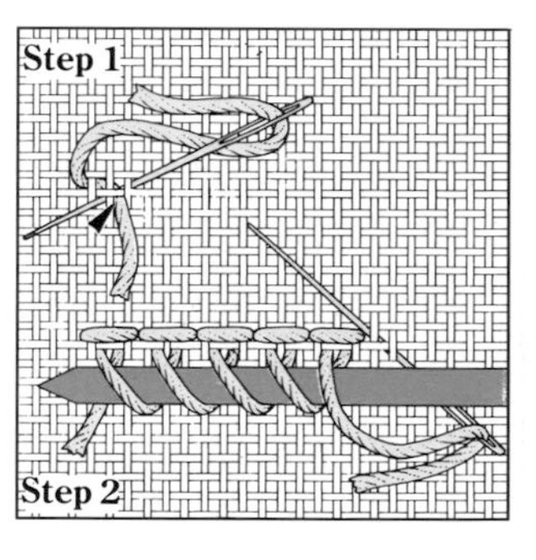

1 Work from left to right, and from the bottom row upwards. Insert needle at arrow and bring out 1 thread up and 2 threads to left. Hold down short end of yarn with left thumb. Insert needle 3 threads to right and bring out 2 threads to left and 1 thread down. Pull yarn tightly downwards to close knot.

2 Continue in this way, taking the yarn around a mesh stick, or a knitting needle, to regulate the size of the loops. Work subsequent rows 1 thread up. Complete the knotting and then cut and trim the loops evenly.

Star stitches

These decorative radiating star stitches are easy to work and cover the canvas fast forming interesting backgrounds or eye-catching motifs.

Star stitch

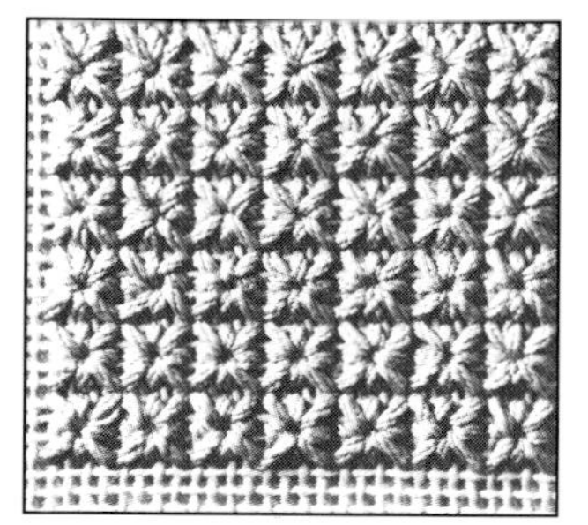

This stitch forms a star within a square and consists of eight stitches all worked into the same central point. It is best worked on single canvas in a coarse thread.

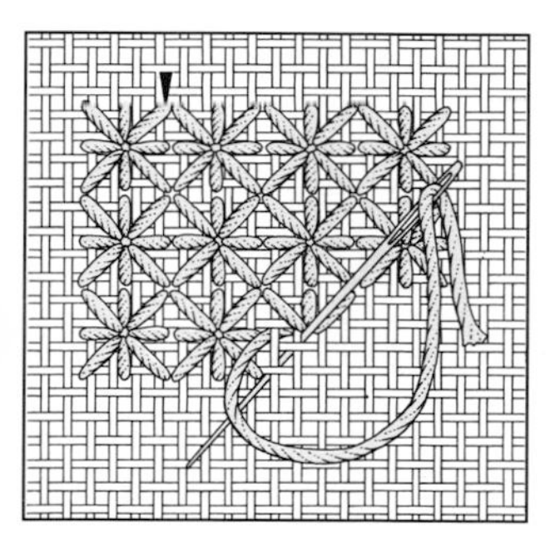

Starting from the outer edge of the square, bring needle out and work each stitch into the centre over 2 canvas threads or over 2 canvas intersections when coming from the corners. Leave 2 canvas threads unworked between each converging stitch so that each star occupies a square 4 horizontal threads by 4 vertical threads.

Work next and subsequent stitches into the side edge of the previous ones.

Rhodes stitch

This stitch consists of diagonal stitches worked around a square in an anti-clockwise direction. It is best worked on a single canvas.

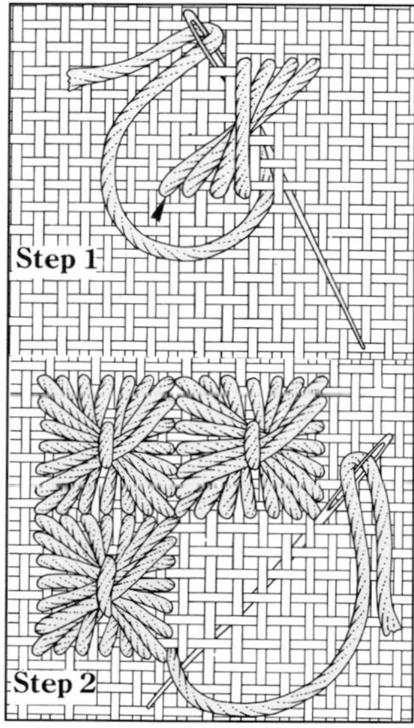

1 Start from the outer edge of the square, bring needle out at arrow. Take it up to right over 6 canvas intersections, insert down to left, bring needle out again 1 vertical thread to right of original starting point.

Work the next stitch over the previous one, inserting needle 1 vertical thread to left at top and bringing it out 1 vertical thread to right again at bottom. Continue in this way as shown, until the square is filled.

2 Finish off each square with a small vertical stitch over 2 horizontal threads at the centre.

Fan stitch

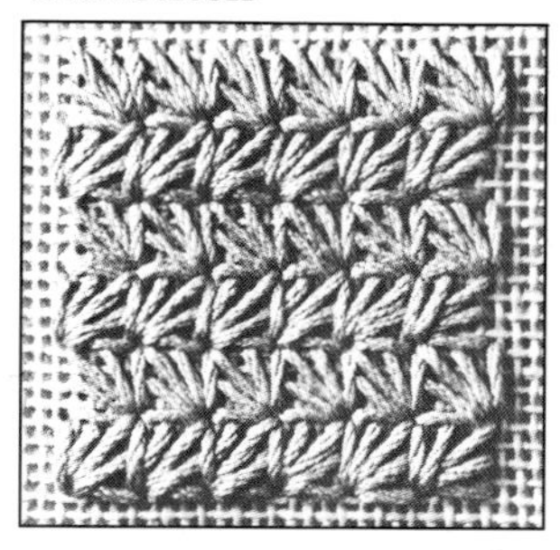

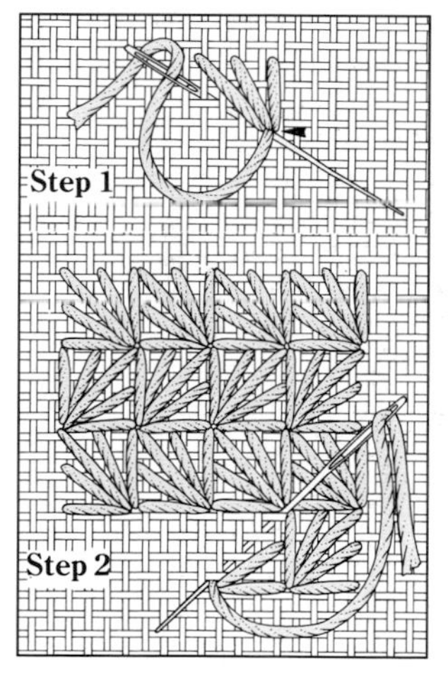

1 Bring needle out at arrow, take it up over 4 horizontal threads, insert downwards and bring it out again at original starting point. Work the next 4 stitches all radiating from the same corner as shown. Leave 2 canvas threads unworked between each stitch.

Continue by working each group of 5 stitches into the side of the previous group.

2 On subsequent rows alternate the fans so that they radiate in the opposite direction.

3

PATCHWORK, QUILTING AND APPLIQUÉ

Fabric, implements and templates

Patchwork is made by joining many small patches of fabric together to make a complete mosaic pattern. The accuracy of joining, the choice of fabrics and the placing of the patches together are the three contributing factors which will make the finished work a thing of beauty. All the patches should be cut into well-defined shapes which will fit together accurately to create the geometric patterns. The colour juxtapositions can either be contrasting or subtly shaded. It is more usual to use alternate dark and light patches so that each shape is clearly defined. Choose fabrics with small prints as they are ideal for the size of most patches. Large patterns used for small patches merge and become meaningless.

Fabrics
Any fabrics can be pieced together but the ideal choices are those which are washable and finely woven so they give crisp fold lines, such as cottons. If you are mixing fabrics, use those of a similar type and weight so they will lie smoothly when joined together.

Implements
It is important to use the correct type of paper for backing the fabric patches to ensure that these are given a smooth even surface and crisp fold lines. Brown wrapping paper is ideal. You will also need adhesive tape, sharp scissors for cutting fabric and paper, pins, fine needles and thread, a pencil and templates.

Templates

Templates are the pattern shapes used to cut out the fabric and paper patches. They can either be made at home or bought at most needlework departments. The bought templates, made of plastic or metal, are usually sold in sets comprising a paper and a fabric template. Window templates are also available, which can be used for both, or simply to line up the print. Crazy patchwork made from randomly-cut shapes, does not, of course, require a template. Home-made templates must be measured accurately and cut precisely so that the edges are straight and the angles correctly formed.

Set of diamond templates for fabric and paper patches

Set of complementary shaped templates for paper patches

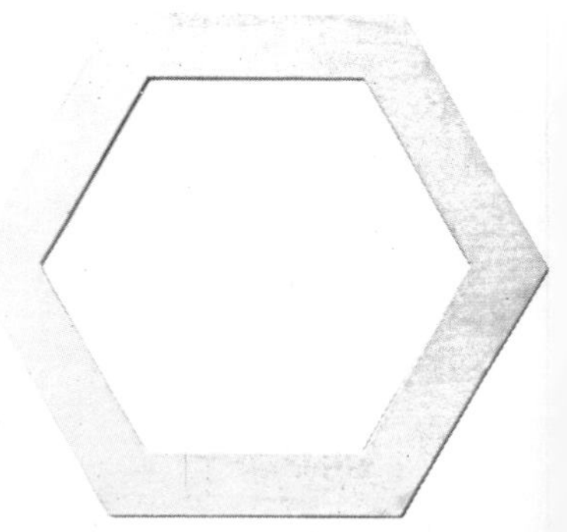

Hexagon window template for both fabric and paper patches

CUTTING TEMPLATES

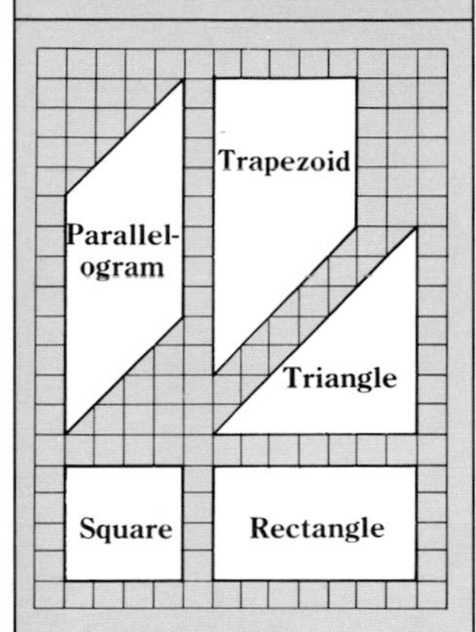

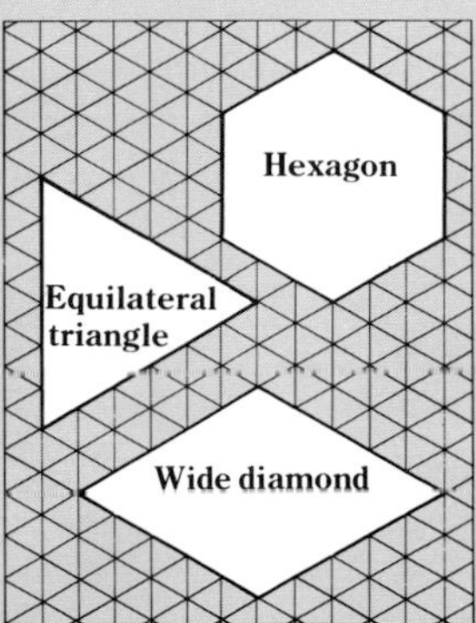

Many shapes can be cut using square and isometric paper. There are two diamond shapes, which are commonly used in patchwork: the 60° - 120° diamond, used for six-pointed stars, hexagons and Tumbling blocks (this can be cut from the triangular grid graph paper); and the long 45° - 135° diamond (below), drawn with ruler and protractor, ensuring that all sides are equal.

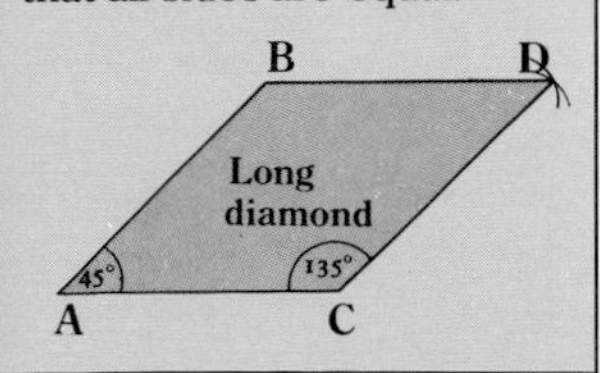

Paper and fabric patches

Although it is not absolutely necessary to use paper backings for the fabric patches it is far better to do so as the paper helps to retain the shape and firmness of the fabric patches and makes the joining together far easier. The paper backings are removed when the patchwork is completed.

Cutting paper backing

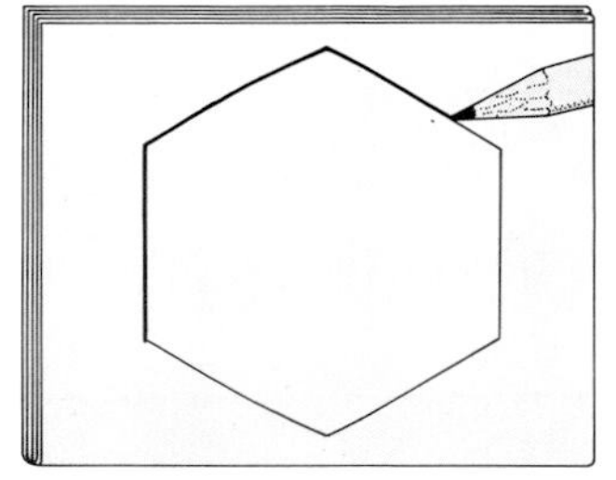

1 Fold a piece of paper so that several layers can be cut to shape at the same time, then place the template on the paper and draw around the edges with a pencil as close to the template as possible.

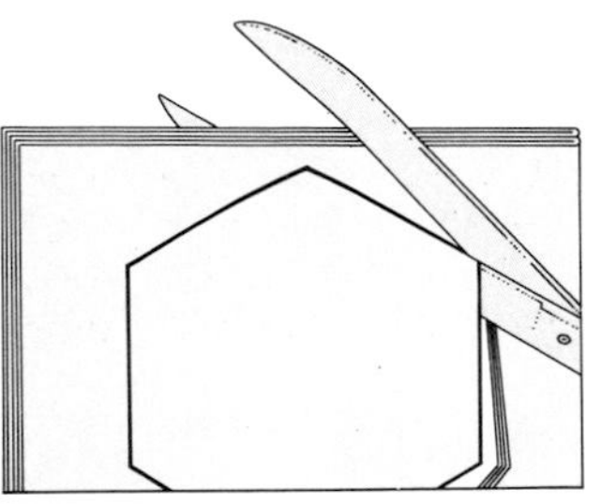

2 Cut through the layers of paper with either an artist's scalpel or scissors, making accurate and identical shapes, with the paper beneath.

Cutting printed fabric patches

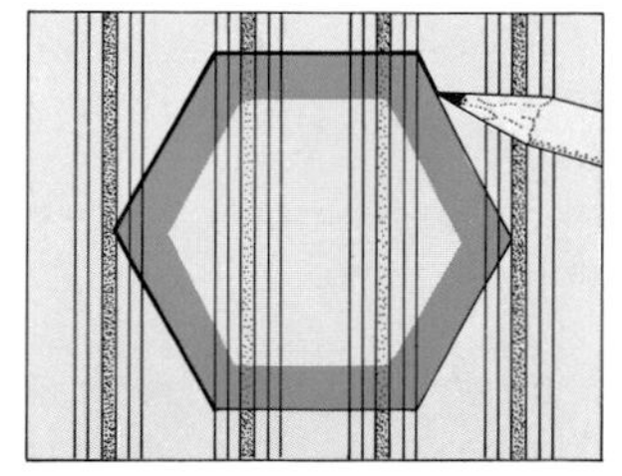

1 Place the window template on top of the fabric and frame the print correctly, making sure that the grain of the fabric always runs in the same direction for each patch. Then pencil around template edges.

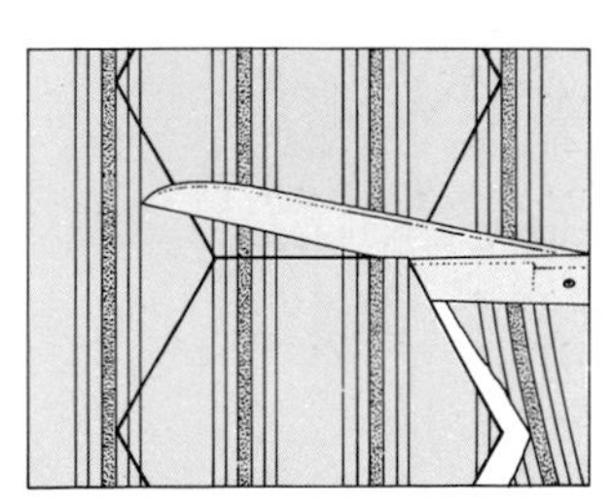

2 Cut along marked lines and when finished collect the various colour, print, shape and size groups together.

Paper patch templates

If a window or fabric template is not being used, then the paper patches themselves can be used as templates. This is done by placing a cut paper patch on top of the fabric, pinning it down and then cutting the fabric underneath ¼in (6mm) larger all round. This is recommended only for simple patchwork shapes.

Traditional patchworks

A careful study of old patchworks is extremely rewarding both as a guide to the placing of the patches and colours, and as a reference to textiles of the past. Indeed one of the ways of dating patchworks is from the textile scraps they contain. When the patchworks were used for quilted bed covers, the quilting stitches were either worked across the surface, ignoring the patched design, or made inside the patches. Sometimes, on plain fabric patchworks, very decorative quilting designs are worked inside the patches and along the borders.

Eighteenth-century English embroidered patchwork of brocades and velvets

Nineteenth-century American crazy patchwork

Nineteenth-century English military patchwork quilt

Nineteenth-century Indian army quilt worked in dyed wool serge

Nineteenth-century English quilt worked in printed cottons

Attaching paper to fabric

After the paper and fabric patches have been cut, the paper backing is attached to the fabric patches. When working with triangles and diamonds make sure that the points are sharply formed. Circles and curved shapes need to be tacked around the edges before they are pinned to the paper to achieve a smooth fit.

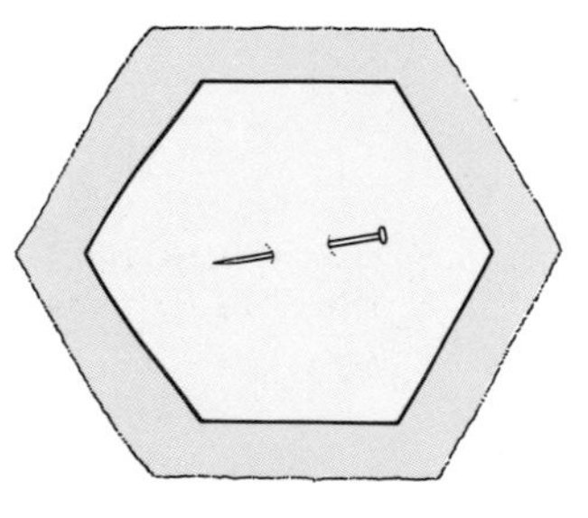

1 Lay fabric patches right side down on a flat surface and pin a paper patch to the centre of each, so that the edges of both patches lie parallel.

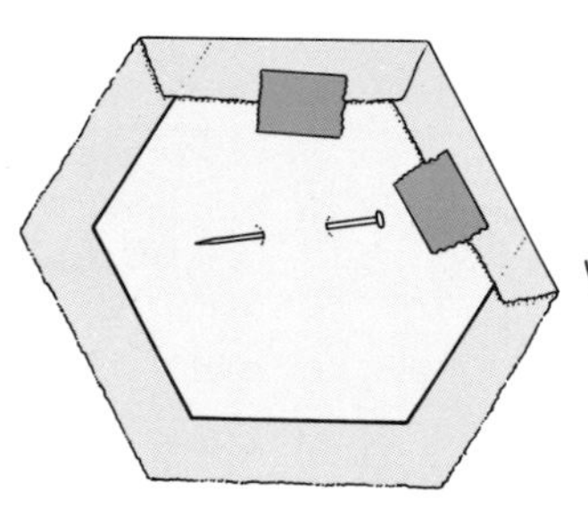

2 Fold the edges over one at a time and secure with a small piece of adhesive tape.

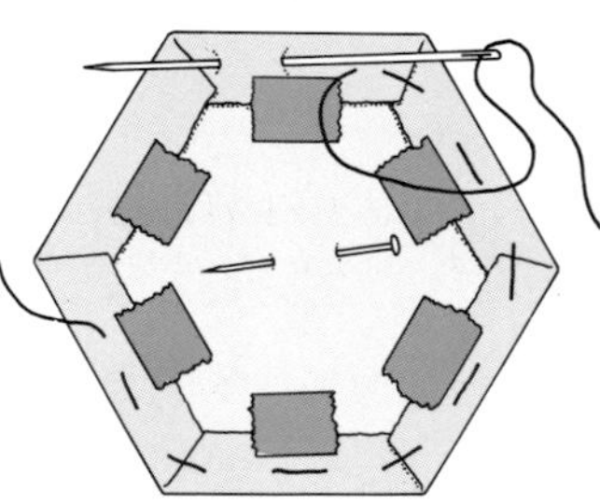

3 Then tack around the edges and remove adhesive tape. Press the folds into position with an iron in order to make clean lines.

TEMPLATE SHAPES

The patches used in patchwork can be made in a vast range of shapes. Below is a selection of template shapes most commonly used.

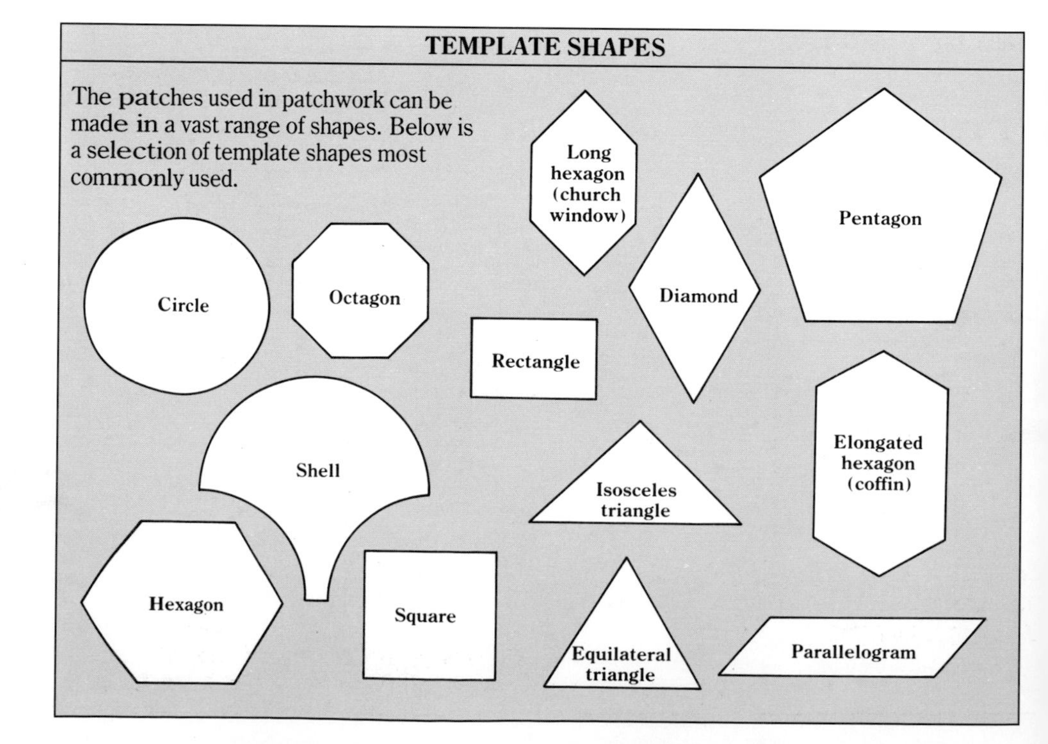

Working with diamonds and triangles

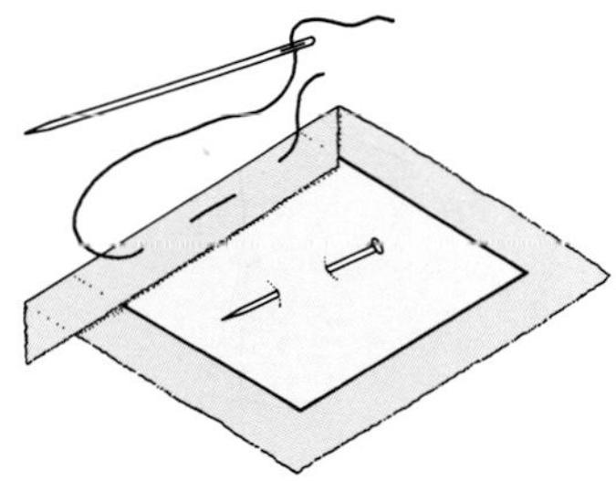

1 Pin the paper backing in position and fold and tack first side of diamond (or triangle).

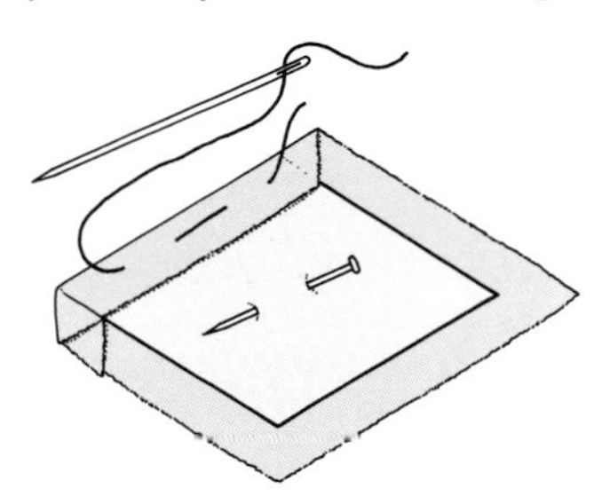

2 Then, before folding 2nd side, fold point of first side down on top of 2nd side.

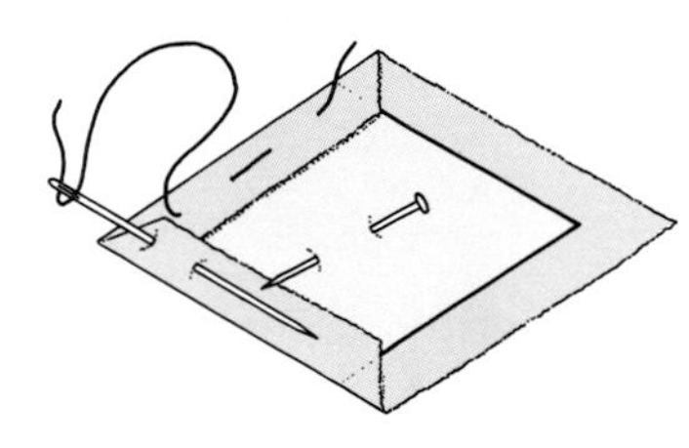

3 Fold and tack down 2nd side.

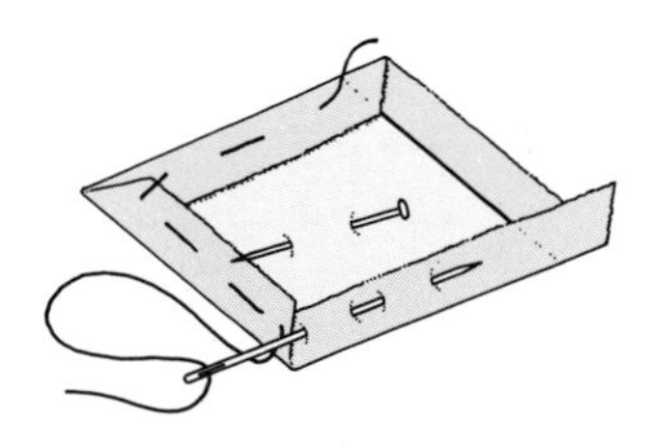

4 Fold back 3rd side, repeating the procedure for the point as in Step 2. Then tack down the final side of the patch.

Working with circles and curved shapes

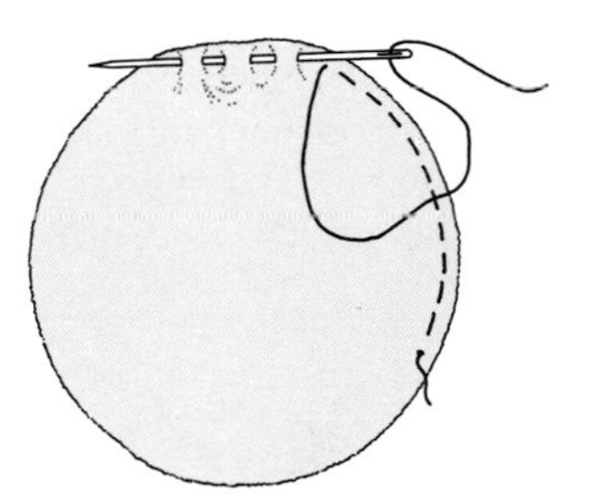

1 Work around the circular fabric patch with running stitches placed 1/8in. (3mm) in from the edge and leave the thread hanging.

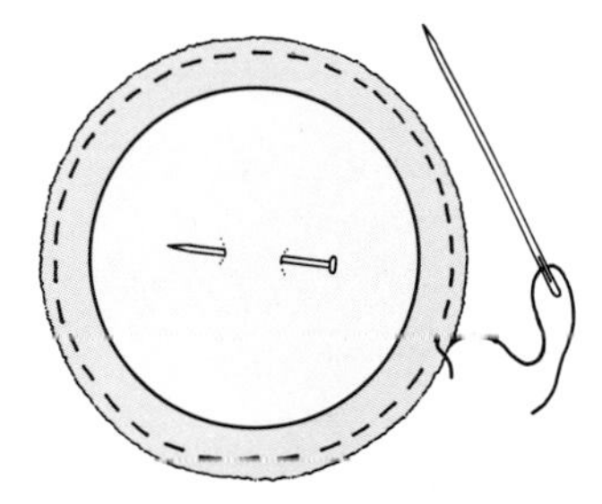

2 Pin paper patch to centre of fabric patch.

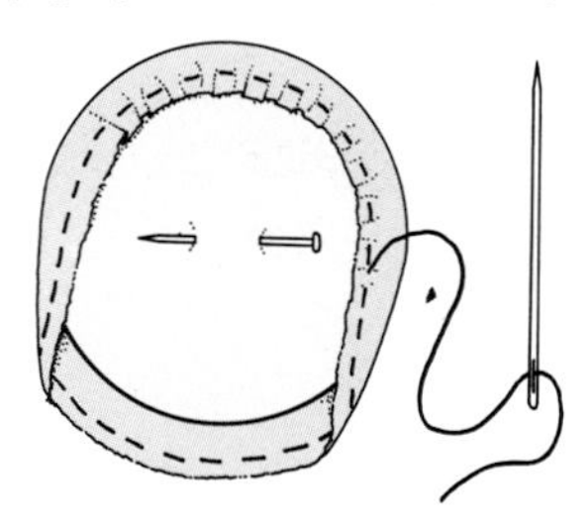

3 Pull thread to gather edge so that it folds neatly over the paper patch.

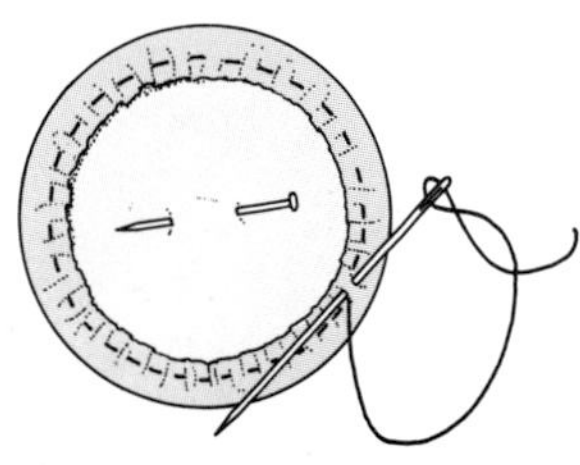

4 When the circle is gathered, knot the thread and cut the end off close to the knot.

One-patch designs

Some of the most traditional patterns are created from single-shape geometric patches. These patches are all the same size and, when repeated, will give an overall mosaic effect. One-patch patterns, because of their simplicity of design, depend upon skilful use of colour and choice of fabric to create an impact. This type of patchwork is traditionally sewn by hand using backing papers.

Pennsylvanian quilt 1880-90

Detail of the quilt showing the dramatic use of contrasting colours

Trip around the world

The bright colours of this Pennsylvanian quilt are typical of those used by the early German settlers who tended to use plain rather than printed fabrics. This pattern is composed of squares sewn together to create an expanding diamond design. To achieve the central square there must be an uneven number of squares and rows. Finished squares of about 2-2½in. (50-65mm) make a reasonable-size quilt and are not too difficult to handle. It is an excellent beginner's pattern.

The success of the design depends on choosing bright colours in tones ranging from light to dark. Cotton fabrics, either plain or with small prints, are the most suitable and offer the widest colour range. Shirting material is also useful for the lighter tones.

Grandmother's flower garden

Shown here is one of a pair of quilts almost identical in design. Each one contains over 6,000 pieces all neatly assembled with the backing papers still intact.

This is a scrap-bag patchwork that successfully uses a great variety of printed fabrics. Generally, hexagon patterns are best made from cotton fabrics of even weights because these can be folded more neatly over the backing papers.

The hexagon, which is always associated with traditional English patchwork, is suitable for small or large projects. The patches can be sewn together in a random pattern or grouped to form individual rosettes.

The best way of making a hexagon pattern is to hand sew it using backing papers. Grandmother's flower garden is usually made up of one central hexagon, encircled by six others in a second colour, surrounded by twelve hexagons in a third colour.

English patchwork 1850-60

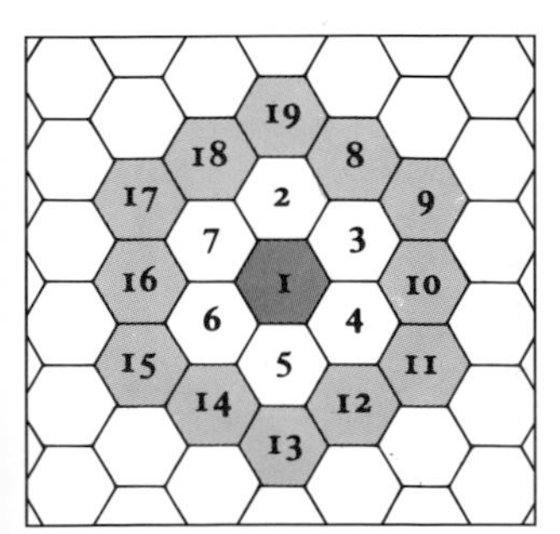

Sewing sequence:
Use 1 as the centre patch. Join 2-7, then 8-19.

Detail from Grandmother's flower garden

Joining the fabric patches

When all the fabric patches have been prepared they are then joined together with small, evenly spaced overcasting stitches, securing the thread at the beginning and end with a back stitch. A fine needle and thread should be used to make the stitches as invisible as possible. The joining can be done in three ways: in rows, sections (or blocks), or in one continuous piece. The method used will depend on the type of patchwork being made.

Slightly different methods are employed for joining more complicated shapes as can be seen on page 102 when making shell patches. Crazy patchwork is stitched to a foundation fabric and its edges overlap.

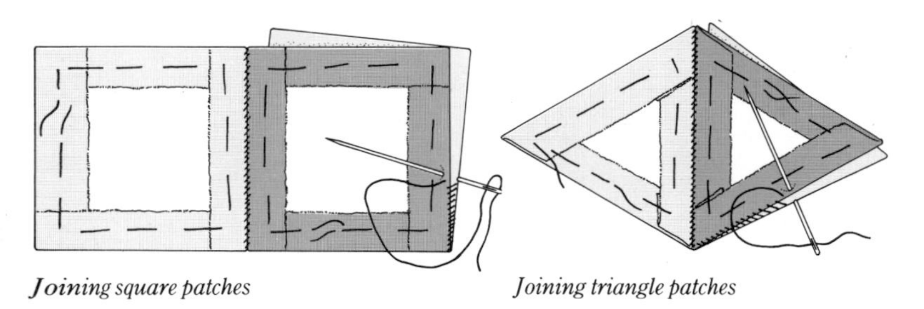

Joining square patches

Joining triangle patches

Joining in rows

This is the best method to use for all-over patterns such as line and diagonal designs. It is worked by placing two patches face to face and oversewing neatly and closely along one edge, catching the fold of the fabric on each patch. Try to avoid sewing the paper patches underneath as it will then be easier to remove them. Join the rows together in the same way, placing first and second rows face to face and oversewing all the side edges together.

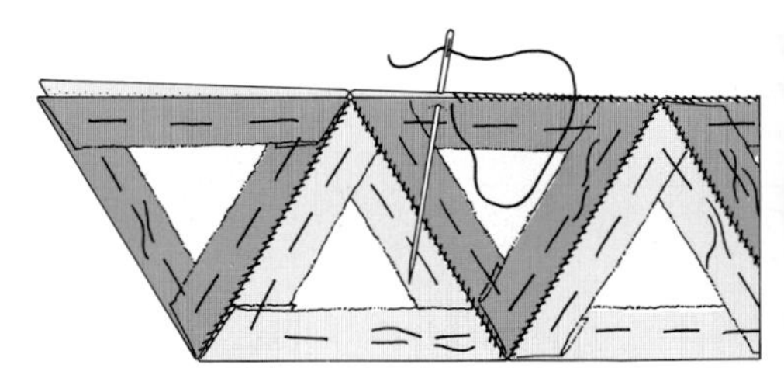

Joining rows of triangle patches

Joining in blocks

Blocks are made by joining a collection of patches together to form individual units. The finished blocks are then joined together. Joining in blocks is the best method to use for medallion and section designs. Block joining is also more convenient if the work is to be carried around as the small blocks are easy to work on.

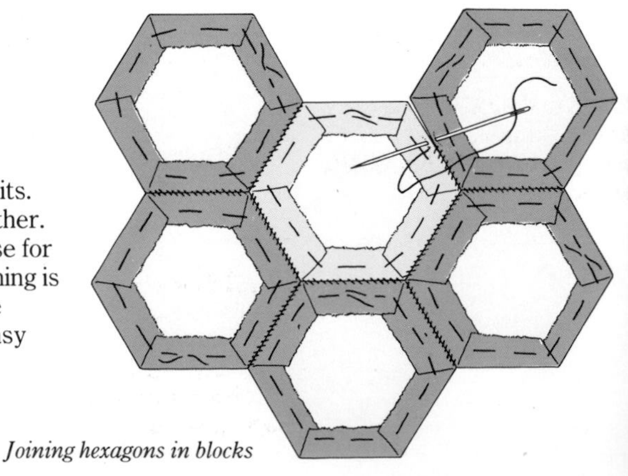

Joining hexagons in blocks

Machine joining

Although small patches need to be joined by hand, larger patches with sides over 1½in. (3.8cm) long can easily be joined by machine. This is especially true of large squares and rectangles which may not require a paper backing but can be machine stitched directly together, side seam to side seam, row by row, in the usual way.

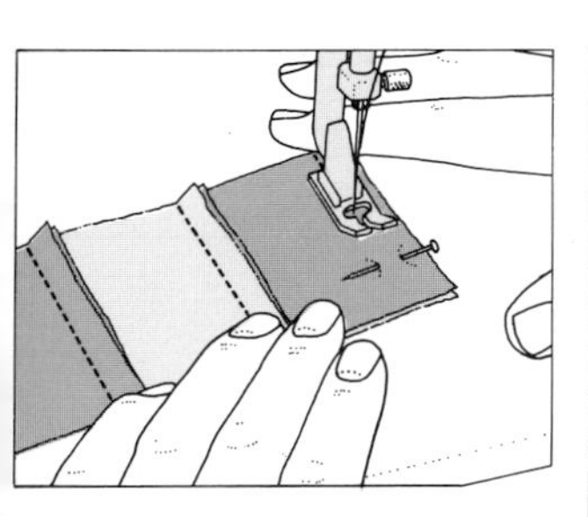

1 Start by pinning the patches together and joining them in rows.

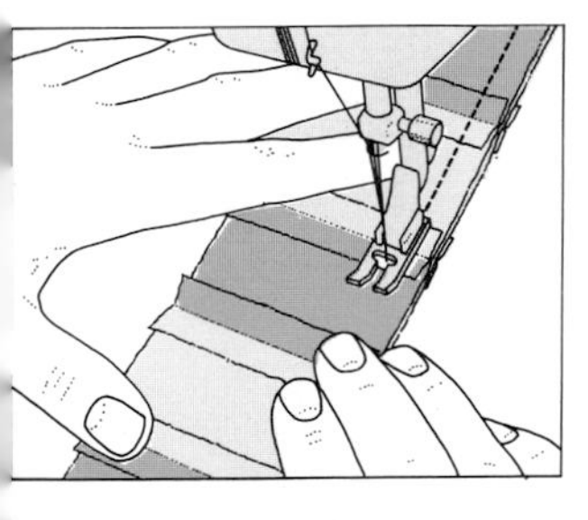

2 When the rows are complete open up the seams and iron them flat. Then machine stitch the rows together.

Finishing

When all the patches have been joined the patchwork must then be finished off and lined (see right). The finishing off process is carried out by pressing the whole patchwork into shape on a padded surface. If the patchwork has been worked in blocks, it may be easier to treat each section in this way first before the final joining.

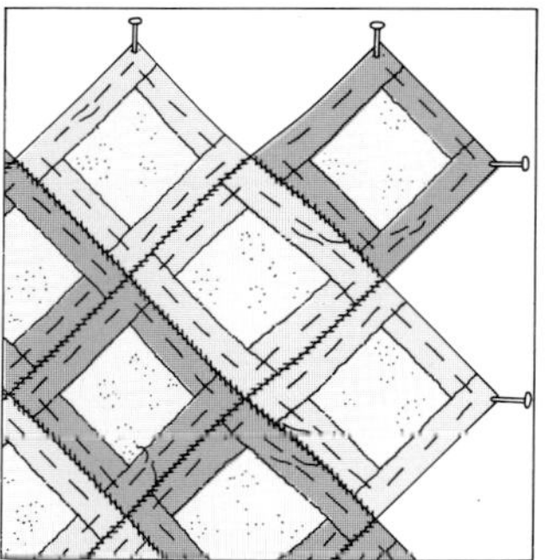

1 Place the patchwork right side down on a padded surface. Stretch it out and pin it at the centre of each side and then at the corners. Continue to pin along the sides until it is the required shape.

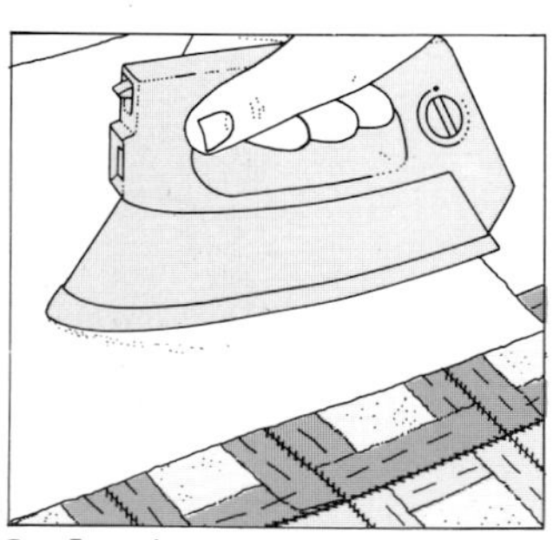

2 Iron it under a damp cloth using a warm iron and leave it until it is dry. Remove pins, tacking stitches and the paper patches.

Lining

When the patchwork is finished it needs to be lined both to strengthen and neaten it. Large patchworks, such as bedcoverings, should also be quilted to keep the original shape and add warmth. The lining fabric should be firm enough to hold the top securely but not so heavy that it will pull away.

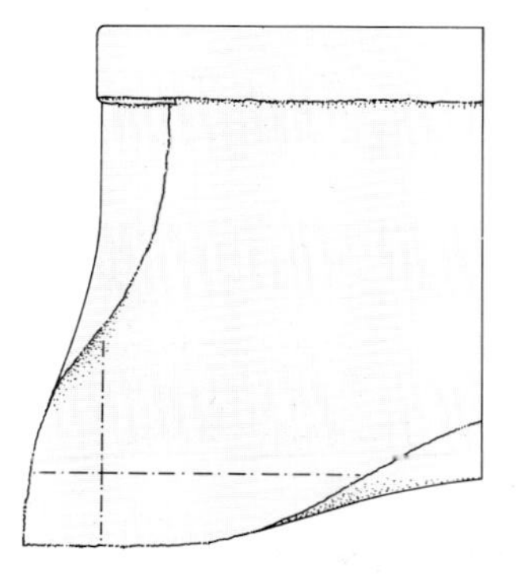

1 Cut the lining fabric to the size of the patchwork plus a ½in. (1.3cm) seam allowance all round. Then lay it right side down, fold in the seam allowance and press flat.

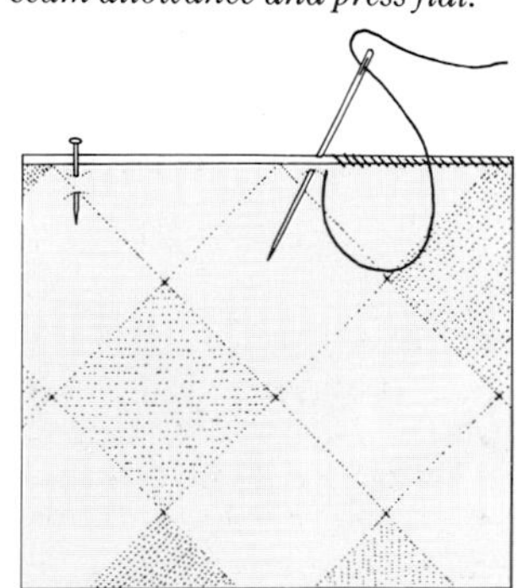

2 Pin the lining fabric and patchwork together wrong sides facing, folding in the edges of the patchwork. Press flat. Tack the two together and slip stitch along all seams.

Patterns in the round

Mennonite quilt, 1880, with sunburst pattern.

The design is made entirely of long diamond shapes

JOINING FROM THE CENTRE OUTWARDS

Patchworks worked in this way can be designed on graph paper first so that the colouring will fall in the correct positions with the centre being the focal point.

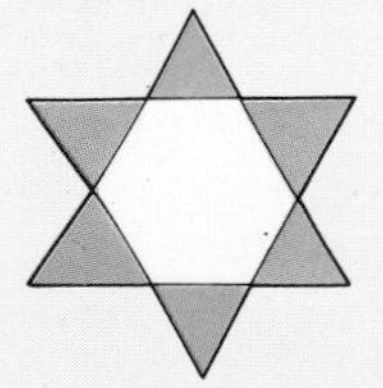

1 Make a star or medallion using either hexagons, triangles or diamond patches and contrasting the colours as desired.

2 Increase outwards, completing one circuit before starting on the next. Sunbursts are made using six- or eight-pointed stars at the centre of the design.

3 Continue until the patchwork is required size. It can be left as a hexagon by placing diamond shapes sideways or cutting them in half.

DECORATIVE BORDERS

The following borders can be used either to edge a plain solid fabric or as a contrast to a completed patchwork. They each form continuous patterns so therefore require a special treatment when the corners are reached. Suggested ways of filling the corners are given below but any block design can be used.

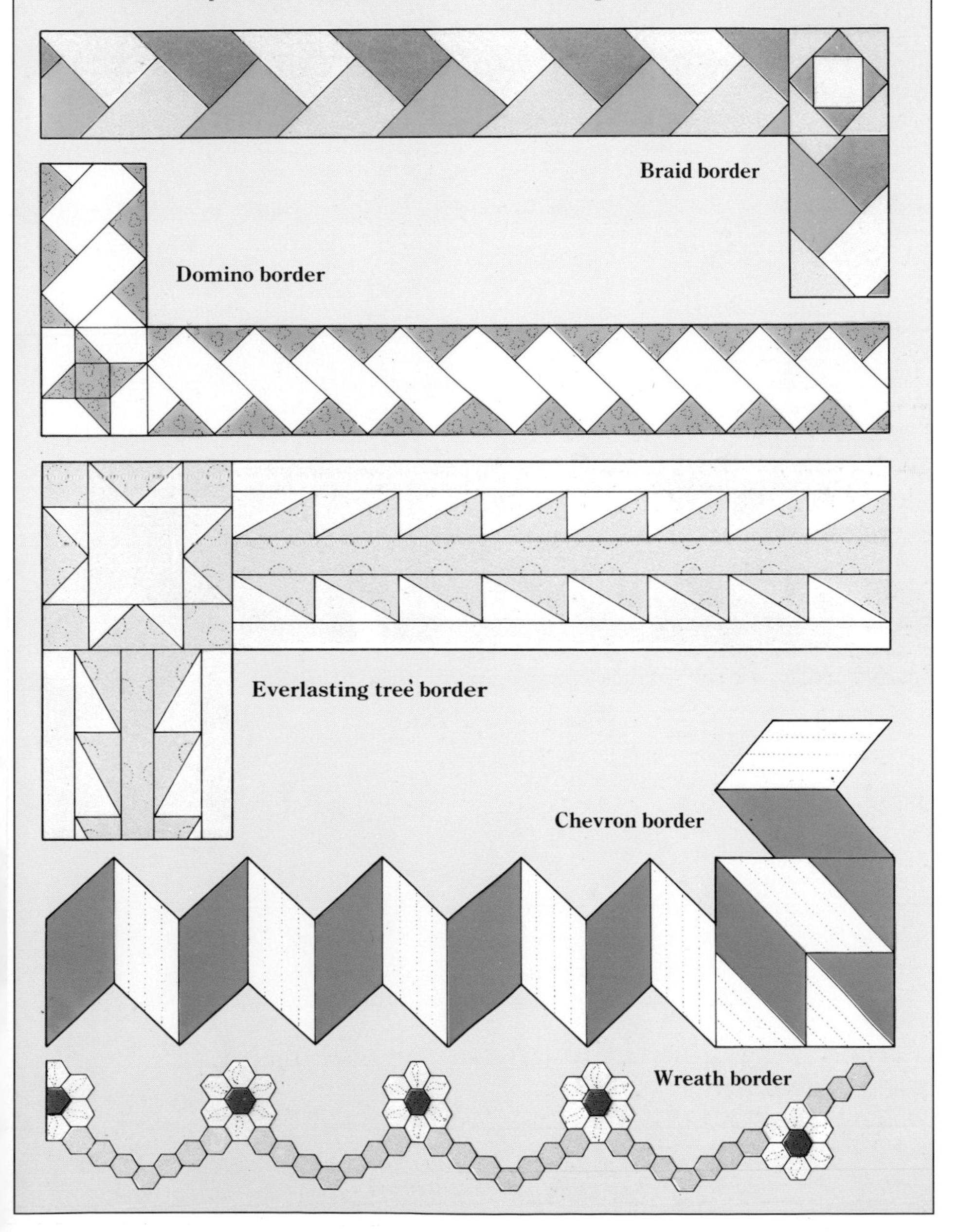

Shell pattern patchwork

In shell pattern patchwork the stemmed shell shape forms the template but when the shell patterns are assembled the stem is concealed. There are two different ways of making the patches: with a fabric lining or with a paper backing. Fabric-lined patches are the most satisfactory as the lining helps to retain the shape of the patches during the joining process. The fabric patches should be cut in the usual way making sure that the grain of the fabric runs straight and parallel to the stem. Use the paper template to cut paper patches or bonded fabric linings.

Making shells

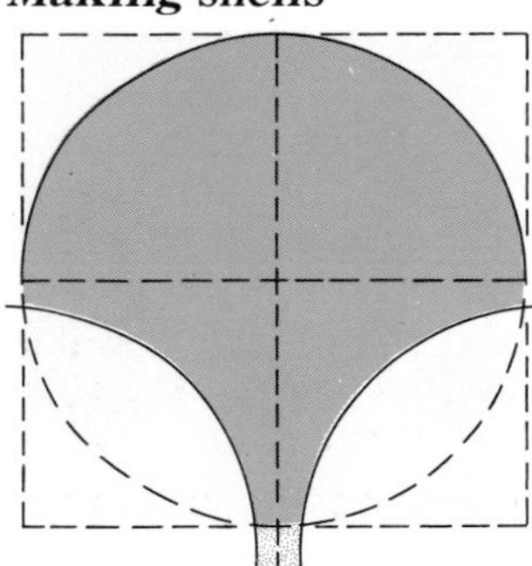

Draw a circle on graph paper and then draw 2 small arcs below and to either side of it so that they cut into the large circle to form the shell.

Fabric-lined patches

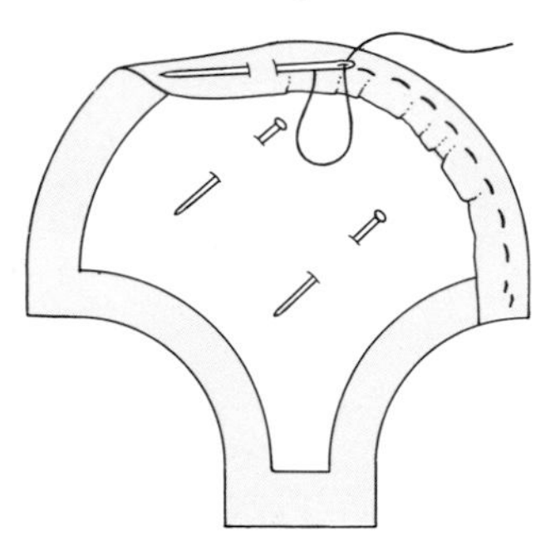

Pin a fabric lining to the back of each patch. Fold over the curved edge and tack into place through hem and lining only.

Paper backed patches

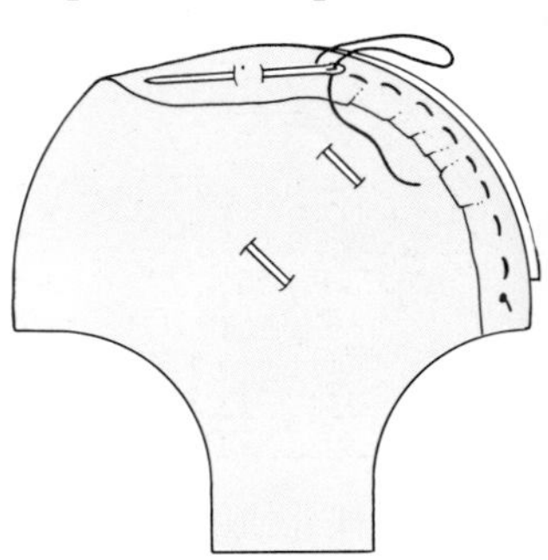

Pin the paper patch to the front of the fabric patch. Fold the edge to the back using the paper patch to indicate the fold line. Tack around curved edge but not through the paper and then remove paper.

Joining shell patterns

Pin the first row of prepared patches onto a cork board. The second row should be placed over these so that they cover the stems. Pin and then tack into position. Remove pins and stitch neatly around curves, as shown, catching the fabric of the first row with each stitch. When the final row has been attached, fold the edges back and then secure with small hem stitches.

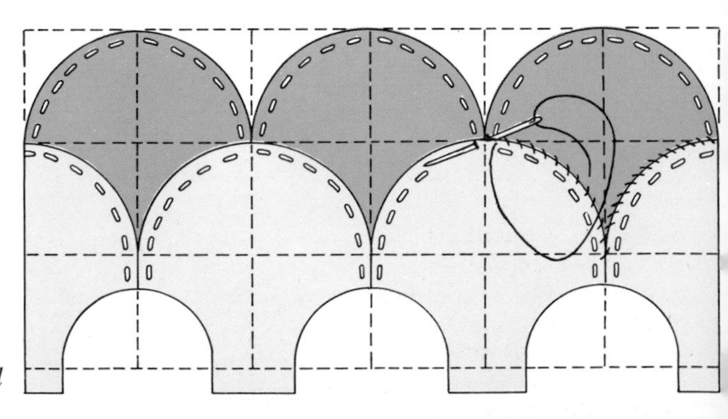

The joining of shell patchwork requires accuracy so that the finished patchwork will be perfectly flat and even.

Log cabin patchwork

Log cabin patchworks were invented entirely for decorative reasons as they use a great deal of fabric. They are very often worked in silks or velvets in square blocks composed of light and dark strips stitched and folded around a small central square.

The central square and strips are sewn one by one onto a foundation fabric. The strips are all cut to the same width which is twice that shown on the template plus ¼in. (6mm) for overlapping. Their length increases with each circuit.

Preparing the strips

The standard log cabin block has strips stitched on to a foundation fabric in the order illustrated above.

Making the templates

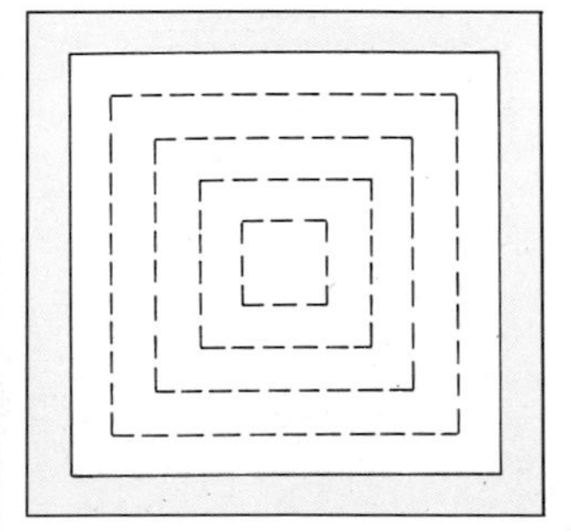

Draw a template as a guide to the width and length of the circuits. The template should be the size of the finished block plus ½in. (1.3cm) seam allowance all round. The squares radiating from the central square should be the same distance apart.

Applying the strips

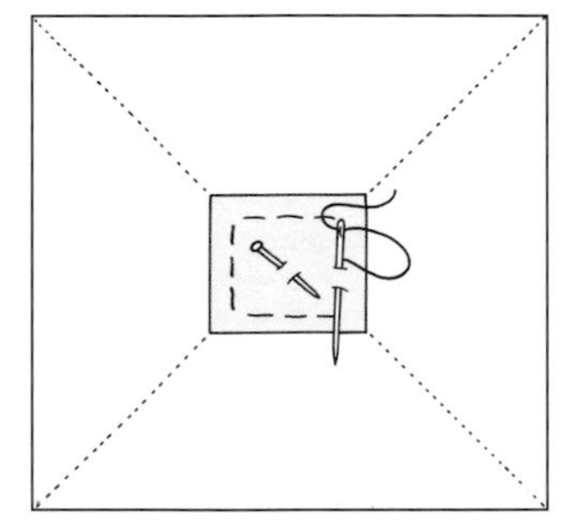

1 Draw 2 diagonal lines on a square of the foundation fabric to help to position the corners of the strips. Cut the small central square with ¼in. (6mm) seam allowance. Pin this to the centre of the large square and secure with running stitches.

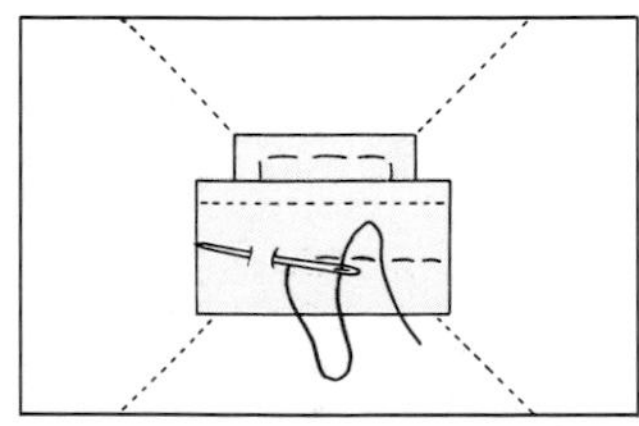

2 Cut the first circuit of dark and light strips allowing an extra ¼in. (6mm) at each end so that the next circuit will overlap it. Then secure the first strip with running stitches, as shown.

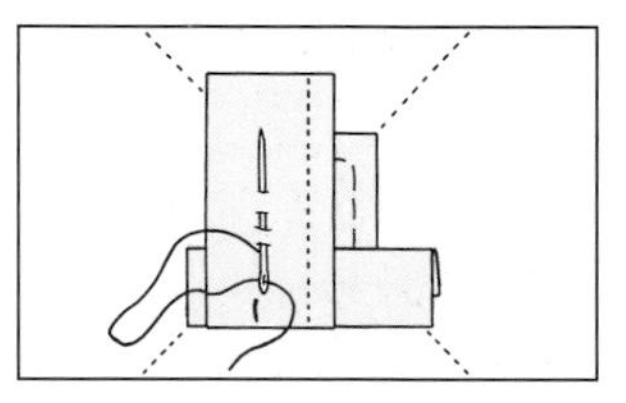

3 Fold back the first strip and secure the second light strip in the same way.

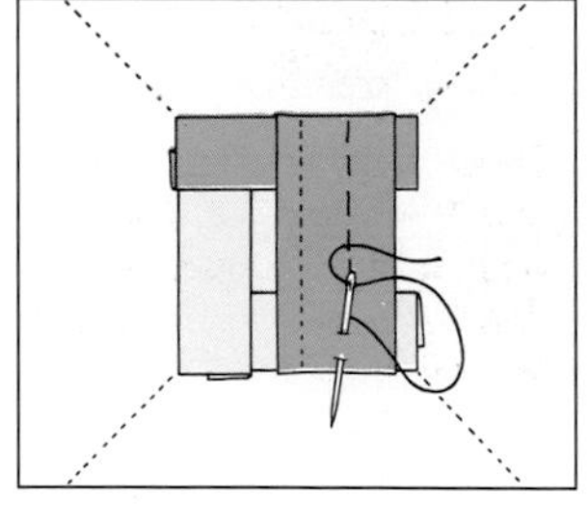

4 Secure and fold the 2 dark strips as shown.

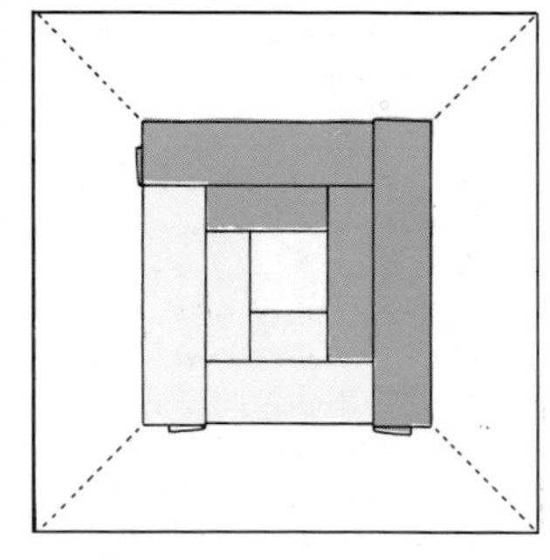

5 Secure the next and subsequent circuits until the square is complete.

Shell and log cabin designs

Shell patchworks look equally attractive made from printed or plain fabrics. More dramatic effects are achieved in log cabin patchworks when contrasting light and dark un-patterned fabrics are used to create a variety of geometric designs.

Eighteenth-century shell patchwork made in printed fabrics from many parts of the world.

Diagonal log cabin

Light and dark squares alternate with light and dark triangles.

PLANNING PATCHWORK DESIGNS

When making an original patchwork it is best to plan it out on graph paper first. Cut the paper to the proposed measurement and then mark in the design with coloured pencils or inks. As a rough guide to estimating the amount of fabric required take the measurements of the design as though it were going to be made in one piece and then add an extra yard for seams. The total is then divided proportionally according to the colours being used. The patchworks illustrated here give combinations of shapes and colours without the use of prints.

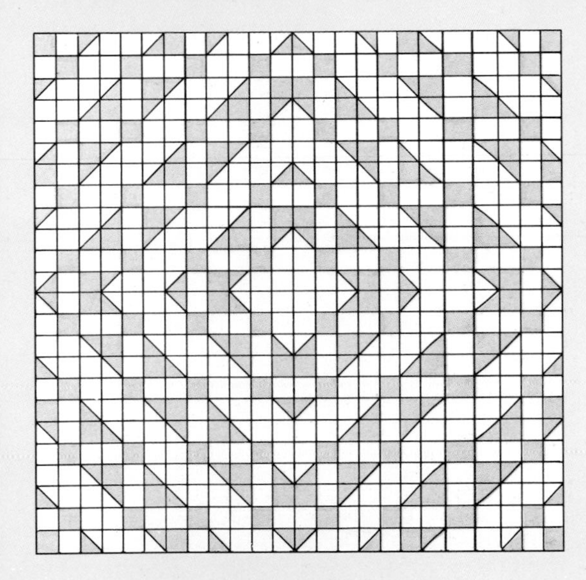

Barn raising variations
This intricate looking pattern is simply formed with light and dark squares and right triangles.

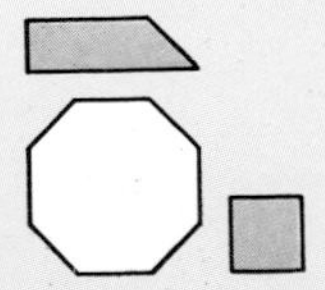

Dutch tile pattern
The pattern, left, is composed of octagons, squares and trapezoids in four tones.

Patchwork designs

There are innumerable designs that can be made from simple geometric shapes. Here are just a few ideas but the possible combinations are endless.

Window pane

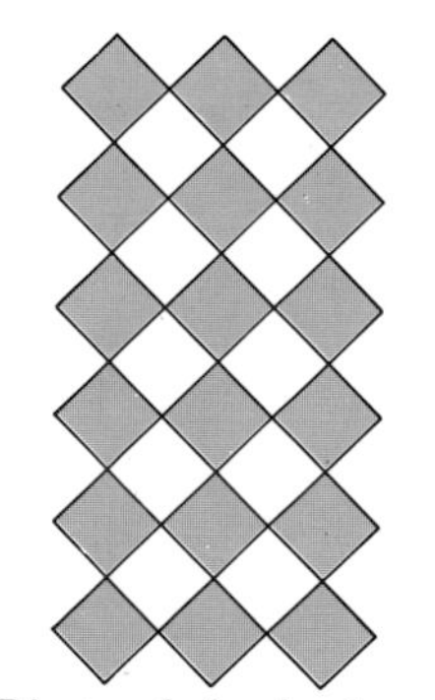

Diagonal checkerboard

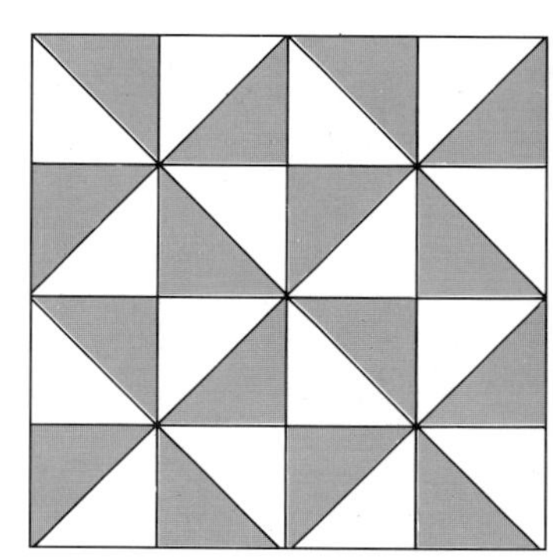

Windmill

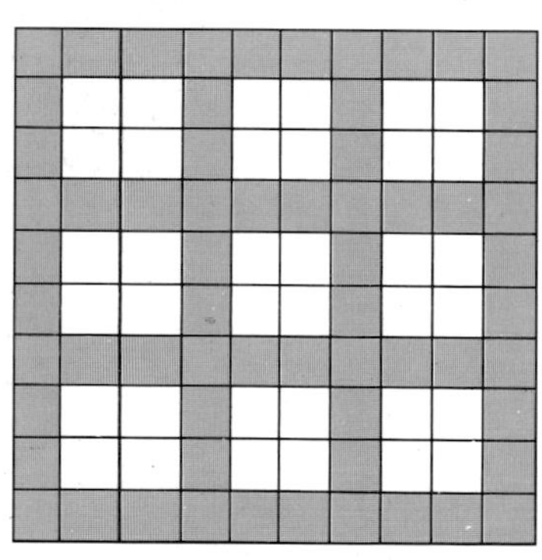

Framed squares

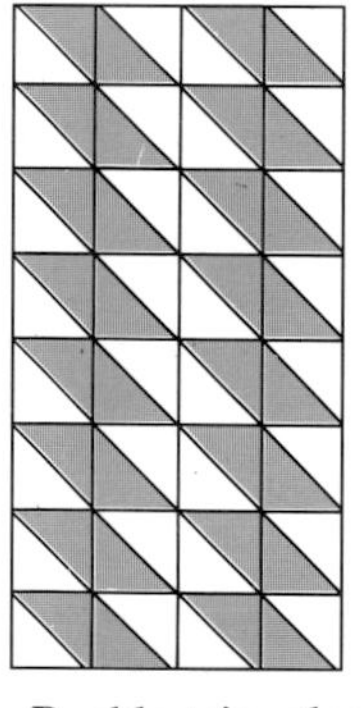

Pueblo triangles

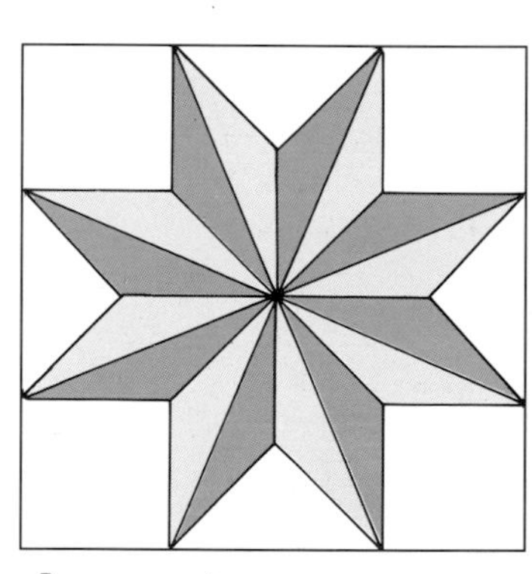

Lemoyne star

Paving pattern

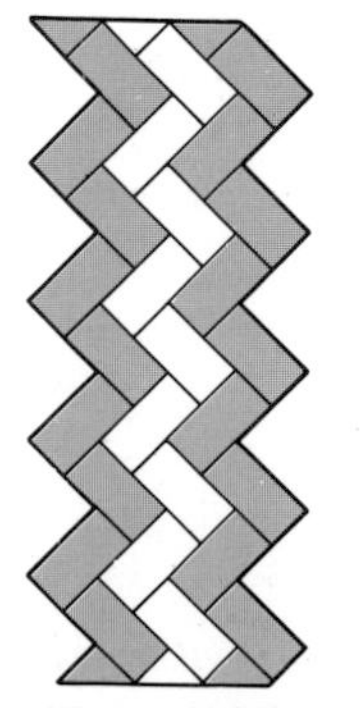

Zigzag bricks

Sunburst

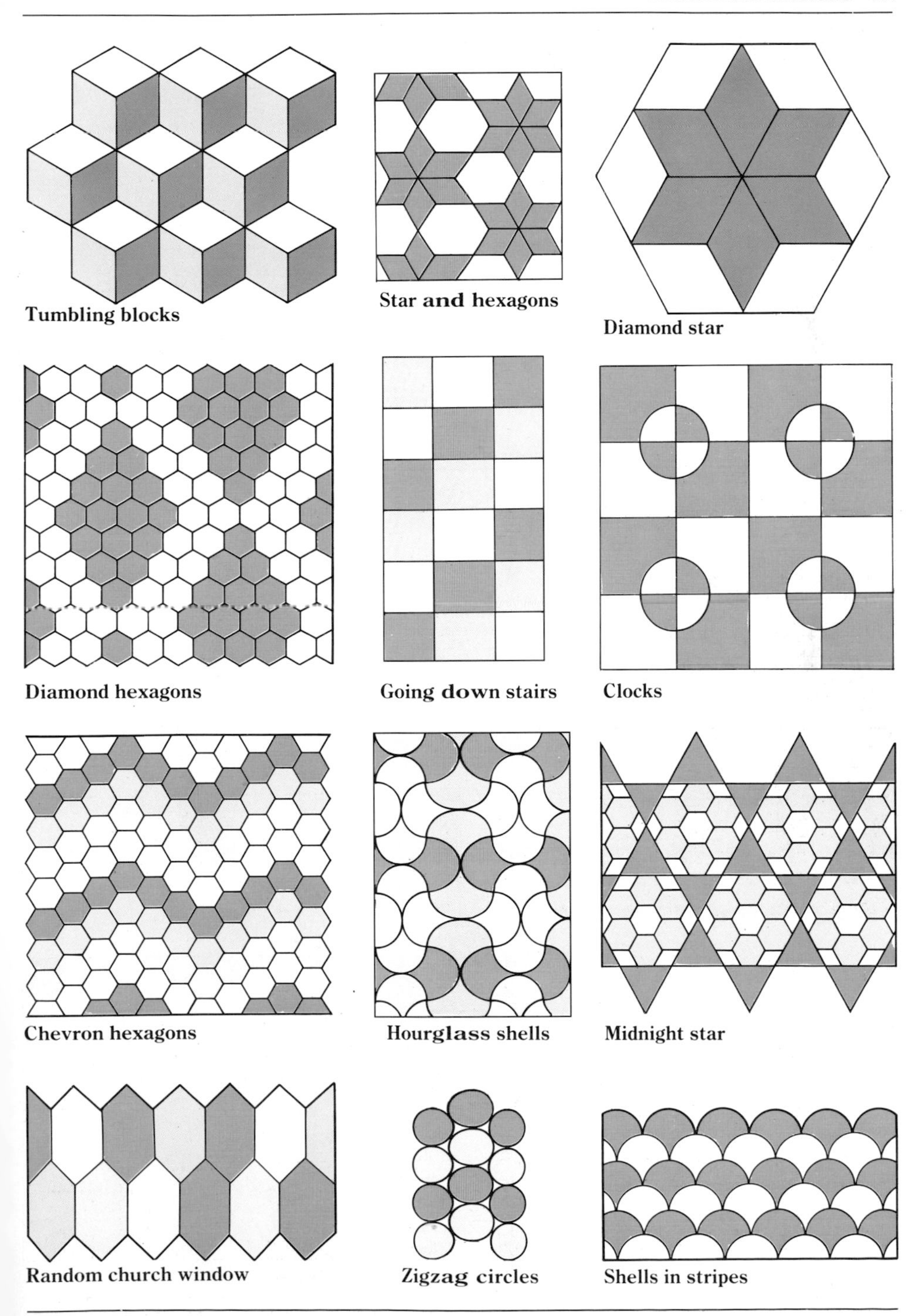
Tumbling blocks
Star and hexagons
Diamond star
Diamond hexagons
Going down stairs
Clocks
Chevron hexagons
Hourglass shells
Midnight star
Random church window
Zigzag circles
Shells in stripes

Birds in the air

Many of the traditional patchwork blocks were based on abstract patterns taken from everyday life. This Mennonite quilt of 1870 shows one of the oldest blocks and is evocative of birds in flight.

Because of its small-sized triangles this pattern was often used for a scrap quilt. A limited colour range as shown gives a more formal design.

The repeat blocks can easily be sewn on a machine. These are set diagonally and alternated with plain squares.

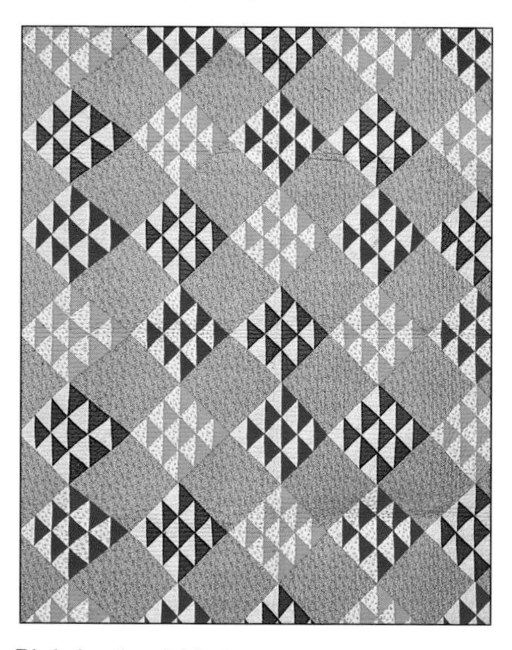

Birds in the air block

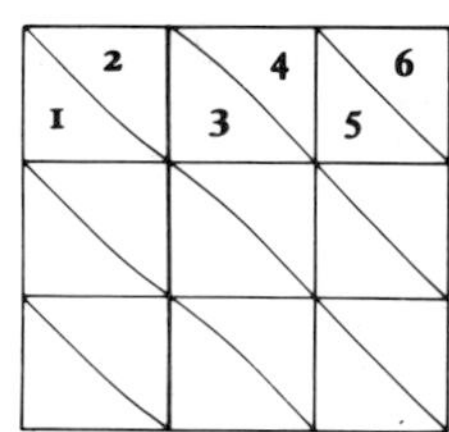

Join 1-2, 3-4, and 5-6. Join into one row. Continue in this way for the next two rows. Join the three rows together, making one block.

Double Irish chain

The two-block pattern used on this late nineteenth-century American quilt is complex in appearance but easy to make.

Plain or small-patterned cotton fabrics are best and the design is most suitable for an allover repeat pattern.

It is much easier to plan this design on graph paper because it can be a confusing pattern to piece. The pattern is a five-patch block alternated with a plain block which has a small square appliquéd onto each corner. Traditionally the plain blocks are quilted following the square patterns on the pieced blocks but other patterns could be used.

Five-patch block **Appliqué block**

1	2	3	4	5
6	7	8	9	10
11	12	13	14	15
16	17	18	19	20
21	22	23	24	25

Sew 1-5, 6-10, 11-15, 16-20, 21-25. Join rows into a block. For the second block take a plain square the same size and appliqué a square onto each corner. Alternate the plain and pieced blocks so as to give a chain pattern.

Patterned bars

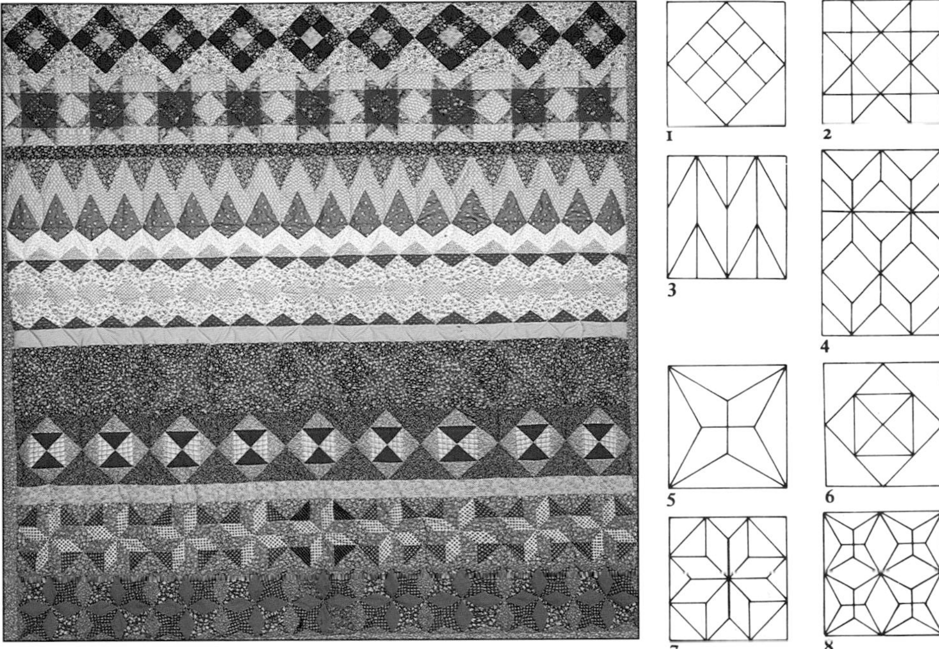

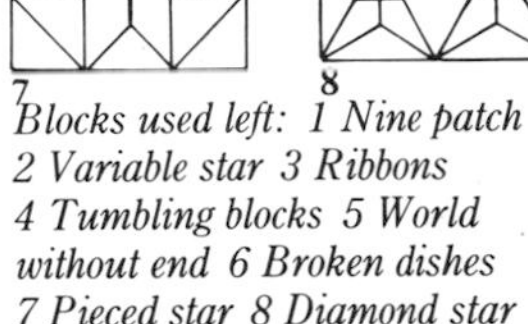

A modern quilt using traditional pieced blocks in an unusual design. This quilt has been sewn by hand using papers but it can be made very easily by machine, with a variety of plain and printed cotton fabrics.

Blocks used left: 1 Nine patch 2 Variable star 3 Ribbons 4 Tumbling blocks 5 World without end 6 Broken dishes 7 Pieced star 8 Diamond star

Houses

A contemporary English quilt which uses the basic house shape in an uncomplicated design. This is reminiscent of the traditional Schoolhouse block.

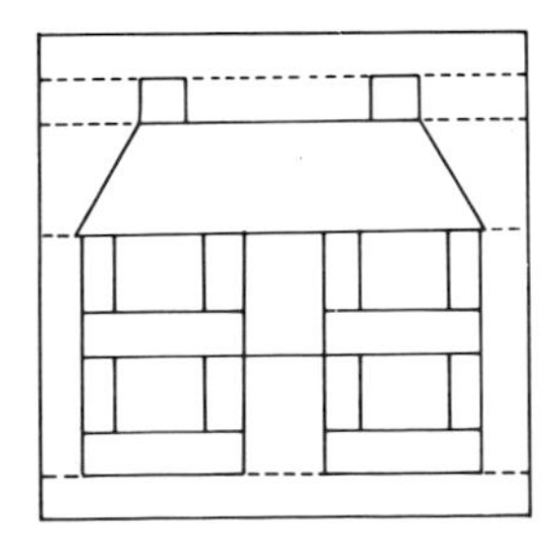

The dotted lines suggest additional seams for easier piecing. Sew the smaller units together into the five rows then join the rows making one block.

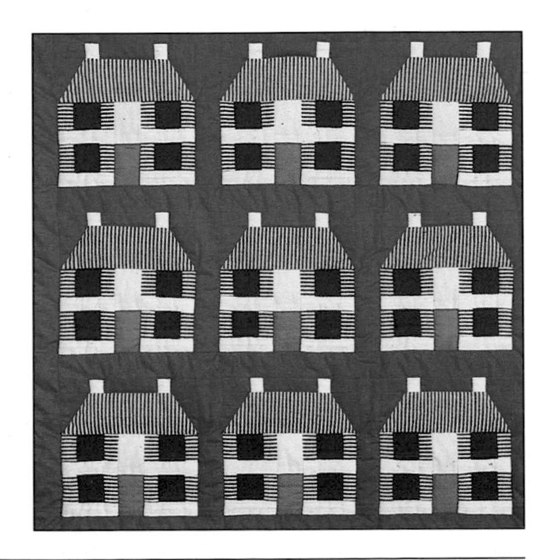

Introduction to quilting

There are two distinctly different types of quilting. In one form, two layers of fabric are separated by a layer of wadding, and all three layers are stitched together. This method of quilting, known as wadded quilting, is sometimes called English quilting and is the earliest type.

In the other form of quilting only two layers of fabric are used and it is purely decorative. The patterns are very often pictorial. When the pattern consists of two narrow lines of stitching, a cord is inserted into the channels to raise the pattern on the surface. This type is known as cord or Italian quilting. In the other variation of this form, the design is stitched in outline through both layers and then raised by inserting a padding from the back of the work. This type is known as padded or trapunto quilting.

Materials and implements

For quilting, a top or ground layer of fabric will be needed, with a backing or lining fabric of a suitable weight for the top fabric. Wadding will also be needed as an interlining or stuffing.

Top and backing fabrics

The fabric chosen should be smooth, soft and closely woven. The most suitable fabrics are cotton, poplin, linen, dull satin and crêpe de chine.

Interlinings

Cotton and synthetic paddings are the most commonly used forms of interlining for wadded quilting as they are cheap and the quilting needle easily passes through them.

Cotton wool is the best padding to use for trapunto work which has to be stuffed with a soft material.

For cord quilting, firm cotton cord gives the best results.

Implements

The needles, pins and thread used for quilting are basically the same as for general sewing. Where they do differ is in their suitability for the fabric and the technique used. A strong thread must be used for quilting stitches.

QUILTING WITHOUT A FRAME

Whether a design is worked on a machine or by hand, it is necessary to ensure that the tension is consistent and that the fabric layers lie together smoothly. The top and backing fabrics are always cut with a 2in. (5cm) seam allowance but the padding is cut to the size of the finished quilt.

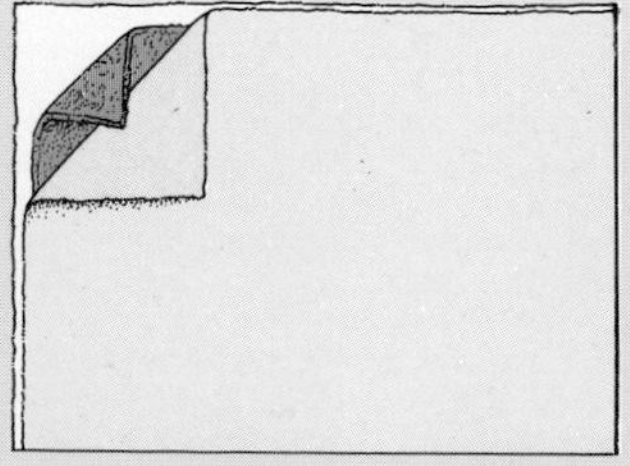

1 Place the backing wrong side up on a flat surface and lay the padding on top. Then place top fabric, right side up, on the other 2 layers.

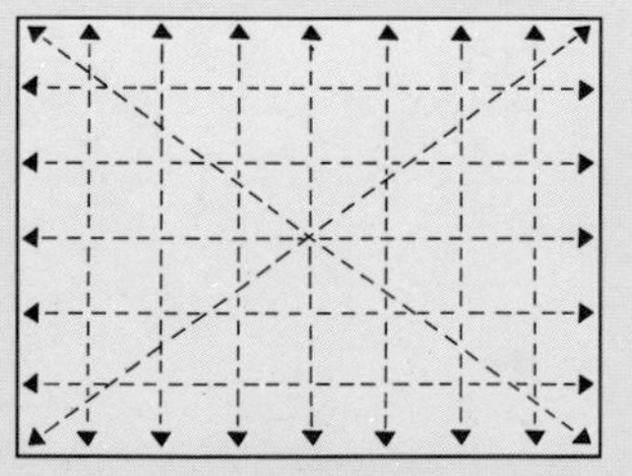

2 Work tacking stitches over the surface starting at the centre and working outwards. Then work 2 diagonal lines as shown, being careful to keep the fabric smooth.

Quilting on a frame

It is advisable to mount large pieces of work on a frame. The fabric should be mounted carefully and slackly or the stitches will not sink deeply into the fabric and the full quilted effect will be lost. Always cut the top and bottom layers with a 2in. (5cm) seam allowance and cut the padding to the size of the finished item. Make sure each layer is smooth and straight.

Mounting the fabric on the frame

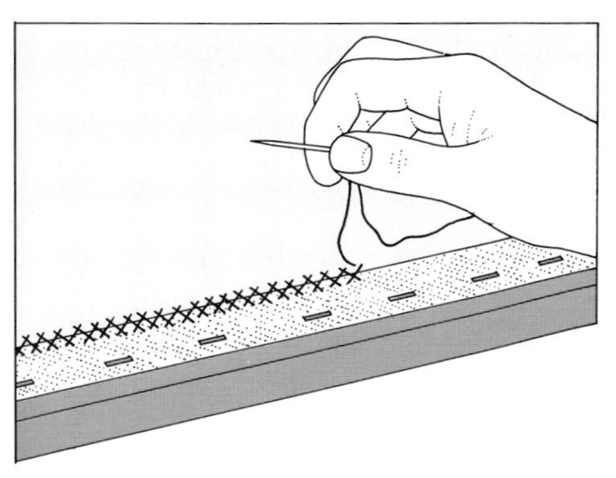

1 Herringbone stitch the side edges of the backing to the webbing on the runners. Roll one side around its runner until a convenient depth for working has been reached. Secure stretchers onto the runners.

2 Position the padding smoothly on top of the backing. Then lay the top fabric, face upwards, on the other 2 layers and allow the end to hang free on the far side. Tack through all 3 layers of fabric along the runner nearest to you. Smooth the cover and padding flat and then pin the 3 layers along the far runner. Be careful not to pull quilting too tight.

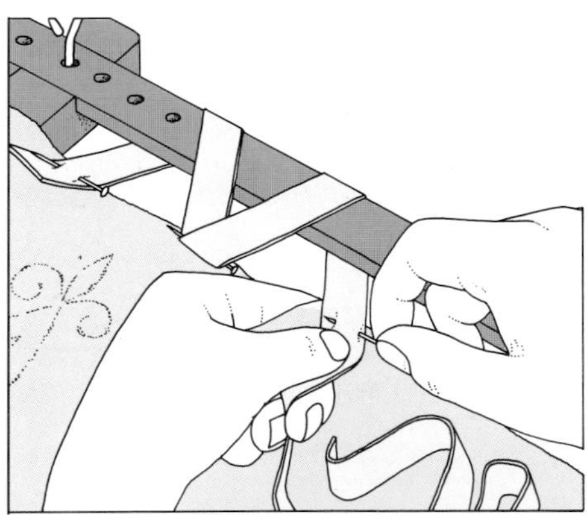

3 Loop tape over stretcher to secure each side and pin through all layers. Remove tapes and pins before rolling the finished area of work on.

FINISHING OFF

Quilted fabrics can be finished in several ways. The edges can be turned under and stitched as here, piping cord can be inserted, or tape attached to the edges.

Running stitch edge

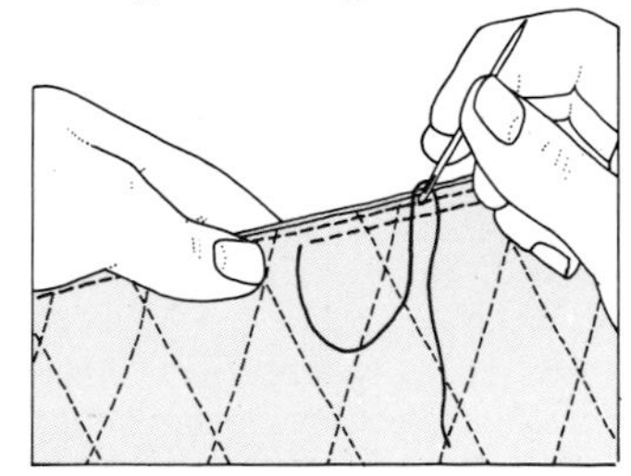

Fold the top and bottom fabrics in to meet over the padding. Then work a line of running stitches as near the edge as possible. Make a second line 1/8in. (3mm) further in to secure the two edges.

Quilting methods

Wadded
The earliest type of quilting was made from two fabric layers enclosing one of wadding and used primarily for warm bed covers and clothing. Wadded quilting designs can be random or decorative, and these North country and Welsh quilts show the regional development of patterns.

Trapunto
Here the technique is used decoratively to give emphasis to enclosed solid areas within a design. The outline of a shape is stitched through two layers of fabric and a padding is inserted from the back of the work. Trapunto can also be combined with other types of quilting.

Italian
This is mainly used for decoration and in combination with other types of quilting or patchwork. Linear patterns are made by stitching two layers of fabric together in narrow parallel lines and threading a cord through from the back to raise the surface. It is also known as cord quilting.

Detail from a typical North country quilt, made in 1930 illustrating a border of curved feather, rose and leaf motifs.

Detail from a typical 1920's Welsh quilt showing the characteristic spiral or snail pattern.

Welsh wedding quilt made by Mary Williams of Monmouthshire in 1888. The design has a large centre circle with a heart in the middle.

Welsh quilt, illustrating a large central design with a rose, tulips and leaves which are repeated in the border.

This American trapunto quilt of 1850 was made from cotton fabric with a cotton filling.

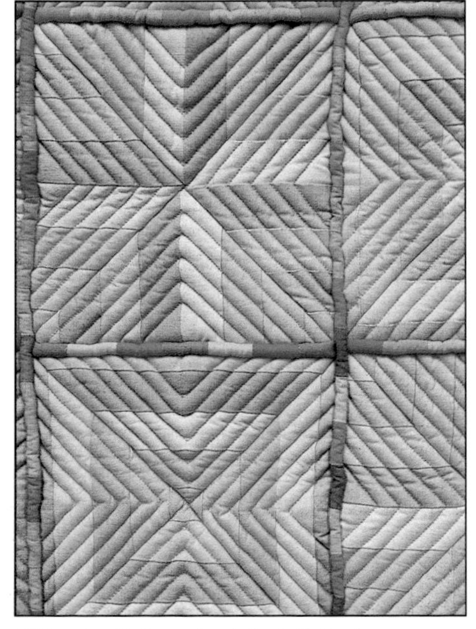

This cot quilt shows clearly the individual squares which combine both patchwork and Italian quilting.

Quilting designs

Quilting was originally used for the purely practical purpose of joining three layers of fabric together. The stitching then followed lozenge, diamond and square patterns without any regard to making it decorative. Circular patterns and motifs were later introduced giving a slightly more elaborate surface to the quilting.

Marking the fabric

It is much easier to mark the design on the top fabric (right side) before assembling the layers together. There are several ways of transferring the design, but first lightly press the top fabric quarters to mark the centre point and main divisions in the area to be filled. The design can be marked with a needle, tailor's chalk or dressmaker's carbon.

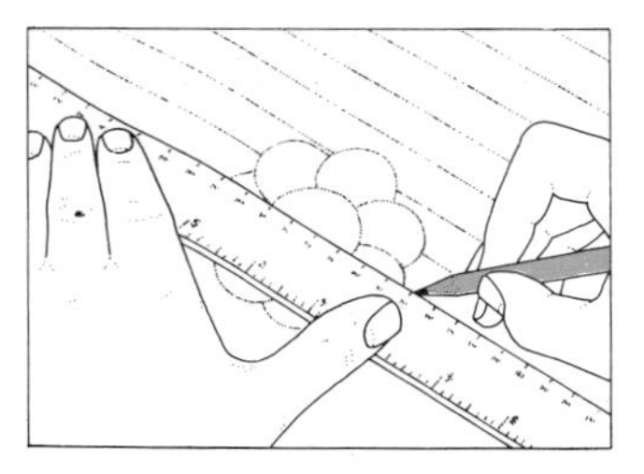

When you have planned your design draw around the templates first with a coloured pencil and then use a long ruler to mark filler patterns.

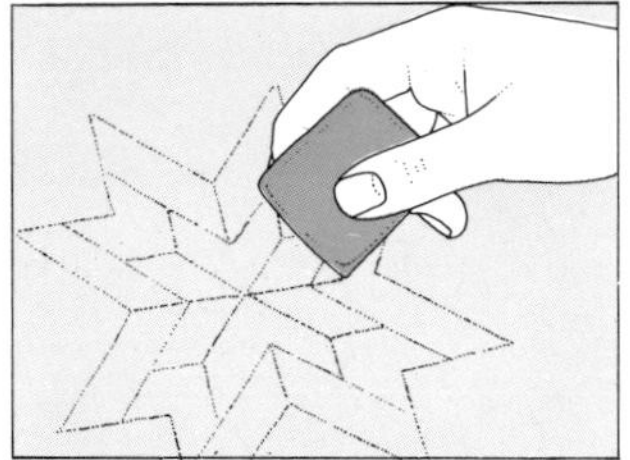

When the outlines of the templates have been marked the details can be filled in with tailor's chalk.

When marking with a needle place the fabric on a padded surface. Hold the needle's blunt end almost parallel to the fabric and press down using a template as your guide.

PATTERNS FOR GROUNDS

These can be worked uniformly over the quilt or in double lines to emphasize the pattern in certain places. A variety of different patterns can be used on the same design but these need to be carefully planned so that they work well together.

There should always be a clear contrast between the template shapes, which are the focal points, and the background patterning. This can best be achieved by using curved motifs against linear pattern backgrounds and vice versa. A central motif can be emphasized by either increasing or decreasing the background patterning.

Trapunto quilting

1 Mark the design onto the backing fabric and tack the 2 layers of fabric together.

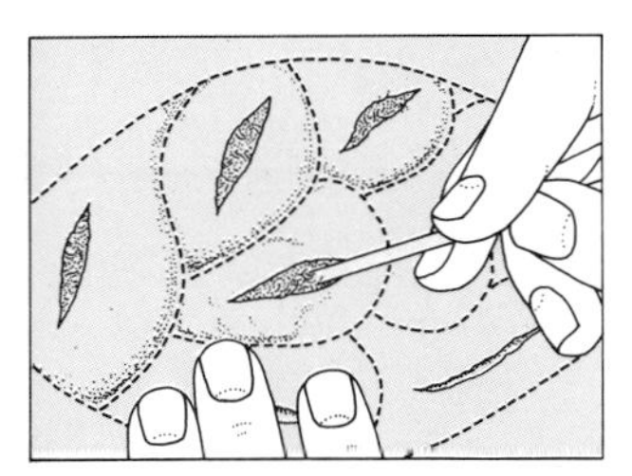

2 Stitch along design outlines, through both layers, with small, even running stitches. Then slit the fabric at the back of the work and insert the padding with a crochet hook or a blunt needle.

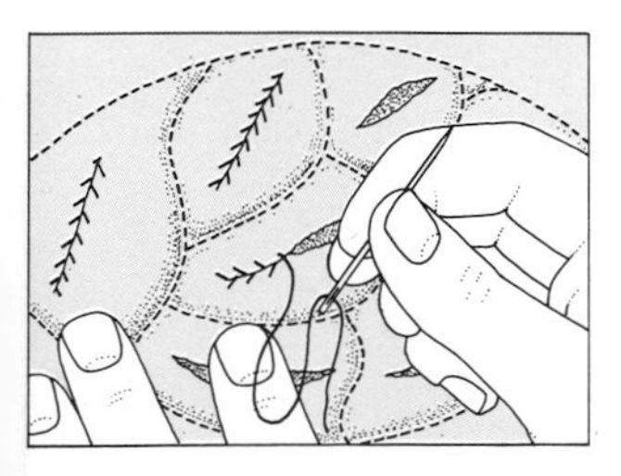

3 Slip stitch over the slits to close them. Stitch a lining to the backing fabric if it is necessary.

Italian quilting

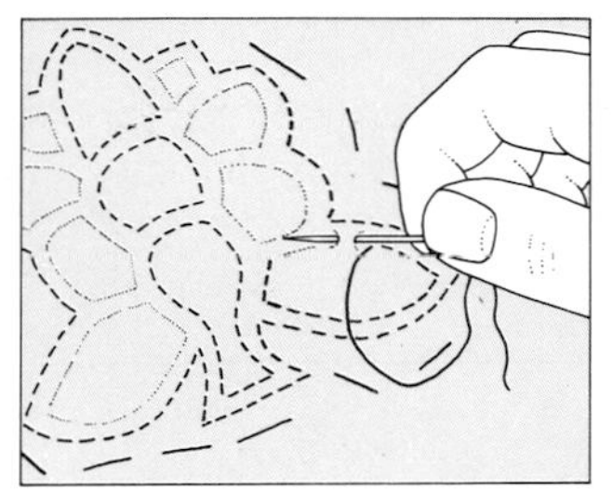

1 Mark the design on the backing fabric and stitch along the double lines.

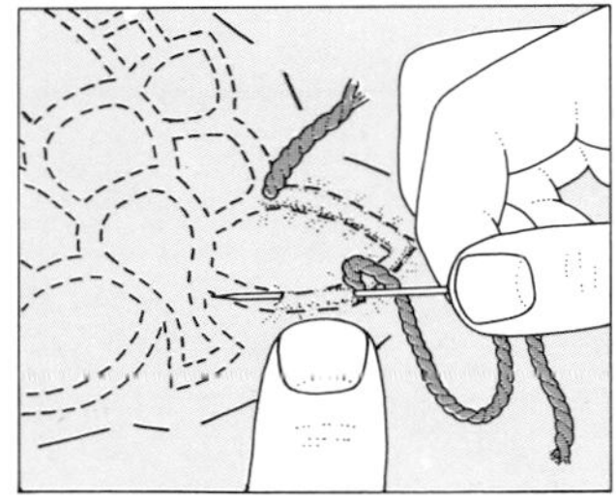

2 Thread the cord onto a needle and insert through back of the work between the 2 lines of stitching and the layers of fabric, pulling it gently along the channels.

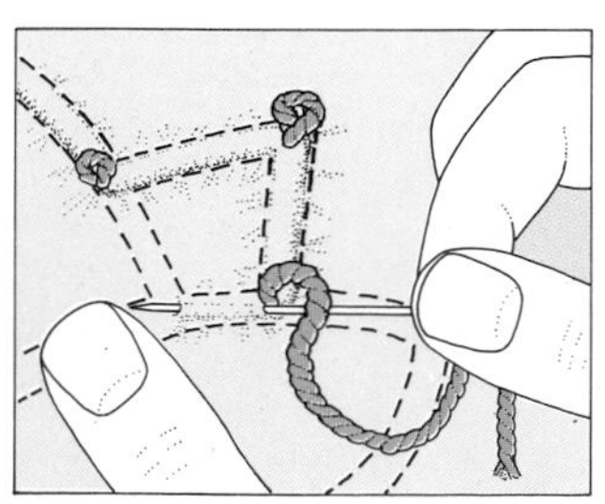

3 At sharp curves bring the needle out at the back of the work and loop the cord a little to prevent puckering.

Tied and buttoned quilting

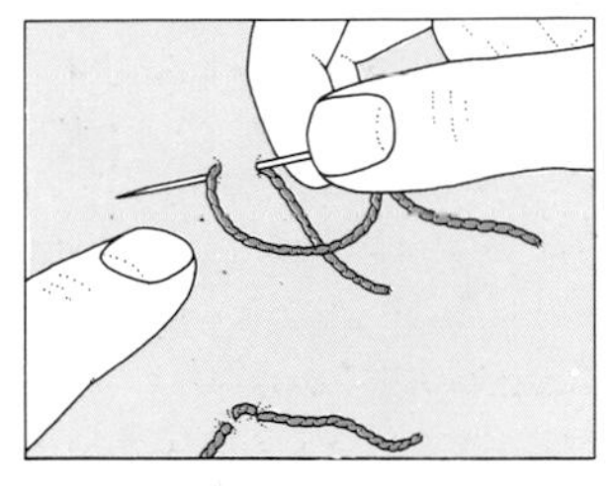

1 Make one stitch through all 3 layers, leaving a long loose end. Then make a back stitch and bring the needle out on the same side of the fabric.

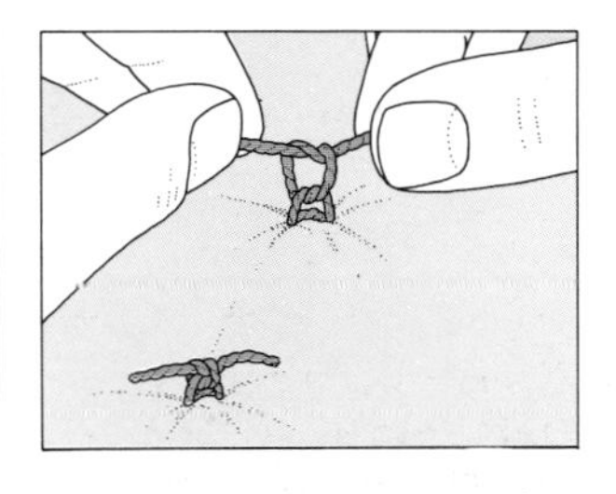

2 Tie the ends together using a reef knot or tie them together in tight bows for a more decorative effect.

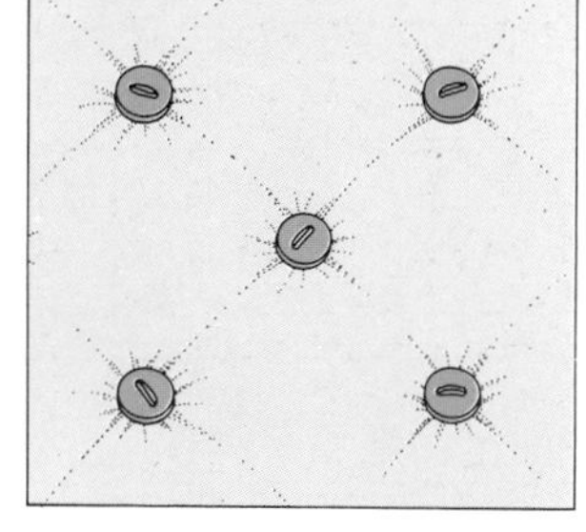

Button quilting is more decorative than tied and almost as quick to work.

Thread a strong needle with buttontwist and secure one button tightly on the top fabric and another directly beneath it on the backing.

Templates for designs

Simple outline shapes can be added to and filled in different ways to create different effects. The shapes illustrated show how they can be built up into richer designs by filling and adding to the original outlines. Interesting designs can be produced by arranging individual motifs into composite shapes such as fans, clusters, stars, or flowers. These can be used as borders or central motifs, but care should be taken to ensure that the overall design is well-balanced and not over-complicated.

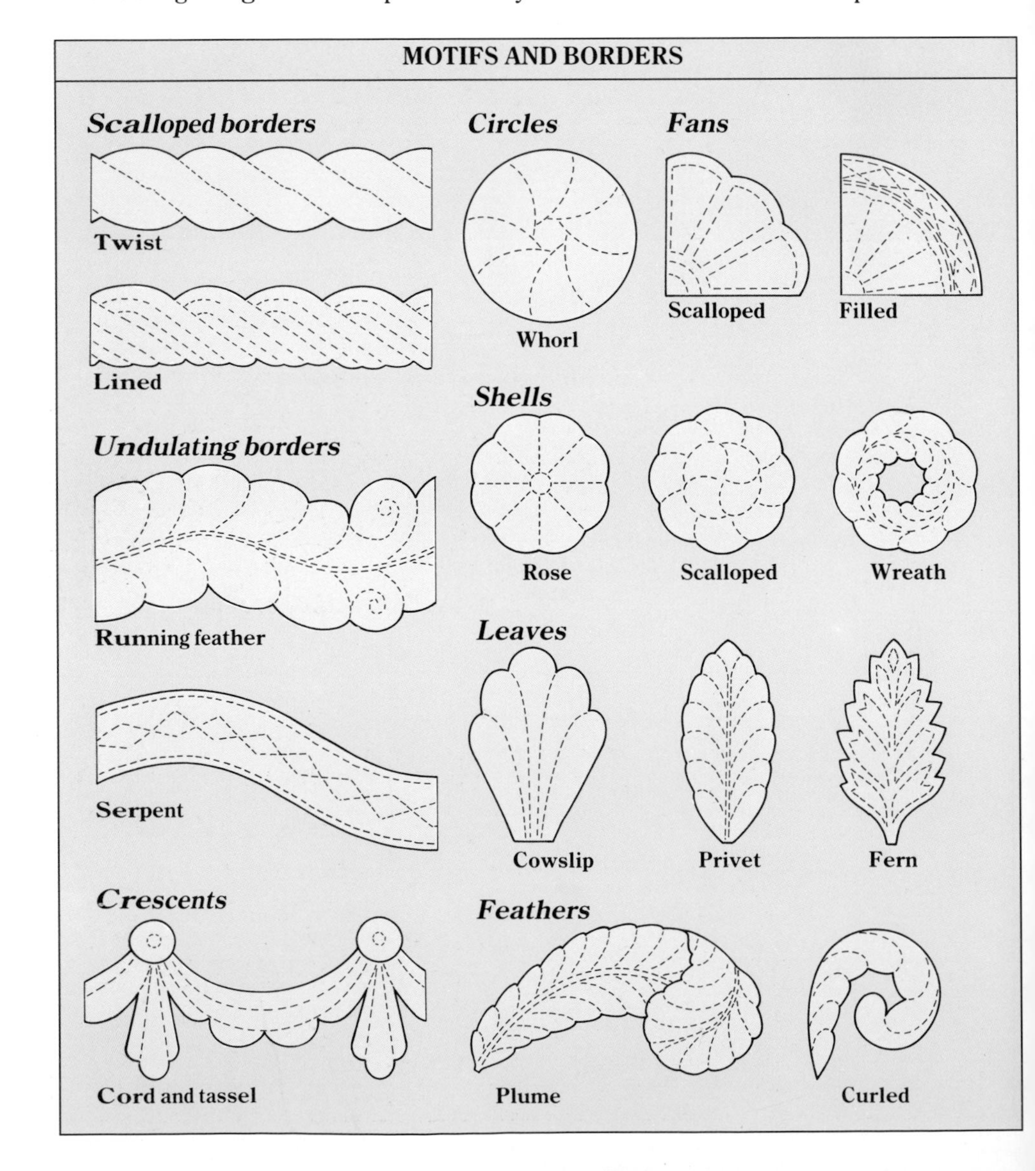

COMPOSITE DESIGNS

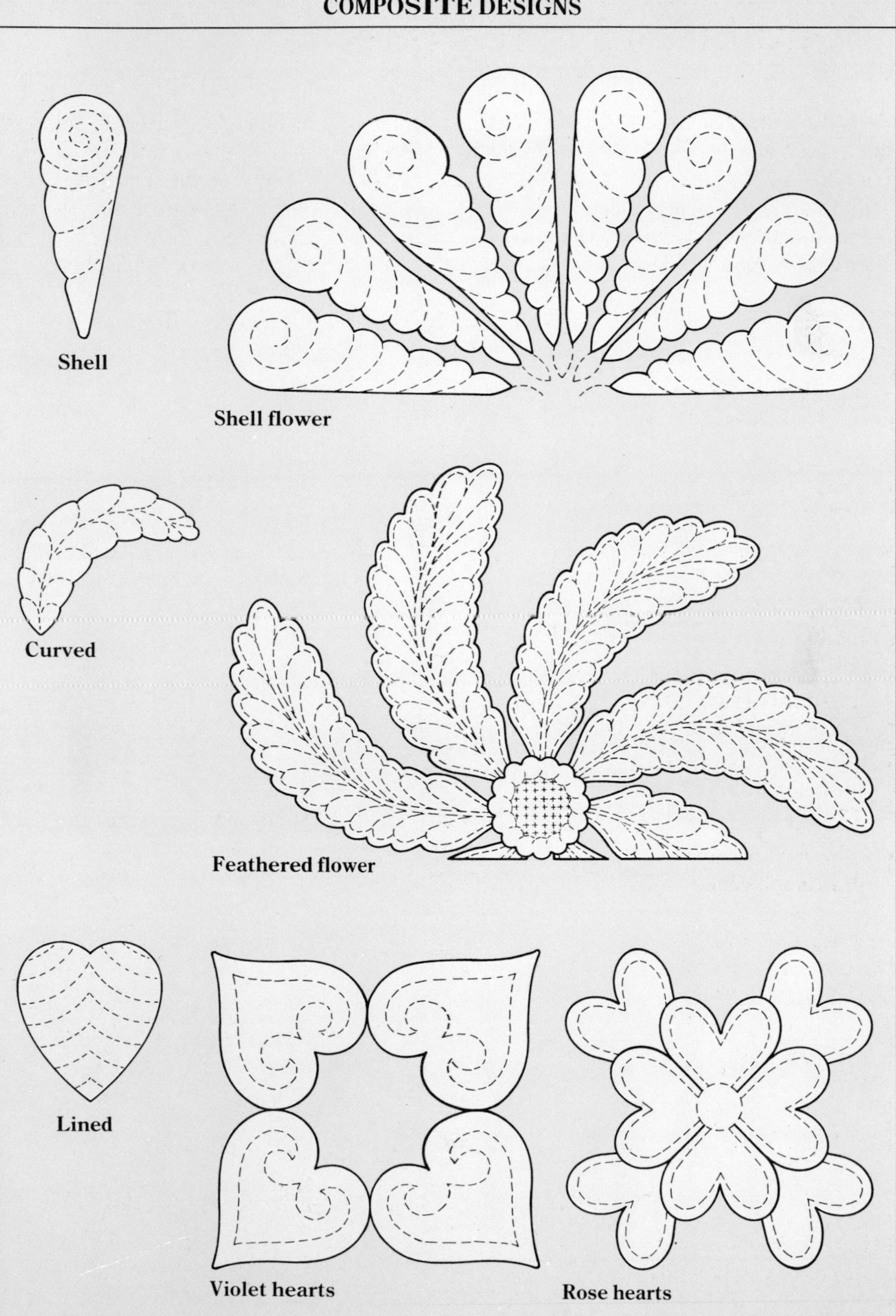

Appliqué

Surface appliqué is the most popular and well known form of appliqué and is worked by applying cut-out fabric shapes, known as motifs, to the surface of the ground fabric to produce an overall design, border pattern or single, dramatic shape.

Before attaching appliqué motifs the edges should be secured to prevent fraying either by folding the edges or by pasting a backing onto them. Surface appliqué should always be worked on a frame to provide sufficient tension.

Applying paste

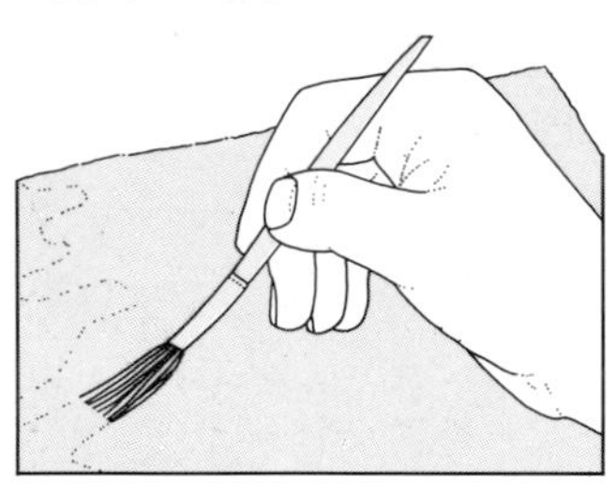

1 Cover the backing evenly with paste without penetrating the other side.

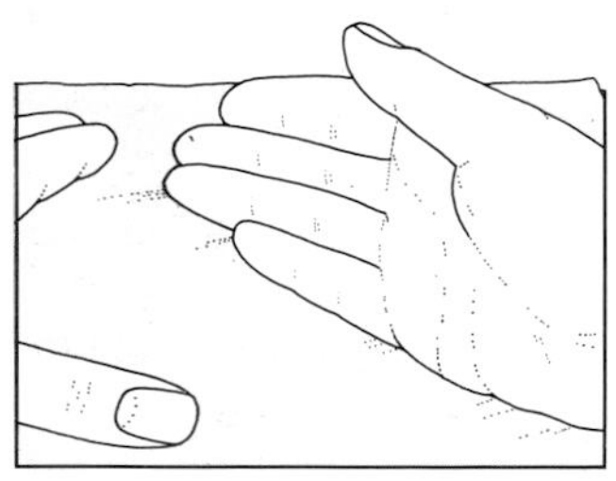

2 Place the appliqué fabric on top and smooth over gently to remove air bubbles.

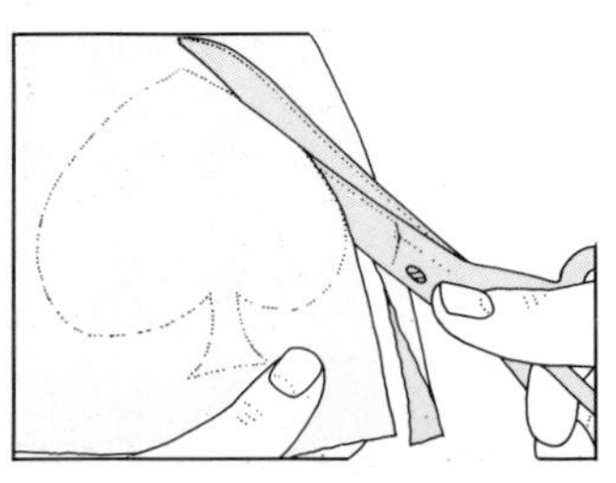

3 When the pasted fabrics are dry mark out the motif and cut along the outlines.

Turning under edges

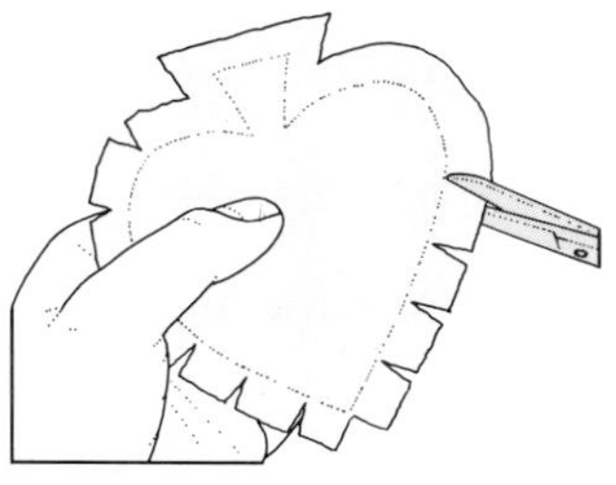

1 Cut out the design allowing an extra 1/4in. (6mm) all round. Then snip the edge of the curved outline to enable it to fold under easily.

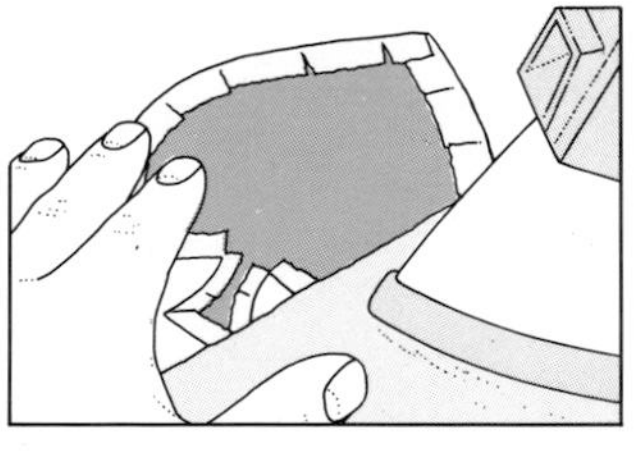

2 When the shapes have been cut fold the raw edges to the back and iron over them using a damp cloth.

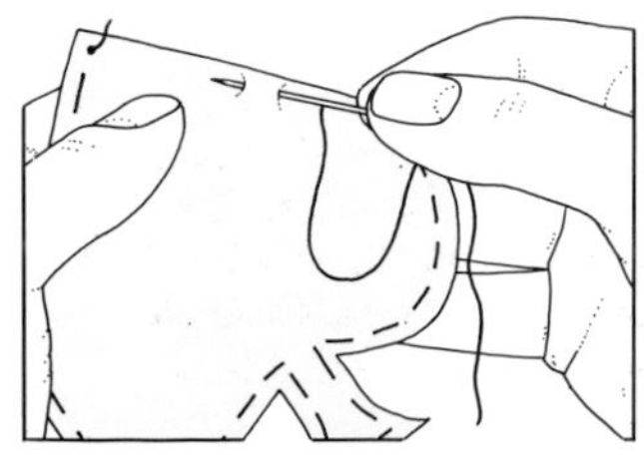

3 Tack around the edges before applying the motif.

Pasting in position

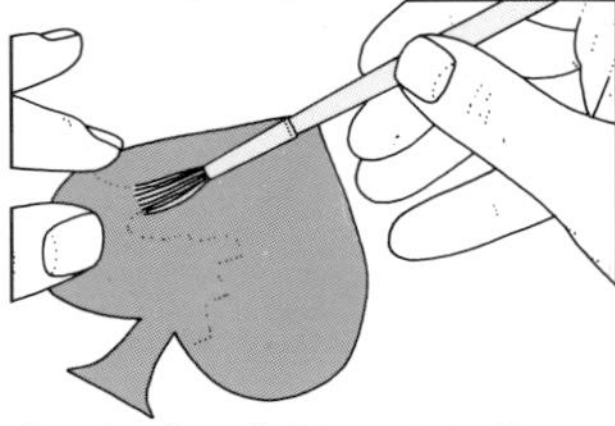

1 Apply a light paste to the back of the motif.

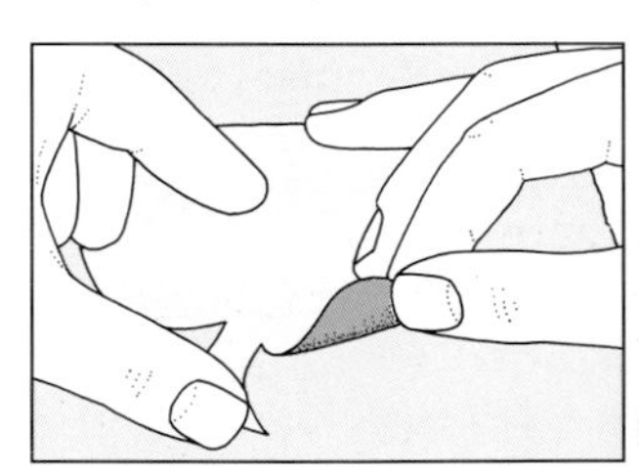

2 Place in position on the ground fabric, pressing it evenly with weights, and leave to dry.

Tacking into position

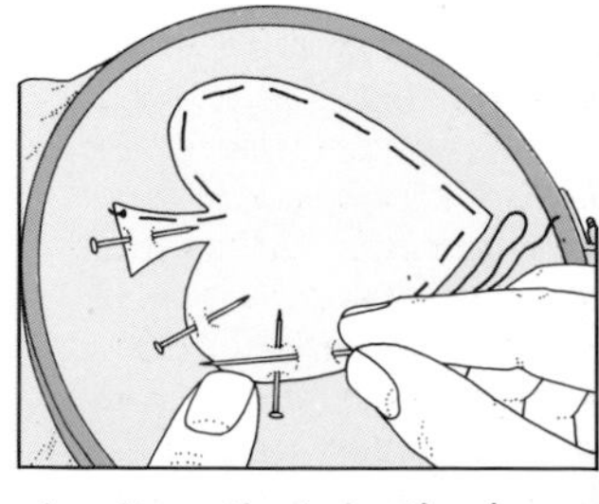

An alternative to pasting is tacking where each piece is positioned on the framed fabric and tacked down.

Stitching the motifs

Once the motifs have been secured on the ground fabric they can be stitched into place. Running stitch, back stitch, overcast stitch or chain stitch are the most commonly used.

Running stitch

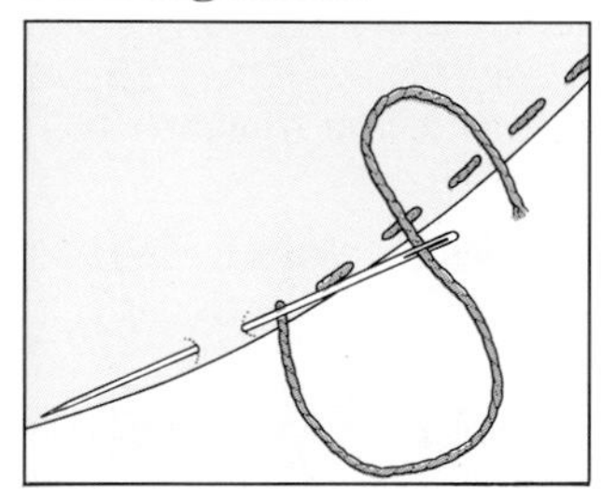

This stitch is useful for securing fabric quickly or for making outlines.

Insert the needle from the back of the work. Take several small stitches onto the point of the needle before drawing the thread through the fabric.

Chain stitch

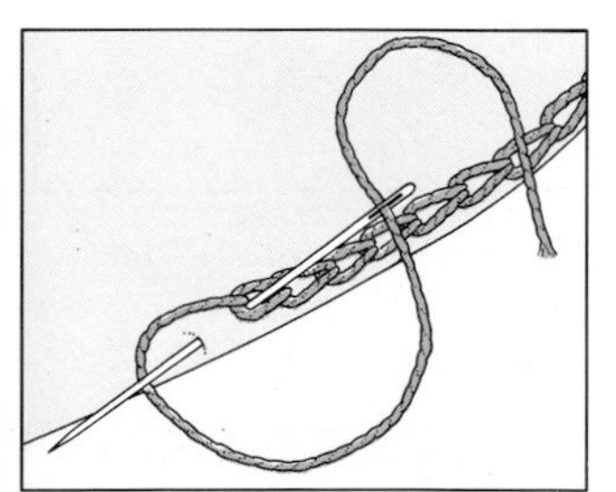

This stitch is more decorative but is also used for securing.

Pull the needle through from the back and make a small stitch forwards. Bring needle out and loop working thread, holding it in place. Pull the needle through, forming one chain. Insert the needle into the hole from which it emerged bringing it out a stitch length further on.

Overcast stitch

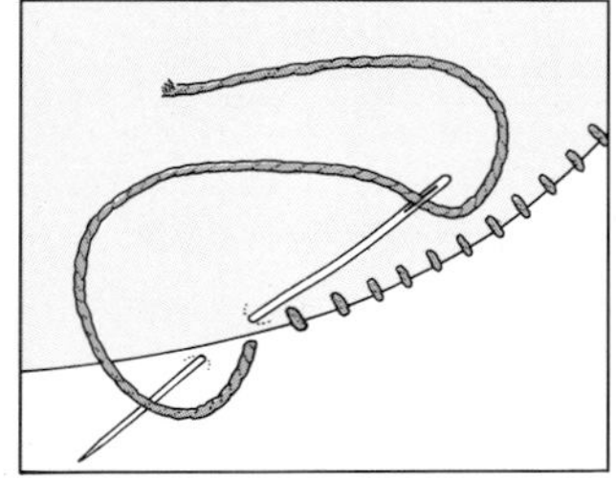

This method of stitching gives an almost invisible stitch on the turned under edges.

Use the same colour thread as the appliqué fabric. Pass the needle through the back of the fabric and into the appliqué motif, making small diagonal stitches. Do not pull them tight.

Back stitch

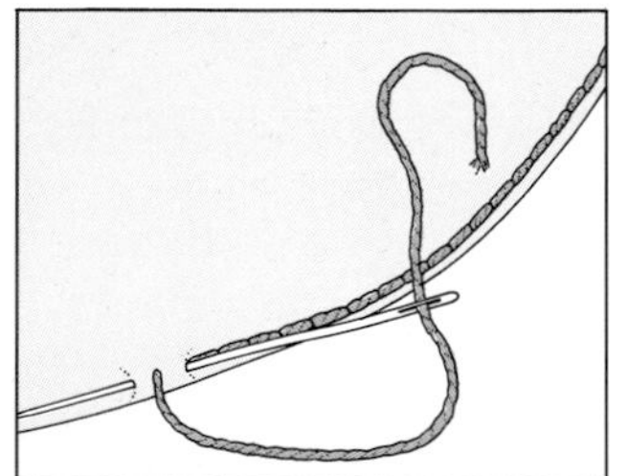

This is good for both turned under edges and raw edges which do not fray.

Make a small stitch from left to right. Then make a double length stitch forwards on the wrong side of the work so that the needle emerges a stitch length in front of the first.

APPLYING FABRICS WITHOUT PREPARATION

Felt, leather and bonded fabrics need no preparation as they do not fray. They are the easiest materials to use when starting to appliqué and are therefore ideal for children.

The shapes are cut out tacked on to the ground fabric and secured with running stitch.

Relief appliqué

Relief effects can be achieved by gathering the appliqué motifs before stitching them to the ground.

Relief rosettes

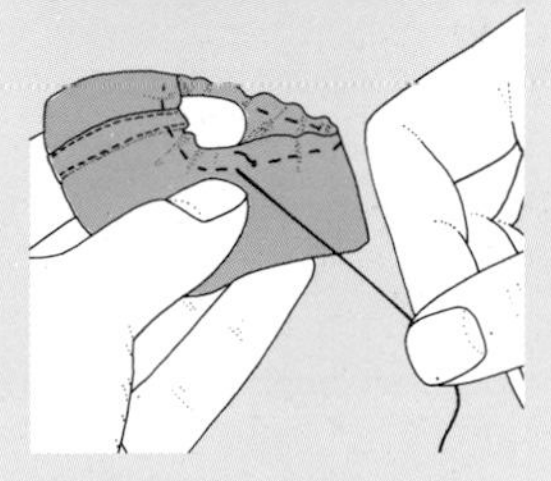

1 Cut out a strip and join into a circle. Work running stitches along one of the edges. Pull together and then knot.

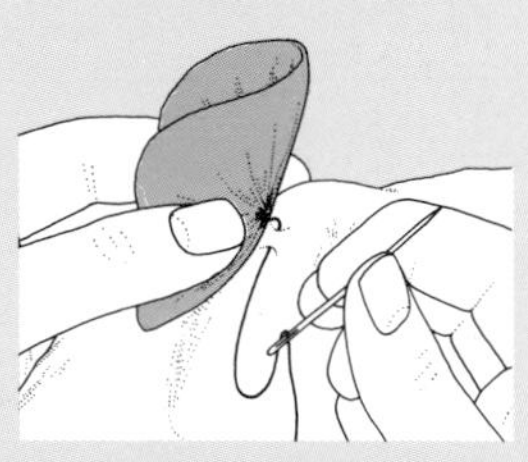

2 Place rosette on the ground fabric and secure edge with overcast stitching.

Plain fabrics for appliqué

The choice of fabrics plays as important a role as the cut shapes in appliqué. On this page all the contemporary designs shown use plain fabrics and the designs are emphasized with the clever choice of graded and contrasting colours. Texture too plays an important part and can be used to bring out a particular feature.

Above *The pansy cushion is worked in two colours of grey, with the outlines machined in white cotton and silver lurex.*

Above right *Machine stitched appliqué with fabric and embroidered lettering. Note the use of gauze for the windscreen.*

Right *The details of the animals and architecture are worked in embroidery, the bears in pile fabrics.*

Printed fabrics for appliqué

Printed fabrics can be used to give a patterned effect within the appliqué motif, or individual motifs can be cut from it and applied to the ground fabric. Embroidery stitches can be used to fill in features or produce textured details. The examples below show the effective use of textured and patterned fabric.

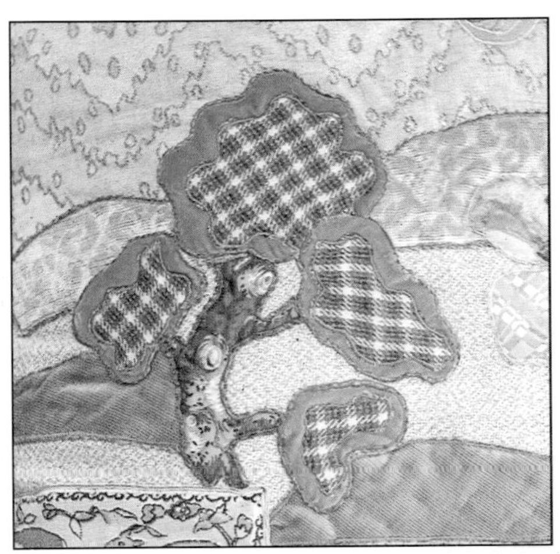

The cushion design is enhanced by the use of checked fabric for the trees and a realistic fabric for the bark.

A detail from a modern wall-hanging based on the formal arrangements of stylized oriental vases.

Left *A small check design is used for the dress, a woven leaf pattern for the trees and a printed motif for the bird. The design, as a whole, seems to float on the velvet, which is stitched with French knots.*

Decorative surface appliqué

Embroidered and needlepoint tapestry motifs and pattern cut fabric can all be used for surface appliqué. A single shape, carefully positioned, can add interest to a plain dress or blouse and will give new life to an old garment.

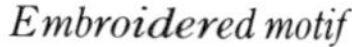

Embroidered motif

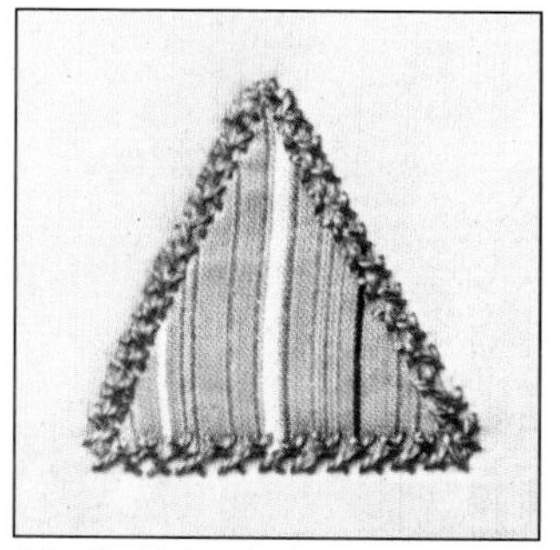

Motif with herringbone stitch

Motif with graded satin stitch

REVERSE APPLIQUÉ

In reverse appliqué several layers are tacked together and the top fabric cut in patterns through different numbers of layers to reveal the fabrics below. This form of appliqué is seen in the designs of the Cuna Indians of the San Blas islands. It requires care and patience to work but the end result is very pleasing.

Fabrics

The best fabric to use in reverse appliqué is lightweight cotton. Because of the intricate cutting, fabrics which fray should be avoided. Very heavy fabrics are also unsuitable because these will be too bulky when cut and turned under. Three to five layers of fabric can be used.

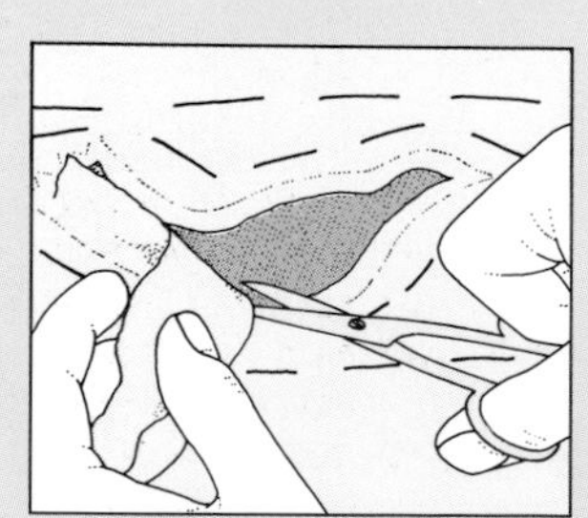

1 Mark the design on the top fabric. Place the layers of fabric on top of each other, in the order in which they appear in the finished design and tack. Cut through the top layer within the outlines using sharp scissors.

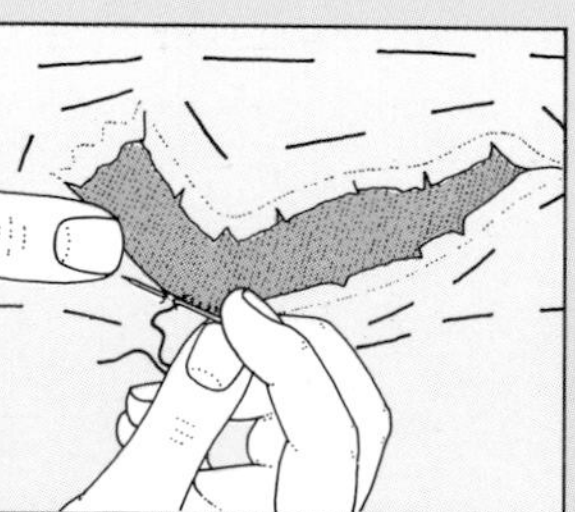

2 Clip around edges. Turn under and stitch to the layer below using small stitches. Always complete stitching before starting another layer.

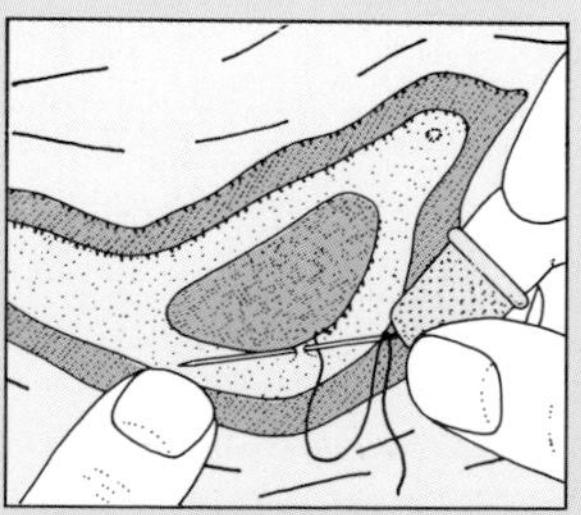

3 Continue to cut and stitch to a lower layer, thus building up the finished design.

Decorating the motif edges

After the motifs have been sewn down they can either be left plain or they can be worked over with embroidery stitches or couching to cover or decorate the edges. A large number of embroidery stitches can be used for edging motifs, the principal ones are shown below.

Buttonhole stitch

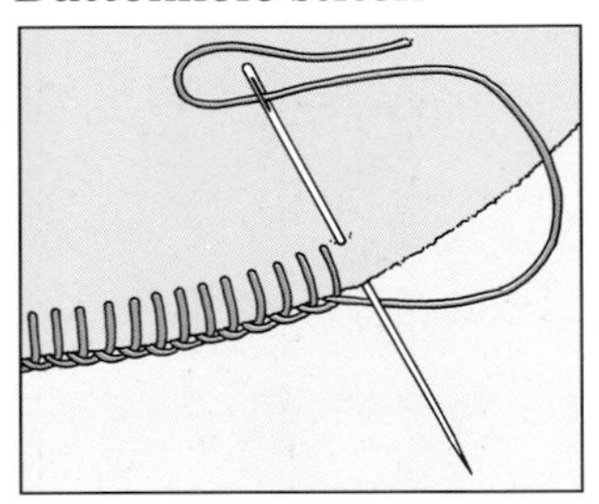

Bring needle through to surface at raw edge of motif. Insert through edge of motif and ground fabric and draw it through at raw edge with thread under needle. Continue in this way around the edge.

Herringbone stitch

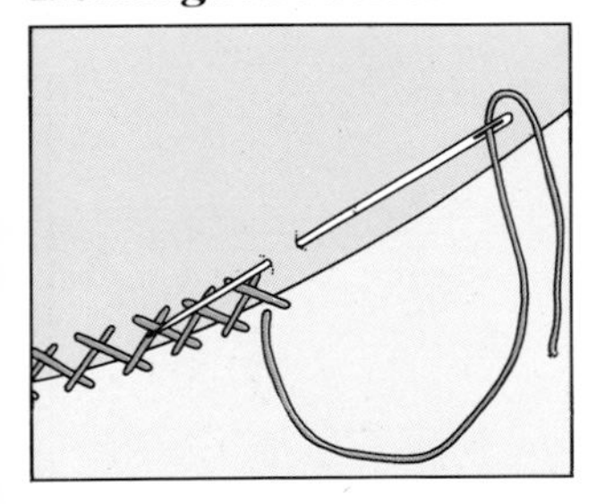

Bring needle through to surface on inner edge of motif then make a back stitch down to right over the raw edge and into the ground fabric. Next make a back stitch up to the right through the motif and the ground fabric.

Graded satin stitch

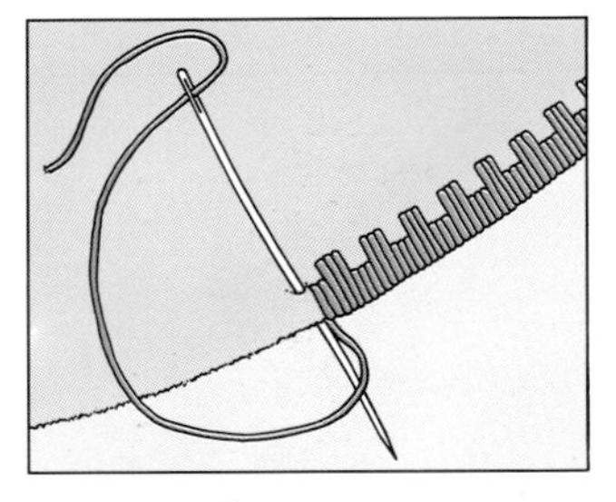

Bring needle to surface of motif and then work graded straight stitches over raw edge in pattern formation.

Padded satin stitch

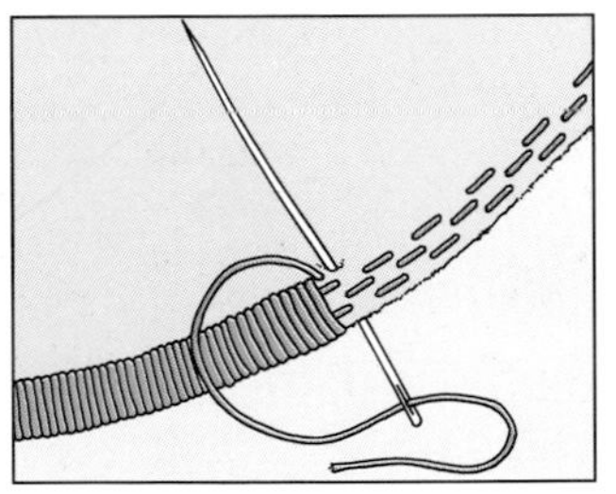

First work 3 or more lines of running stitches along the edge of the motif through both layers of fabric. These stitches act as a padding. Then cover them with closely worked satin stitches around the motif.

Coral stitch

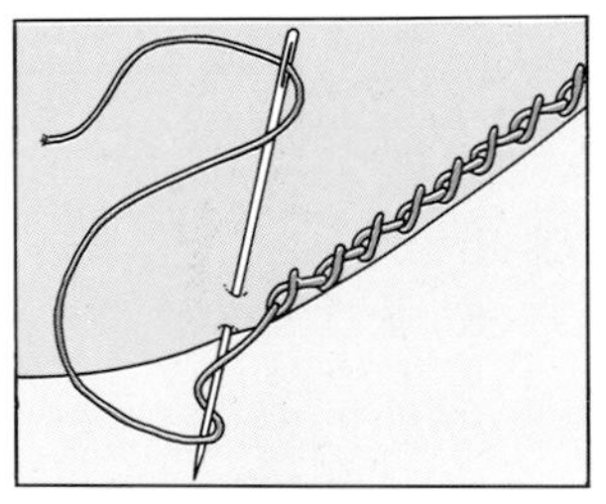

Bring needle to surface through the motif and make a small stitch downwards through both layers of fabric with thread over the needle. Bring the needle out with thread twisted as shown.

Feather stitch

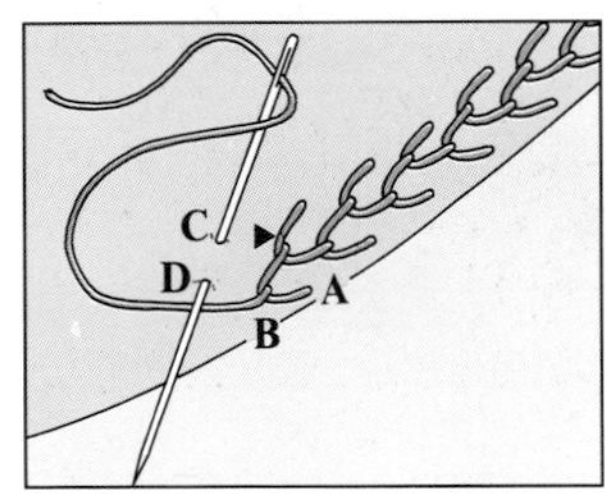

Bring needle out at arrow and insert at A. Hold thread down to left and bring needle out at B over thread. Next insert needle at C, hold thread down and bring needle out at D over thread. Continue in this wa

Traditional appliqué

Pennsylvanian Dutch quilt 1920 with flower basket.

Egyptian appliquéd tent wall hanging.

The Rose of Sharon, used in this American quilt of 1850, is one of the most popular and oldest of all appliqué patterns.

American quilt 1850 with Turkey track design.

Reverse appliqué

The rabbits are worked from red to green, black to yellow and the bird and cat are applied on top in two reverse layers. Teeth, eyes and squares are of surface appliqué.

This design is worked on a printed background. In certain areas further layers of reverse appliqué have been worked.

San Blas Molas
The simple two-layered Mola below uses pink as the top and blue for the backing.

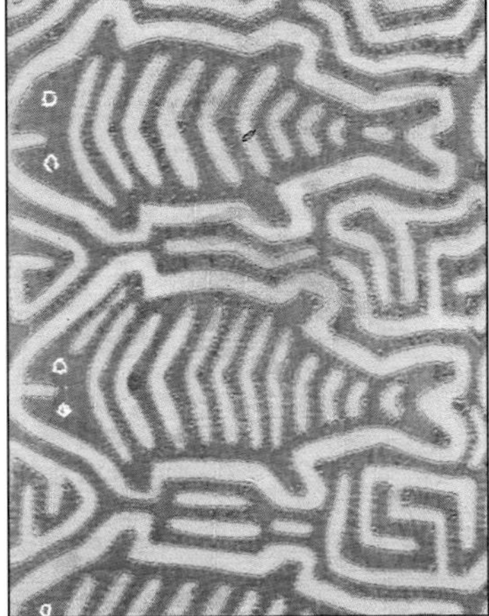

4

KNITTING

Knitting implements

Types of needles

Modern knitting needles are double pointed or knobbed at one end and are made of steel, aluminium, plastic or wood. They are available in different sizes and types for different jobs and have been internationally standardized into 17 graded sizes, from 2 mm to 17 mm.

Double pointed

Double pointed needles are sold in sets of four or six and sized in the usual way. They are used for knitting in the round.

Circular

Circular needles are pointed and joined by a flexible length of wire or plastic. They are used for knitting large tubular shapes.

Cable

Cable needles are much shorter than double pointed needles. They are used for holding stitches when working twisted cable patterns.

Other equipment

The following additional accessories are essential for successful knitting.

Needle gauge

A needle gauge is a piece of metal or plastic punched with holes which correspond to the standard sizes of needles.

Row counter

This is pushed onto the end of a knitting needle, and used to count rows or stitches.

Stitch holder

Resembling a large safety pin, this is used to hold stitches not being worked.

Sewing needle

A blunt-ended wool sewing needle is used to sew pieces of knitting together.

Tape measure

A tape measure or a rigid ruler is essential for measuring stitch gauge and for checking the length of a piece of knitting.

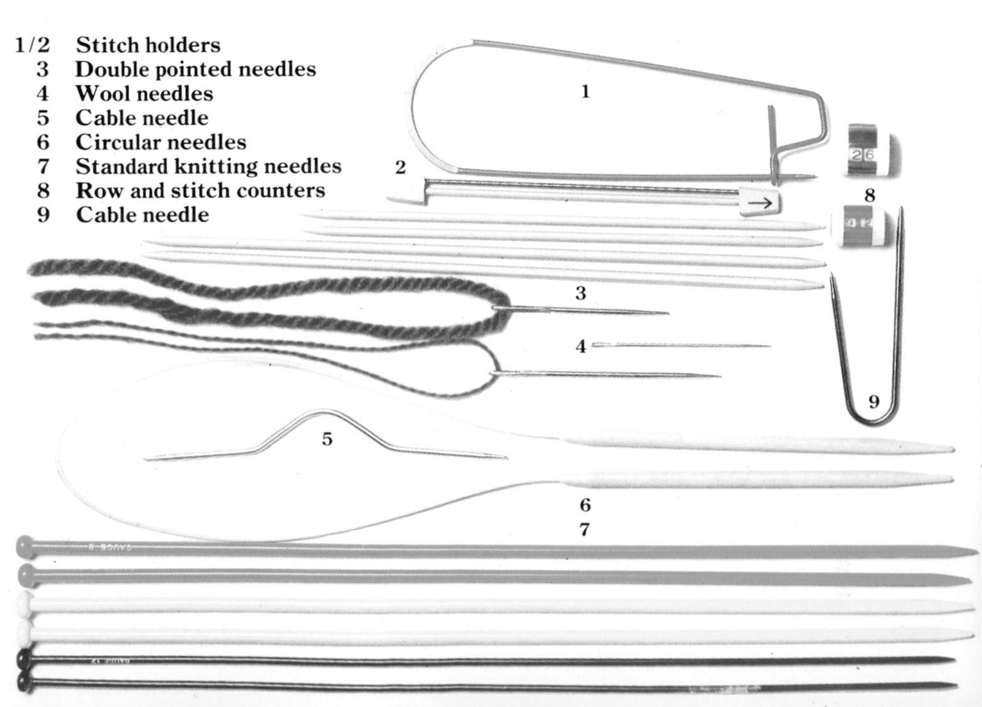

1/2 Stitch holders
3 Double pointed needles
4 Wool needles
5 Cable needle
6 Circular needles
7 Standard knitting needles
8 Row and stitch counters
9 Cable needle

Knitting yarn

Yarn is the name for spun strands of fibre which can either be animal, vegetable or mineral. The most common types of yarn fibre are shown below.

Each strand of knitting yarn is known as a ply. Two or more strands can be combined to form yarns of different thicknesses. There are also many interesting textures available.

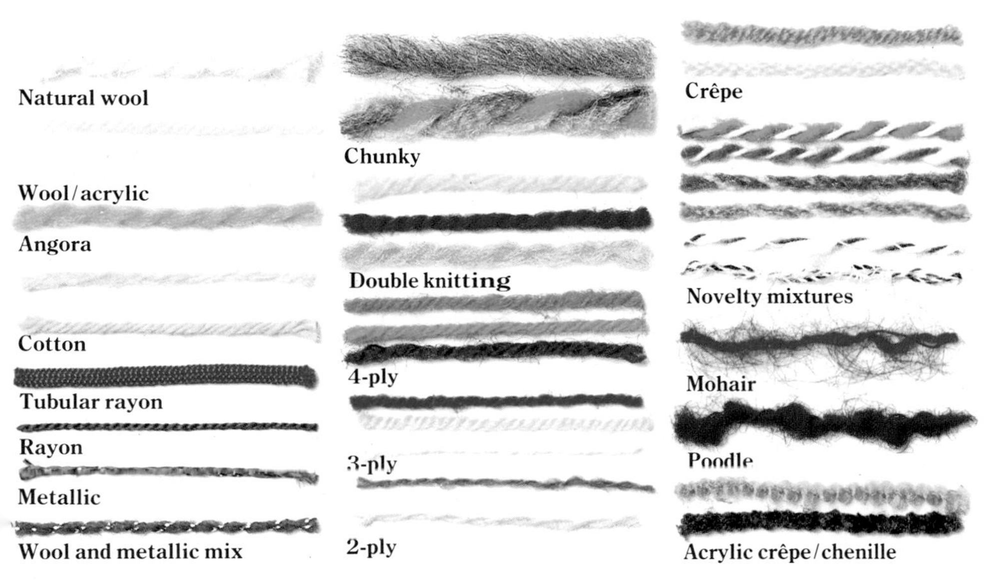

WINDING KNITTING YARNS

Most yarn is sold wound ready for use, but occasionally it is necessary to wind a ball from the coiled hank or skein. Carefully unfold the hank then stretch it around 2 chairs placed back to back, or loop it over the fingers of a helper, leaving the thumbs free to manoeuvre the yarn. Begin winding with the end of the hank: winding from the inside causes tangles.

Wind all yarns, especially natural ones, loosely or they will stretch.

Winding so that the working end is on top

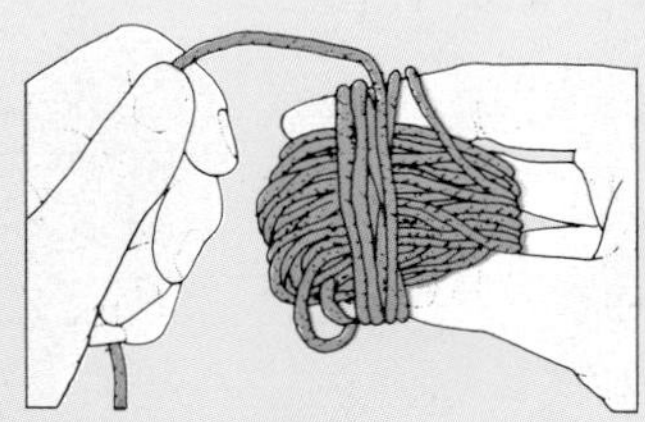

Wrap wool tightly around 3 fingers. Slip the coils off. Change position of wool and continue, adding more layers and forming a well-shaped ball.

Winding so that the working end comes from the centre

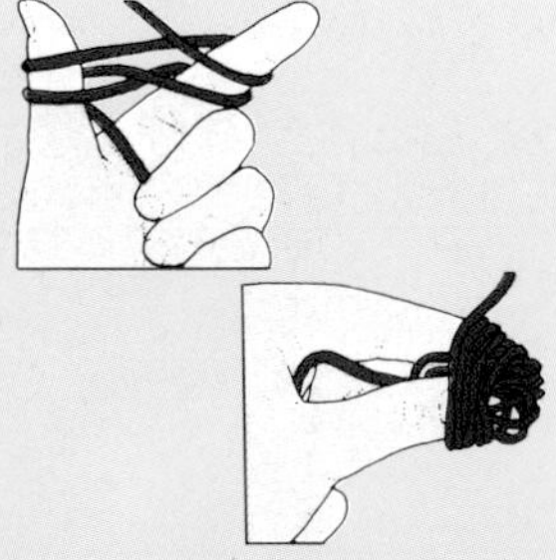

Hold the end of yarn across the palm. Wind the yarn in a figure of eight over thumb and fore-finger. Slip yarn off, fold over and wind loosely into a ball.

Starting to knit

All hand knitting starts with two needles and a ball of yarn. A number of loops are cast on to one needle and further rows are then worked into these loops.

Casting on

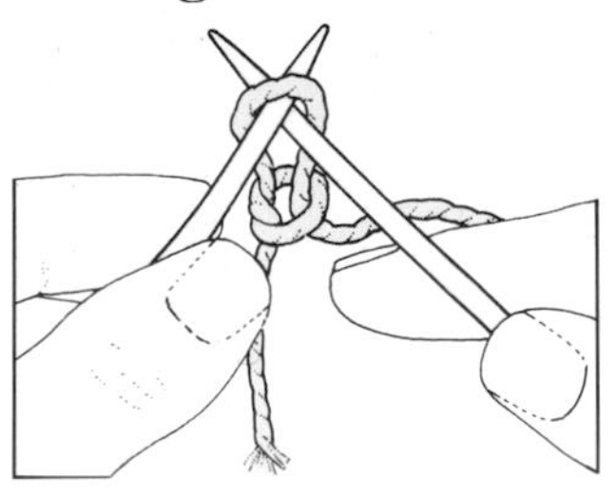

1 Make a slip loop on the left needle. Insert the right needle through the loop from front to back.

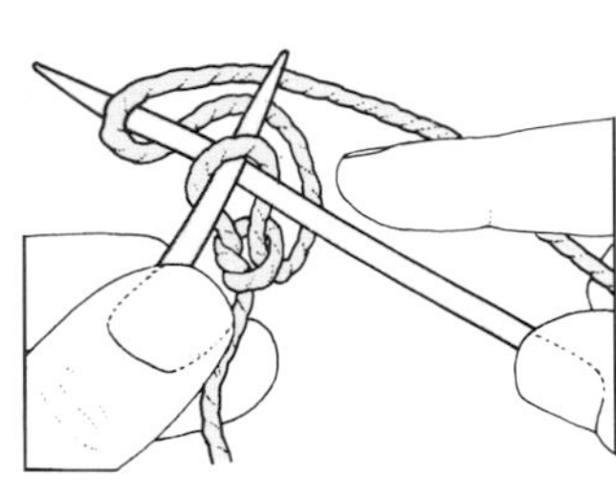

2 Pass the working yarn under and over the right needle.

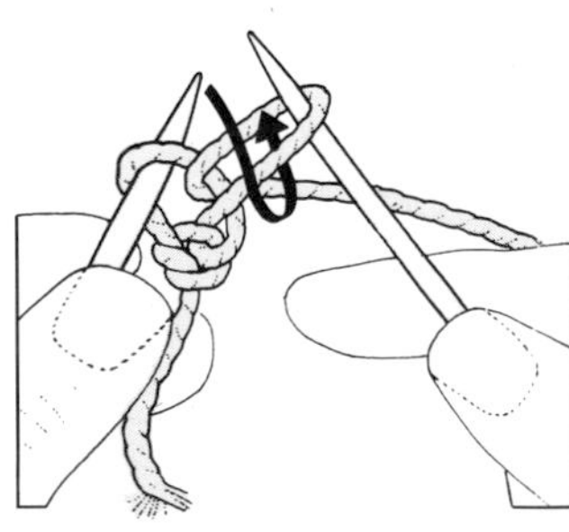

3 Draw loop through slip stitch and transfer to left needle. Repeat steps 2 and 3, now working through the first knitted stitch.

The basic knit stitch

1 With yarn at back, insert right needle through the front of the first stitch on the left needle.

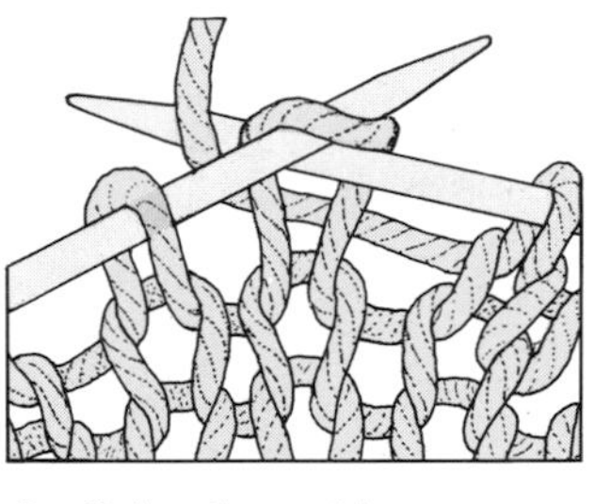

2 Bring the working yarn up and over the right needle.

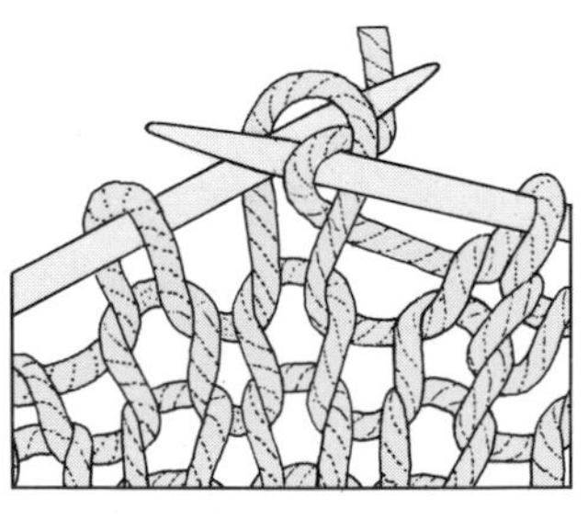

3 Draw loop through, discarding worked stitch on left needle. Continue to end of row.

The basic purl stitch

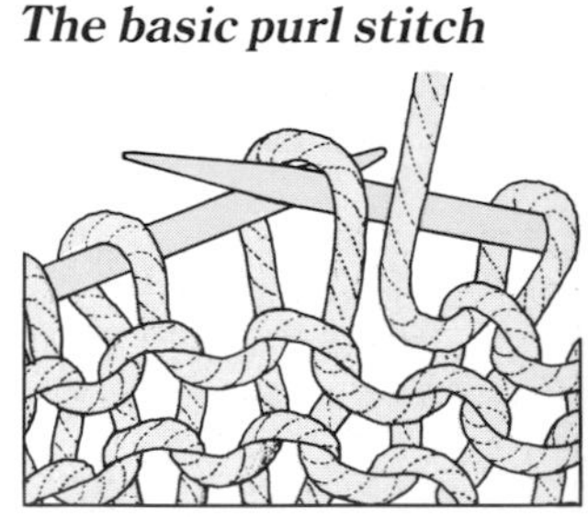

1 With yarn at front, insert the right needle from back to front into the first stitch on the left needle.

2 Bring working yarn over and around the right needle.

3 Draw loop through discarding the worked stitch on the left needle and at the same time forming a new stitch on the right needle. Continue to end of row.

Knitting the second row

When the first row of knitting is complete, turn the work around and take the needle carrying the stitches in the left hand. The empty needle is now ready to begin a new row of knitting. The back of the work now faces the knitter.

Garter stitch

When every row is knitted back and forth on two needles, this pattern (above), called garter stitch, is formed.

Stocking stitch

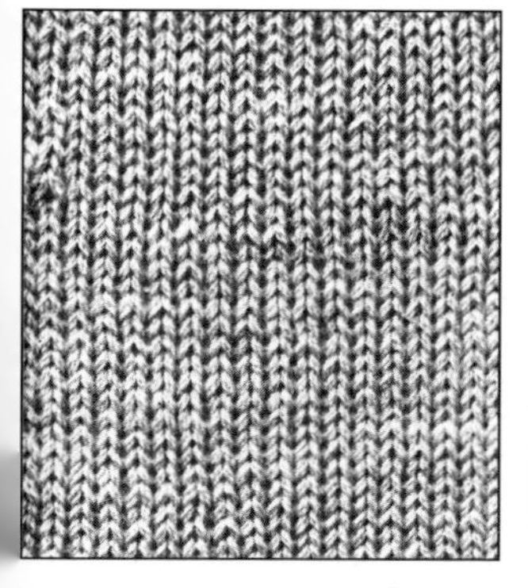

Stocking stitch (above) is made by knitting the first and every alternate row and purling the second and every alternate row.

Knit and purl stitches combined

Once the basic knit and purl stitches have been mastered, many patterns can be worked using these two stitches in combination. The fabric on the right has been made by working rows of stocking stitch and rows of garter stitch. Stitches for rib patterns on the following two pages can be used to edge garments or as overall patterns.

HOLDING NEEDLES AND YARN

There are many ways of holding needles and yarn. Some methods make knitting faster, but all that matters is that each knitter finds a comfortable personal style. Threading the working end of yarn through the fingers controls tension and helps produce a firm, even fabric.

Yarn in right hand

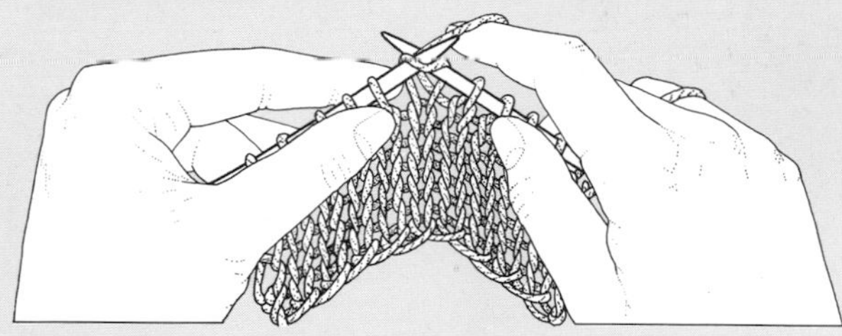

Hold the needles as shown with the working yarn in the right hand. Use the right forefinger to wrap the working yarn over the needles.

Working purl stitch

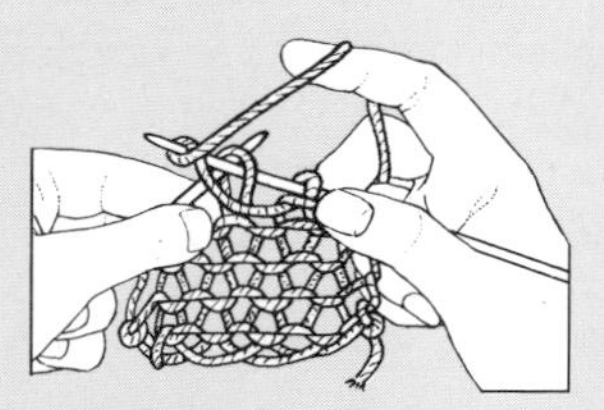

The right forefinger wraps the yarn around the needle. The right needle should be held like a pen.

Threading yarn

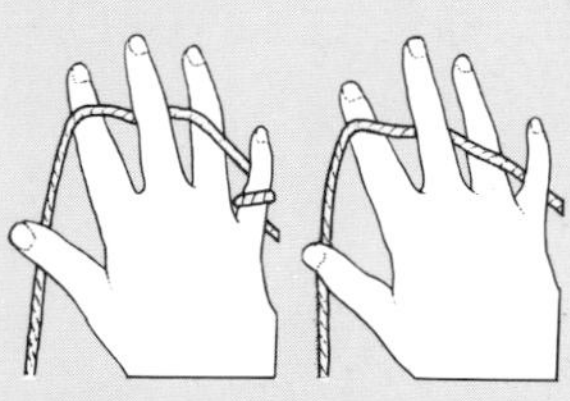

Thread the working yarn through the fingers of the right hand in either of the ways shown here.

Ribbing

Ribbing is most commonly used for collars, cuffs and edges of cardigans and pullovers, but it can be worked over the whole garment.

Before trying any of these patterns, look at the notes for reading knitting instructions and abbreviations which appear on page 139.

Sailor's rib

Work in a chunky or Aran-type wool for warmth or a novelty or random-dyed yarn for a sporty effect.

Use for coat or sweater inset panel; all-over repeat for cardigan, waistcoat, toddler's togs or child's knee socks.

Multiple of 5 sts plus 1.
Row 1 (RS) k1-b, *p1, k2, p1, k1-b; rep from *.
Row 2 P1, *k1, p2, k1, p1; rep from *.
Row 3 K1-b, *p4, k1-b; rep from *.
Row 4 P1, *k4, p1; rep from *.
Repeat rows 1 to 4.

Seeded rib check

Work in a medium-weight yarn for a dense-textured fabric and warm casual wear.

Use for jersey or pullover inset panel; all-over design for toddler's togs or blanket square.

Multiple of 4 sts plus 3.
Row 1 K3, *p1, k3; rep from *.
Row 2 K1, *p1, k3; rep from *, end P1, K1.
Rows 3 and 5 Repeat row 1.
Rows 4 and 6 Repeat row 2.
Rows 7,9 and 11 Repeat row 2.
Rows 8,10 and 12 Repeat row 1.
Repeat rows 1 to 12.

Basket rib

Work in a chunky knitting or double crêpe wool mixture for a rich nubbly texture and warmth; synthetic yarn for washability.

Use for a sweater or slipover inset panel; all-over repeat for baby's coat or sleeping bag.

Multiple of 4sts plus 1.
Row 1 (RS) K1, * p1, k1; rep from *.
Row 2 K2, * p1, k3; rep from *, end P1, K2.
Row 3 P2, * k1, p1; rep from *, end k1, p2.
Row 4 P1, * K1, p1;rep from *.
Row 5 K1, *p3, k1; rep from *.
Row 6 P1, *k3, p1; rep from *.
Repeat rows 1 to 6.

Steep diagonal rib

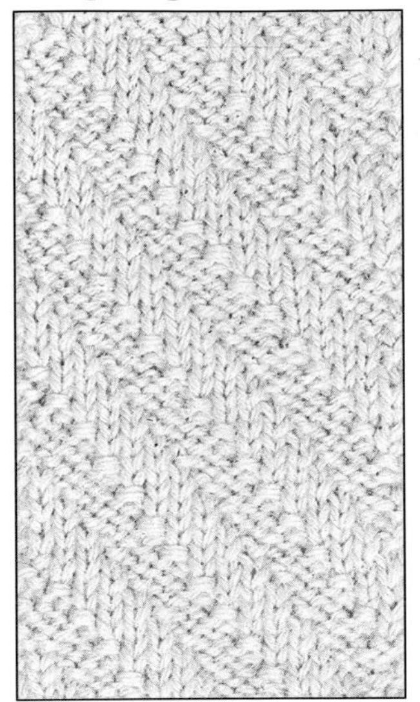

Work in a double knitting or tweedy wool for a sporty, deep-textured fabric.

Use for an all-over design for father and son pullover, tie or zipped blouson jacket.

Multiple of 6 sts.
Row 1 ★P3, k3; rep from ★.
Row 2 and all other even-numbered rows. Knit all knit sts and purl all purl sts.
Row 3 P2, ★k3, p3; rep from ★, end k3, p1.
Row 5 P1, ★k3, p3; rep from ★, end k3, p2.
Row 7 ★K3, p3; rep from ★.
Row 9 K2, ★p3, k3; rep from ★, end p3, k1.
Row 11 K1, ★p3, k3; rep from ★, end p3, k2.
Row 12 See row 2.
Repeat rows 1 to 12.

Long rib check

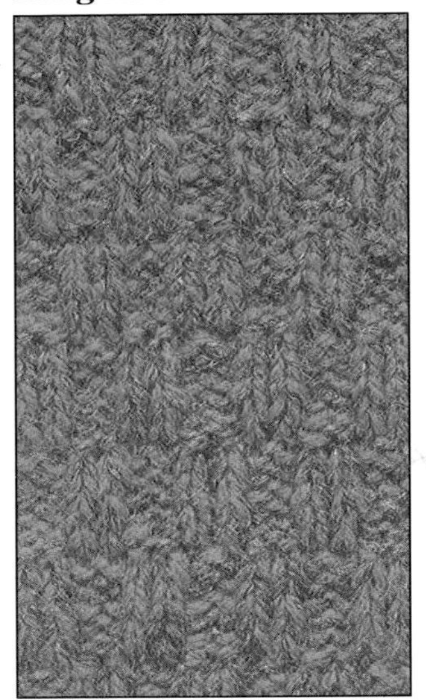

Work in a double knitting wool, crêpe or acrylic yarn for everyday wear.

Use for an all-over pattern for full-size cardigan, baby togs or school wear.

Multiple of 4 sts plus 2.
Rows 1,3 and 5 K2, ★p2, k2; rep from ★.
Rows 2,4 and 6 P2, ★k2, p2; rep from ★.
Rows 7,9 and 11 P2, ★k2, p2; rep from ★.
Rows 8,10 and 12 K2, ★p2, k2; rep from ★.
Repeat rows 1 to 12.

Basketweave

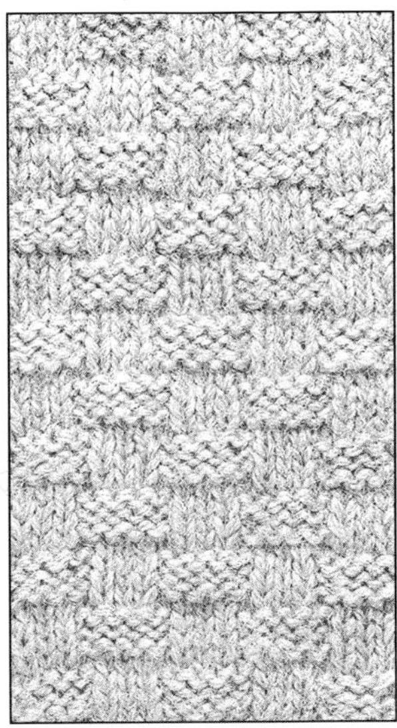

Work in a double knitting or random-dyed yarn for a sporty look; synthetic or cotton for wash and wear.

Use for an all-over pattern for bomber-style jacket, tabard or baby's bed cover; cushion cover, place-mat or bathroom set.

Multiple of 8 sts plus 5.
Row 1 (RS) Knit.
Row 2 K5, ★p3, k5; rep from ★.
Row 3 P5, ★k3, p5; rep from ★.
Row 4 Repeat row 2.
Row 5 Knit.
Row 6 K1, ★p3, k5; rep from ★, end last rep k1 instead of k5.
Row 7 P1, ★k3, p5; rep from ★, end last rep p1 instead of p5.
Row 8 Repeat row 6.
Repeat rows 1 to 8.

Basic techniques

These two pages contain useful information to enable you to correct the inevitable mistakes when they occur. Instructions for casting off are also given so you can now tackle your first piece of knitting with confidence.

Casting off a knit row

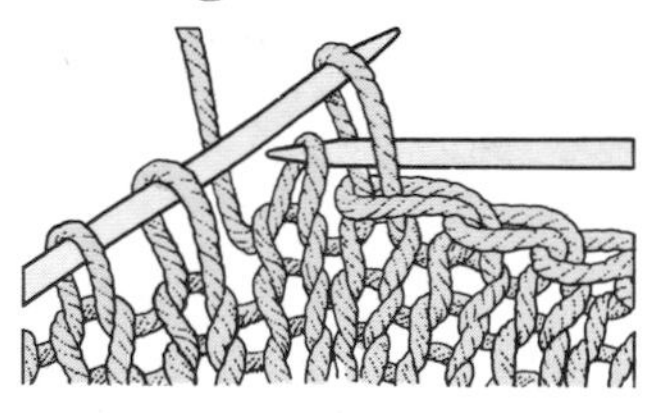

1 Knit the first 2 stitches and insert the tip of the left needle through the first stitch.

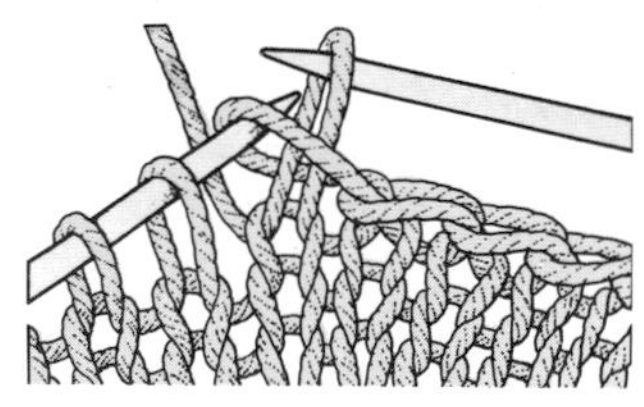

2 Lift the first stitch over the second stitch and discard it. Knit one stitch and continue to lift one stitch over the other to end of row. Cut yarn and pull it through last stitch.

Casting off a purl row

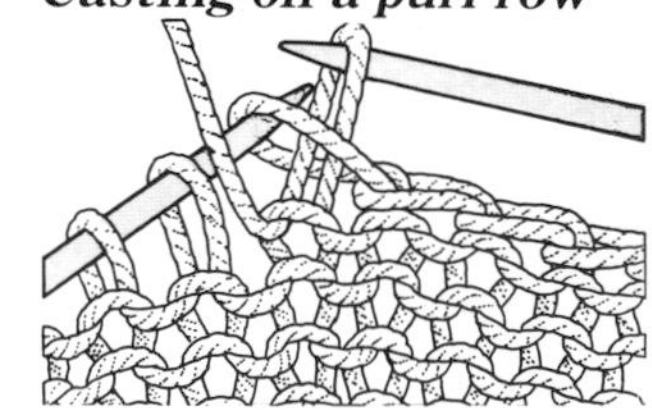

The method is exactly the same as for a knit row. Purl the first 2 stitches and continue as for knit row (left). When casting off in rib, knit stitches are knitted and the purl stitches are purled.

Correcting a ladder

When a dropped stitch is not picked up it forms a ladder. Any patterned stitches using knit and purl combinations will need both pick-up methods.

Picking up a knit stitch

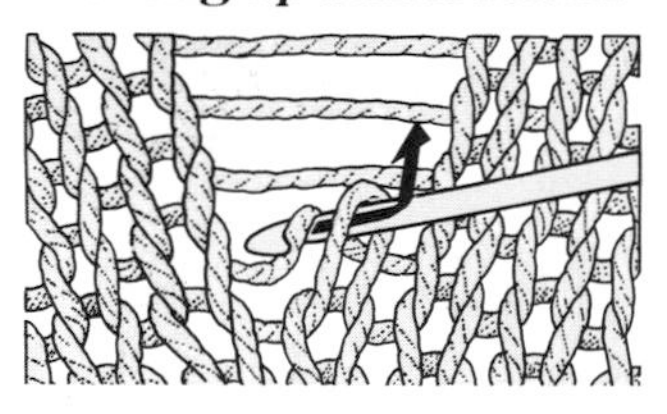

Insert a crochet hook through the front of the fallen stitch. Hook up one strand, pulling it through the stitch to form a new stitch one row further up. Continue to top of ladder.

Picking up a purl stitch

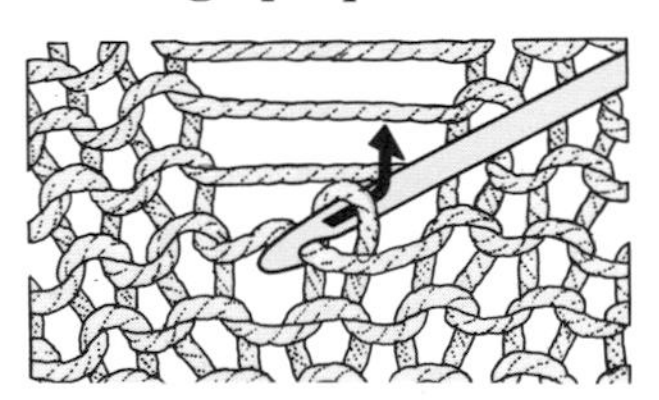

This is rather more difficult than on a knit row. After each strand has been picked up the hook must be taken out and re-inserted for the next stitch.

UNPICKING MISTAKES

Mistakes can easily occur when following a pattern and remain unnoticed for several rows.

Knit row

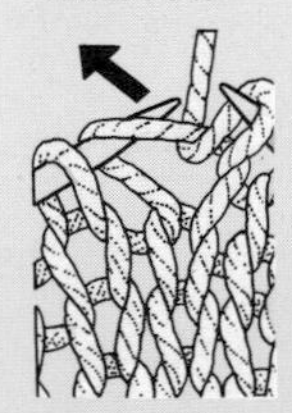

Purl row

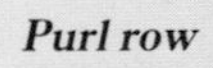

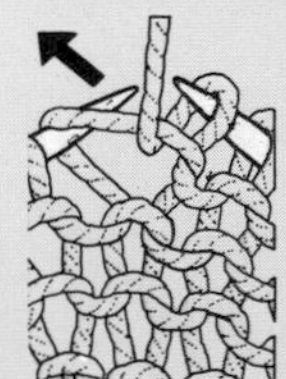

Carefully, unpick the stitches, putting the needle into the row below and undoing the stitch above until the mistake is reached. The needle position is shown for a knit row (above left), a purl row (above right).

Picking up a dropped knit stitch

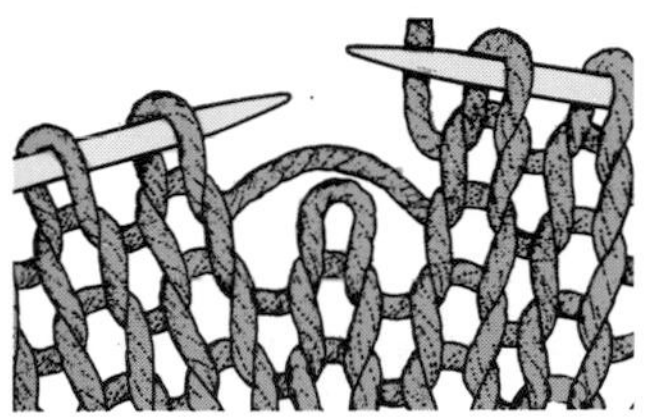
A dropped knit stitch

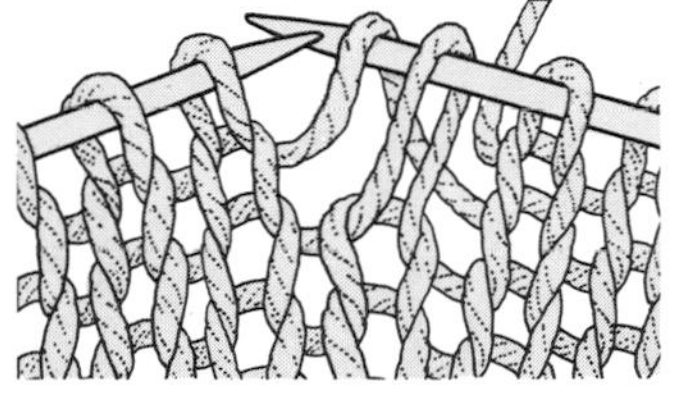
1 Pick up the stitch and the strand on the right needle, inserting the needle from the front to the back.

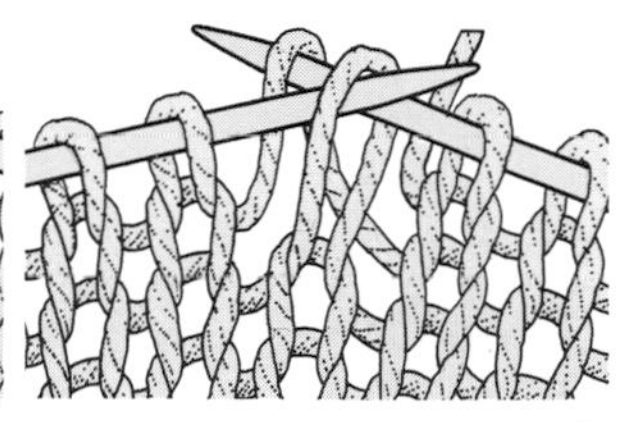
2 Insert left needle from back to front through the stitch only.

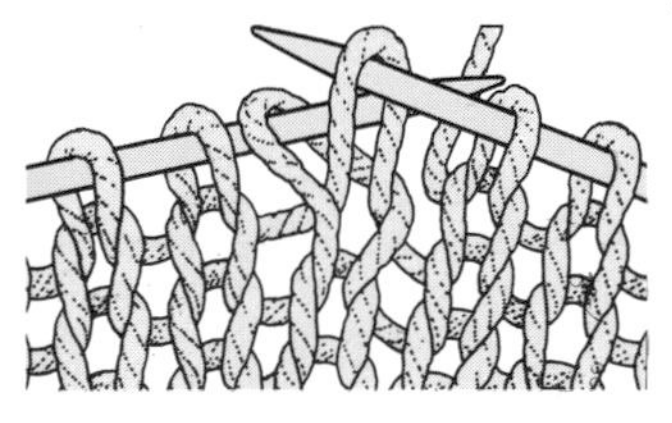
3 With the right needle, pull the strand through to re-form the stitch on the row above.

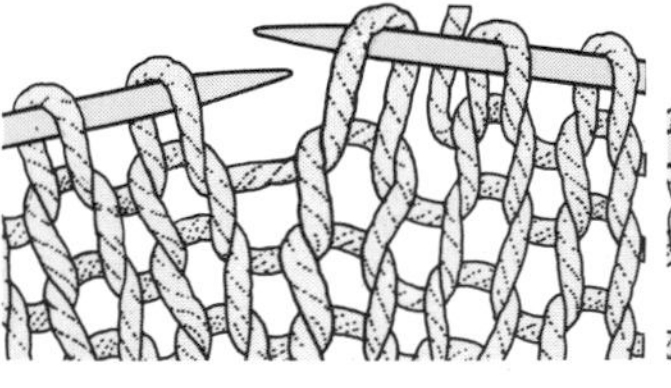
4 The stitch is on the right needle, but it is twisted.

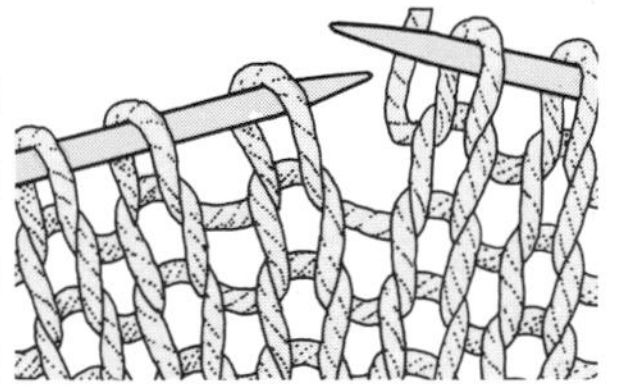
5 Place the stitch in the correct position on the left needle ready to begin knitting.

Picking up a dropped purl stitch

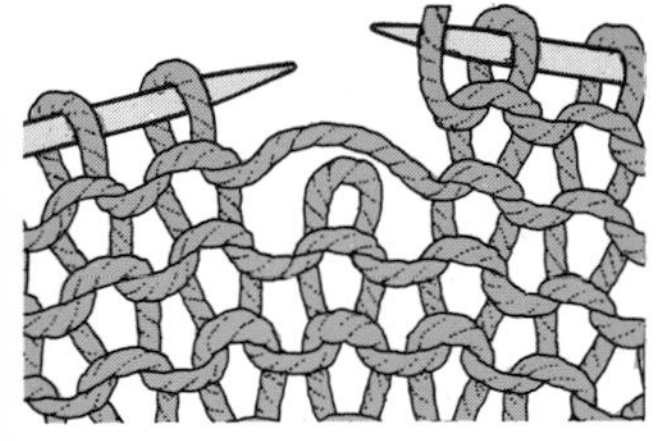
A dropped purl stitch

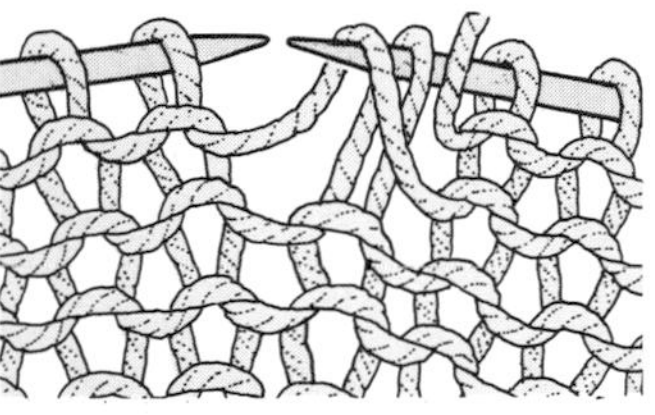
1 Pick up the stitch and the strand on the right needle, inserting the needle from the back to the front.

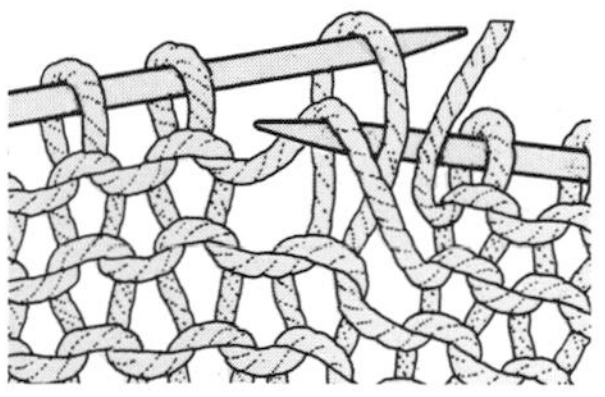
2 Insert the left needle from the front to back through the stitch.

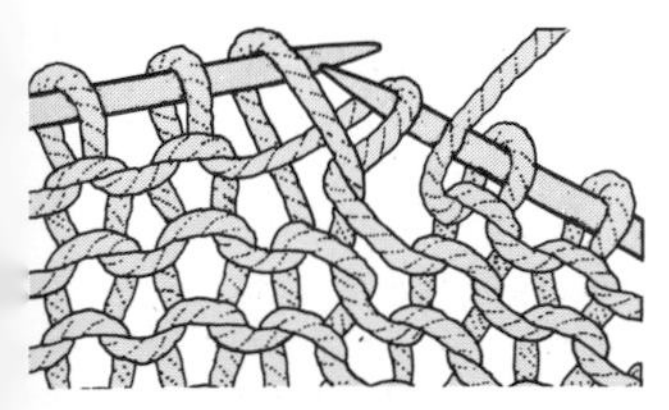
3 With the right needle, pull the strand through the stitch. Drop stitch from left needle.

4 The re-formed stitch is now on the right needle.

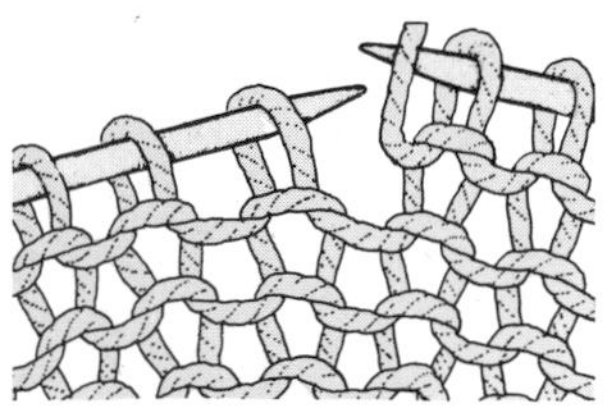
5 Place the re-formed stitch on the left needle, ready to begin purling.

Knit and purl patterns

These two simple stitches form the basis of all knitting stitch patterns. There are innumerable patterns you can make by using either one or a combination of both stitches and these may be smoothly or richly textured. Beginners could knit a trial sample square first.

Reversible diagonal

Chevron

Work in a chunky or double crêpe for stitch clarity; tweedy wool for country wear.

Use for an all-over design for jacket, poncho or chequered travelling rug; inset cape panel or all-over pattern for sporty knee socks.

Multiple of 8 sts.
Row 1 *K1, p1, k1, p5; rep from *.
Row 2 and all other even-numbered rows. Knit all k sts and purl all p sts.
Row 3 K1, p1, *k5, p1, k1, p1; rep from *, end k5, p1.
Row 5 K1, *p5, k1, p1, k1; rep from *, end p5, k1, p1.
Row 7 *K5, p1, k1, p1; rep from *.
Row 9 P4, *k1, p1, k1, p5; rep from *, end (k1, p1) twice.
Row 11 K3, *p1, k1, p1, k5; rep from *, end p1, k1, p1, k2.
Row 13 P2, *k1, p1, k1, p5; rep from *, end k1, p1, k1, p3.
Row 15 K1, *p1, k1, p1, k5; rep from *, end p1, k1, p1, k4.
Row 16 See row 2.
Repeat rows 1 to 16.

Chevron

Work in 4-ply, novelty mix or tweedy wool for a sporty look; bouclé or angora for warmth.

Use for an inset dress or sweater panel or all-over design for a classic slipover.

Multiple of 8 sts.
Row 1 *K1, p7; rep from *.
Row 2 and all even-numbered rows. Knit all k sts and purl all p sts.
Row 3 K2, *p5, k3; rep from *, end p5, k1.
Row 5 K3, *p3, k5; rep from *, end p3, k2.
Row 7 K4, *p1, k7; rep from *, end p1, k3.
Row 9 *P1, k7; rep from *.
Row 11 P2, *k5, p3; rep from *, end k5, p1.
Row 13 P3, *k3, p5; rep from *, end k3, p2.
Row 15 P4, *k1, p7; rep from *, end k1, p3.
Row 16 See row 2.
Repeat rows 1 to 16.

Dotted chevron

Work in a chunky or double knitting wool for wind cheating; tweedy wool for cruiser furnishing.

Use for an inset sweater or coat panel; Aran-style cushion cover or bunk-bed set.

Multiple of 18 sts.
Row 1 (RS) *K8, p2, k8; rep from *.
Row 2 *P7, k4, p7; rep from *.
Row 3 *P1, k5, p2, k2, p2, k5, p1; rep from *.
Row 4 *K2, p3, k2, p4, k2, p3, k2; rep from *.
Row 5 *P1, k3, p2, k6, p2, k3, p1; rep from *.
Row 6 *P3, (k2, p3) 3 times; rep from *.
Row 7 *K2, p2, k3, p4, k3, p2, k2; rep from *.
Row 8 *P1, k2, (p5, k2) twice, p1; rep from *.
Row 9 *P2, k14, p2; rep from *.
Row 10 *K1, p16, k1; rep from *.
Repeat rows 1 to 10.

Zigzag stitch

Work in a smooth medium-weight yarn for a classic style.

Use for an all-over pattern or inset panel for boy or girl sweater, jacket or dress.

Multiple of 6 sts.
Row 1 (WS) and all other WS rows. Purl.
Row 2 *K3, p3; rep from *.
Row 4 P1, *k3, p3; rep from *, end last rep p2 instead of p3.
Row 6 P2, *k3, p3; rep from *, end last rep p1 instead of p3.
Row 8 *P3, k3; rep from *.
Row 10 P2, *k3, p3; rep from *, end last rep p1 instead of p3.
Row 12 P1, *k3, p3; rep from *, end last rep p2 instead of p3.
Repeat rows 1 to 12.

Double moss stitch

Work in a 3- or 4-ply wool or synthetic mixes for school wear.

Use for an all-over pattern for child's button-through cardigan, pullover or snug-fitting hat with matching scarf and gloves.

Multiple of 4 sts.
Rows 1 and 2 *K2, p2; rep from *.
Rows 3 and 4 *P2, k2; rep from *.
Repeat rows 1 to 4.

Selvedges

Selvedges can be worked in several ways to produce neat edges. When care is taken to make the sides straight and even, the sewing up of a piece of knitting is so much easier.

Stocking stitch selvedge

The most common edge of all. The first and last stitches must be knitted firmly to keep the edge straight.

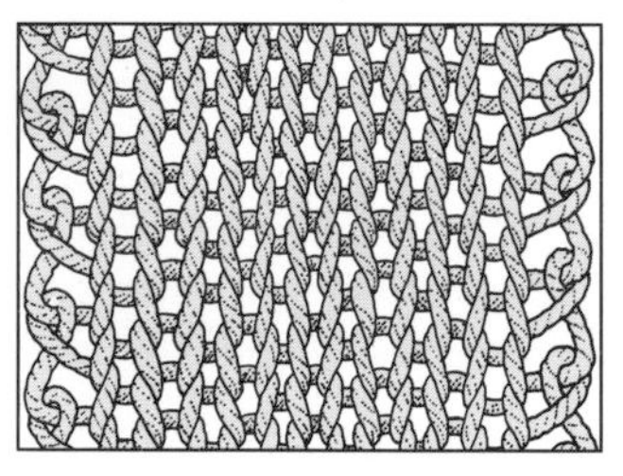

All knit row stitches are knitted and all purl row stitches are purled.

Slip stitch selvedge

Use when a neat edge is required on cardigans.

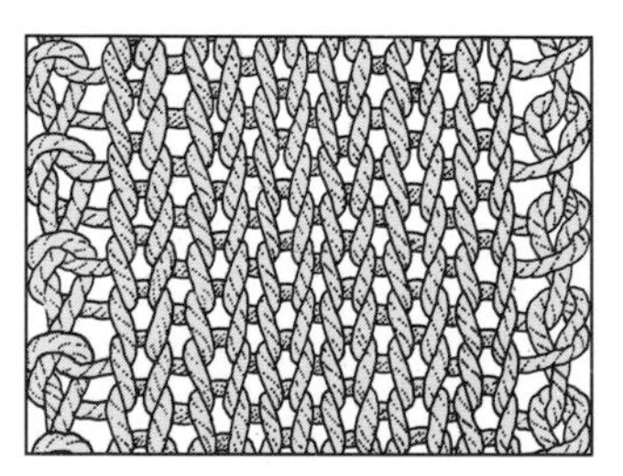

Slip the first stitch of each row knitwise then knit the last stitch of each row. This forms even 'pips' along the edge which look neat and make row counting easier as each 'pip' counts for 2 rows. Sewing up is also made easy.

Open selvedge

This makes a neat but decorative edge.

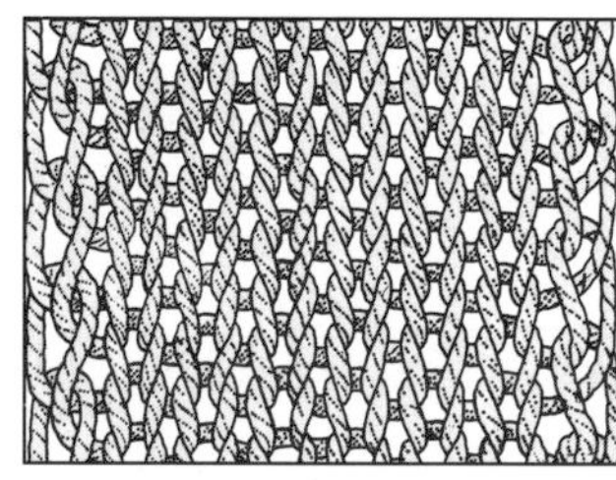

Slip the first and last stitches of every knit row knitwise. Purl all the edge stitches in the purl row.

Fancy selvedge

Use on openwork and lace knitting patterns.

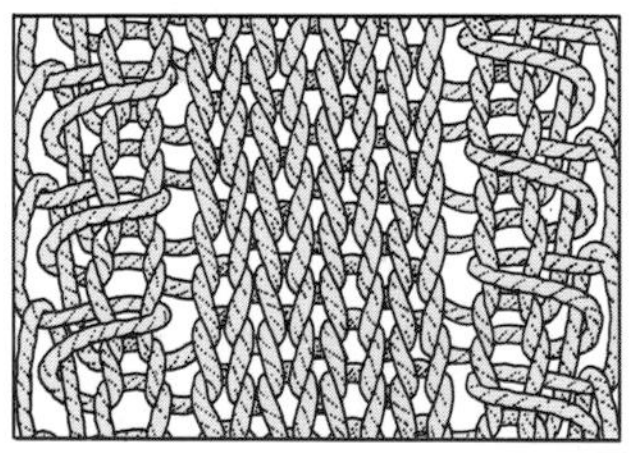

First row *Take yarn to front of work and once over needle to make a stitch (yarn over increases, page 142). Slip next stitch, knit one, pass slipped stitch over. Continue in pattern.*
Second Row *Take yarn to back of work and once around needle, purl 2 stitches together. Continue in pattern.*

Flat selvedge

Prevents edges curling on ties, scarves, mats and shawls.

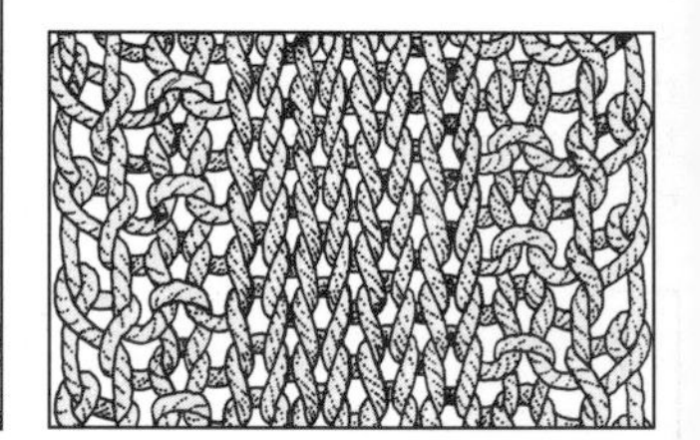

Purl the second and next to last stitches on all knit rows. The purl rows do not alter.

Sewing up selvedges

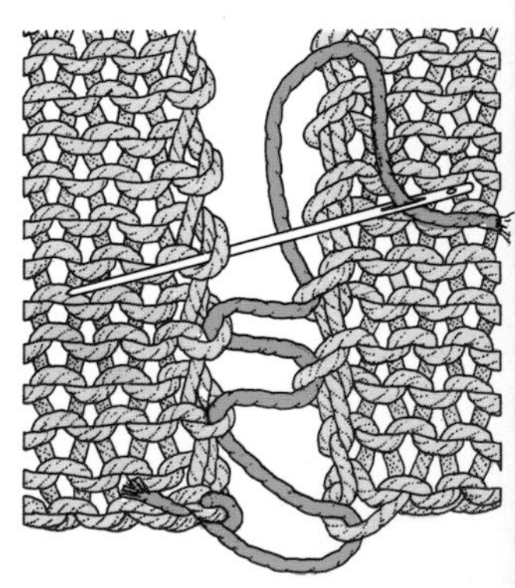

Sew into the 'pips' of the slip stitch selvedge when sewing up. A neatly worked selvedge makes sewing up much easier.

Reading knitting instructions

Knitting patterns may appear incomprehensible at first, but they are in fact a very logical shorthand. Instructions usually guide the knitter through a pattern row by row, if the instructions were written out in full even the simplest pattern would run for pages. So a standard set of abbreviations has evolved. An instruction reading k5, p3 means knit five stitches then purl three. An asterisk, *, means the following instructions must be repeated: for example; p1, *k5, p3; repeat from *, end p2. This means purl the first stitch in the row then repeat the k5, p3 sequence up to the last two stitches which are purled. Brackets are also used to indicate repeats: for example; k1, p1 (k5, p3) twice, k1, p1. This means that k5, p3 must be repeated twice before you move on to k1, p1. Each stitch pattern is preceded by the words 'multiple of x sts'. This indicates the number of stitches required to complete one repeat of the pattern in each row. Thus, 'multiple of 8 sts plus 5', means cast on 16 + 5, 24 + 5, or 32 + 5, and so on. A complete list of abbreviations appears below.

KNITTING ABBREVIATIONS	
BC	Back cross: in cabling, the cn is held to the back of the work while other stitches are worked in front
beg	Beginning
col	Colour
cont	Continue or continuing
cn	Cable needle
dec	Decrease
dpn	Double pointed needle
FC	Front cross: in cabling, the cn is held to the front of the work while other stitches are worked behind
foll	Following
gm	Gram
g-st	Garter stitch
inc	Increase
Inc 1	Increase one stitch by knitting into the front then the back of a stitch
k	Knit
k1-b	Knit one into the back of the stitch
k2tog	Knit two stitches together
Kssb	Knit slip stitch through the back
k up 1	Pick up and knit the stitch in the row below
k-wise	Knitwise
LN	Left needle
M1, M1-b	Make one. Pick up loop or running thread below and knit into back of it
MB	Make bobble
m-st	Moss stitch
no	Number
nos	Numbers
oz	Ounces
()	Parentheses: Repeat all the material between parentheses as many times as indicated
pnso	Pass next stitch over
psso	Pass slipped stitch over
p2sso	Pass two slipped stitches over
patt	Pattern
p	Purl
pl-b	Purl into back of stitch
p2tog	Purl two stitches together
p-wise	Purlwise
rem	Remain or remaining
rep	Repeat
Rep from *	Repeat all the instructions that follow *
RN	Right needle
RS	Right side
sl	Slip
sl st	Slip stitch
sl 1f	Slip a stitch onto a cable needle at the front of the work
sl 1b	Slip a stitch onto cn at back of work
st	Stitch
sts	Stitches
st-st	Stocking stitch
tbl	Through back of loop
throw	To make an elongated stitch, yarn is thrown, or wrapped, twice or more around point of needle. Throws are dropped in the subsequent row
tog	Together
turn	Turn the work around at the point indicated, *before* the end of the row
WS	Wrong side
Wyib	With yarn in back
Wyif	With yarn in front
ybk	Yarn back
yfwd	Yarn forward
yrn	Yarn around needle
y2rn	Yarn twice around needle
yo	Yarn over
yo2	A double yarn over
yon	Yarn on needle

Cable patterns

In cable patterns stitches are moved from one position to another in the same row. The knit and purl patterns are made by knitting the stitches in the order in which they come off the needle. Cabling alters this order, because a number of stitches are slipped on to a cable needle and are held at the back or the front of the work while the next few stitches are worked. The held stitches are then knitted off the cable needle.

Left over right cable

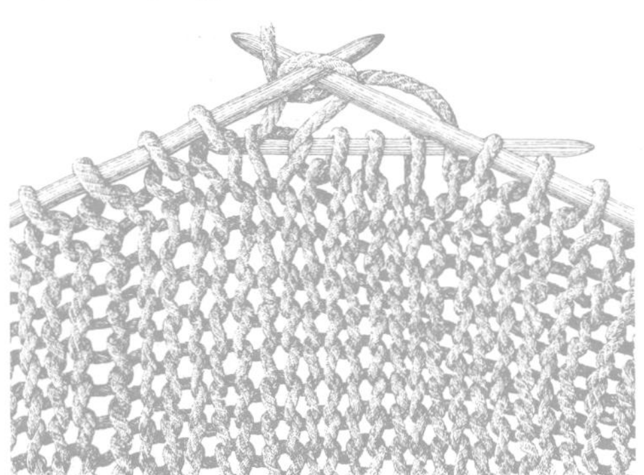

To twist a six stitch cable slip the first 3 stitches on to the cable needle, abbreviated as cn, and hold at back of work. Knit the next 3 stitches. Then knit the first 3 stitches off the cn.

Left over right cable *Here the cable needle is held at the back of the work.*

Right over left cable

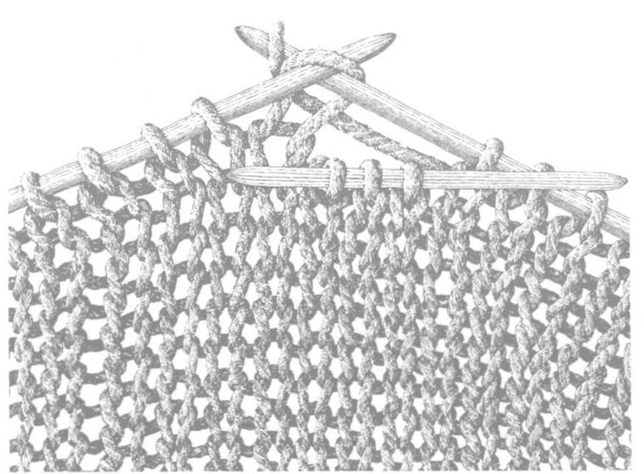

Slip the first 3 stitches on to the cn and hold at the front of the work. Knit the next 3 stitches and then knit the 3 stitches from the cable needle. This right over left cable is the best one to use when knitting in the round as it is more convenient to hold stitches to the front.

Right over left cable *This is formed by holding the cable needle at the front of the work.*

Six stitch cable

Work in an oiled wool, Aran-type or double knitting for an authentic nautical look; angora or mohair for wintry days.

Use for a jersey or jacket inset panel; all-over design for mother and daughter button-through cardigan.

Centre panel of 10 sts.
Rows 1 and 3 (WS) K2, p6, k2.
Row 2 P2, k6, p2.
Row 4 P2, sl next 3 sts to cn and hold at back (or at front); k3, then k3 from cn, p2.
Rows 5 and 7 As rows 1 and 3.
Rows 6 and 8 As row 2.
Repeat rows 1 to 8.

Bobble cable

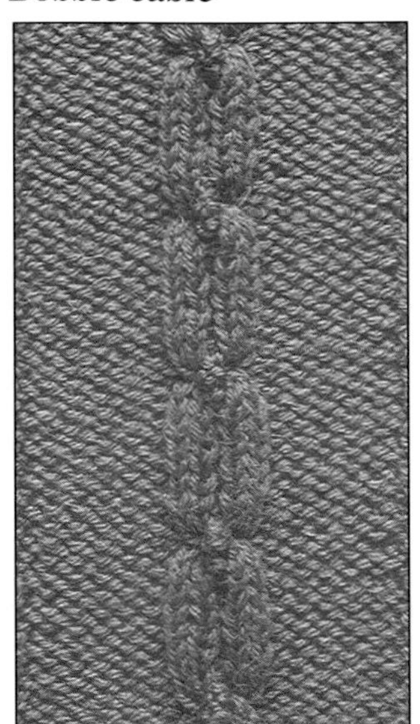

Work in an Aran-type yarn for an authentic fisherman style; tweedy wool for a sporty look.

Use for a double stripe for sweater inset panel, hat or scarf; single stripe for socks or mittens.

Centre panel of 10 sts.
Row 1 (RS) (P2, k2) twice, p2.
Row 2 (K2, p2) twice, k2.
Row 3 P2, sl next 4 sts to cn and hold at front, k2, then sl the 2 purl sts from cn back to left-hand needle, then pass the cn with 2 remaining knit sts to back of work; p2 from left-hand needle, then k2 from cn; p2.
Rows 4,6 and 8 Repeat row 2.
Rows 5,7 and 9 Repeat row 1.
Row 10 Repeat row 2.
Repeat rows 1 to 10.

Double cable

Work in a medium to heavy-weight yarn for snug seaside holiday wear.

Use for an all-over design for polo neck sweater, or combine with Aran patterns for sou'wester and cape or country-style coat.

Centre panel of 12 sts.
Rows 1,3,5 and 7 (WS) K2, p8, k2.
Row 2 P2, sl next 2 sts to cn and hold at front, k2, then k2 from cn; sl next 2 sts to cn and hold at back, k2, then k2 from cn; p2.
Rows 4, 6 and 8 P2, k8, p2.
Repeat rows 1 to 8.

Aran lattice

Work in a double knitting yarn for warm, densely textured Arans.

Use for a sweater inset panel, or classic fisherman's jersey.

Multiple of 6 sts plus 2.
Rows 1 and 3 (WS) K1, *k2, p4; rep from *, end k1.
Row 2 K1, *sl next 2 sts to cn and hold at front, k2, then k2 from cn; p2; rep from *, end k1.
Row 4 K1, p2, *k2, sl next 2 sts to cn and hold at back, k2, then p2 from cn; rep from*, end k5.
Rows 5 and 7 K1, *p4, k2; rep from *, end k1.
Row 6 K1, *p2, sl next 2 sts to cn and hold at back, k2, then k2 from cn; rep from *, end k1.
Row 8 K5, *sl next 2 sts to cn and hold at front, p2, then k2 from cn, k2; rep from *, end p2, k1.
Repeat rows 1 to 8.

Increasing and decreasing

To increase is to add, or to make stitches. To decrease means to lose stitches. Increasing and decreasing serve two purposes, either to shape the knitted fabric into a piece of clothing – a sweater front, sleeve or sock, or to make the decorative texture in lace, embossed and fancy stitches. For shaping clothes, increases or decreases are worked in pairs, so that the garment widens or narrows equally on both sides. Methods of using increases and decreases for shaping are explained on page 160.

An increase can be made visible or invisible. Visible increases are usually used in lace and fancy patterns where the increase itself makes the open-work pattern by the hole or gap it creates in the knitting. Invisible increases are worked by making one stitch from another so that no hole or gap is left in the fabric.

Decreases are always visible with the decreased stitch slanting at an angle. A slip stitch decrease slants from right to left whereas knitting two stitches together results in a slant from left to right.

Visible increases

Yarn over in a knit row

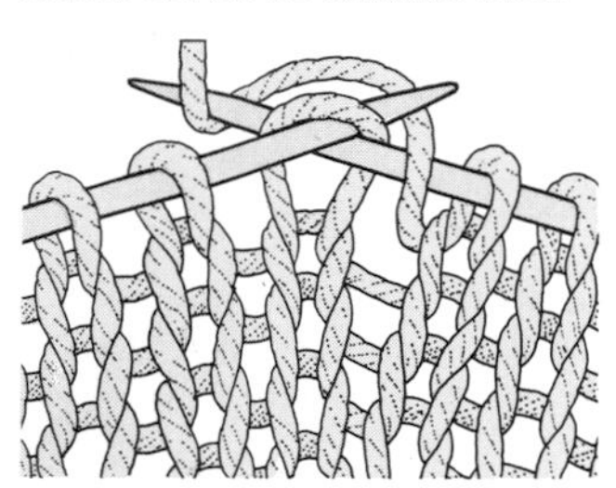

1 Bring the yarn forward to the front, loop it over the right needle, knit the next stitch.

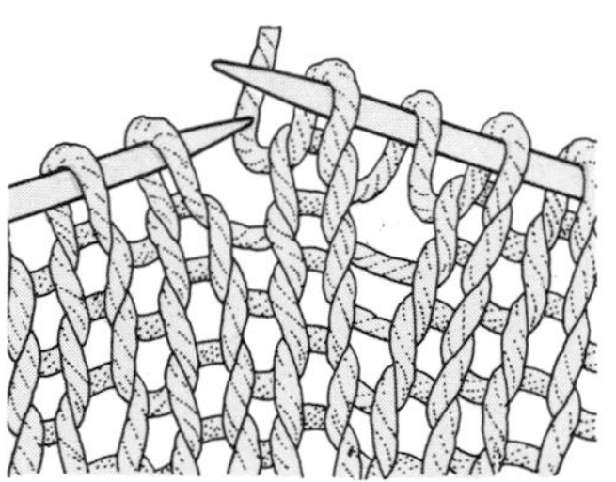

2 With the loop and the new stitch on the right needle, knit to the end of the row.

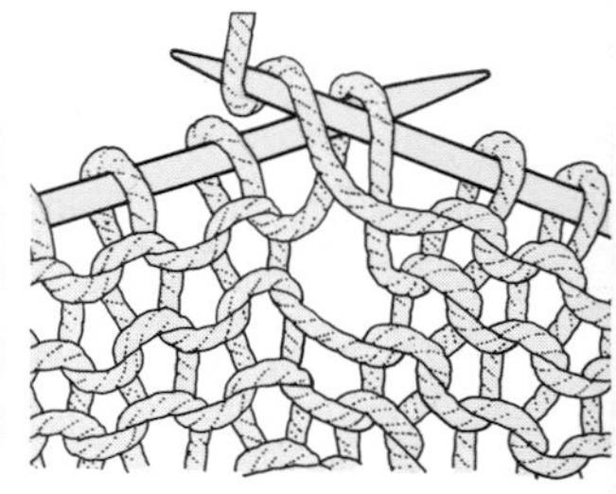

3 On the following row purl the yarn over loop in the usual way.

Yarn over in a purl row

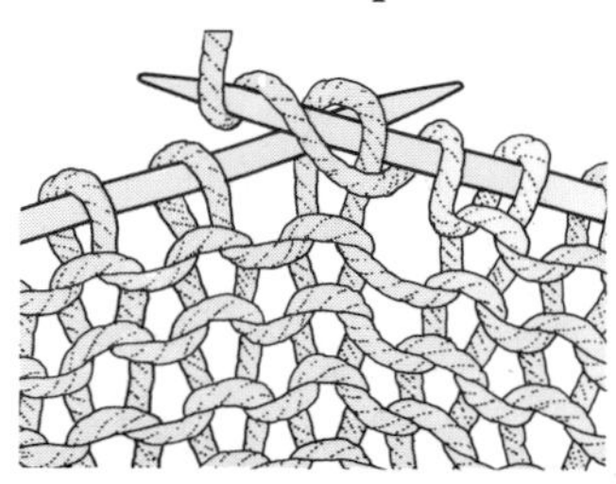

1 Take the yarn round right needle to the front of the work. Purl next stitch.

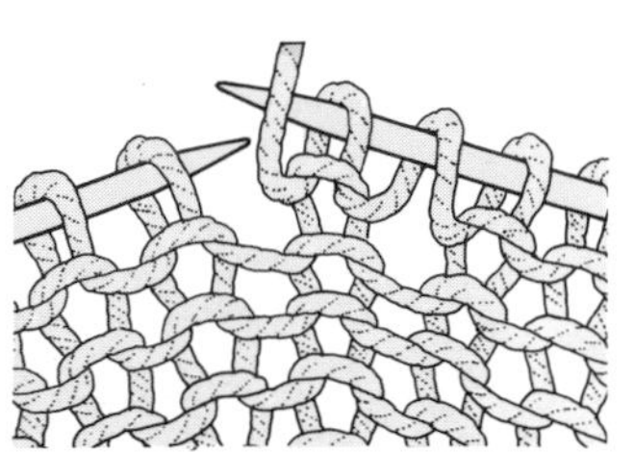

2 With the loop and the new stitch on the right needle, purl to the end of the row.

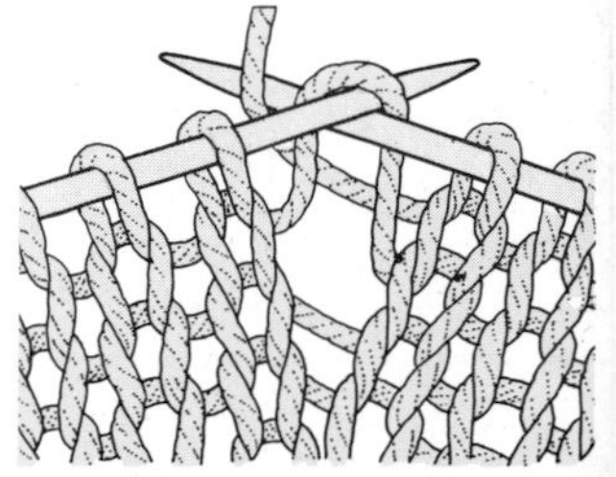

3 On the following row knit the yarn over loop in the usual way.

Lacy motifs

The patterns on the two panels below are both made using the visible increasing and decreasing techniques.

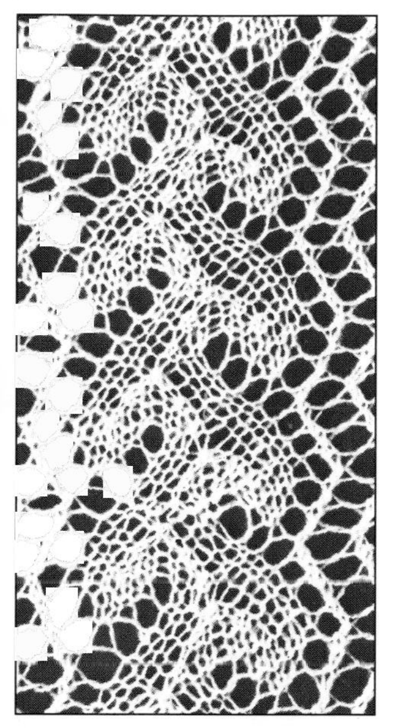

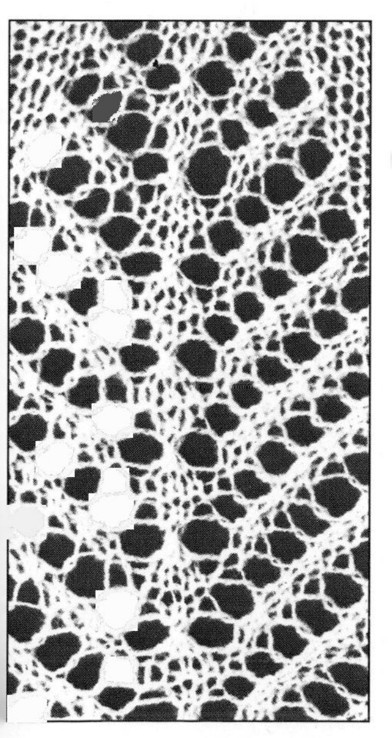

Yarn over between knit and purl stitches

The abbreviation for this yarn over needle movement is yo or yon.

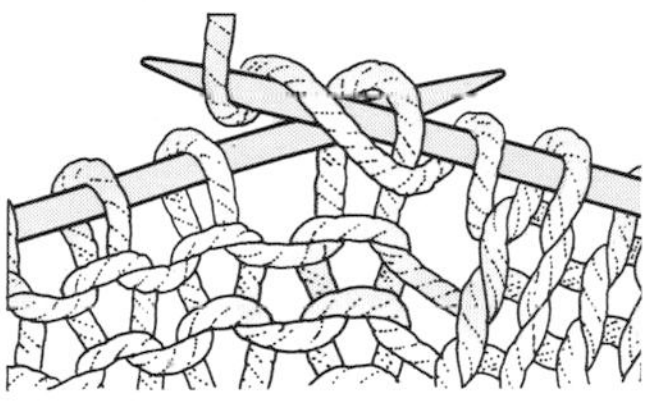

1 After a purl stitch and before a knit stitch, the yarn is already in the correct position at the front of the work. Knit the next stitch in the usual way.

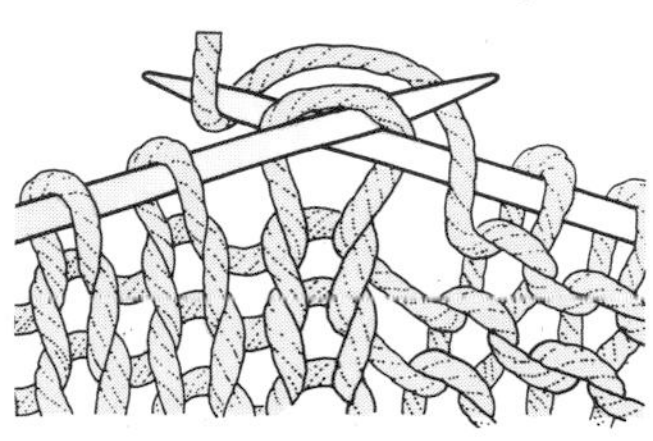

2 After a knit stitch and before a purl stitch, bring the yarn forward and under the needle then back over and around the needle again to the front. Purl the next stitch.

Yarn over on a selvedge

This increase can be used to form looped or picot edges, as well as selvedge increases.

Yarn over in a knit row

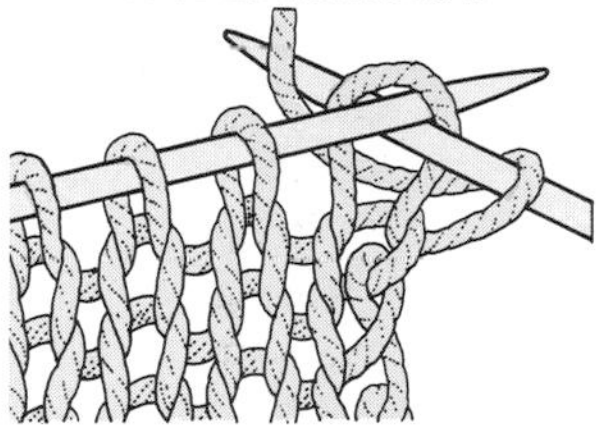

With yarn forward, knit the first stitch in the usual way.

Yarn over in a purl row

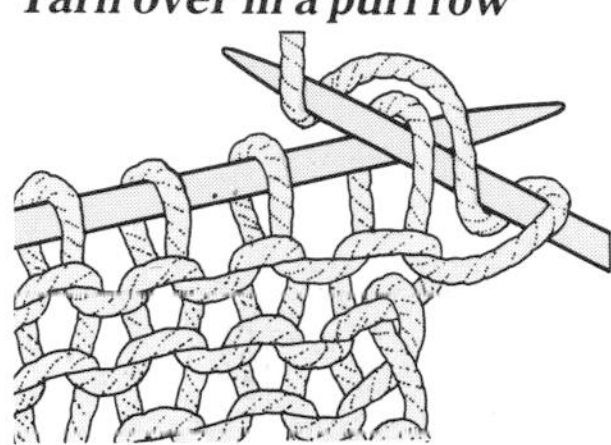

Loop the yarn around the right needle from front to back. Purl the first stitch in the usual way.

VISIBLE DOUBLE INCREASES

Any number of stitches may be increased by the yarn over method.

Double increase in a knit row

This increase is abbreviated as yo2 or yfwd2. Take the yarn forward then take it around the needle, knit the next stitch and complete the row. On the subsequent purl row the first new stitch is purled and the second stitch is knitted.

Double increase in a purl row

This is abbreviated as yo2 or yrn2. Take the yarn around the needle as for a single yarn over, then take it completely around a second time and complete the purl row. On the subsequent knit row, the first new stitch is knitted and the second purled.

Patterns made by visible increases

The lace effect on both of these patterns has been created by using the visible increasing technique. They show how the same basic method can produce two different designs.

Travelling leaf

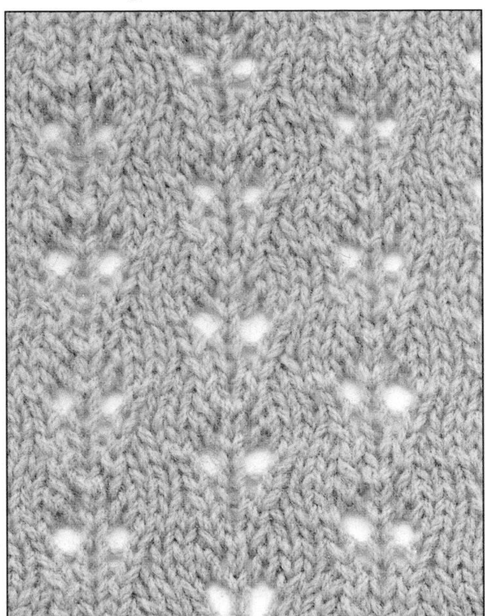

Willow

Work in a lightweight crochet cotton to bring out the pattern; mohair or angora for a fluffy look.

Use for an inset panel for evening blouse or gloves; all-over pattern for poncho, baby's blanket or loose-fitting jacket.

Multiple of 12 sts plus 5.
Row 1 (WS) and all other WS rows. Purl.
Rows 2 and 4 K2, *k1, yo, k3, k2tog, k1, sl 1, k1, psso, k3, yo; rep from *, end k3.
Rows 6 and 8 K2, *k1, sl 1, k1, psso, k3, yo, k1, yo, k3, k2tog; rep from *, end k3.
Repeat rows 1 to 8.

Willow

Work in mohair and lightweight yarns for softness; lurex mix for a glittery effect.

Use for an all-over pattern for baby's blanket or shawl; inset panel for socks or evening jacket.

Multiple of 10 sts plus 3.
Row 1 K2, *yfwd, k3, sl 1, k2 tog, psso, k3, yfwd, k1; rep from *, end k1.
Row 2 and all other even-numbered rows. Purl.
Row 3 K2, *k1, yfwd, k2, sl 1, k2tog, psso, k2, yfwd, k2; rep from * end k1.
Row 5 K2, *k2, yfwd, k1, sl 1, k2tog, psso, k1, yfwd, k3; rep from *, end k1.
Row 7 K2, *k3, yfwd, sl 1, k2tog, psso, yfwd, k4; rep from *, end k1.
Row 8 Purl.
Repeat rows 1 to 8.

Invisible increases

Invisible increases are most often used for shaping garments. They can be made in several ways as shown below. If you are following a printed pattern the instructions will tell you which of the three methods described here to use.

Knitting two stitches from one

This increase is abbreviated as Inc 1, increase 1.

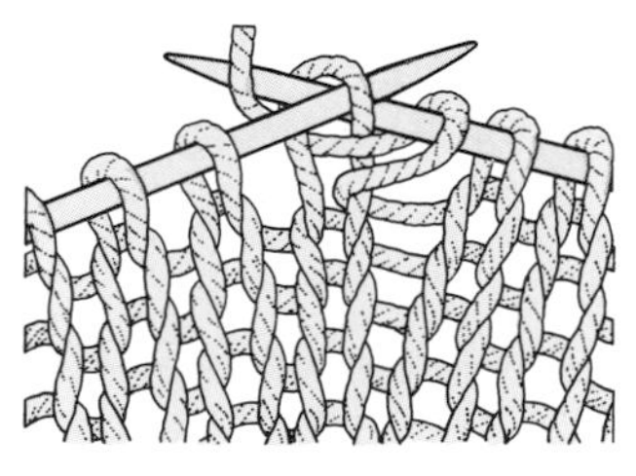

In a knit row, knit into the front of the stitch in the usual way, then knit into the back of it and discard it.

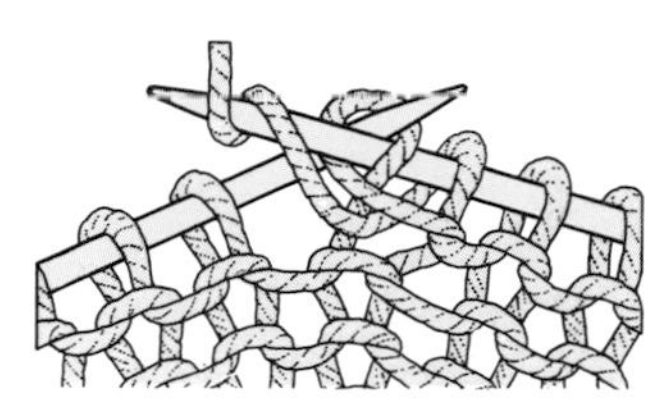

1 In a purl row, purl into the front of the stitch in the usual way, then purl into the back of it and discard it.

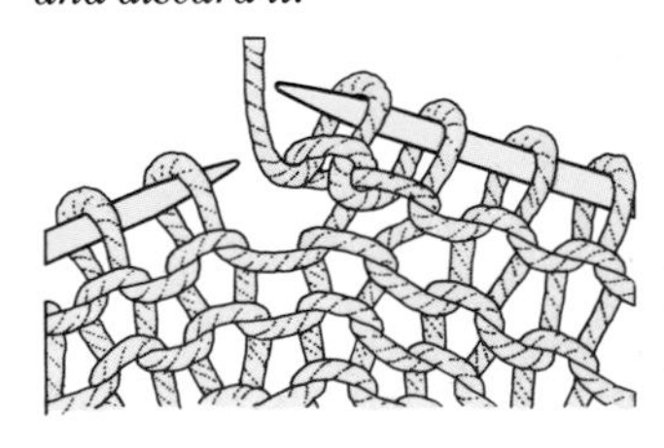

2 Two stitches have been made from one.

Knitting into the stitch below

This increase, which is often called a 'lifted increase', is abbreviated as K up 1 or P up 1.

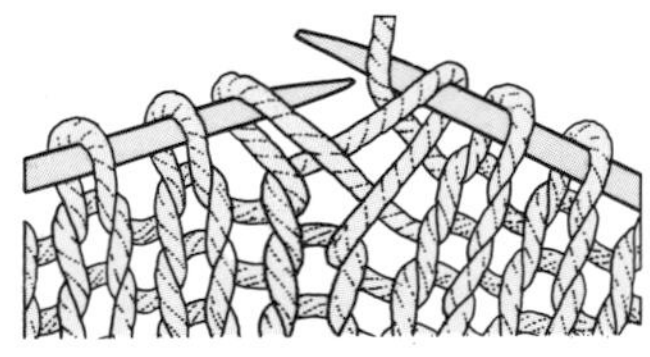

1 In a knit row insert right needle from front to back into top of stitch below the next one to be knitted. Knit the stitch in the usual way.

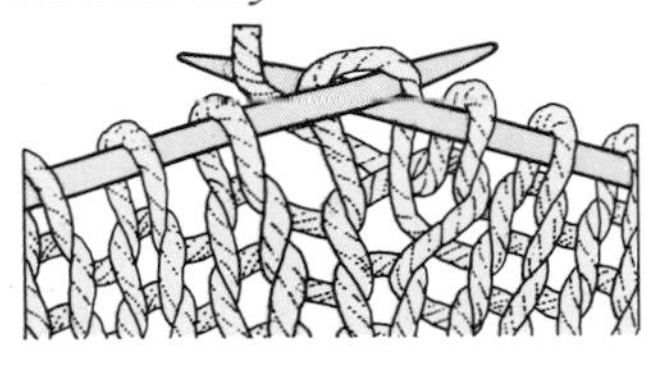

2 Knit the next stitch and continue to the end of the row.

In a purl row insert right needle from back to front into top of stitch below the next one to be purled. Purl it in the usual way to end of row.

Knitting into the running thread below

This increase, which is often called a 'raised increase', is abbreviated as M1, make one.

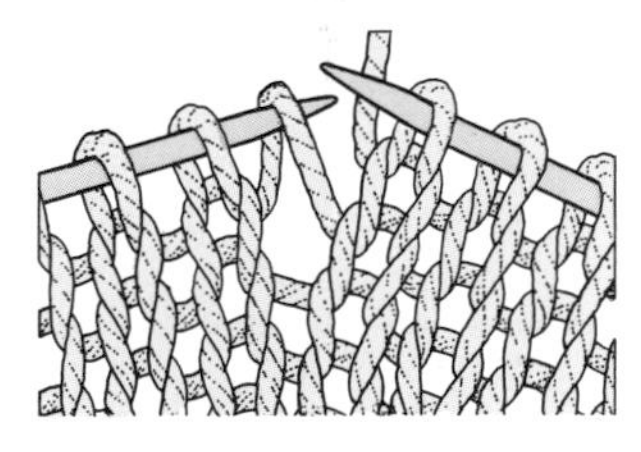

1 In a knit row insert the left needle under the running thread between the 2 stitches.

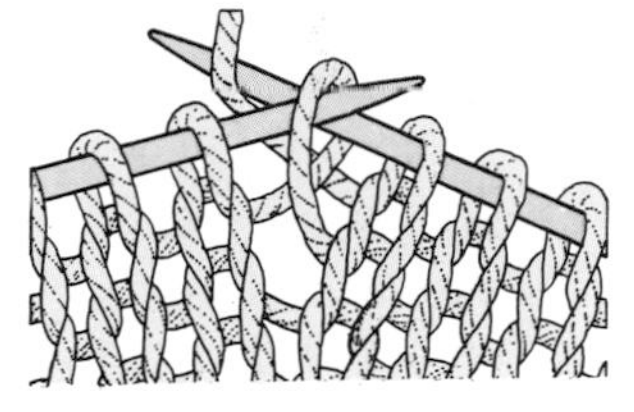

2 Knit into the back of the raised running thread.

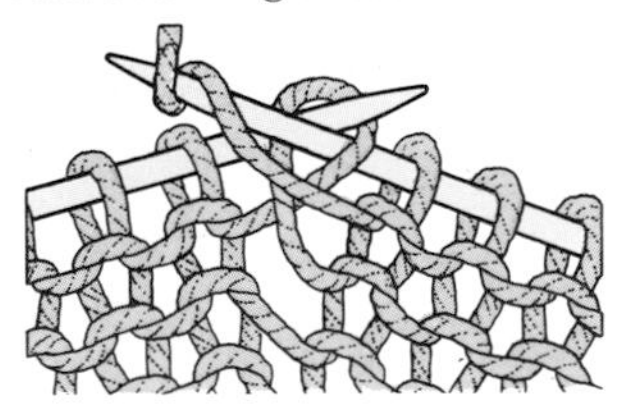

In a purl row insert left needle under the running thread between the 2 stitches and purl into the back of the raised running thread.

Shaping

Simple garments can be created by using a very basic knowledge of knitting techniques. The results are just as satisfying as thos achieved by more complicated patterns.

Short-sleeved sweater
This sweater has been shaped using invisible increasing (page 145) and decreasing (page 148) on the neck and sleeves. The inset patterned panel adds interest to the sweater which has been knitted in a wide rib. A lace-effect panel created by visible increases, as shown on page 144, would also look very effective here.

Knitted poncho
This poncho uses increases and decreases to create a garment shape. On page 160 there is an explanation of how increases and decreases can be used to create different shapes.

Adding fringe to the poncho
Use odd balls of yarn to decorate the poncho with a bright multi-coloured fringe. Loop the yarn through the edge of the poncho with a crochet hook. The fringe can be also knotted into patterns for a more decorative effect.

Decreases

As with invisible increases, there are several ways of decreasing. Again your pattern instructions will tell you which method to use. It is, however, useful to try out the different methods of decreasing with an oddment of wool before starting a complete garment.

Knitting two stitches together

This decrease is abbreviated as K2 tog or P2 tog.

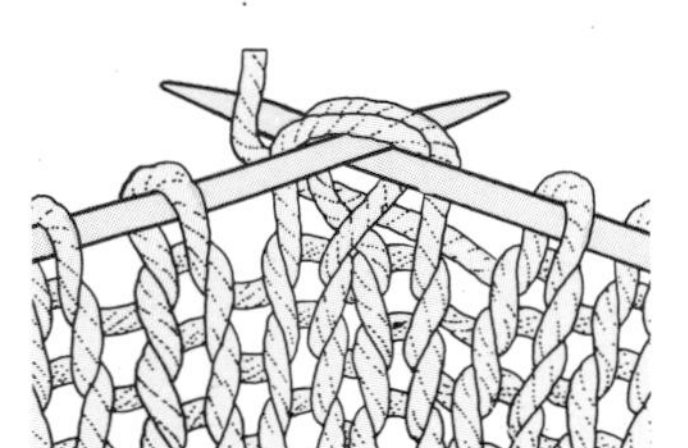

In a knit row insert right needle through the front of the first 2 stitches. Knit them together.

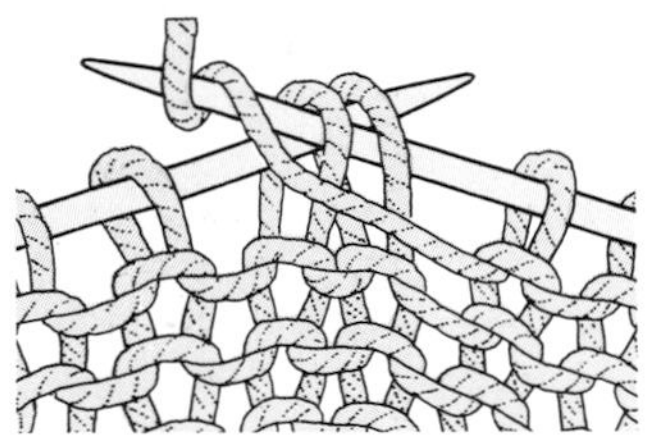

1 In a purl row, insert right needle through the front of the first 2 stitches. Purl them together.

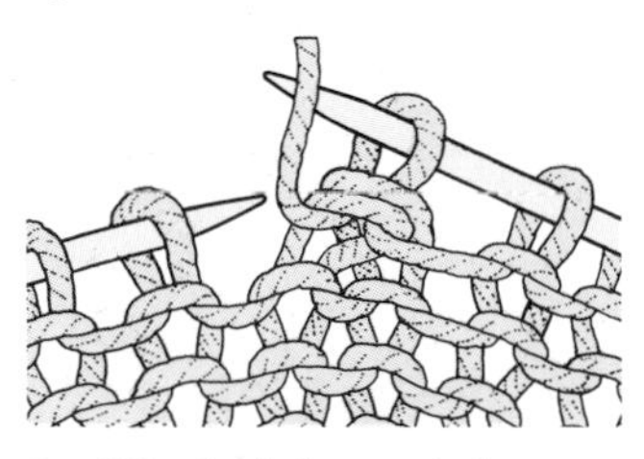

2 The 2 stitches purled together through the front slant from left to right. If purled together through the back, the decrease slants from right to left.

The slip stitch decrease

This decrease is abbreviated as Sl 1, k1, psso: slip one, knit one, pass slipped stitch over. On a purl row the abbreviation is Sl 1, p1, psso. The decrease slants from right to left on the front of the knitting.

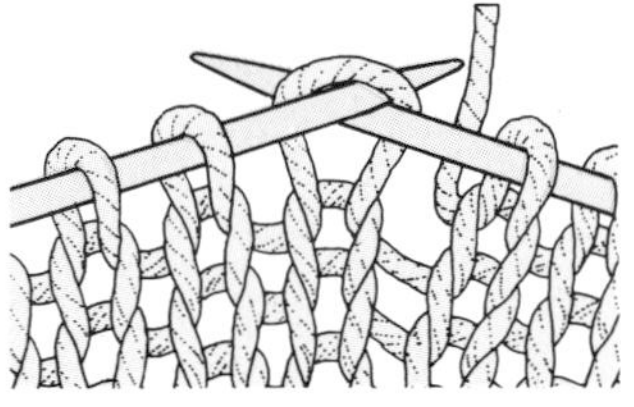

1 In a knit row insert the right needle knitwise into the stitch on the left needle and then slip the stitch onto the right needle.

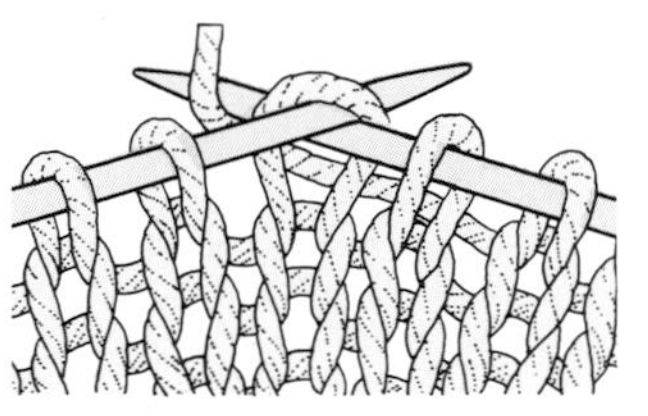

2 Hold the slipped stitch and knit the next stitch in the usual way.

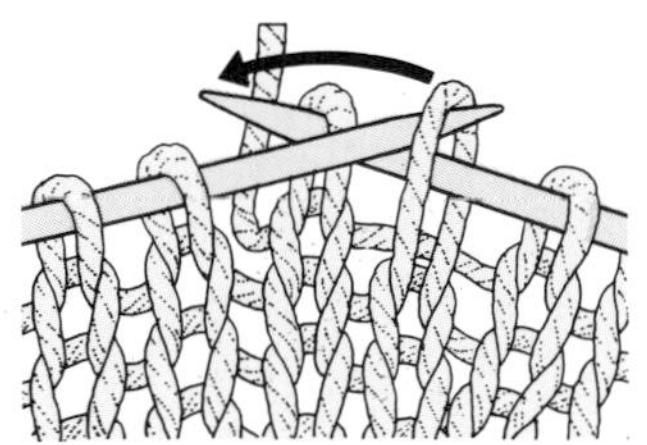

3 Insert the left needle through the front of the slipped stitch and lift it over the stitch just knitted.

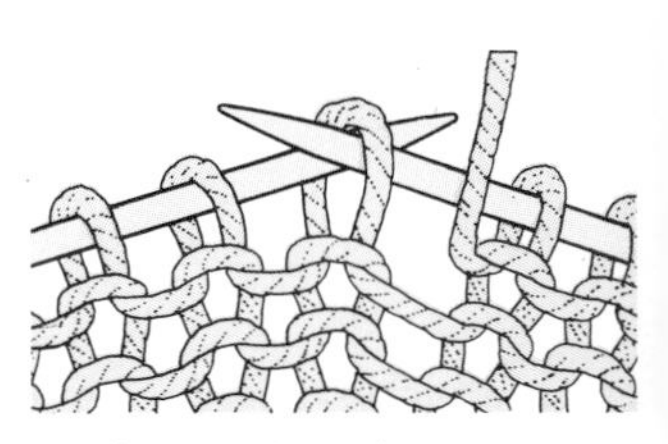

1 In a purl row insert the right needle purlwise into the first stitch on the left needle and slip it onto the right needle.

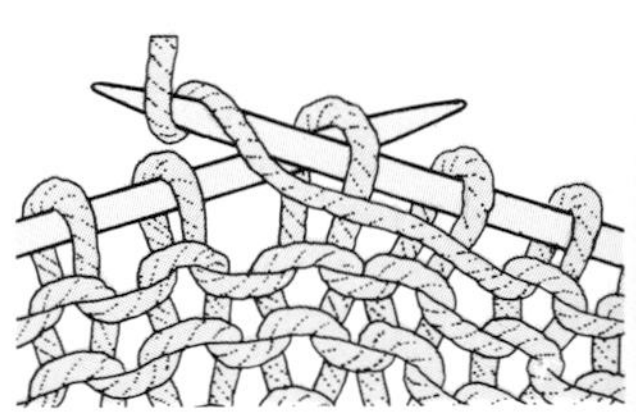

2 Hold the slipped stitch and purl the next stitch in the usual way.

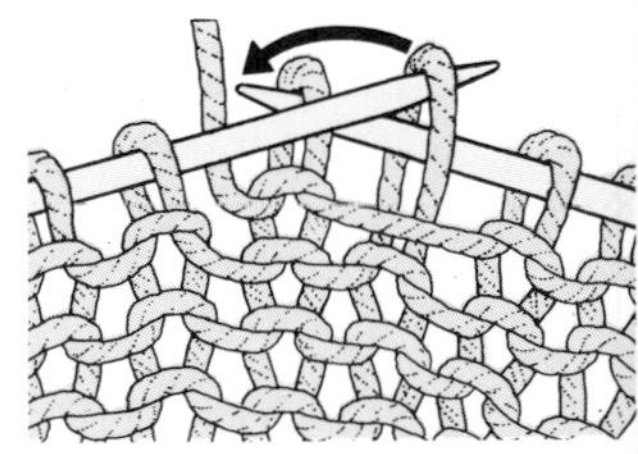

3 Insert the left needle through the front of the slipped stitch, and lift it over the stitch just purled.

BOBBLE AND EMBOSSED PATTERNS

In bobble and embossed patterns a single stitch is used repeatedly, and increases are made into it to form a cluster of stitches. This cluster is knitted in a variety of ways according to the pattern. The stitches are then decreased and all but one stitch discarded. In this way the surface of the knitting is raised to a greater or lesser extent depending on whether the pattern calls for a round fat bobble or an embossed leaf design.

On the next two pages there are five bobble and embossed patterns to work, each giving a rich textured effect.

Making a simple bobble

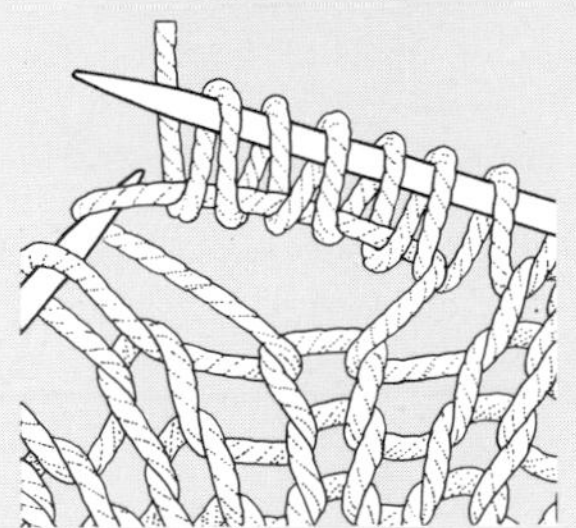

Row 1 Knit two, take the yarn forward to the front of the work and over the needle, knit one but do not discard the stitch, instead continue working into the stitch twice more. In a knitting pattern this instruction would read:
K2, *yo, k1*; rep from * twice more.

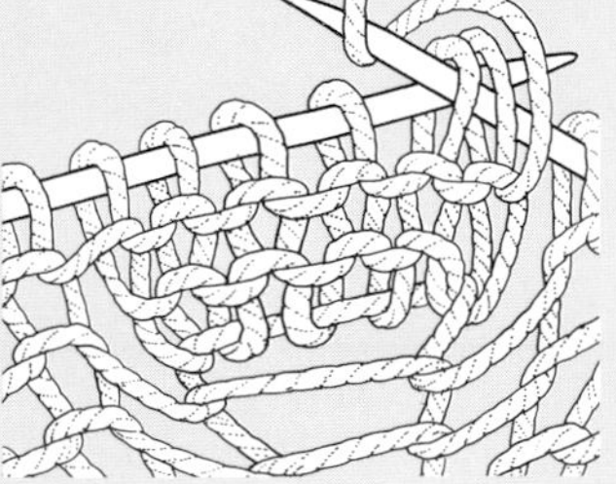

Row 2 Turn the work. Slip the first stitch purlwise onto the right needle and purl 5 stitches. Turn. Sl 1 pwise, p5.

Row 3 Turn. Slip the first stitch knitwise onto the right needle and knit 5. Turn. Sl 1, kwise, k5.

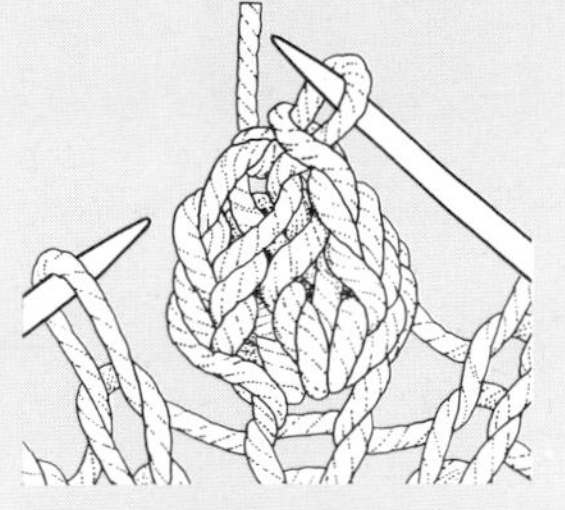

Row 4 Turn. Purl 2 stitches together 3 times. Turn. P2 tog 3 times.

Row 5 Turn. Slip 1 stitch knitwise, knit 2 stitches together pass the slipped stitch over. One stitch remains on the needle. Turn. Sl 1 kwise, k2tog, psso. 1 st rem.

The finished bobble

These five rows form a simple bobble. In the patterns which follow, different types of bobble and embossed stitches are produced, but the basic principle remains the same.

Detail from bobble and diamond cable

Bobble and embossed

Deeply textured bobble and embossed patterns are created by raising and lowering the surface of the knitting. This group of stitch patterns offers one of the widest ranges of surface decoration and texture, from small berry-like repeats to flowing vine, bead and bouquet patterns, ideal for a wide variety of garments for both children and adults.

Gooseberry stitch

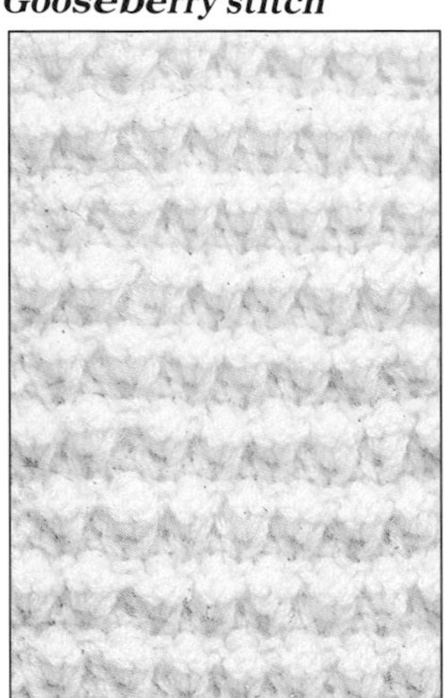

Work in an oiled or double knitting wool for a traditional Aran look; baby wool for nursery wear.

Use for a mix panel with Aran patterns for fisherman's jersey; all-over design for baby's pram set or shawl.

Odd number of sts.
Row 1 (RS) Knit.
Row 2 K1, *(p1, yo, p1, yo, p1) in next st, making 5 sts from one; k1, rep from *.
Row 3 Purl.
Row 4 K1, *sl 2 wyif, p3 tog, p2sso, k1; rep from *.
Row 5 Knit.
Row 6 K2, *(p1, yo, p1, yo, p1) in next st, k1; rep from *, end k1.
Row 7 Purl.
Row 8 K2, *sl 2 wyif, p3 tog, p2sso, k1; rep from *, end k1.
Repeat rows 1 to 8.

Berry stitch

Work in a thick or medium-weight wool for a fisherman look; 4-ply wool or acrylic mix for everyday wear.

Use for a sweater inset panel or alternate with cables for Arans; all-over design for mother and daughter cardigan.

Multiple of 4 sts.
Row 1 (WS) *(K1, yo, k1) in same st, p3tog; rep from *.
Row 2 *K1, p3; rep from *.
Row 3 *K3, p1; rep from *.
Row 4 *P1, k3; rep from *.
Row 5 *P3 tog, (k1, yo, k1) in same st; rep from *.
Row 6 *P3, k1; rep from *.
Row 7 *P1, k3; rep from *.
Row 8 *K3, p1; rep from *.
Repeat rows 1 to 8.

Puffball pattern

Work in a thick, medium-weight wool or novelty mix for outdoor wear; angora or mohair for light-weight warmth.

Use for a fisherman's sweater inset panel; all-over pattern for slipover or V-neck button-through cardigan.

Multiple of 10 sts plus 2.
Rows 1 and 3 (WS) Purl.
Row 2 Knit.
Row 4 K1, *(k5, turn, p5, turn) 3 times, k10; rep from *, end k1.
Rows 5, 6 and 7 Repeat rows 1, 2 and 3.
Row 8 K6, rep from * of row 4; end last repeat k6 instead of k10.
Repeat rows 1 to 8.

Clam shells

Sheaf stitch

Work in a lurex mix or flecked yarn for a sophisticated look; angora or baby yarn for infant's wear.

Use for an all-over pattern for evening jacket, bolero or bag; or baby's bonnet and cardigan set.

Multiple of 4 sts plus 1.
Row 1 (WS) K2, *(p1, yo, p1, yo, p1) in next st, k3; rep from *, end last repeat k2.
Row 2 P2, *k5, p3, rep from *, end last repeat p2.
Row 3 K2, *p5, k3; rep from *, end last repeat k2.
Row 4 P2, *k5tog-b, p3; rep from *, end last repeat p2.
Row 5 K4, *(p1, yo, p1, yo, p1) in next st, k3; rep from *, end k1.
Row 6 P4, *k5, p3; rep from *, end p1.
Row 7 K4, *p5, k3; rep from *, end k1.
Row 8 P4, *k5tog-b, p3; rep from *, end p1.
Repeat rows 1 to 8.

Sheaf stitch

Work in a 3- or 4-ply yarn, crêpe or double knitting wool for a deep-textured fabric with a young look.

Use for a mother and daughter sweater or coat yoke, toddler's tops or baby's crib cover.

Multiple of 8 sts plus 2.
Rows 1 and 3 (WS) K2, *p2, k2; rep from *.
Row 2 P2, *k2, p2; rep from *.
Row 4 P2, *insert right needle from front between 6th and 7th sts on left needle and draw through a loop; sl this loop onto left needle and knit it together with first st on left needle; k1, p2, k2, p2; rep from *.
Rows 5 and 7 Repeat rows 1 and 3.
Row 6 Repeat row 2.
Row 8 P2, k2, p2, *draw loop from between 6th and 7th sts as before and knit together with first st, then k1, p2, k2, p2; rep from *, end k2, p2.
Repeat rows 1 to 8.

Working in colour

Colour in knitting can be as flexible as colour in painting. There is no limit to the number of effects you can achieve once you have mastered the techniques that make it possible to combine colours in any way you choose. The simplest way to start working with colour is to make horizontal stripe patterns for which the new colour is added at the beginning of a row and the unused colours are either broken off or carried up the side of the work until they are needed again. For more complicated colourwork designs, the new colour or colours can be added either at the beginning of a row or during a row, depending on where they are needed.

Adding a new colour at the beginning of a row

Use this method to knit horizontal stripe patterns.

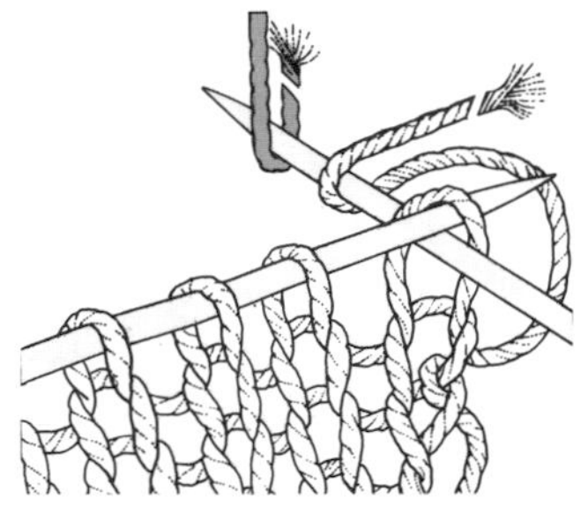

1 Insert the right needle into the first stitch on the left needle. Knit one stitch using old and new yarns together.

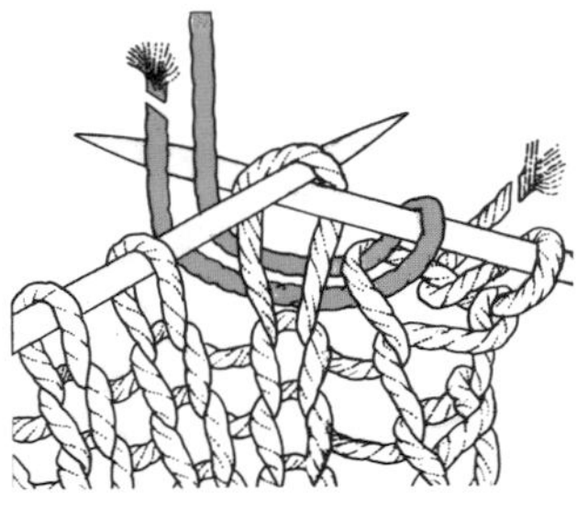

2 Leave the old yarn at the back and knit the next 2 stitches using the doubled length of new yarn.

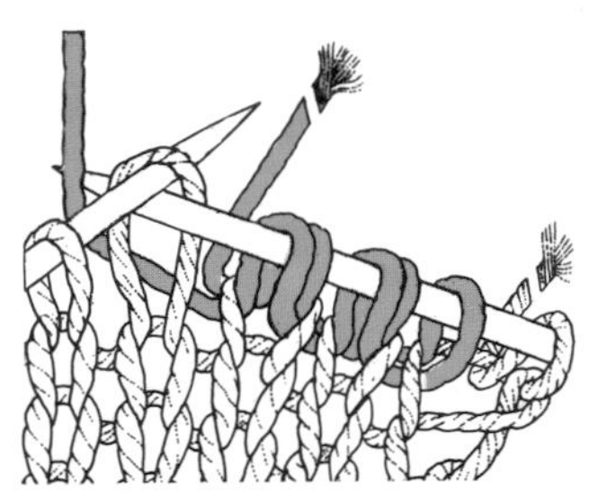

3 Then discard the short end of new yarn and continue to knit. On the following row, the 3 double stitches are each treated as single stitches. Pick up old yarn from side edge if required later.

Adding a new colour in the middle of a row

Use this method for patterns where the old colour will be used again in the same row.

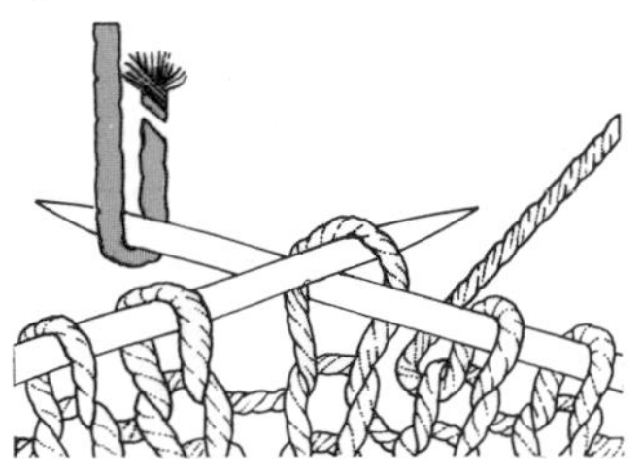

1 Insert the right needle into next stitch on the left needle. Wrap the new yarn over the right needle and knit the stitch with the new yarn.

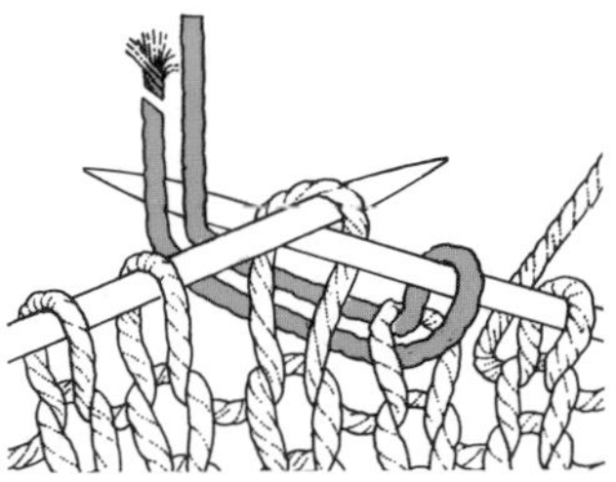

2 Leaving old yarn at back of work, knit the next 2 stitches using the new yarn double.

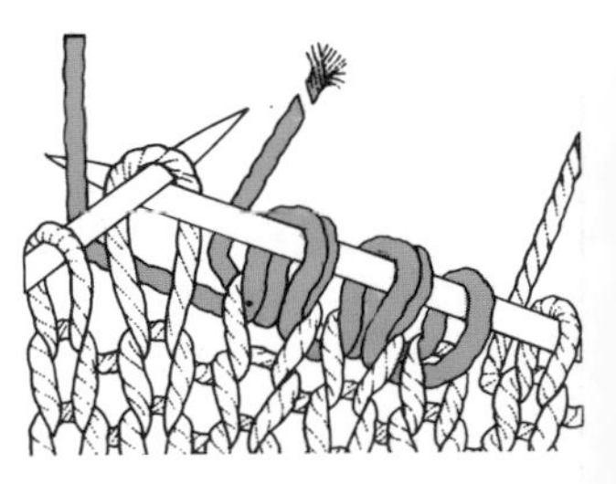

3 Discard the short end and continue knitting with the new colour. Use the new and old yarns as required by the pattern.

Slip patterns

These patterns are formed by knitting some stitches and slipping others. You slip a stitch by transferring it from one needle to another without working it. Stitches are always slipped purlwise unless the pattern specifically states knitwise. When the yarn is brought to the front of the slipped stitches the pattern reads: With yarn in front (Wyif). When the yarn is brought behind, the pattern reads: With yarn in back (Wyib).

A selection of slip patterns is shown over the page, with their pattern instructions.

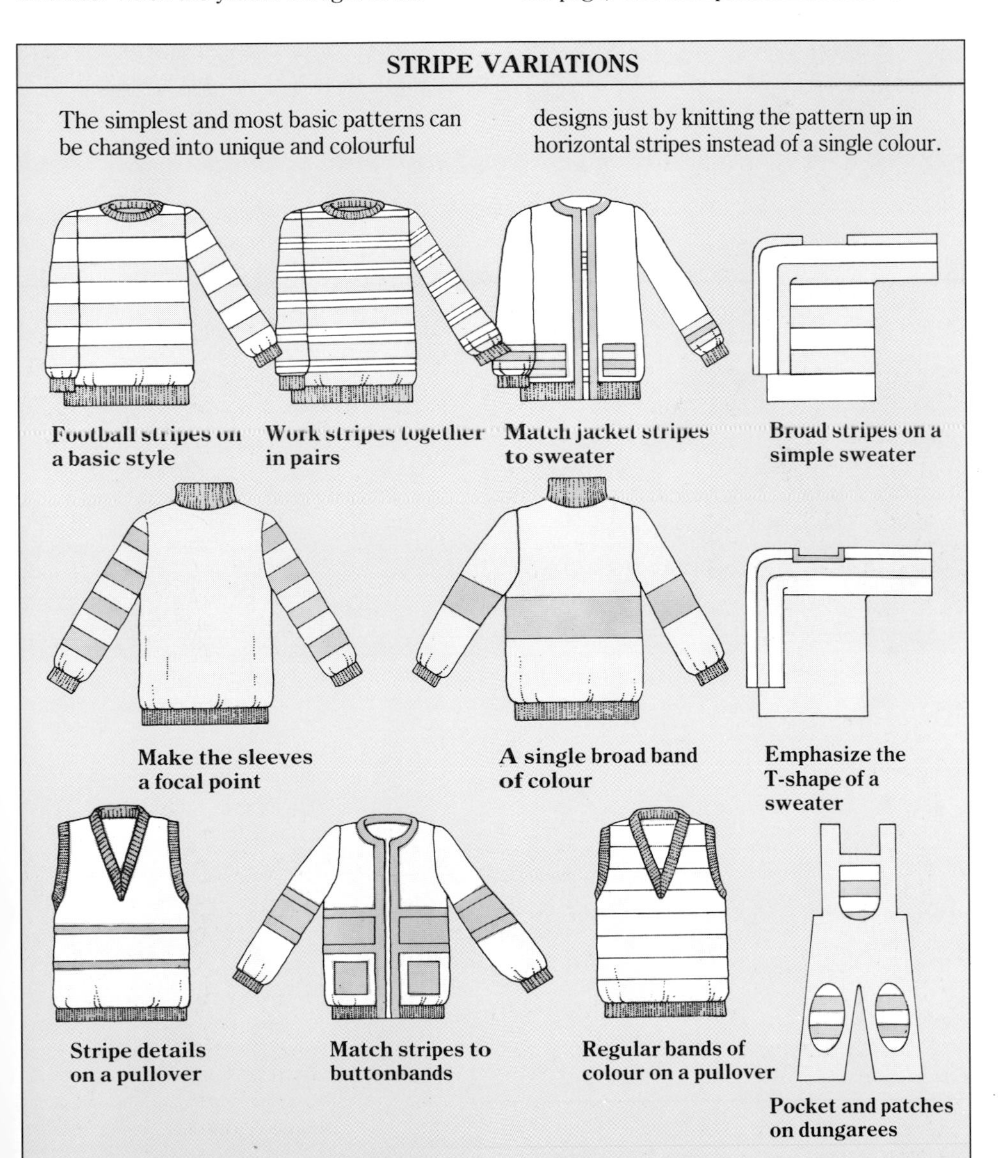

STRIPE VARIATIONS

The simplest and most basic patterns can be changed into unique and colourful designs just by knitting the pattern up in horizontal stripes instead of a single colour.

Football stripes on a basic style

Work stripes together in pairs

Match jacket stripes to sweater

Broad stripes on a simple sweater

Make the sleeves a focal point

A single broad band of colour

Emphasize the T-shape of a sweater

Stripe details on a pullover

Match stripes to buttonbands

Regular bands of colour on a pullover

Pocket and patches on dungarees

Colourslip

This is one of the easiest methods of introducing stitch texture into two-colour or multi-colour work. Such patterns look intricate but are quick and easy to knit and include tweeds, stripes and chevrons through interlaced bands to basketweave.

Chevron stripes

Work in 4-ply, double-knitting or acrylic yarn for a bright, sporty effect; loosely twisted chunky yarn for a bolder look.

Use for a sweater yoke or inset panel; mix with other pattern bands across man's waistcoat front or on a blouson jacket.

Multiple of 4 sts.
Colours A, B and C.
Cast on with A and purl one row.
Row 1 (RS) with B, *k1, sl 3 wyib; rep from *.
Row 2 With B, *p1, sl 1 wyif, p3; rep from *, end sl 1, p2.
Row 3 With B, knit.
Row 4 With B, purl.
Rows 5 to 8 With C, repeat rows 1 to 4.
Rows 9 to 12 With A, repeat rows 1 to 4.
Repeat rows 1 to 12.

Greek tile

Work in a smooth, medium-weight yarn for colour contrast; poodle or mohair for a softer image.

Use for a man's classic style V-neck slipover or child's hat; sweater yoke and inset sleeve band.

Multiple of 10 sts plus 2.
Colours A and B.
Note On all RS (odd-numbered) rows slip all sl sts wyib; on all WS (even-numbered) rows slip all sl sts wyif.
Row 1 (RS) With A, knit.
Row 2 With A, purl.
Row 3 With B, k1, *k8, sl 2; rep from *, end k1.
Row 4 and all subsequent WS rows. Using the same colour as previous row, purl across, slipping wyif all slipped sts on previous row.
Row 5 With A, k1, * sl 2, k4, sl 2, k2; rep from *, end k1.
Row 7 With B, k1, *k2, sl 2, k4, sl 2; rep from *, end k1.
Row 9 With A, k1, *sl 2, k8; rep from *, end k1.
Row 11 With B, knit.
Row 13 With A, *k4, sl 2, k4; rep from *, end k2.
Row 15 With B, k2, *sl 2, k2, sl 2, k4; rep from *.
Row 17 With A, *k4, sl 2, k2, sl 2; rep from *, end k2.
Row 19 With B, *k6, sl 2, k2; rep from *, end k2.
Row 20 See row 4.
Repeat rows 1 to 20.

Florentine

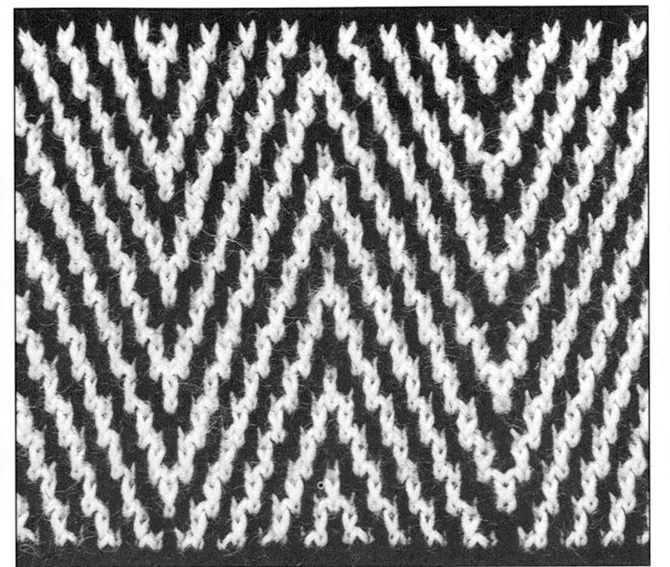

Work in a medium-weight wool, double crêpe or rayon for a figure-flattering effect; rug wool for wear.

Use for an all-over pattern for mother and daughter short jacket, skirt and matching scarf; sofa upholstery or floor cushion.

Multiple of 24sts plus 2.
Colours A and B.
Note On all RS (odd-numbered) rows all sl sts are slipped wyib. On WS (even-numbered) rows all sl sts are slipped wyif.
Cast on with A and purl one row.
Row 1 (RS) With B, k1, *sl 1, k2; rep from *, end k1.
Row 2 With B, k1, *p2, sl 1; rep from *, end k1.
Row 3 With A, k1, *k1, sl 1, (k2, sl 1) 3 times, k3 (sl 1, k2) 3 times, sl 1; rep from *, end k1.
Row 4 With A, k1, *sl 1, (p2, sl 1) 3 times, p3, (sl 1, p2) 3 times, sl 1, p1; rep from *, end k1.
Row 5 With B, k1, *k2, (sl 1, k2) 3 times, sl 1, k1, sl 1, (k2, sl 1) 3 times, k1; rep from *, end k1.
Row 6 With B, k1, *p1, (sl 1, p2) 3 times, sl 1, p1, sl 1, (p2, sl 1) 3 times, p2; rep from *, end k1.
Rows 7 and 8 With A, repeat rows 1 and 2.
Rows 9 and 10 With B, repeat rows 3 and 4.
Rows 11 and 12 With A, repeat rows 5 and 6.
Repeat rows 1 to 12.

Rainbow zigzag

Work in a 4-ply wool or synthetic yarn for a figure-flattering finish; chunky yarn for furnishing.

Use for an all-over pattern for matching jacket, skirt and scarf or sleeveless slipover; bed cover or cushion set.

Multiple of 12 sts plus 3.
Colours A and B.
Cast on with A and knit one row.
Row 1 (RS) With B, k1, sl 1, k1, psso, *k9, sl 2, k1, p2sso; rep from *, end k9, k2tog, k1.
Row 2 With B, k1, *p1, k4 (k1, yo, k1) in next st, k4; rep from *, end p1, k1.
Rows 3 and 4 With A, repeat rows 1 and 2.
Repeat rows 1 to 4.

Embroidery on knitting

There are many ways of using embroidery on knitting. All are simple to work and all turn plain knitting into something far richer. The most common ways of decorating knitting are with Swiss darning and cross stitch embroidery, both of which add more colour and pattern to knitting. Embroidered bullion knots add texture and look particularly effective worked on lacy patterns. The eyelet holes in lace patterns can be decorated by surrounding them with stitching in a contrast colour. Ladder weaving is useful for decorating dropped stitches and dropped stitch patterns. Finally, with appliqué you can make intricate patterns by applying one piece of knitting on top of another.

When embroidering on knitting, always use a blunt-ended wool or tapestry needle to avoid splitting the yarn, and make sure that the embroidery stitches are worked to the same tension as the knitting.

DECORATING KNITTING

Here are three unusual but very easy ways of decorating knitting. Use them to emphasize features of the knitted fabric and make your knitting more colourful.

Ladder weaving

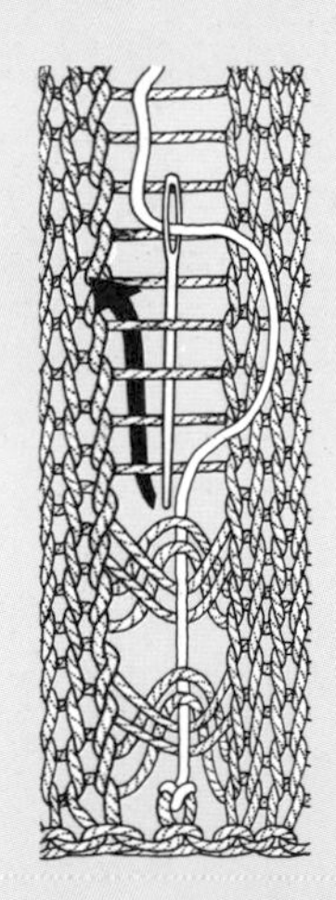

Secure yarn to the dropped stitch. Insert the needle downwards under the second two strands then over the lower two strands. Invert the needle, twisting the two pairs of strands around the embroidery yarn.

Embroidering eyelets

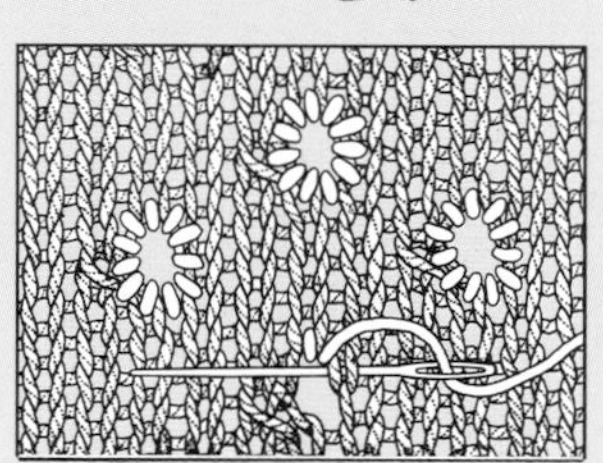

Knitted eyelets can be emphasized and finished off in a different colour simply by stitching around each one.

Bullion knots

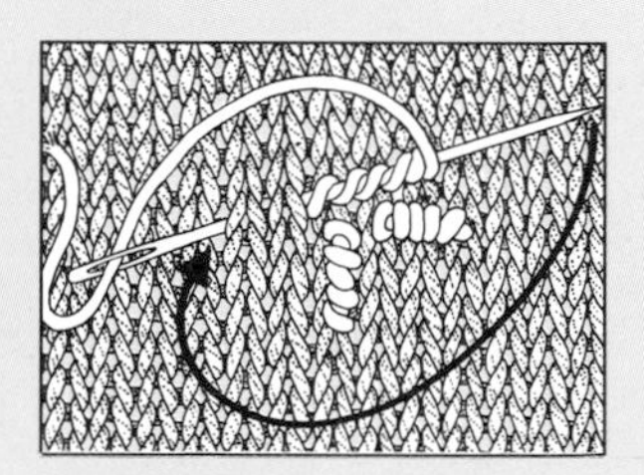

Push the needle through as far as possible twisting the yarn around it and then invert needle as shown.

Freestyle embroidery

Freestyle motifs can be worked in any combination of stitches on a finished knitted garment. Use stranded or soft embroidery cotton.

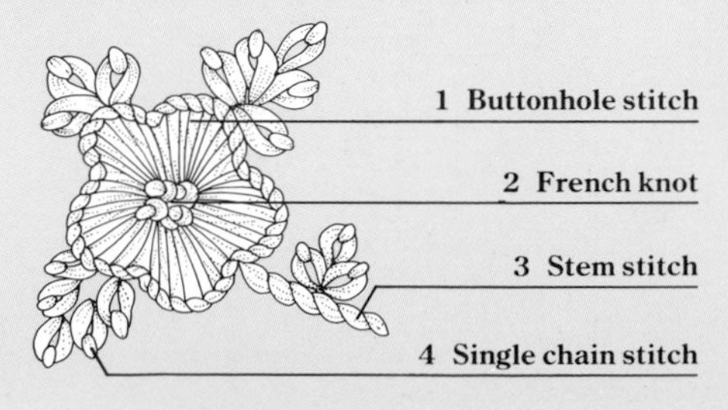

Swiss darning

Swiss darning embroidery imitates knitting and colour can be added to a piece of knitting easily and in far less time than it takes to knit it in. It can be used for any design given in chart form.

Embroidery on knit stitches in horizontal rows

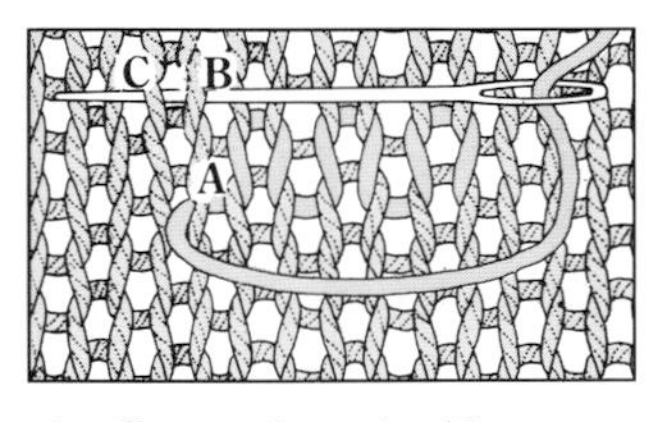

1 Secure the embroidery yarn at the back of the work. Bring needle out to the front of the work at A. Insert the needle at B, under the base of the stitch above, to emerge at C.

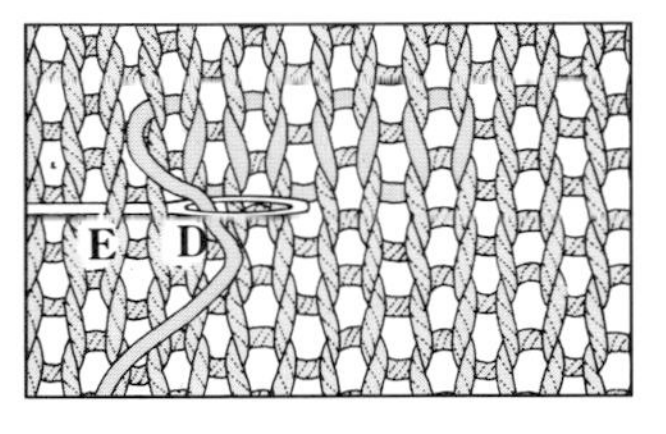

2 Insert the needle at D and emerge at E ready for the next stitch.

Embroidery on knit stitches in vertical rows.

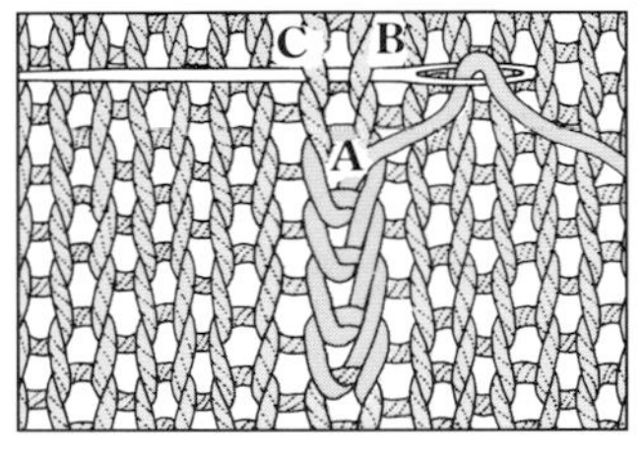

1 Bring the needle out to the front of the work at A. Insert the needle at B, bringing it out at C.

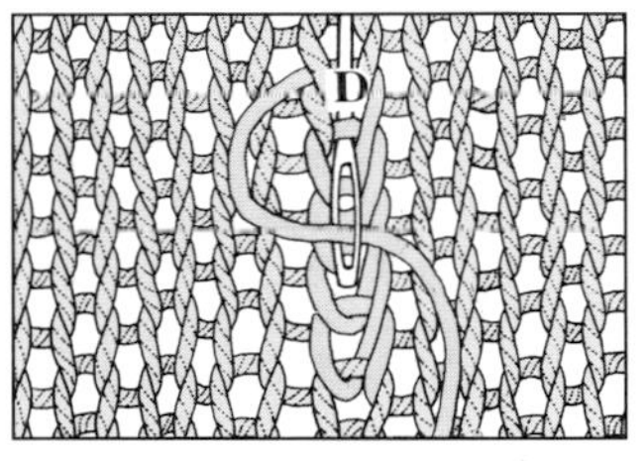

2 Then take the needle under the head of the stitch below and emerge above it at D ready to form the next stitch.

Embroidery on purl stitches in horizontal rows

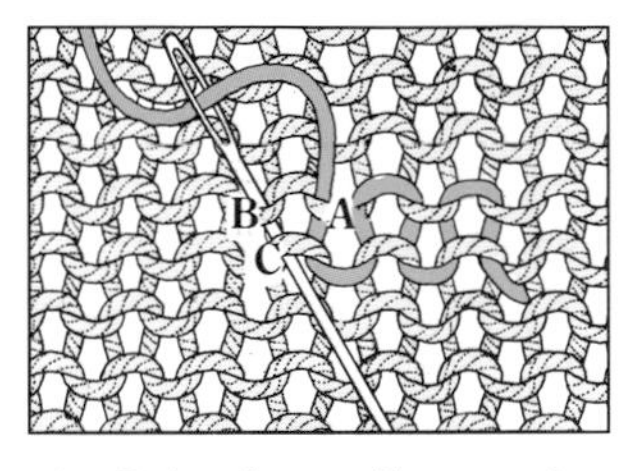

1 Bring the needle out at A. Take it across the head of the stitch and insert at B. Bring it out at C, under the head of the stitch, in the row below.

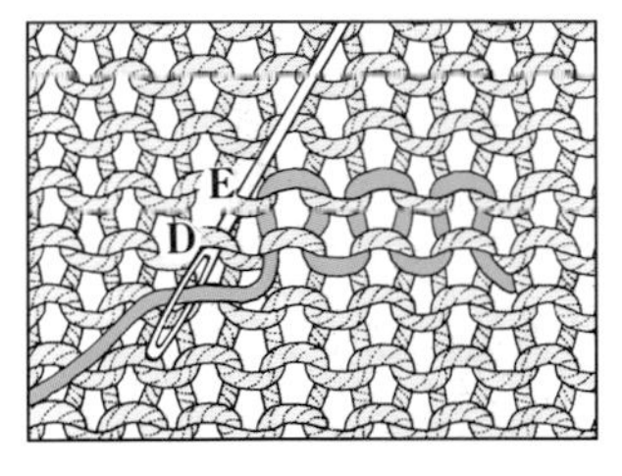

2 Insert the needle at D, take it up to the row above, to emerge at E.

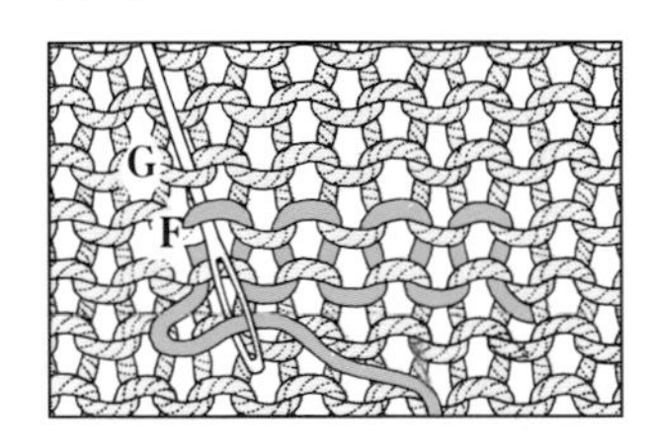

3 To complete the embroidery insert the needle at F under the head of the last stitch to be embroidered and bring it out 1 row above at G. Work from left to right in the same way.

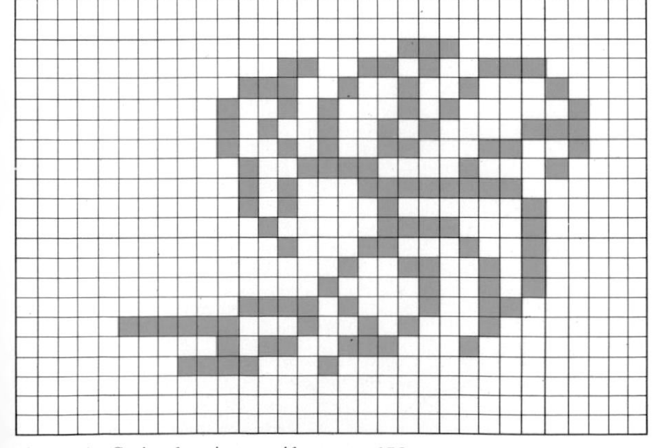

Chart for Swiss darning motif on page 158

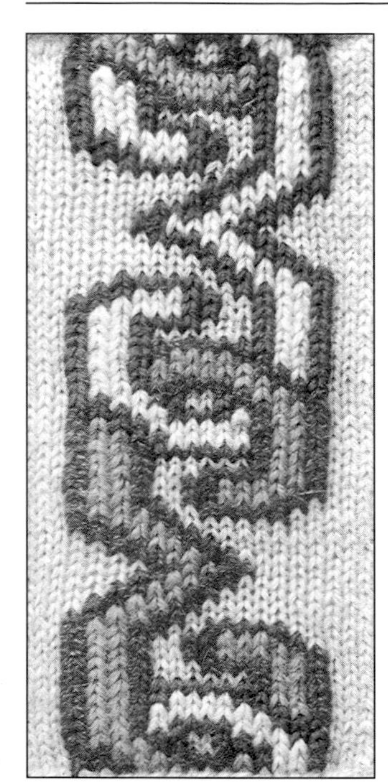
Swiss darning with linking numerals

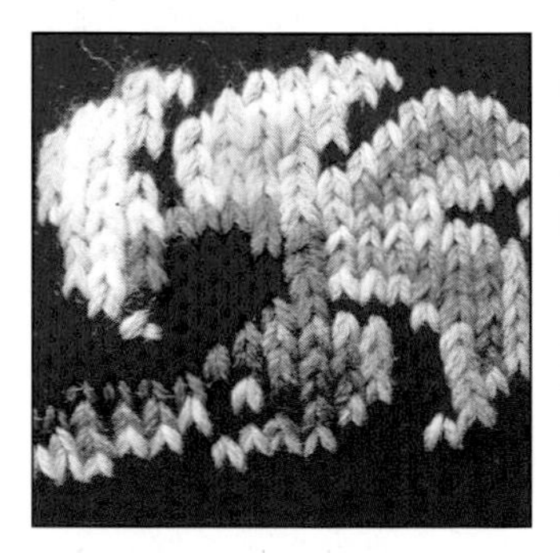

The embroidery motif
Swiss darning is such excellent knitting forgery, even a simple motif can be most impressive. A graph chart for this stylized flower pattern can be found on page 157.

Swiss darning motif with ribbon bow

CROSS STITCHING

Cross stitch is best worked on a stocking stitch background. Each cross should be square, counted over, for example, two stitches and two rows (blocked), or two stitches and three rows (unblocked).

Cross stitch motif on a stocking stitch background

Work a row of diagonal stitches from R to L first, and complete the crosses by working back along the row in the opposite direction.

Bullion knots on lace knitting

Lace knitting decorated with embroidered bullion knots is an old idea dating from the eighteenth century when it was worked in imitation of expensive needlemade lace. For a modern adaptation, sew several squares together to make a bedspread. Diagrams showing how to make bullion knots are on page 156.

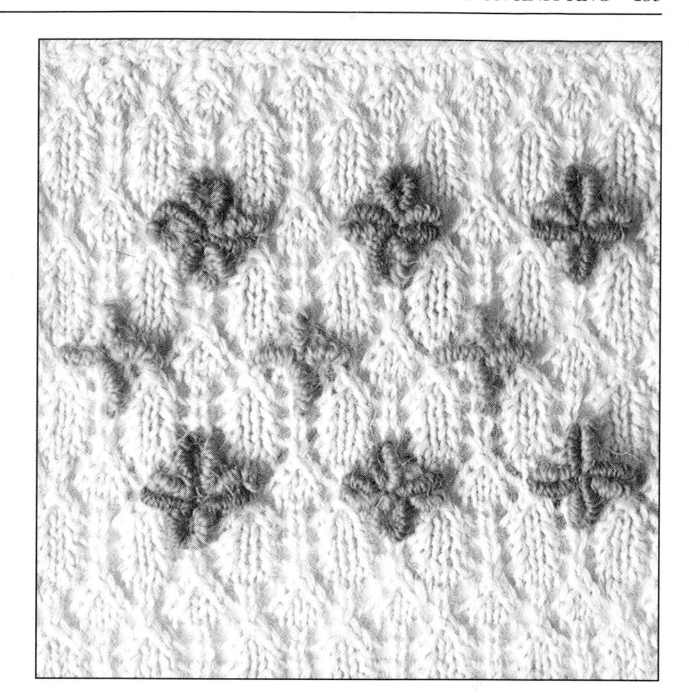

Appliqué with knitted shapes

Plain stocking stitch squares can be built up into extravagant designs by applying simple knitted shapes like squares, diamonds and triangles. Strips of striped knitting on the sample (right) have been arranged into a Celtic motif. Apply the shapes using the running stitch of Swiss darning.

Increasing and decreasing for shape

Increasing invisibly by making two stitches from one is shown on page 145 and to shape garments equally on both sides, increases and decreases must be paired, with one placed on either side of the knitting.

Triangular shapes

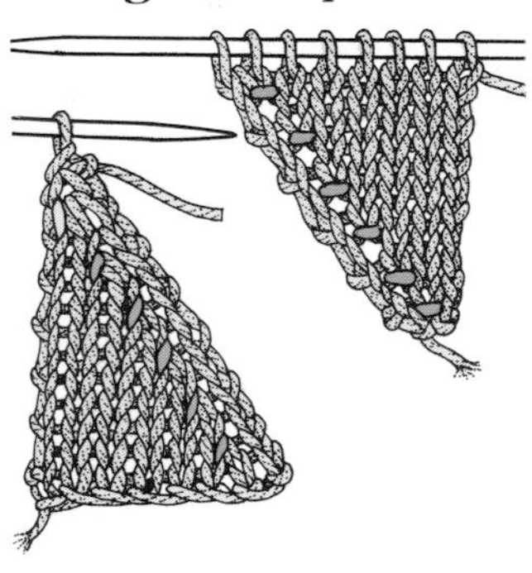

For a right angle triangle cast on 2 stitches. Increase 1 at the end of every knit row.

For a left angle triangle cast on stitches for the base. Sl 1, k1 psso at the beginning of every knit row.

Double triangle made by increasing

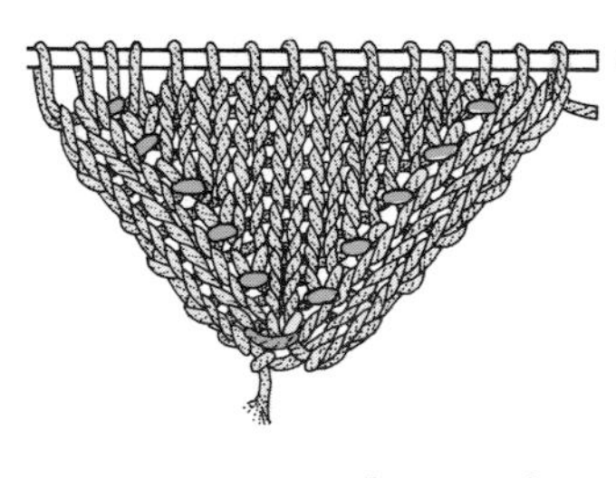

Cast on 3 stitches. Increase 1 on the second stitch at the beginning of every row.

Double triangle made by decreasing

Cast on the required number of stitches. Decrease on the second stitch at the beginning of every row.

TENSION

Before you begin to knit any item you should always work a tension sample first. This is necessary whether you intend to use a printed pattern, substitute the given stitch and/or yarn, with another, or use a design that you have created.

Printed patterns give a tension guide stating the number of stitches and rows to a 4in. (10cm) square using the recommended yarn and needles.

Making a tension sample

Work a square slightly larger than 4in. (10cm). Mark out with pins the tension measurement given in the pattern. Count the rows and stitches between the pins and if they are the same as in the pattern, then your tension is correct. If there are too many stitches between pins, then your tension is too tight and you should try one, or more, size larger needles. Too few stitches, and you should try one, or more, size smaller.

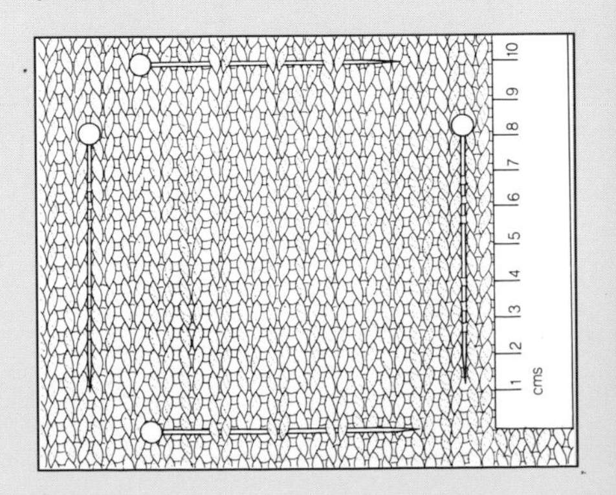

Blocking and pressing

Before the knitting can be sewn up into a garment, it should be blocked and pressed. When you have finished any piece of knitting, first darn in all loose ends to the back of the work.

Blocking a piece of knitting

To block a piece of knitting, pin it out to the correct size and shape on a padded surface. A table covered with a folded blanket under a sheet is ideal. Using rustless pins, pin each piece of knitting wrong side up to the padding. Do not stretch or distort the fabric. Check the length and width of each piece against the pattern measurements. Make sure that all the rows run in straight lines, then pin closely all around the knitting.

Pressing the knitting

Wool should be pressed lightly under a damp cloth with a warm iron. Do not move the iron over the surface, but lay it on the cloth and lift it up again. Leave the knitting pinned in position until it has cooled and dried completely. Some yarns other than wool may need to be treated differently, if so, the ball band will give pressing instructions. Highly textured knitting like embossed, cable and rib patterns should be treated differently from flat fabrics like stocking stitch and garter stitch. They need gentle pressing and careful treatment.

Pressing embossed patterns

Press raised and embossed patterns under a damp cloth. Remove the cloth and the pins, and immediately adjust the knitting, easing and patting it into shape while it is still hot. Swift action will prevent the raised patterns being flattened.

Pressing ribbing

Ribbing should be lightly stretched and pinned before ironing. Iron it under a heavy cloth and remove the cloth and pins immediately afterwards then gently ease the ribbing into its correct position while it is still warm.

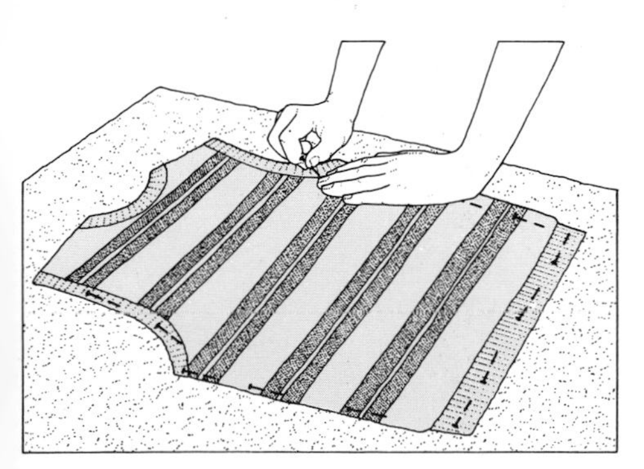

Blocking the knitting

Pin the knitting at the corners, check the length and width against the measurements given in the pattern, then pin all around.

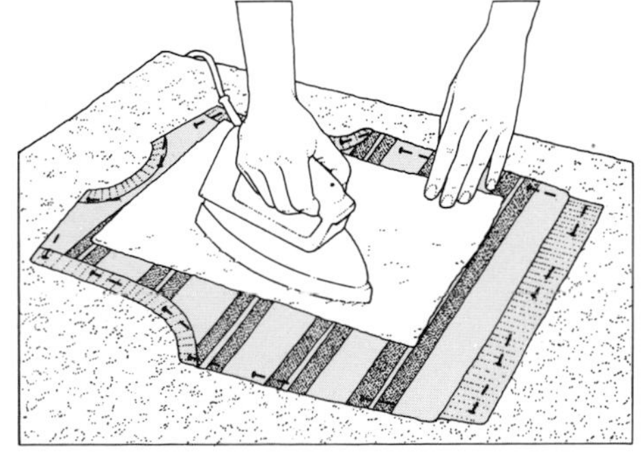

Pressing the knitting

Press each section of the blocked piece of knitting evenly under a damp cloth.

5
CROCHET

Crochet hooks and yarns

The word "crochet" comes from the French *croc* meaning a hook. Like all textiles, its origins are difficult to trace and few examples of early crochet remain.

It is formed, like knitting, into a looped fabric from one continuous length of yarn. But whereas knitting uses two or more needles onto which a number of stitches are cast, crochet uses only one hook on which one stitch at a time is worked. There is a different form of crochet, known as *Tunisian crochet,* which is worked in much the same way as knitting – on a long hook onto which a number of loops are cast, then worked off and cast on again for the next row. As it seems more than likely that the origins of knitting and crochet are the same, possibly Tunisian crochet was the point of departure between the two.

Crochet has two very distinctly different appearances: it can be worked using very fine yarns and the finest hooks to form a delicate, open fabric that is very similar to lace or it can be worked with thicker yarn on larger hooks to make a dense fabric. The crochet fabric can either be worked in flat pieces or in rings from which tubular shapes and medallions can be made.

The simplest forms of crochet are very easy to work once the basic technique has been mastered. Because only one loop is on the hook at a time, it will not unravel and can therefore be carried around more easily than knitting. Crochet is very useful as an edging fabric because it is easy to pick up stitches on an existing piece of fabric. Knitting and crochet could easily be combined to provide a crochet border on a knitted blanket for example. Crochet can, of course, be worked using a variety of fabrics from cotton and silk ribbon to thick wool yarn.

HOOKS AND YARNS

There are 19 different sizes of crochet hook, ranging from 0.60 mm to 10.00 mm and the two ends of that range are illustrated here. The table shows which size of hook is most suitable for a particular yarn.

Hook	Yarn
0.60 mm	very fine cotton
0.75	
1.00	
1.25	fine cotton and equivalent yarns
1.50	
1.75	
2.00	light-weight yarns
2.50	
3.00	
3.50	
4.00	medium-weight double knitting yarn
4.50	
5.00	
5.50	double crêpe, mohair
6.00	
7.00	Aran-type double, double yarn
8.00	
9.00	chunky, heavy-weight
10.00	

0.60 mm

10.00 mm

Crochet cottons

Knitting cottons

Knitting wools

Novelty yarns

Holding the hook and yarn

Threading yarn

Threading the yarn through the fingers is important as this helps to give extra tension, controlling the yarn while allowing it to flow easily from hand to hook. If you are left-handed the method is exactly the same.

Threading yarn around the little finger

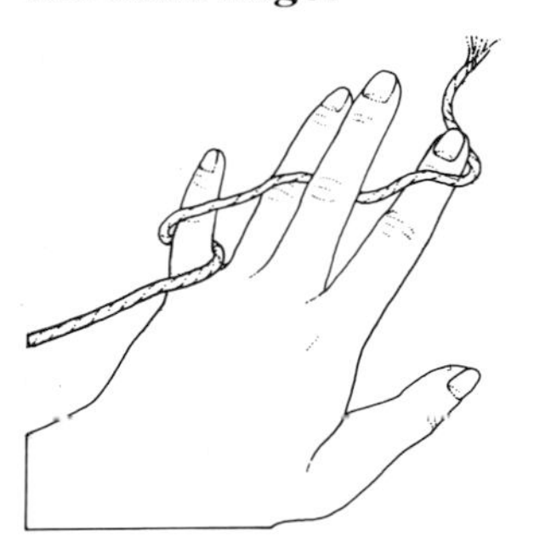

Pass the working end of yarn around the little finger, over the next finger, under the middle finger and finish with it resting over the forefinger.

Threading yarn over the little finger

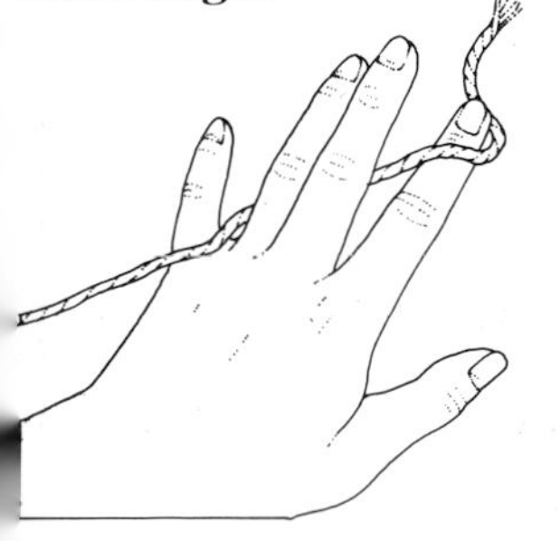

Pass the working end of yarn over the little finger, under the next 2 fingers and finish with it resting over the forefinger.

Holding the hook

The crochet hook can be held in either the knife or the pencil position. Both ways are equally good and the choice depends on which position feels most comfortable.

Holding the hook in the pencil position

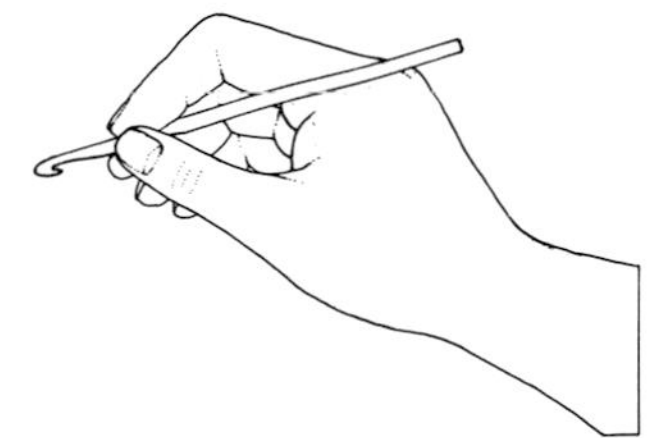

1 Hold the hook in the right hand like a pencil. If you are left-handed hold the hook in the same way, but in the left hand.

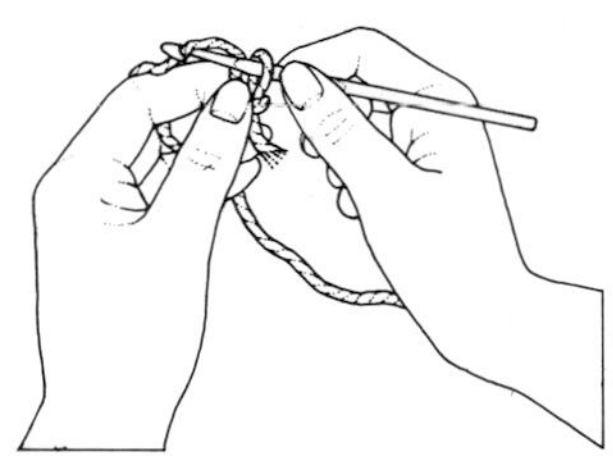

2 Prepare to make the first chain by drawing the yarn from the left forefinger with the hook through the slip loop.

Holding the hook in the knife position

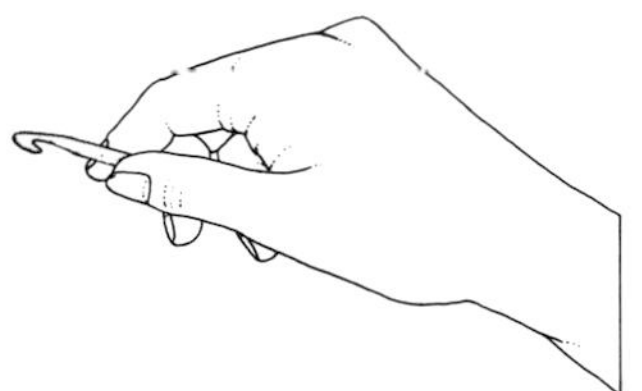

1 Hold the hook in the right hand like a knife. If you are left-handed hold the hook in the same way, but in the left hand.

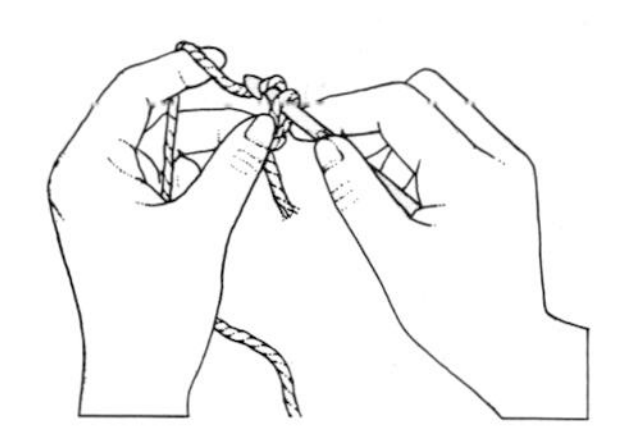

2 Prepare to make the first chain by drawing the yarn from the left forefinger with the hook through the slip loop.

PUTTING THE STITCH PATTERNS TO USE

Before beginning to crochet make a tension sample first.

Work a test piece slightly larger than 10 cm (4 in.) square. Mark out the tension measurement given in pattern with pins. If there are too many stitches between pins try a larger hook; if too few, try a smaller hook.

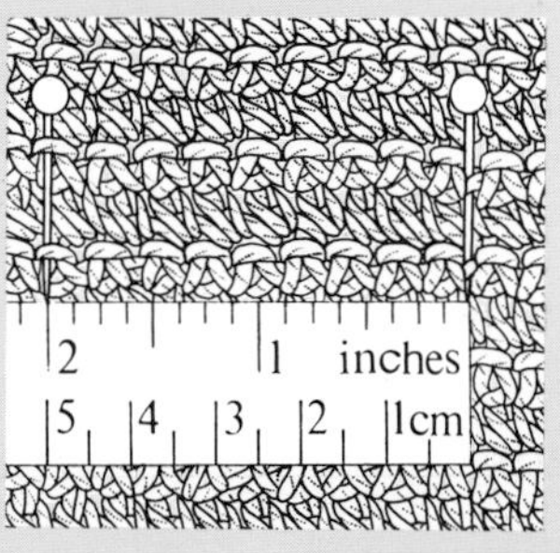

The foundation chain

To begin to crochet, a slip loop is placed on the hook and the yarn is then threaded through the left hand. Both hands are then brought together so that the hook in the right hand and the yarn threaded over the left forefinger are in easy contact.

Making a slip loop

The slip loop is the first crochet stitch and is made in the same way as the slip loop in knitting using a hook instead of a knitting needle to draw the loop through.

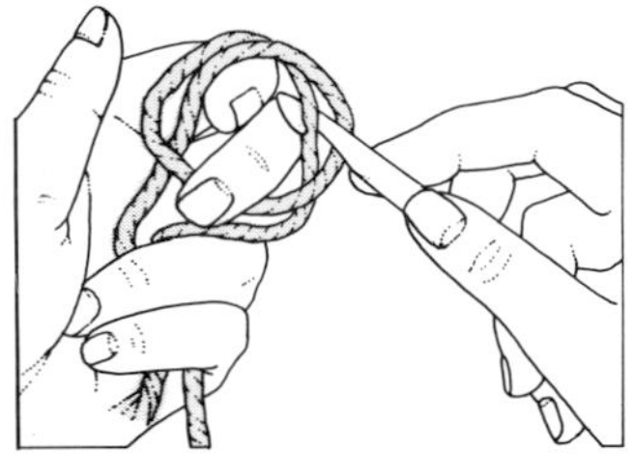

1 Twist the yarn twice around 2 fingers and insert the hook between the 2 twists of yarn.

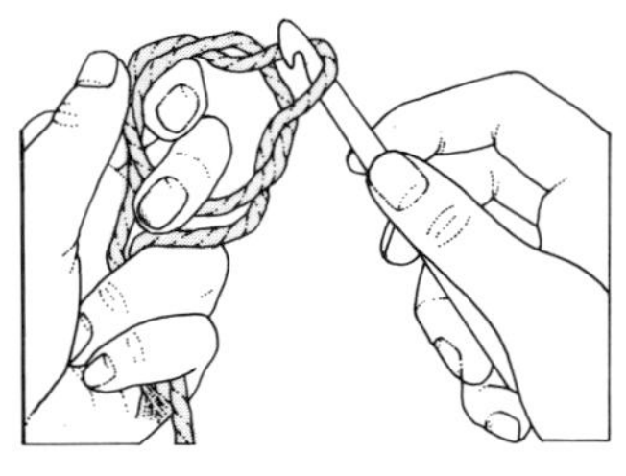

2 Using the hook, draw one twist through the other.

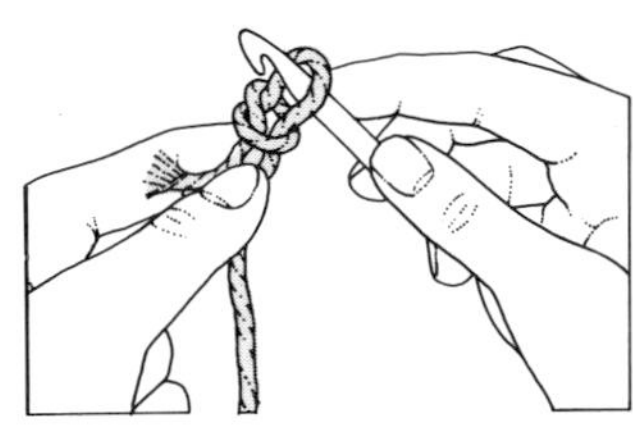

3 Pull both ends of yarn to tighten the slip loop and secure it on the hook.

Making a chain stitch

Chain stitch is used for the foundation row, upon which the next row or round will be worked. It is also used to make spaces between stitches, and for bars in open and lace work. All crochet patterns give the hook size, type of yarn to use and number of chains to cast on. When learning the basic stitches, 20 chain stitches are sufficient.

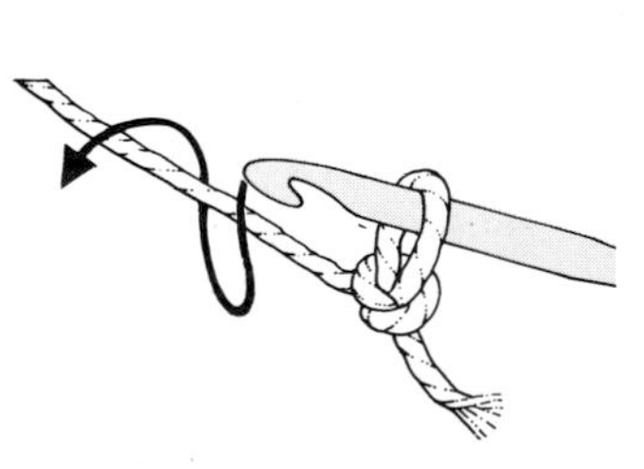

1 Thread the yarn in the left hand and hold the hook with the slip loop in the right hand. Twist the hook first under and then over the yarn to wind yarn around the hook.

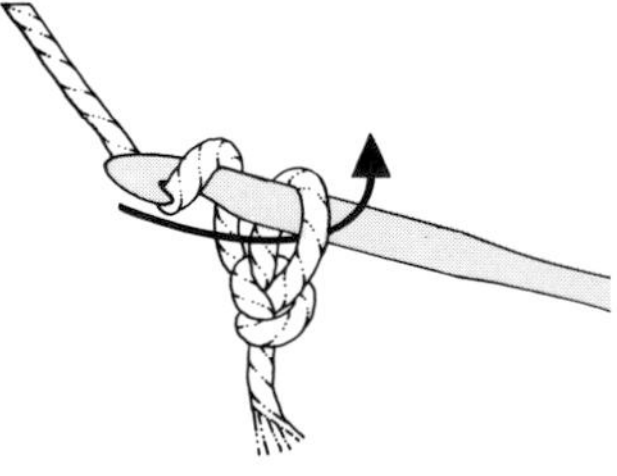

2 Draw the hook with the yarn on it through the slip loop to form a chain stitch. The chain stitch is now complete. Repeat this process until the movement becomes easy and feels quite natural to work.

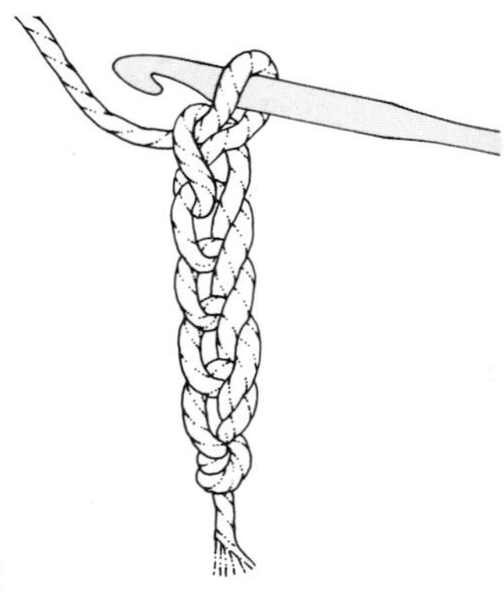

A length of chain stitches.

Making a double chain stitch

For garments which will have to endure strain on the edges, such as socks, hats and gloves, a firmer foundation row can be made by working a double chain stitch.

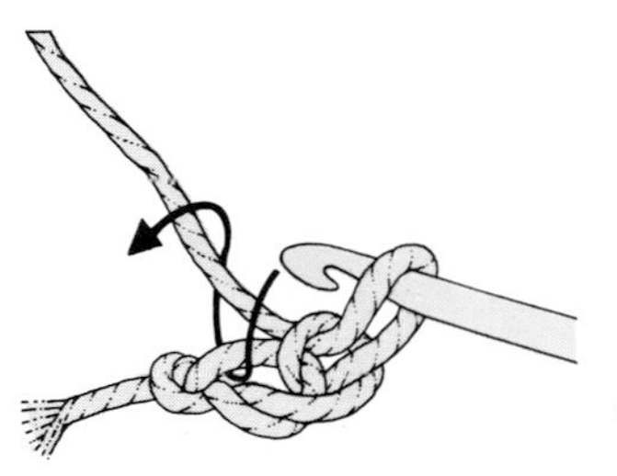

1 Make a slip loop and work 2 chain stitches. With the yarn at the back insert the hook between the 2 halves of the first chain stitch, twist the hook around the yarn and draw it through. There are now 2 loops on the crochet hook.

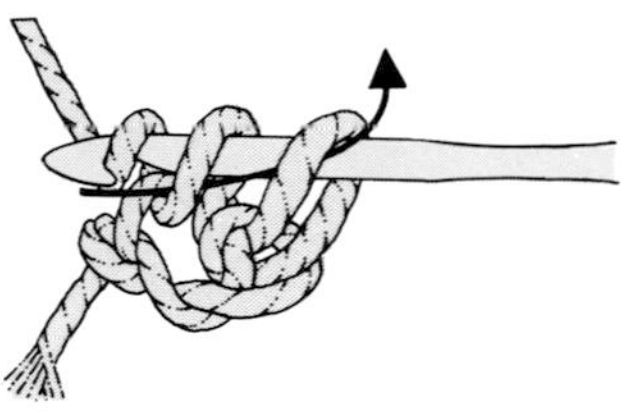

2 Twist the hook around the yarn and draw through both loops to form a double chain. Continue in this way to form more double chain stitches, each time inserting the hook into the left side of the stitch just made.

A foundation row of double chain stitches.

Finishing off

When the work has been completed the yarn must be finished off properly, otherwise it will come undone. This is also known as casting off.

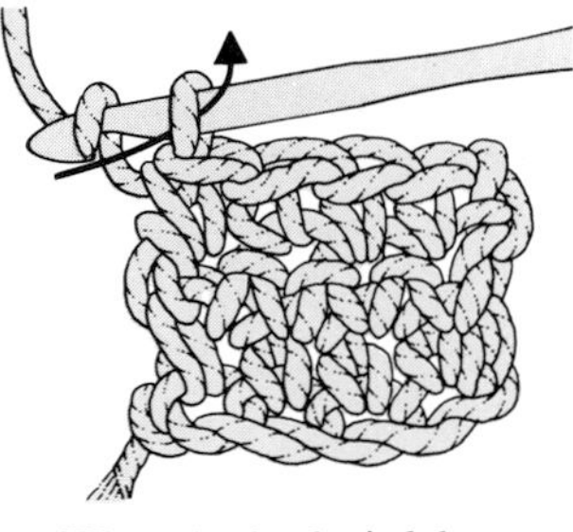

1 When the final stitch has been completed, cut the working yarn and pull it through the last loop on the hook. Pull it tight to close the loop.

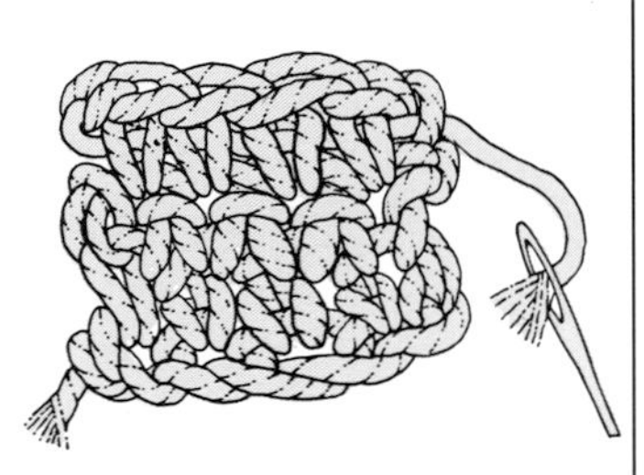

2 Thread the working end of the yarn into a sewing needle and darn it neatly into the back of the work.

COUNTING STITCHES

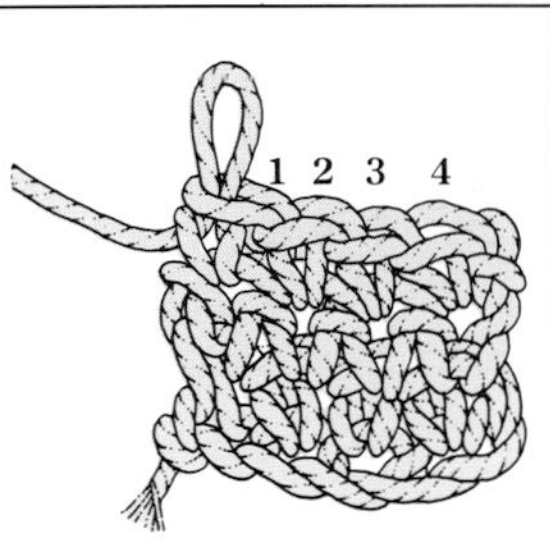

Counting stitches in crochet is more difficult than in knitting, for the stitches are not left on the hook. The sample above is worked in double crochet.

Each stitch is numbered to show how to count the stitches. Counting treble stitches is easier, because each treble forms 1 upright or post which is counted as a single stitch. A chain stitch counts as 1, and if between 2 trebles, 3 stitches should be counted.

Basic stitches

Crochet stitches are always made in the same way, whether the work is flat and turned at the end of each row, or circular and never turned at the end of the round. The texture of some stitches does, however, differ, according to whether they are worked flat or in a circle. In flat work because the work is turned the direction of the stitches is also turned, whereas for work in the round the direction of the stitches always remains the same. This texture change is more apparent in stitches which are based on single and double crochet stitches.

Before beginning to work the basic stitches you should remember that all first row stitches are worked through the back half of the chain stitch foundation row. On subsequent rows, unless instructed otherwise, all the stitches are worked through both halves of the stitches below, and the hook is inserted from front to back.

Turning chains

Extra chains are worked at the end of a row before turning to bring the hook to the correct depth of the stitch being worked, so that the first stitch can be made evenly. The number of turning chains that you will need for each stitch is given below.

Double crochet: 1 turning chain
Half treble: 2 turning chains
Treble: 3 turning chains
Double treble: 4 turning chains
Triple treble: 5 turning chains

Substituting one stitch for another

Make sure that your substitute stitch is of a similar type to the one suggested in the pattern, and that the stitch multiple will divide evenly into the foundation chain. Stitch multiples in crochet are generally small and can usually be adjusted at the tension sample stage.

WORKING FROM PATTERNS

To save space all crochet instructions are written with the following symbols and abbreviations.

alt	alternate(ly)	**no.**	number
B	back	**patt**	pattern
beg	begin(ning)	**pc**	picot
bet	between	**rem**	remain(ing)
ch(s)	chain(s)	**rep**	repeat
cl	cluster	**reqd**	required
col	colour	**RS**	right side
cont	continu(e)(ing)	**rnd**	round
dec	decreas(e)(ing)	**RTF**	round treble front
dc	double crochet	**ss**	slip stitch
dch(s)	double chain(s)	**sp(s)**	space(s)
dtr	double treble	**st(s)**	stitch(es)
F	front	**tog**	together
foll	follow(ing)	**tr**	treble
gr(s)	group(s)	**tr tr**	triple treble
htr	half treble	**t-ch(s)**	turning chain(s)
inc	increas(e)(ing)	**WS**	wrong side
lp(s)	loop(s)	**yrh**	yarn round hook

Symbols

A star ⋆ shown in a pattern row denotes that the stitches shown after this sign must be repeated from that point.
Round brackets ( ), enclosing a particular stitch combination, denote that the stitch combination must be repeated in the order shown.
Hyphens refer to those stitches which have already been made but which will be used as the base for the next stitch, eg. you would work 2tr into 2-ch sp, by making 2 trebles into the space created by the chain stitches worked in the previous row.

Single and double crochet

Slip stitch

Also known as single crochet.

1 Make a foundation row of chs. Insert hook through back of 2nd chain from hook.

2 Twist the yarn around the hook (yrh) and draw through the 2 loops now on hook, making an ss. Continue working into the next and following chains.

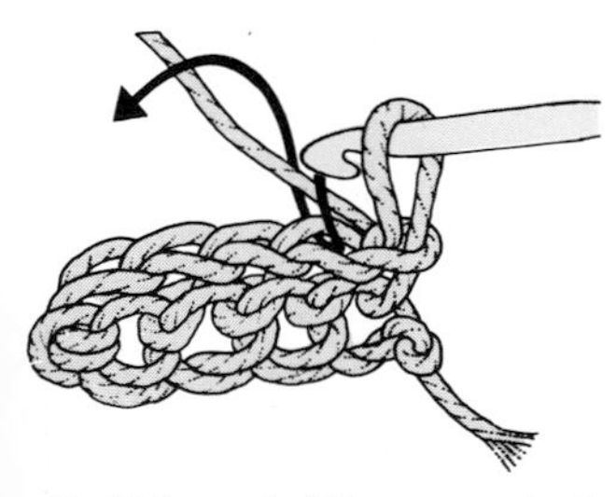

3 At the end of the row make 1 t-ch, turn work and insert hook through back half of first stitch in row below to make first ss. Continue in this way for all the following rows.

Double crochet

Also known as plain stitch.

1 Make a foundation row of chs. Insert hook through back of 2nd chain from hook, yrh and draw through.

2 With 2 loops now on hook, yrh and draw through both loops, making a dc.

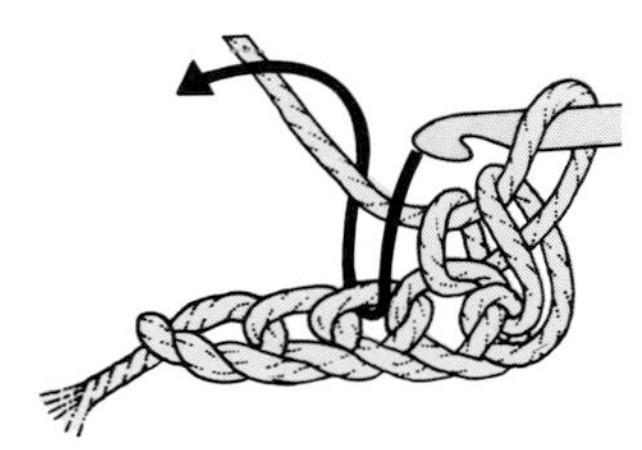

3 Continue working dc into the next and following chains to end of row.

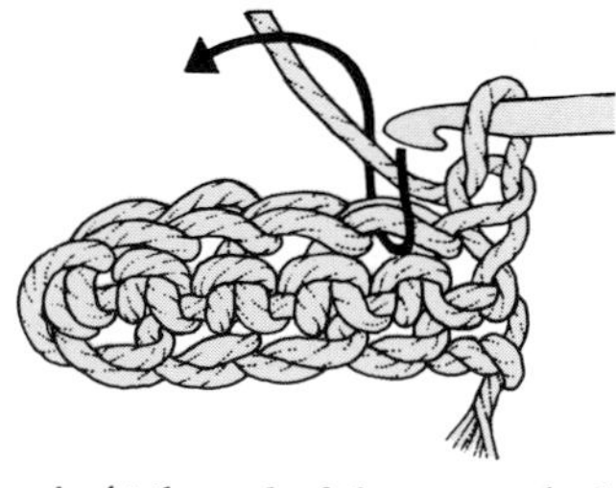

4 At the end of the row make 1 t-ch, turn the work and insert the hook through both halves of the first stitch in the row below to make the first dc.

TUNISIAN CROCHET

Like knitting, this type of crochet is worked with many stitches at once. They are worked from a foundation row of chains and are picked up on the first row, made into stitches and discarded on the next row.

1 With yarn at back of work insert hook into 2nd ch from hook, yrh and draw 1 loop through. Continue making loops into each ch to end of row.

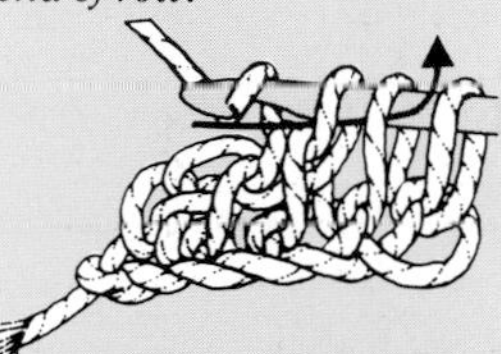

*2 With yarn at back of work, yrh and draw hook through first loop, *yrh and draw hook through next 2 loops. Repeat from * to end.*

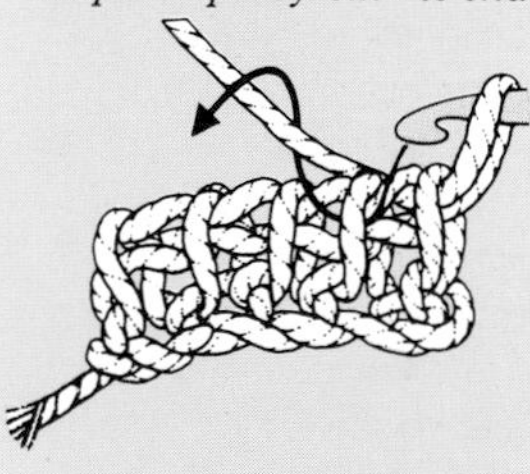

3 With yarn at back of work insert hook through vertical loop of 2nd stitch in previous row, yrh and draw through 1 loop. Continue making loops to end of row. Repeat from Step 2 making loop rows and return rows.

Treble crochet

Half treble

1 Make a foundation row of chs. Yrh and then insert hook through back of 3rd chain from the hook.

2 Yrh and draw through. There are now 3 loops on hook. Yrh and pull through all 3 loops, making a htr.

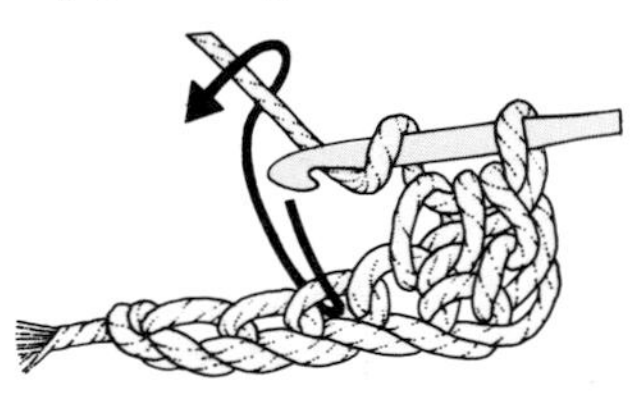

3 Continue working htr into every chain.

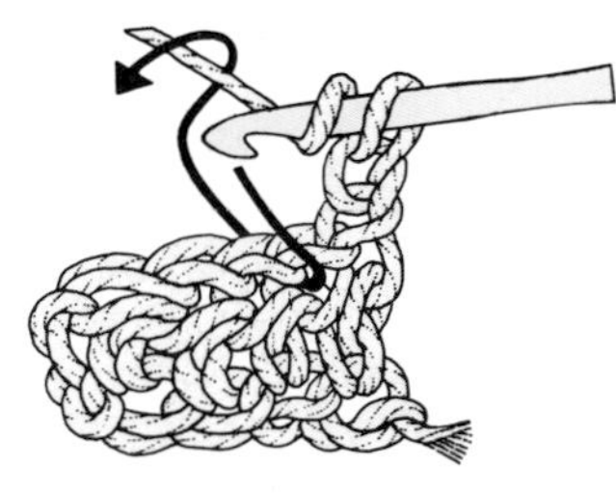

4 At the end of the row make 2 t-ch, turn work and make first htr into first stitch in row below. Continue in this way for all the following rows.

Treble

1 Make a foundation row of chs. Yrh and insert hook through back of 5th chain from the hook.

2 Yrh and draw through (3 loops on hook), yrh and draw through first 2 loops.

3 There are now 2 loops on hook. Yrh and draw through these 2 loops to complete the tr.

4 Continue to make tr to end of row. Then make 3 t-ch, turn work and make first tr into 2nd stitch in row below.

Double treble

1 Make a chain row. Yrh twice and insert hook into back of 6th chain from hook.

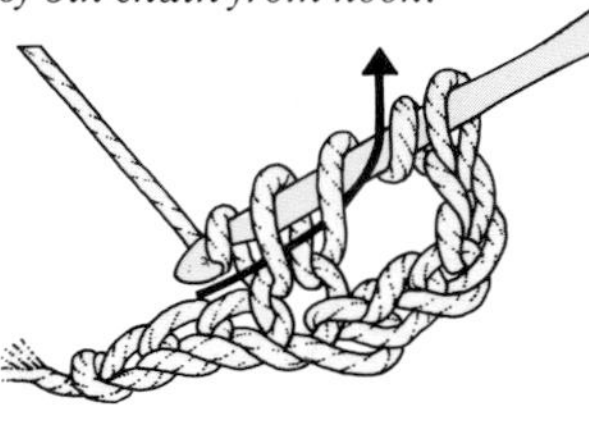

2 Yrh and draw through. There are now 4 loops on hook. Yrh and draw through first 2 loops.

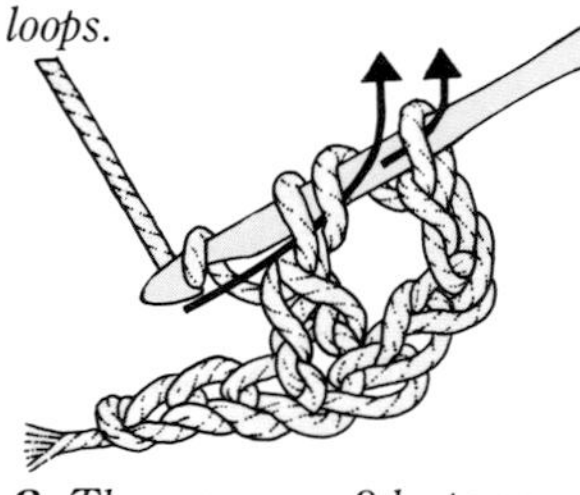

3 There are now 3 loops on hook. Yrh and draw through first 2 loops, yrh and draw through rem 2 loops to complete the dtr.

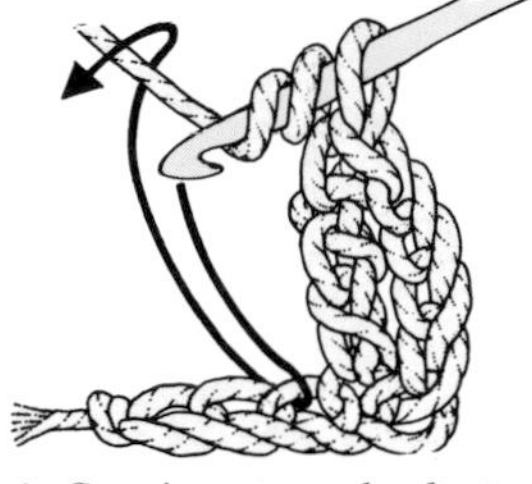

4 Continue to make dtr to end of row. Then make 4 t-ch, turn work and make first dtr into 2nd stitch in row below.

Triple treble

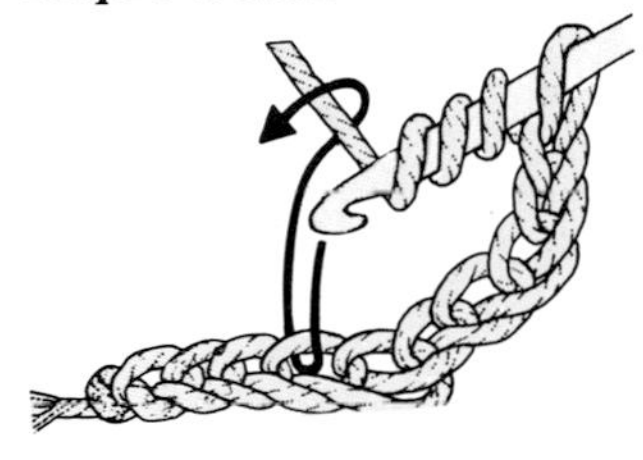

1 Make a foundation row of chs. Yrh 3 times and insert hook through back of 7th chain from hook.

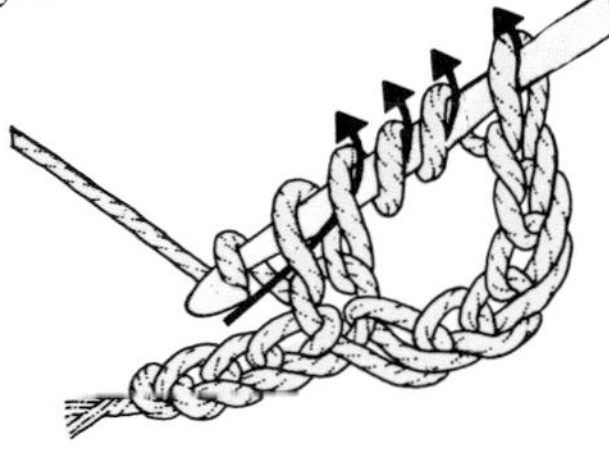

2 Yrh and draw through. There are now 5 loops on hook. Yrh and draw through first 2 loops. Then repeat this process 3 more times.

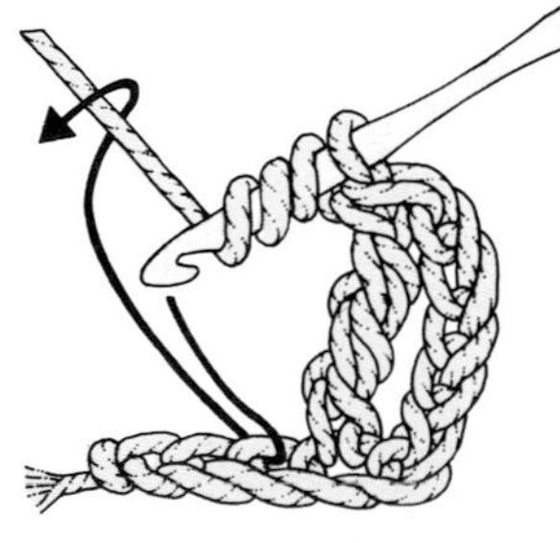

3 Continue to make tr tr to end of row. Then make 5 t-ch, turn work and make first tr tr into 2nd stitch in row below.

BASIC STITCH VARIATIONS

Variations to basic stitches are made by inserting the hook into different parts of the stitches below and manipulating the yarn in different ways. The following diagrams illustrate some of the variations.

Making crossed double crochet

By reversing the normal hook under yarn process, crossed double crochet is made.

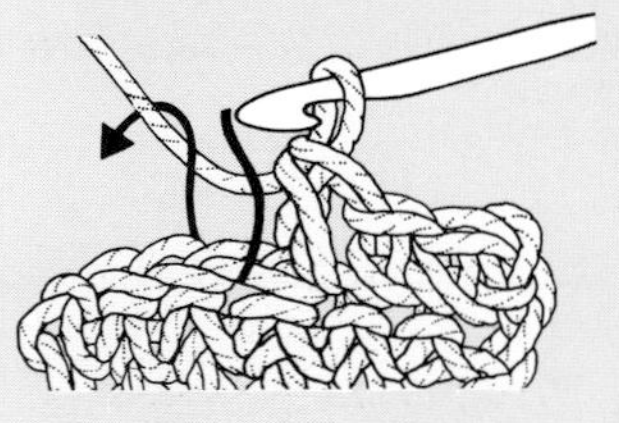

Take the hook over the yarn each time a loop is drawn through.

Working into the chain space

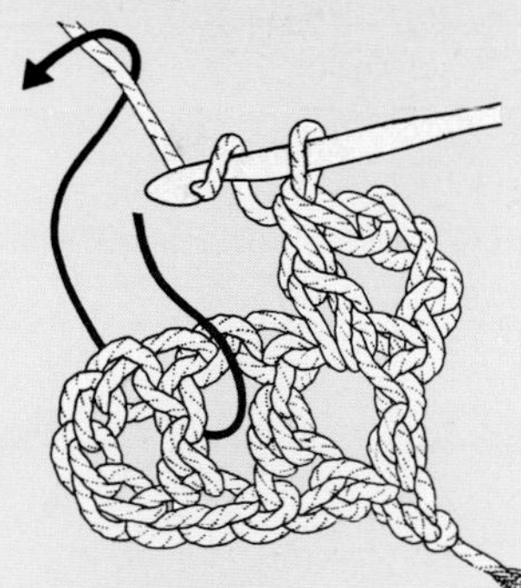

Insert the hook into the space made by the chain in the row below.

Working between two stitches

Many different effects can be achieved by working into the spaces between the stitches rather than by working into the stitches themselves.

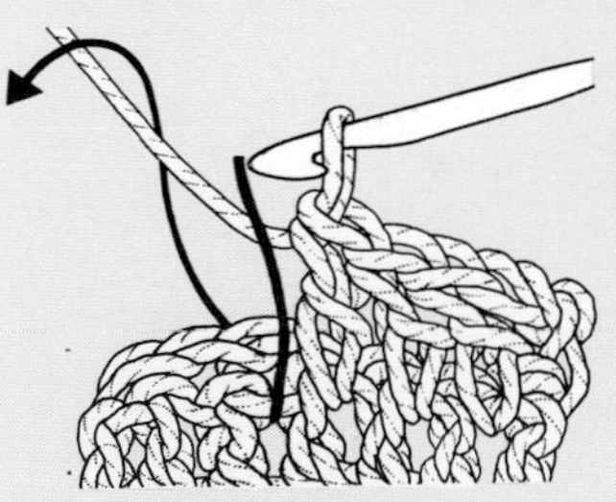

Insert the hook through the space between the 2 stitches in the row below.

Making a raised or indented effect

Crochet stitches can be given a raised appearance by working around the stitches below from the front or an indented effect by working around stitches from back.

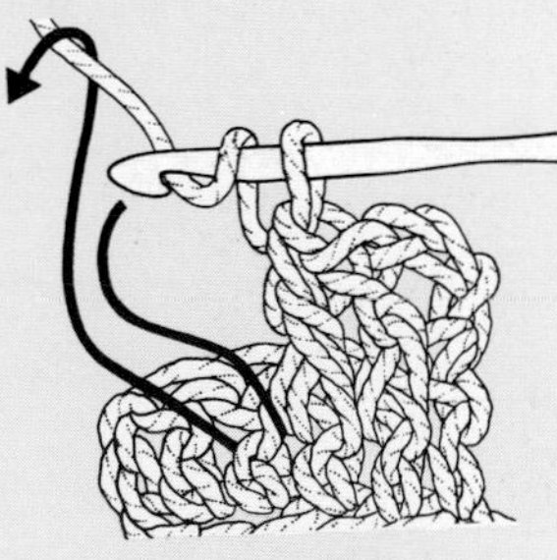

Insert the hook from the front around the stitches below. To obtain an indented effect, work around stitches from back.

Textured stitches

Textured effects are created in crochet either by working into the same stitch several times or by wrapping the yarn around the hook several times and then drawing a loop through the wrappings. Here are five standard techniques.

Pineapple stitch

Each pineapple (or bobble) stitch is made into every other stitch on a row of chains.

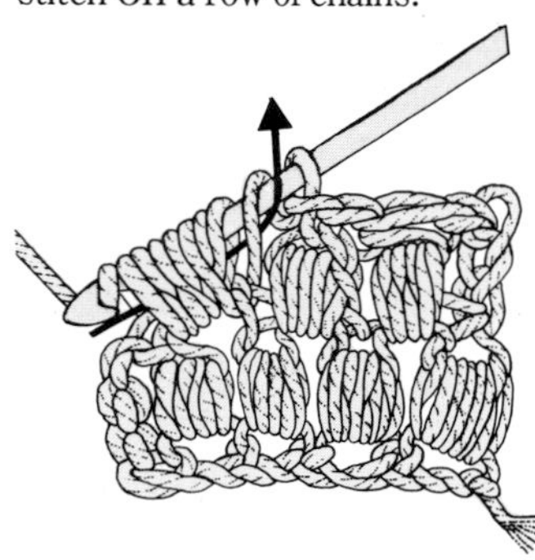

(Yrh, insert hook into ch, yrh, draw through) 4 times into same st, 9 loops on hook, yrh, draw through 8 loops, yrh, draw through rem 2 loops, 1ch.

Popcorn stitch

Each popcorn stitch is separated by trebles and made on a row of chains.

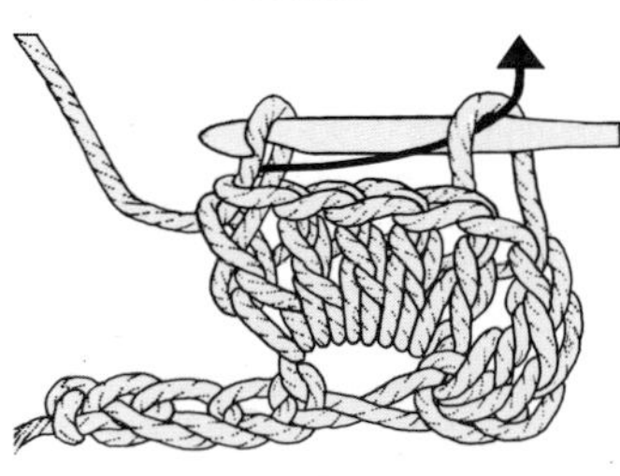

5tr into next st, withdraw hook from loop, insert hook into first of 5tr, pick up dropped loop and draw it through. Finish with 1ch.

Cabling around the stitch

Each cable is made by wrapping the hook around the treble below.

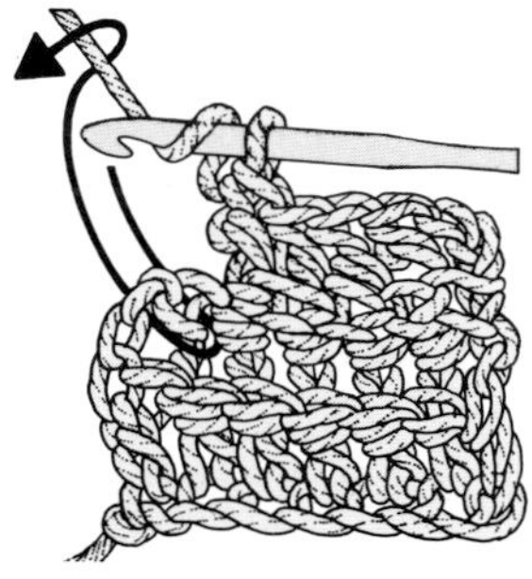

Yrh, insert hook from back to front and through to back again around the tr of previous row, yrh, draw through 3 loops on hook, yrh, draw through 2 loops on hook, yrh, draw through rem 2 loops.

Bullion stitch

Begin with a row of loose chain stitches and make one bullion into each stitch.

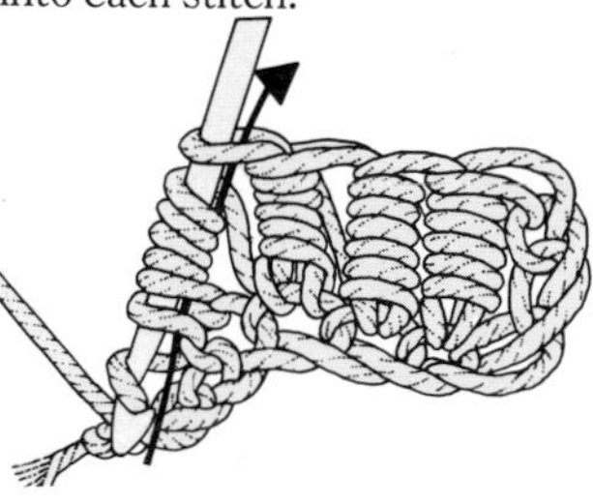

Yrh evenly several times, insert hook into ch, yrh, draw through, yrh and draw through all loops on hook.

Loop stitch

Begin by making a row of double crochet.

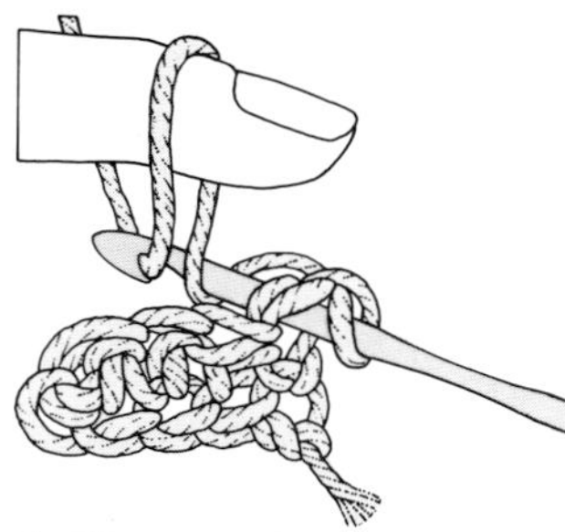

1 Wrap yarn from back to front around left forefinger, insert hook through first st and pass it behind yarn on forefinger. Catch both strands on finger.

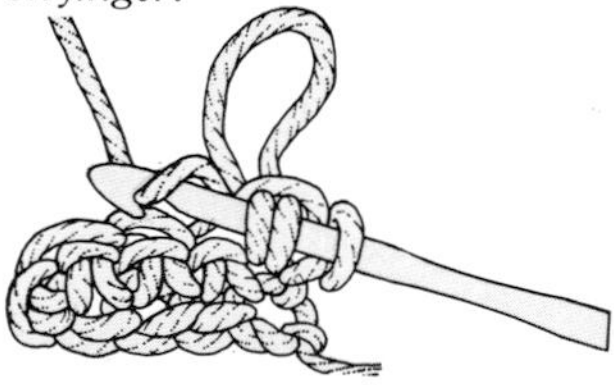

2 Draw both loops through and drop loop from forefinger, 3 loops on hook, yrh.

3 Draw through all 3 loops on hook to complete loop stitch. Continue to end. Work one row of dc before next loop row.

Openwork techniques

Openwork crochet is formed by missing stitches and making chains over the spaces left. Various patterns can be made with openwork by altering the combinations of stitches and spaces. For example, chains can be used to make a simple net ground. They can also be used to form bars onto which subsequent stitches are worked to make more intricate patterns, the simplest of which are worked with double crochet and trebles to form lattices. Other openwork patterns can be made by connecting trebles and crossing them to give a fretwork effect.

Making a simple openwork pattern

The spaces in the pattern below are formed by missing stitches and making chains over them.

Work 1tr, 2ch, miss 2ch in previous row, 1tr into next ch in previous row.

Making a simple net ground

The net ground below is made with chain and double crochet stitches.

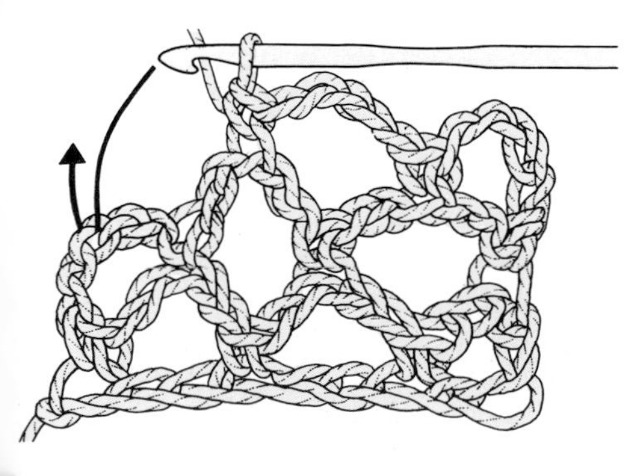

Work 1dc into middle of 5ch of previous row, 5ch, 1dc into middle of 5ch of previous row.

Making crossing trebles

A fretwork effect is formed by making a row of crossing trebles on a foundation chain.

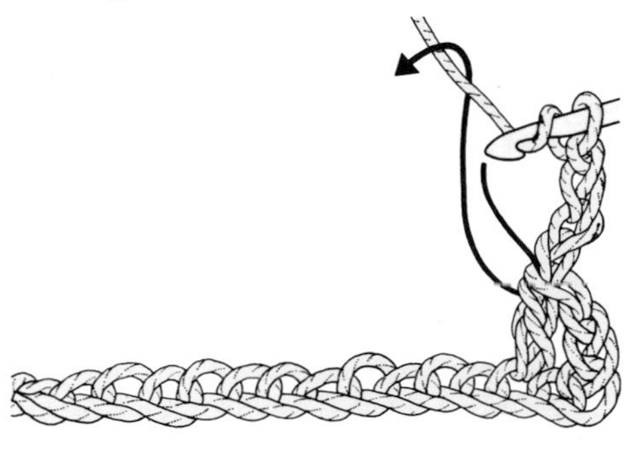

1 *Work 3ch (to act as 1tr), 1tr into 5th ch from hook, 4 ch, yrh, insert hook into junction of tr and 3ch as shown in diagram above.*

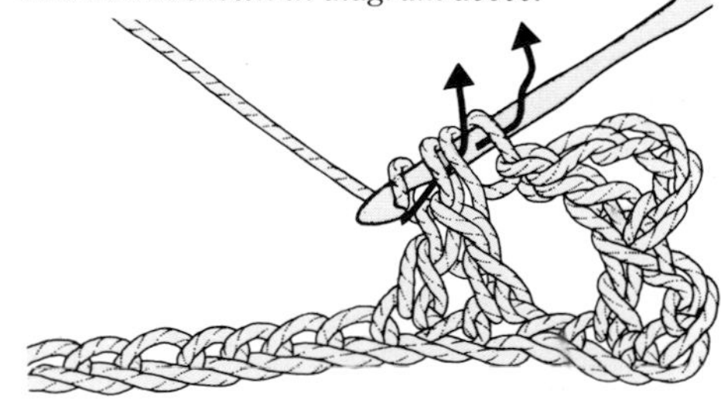

2 *Complete tr in usual way, 1ch, ⋆ yrh twice, miss 1ch, insert hook into next ch, yrh, draw through, yrh, draw through 2lps, 3lps now on hook, yrh, miss 1ch, insert hook into next ch, yrh, draw through, 5lps now on hook, (yrh, draw through 2lps) 4 times as shown in diagram above. Then 1ch, yrh, insert hook through upper part of connected trebles, complete tr in usual way, 1ch, rep from ⋆ to complete row.*

Textured patterns

Deeply-textured patterns are made by raising and lowering the fabric in such a way as to create a regular stitch repeat (see p. 172). These can be arranged as borders, large spot repeats or all-over patterns for both garments and furnishings.

Pineapple stitch

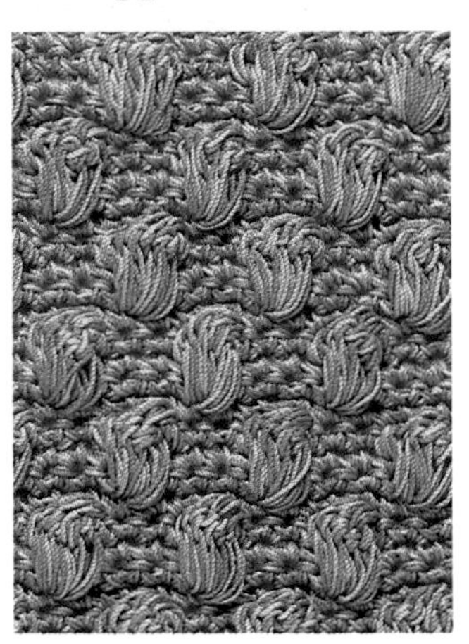

Work in a synthetic yarn for wash and wear.

Use for all-over repeat for sweater or shawl.

Make a number of ch divisible by 4 plus 3, 1ch, turn.
Work 3 rows in dc, 1ch, turn.
Row 4 1dc into each of first 3sts, ★ insert hook into next st, yrh, draw lp through, (yrh, insert hook into the same st 2 rows below – i.e. first row – yrh, draw lp through, yrh, draw through 2lps) 6 times, yrh, draw through all 8lps on hook – called 1 pineapple – 1dc into each of next 3dc, rep from ★ to end, 1ch, turn.
Work 3 rows in dc, 1ch, turn.
Row 8 1dc into first dc, ★ 1 pineapple into next dc, 1dc into each of next 3dc, rep from ★ to last 2sts, 1 pineapple into next dc, 1dc into next dc, 1ch, turn.
Rep rows 1 to 8 throughout.

Spray stitch

Work in a very fine cotton or silky yarn for special occasions; 2-ply wool for light warmth.

Use for bridesmaid's purse, party dress insertion or necktie; baby's shawl inset panel, or all-over repeat for bride's cape.

Make a number of ch divisible by 3 plus 1, 2ch, turn.
Row 1 2tr into 3rd ch from hook, ★ miss 2ch (1dc, 2tr) into next ch, rep from ★ to last 3ch, miss 2ch, 1dc into last ch, 2ch, turn.
Row 2 2tr into first dc, ★ (1dc, 2tr) into next dc, rep from ★ to end, 1dc into t-ch, 2ch, turn. Rep row 2 throughout.

Blossom stitch

Work in a medium-weight crochet cotton or fine wool for a close textured fabric.

Use for cushion, blanket border or straw hat band; sweater, bed-jacket inset panel or cape.

Make a number of ch divisible by 4 plus 3, 2ch, turn.
Row 1 (1tr, 1ch, 1tr) into 3rd ch from hook, miss 1ch, 1dc into next ch, ★ miss 1ch (1tr, 1ch, 1tr) into next ch, miss 1ch, 1dc into next ch, rep from ★ to end, 2ch, turn.
Row 2 ★ 1tr into dc, 1ch, 1dc into ch sp, 1ch, rep from ★ to end, 1tr into t-ch, 2ch, turn.
Row 3 ★ (1tr, 1ch, 1tr) into dc, 1dc into tr, rep from ★ to end, working last dc into t-ch, 2ch, turn.
Rep rows 2 and 3 throughout.

Honeycomb stitch

Work in a 3- to 4-ply wool or double knitting yarn.

Use for jacket or sweater inset panel or all-over repeat for slipover, beret, blanket square or shawl.

Make a number of ch divisible by 3, 1ch, turn.
Work a row of dc on foundation ch, 1ch, turn.
Row 1 ★ Yrh, insert hook into next st, (yrh, draw lp through, yrh, draw through 2lps) 5 times, yrh, draw through 6lps, 1dc into each of next 2dc, rep from ★ to end, 1ch, turn.
Row 2 1dc into each st to end, 1ch, turn.
Row 3 ★ 1dc into each of next 2dc, yrh, insert hook into next st (yrh, draw lp through, yrh, draw through 2lps) 5 times, yrh, draw through 6lps, rep from ★ to end, 1ch, turn.
Row 4 As row 2.
Rep rows 1 to 4 throughout.

Sweetpea stitch

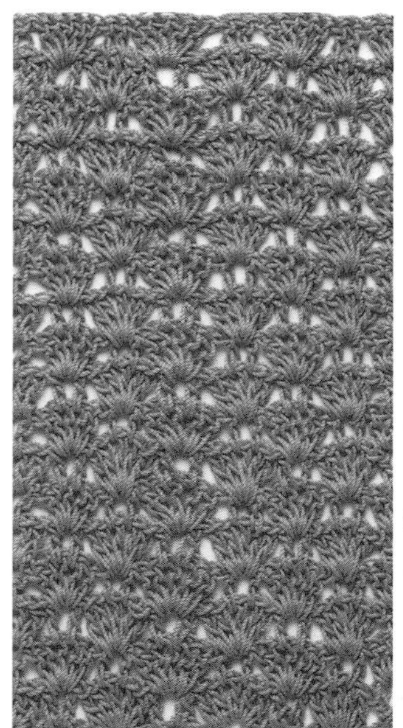

Work in a medium-weight crêpe-rayon, cotton, silk or acrylic yarn for a lacy effect.

Use for inset panel for child's dress or baby's pram set; all-over design for classic cardigan, sleeveless pullover or dress bodice.

Make a number of ch divisible by 7 plus 4, 3ch, turn.
Row 1 1tr into 4th ch from hook, ★ miss 2ch, 5tr into next ch, miss 2ch, 1tr into each of next 2ch, rep from ★ to last 3ch, miss 2ch, 3tr into last ch, 3ch, turn.
Row 2 1tr bet first 2tr, ★ 5tr bet the 2 single tr, 1tr bet 2nd and 3rd of 5tr, 1tr bet 3rd and 4th of 5tr, rep from ★ to end, 3tr bet last tr and t-ch, 3ch, turn.
Rep row 2 throughout.

Loop stitch

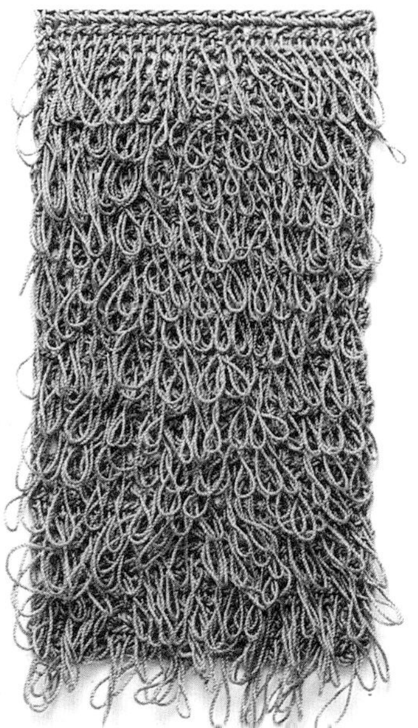

Work in a cotton or synthetic yarn for easy care; 4-ply yarn, double knitting or chenille for warmth.

Use for jacket trim or all-over pattern for bathroom set, full-length coat and matching beret, egg or teapot cosy, pram cover or furry toys.

Make any number of ch, 1ch, turn. Work a row of dc on the foundation ch, 1ch, turn.
Row 1 (wrong side of work) ★ Yrh, insert hook into next st, take yarn round finger, yrh, draw lp through, yrh, draw through 3lps on hook, rep from ★ to end, 1ch, turn.
Row 2 1dc into each st to end, 1ch, turn.
Rep rows 1 and 2 throughout.

Using increasing to shape

By increasing the number of stitches in a row you can widen the crochet. Increases are usually worked on basic stitches but when they are used in conjunction with a special stitch, the instructions will be given in the pattern you are using.

Increasing by working twice into one stitch

The simplest form of increasing is to work twice into the same stitch, making 2 stitches from one.

Single increases

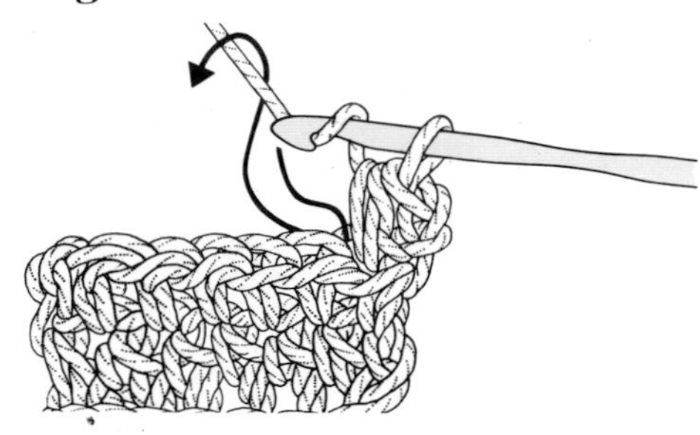

Where the increase is required, insert the hook into the stitch in the row below. Make a stitch; insert the hook again into the same stitch and make a second stitch.

When increasing at the beginning of the row, work twice into the first stitch and at the end of the row twice into the last stitch.

Double increases

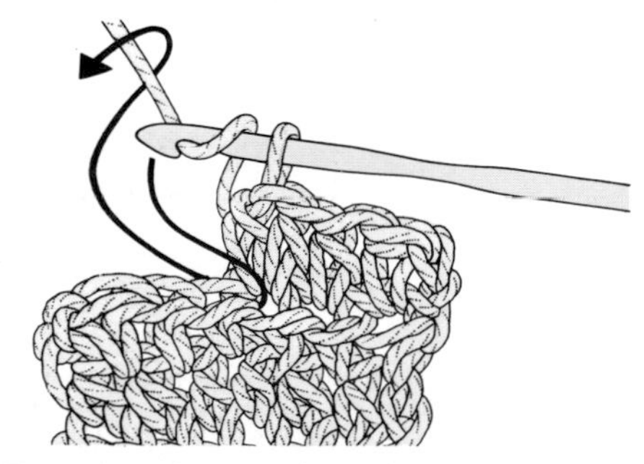

To make 2 increases instead of one, work three times into the same stitch where the double increase is needed.

Multiple increases

If several stitches need to be added at edge of work, additional chain stitches are made.

Beginning of the row

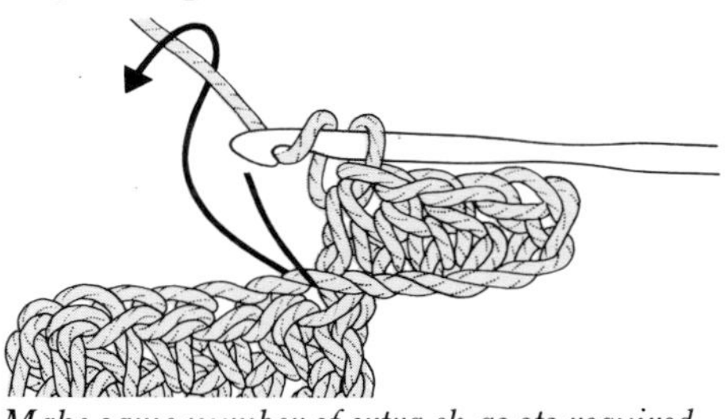

Make same number of extra ch as sts required plus t-chs, turn. Work new sts in pattern.

End of the row

To keep increases made at both ends of row level, make provision for these stitches on previous row.

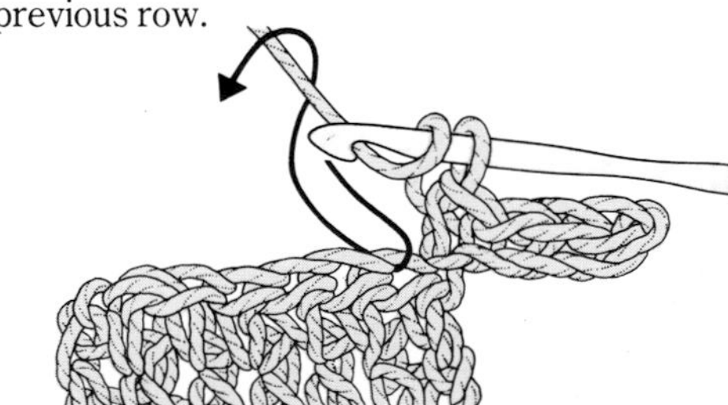

1 *Make same number of extra ch as sts required plus t-chs. Work ss over new ch, cont. in pattern.*

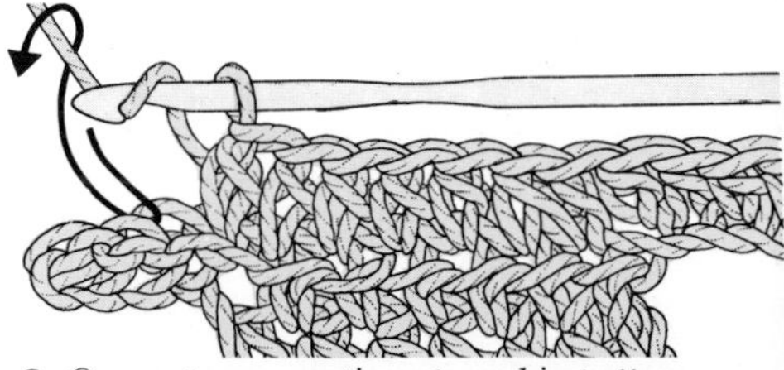

2 *On next row, continue to end in pattern working through slip sts.*

Using decreasing to shape

Decreasing the number of stitches in a row or round narrows the crochet. The simplest method is to miss a stitch either at the beginning, middle or the end of a row. Like increases decreases are usually worked in basic stitches.

Decreasing by missing a stitch

One stitch is missed for a single decrease and two for a double decrease.

Beginning of the row

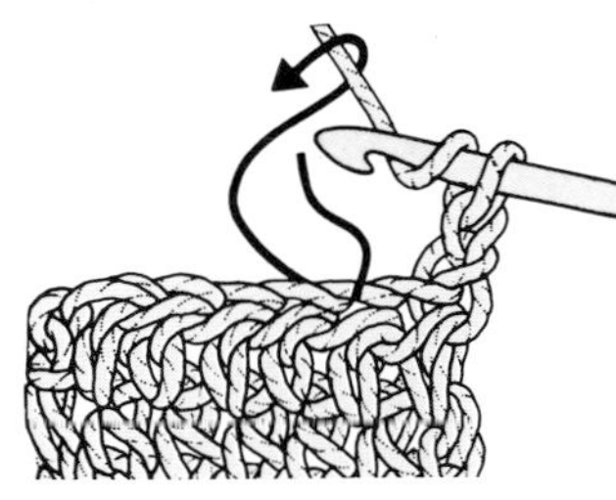

Miss one stitch, leaving it unworked, and then work into the next stitch.

End of the row

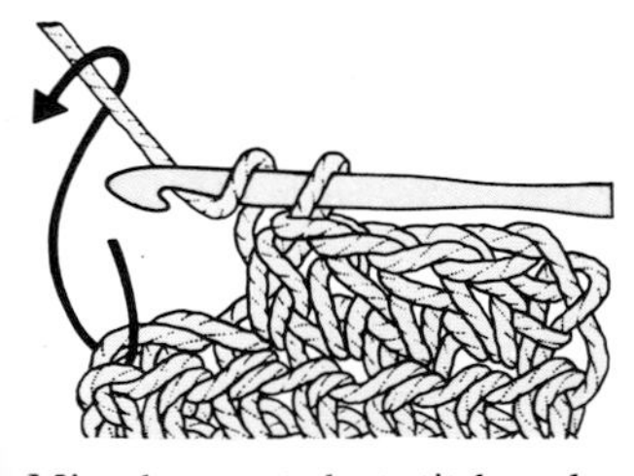

Miss the next to last stitch and work into the final stitch.

Middle of the row

The method is the same, but the decreases must be evenly spaced. The abbreviation is dec evenly.

Decreasing by working two stitches as one

Another method of decreasing is to work two stitches as one. This method can be used on all the basic crochet stitches either at the beginning, the middle or the end of the row.

In double crochet

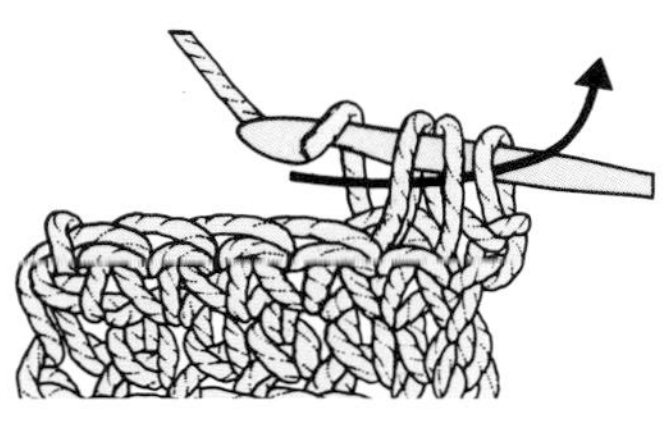

Make t-ch, insert the hook into the first stitch, yrh and draw through. Repeat into next stitch, yrh, draw through all loops.

In middle of row

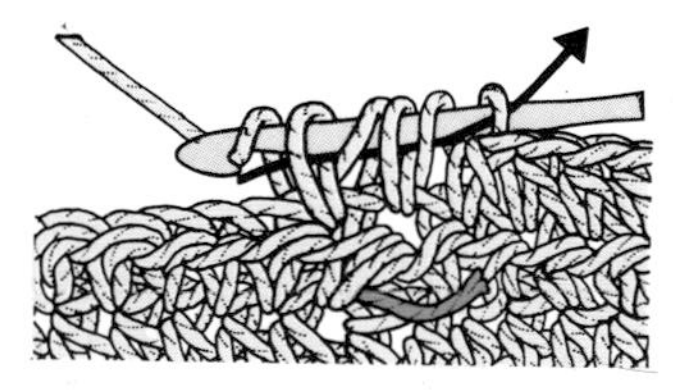

Work 2sts tog. as 1. As guide for further decreasing, mark position of dec sts with coloured yarn.

Decreasing several stitches at row ends

At the beginning of a row work ss over stitches to be decreased, make t-chs. Continue in pattern. At end, leave stitches to be decreased unworked, make t-chs.

SHAPING BY USING DIFFERENT STITCH LENGTHS

Each of the basic stitches is of a different height. Used in the same or subsequent rows, they automatically shape the crochet as shown here.

This technique is often used in shaping medallions.

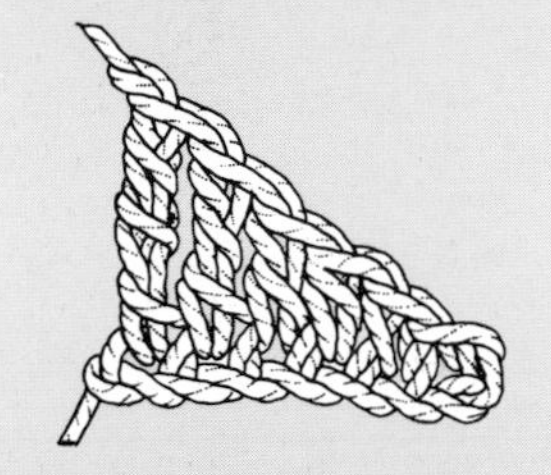

Wedge shape worked in slip stitch to triple treble.

Openwork

Openwork stitch patterns are some of the quickest and easiest to crochet (see p. 173). As all openwork is made by leaving large spaces between stitches, the work grows rapidly. This group of lacy stitch patterns, combined with the variety of crochet yarns available, offers one of the widest ranges of decorative textures – from a simple bar and lattice to intricate star and peacock patterns.

Bar and lattice

Work in a fine to medium-weight wool or synthetic yarn.

Use for dress yoke, inset panel or curtains.

Make a number of ch divisible by 4 plus 1, 5ch, turn.
Row 1 1tr into 10th ch from hook, ★ 3ch, miss 3ch, 1tr into next ch, rep from ★ to end, 4ch, turn.
Row 2 ★ 1dc into 2nd of 3ch, 2ch, 1tr into tr, 2ch, rep from ★ to end, ending with 2dc into 2nd ch, 2ch, 1tr into t-ch, 5ch, turn.
Row 3 1tr into next tr, ★ 3ch, 1tr into next tr, rep from ★ to end, working last tr into t-ch, 4ch, turn.
Rep rows 2 and 3 throughout.

Star stitch

Work in a fine wool, silk crêpe or rayon for a soft, pretty look; medium-weight yarn for a rich textured effect.

Use for dress inset panel, cardigan, cushion set or bedspread border.

Make a number of ch divisible by 4 plus 1, 3ch, turn.
Row 1 1tr into 8th ch from hook (1ch, 1tr) 3 times into same ch, ★ miss 3ch, 1tr into next ch (1ch, 1tr) 3 times into same ch, rep from ★ to last 4ch, miss 3ch, 1tr into last ch, 3ch, turn.
Row 2 1tr into 2nd ch sp of shell (1ch, 1tr) 3 times into same ch sp, rep from ★ to end, 1tr into t-ch, 3ch, turn.
Rep row 2 throughout.

Irish net stitch

Work in a fine crochet cotton for a lacy look; medium-weight yarn for furnishing.

Use for all-over pattern for classic-style cardigan, bedcover or buffet runner.

Make a number of ch divisible by 4 plus 1, 5ch, turn.
Row 1 (1dc, 3ch, 1dc) into 10th ch from hook, ★ 5ch, miss 3ch (1dc, 3ch, 1dc) into next ch, rep from ★ to last 4ch, 5ch, miss 3ch, 1dc into last ch, 5ch, turn.
Row 2 ★ (1dc, 3ch, 1dc) into 3rd of 5ch, 5ch, rep from ★ to end, 1dc into t-ch, 5ch, turn.
Rep row 2 throughout.

Ladder stitch

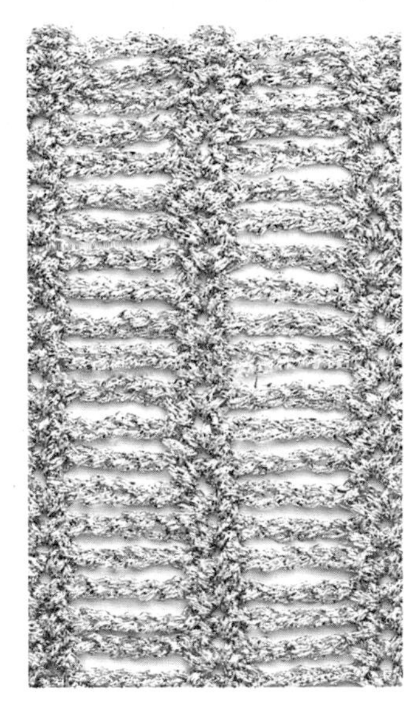

Work in cotton for sunshine, lurex for moonlight; double knitting wool, mohair or angora for warmth.

Use for all-over pattern for beach wrap or blouson, cape or camisole top; jerkin, long, belted cardigan or scarf.

Make a number of ch divisible by 6 plus 1, 1ch, turn.
Row 1 1dc into 2nd ch from hook, ⋆ 5ch, miss 5ch, (1dc, 3ch, 1dc) into next ch, rep from ⋆ to last 6ch, 5ch, miss 5ch, 1dc into last ch, 1ch, turn.
Row 2 1dc into first dc, ⋆ 5ch (1dc, 3ch, 1dc) into 3ch lp, rep from ⋆ to end, ending with 5ch, 1dc into last dc, 1ch, turn.
Rep row 2 throughout.

Reseau stitch

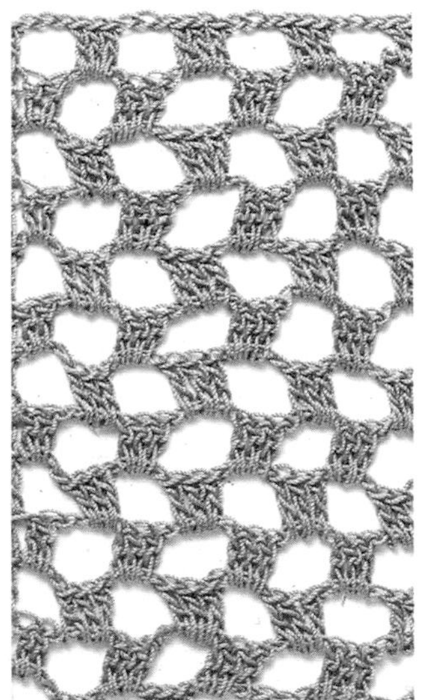

Work in a silk, rayon or cotton yarn for summer wear; chunky or double knitting wool for winter warmth.

Use for evening wrap or shawl inset panel; all-over repeat for blanket with contrast needle-weaving using fur strips or thick wool.

Make a number of ch divisible by 6 plus 1, 3ch, turn.
Row 1 1tr into 4th ch from hook, 1tr into next ch, ⋆ 3ch, miss 3ch, 1tr into each of next 3ch, rep from ⋆ to last 4ch, 3ch, miss 3ch, 1tr into last ch, 3ch, turn.
Row 2 2tr into first 3ch sp, ⋆ 3ch, 3tr into next 3ch sp, rep from ⋆ to end, ending with 3ch, 1tr into t-ch, 3ch, turn.
Rep row 2 throughout.

Peacock stitch

Work in a medium-weight cotton or acrylic for wash and wear; Shetland wool or mohair for lacy softness.

Use for bedspread or curtain border; shawl inset panel, loose-fitting blouson top or scarf.

Make a number of ch divisible by 14 plus 1, 1ch, turn.
Row 1 1dc into 2nd ch from hook, ⋆ miss 6ch, 13 long tr into next ch (drawing lp up to 1.3cm to form a long tr), miss 6ch, 1dc into next ch, rep from ⋆ to end, 4ch, turn.
Row 2 1 long tr into dc, ⋆ 5ch, 1dc into 7th of 13 long tr, 5ch, 2 long tr into dc, rep from ⋆ to end, 1ch, turn.
Row 3 ⋆ 1dc bet 2 long tr, 13 long tr into dc, rep from ⋆ to end, 1dc bet long tr and t-ch, 4ch, turn.
Rep rows 2 and 3 throughout.

Working with colours

Colours can be introduced at any point and either carried along the top of the previous row and passed over until they are needed, or introduced in the middle of a row. Horizontal stripes are made by joining in a new colour at the beginning of rows or rounds, and vertical stripes are worked with the colours being carried along the top when not in work. They are then exchanged with the original colour which itself is now carried along the top while the second colour is in work. Diagonals and chevrons are worked in the same way as striped patterns.

Random patterns can be created by introducing the colours as required and either carrying them along the top of the work and using them when needed, or by introducing them and leaving them hanging at the back of the work, picking them up on the subsequent row at the same point and working them from that position.

Adding new yarn in double crochet

This is done to replace an old yarn which has run out or to introduce a new colour.

Before a stitch

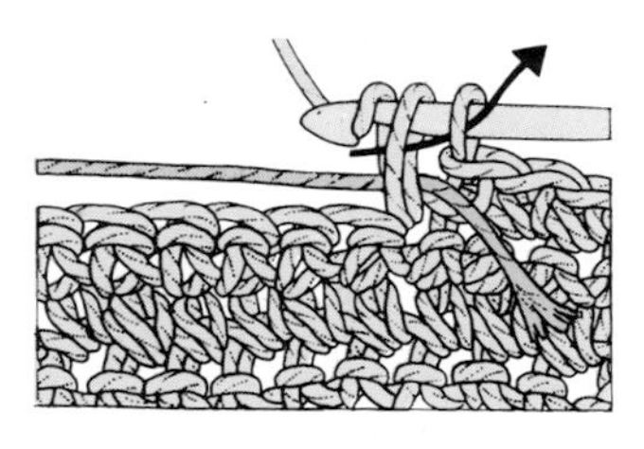

1 Carry new yarn loosely along top of previous row and work over it as though it were part of row. When needed new yarn is introduced with final yrh of dc.

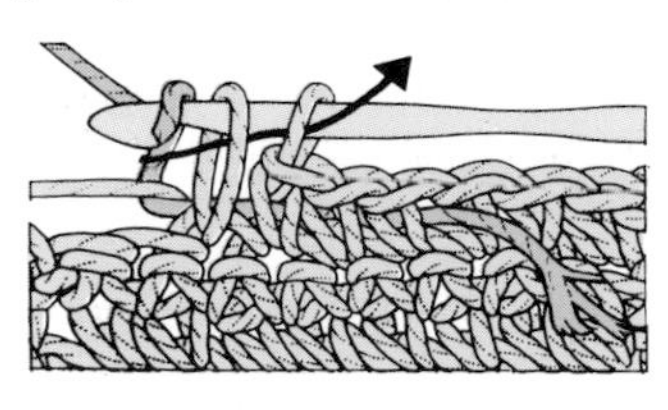

2 If old yarn is to be used again in this row carry it along top of previous row. If not, carry it along top of row for a few stitches and snip off end.

After a stitch

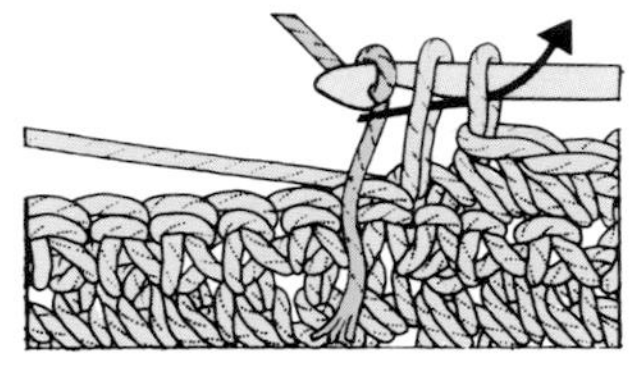

1 Work stitch with old yarn to final yrh and then introduce the new yarn.

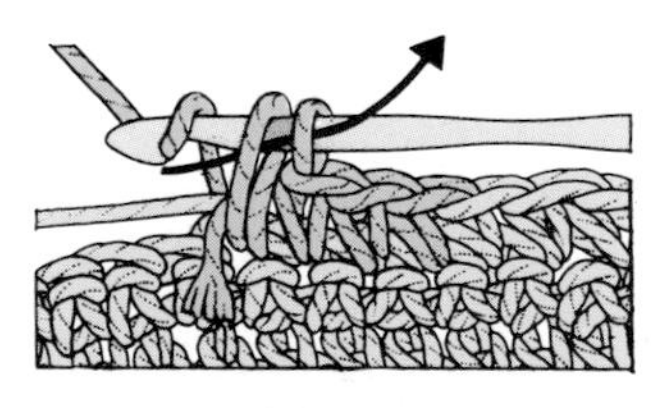

2 Lay loose end of new yarn along top of row and work over it. If old yarn is required again in this row lay it along the top and work over it until needed.

Changing colours

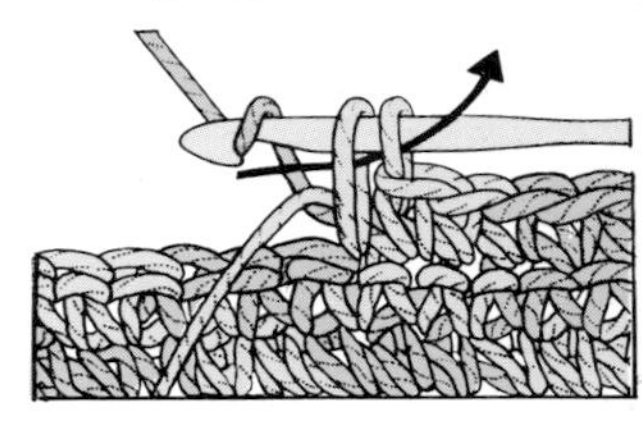

1 Introduce the second colour with final yrh of previous stitch. The first colour is then carried along top of previous row.

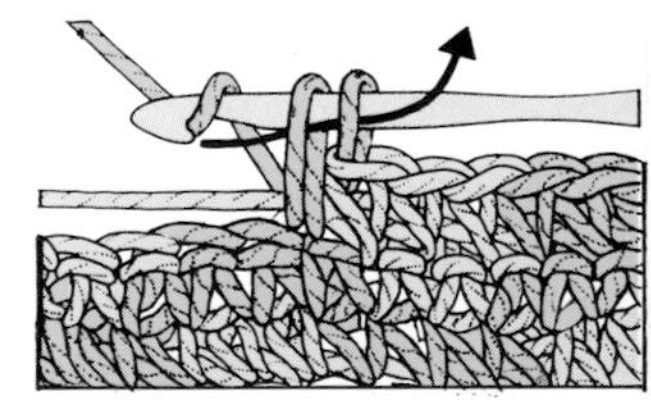

2 The 2 yarns exchange roles when the old colour is required again. When several colours are worked in this way a dense stitch such as dc must be used if the carried yarns are to remain hidden behind the work.

Working in the round

Working in the round instead of in rows means that the foundation row of chains is made into a circle or ring, and the crochet stitches are then worked from this circle in a continuous round without turning and working back and forth. Many different shapes can be made from this simple foundation ring: round medallions are made by increasing evenly around the circle, square medallions by increasing at four regular intervals and hexagons by increasing at six regular intervals.

Single chain ring

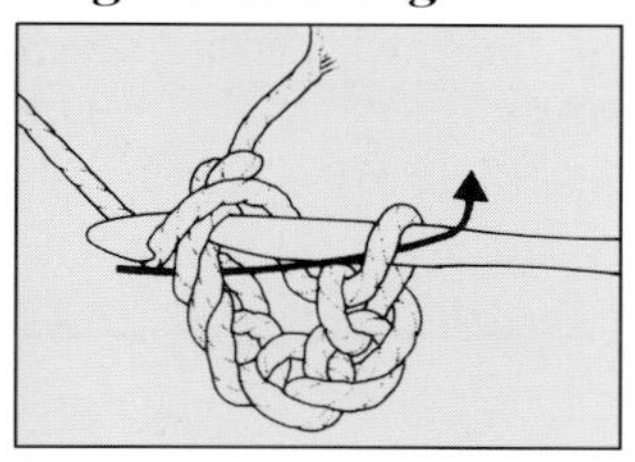

Make a foundation chain to required length and then close ring with a slip stitch into the first chain.

Double crochet ring

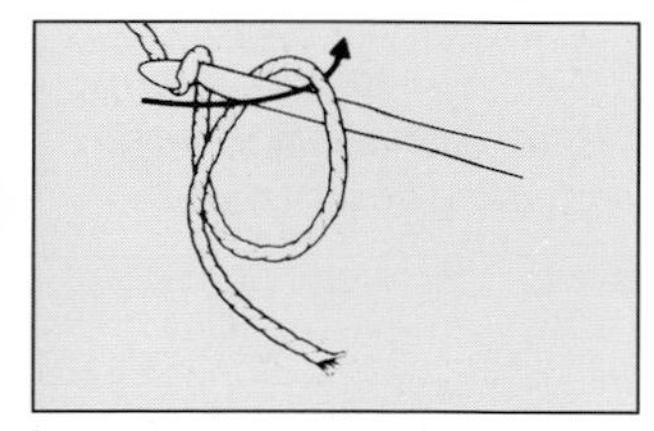

1 Make a circle with yarn as shown. Insert hook, yrh, draw through circle, yrh, draw through loop.

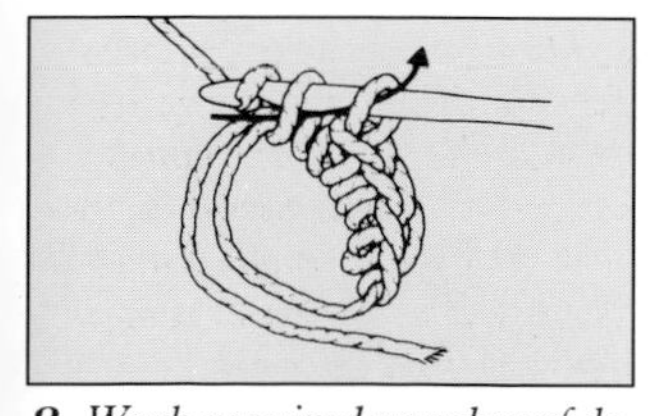

2 Work required number of dc around circle over both strands.
3 Pull loose end firmly to draw circle together. Close ring with a slip stitch.

Beginning a round

In many of the patterns, the first instruction in round 1 is to chain 1, 2, 3 or more. These chains bring the hook up to the height of the stitches which will then be made into the ring. Although they do not resemble a stitch, these chains are the equivalent of the first stitch of the round. For example:

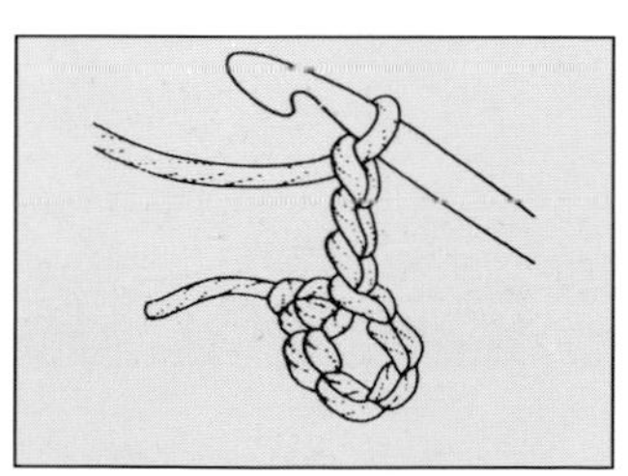

***Round 1** 3ch, 11 tr into ring.*

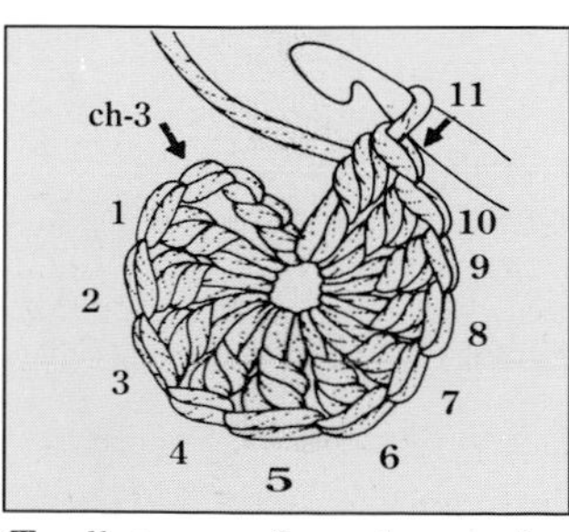

To allow room for subsequent stitches to fit into the ring, slide the stitches along the ring.

Ending a round

When all the stitches of a round have been made, the first and last stitches are joined with a slip stitch.

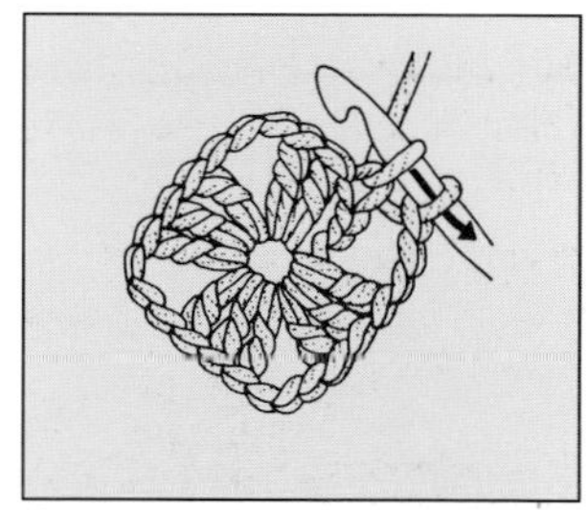

Insert the hook into the third (top) chain of the initial ch-3, pull through a loop, pull the new loop through the loop on the hook, thereby making a slip stitch.

Colourwork medallions

Colourwork medallions are composed of two or more colours. As well as being decorative, they are an economic way of using up odd scraps of yarn. In colourwork medallions, new colours are added at the beginning of rounds. When breaking off the old yarn at the end of a round and joining in the new colour, secure the ends carefully by working stitches over the loose ends.

Colour patterns

Many attractive and intricate effects can be crocheted simply by introducing two or more colours into patterns (see page 180). As the technique for working colour patterns produces a close fabric, it is generally advisable to use a hook one size larger than the normal choice for the chosen yarn. Patterns vary from a single dot repeat through speckle and petal patterns to undulating peaks and pinnacles.

Petal stitch

Work in a medium-weight wool, silk, crêpe or acrylic yarn for softness; crochet cotton for a finer fabric.

Use for dress yoke, slipover inset panel or all-over pattern for bed-jacket or shawl; scatter cushion border, deep collar and cuffs or decorative trim for a waistcoat.

This pattern uses 2 colours, A and B.
Using A make a number of ch divisible by 6 plus 1, 3ch, turn.
Row 1 2tr into 4th ch from hook, ⋆ miss 2ch, 1dc into next ch, miss 2ch, 5tr into next ch, rep from ⋆ to end, ending with 3tr into last ch instead of 5.
Row 2 Join B to top of 3ch at beg of row 1, 1dc into this st, ⋆ 2ch, ⋆⋆ yrh, insert hook into next tr, yrh, draw lp through, yrh, draw through 2lps ⋆⋆ rep from ⋆⋆ to ⋆⋆ into next tr, into dc, then into each of next 2tr, yrh, draw through 6lps on hook, 2ch, 1dc into next tr, rep from ⋆ to end, drawing through A on last dc.
Row 3 Using A, 3ch, 2tr into first dc, ⋆ 1dc into top of gr, 5tr into next dc, rep from ⋆ to end, but ending with 3tr into last dc.
Row 4 Return to beg of row 3, draw B through top of 3ch and work as row 2.
Rep rows 3 and 4 throughout.

Dot stitch

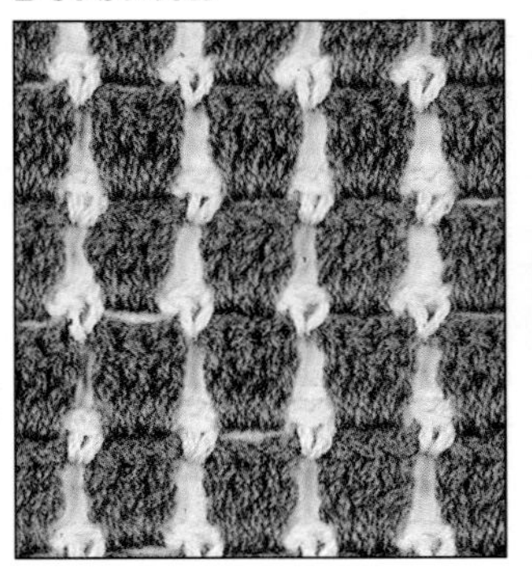

Work in a fine to medium-weight yarn.

Use for classic twinset or matching gloves and hat.

This pattern uses 2 colours, A and B.
Using A, make a number of ch divisible by 3 plus 1, 1ch, turn.
Row 1 1dc into 2nd ch from hook, ⋆ 2ch, miss 2ch, 1dc into next ch, rep from ⋆ to end, joining in B on last dc.
Row 2 Using B, 4ch, ⋆ 3tr into 2ch sp, 1ch, rep from ⋆ to end, 1tr into last dc.
Row 3 Return to beg of row 2, draw A through under 4th of 4ch, 1ch as first dc, ⋆ 2ch, 1dc into 1ch sp, rep from ⋆ to end, drawing B through on last dc.
Row 4 Using B, work as row 2. Always starting each row at the end where the correct colour was left, rep rows 3 and 4 throughout.

Speckle stitch

Work in a medium-weight wool or synthetic yarn for a rich tweedy effect.

Use for sweater inset panel or all-over pattern for man's sleeveless cardigan or deer-stalker cap.

This pattern uses 3 colours, A, B and C.

Using A, make a number of ch divisible by 3 plus 2, 1ch, turn.

Row 1 1dc into 3rd ch from hook, 1dc into each ch to end.

Row 2 1ch, 1dc, into each dc to end. Do not break off A.

Row 3 Join in B, 1ch, 1dc into each dc to end.

Row 4 As row 2. Do not break off B.

Row 5 Return to beg of row 4, join in C, 1ch, 1dc into each dc to end. Do not break off C.

Row 6 Draw A through first st, 1ch, 1dc into next dc, ⋆ 1dtr inserting hook from right to left in front of corresponding st on row 2, 1dc into each of next 2dc, rep from ⋆ to end.

Row 7 As row 2.

Row 8 Draw C through first st, 1ch, 1dc into each dc to end.

Row 9 Return to beg of row 8, draw B through first st, 1ch, 1dc into next dc, ⋆ 1dtr, inserting hook from right to left in front of dtr on row 6, 1dc into each of next 2dc, rep from ⋆ to end.

Row 10 As row 2.

Always starting each row at the correct end where yarn was left, rep rows 5 to 10 throughout.

Pinnacle stitch

Work in a shetland, double knitting wool or mohair.

Use for all-over repeat for throwover bedspread, cushion set or travel rug; dress, shawl or scarf border.

This pattern uses 2 colours, A and B.

Using A, make a number of ch divisible by 14 plus 1, 2ch, turn.

Row 1 1dc into 3rd ch from hook, ⋆ 1dc into each of next 5ch, miss 3ch, 1dc into each of next 5ch, 3dc into next ch, rep from ⋆ to end, but ending with 2dc into last ch instead of 3.

Row 2 1ch, 1dc into same place, ⋆ 1dc into each of next 5dc, miss 2dc, 1dc into each of next 5dc, 3dc into next dc, rep from ⋆ to end, but ending with 2dc into t-ch. Rep row 2 throughout, working 2 more rows in A, then 4 rows in B and 4 rows in A throughout.

Finishing details

The finishing details of a crochet design are as important as the actual working of the crochet. You can, if you choose, make a design entirely of crochet from the buttons to the loops, cords and final seaming together. But you can, of course, also use bought buttons and the seams can be stitched together with needle and yarn.

Buttonholes

There are two methods of making vertical buttonholes: one for small stitches (up to half trebles); the other for larger stitches. Making horizontal buttonholes is also quite simple.

Vertical buttonholes for small stitches

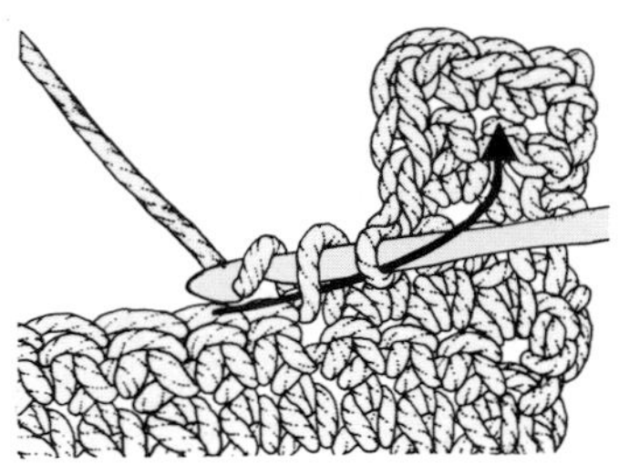

1 Work to the buttonhole position and turn. Work back and repeat on this and all the subsequent rows until buttonhole is of required length, ending at inner edge. Work ss down inner edge to last complete row.

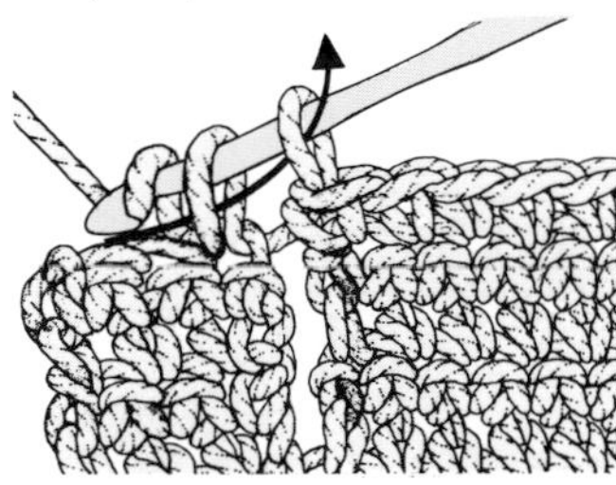

2 Continue working these stitches to and fro until they are level with the first side. Then continue across all stitches in the pattern, closing the slit to form the buttonhole.

Vertical buttonholes for large stitches

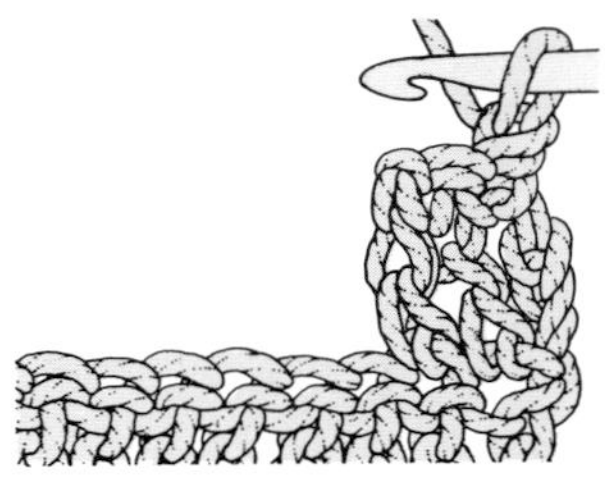

1 Work to the buttonhole position and complete the first side of the buttonhole in the same way as for smaller stitches ending at outer edge.

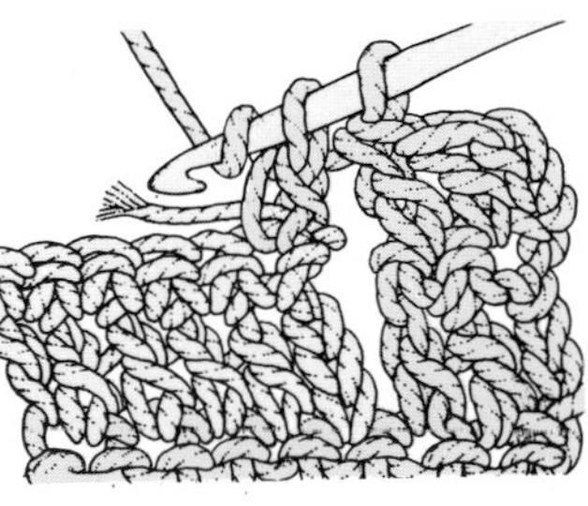

2 Using a separate ball of yarn, begin working from inner edge of buttonhole and form second side to match first. Break off new yarn and continue with original yarn across all stitches to complete buttonhole.

Horizontal buttonholes

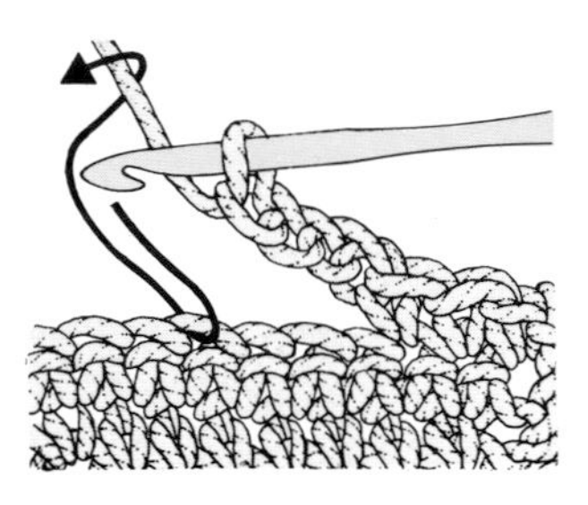

1 Work from the side edge to the buttonhole position – 3 to 4 stitches is usually enough. Make 2 or more chains, depending on the size of the button. Miss the same number of stitches in the row below.

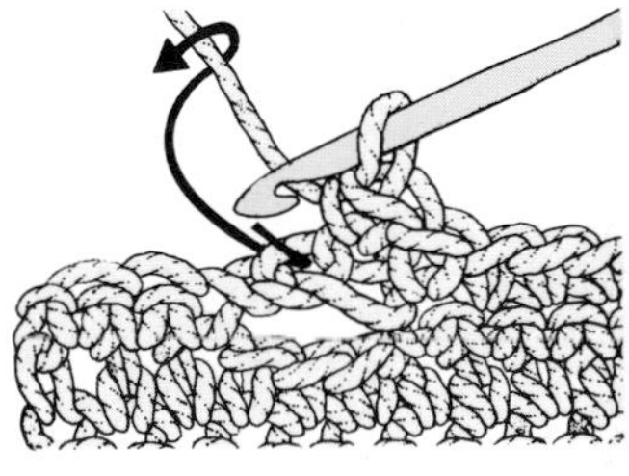

2 Work in pattern to the end of the row. On the following row work in pattern over the chains to the end of the row.

Crochet cords

Crochet cords or chains are made in several ways and are used for gathering, tying and for belts. They can be made in various colours to add decorative interest.

Coloured chains

A simple two-coloured chain is worked like a single chain but using each colour alternately.

Place both colours in the left hand and over the left forefinger. Pick each one up and drop it alternately, making one chain with each colour.

Using single chains

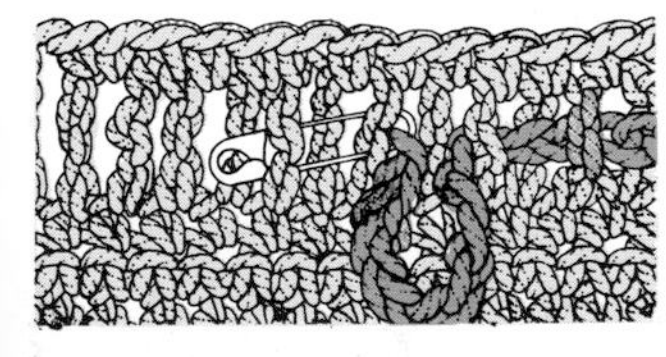

Make a single chain as shown on page 166. Then, with a safety pin fixed at one end, thread the chain as shown, through a row of double trebles, to gather up a cuff, neckline or waistline.

Seams and edges

Crochet sections may be joined together by sewing, using a blunt-ended wool needle or by working crochet stitches to give a firm seam.

Slip stitch seams

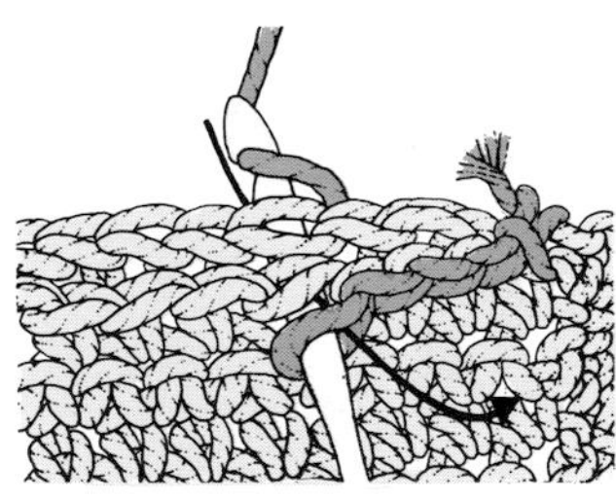

Insert the hook from front to back through the edge stitches of both pieces, yrh and draw through. Work 1ss in the usual way, then insert the hook into the next stitch along, ready to make the next ss. Continue in this way to end and fasten off.

Back stitch seams

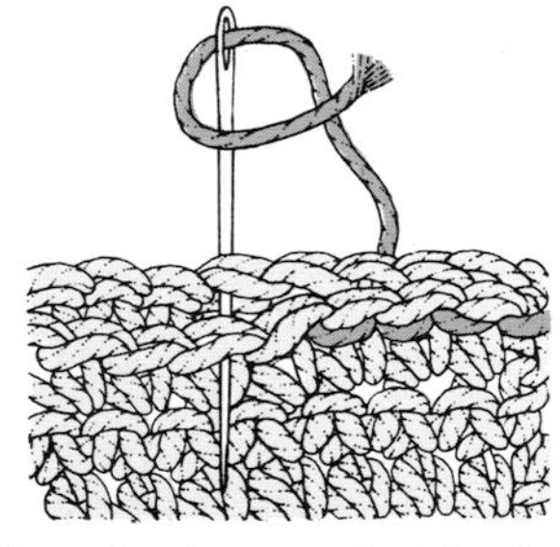

Place the pieces to be joined with right sides facing. Thread a wool needle with matching yarn and work back stitch as shown, inserting the needle between two crochet stitches.

Woven seams

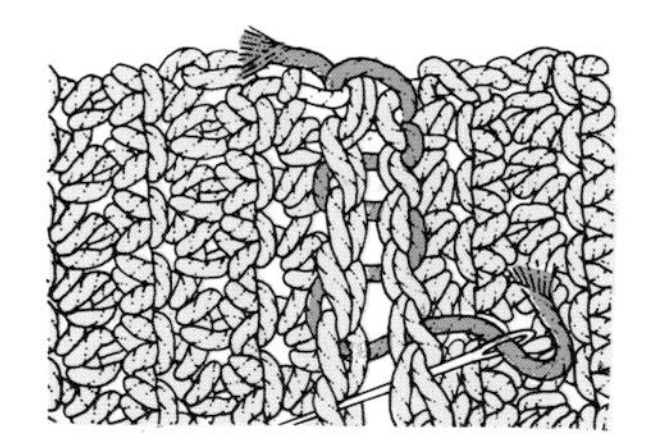

Woven seams are best for fine work and baby clothes. Lay the pieces wrong side up with edges touching. Thread a wool needle with matching yarn and weave it loosely around centres of the edge stitches of both pieces as shown in the diagram above.

Double crochet edging

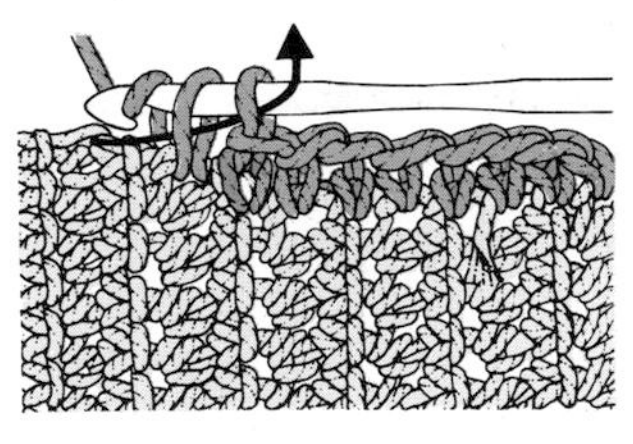

Double crochet edging is used mainly for necklines or borders. Insert the hook from front to back through the edge. Yrh and draw through. Work a double crochet and then continue along the edge, inserting the hook row by row.

Simple medallions

These are worked from the centre and increased outwards. The positioning of the increase forms the shapes. Medallions can be plain, multicoloured, relief or lacy. By working in different weight yarns the same medallion shape and pattern can be used either for everyday household items or articles of clothing.

Scalloped circle

Work in a fine to medium-weight crêpe, rayon or cotton for a lacy look.

Use for single motifs for applying to bridesmaid's sash or hairslide; all-over repeat for placemat or tablecloth.

Make 6ch and join into a ring with a ss into first ch.
Round 1 3ch, 23tr into ring, join with a ss to 3rd of the first 3ch.
Round 2 5ch, 1tr into ss, 1ch, ⋆ miss 2tr (1tr, 2ch, 1tr) into next tr, 1ch, rep from ⋆ 6 times more, join with a ss to 3rd of first 5ch.
Round 3 Ss into 2ch sp, 3ch (1tr, 2ch, 2tr) into same sp, ⋆ 1dc into 1ch sp (2tr, 2ch, 2tr) into 2ch sp, rep from ⋆ 6 times more, 1dc into 1ch sp, join with a ss into 3rd of first 3ch.
Round 4 Ss into 2ch sp, 3ch (2tr, 1ch, 3tr) into same sp, ⋆ 1dc before next dc, 1dc after the same dc (3tr, 1ch, 3tr) into 2ch sp, rep from ⋆ 6 times more, 1dc before next dc, 1dc after the same dc, join with a ss to 3rd of first 3ch.
Fasten off.

Spiral hexagon

Work in a medium-weight yarn or space-dyed cotton for town wear; use fine string for a country look.

Use for beret, bedspread and bolster module, or scatter cushion.

Make 5ch and join into a ring with a ss into first ch.
Round 1 ⋆ 6ch, 1dc into ring, rep from ⋆ 5 times more, ss over first 3ch of first lp.
Round 2 ⋆ 4ch, 1dc into 6ch lp, rep from ⋆ 5 times more, working the last dc into ss before the first 4ch.
Round 3 ⋆ 4ch, 2dc into 4ch lp, 1dc into dc, rep from ⋆ 5 times more, working last dc into last dc at end of last rnd.
Round 4 ⋆ 4ch, 2dc into 4ch lp, 1dc into each of next 2dc, rep from ⋆ to end.
Round 5 ⋆ 4ch, 2dc into 4ch lp, 1dc into each of next 3dc, rep from ⋆ to end.
Cont in this way, working 1 more dc in each group on each rnd until motif is the required size, ending with a ss into next dc. Fasten off.

Eternal triangle

Work in a double knitting wool or chunky yarn.

Use for pot holders or coasters.

Make 4ch and join into a ring with a ss into first ch.
Round 1 3ch to count as 1tr, 11tr into ring, join with a ss into 3rd of first 3ch.
Round 2 (5ch, ss into 4th tr of previous round) twice, 5ch, join with a ss to base of first 5ch.
Round 3 Ss into 5ch sp, 3ch to count as 1tr, 6tr, 2ch (7tr, 2ch) twice, join to top of 3ch.
Round 4 2ch, 6htr, 9tr in 2ch sp, (7htr, 9tr in 2ch sp) twice, ss in top of 2ch.
Round 5 4ch (miss htr, 1tr, 1ch), 5 times, ⋆ 1tr, in next tr, 4ch, miss 1tr, 1tr in next tr, 1ch, 1tr (1ch, miss 1tr, 1tr), 6 times, 1ch, repeat from ⋆ once more, 1tr, 4ch, miss 1tr, 1tr, 1ch, 1tr, 1ch, ss in 3rd ch at start.
Round 6 3ch, 1tr in 1ch sp, 1tr in each tr to 4ch sp, 3tr, 2ch, 3tr, into corner sp, all round, ss in top of 3ch. Fasten off.

Plain square

Work in a warm, chunky wool.

Use for blankets or cushion covers.

Make 4ch.
Round 1 (1tr, 1ch, 4tr, 1ch, 4tr, 1ch, 4tr, 1ch, 2tr) into the first ch st, ss into top of starting chain.
Round 2 3ch, tr into next tr, (2tr, 1ch, 2dc) into corner st ch, ⋆ 4tr into 4tr, (2tr, 1ch, 2tr) into corner st; repeat from ⋆ twice more, 2tr, join with a ss. Continue in this way, working 1tr into each tr and working the corners (1tr into corner st ch, 2tr, 1ch, 2tr), until square is the required size. Fasten off.

Lazy daisy

Work in a silky yarn for evening wear or an acrylic yarn for tableware.

Use for a lady's shawl or a luncheon set.

This square uses 2 colours, A and B. Using A, make 10ch and join into a ring with a ss into first ch.
Round 1 (10ch, dc into ring) 12 times. Break off A.
Round 2 Join in B to any 10-ch loop, 3ch, (2tr, 2ch, 3tr) in same loop, ⋆ 3htr in each of next 2 loops, (3tr, 2ch, 3tr) in next loop; repeat from ⋆ twice more, work 3htr in each of last 2 loops, join with a ss to 3rd ch of 3ch. Fasten off.

JOINING MEDALLIONS

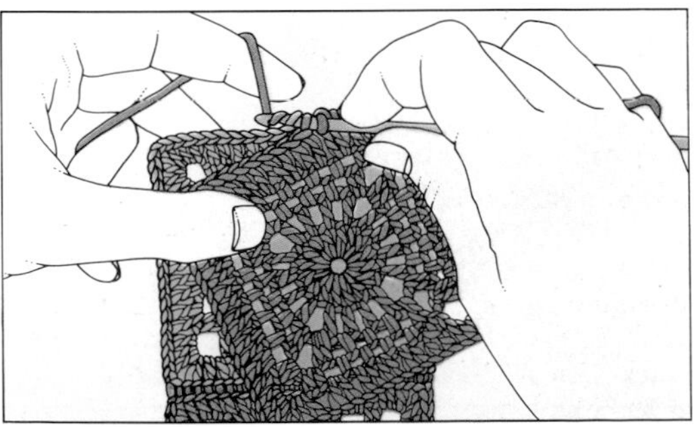

Place the patches face to face and join with slip stitch or with one of the methods shown on page 185.

Crochet edgings

Crochet edgings at their most decorative were designed to resemble as closely as possible the needle- and bobbin-made laces and were originally worked in the finest cottons on the smallest gauge hooks. However, they can look just as good though not so lace-like when worked in wools on larger gauge hooks. They are used to finish off or decorate a piece of work and can be made directly onto the crocheted or knitted fabric or worked separately and then joined to the fabric.

Working the edging direct

When working an edging directly onto a piece of crochet or knitting the first row is worked into the existing stitches.

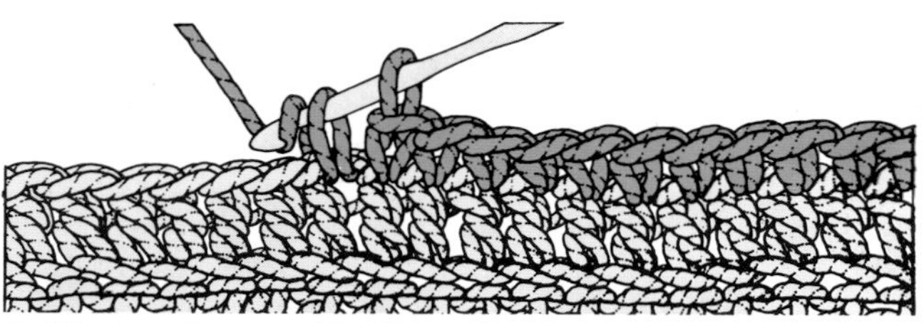

1 First work a row of double crochet in same or contrasting yarn along edge to serve as a base to edging.

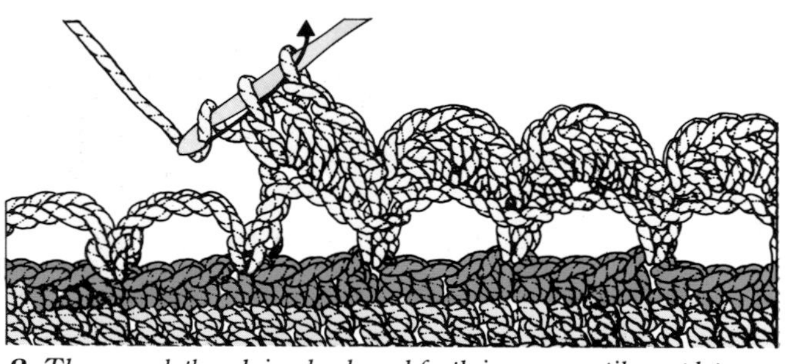

2 Then work the edging back and forth in rows until complete.

Joining the edging with slip stitch

When an edging is worked vertically along the strip it can only be joined to a fabric after completion. It should be applied to ordinary fabric with overcast or running stitch and to a piece of crochet or knitting with double crochet or with slip stitch (see page 169).

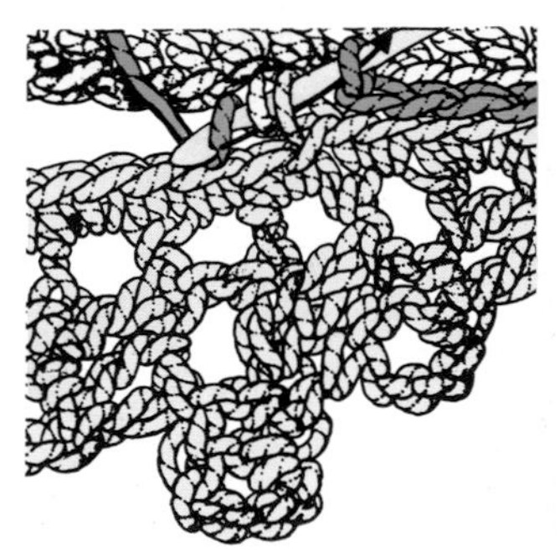

Make slip stitches passing hook through edging and fabric.

FRINGED BORDER

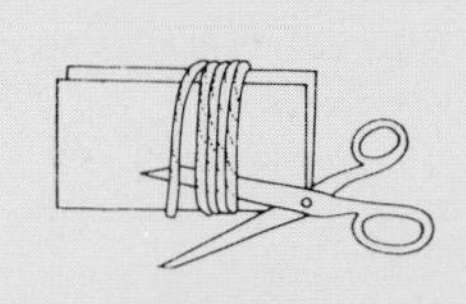

1 Wind yarn around a cardboard gauge which is the desired depth of the completed fringe. Cut ends at one side.

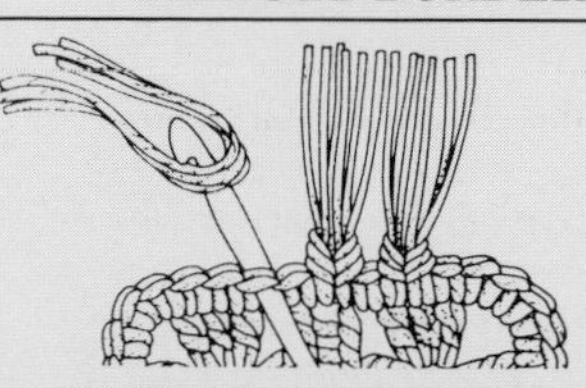

2 Fold 3 or 4 strands in half, insert hook in stitch and pull the loop of the strands through the stitch.

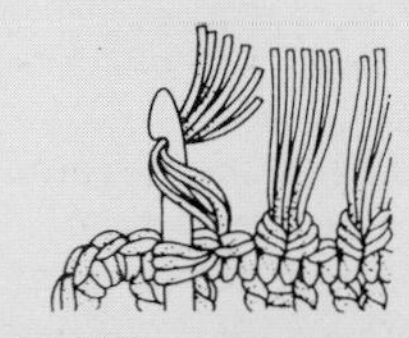

3 Pull the strands through the loop, and then, to tighten the knot, pull the strands away from the edge.

Edging patterns

These narrow edging patterns can be used in many different ways either to decorate collars, cuffs and pockets or furnishings such as lamp shades and cushion covers.

Arch edging

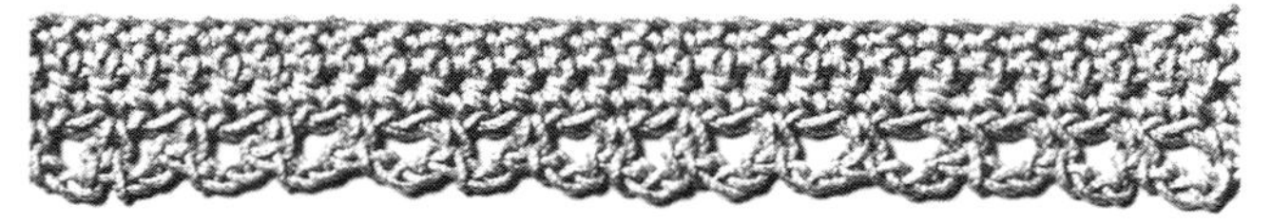

Worked into a row of dc on edge of work.
1dc into next dc, ⋆ 3ch, miss 1dc, 1dc into next dc, rep from ⋆ to end.

Wave edging

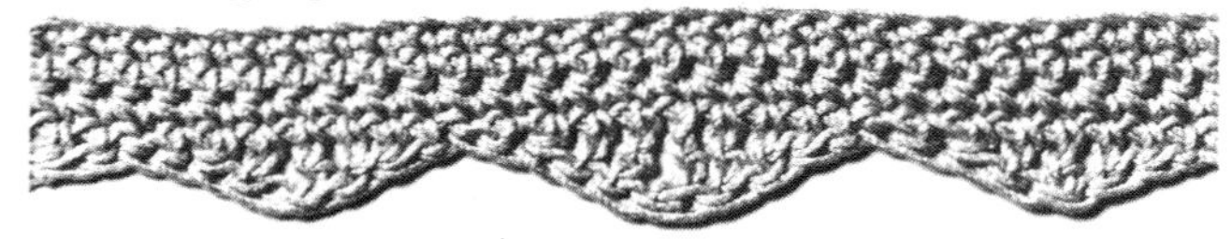

Worked into a row of dc on edge of work, having a number of dc divisible by 18, plus 1.
Ss into first st, ⋆ 1dc, 1htr, 1tr, 1dtr, 1tr, 1htr, 1dc, 1ss, 1dc, 1htr, 1tr, 1dtr, 1tr tr, 1dtr, 1tr, 1htr, 1dc, 1ss, rep from ⋆ to end.

Bicolour loop edging

Worked into a row of dc on edge of work, having a number of dc divisible by 4, plus 1.

This border uses 2 colours, A and B.
Row 1 Using A, work in dc to end of row. Break off yarn and return to beg of row.
Row 2 Using B, work in dc to end of row. Break off yarn and return to beg of row.
Row 3 Using A, 1dc into first dc, ⋆ 6ch, miss 3dc, 1dc into next dc, rep from ⋆ to end. Break off yarn and return to beg of row.
Row 4 Using B, 1dc into first dc, ⋆ 1ss into back half only of each of next 6ch, 1dc into next dc, rep from ⋆ to end.
Fasten off.

Picot loop edging

Make a length of ch as reqd, 1ch, turn.
Row 1 1dc into 2nd ch from hook, ⋆ 1ch, draw this ch up to the reqd length, and to keep the lps even put onto a pencil or a thick knitting needle, take hook out of lp, insert hook into the st below the lp, then into next ch along foundation ch, yrh, draw lp through ch, yrh, draw through 2lps on hook, rep from ⋆ to end.
Fasten off.

Crescent border

Make a ch the length reqd, having a number of ch divisible by 8, plus 5, 2ch, turn.
Row 1 1tr into 4th ch from hook, 1tr into each ch to end.
Row 2 ⋆ 5ch, miss next 3tr, 1tr into next tr, rep from ⋆ to end.
Row 3 Ss into first lp, ⋆ 3ch, 1tr into next lp, (5ch, 1tr into same lp) 3 times, 3ch, 1dc into next lp, rep from ⋆ to end.
Fasten off.

6

BASIC SEWING

Including Garment and Household Applications

Basic sewing techniques

Most people want to sew in order to make clothes or household items for themselves and their families. If you have never sewn before, begin by acquiring the basic skills and practising on simple projects. As a beginner it is best to choose a simple item with one major pattern piece.

Whether you are making a simple or a complicated item you should always work methodically.

Implements

There are certain essential implements for measuring, marking and cutting and these are illustrated below. A tape measure, preferably marked on both sides, is essential for taking body measurements. A metre stick is useful for taking straight measurements or marking hems.

Cutting equipment

Good quality cutting implements are necessary to avoid damaging your fabric. Dressmaker's shears, with a bent handle, are best for cutting out patterns. The angled handles allow you to cut but still leave the fabric flat. Pinking shears are necessary for finishing raw edges on fabrics liable to fray. Do not use them to cut out patterns. Sewing scissors are useful for more delicate cutting and trimming. Embroidery scissors should be kept for needlework and buttonhole cutting.

Marking equipment

The most common method of marking your fabric is with carbon and a tracing wheel. Tailor's chalk is ideal for fitting but can also be used for construction marks.

MEASURING, MARKING AND CUTTING IMPLEMENTS

Below are the essential implements for measuring, marking and cutting.

Make sure that your scissors are well maintained by regular oiling and sharpening.

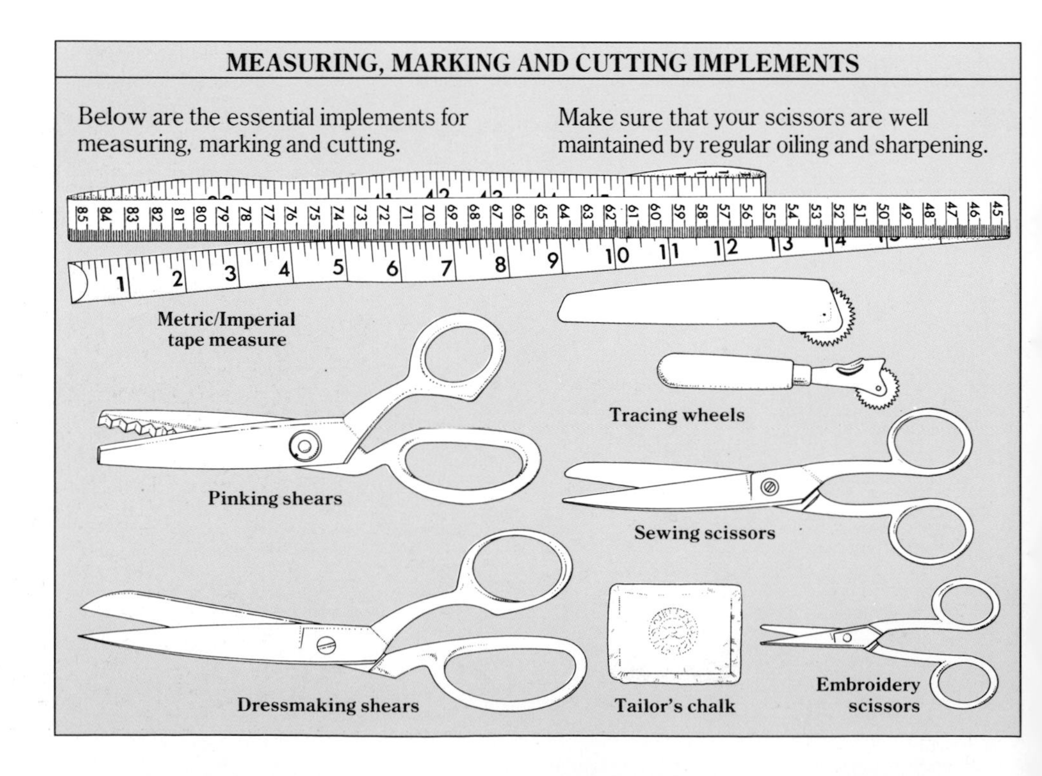

Stitching implements

The most important implements you will need for hand sewing are needles and threads. The criteria which will affect your choice of these are given in the table below: for example, the type of fabric being sewn and the fabric weight and texture. Implements such as unpickers or thimbles, while not essential, are aids to easier and speedier sewing.

Needles

Needle design varies according to purpose. Sharps, of medium length, can be used on most fabric weights. Betweens are smaller, allowing them to take fine stitches. Use long milliner's needles for tacking.

Sharp

Between

Milliner

Pins

It is best to buy dressmaker's rustless, brass or stainless steel silk pins. Use extra fine pins for delicate fabrics.

1in. (2.5cm) fine pin

Dressmaker's pin

Unpicker

An unpicker has a sharp, curved head and is used to unpick seams. Insert the head into the seam to be undone, slitting threads as you do so.

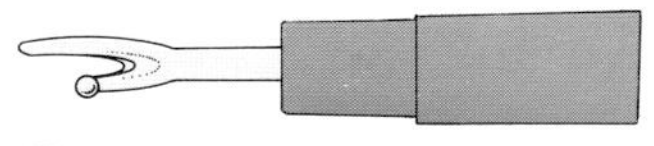

Unpicker

Thimbles

Thimbles fit on the middle finger of the hand which holds the needle enabling you to push the needle through the fabric painlessly.

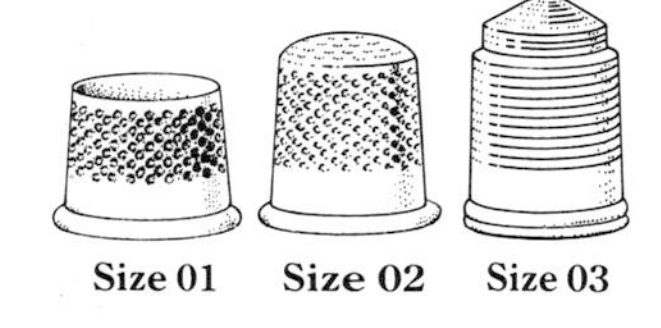

Size 01 Size 02 Size 03

Threads

Select your thread according to fabric weight, colour and purpose. For example, do not use a fine silk thread on a heavy canvas because the threads will break too easily. Thread should be the same colour or a darker shade than your fabric. Use the following as a guide.

Tacking cotton: The loose twist allows easy breaking and is ideal for tacking.

General purpose cotton, size 50: Machine and hand sewing on cottons, rayons, linens. When mercerized, it is smooth and silky.

General purpose silk, fine (size A): Strong but flexible, used for silk or wool. It is fine enough to leave no holes or impressions after pressing.

General purpose nylon, fine (size A): Use on light- to medium-weight synthetics (especially nylon knits).

General purpose polyester, size 50: Suitable for most fabrics, especially woven synthetics, knits or stretch fabrics.

General purpose cotton-wrapped polyester, size 40: Use on heavy vinyl or upholstery fabrics.

Pressing equipment

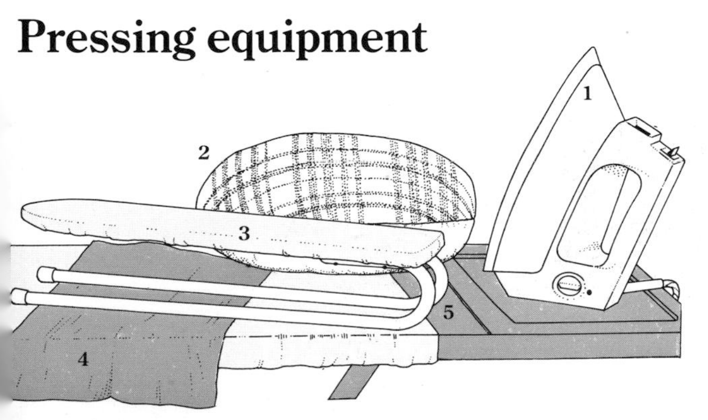

Basic pressing equipment 1 Steam iron 2 Tailor's ham (used for curved areas) 3 Sleeve board 4 Pressing cloth 5 Ironing board

Introduction to machine sewing

A number of different types of sewing machine are available, from the simplest hand-operated models to the latest electric ones which have a number of sophisticated attachments.

Choose a machine depending on the type of sewing you do and on whether you want to progress from simple sewing to more complicated tailored and embroidered garments. The principle of operation is the same for all types of machines. An instruction book is always included with the machine which will tell you exactly how it works.

How the machine works

A sewing machine combines two separate threads to make stitches. The top reel of thread is fed through the fabric by a needle and looped with the bobbin thread to form a stitch. The fabric is guided through the machine by hand, and is held firm by a presser foot.

1 Spool pin
2 Thread guide
3 Take-up lever
4 Tension disc and regulator
5 Presser foot
6 Feed
7 Bobbin case
8 Stitch length regulator
9 Stitch width regulator
10 Handwheel

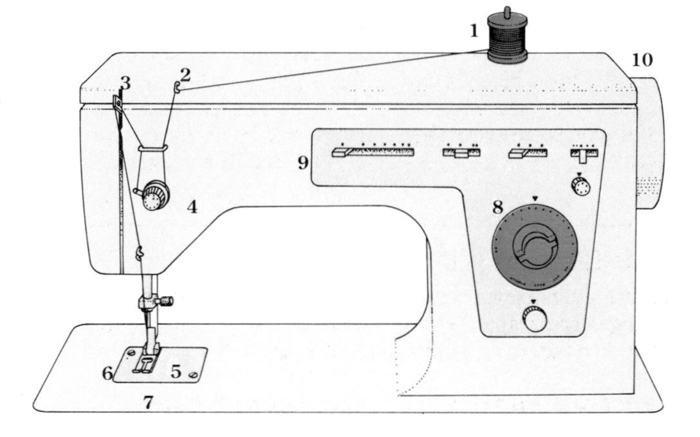

Winding the bobbin

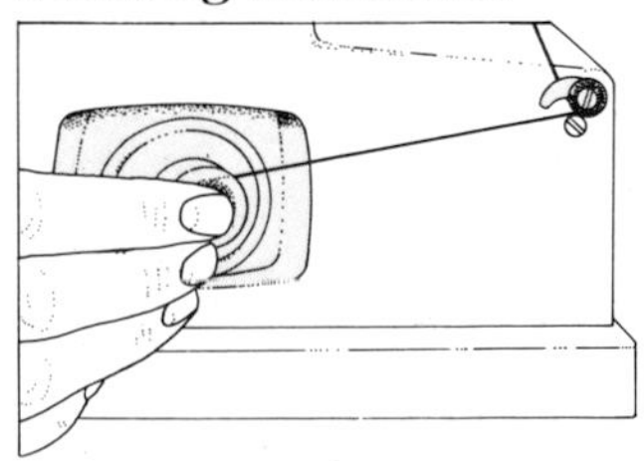

The bobbin on the machine will always need to be wound, but the position of the bobbin winder can vary. Make sure it is evenly wound and not too full or the thread will break.

Threading the needle

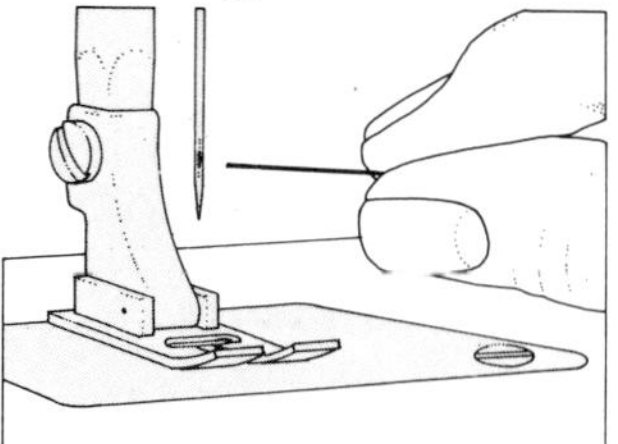

First raise the needle to expose the eye. The thread guide should be at its highest position so the needle will not unthread when you start machining. Follow the instructions for your machine.

Drawing up the thread

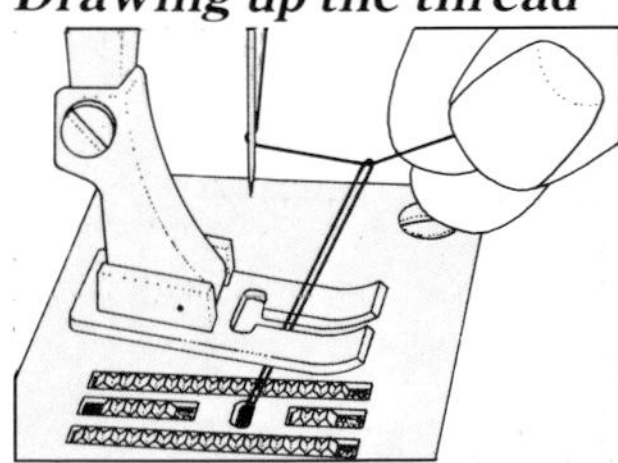

Turn the handwheel until the needle enters the bobbin case and returns to its highest position. As the needle rises it will pull up a loop of bobbin thread. Pull the loop to bring up the bobbin thread.

Tension

Most machines have tension controls for the needle and bobbin threads. A perfect stitch can only be formed if the tensions balance drawing the threads evenly into the fabric.

Correct tension

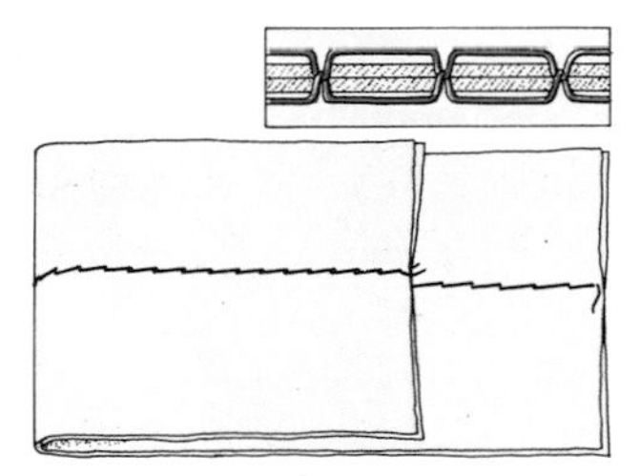

When the pressure is correct on both threads the link formed with each stitch is centred between the fabric layers. Equal amounts of top and bottom thread should have been used to produce the stitches, and there should be no puckering of the fabric.

Top thread too tight

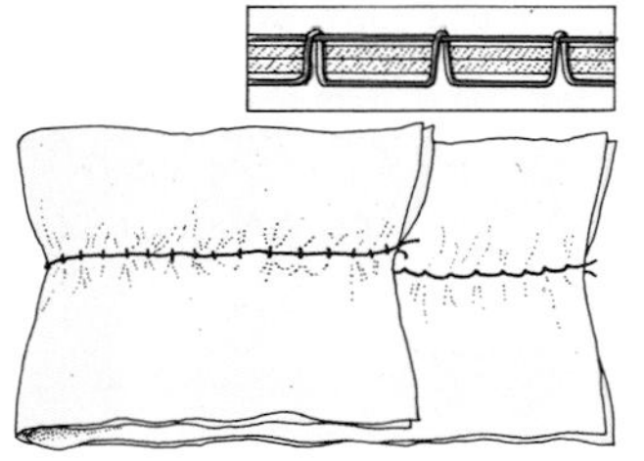

Look at the position of the stitch links. With too much tension these will be nearer the top fabric. Excessive top tension results in too little thread for the stitch causing the fabric to pucker and the stitches to break easily. To correct, turn the tension dial to lower number.

Top thread too loose

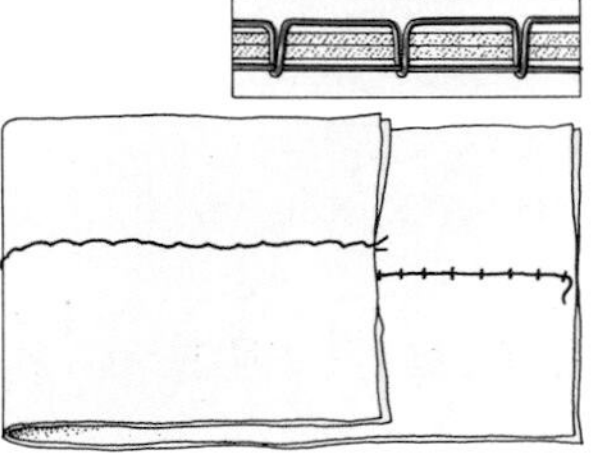

When the stitch links appear near the bottom layer of fabric the top thread tension is too loose. Too little tension results in too much thread, producing a floppy and imprecise seam. The fabric may also pucker. To correct this, turn the tension dial to a higher number.

Pressure and feed

Pressure and feed interact to produce even stitching. The presser foot exerts downward pressure on the fabric, so that the layers move through evenly. The feed plate exerts an upward force to move the fabric under the presser foot.

Correct pressure

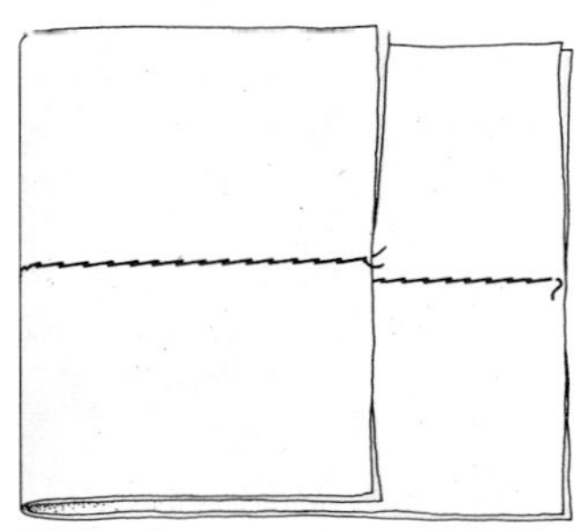

Under the correct pressure, the fabric layers feed through the machine evenly and easily. The stitches are of an even length and tension and the fabric therefore shows no sign of damage.

Too much pressure

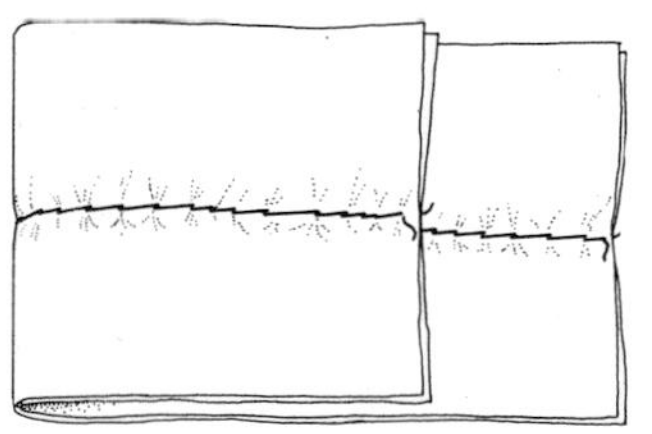

With too much pressure the top fabric may slip while the bottom puckers up. The stitches may appear uneven in length and tension, or the fabric itself may be pinched up. Correct by dialling pressure regulator to a lower number.

Too little pressure

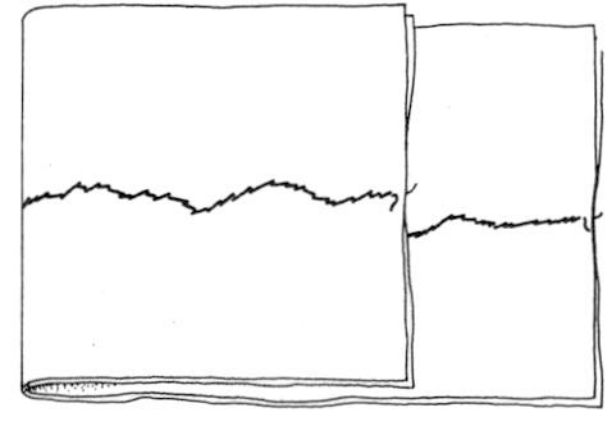

Too little pressure causes irregular feeding. Stitches may be of uneven length and tension and in some cases the fabric may be caught and pulled into the bobbin area. Rectify by dialling pressure regulator to a higher number.

Machine stitching

A well-maintained machine will produce perfect stitches providing you use the right needle and thread for the fabric, with the correct tension.

The basic machine stitch is a running stitch. Use a short stitch length for sewing seams on lightweight fabrics; regular stitch length for general household sewing, and long stitch length for tacking, easing and gathering.

Special stitches
Most machines are capable of special stitches. Multistitch, in which both length and width can vary, is used for edging, mending and attaching elastic. Overcasting stitch is used to produce neat durable seams on bulky fabrics and those which fray. Satin stitch is used for buttonholing or edging.

Fine stitch length

Regular stitch length

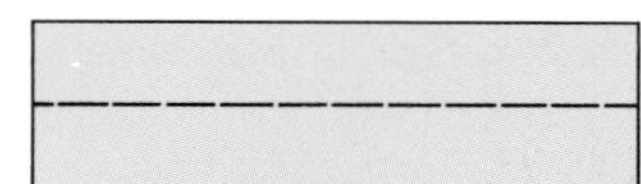
Long stitch length

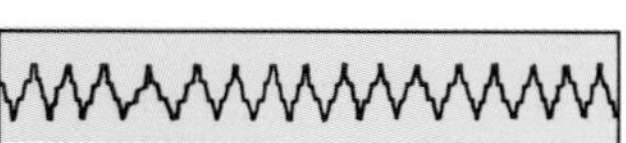
Multistitch

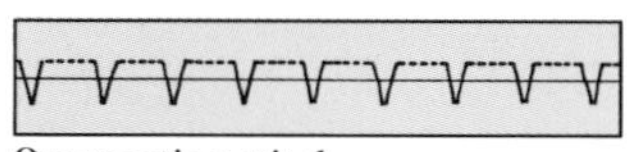
Overcasting stitch

Satin stitch

Learning to stitch

If you have never used a machine before, practise on a piece of paper, with the machine unthreaded. Always start to sew slowly, learning to control starting and stopping.

Starting to stitch

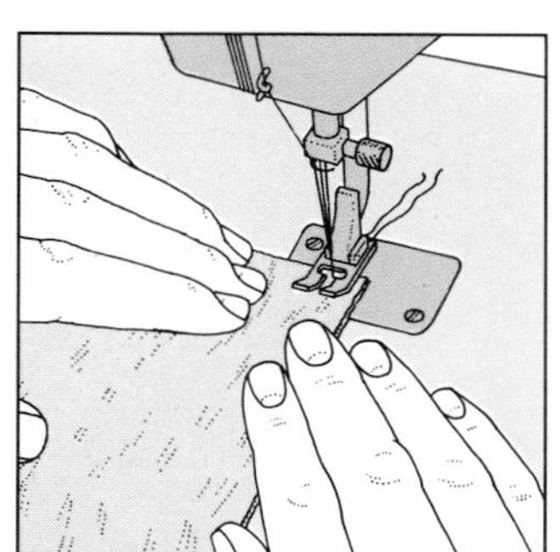

Raise the take-up lever to its highest position, pull the bobbin and top threads underneath and behind the presser foot. Then put the fabric underneath with the bulk of the fabric to the left and the seam edge to the right. Put the needle into the fabric where you want to begin. Lower the presser foot and start to sew.

Finishing off

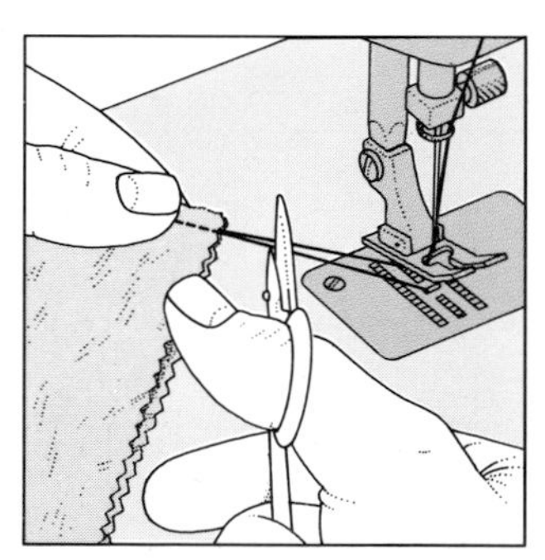

When you come to the end of your stitching line take the needle to its highest position and raise the presser foot. Withdraw your work by pulling it back and away from the needle. Leaving a short length, cut the two threads. Pull the needle thread through to the underside and then fasten the threads securely. Trim ends.

Corners and curves

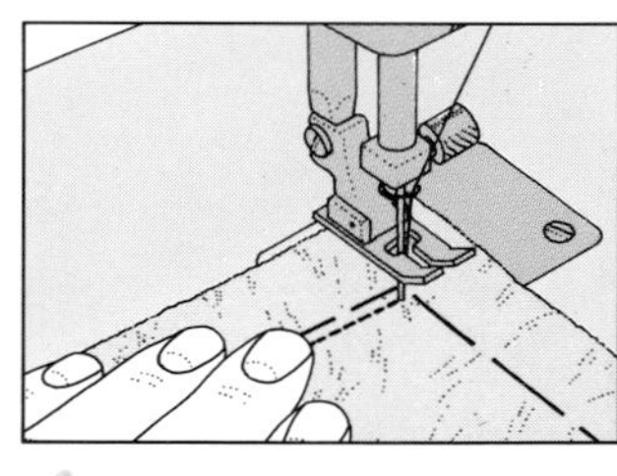

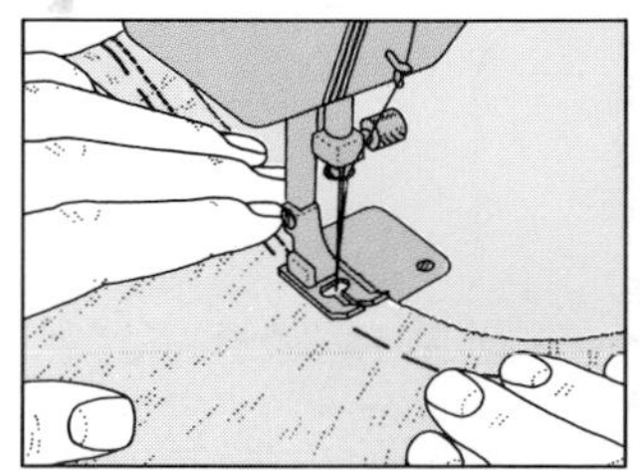

To stitch corners or curves you will need to "pivot" the fabric. Stitch up to turning point. Raise the needle until it is about to leave the fabric. Raise the presser foot and pivot the fabric. Then lower the presser foot and continue.

Choosing machine needles

The size and type of point are the determining factors in needle choice. Sizes range from 9 to 18 (the lower the number, the finer the needle). To prevent damage to light-weight fabric use a fine needle. A heavier fabric will require a thicker needle to prevent needle deflection or breakage. The type of point is very important. A sharp-point is most commonly used and is recommended for all types of woven fabric. A ball-point needle has a round tip and is used when sewing knitwear because the point slides between the yarns instead of piercing them. A wedge-point needle is designed specifically for leathers and vinyls to minimize the risk of the fabric splitting.

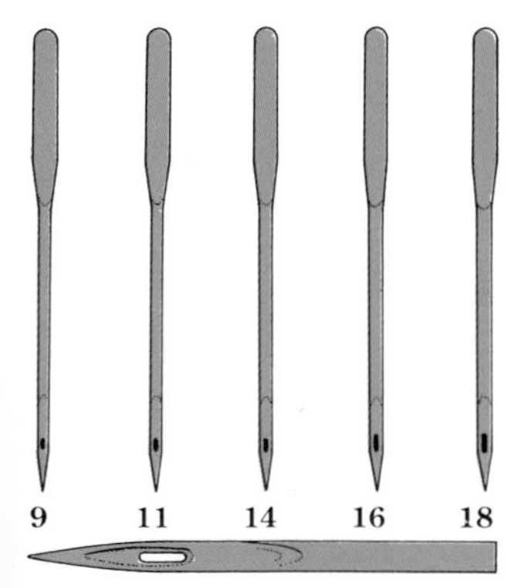

A sharp-point needle is recommended for woven fabrics

A ball-point needle should be used for knitted fabrics

A wedge-point needle is needed for leathers and vinyls

Selecting threads

Choose thread according to the type of fabric being used. Use synthetic threads with man-made fibres and mercerized cotton or silk thread with cotton or linen. Woollen fabrics should be sewn with silk or synthetic threads as they are capable of stretching with the fabric. On all types of thread the higher the number on the label, the finer the thread.

Needle and thread selection chart

Fabric	Thread	Needle	Stitches per in. (2.5cm)
Light-weight Chiffon, organza, fine lace, lawn, voile	Silk, size A, nylon, size A, mercerized cotton, extra fine (any fibre), size 60–100	9 or 11	10–15
Medium-weight Velvet, gingham, crepe, corduroy, stretch terry, brocade, linen, some denims	Polyester, cotton-wrapped polyester, mercerized cotton, size 50–60	11 or 14	10–12
Heavy Wide rib corduroy, terry cloth	Polyester, cotton-wrapped polyester, heavy duty (any fibre), size 30–40	16 or 18	8–12
Very heavy Canvas, upholstery fabric	Polyester, cotton-wrapped polyester, heavy duty (any fibre), size 20	16 or 18	8–12

TOP STITCHING YOUR GARMENT

Top stitching is used for decorative as well as functional purposes. Make all alterations to your garment before you top stitch it and tack close to the proposed sewing line. Use thicker or contrasting thread and the longer stitch setting when using as decoration. When using as a strengthener, set for the regular stitch length and sew through the seam allowances.

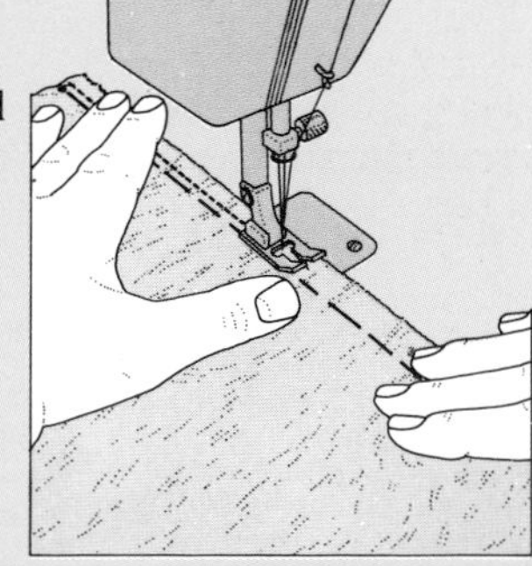

Dressmaking

Taking measurements
Personal measurements must be taken before you buy or alter your pattern. Ask a friend to measure you, as this is easier and more accurate. Keep the tape pulled taut.

Bodice
Measure your waist, then from neck to waist and from the centre of your shoulder, over the bust point to the waistline. From the centre of the shoulder measure to the point of the bust. Measure from the neckline to the top of the sleeve and from the back shoulder to the waist. Measure your bust with the tape slightly higher at the back. Take the back measurement from side to side at mid-armhole point.

Skirt
Take the waist measurement as for the bodice. Then the centre front waist to the desired hemline. Also the centre back waist to the hem and side waist to hem. Take your hip measurement around the fullest part.

Sleeve
Measure from your shoulder to the wrist, with your arm bent to waist height. Also measure shoulder to elbow and elbow to wrist. With the arm straightened, take your inside arm length from under the armhole to the wrist. Measure your upper arm around the widest part and around the elbow with the arm bent to waist length. Lastly, take your wrist measurement.

Bodice and skirt measurement

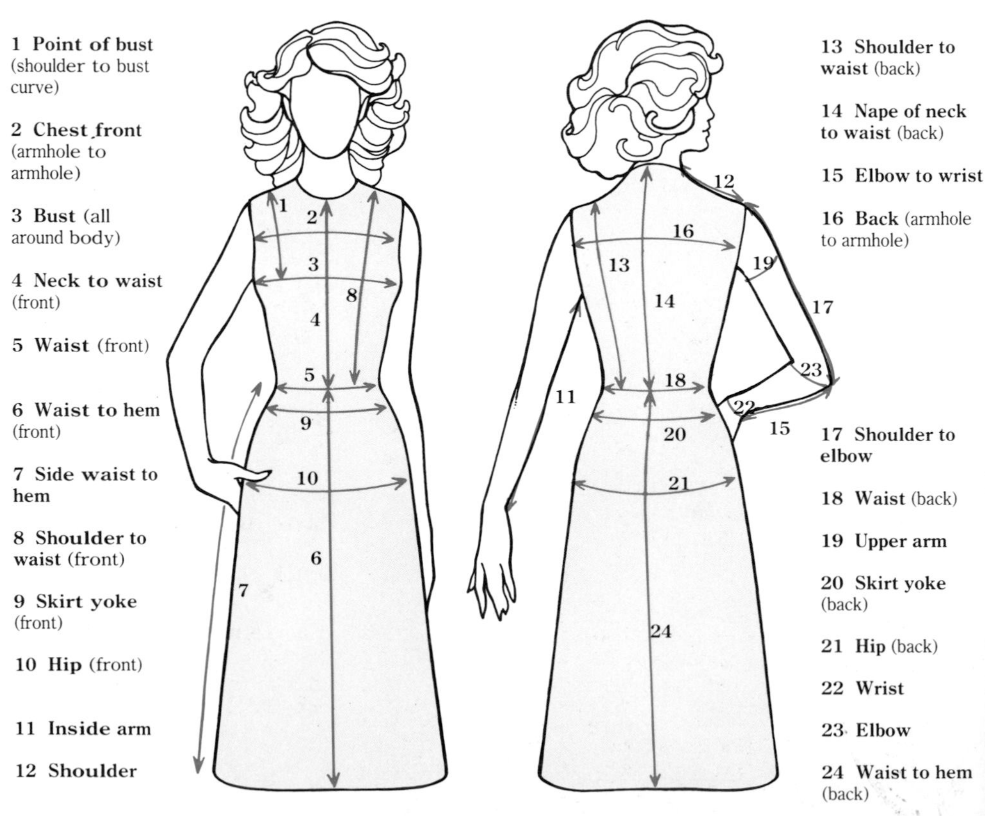

Choosing fabric

If you are using a bought pattern the pattern envelope usually contains a chart giving details of the amount of fabric you will need to buy. Advice on which type of fabric to buy is sometimes included. The fabric should be as crease resistant as possible. Take a corner of the fabric and crush it in your hand. The wrinkles should fall out. If they do not, any garment using such fabric will display the same amount of "wrinkle". Buy only the amount specified on the pattern envelope.

Hints for beginners

Beginners should make garments using light- to medium-weight, non-slip fabrics such as cottons, brushed rayon, Viyella, polyester, light wool. Avoid very light-weight fabrics such as chiffon or georgette and heavy-weight, loosely woven fabrics such as tweeds. Do not use heavily patterned fabric or fabric with a napped surface (where the pile runs in one direction only).

Checking for suitability

Check the fabric's suitability for the pattern: ie. if the pattern is gathered or pleated ensure that the fabric will adapt to the design. If in doubt ask the sales assistant for advice.

Check the fabric's suitability for you by draping the fabric near your face to see if the colour suits you.

Simple garments and suitable materials for beginners		
Garments	**Material**	**Linings**
Dresses and skirts Pleated	Light-weight, firm woven without print	Lining helps give a light, soft fabric more body
Seamed	Light-weight, firm woven without print, or knitted	Lining can be a simple 'A' shape
Plain	Light-weight or firm woven in any pattern, or knitted	
Gathered	Light-weight or soft fabric, any pattern or knitted	
Tops and shirts Loose fitting	Light-weight, firm, soft or knitted	
Fitted	Large patterned fabric unsuitable. Firm woven or knitted best	
Trousers	Medium-weight. Knits unsuitable. Strong zips needed for openings	Unlined

Construction marks

Every bought pattern has construction marks and it is essential to follow them.

Cutting line This is a continuous line on the outer edge of the pattern.

Stitch line This is a broken line near the cutting line.

Alteration line This double line indicates where the pattern should be shortened or lengthened.

Fold line This is represented by a line with arrows at right angles at either end, pointing to the pattern edge. It is always placed on a fold of material so that a double piece of fabric can be cut.

Grain line This appears as a line with arrows at either end. It always runs parallel to the selvedge, following the true grain of the fabric.

Easing line This appears as a row of short broken lines with an arrow and a dot at each end.

Gathering line Two rows of short broken lines with arrows at each end. Dots mark the gathering points.

Balance marks These are generally represented by notches, either single or double. Use these to match one piece of fabric to another.

Darts These are represented by broken lines meeting at a point.

Zip position This is noted by a line of small triangles, showing the exact position of the zip.

Buttonholes The position and size of buttonholes is represented by a circle or dot with a horizontal line.

Working from a pattern

If you are working from a bought pattern, your envelope will state how much fabric you need to buy, according to your size, the fabric width and whether it is napped or not. Having obtained the fabric, assemble all the equipment you will need for cutting and prepare a clear surface.

Inside the pattern envelope, you will find a guide on how to lay out the fabric and deal with different fabric widths. Remember to leave enough space for turnings and facings.

Check that you have all the pattern pieces before you start work.

Narrow fabric

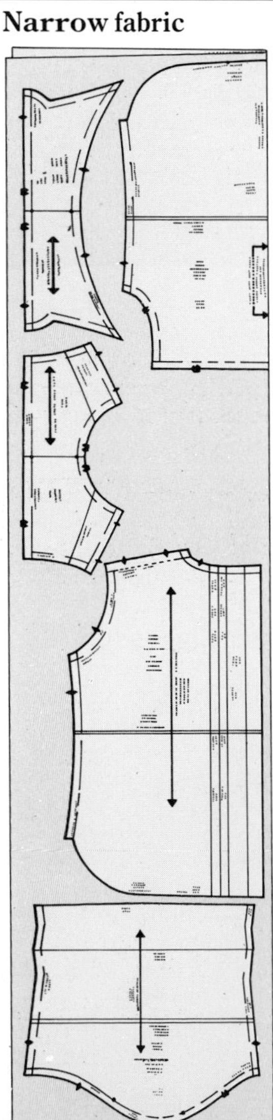

Wide frabric

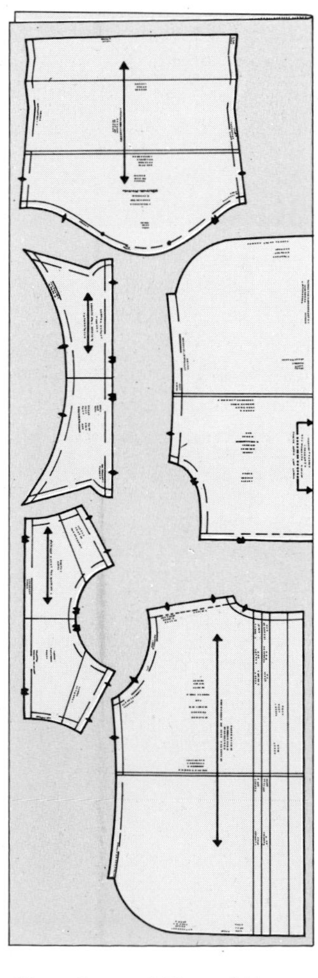

Above *Pattern laid on a fold on wide fabric*
Left *Pattern laid on a fold on narrow fabric*

Cutting the fabric

Having laid out your pieces correctly, pin them securely to the fabric. Place the pins, using as few as possible, diagonally well within the seam lines.

Cutting

Before you begin, look at the cutting checklist. Always cut on a flat surface with sharp scissors. Follow the seam allowance line, securing the fabric with one hand as you cut. Cut all the main pattern pieces first. Make sure that all necessary marks are transferred before unpinning.

Cutting checklist

1 Do you have all the pattern pieces for the design?
2 Are the pattern pieces straight on the grain of the fabric? Make sure there are no flaws or creases in the fabric.
3 If the fabric has a nap, are the pattern pieces lying in one direction only?
4 If the fabric is printed, are the pattern pieces arranged so that the fabric design matches when joined together?
5 If the pattern is to be used double, have you the right pattern edge on the fold?
6 Is the fabric folded with the correct sides together?
7 Is the fabric lying on an even surface?

Laying out napped fabrics or one-way designs

If you use a napped fabric like velvet, the pile must run the same way on each piece of the garment. Therefore the pattern pieces must be laid out so that they all follow the same direction. The pattern will take more fabric than one without nap because you cannot lay pattern pieces top to toe. You can test for nap by smoothing the fabric with your hand. If in doubt, ask the sales assistant. One-way designs are similarly laid out.

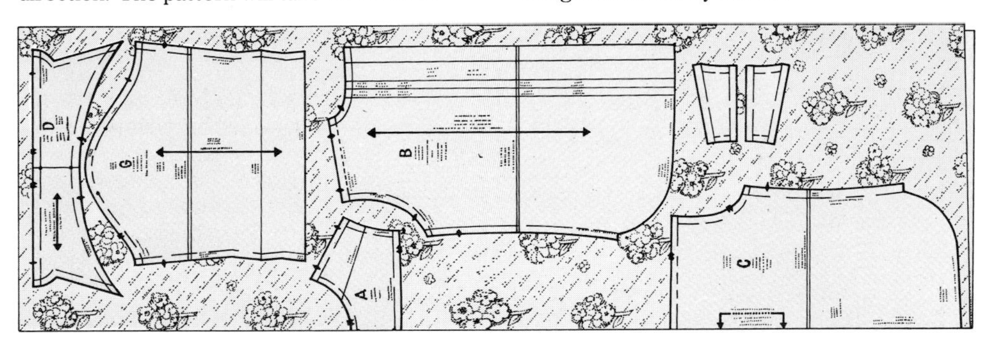

Laying out fabric with checks and stripes

Checks and stripes must match exactly at the side seams, centre seams or openings, waistlines, armholes and sleeves. The pattern pieces will need careful positioning. The key to this is the notches. Shift pattern pieces so they align on the same check or stripe. Be careful to match the checks and stripes at the line where the seam is stitched, rather than on the edge of the seam allowance and make any alterations to the pattern before laying out.

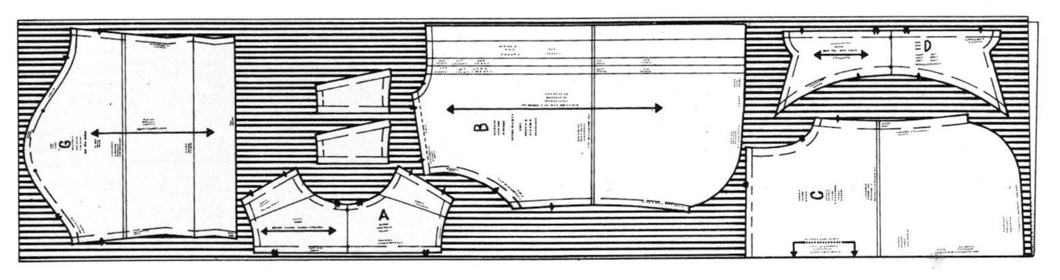

MARKING THE FABRIC

Once you have cut out the pattern pieces, leave them pinned to your fabric so that you can transfer any marks.

If you are using a tracing wheel you will also need dressmaker's carbon paper. Put the carbon paper, coloured side down, on the wrong side of the fabric. With the pattern on top of the carbon paper, trace along the markings using a ruler as a guide. It is helpful to mark the ends of the darts, points of slashes and other small symbols with horizontal bars. Transfer marks with short firm strokes using a ruler as an accurate guide.

Hand sewing

Almost everything you sew needs some hand stitching, so you must be able to handle a needle and thread competently. The stitch tension should always be even, and the work finished off securely. Unless directed otherwise you should work from right to left. Start by inserting the needle into the wrong side of the fabric.

Tacking stitch

Tacking is used to hold fabric together temporarily, but quite securely.

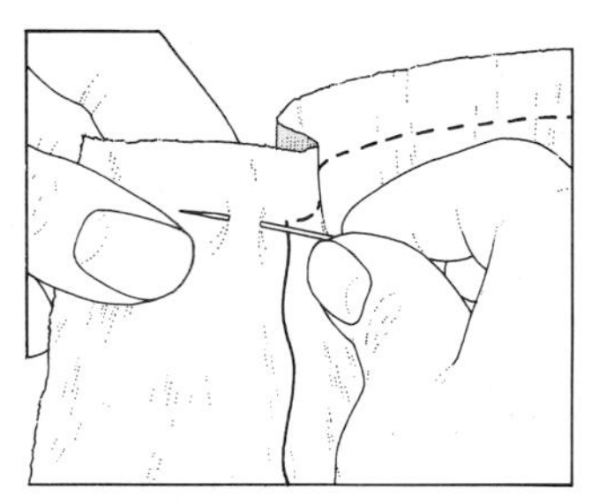

Make even stitches about 1/4in. to 3/8in. (6mm to 10mm) long.

When easing one layer of fabric to another, hold the layer to be eased on top and gather this top layer of fabric gently as you stitch.

Oversewing

Oversewing is used to finish seam edges on fabrics which fray easily.

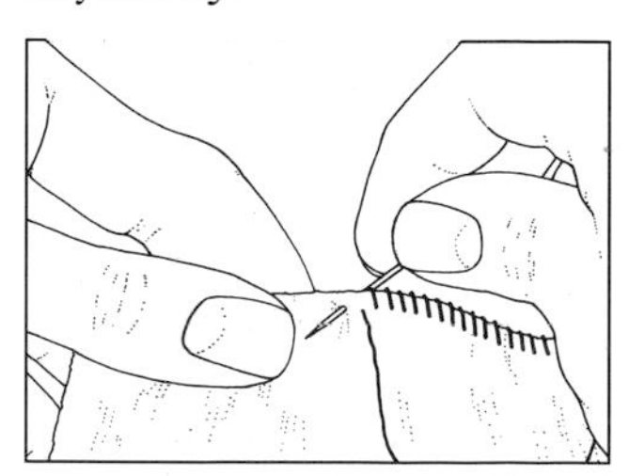

Hold the fabric with the edge to be worked away from you. Insert the needle 1/8in. to 1/4in. (3mm to 6mm) from the edge and bring the thread over the edge of the fabric. Make the next stitch 1/4in. (6mm) further on.

Running stitch

Running stitch is mainly used for gathering fabric. Make sure you have enough thread in the needle to make an unbroken line of stitches.

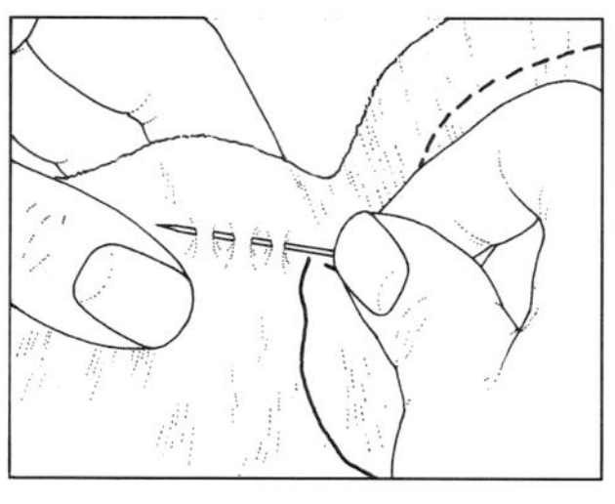

Take several very small stitches on to the needle before drawing the thread through.

Buttonhole stitch

Buttonhole stitch is worked with the needle pointing towards you, and the fabric edge away from you.

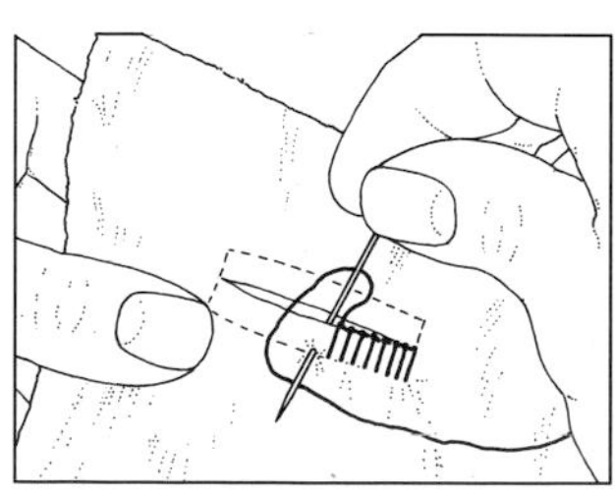

Insert the needle into the right side of the edge of the buttonhole. Bring it out 1/8in. (3mm) below. Loop the thread hanging from the eye of the needle from right to left under the point of the needle and draw the needle upwards to knot the thread at the buttonhole edge.

Back stitch

Back stitch is useful for making strong seams and for finishing off a line of stitching.

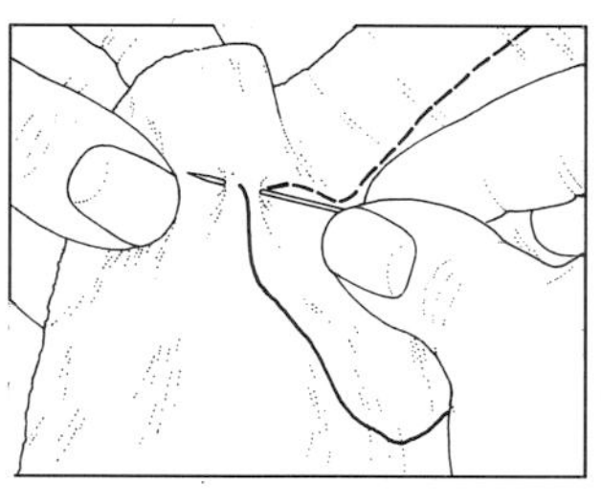

Make a small stitch back from left to right. Then make a double length stitch forwards on the wrong side of the work so the needle emerges a stitch's length in front of the first one.

Hem stitch

Hem stitch is used for hems on medium-weight or lightweight fabrics. The stitch size will depend on the fabric. The thread should not be pulled taut or the fabric will pucker.

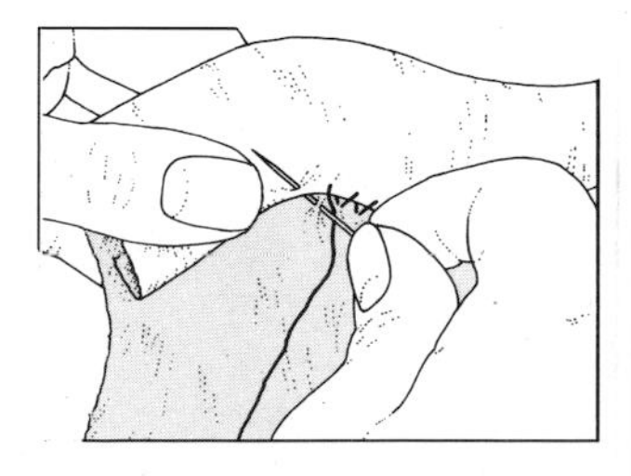

With the work held as shown, pick up a thread of the single fabric on the needle point and then catch a thread of the fold on the point of the needle before pulling through.

Blind hemming stitch

Blind hemming is worked on the inside fold of the hem so that the stitches are almost invisible. The thread should not be pulled taut.

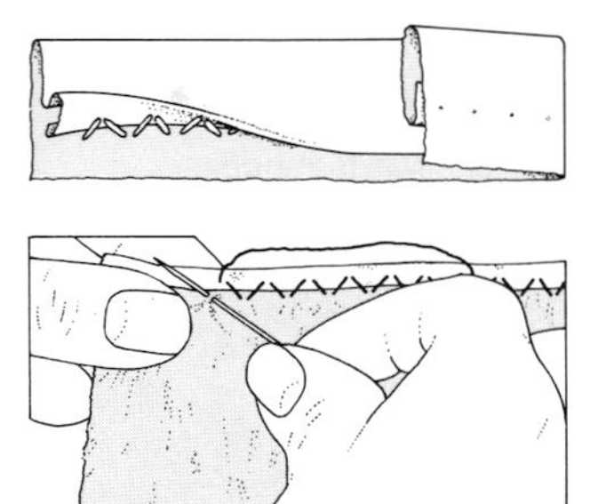

Holding the work with the fold of the hem towards you as shown, take a very small stitch inside the hem fold edge, picking up a thread of the single fabric on the point of the needle before taking another stitch on the inside hem fold of the garment you are making.

Slip stitch

Slip stitch is used for flat hemming with a turned-in edge on lightweight to medium-weight fabrics. The thread should not be pulled taut, and the stitches should be worked about ¼in. (6mm) apart.

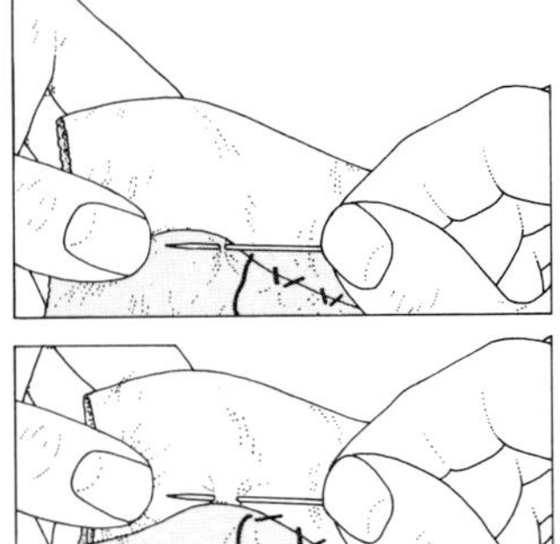

Pick up 1 or 2 threads of the single fabric and then slide the needle through the hem fold for about ¼in. (6mm). Draw the thread through.

Herringbone stitch

Herringbone is used for securing hems on heavy fabrics which do not fray easily and on stretch fabrics. It is worked from left to right.

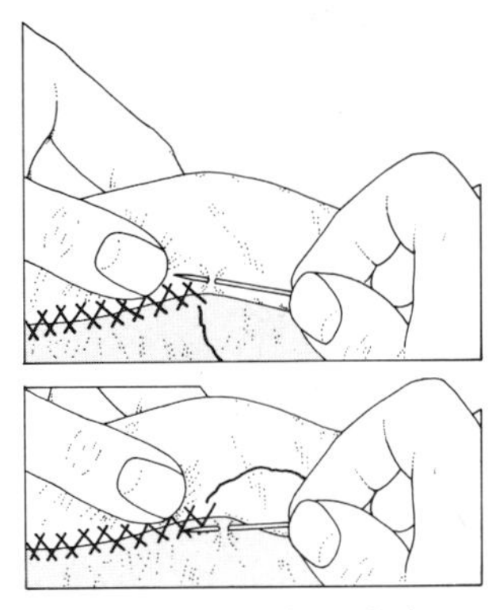

Insert the needle through the inside of the hem turning, then right and down to make a small stitch in the single fabric. Move the needle diagonally up and right and take a small stitch from right to left in the hem fold, but not through it.

TYING A KNOT

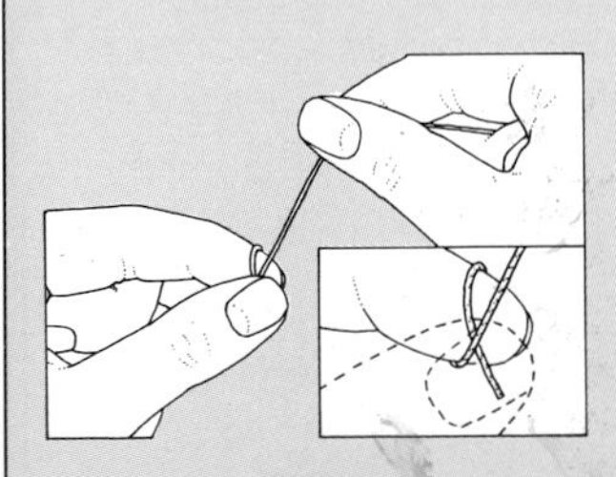

1 Hold the end of the thread between the thumb and forefinger of your left hand. With your right hand, bring the thread over and around the tip of the left forefinger, crossing the threads over.

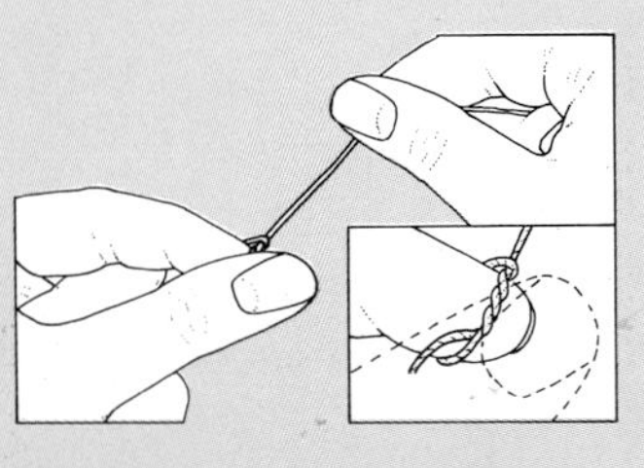

2 With the long end of thread held taut in your right hand, roll the thread around the loop by pushing the thumb of your left hand up towards the tip of your left forefinger.

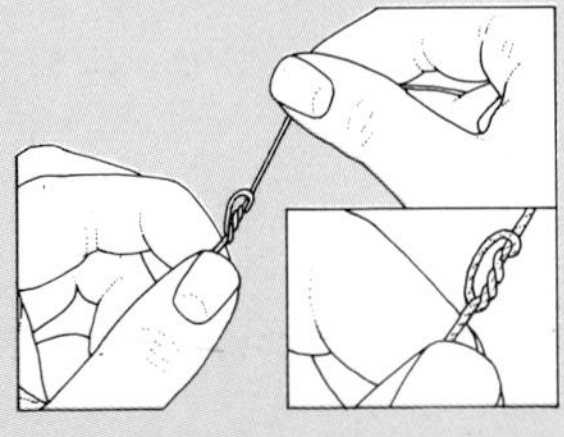

3 Slip the loop off your left forefinger, still holding the thread taut in your right hand. Pinch the loop with the thumb and forefinger of the left hand and pull the knob tight.

Seams

A seam is made when you join two or more pieces of fabric together, usually with a line of machine stitching. You can sew by hand, if you wish, using back stitch (see page 202).

Always make sure that the needle and thread used are appropriate for the fabric weight and texture (see page 197). Because the seams of a garment must withstand wear and tear, the beginning and end of the line of stitching should be secured with a few back stitches. Enough fabric should always be left between the line of stitching and the fabric edge to prevent fraying.

The type of fabric and garment should determine the seam you choose. A flat seam can be used on most garments and the seam edges should always be finished as appropriate for the fabric you are using.

Flat seam

A flat seam is the basic seam, joining the edges of two pieces of fabric. It is used on normal weight fabrics where there is no special strain on the seam.

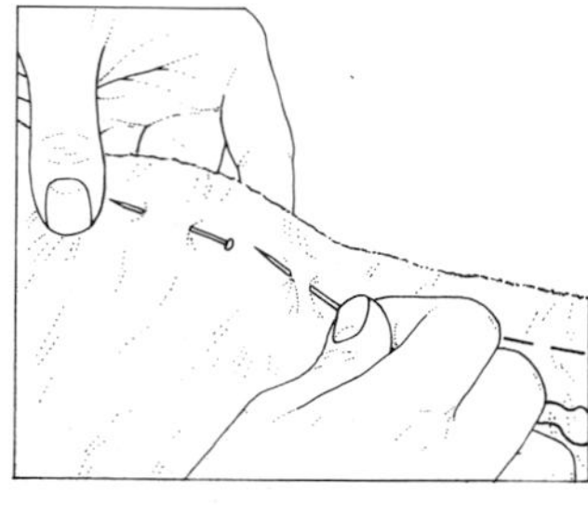

1 With the right sides of the fabric facing, pin the fabric together at both ends of the seam line and at intervals along the seam line, leaving an allowance of ¾in. (2cm).

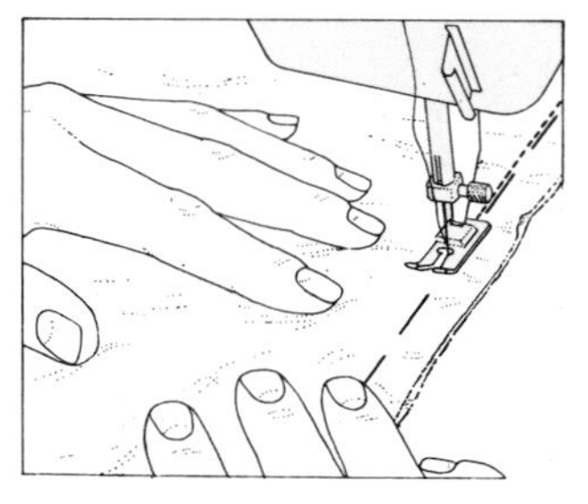

2 Tack close to the seam line and remove the pins. Then stitch along the seam line, back stitching a couple of stitches at each end to secure.

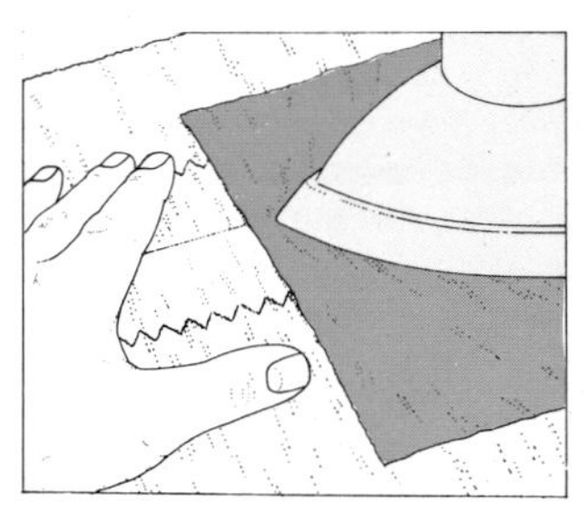

3 After removing the tacking stitches finish the seam edge by pinking it or as necessary for the fabric. Press the seam as stitched and then press it open as shown.

French seam

A French seam is generally used for fine fabrics or for those which fray easily. It is a seam within a seam and when finished should be about ¼in. (6mm) or less in width.

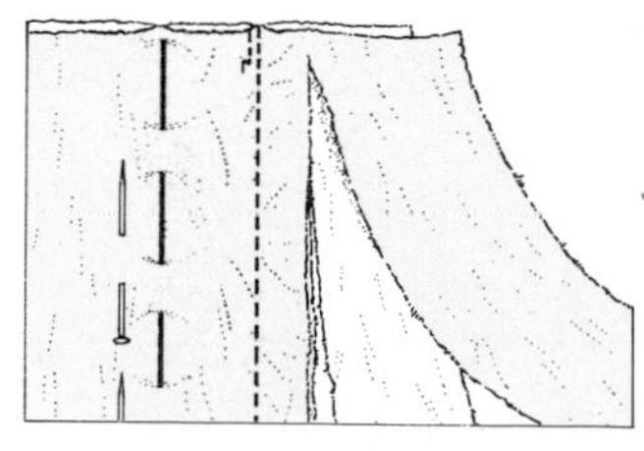

1 Place the wrong sides of the fabric together. Pin and tack close to the seam line. Then stitch ¼in. (6mm) to the right of it. Press and trim seam allowance.

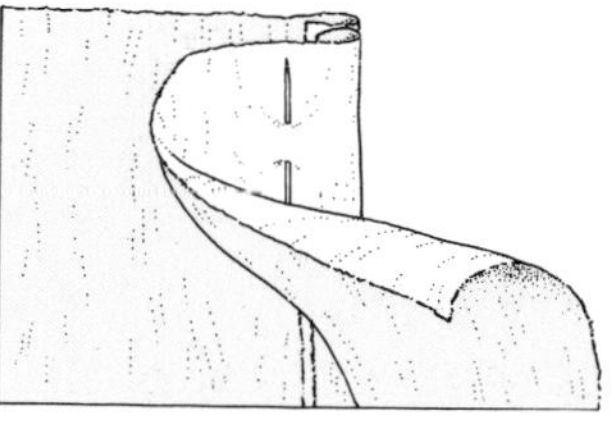

2 Press the seam open. Then turn the right sides of the fabric together. Fold on the stitch line and press. Tack in position.

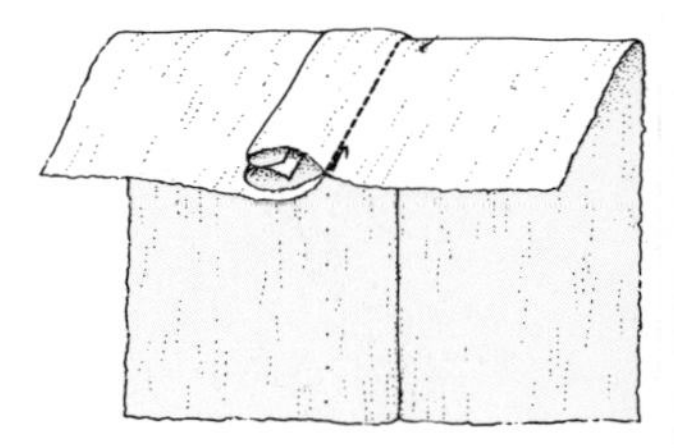

3 Stitch along the seam line and press as stitched.

Curved and corner seams

Curved pieces of fabric can be stitched together using a flat seam. However, special attention has to be paid to easing the curved pieces of fabric together as they are being sewn (see page 196 for instructions on machining curves and corners).

Making a curved seam

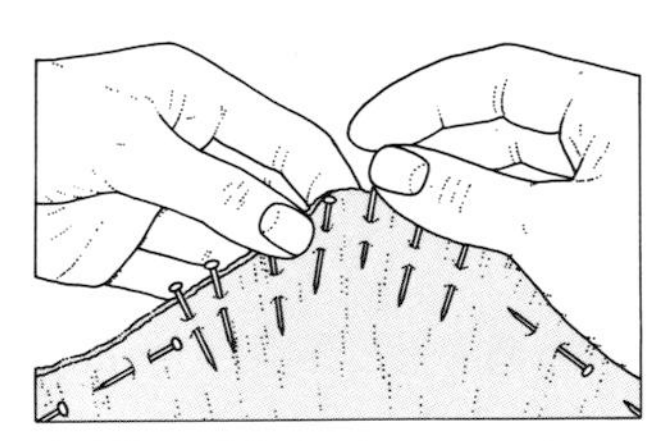

1 Place fabric pieces together, right sides facing, and pin along seam line, easing fabric along the inside curve. Stitch along the seam line using a shorter stitch length than normal for your fabric.

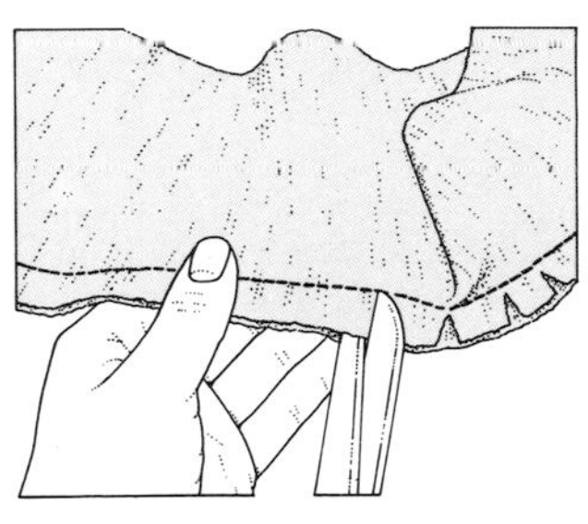

2 Clip the seam allowance on the outside curve and notch the seam allowance on the inside curve so that it lies flat.

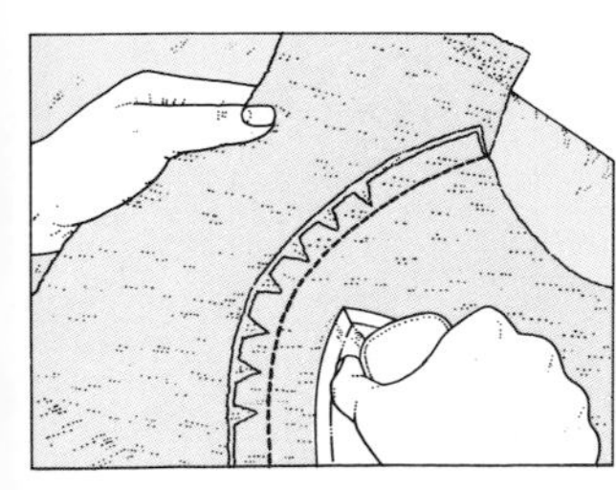

3 With the iron correctly set, press seam flat to one side and then press it open.

Making a corner seam

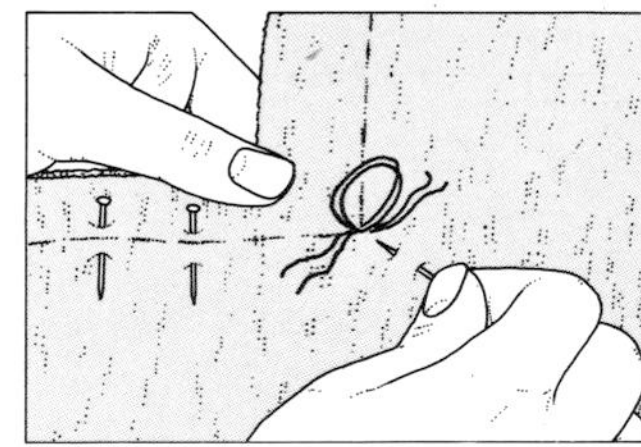

1 Mark the corner points of your fabric pieces. With right sides facing, pin the corner point and one seam in place.

2 Clip the top piece of fabric to the corner point. Stitch right to this point.

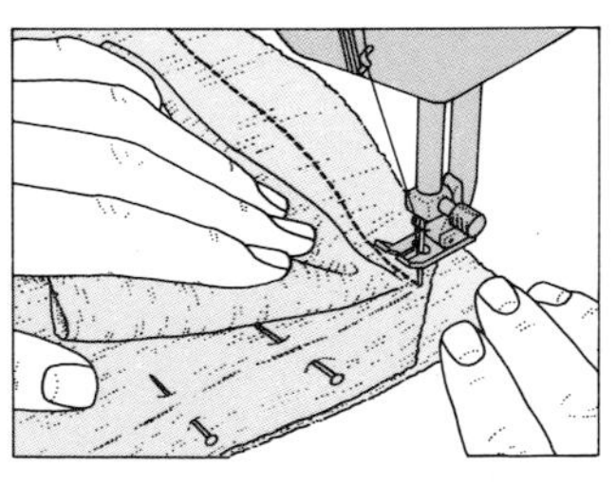

3 Pivot the work. Pull the top layer of fabric around to align with the lower layer. Pin it into place and stitch to the end of the seam. Remove the marking thread and pins and press flat into place. Finish seams in the appropriate way.

TAILOR'S TACKS

Tailor's tacks are used to mark double layers of fabric, as in pleats, darts and tucks.

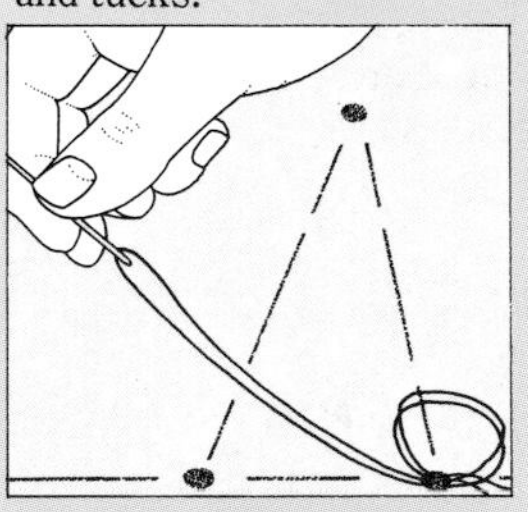

1 Using doubled thread make a small stitch through the pattern and both layers of the fabric, leaving a 1in. (2.5cm) end. Make another stitch at the same point and leave a 2in. to 3in. (5cm to 7.5cm) loop and a 1in. (2.5cm) end.

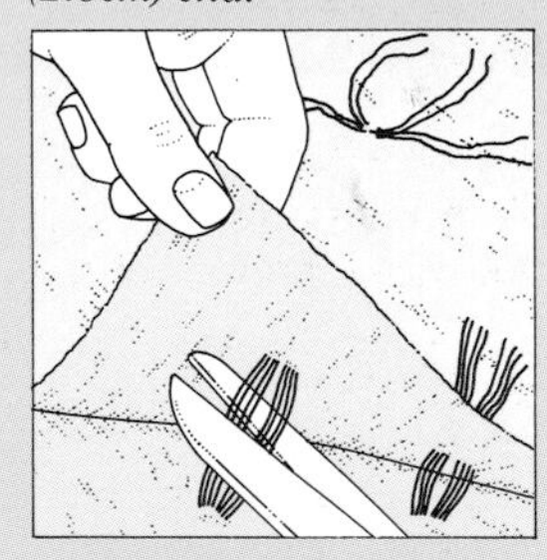

2 When all the symbols have been marked in this way, lift the pattern off the fabric, taking care not to pull out the thread markings. Separate the layers of fabric to the limits of the thread and cut the loop joining the 2 pieces of fabric together.

Darts

Darts are used to provide fullness at the bust, hip, shoulder and elbow. They can be curved or straight, single or double pointed but they must finish just short of the curve.

Unless used as a decorative feature, darts are made on the wrong side of the garment. They should taper to a fine point. Slashed darts should be pressed flat. Other darts should be pressed as stitched, over an ironing ham if necessary and available.

Making a dart

Darts used to give shape to a bodice.

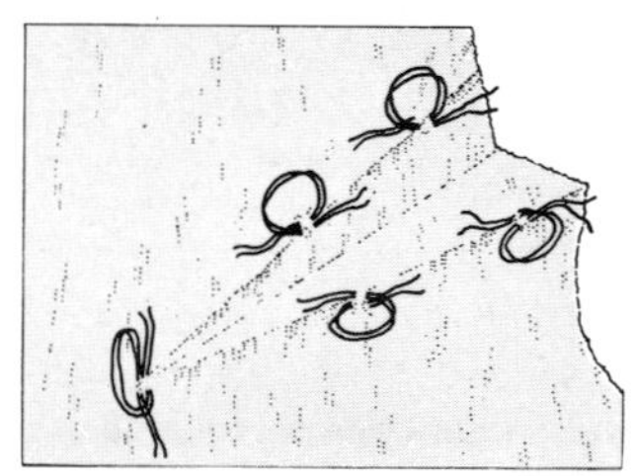

1 Mark the dart with tailor's tacks or with a tracing wheel. Fold the dart carefully so that the markings match.

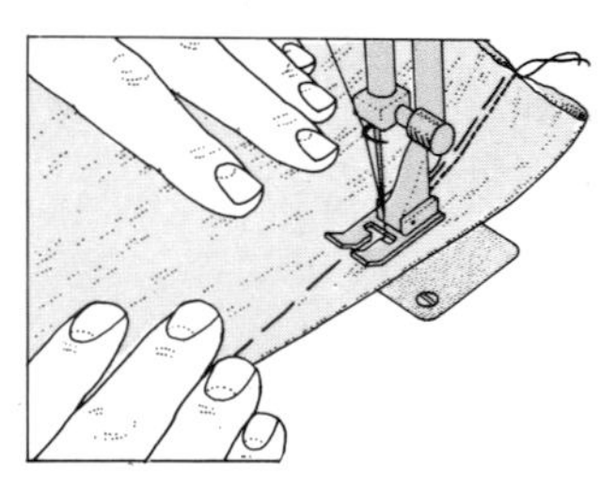

2 Pin the dart and tack in position, starting at the seam edge and tapering the dart to a fine point. Remove any markings. Machine stitch starting at the seam edge, reinforcing at the point for a couple of stitches.

Dart finishes

Although there is usually no special finish to a dart before it is pressed, there are a few exceptions: for example deep darts, used on heavy fabrics and contour and curved darts, used on light- to medium-weight fabrics, are slashed or clipped to ease the fabric.

Deep dart

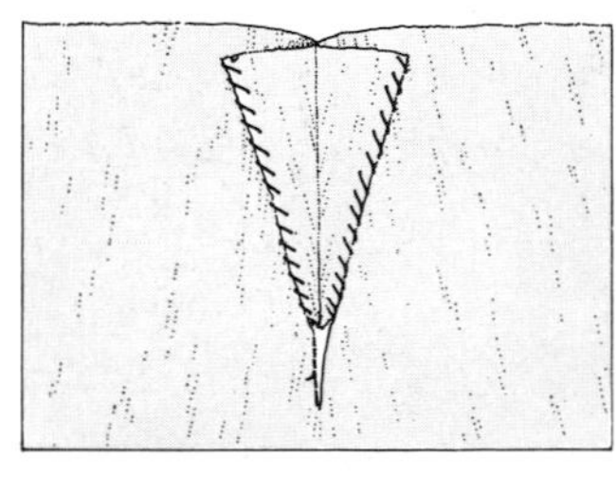

A dart which is made with a deep fold should be slashed through the fold to within ½in. (1.3cm) from the point and pressed open. If the fabric frays, overcast the edges.

Contour darts

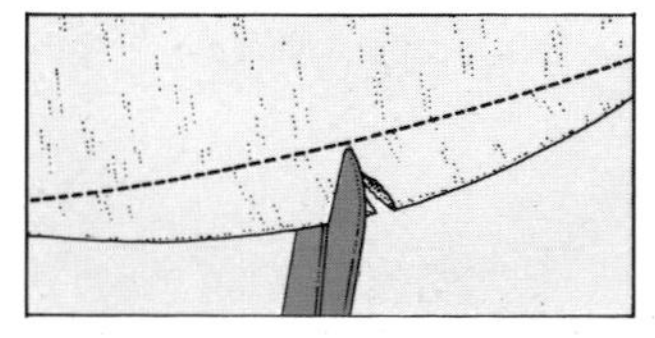

Contour darts are pointed at each end. They should be clipped through almost to the stitching line at the widest point of the curve.

Curved dart

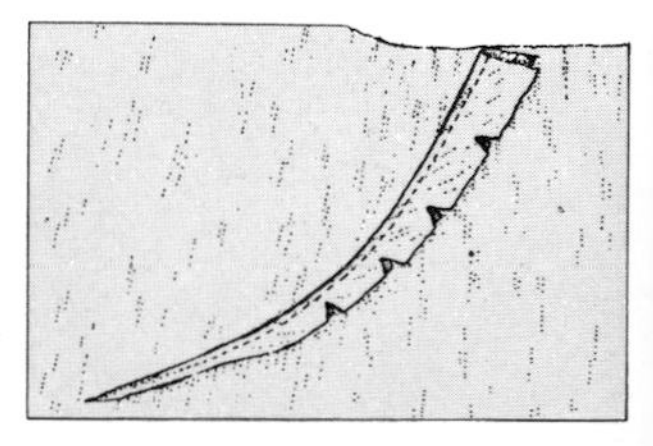

A curved dart should be trimmed to ⅝in. (1.5cm) from the point, and clipped at the curve. Reinforce the curve with a second line of stitching.

Necklines and facings

Most necklines will need a facing to finish them. Usually the facing is cut from a piece of the garment fabric to match the exact shape of the neckline. A second layer of fabric, known as an interfacing, can be applied to give the neckline edge a crisp finish.

Facing a round neckline

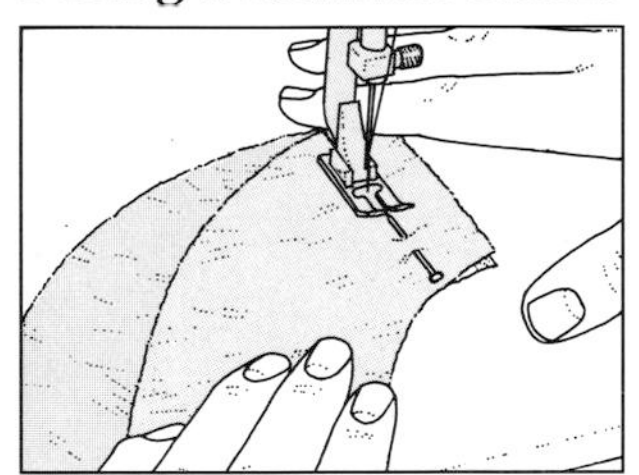

1 Join the facing at the shoulder seams and finish the seam edges. Press the seams open. Turn the facing edge under by ¼in. (6mm) and edge stitch it.

2 Pin the facing to the garment, right sides together. Stitch with short stitches around the edge of the neckline.

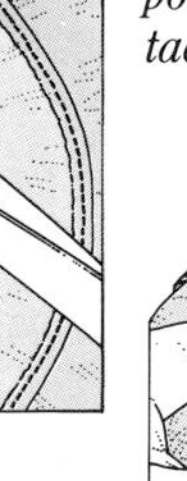

3 Trim the facing seam allowance and the garment neckline allowance. Clip into the seam allowance at regular intervals. Trim corners where the seams cross. Press.

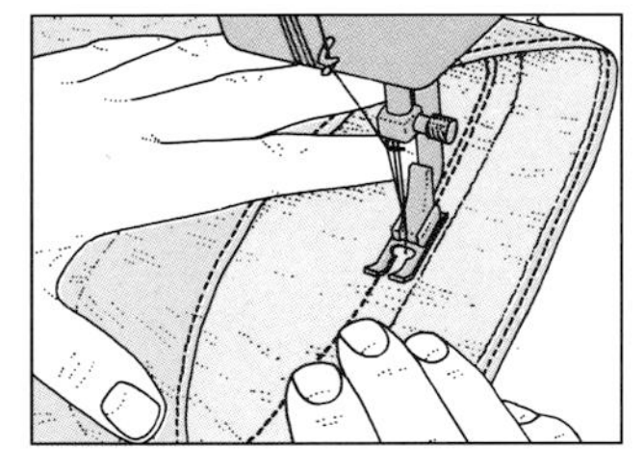

4 Pull the facing outside the neckline. On the right side of the facing stitch around the neckline as close to the seam line as possible and press.

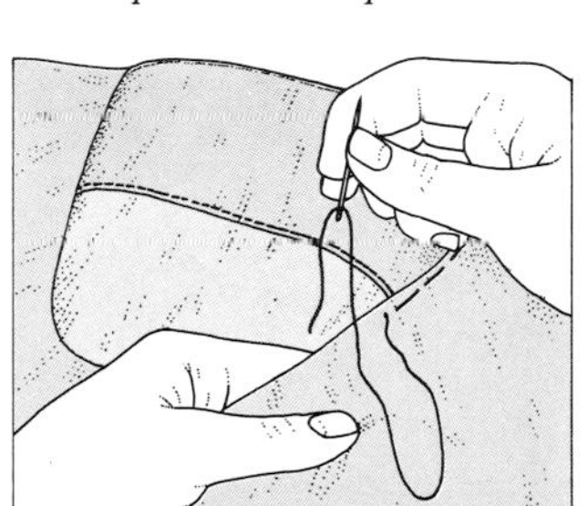

5 Turn the facing to the inside, rolling it under gently so that the seam line lies just to the inside of the neckline. Tack in position and press. Remove the tacking threads.

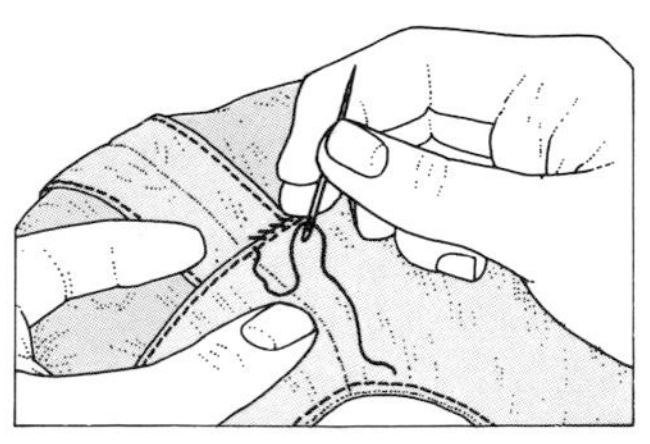

6 Catch the facing to the garment at the shoulder line seam with a few small slip stitches to hold it in place.

Facing a square neckline

Follow the instructions for attaching a round facing. When stitching around the neckline, pivot the fabric on the needle at the corners and clip into the corners to within ⅛in. (3mm) of the seam line.

Facing a V neckline

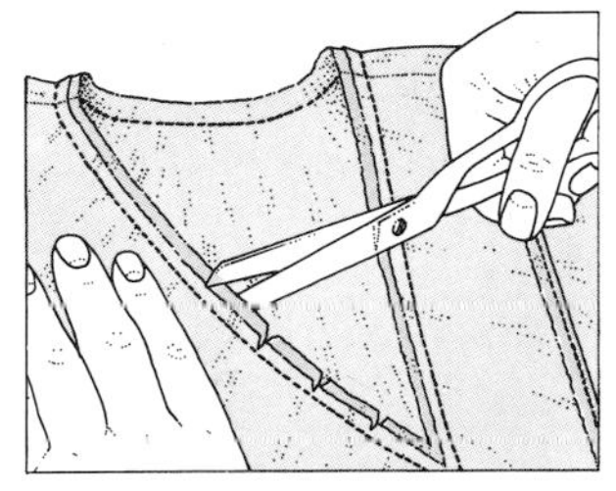

Follow the instructions for attaching a round facing, pivoting the fabric on the needle at the point of the V. Clip into the V as above.

Finishing off

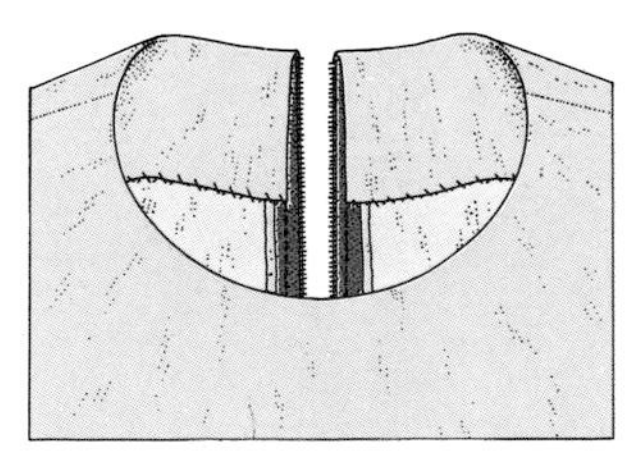

If a zip fastener is to be inserted into the opening, attach it before finishing off the facing. Then turn the ends of the facing seam allowance to the inside and catch it down to the zip with a few slip stitches.

Constructing collars

The collar must fit perfectly, so the neckline of the garment and the neck-edge of the collar must match exactly. All matching notches should align and they should be clearly marked. Collar seam allowances are trimmed to the minimum to prevent bulk.

Making a two-piece collar

A two-piece collar consists of an upper and under collar and an interfacing which exactly matches the collar shape.

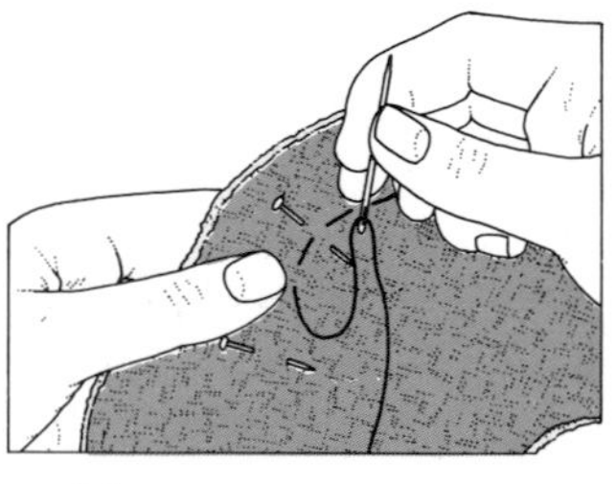

1 Pin and tack the interfacing securely to the wrong side of the upper collar.

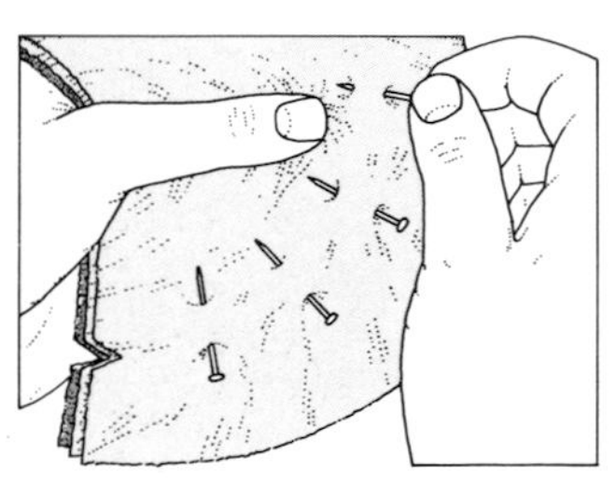

2 With the right sides facing, pin and tack the interfaced upper collar to the under collar around the outside edge only, leaving the neckline edge open.

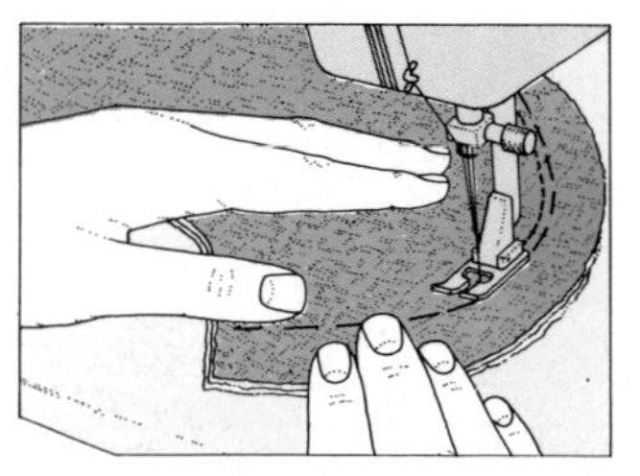

3 Stitch along the outside edge seam line, using a shorter stitch on any curved part of the collar to strengthen it.

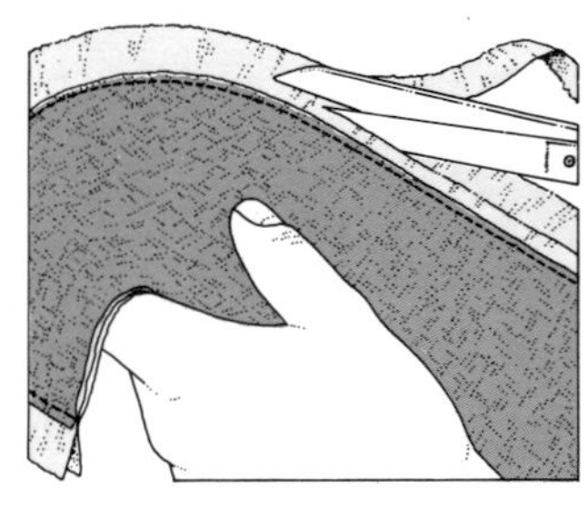

4 Trim the interfacing close to the stitching line. Then trim the seam allowance on the under collar to 1/8in. (3mm) and on the upper collar to 1/4in. (6mm). Clip the curved part of the collar through the seam allowance almost to the stitching line.

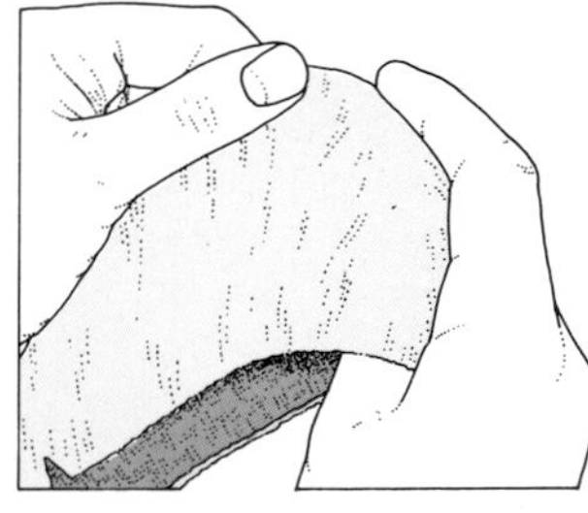

5 Press the collar, paying attention to the seam edges and turn it to the right side. Work the seam edges between the fingers and ease the seam line slightly to the underside. Tack close to the collar edge to hold it in place and press.

Roll collar

A roll collar is made from one piece of fabric cut on the bias and folded in half before stitching. It is then worn folded in half again to give a soft neckline.

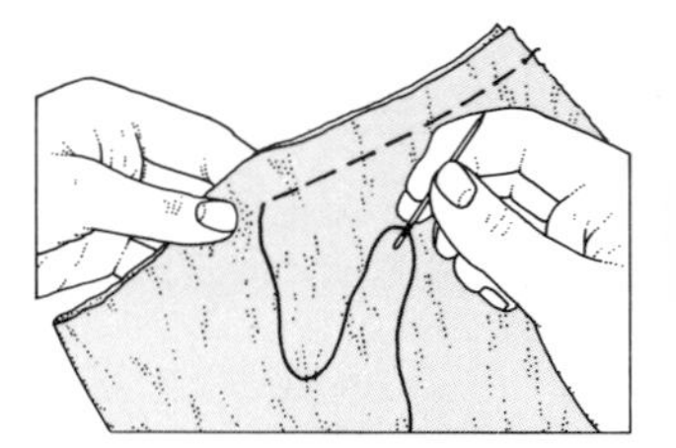

1 Fold the collar in half with the right sides together. Match the notches at the neckline edge and tack the two ends.

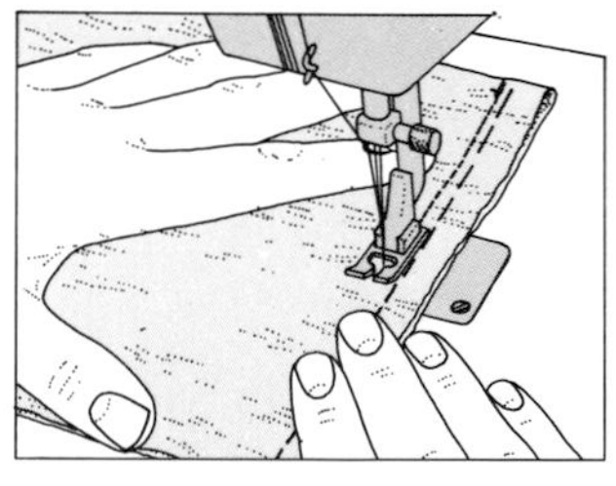

2 Stitch the ends together, leaving the neckline edge open. Trim the seam allowance of the inner collar to 1/8in. (3mm) and the outer collar seam allowance to 1/4in. (6mm) and then cut across the seam allowances at the corners. Turn the collar through to the right side taking care to push the corners out well. Press stitched seams but not the fold of the collar.

Stand collar

This is a close-fitting collar which stands up stiffly against the neck. It is cut on the bias in two pieces with an opening at the front or the back. The interfacing should be pinned to the wrong side of the outer collar. With right sides facing, the outer collar should be pinned and tacked to the inner collar. Stitch along the seam line. Leave neck edge open.

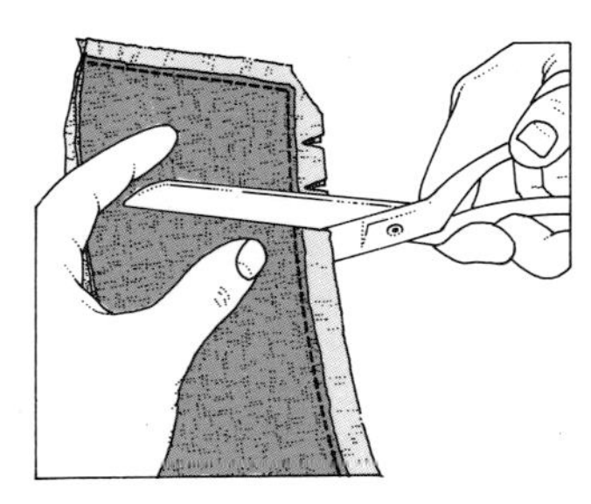

1 Trim the interfacing close to the stitching line. Trim the collar to 1/4in. (6mm) on the seam edges. Trim the seam across and close to the stitching line at corners. Clip into the curved edge almost to the stitching line.

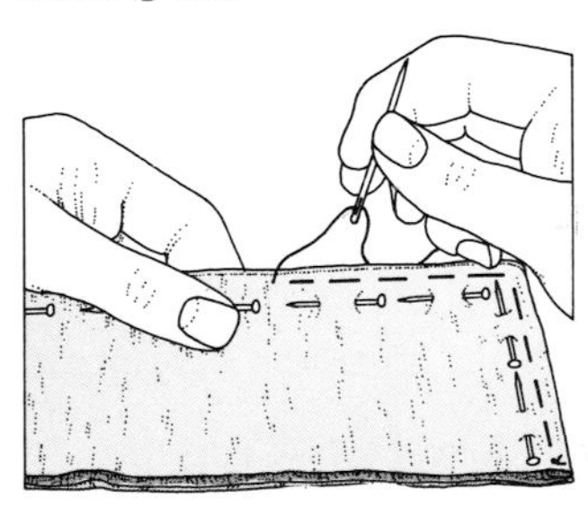

2 Turn the collar through to right side. Roll the seam slightly to the inside and pin and tack in position, then press. Remove tacking and press; attach to garment.

ATTACHING COLLARS

Without a facing

This is used to attach a collar to a garment without a neck facing.

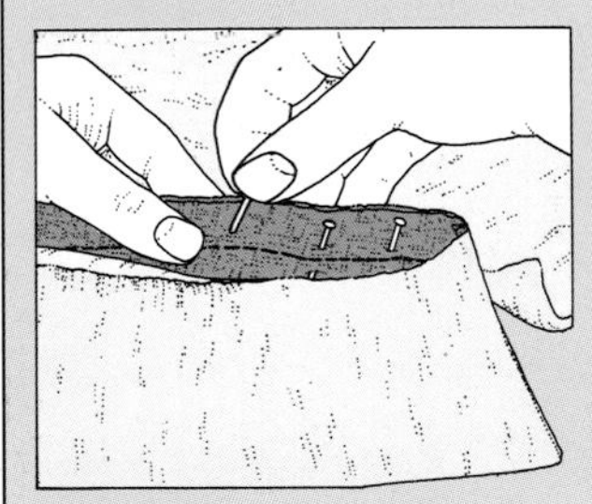

1 Pin the collar on garment neckline, right sides and raw edges together.

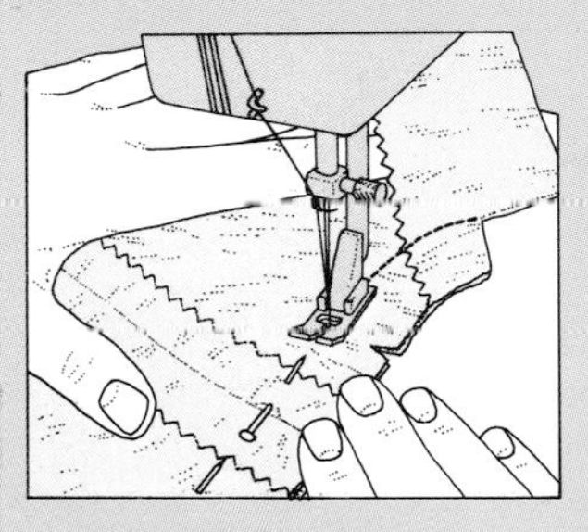

2 Stitch, then trim the seams to 1/4in. (6mm) and press. Fold the collar up to a stand position. Press the seam again to tuck allowance into collar.

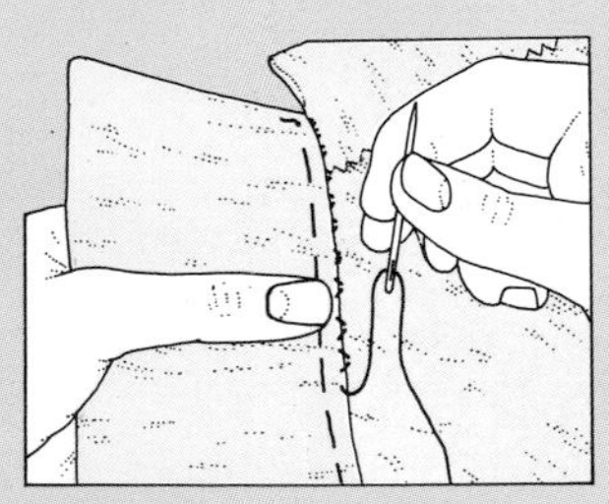

3 Turn under the seam allowance on the top collar. Pin and tack into place, then slip stitch and press along original stitching line.

With a facing

Lay the facing over the outer collar with right sides together.

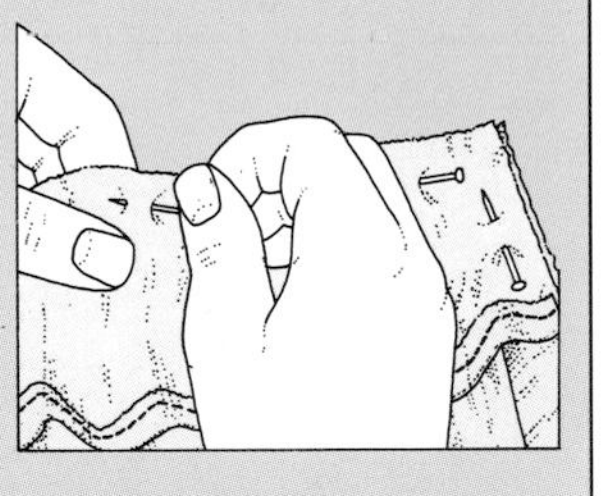

1 Pin into place and tack through all the thicknesses of fabric. Then stitch along the neckline.

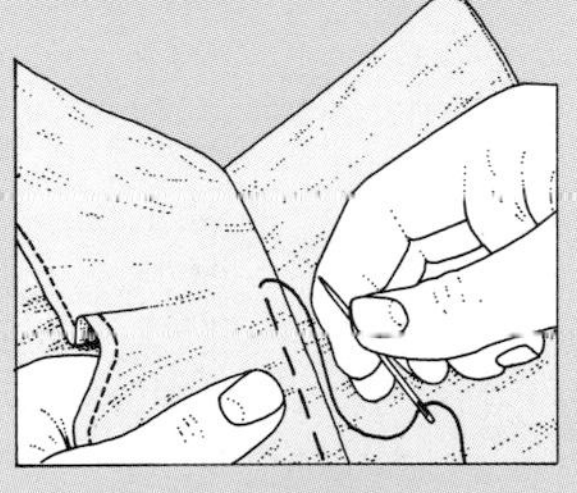

2 Trim turnings to 1/4in. (6mm) then trim the corners and clip into the curve of the neckline, almost to the stitching line. Fold the facing to the inside of the garment and ease out the corners. Bring the stitched line onto the fold and press. Tack facing.

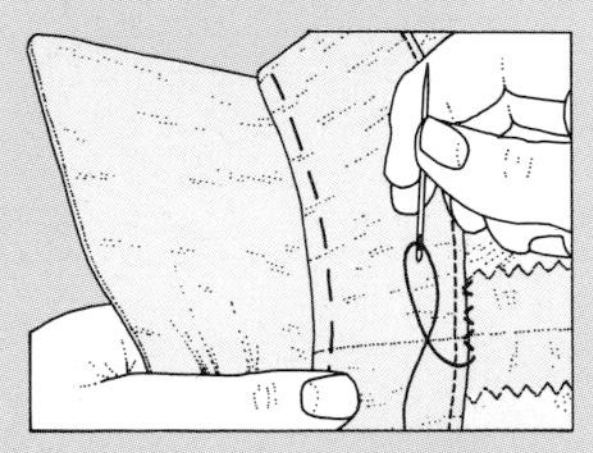

3 Slip stitch the facing to the seam allowances of the shoulder seams.

Sleeves

There are several different styles of sleeve but they have all evolved from the same basic sleeve shapes. Follow the instructions closely and sleeves should not be a problem.

TYPES OF SLEEVE

The most common type of sleeve is the set-in one, where the sleeve is inserted into the armhole. The raglan sleeve is joined to the bodice by a seam running from the underarm to the neckline.

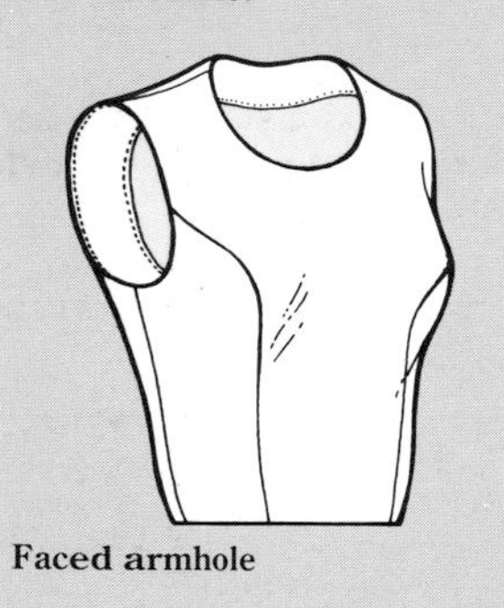

Faced armhole

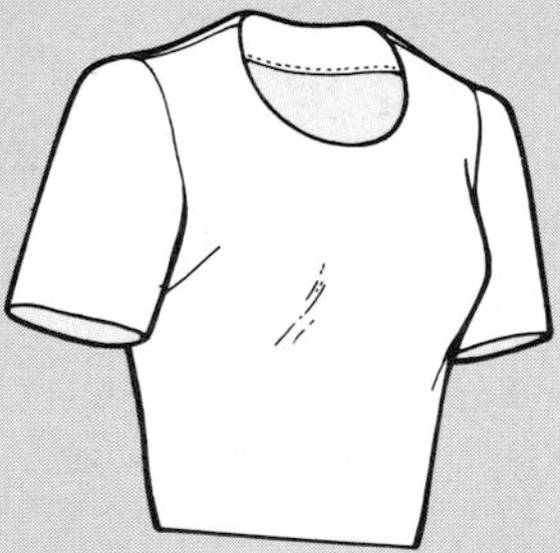

Set-in sleeve

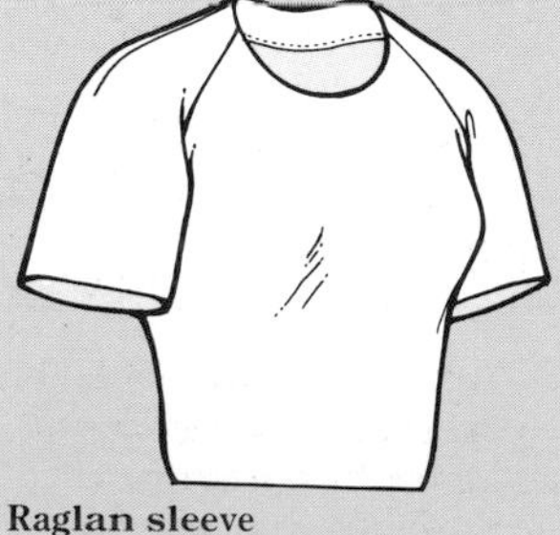

Raglan sleeve

Applying a facing

The armhole of a sleeveless garment will need to be finished with a piece of the same fabric, cut to match the armhole shape.

Before applying the facing, join the shoulder and side seams of the bodice. Then join the shoulder and underarm seams of the facing. Finish all the seam edges and press the seams open.

Turning the garment to the right side, pin the facing to the armhole, right sides together, matching any notches and the seams. Tack in position.

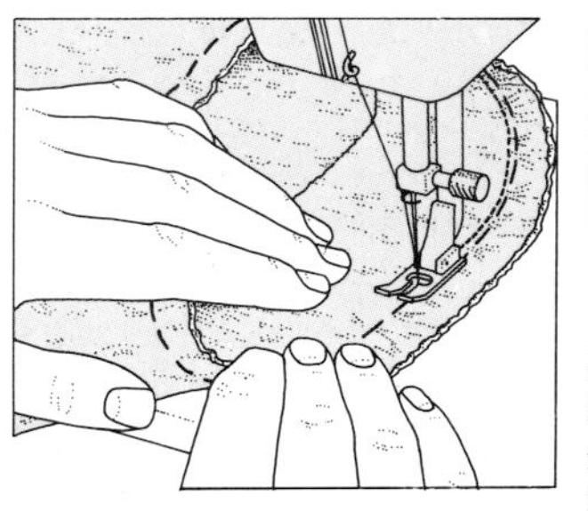

1 Stitch around the armhole and overlap a few stitches at the starting point. Press.

2 Trim the facing seam allowance to 1/8in. (3mm) and the garment seam allowance to 1/4in. (6mm). Slash the seam allowance on the inside curve and cut off corners where seams cross.

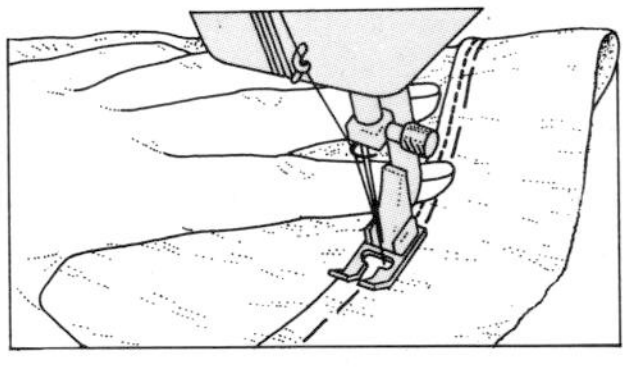

3 Pulling the facing outside the garment, understitch on the right side close to the seam line, through seam allowance.

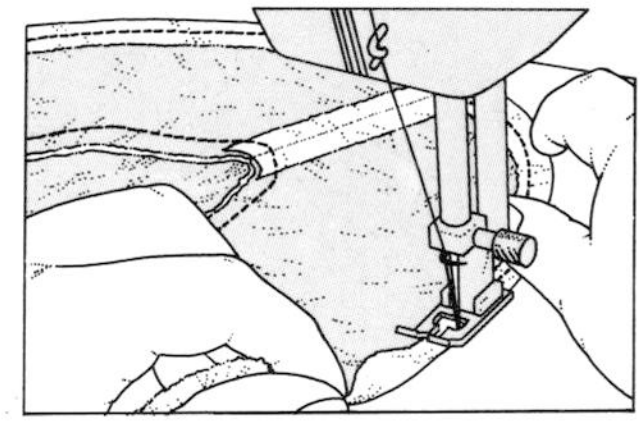

4 Turn the facing edge under along the outer edge and neaten it by edge stitching.

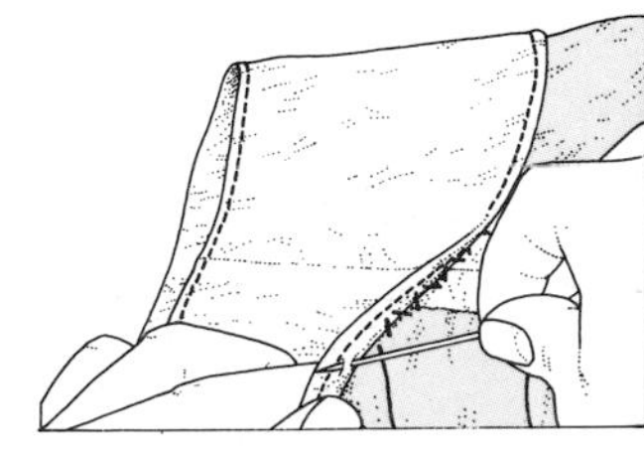

5 Turn the facing back into the armhole. Using a blind hemming stitch, catch the facing to the shoulder and underarm seams.

Set-in sleeve

The set-in sleeve is cut separately from the garment and inserted into the armhole. The width and length of the sleeve can vary, but the principle of application remains the same.

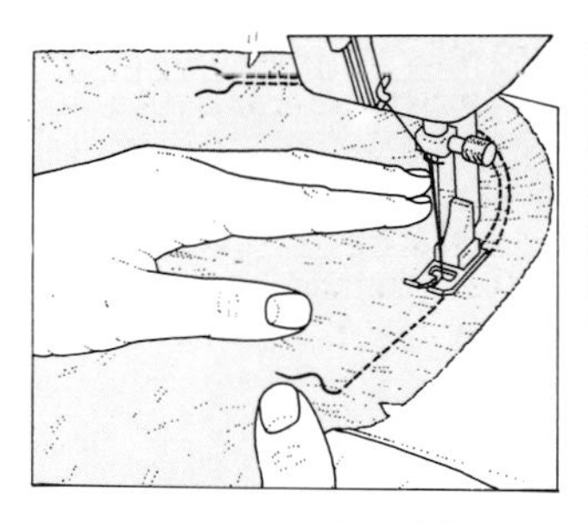

1 On the wrong side of the sleeve make 1 or 2 rows of gathering stitches within the seam allowance between the notches on the crown of the sleeve. Turning the sleeve to the right side, slip it into the armhole, right sides facing.

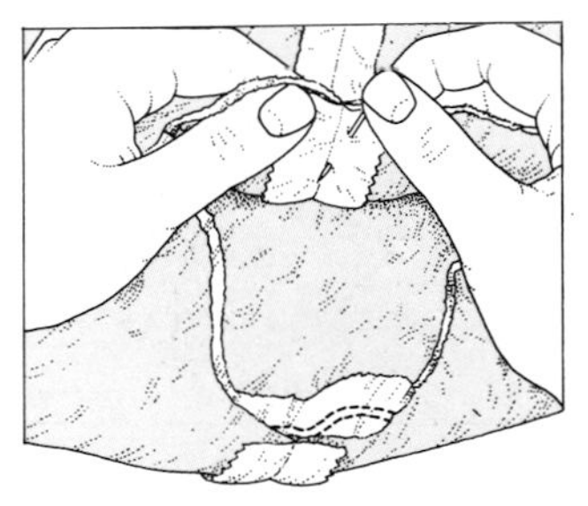

2 From the inside pin at the underarm and shoulder seam points and at the notches.

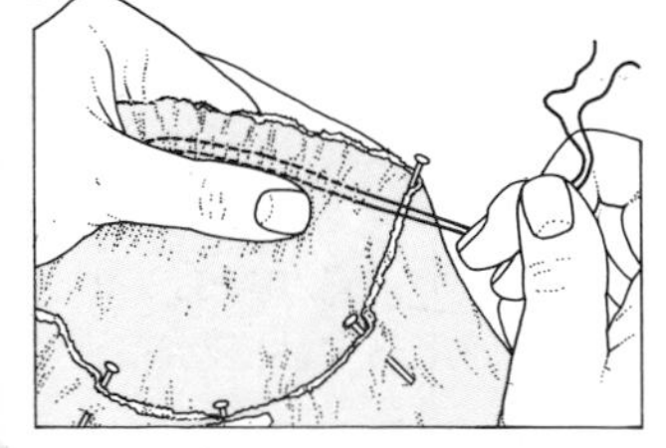

3 Gather up the fullness in the sleeve evenly towards the shoulder line until it fits exactly into the armhole.

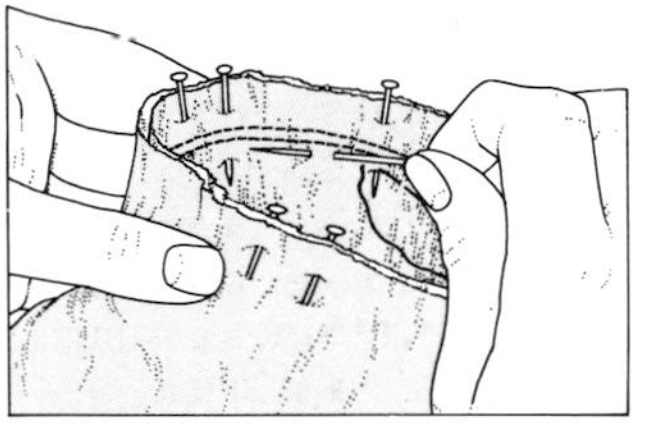

4 Distribute the gathers evenly and pin across the seam line at close intervals and tack the sleeve in position. Fasten the gathering threads.

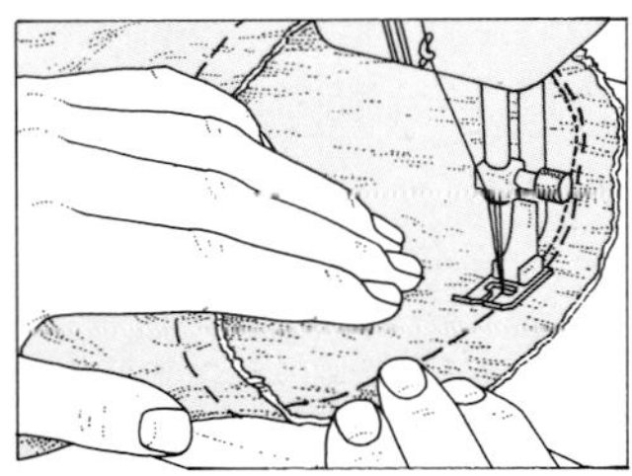

5 From the sleeve side, stitch along the seam line starting at the underarm seam and overlapping a few stitches at the end. Remove the gathering threads from the sleeve.

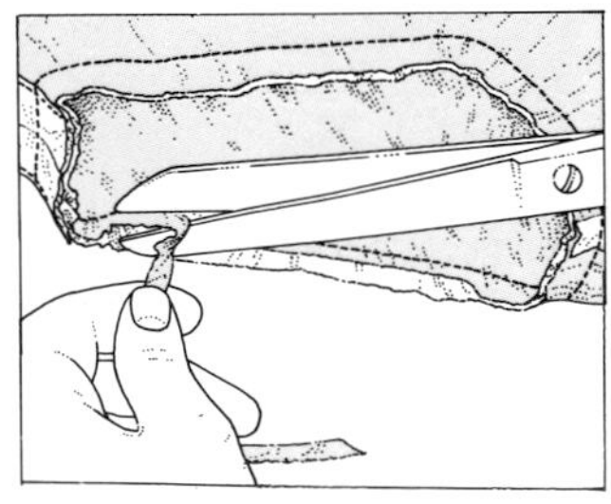

6 Trim and grade the seam allowances and cut off the corners where the seams cross at the shoulder and underarm points. Neaten the seam edges.

Raglan sleeve

The raglan sleeve is cut separately and is attached to the bodice at the back and front of the garment with a seam from the neckline to the underarm sleeve.

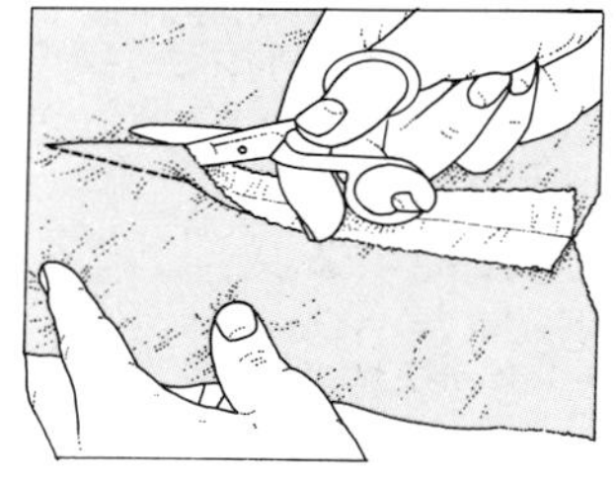

1 Pin, tack and stitch the dart at the shoulder. Slash the dart nearly to the point and press it open. Stitch the underarm seams of the sleeve and bodice. Press seams open.

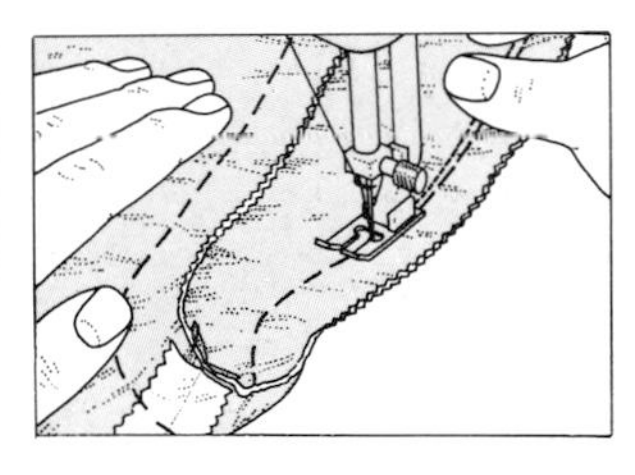

2 Turn the sleeve to the right side and pin to the bodice along the seam line with the right sides facing. Tack and then stitch in one continuous line from one neck edge to the other.

3 Slash the seam allowance at intervals on the inside curve and notch it on the outside curve. Press the seams.

Cuffs

Long sleeves finished with a cuff need a slashed side opening to allow the hand to pass through easily. This opening must always be made and finished before the cuff is attached.

TYPES OF CUFF

Sleeves must be neatened to finish them. This can be done with either a simple hemmed finish or with a cuff, the design of which can vary considerably. The most common sleeve finishes are shown below.

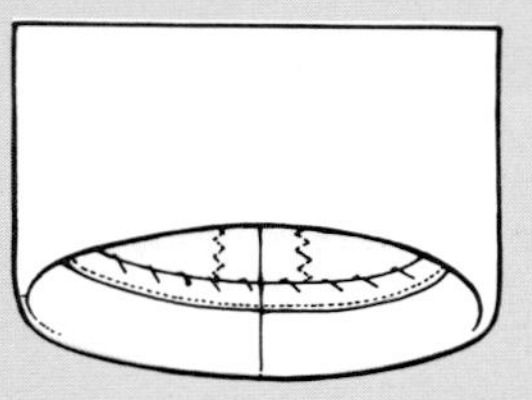

Basic hemmed edge

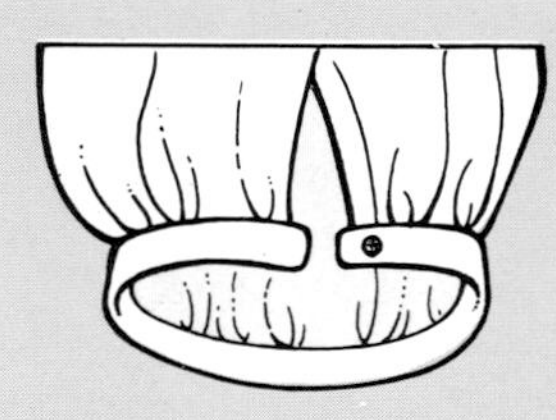

Rouleau strip cuff

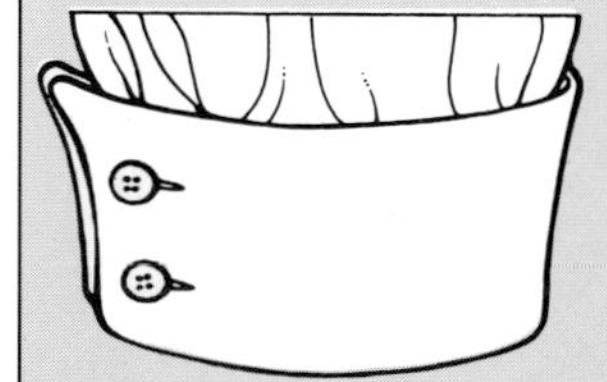

French cuff

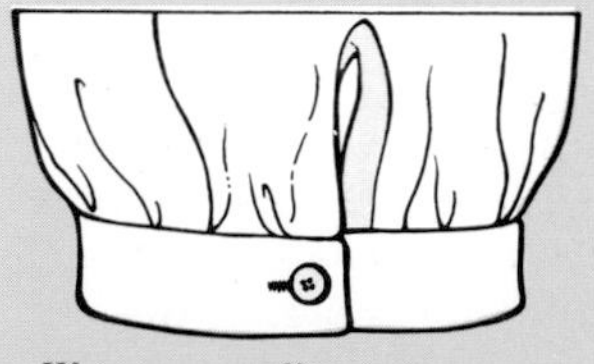

Wrapover cuff

Making a facing strip

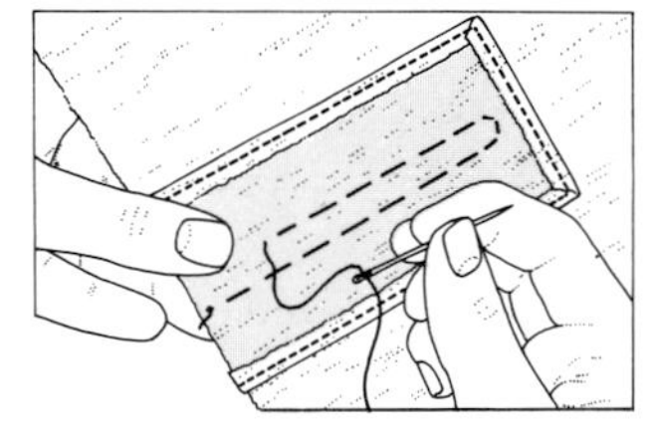

1 Cut a strip of fabric as long as the opening, plus 1¼in. (3cm), and 2½in. (6.3cm) wide. Edge stitch on 3 sides. With the centre of the strip over the slash line, tack to sleeve with right sides facing.

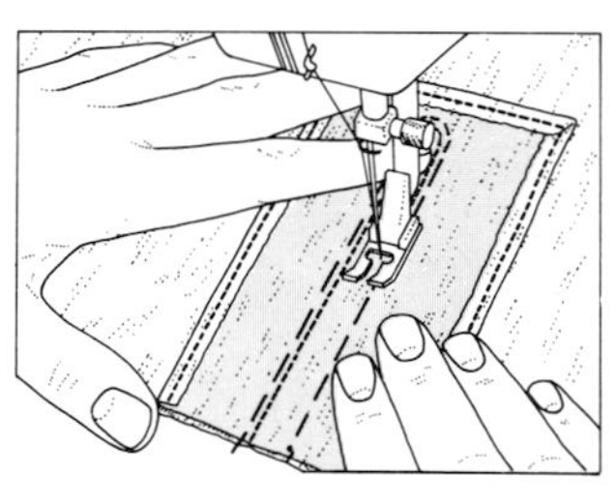

2 Start stitching at the bottom of the sleeve. Keeping ¼in. (6mm) out from the tacking row, stitch along the V of the slash line.

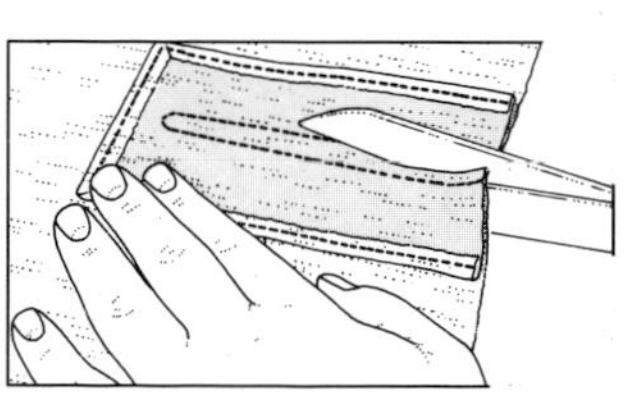

3 Cut down the line of tacking to the point of stitching. Roll the facing to the wrong side of the sleeve, tack and then press into position. Slip stitch the facing to the sleeve.

Making a rouleau strip

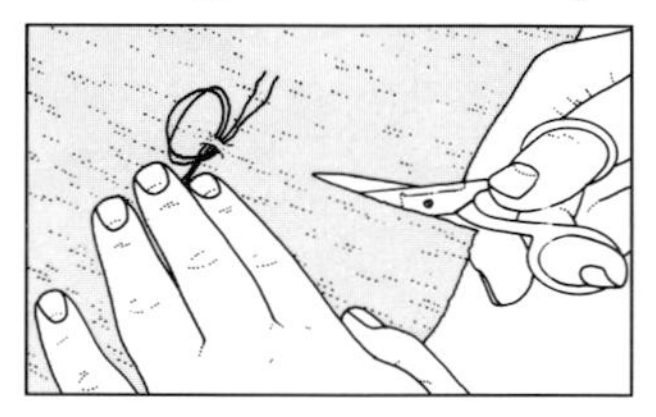

1 Slash the opening to within ¼in. (6mm) of its top. Cut a strip of fabric on the true bias, twice as long as the opening plus ¾in. (2cm) and 1¾in. (3.2cm) wide. With right sides facing, place edge of the strip on left edge of opening.

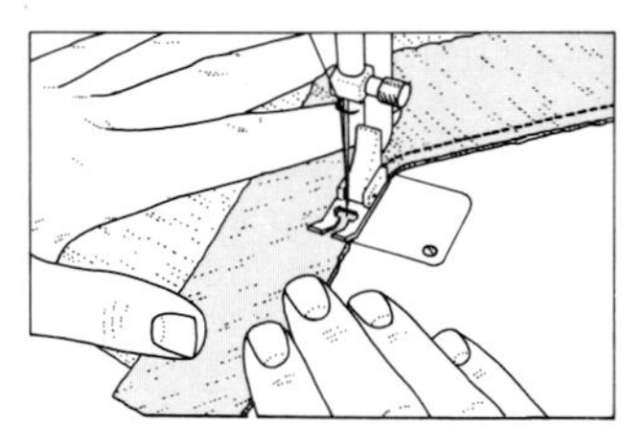

2 Stitch ¼in. (6mm) from the raw edge. Curve the bias at the top of the opening to stitch around the point. Stitch to end.

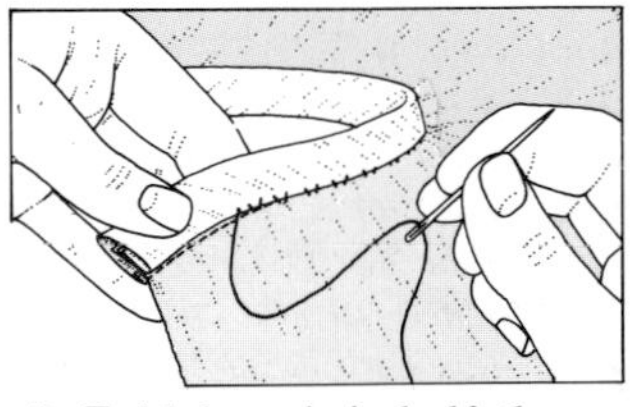

3 Fold the strip in half, then over the raw edge of the opening to the wrong side of the sleeve. Pin and slip stitch to the row of machine stitching. Trim the ends to the edge of the sleeve. Fold rouleau strip to inside of sleeve on front edge only. Press.

Wrapover cuff

This cuff is often used on blouses and shirts. It is cut from a straight piece of fabric, and wraps over at the opening to be fastened with buttons or cuff links.

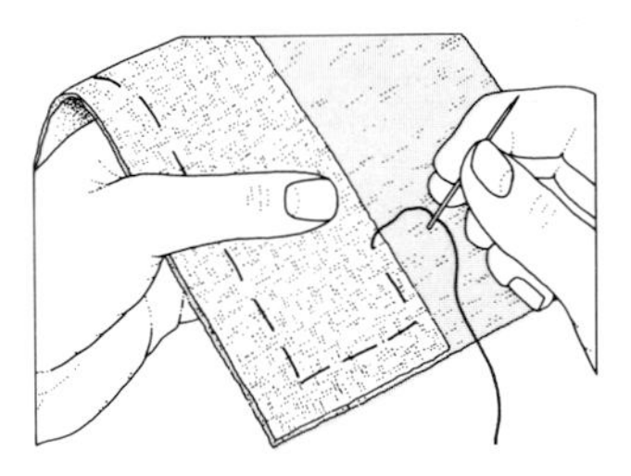

1 Tack the interfacing to the wrong side of the cuff. Fold the cuffs in half lengthwise, right sides facing. Tack the ends and stitch. On one end, stitch to mark for wrapover. Backstitch ½in. (1cm).

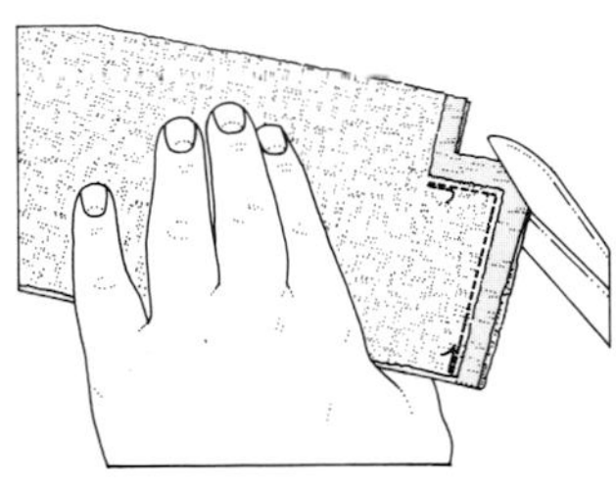

2 Trim the interfacing close to the stitching. Trim the seam allowance on the inner cuff to ⅛in. (3mm) and on the outer cuff to ¼in. (6mm). Cut diagonally across the corners, close to the stitching. Press the seams, then turn the cuff to the right side. Pull the corners out to square them. Cut into the seam allowance at the wrapover mark, almost to the stitching. This will ease the stitching of cuff to sleeve. Press the seams again.

French cuff

This is made from two pieces of fabric cut to twice the finished width. It folds back on itself to form a double cuff. It has four buttonholes for cuff links or button links.

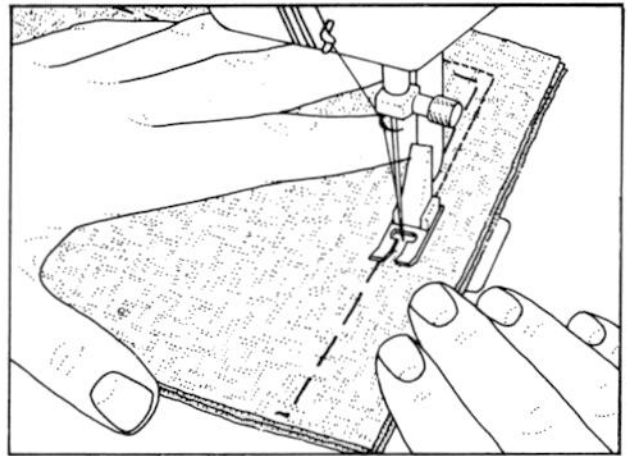

1 Tack the interfacing to the wrong side of the upper cuff. With right sides facing and notches matching, pin the outer to the inner cuff. Tack, then stitch around 3 sides, leaving open the edge to be stitched to the sleeve. Take one stitch across the corners and backstitch seam ends. Remove tacking; press.

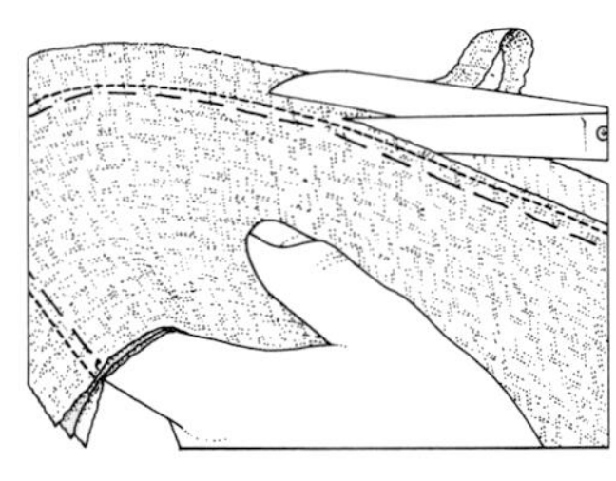

2 Trim the interfacing close to stitching. Trim the inner cuff seam edge to ⅛in. (3mm) and the outer cuff seam edge to ¼in. (6mm). Press seams. Turn cuff through to the right side. Pull out the corners to square them. Roll the seam between thumb and forefinger, easing inner cuff. Tack and press.

Attaching a basic cuff

Before attaching a cuff to the sleeve, the sleeve seams must be stitched and the length of the sleeve checked. As the sleeve will be fuller than the cuff the fabric is usually gathered up to fit its width.

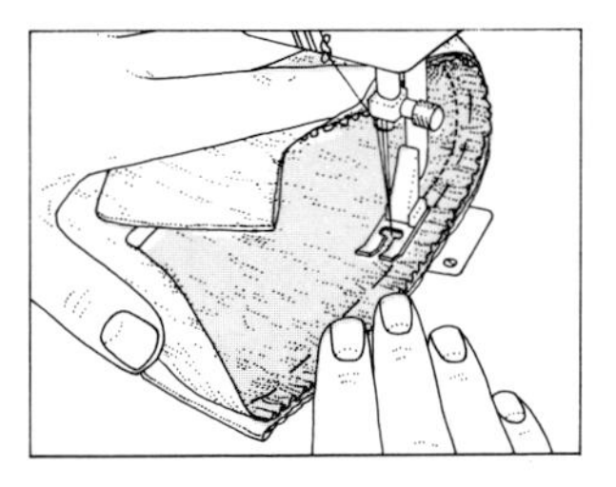

1 With the sleeve turned right side out, run a row of gathering stitches along the seam line at the bottom of the sleeve. Sew a second row ¼in. (6mm) nearer the raw edge. Draw up the gathering threads until sleeve edge fits the cuff. With right sides facing, pin the interfaced half of the cuff to the sleeve. Match the notches and adjust the gathers evenly. Tack and stitch the cuff to the sleeve from the sleeve side. Trim seam allowance.

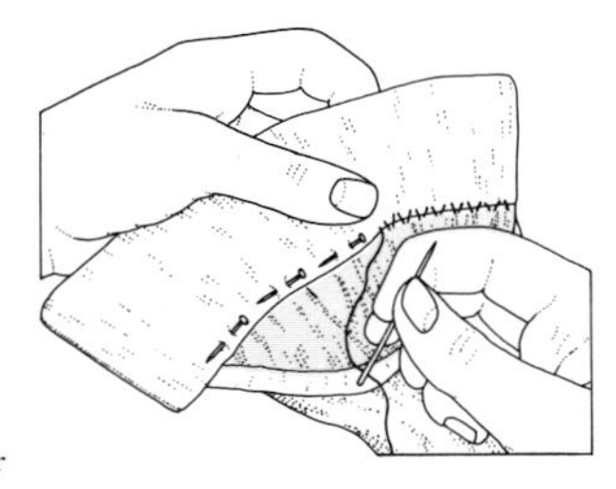

2 Press the seam. Turn the cuff up and press the seam edges towards the cuff. Working from the wrong side, fold the edge of the cuff under and slip stitch to the row of machine stitching.

Pockets

Pockets should be large enough for the hand to fit into comfortably and they should always be firmly attached to the garment. They can also be decorative and often add a finishing touch to the garment. There are two basic ways of making pockets: either they are stitched up onto the outside of the garment or they can be concealed within the seam.

Making a patch pocket

A patch pocket is made from one piece of fabric folded in two and stitched before being attached to the garment. It can have square or rounded edges at the base.

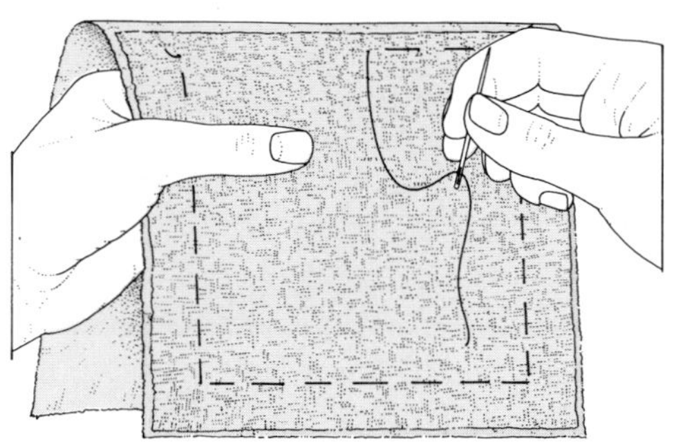

1 Pin and tack the interfacing to the wrong side of the outer pocket. Fold the pocket over so the right sides are together and pin into place. Stitch the pocket, leaving an opening for turning it right side out in the centre of the bottom edge. Backstitch ends of stitching.

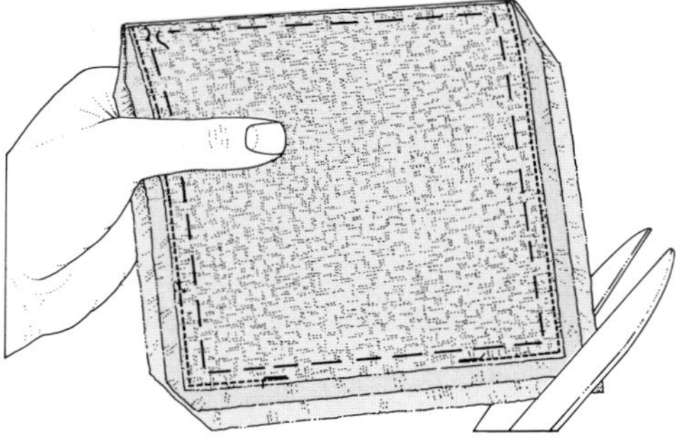

2 Trim the interfacing close to the stitching line and trim and grade the pocket seam allowances. Wedge-trim the corners or, if the corners are rounded, notch into the seam allowance at the curve. Pull the pocket through the opening, turning right side out and press. Slip stitch the hem of the opening.

Making a pocket in a seam

A concealed pocket is constructed from two pieces of fabric and is made in one with the garment. It is usually made of the garment fabric but stronger material may be used.

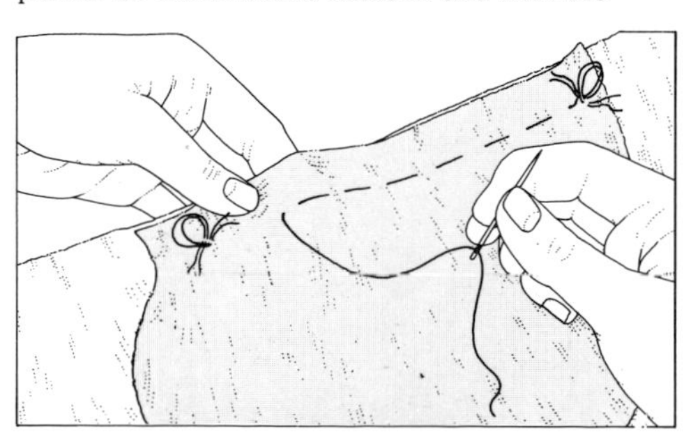

1 Place one piece of the pocket in position on the garment. Pin and tack into place. Stitch ½in. (1cm) from the edge between the marks. Press then fold the pocket piece outside the seam line and press again. Repeat the process with the other pocket half.

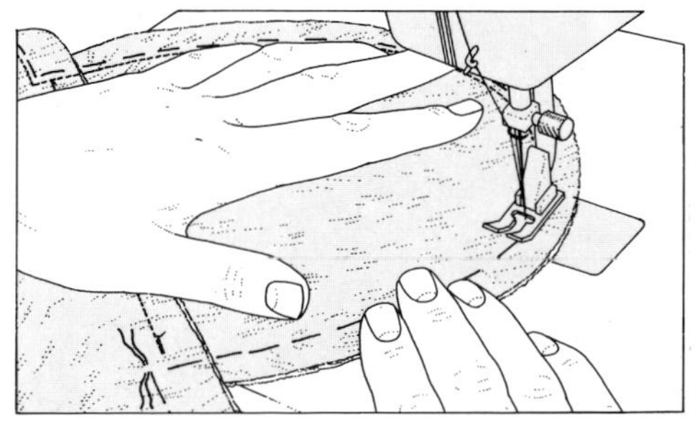

2 With right sides together, and markings matched, pin and tack along the seam line. Stitch on garment seam line to first mark, then stitch around the pocket to second mark. Pivot fabric on needle and stitch to end of seam. Press. Pink seams to prevent fraying.

TYPES OF POCKET

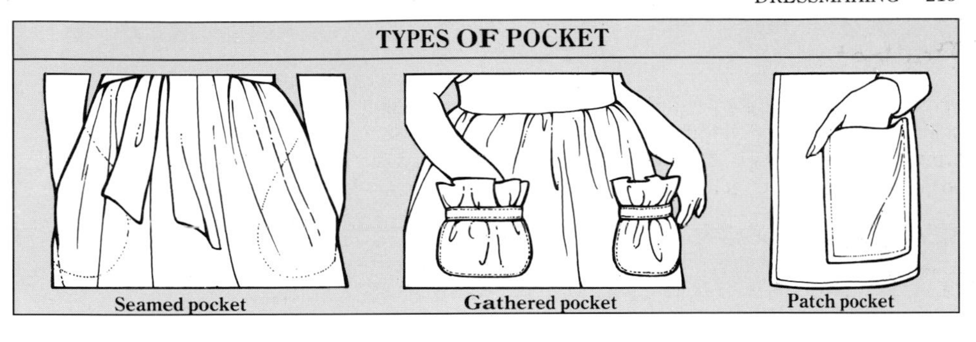

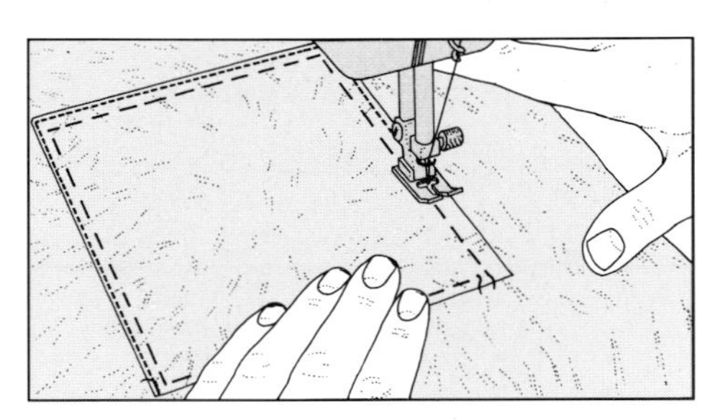

3 Pin and tack the pocket onto the garment. Start to stitch 3/8in. (1cm) from the top right hand corner and backstitch just into garment fabric to reinforce. Stitch close to pocket edge on 3 sides, finishing securely.

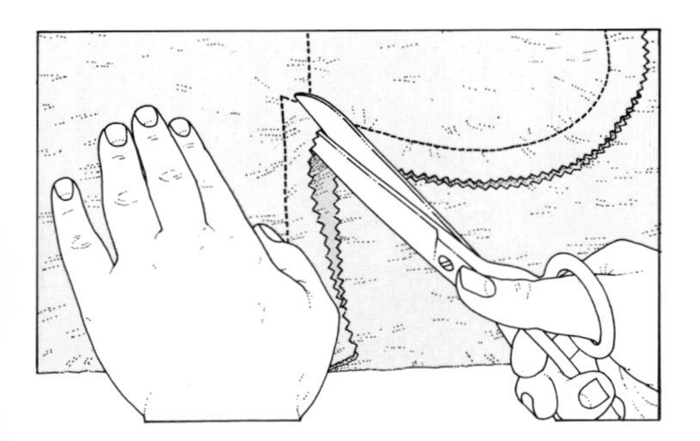

3 Turn the pocket towards the front of the garment and clip into the angle of the seam allowance of the back of the garment and the pocket. Press the seams open.

GATHERED POCKET

This is a decorative patch pocket, made of a single layer of fabric.

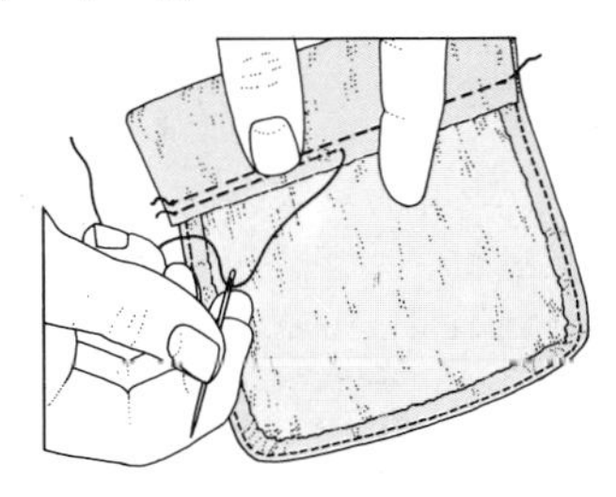

1 Finish all raw edges by turning under 1/4in. (6mm), and run one row of gathering stitches just outside the seam line of the curved edge of the pocket. Fold over 2in. (5cm) at the top of the pocket for the frill and tack into place. Run 2 rows of gathering stitches through both layers of fabric at the bottom edge of the frill and draw up to the required width.

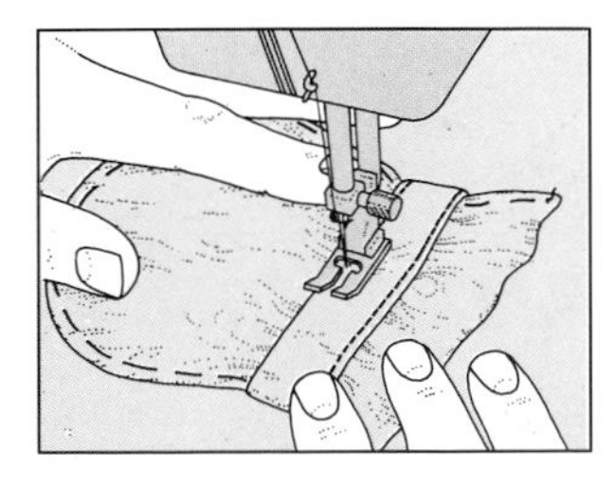

2 Tighten the gathering thread slightly on the curve. Turn in 1/2in. (1.3cm) seam allowance around the pocket. Tack and press. Stitch fabric band or ribbon over gathering for frill. Attach as for a patch pocket.

Waistbands

The simplest finish for skirts and trousers is a waistband. This must fit snugly and be firm enough to ensure that the garment hangs well from it. It can either be a plain, stiffened strip or it can be threaded with elastic. It is always attached after the garment is finished.

TYPES OF WAISTBAND

Belts and waistbands can be decorative or purely functional. A few basic types are shown here which will fulfil the requirements of most garments.

Elasticated waistband

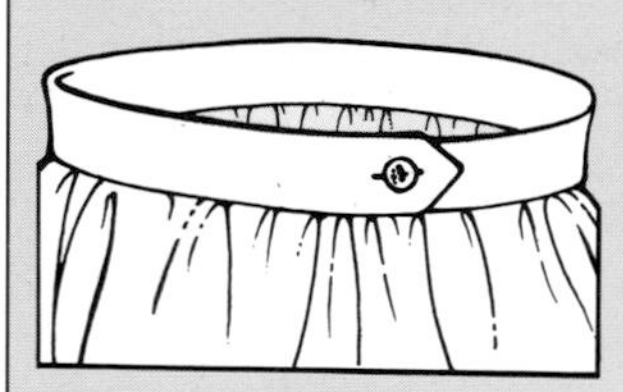

Stiffened waistband

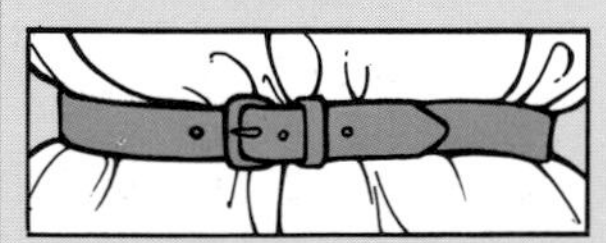

Stiffened belt

Tie belt

Elasticated waistband

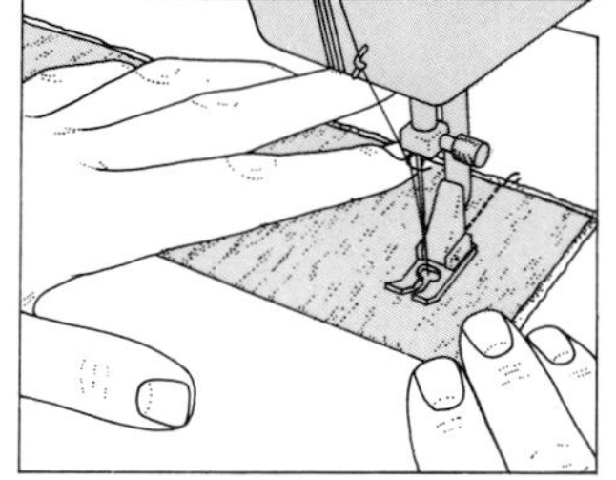

1 Find the correct length of elastic by tying it around your waist so that it fits comfortably. Add 1in. (2.5cm). The casing should be twice the width of the elastic plus 1/8in. (3mm) and sufficient fabric for turnings. Stitch the ends of the waistband together and press the seams open. With right sides facing, pin and tack it to the waistline and stitch. Press. Trim the skirt seam to 1/8in. (3mm) and trim the waistband seam to 1/4in. (6mm).

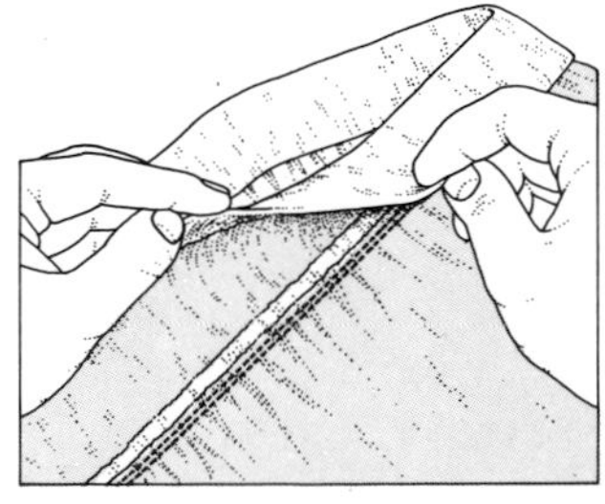

2 Fold the waistband down. Turn under seam allowance to the line of stitching and pin in place. Slip stitch, leaving a gap at the joining seam through which the elastic will be threaded.

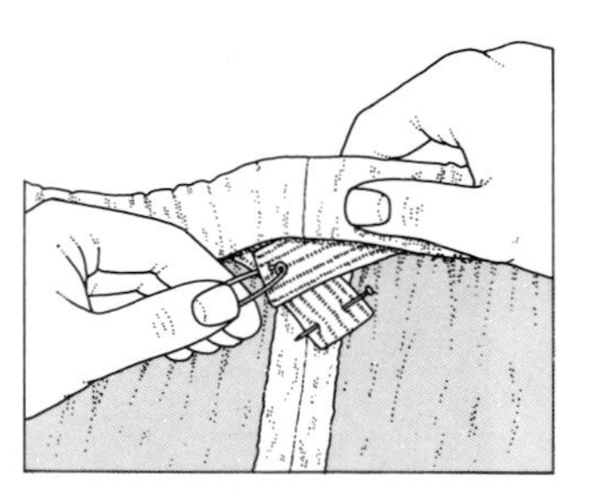

3 Attach a safety pin to the elastic to guide it through the casing. Secure the free end of the elastic to the casing with a pin. Hold the front of the safety pin firmly between the 2 layers of casing fabric. Gather the casing up onto the elastic. Continue until all the elastic has been threaded through the waistband casing and the 2 ends overlap.

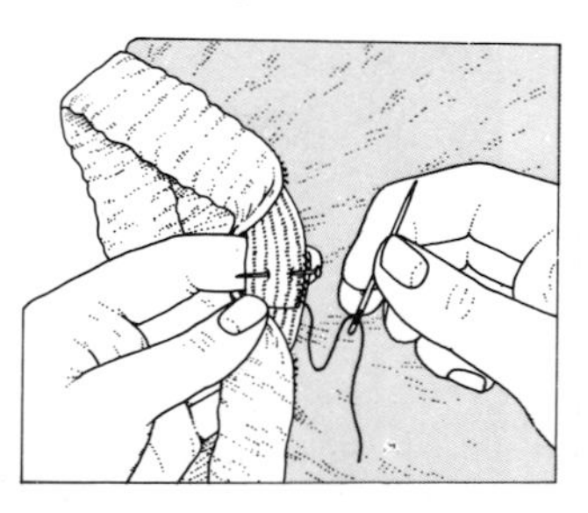

4 Unpin the ends of the elastic and overlap them by 1in. (2.5cm) and pin. Either oversew the edges very firmly or make two or three rows of zigzag stitches. Pull the casing back over the elastic and slip stitch neatly into place.

Stiffened waistband

A plain waistband must be strengthened with interfacing to maintain its shape.

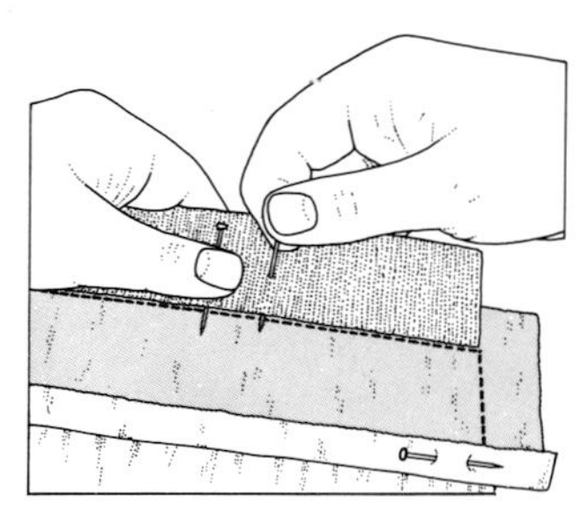

1 Lay the waistband onto the skirt with right sides facing. Match the notches at the centre front, back and side seams. Pin and tack into place, then stitch. Pin the stiffening to the waistband as shown, with the edge on the line of stitching. Tack, then stitch close to edge from other side.

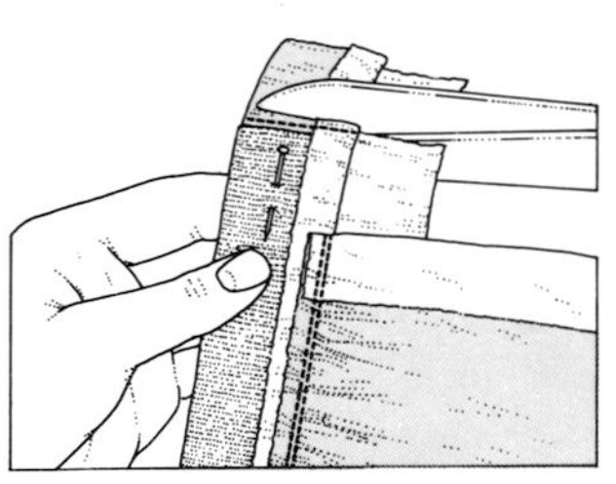

2 Trim skirt seam close to the stitching. Trim waistband allowance 1/8in. (3mm) wider. Fold waistband against stiffening. Press the seams and the band away from the skirt. Fold band back on itself, against stiffening. Stitch each end of the band then trim the ends. Turn waistband to the right side. Trim seam allowance from inside edge and turn under. Pin into place on top of the row of stitching. Slip stitch the edge.

BELTS

Belts are traditionally used to hold loose garments in place, but they also add a finishing touch to a tailored garment.

Stiffened belt

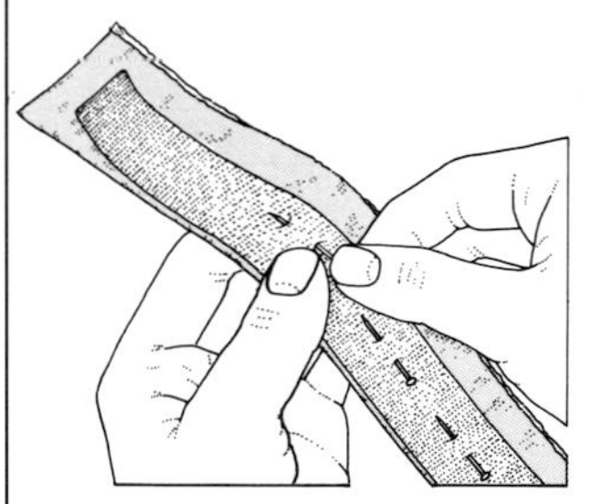

1 Fold the fabric in half lengthwise, right sides facing. Lay the stiffening, which is shaped at one end, with the edge along the folded edge and pin in place. Using the stiffening as a template, stitch around it. Do not stitch the stiffening. Trim fabric to 1/8in. (3mm) and cut corners diagonally. Unpin stiffening and turn through to right side.

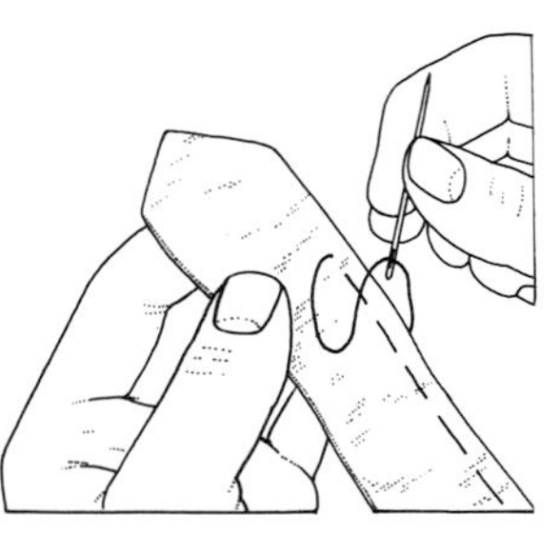

2 Insert stiffening, making sure the seam runs along its edge. Turn under and slip stitch the opening. Press. Tack and stitch close to the edge on the long sides and the shaped end. Attach buckle to other end.

Tie belt

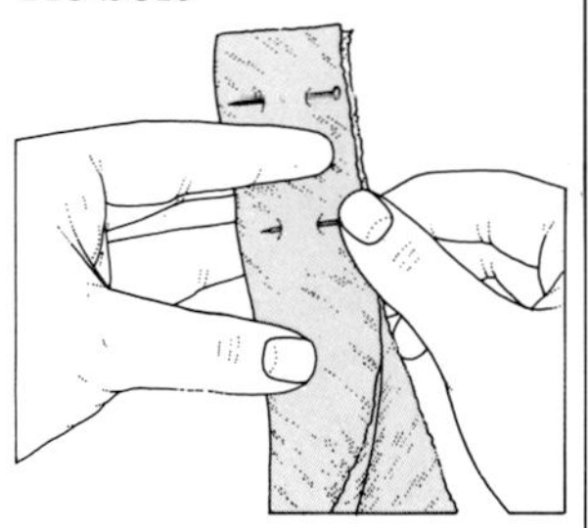

1 Cut the belt on the bias, making it long enough so that the ends can be tied. Decide on a width to suit the garment. Fold the fabric in half lengthwise, with right sides facing. Pin and tack 1/4in. (6mm) from the raw edge, leaving one end open. Take care not to stretch the fabric. Stitch along the length of the belt and across one of the ends.

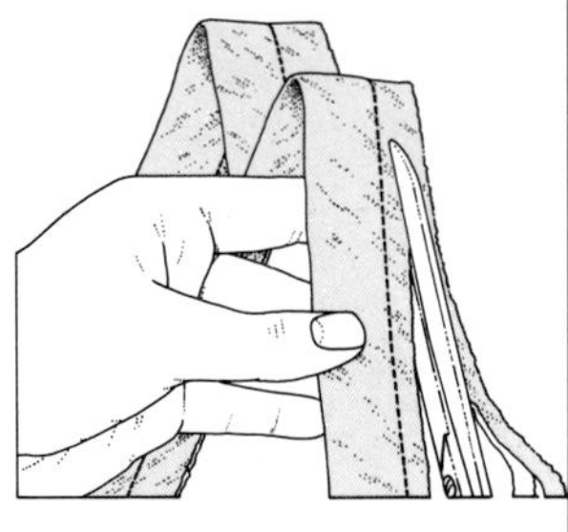

2 Trim the excess seam allowance and cut the corners diagonally. Turn the belt through to the right side. Turn under the raw edges at the open end and slip stitch into place. Press the finished belt.

Fastenings

All garments will need openings at various points so that they can be put on and taken off easily. The openings can be fastened in a variety of ways – which type of fastening you choose will depend on the position of the fastening, the amount of strain put on it and whether the fastening is to form a decorative feature on the garment.

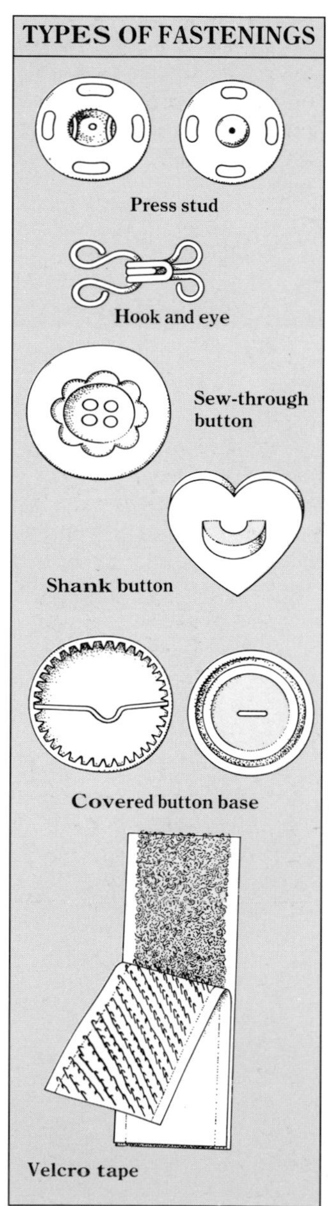

Hooks and eyes

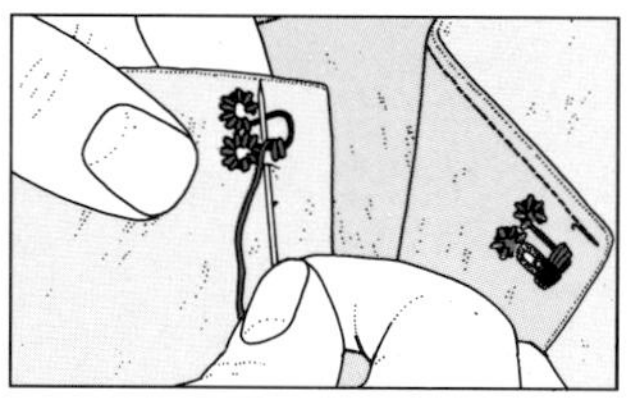

Position the hook on the underside of the overlap 1/8in. (3mm) from the edge. Buttonhole stitch both holes on the hook and overcast the neck of the hook. Then position the eye on the other side of the opening and stitch in place.

Press studs

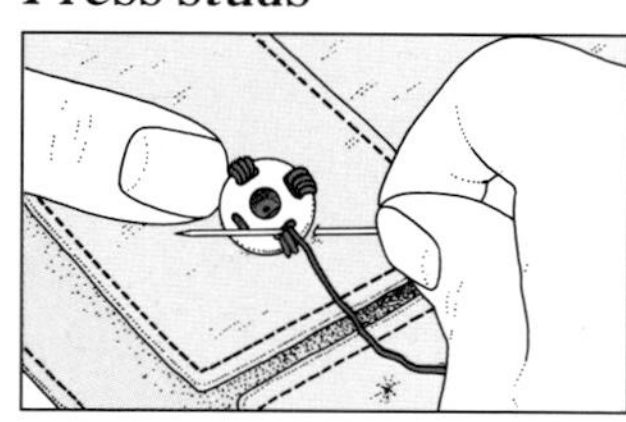

1 *Mark the position for the stud taking care to match the lap of the opening. Make at least 4 stitches into each hole.*

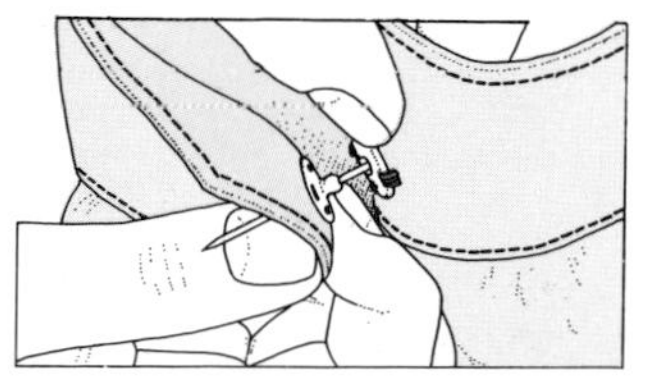

2 *To sew on the socket, align the 2 parts of the press studs by putting the needle through the centres of both studs. Then stitch as in step 1.*

Sew-through buttons

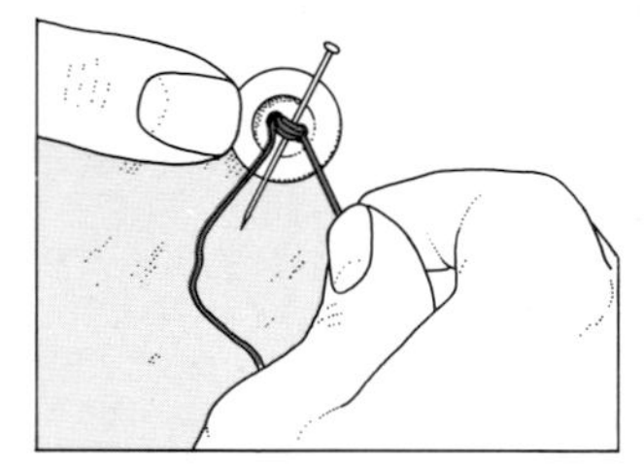

Knot the thread and make a small stitch underneath the button to hide the knot. Then stitch in and out of the holes over a pin, leaving the thread fairly loose under the button. Wind the thread securely around the under threads and fasten off.

Shank buttons

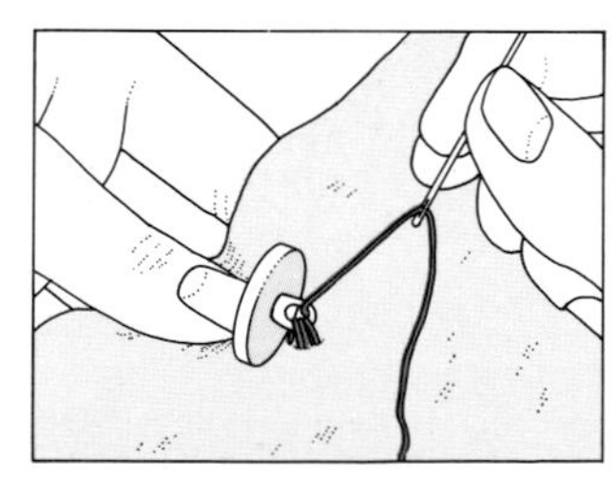

Place the button at right angles to the fabric and then stitch through the loop of the shank and the garment several times before fastening off on the wrong side of the garment.

Buttonholes

Buttonholes can either be hand-stitched or machine-stitched using a buttonhole attachment. Always make a test buttonhole first to check that it will fit the button. The size of the buttonhole will depend on the size and shape of the button.

Making the buttonhole

1 Mark one end of the buttonhole with vertical tacking and mark centre.
2 Using a short stitch sew 1/8in. (3mm) along each side of this horizontal line and across the other end of the buttonhole.
3 Slash carefully between the stitching. Overcast the raw edges. Work from right to left on the lower edge of the slash. Insert the needle into the slash and bring it out at the line of tacking stitches below. Loop the thread around the needle point from left to right. Pull the needle away from you through the fabric, so that a knot forms exactly on the slash edge.
4 Stitch along the length of the slash using this technique. Make the stitches very close together. When you get to the corner, fan the stitches out. Make a bar of satin stitches at the other end of the buttonhole to reinforce it.

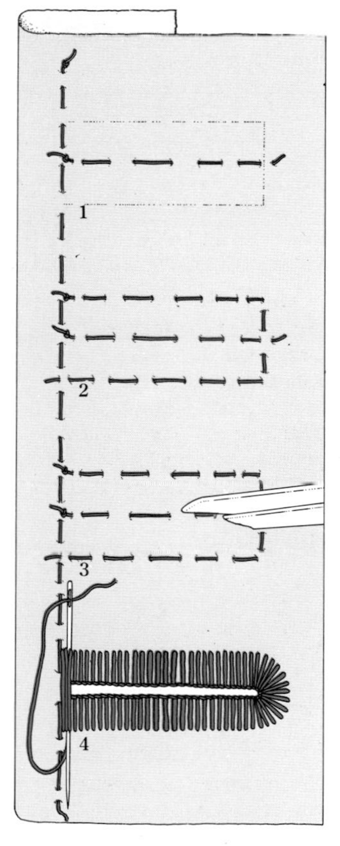

MACHINE WORKED BUTTONHOLES

Mark the buttonhole or buttonholes in the same way as for a handstitched buttonhole. Then, using the buttonhole attachment on the machine, work around the buttonhole position and slash carefully through the centre.

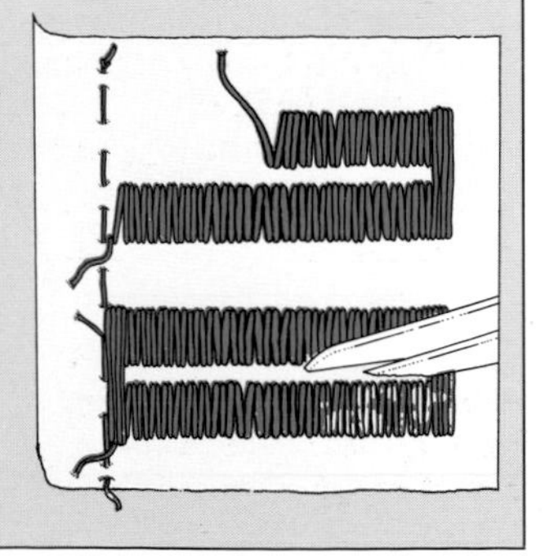

Covering metal buttons

Covered buttons can make a decorative finish to a garment. The buttons, which come in two parts and are made of metal, are sewn on as for shank buttons (see left).

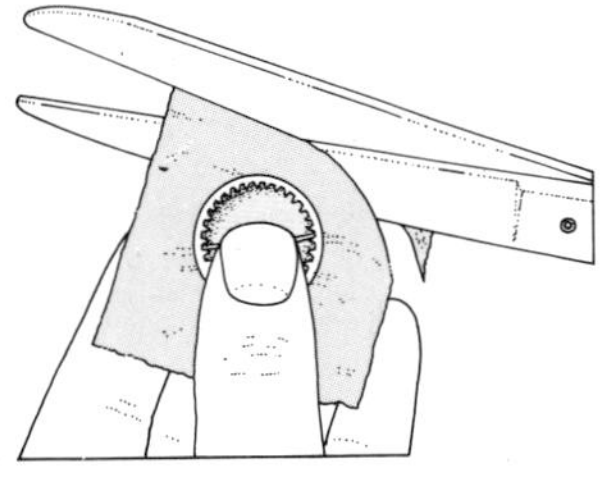

1 Cut a circle of fabric half as large again as the button to be covered and place it over the top half of the button.

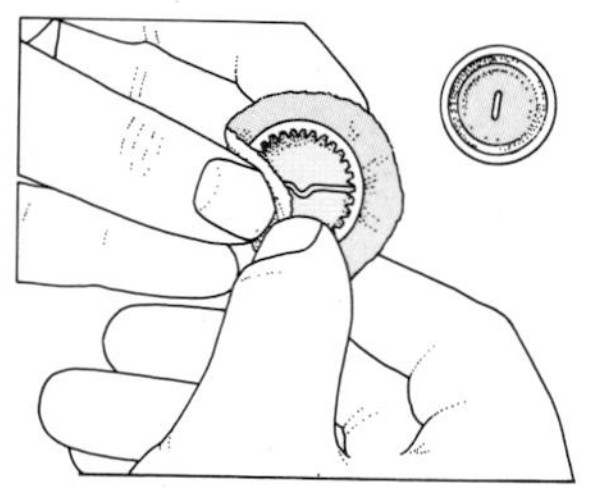

2 Fold the surplus fabric under the button and clip the bottom half to the top half, firmly securing the fabric.

Zip fastenings

Zips are made in different weights for use on different types of garments and fabrics. The heavier zips with metal teeth are naturally the strongest and should be used on garments which will receive the heaviest wear.

A standard zip is the type most commonly used on skirts, dresses and trousers. It can either be lapped or centred. The invisible zip is sometimes used on tailored skirts and dresses, where a standard zip opening might spoil the line of the garment. Open-ended zips (not illustrated) are used, for example, on anoraks and sleeping bags because they unfasten to completely separate the zip.
Three zip types are shown right.

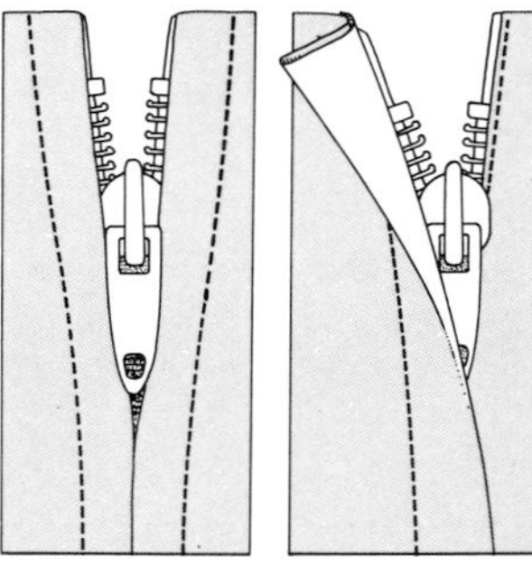

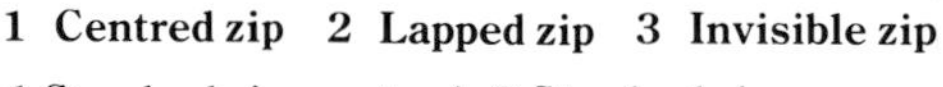

1 Centred zip 2 Lapped zip 3 Invisible zip

1 Standard zip, centred. **2** Standard zip, lapped. **3** Invisible zip.

Centred zip

This standard zip is placed in the seam with an equal width of seam allowance on each side. It is the easiest method of inserting zips and can be used on centre and back seams.

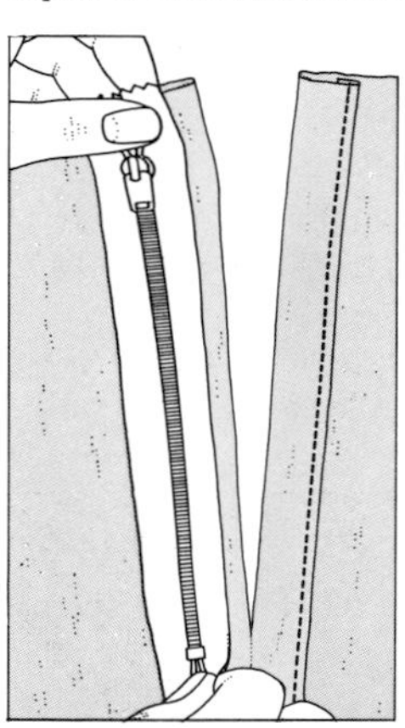

1 Aligning the zip

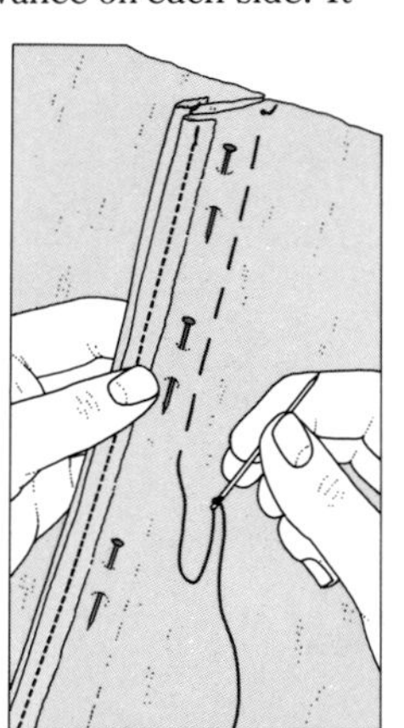

2 Tacking fold lines

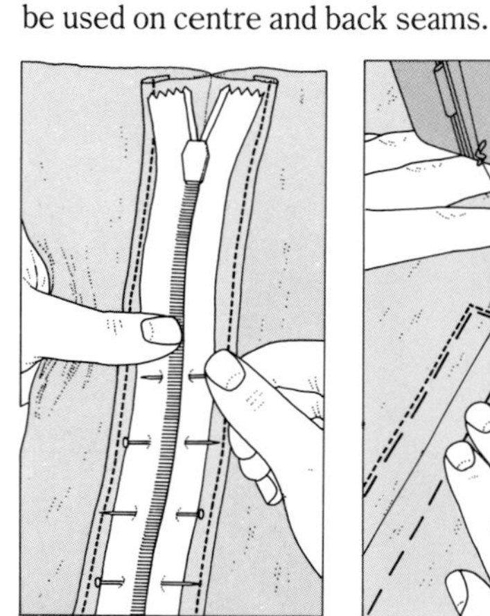

3 Pinning the zip

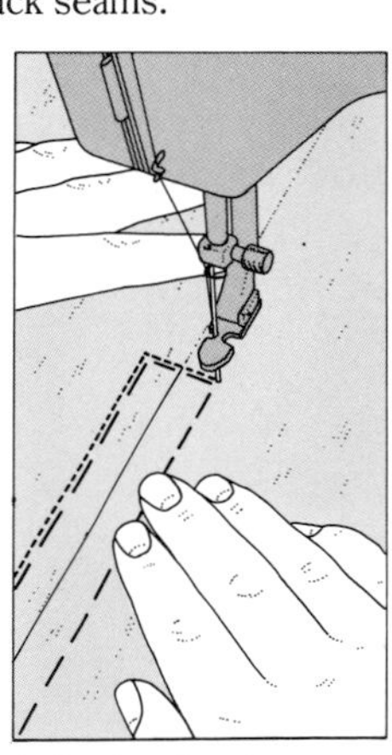

4 Sewing the zip

OPEN-ENDED ZIP

This zip is best inserted before the garment has been hemmed. Usually centred, the teeth can be semi-concealed in the usual way, or exposed for a decorative finish.

Align the lower end of the zip so that it tucks into the hem. Tack the zip in place and turn the tape ends over at the top. Fold the facing and hem down over the tapes. Slip stitch into place, making sure that they do not interfere with the action of the zip.

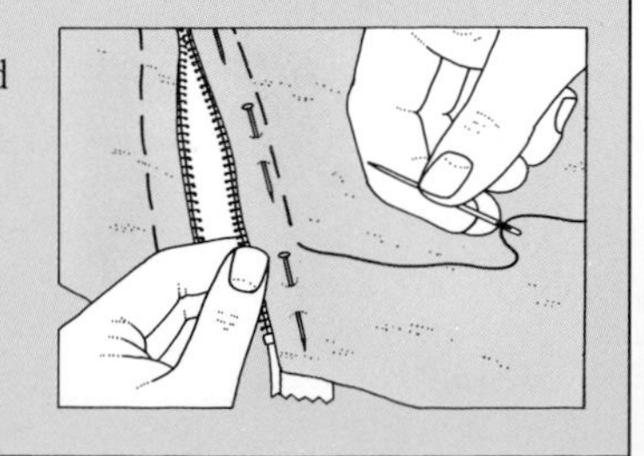

Lapped zip

This zip lies behind a flap formed by the seam allowance on one side. It is suitable for use on side and centre seams.

Inserting the zip

Stitch seam up to the opening for the zip. This should be the same length as the teeth of the zip. Press the stitched seam allowance open as well as the overlapping section of the opening so that the fitting line lies on the fold (fig. 1). From the right side of the garment place the zip under the seam opening (fig. 2). Pin and tack the unpressed edge close to the teeth of the zip (fig. 3). Lap the opposite seam allowance over the zip teeth, ensuring they are covered. Tack and stitch (fig. 4).

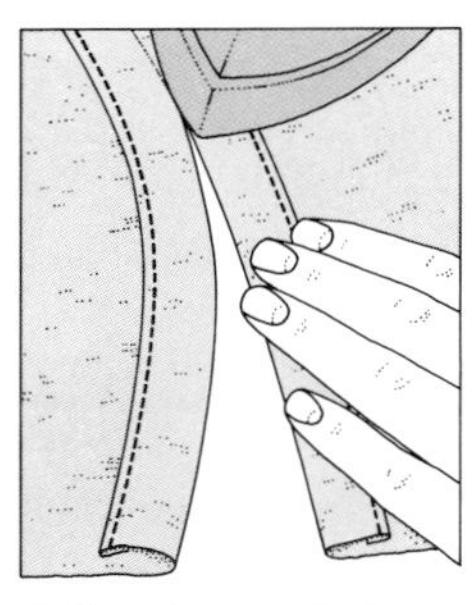

1 **Pressing opening**

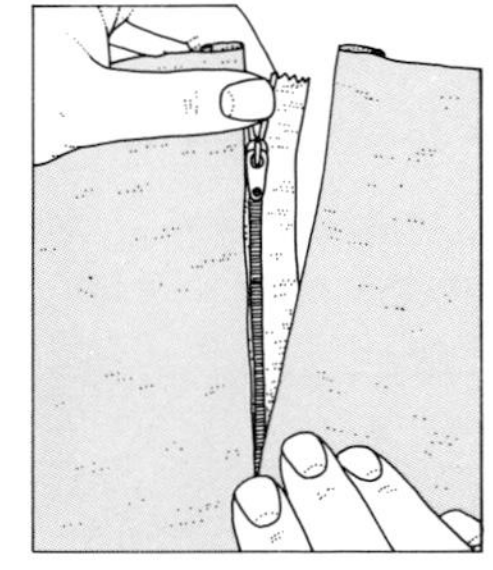

2 **Positioning zip**

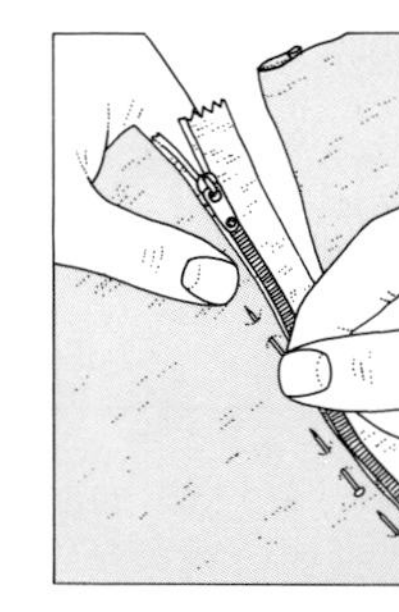

3 **Pinning in zip**

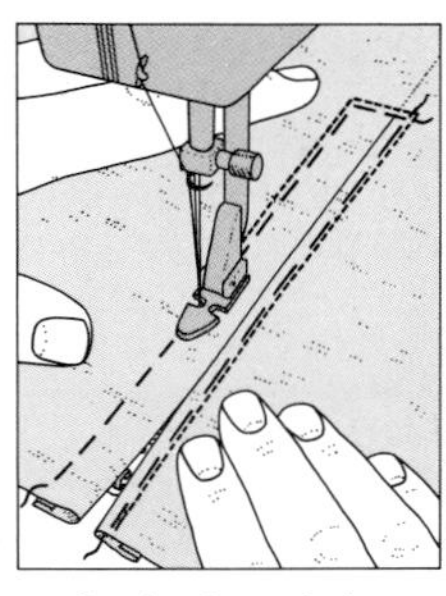

4 **Sewing lapped zip**

Invisible zip

This zip provides an invisible fastening. All that shows from the right side of the garment is a plain seam and a pull tab, but no stitching. This is because the zip tapes are only stitched to the seam allowance of the open seam using a special zip foot attachment (the zip foot must be the one recommended for the brand of the zip that you buy).

The zip is stitched in place before the remainder of the seam has been sewn.

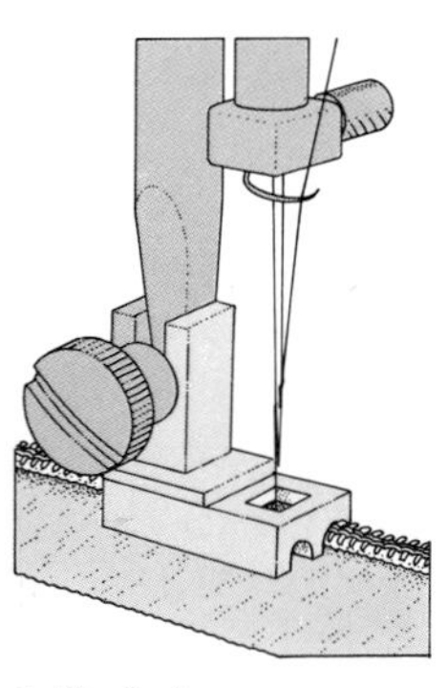

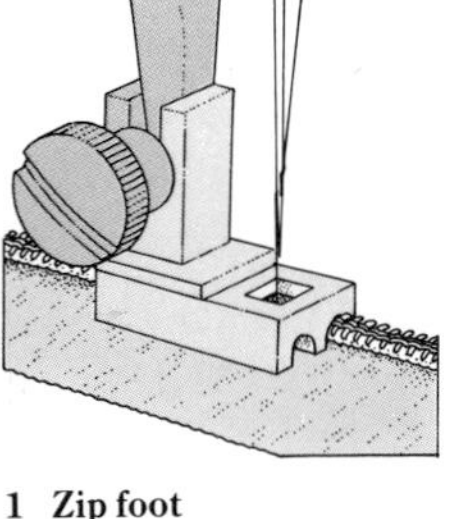

1 **Zip foot**

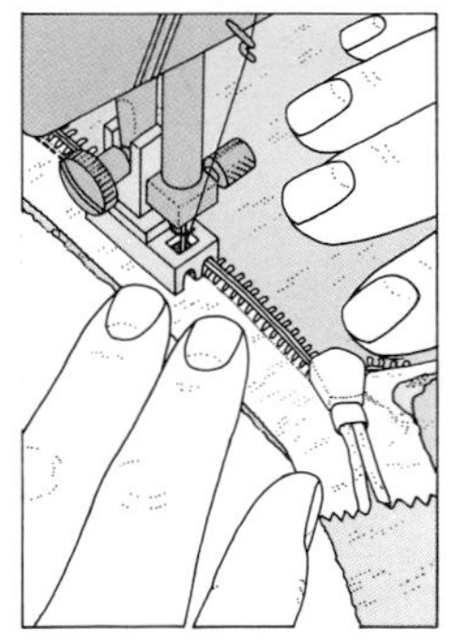

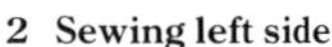

2 **Sewing left side**

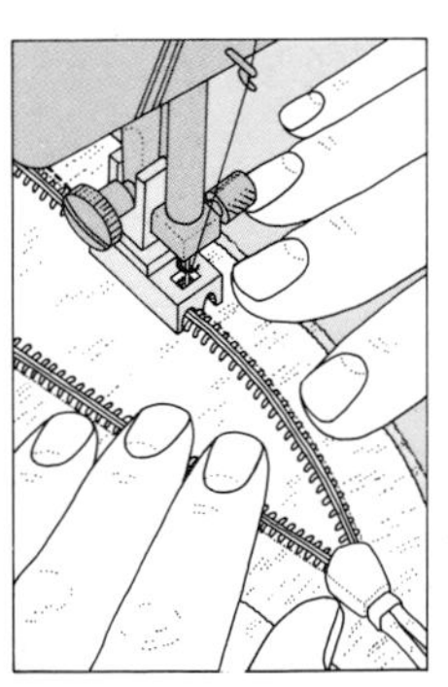

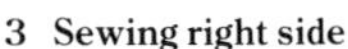

3 **Sewing right side**

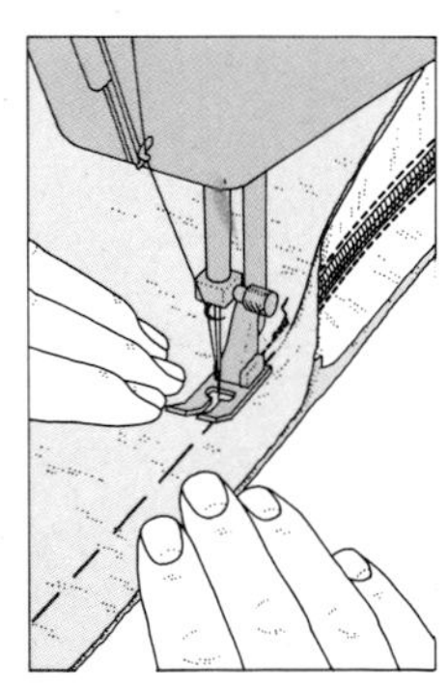

4 **Finishing seam**

Hems

The hem is the last step in garment making and is usually hand-stitched. To achieve a perfectly smooth hem use the right stitch for your fabric, never tighten the thread or the fabric will pucker, and always match seam and centre lines after turning up the hem. Stitches should never show on the right side (instructions for hand stitches are on pages 202–203).

Marking the hemline

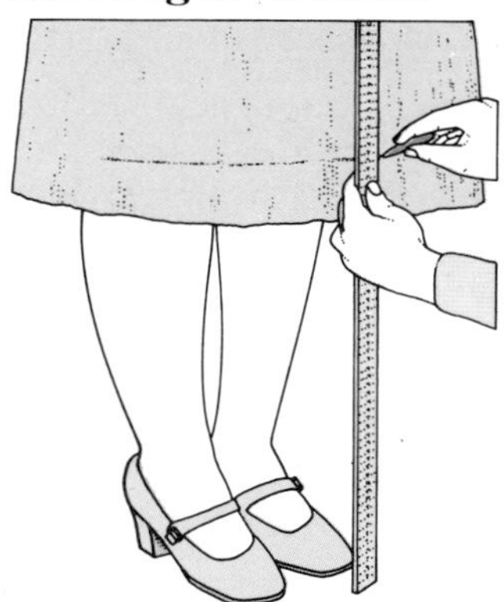

Before marking the hem, make sure that the garment fits perfectly and hangs correctly. It is best to find someone to mark the hem for you. Use a chalk marker or a metre stick, measuring an even distance from the floor. The marker should move around the wearer to avoid any change in the hang of the skirt caused by movement. For full length skirts stand on a stool.

Turning the hem

Fold the hem on the chalk line and pin at right angles to the folded edge. When you are sure the hem is level tack ¼in. (6mm) from the folded edge. Press to sharpen the creases, sliding the iron along the crosswise grain.

Always sew the hem using the appropriate stitch, and make sure that only a thread of the garment fabric is taken onto the needle.

Hem finishes

Having taken trouble to ensure the correct fit and hang of your garment you must choose the most appropriate method for finishing the hem.

Edge stitched hem

Suitable for garments which are frequently laundered.

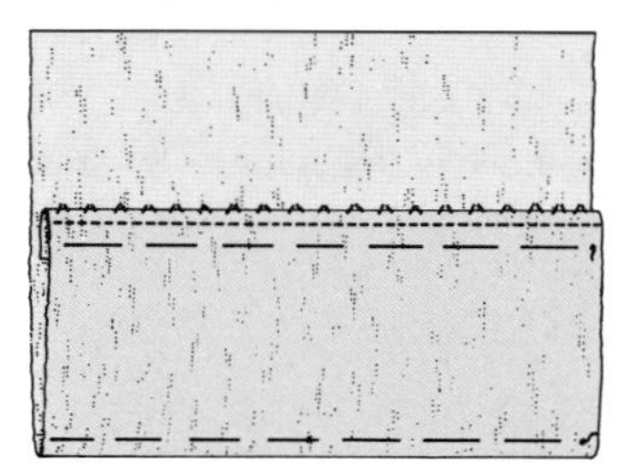

Fold raw edge of the hem under ¼in. (6mm). Stitch near the edge of the fold and press. Pin the hem edge in place, then tack. Finish with slip stitch.

Blindstitched hem

This is suitable for children's clothes and curtains.

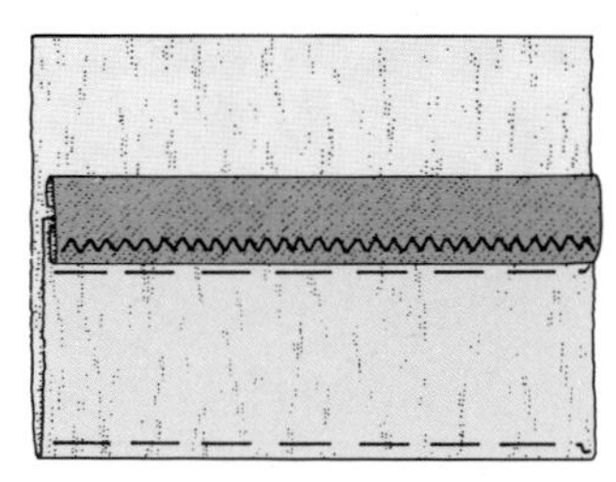

The hem may be bound with straight or bias binding. Sew this ¼in. (6mm) from the raw edge of the hem using narrow zigzag stitch, then press. Tack the hem then stitch using blind hemming stitch (see page 203).

Herringbone hem

This is suitable for loosely woven fabrics. Bind the raw edge, if necessary.

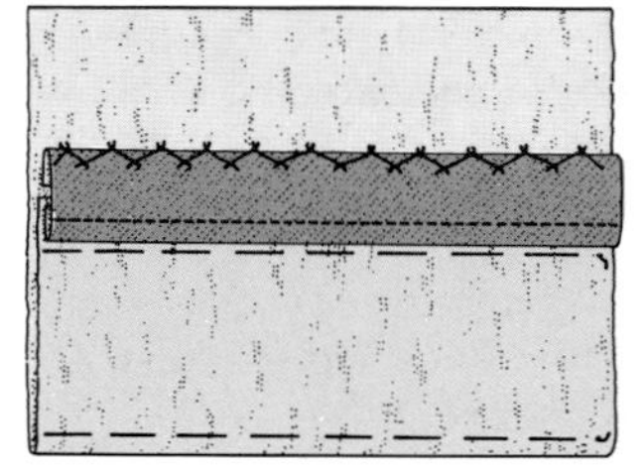

Stitch hem using herringbone stitch (see page 203), working from left to right.

Zigzag hem

This is most suitable for double knit fabrics because it prevents fraying.

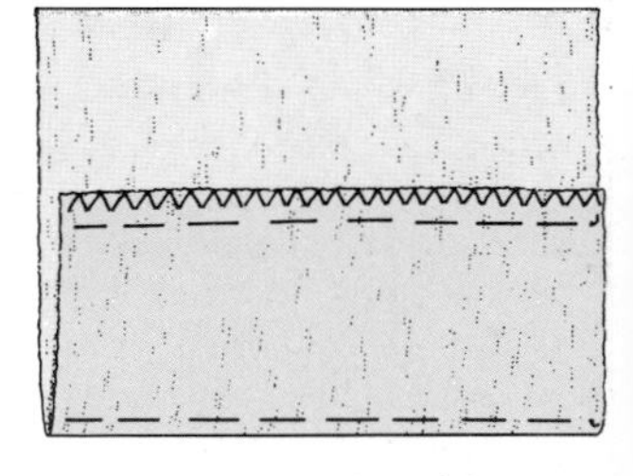

Neaten the raw edge with multistitch. Press, then trim close to the stitching. Pin and tack the raw edge to the skirt, matching seam and centre lines. Finish with blind hemming stitch (page 203).

Flared and gored skirts

The following method is suitable if the skirt is slightly flared or gored.

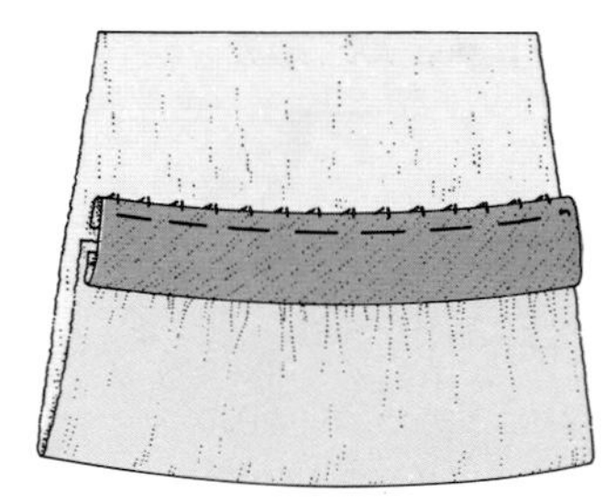

Run gathering stitches ¼in. (6mm) from the raw edge. Pin the hem to the skirt, matching centre and seam lines. Draw the gathering thread up slightly to ease the fullness and fit the skirt shape. Do not draw the hem in too much or the shape will be lost. Place the hem over a pressing mitt and shrink out fullness with a steam iron. Place bias binding over the gathering. Pin and tack the hem to the skirt. Press, shrinking the bias binding to the curve. Finish with blind hemming stitch (see page 203).

Circular hem

For a smooth finish this hem should be made narrow. If the hem is left deep, there will be too much bulk for the hem to lie flat.

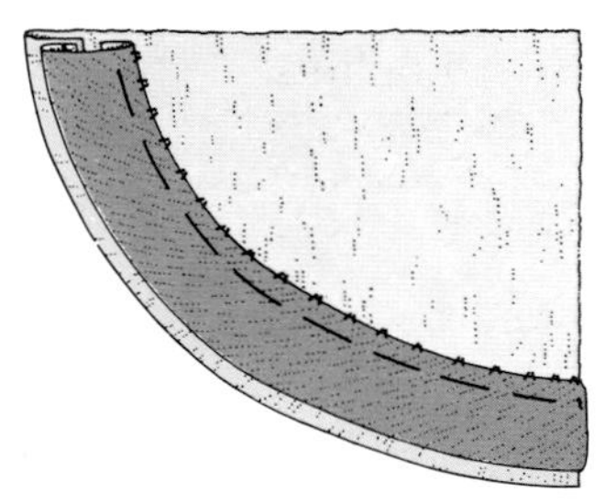

After marking the hemline, trim away excess fabric to leave a turning of ½in. (1.3cm). Pin and stitch the bias binding, ¼in. (6mm) from the raw edge. Take care not to stretch the bias binding as you stitch. Press. Fold the fabric on the marked line. Pin and tack close to the fold, then press. Tack the raw edge to the skirt, close to the edge of the binding. Finish with blind hemming stitch or slip stitch (page 203).

Finishing corners

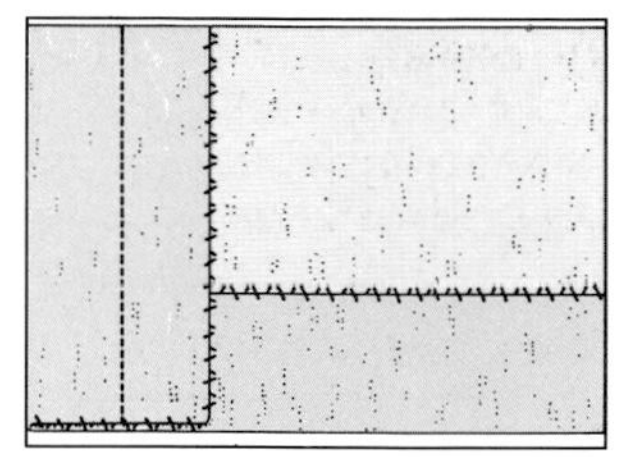

It is worth taking trouble, when turning hem corners, to ensure there is no excess bulk and that you have sharp, square corners.

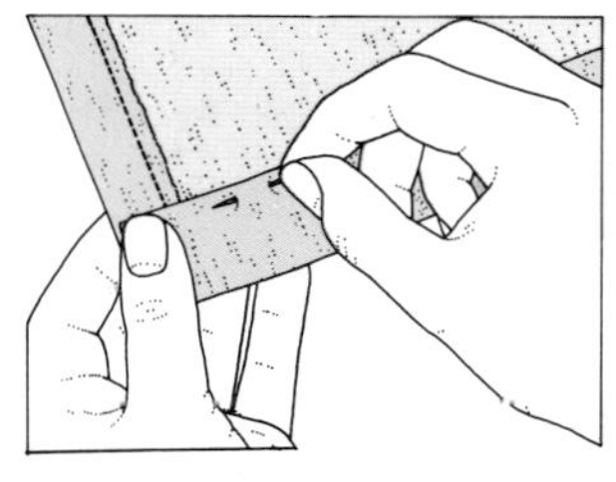

1 *Before turning up the hem, fold the raw edge of the facing under ¾in. (2cm) then stitch. Pin and stitch the hem into place at the required depth.*

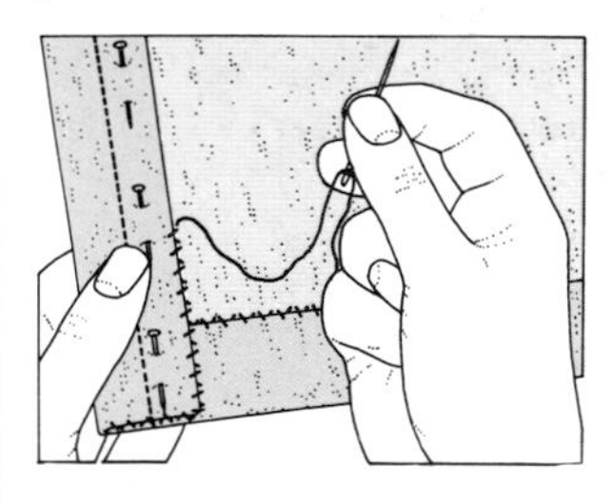

2 *Turn facing back over hem to required width and slip stitch into place by first stitching along the bottom of the facing to secure it to the hem, and then stitching up the side of the facing for a neat finish.*

PRESSING HEMS

Hems should be steam pressed from the folded edge to the cut edge to shrink out any fullness at the cut edge and avoid wrinkles. Press the hem when it has been tacked in place, and press again after stitching to remove thread marks. It is worthwhile spending a little time pressing the garment to achieve a sharp finish.

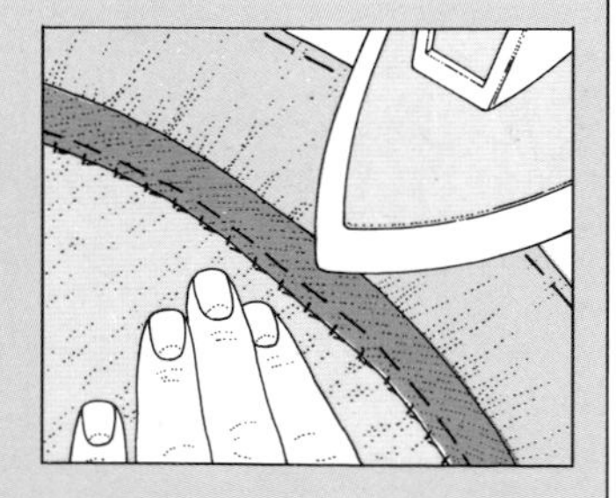

Interfacings and linings

Interfacings and linings add strength to a garment and help it to keep its natural outline. Interfacings will reinforce collars, cuffs and waistbands, and linings are especially necessary when a jersey, knitted or stretchy fabric is being used.

Interfacing

An interfacing is an extra piece of fabric placed between the garment fabric and the facing.

If you are using a bought pattern, it will include instructions for using an interfacing.

The type of interfacing you use will depend on the fabric and the type of garment. It should never be heavier than the garment fabric. As well as the standard interfacing fabric you can buy an iron-on interfacing which can be applied by pressing it onto the fabric using a warm iron; the heat bonds the two layers together.

Lining

A lining neatens the inside of a garment by covering the seam edges. It also helps to prolong the life of a garment because it prevents the fabric from pulling out of shape. Lining is therefore particularly important when making garments from knitted or stretch fabrics, and on garments, or parts of garments, which will have a lot of hard wear.

Most outer garments, such as coats and jackets, need a lining both to hide the seam edges and to make sure that the fabrics of the inner and outer garments do not rub together.

Lining fabrics should ideally be slippery and pliable. The most commonly used fabrics are imitation silks such as man-made crepe and taffeta. The lining's suitability regarding the weight and laundering needs should be considered when buying the fabric.

Making up the lining

Cut the lining pattern pieces from the garment pattern but omit the parts which do not require lining such as collars, cuffs and facings. Pleated or gathered garments will not require pleated or gathered linings, but the lining should be full enough to allow room for movement. Remember to transfer any markings onto the lining fabric and incorporate any alterations that are necessary.

Finishing a lining hem

On skirts and dresses the lining will need to be hemmed separately from the garment. Before the lining is hemmed, the garment hem should be finished in the appropriate way. The hem linings on jackets and some coats are not hemmed separately. They are slip stitched to the finished hem of the outside fabric.

Hemming the lining

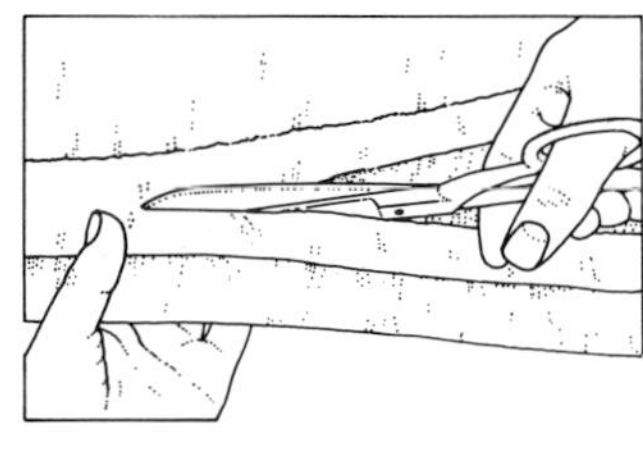

1 Turn the garment inside out and fold the excess lining fabric back at the hem, so that the hem of the lining is 1in. (2.5cm) from the hemline. Trim surplus fabric.

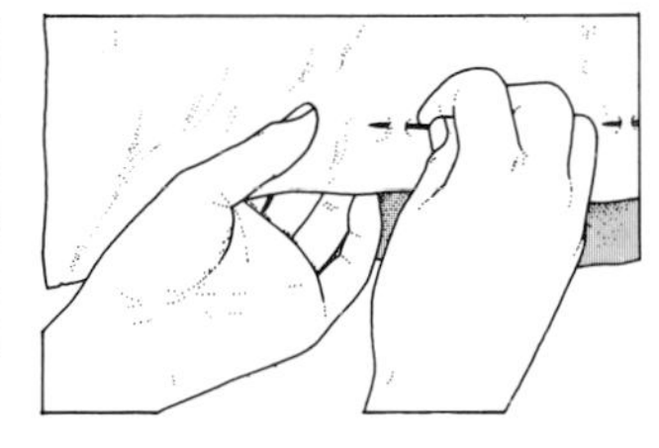

2 Pin the hem of the lining into position, easing any surplus fabric at the raw edge. Tack it into position. Then machine stitch around the hem.

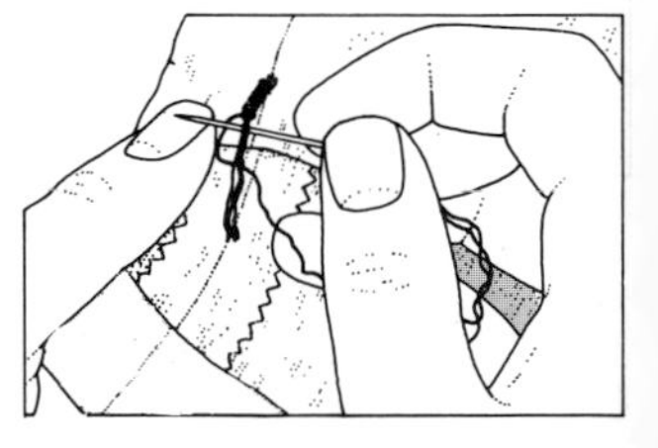

3 If you want to secure the lining hem to the garment at the side seams make several long stitches and reinforce these by working over them with blanket stitch.

Lining a garment

The lining should be made exactly the same size as the garment, minus the details such as pleats or gathers, and should fit without pulling or straining.

Make up the bodice and skirt of the lining separately but do not stitch the hems. Press all the seams open and the darts in the opposite direction to those on the outer garment.

Bodice lining

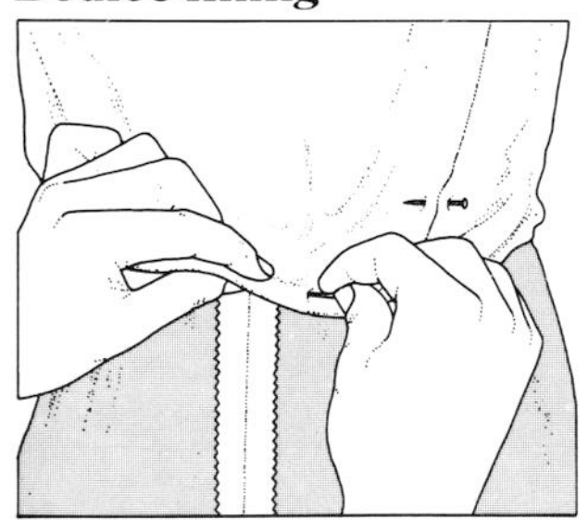

1 Pin the bodice onto the garment, wrong sides facing, matching the shoulder, side, centre and back seams, and all dart and style lines. Tack the lining to the seam allowance of the garment at the waistline and the armholes.

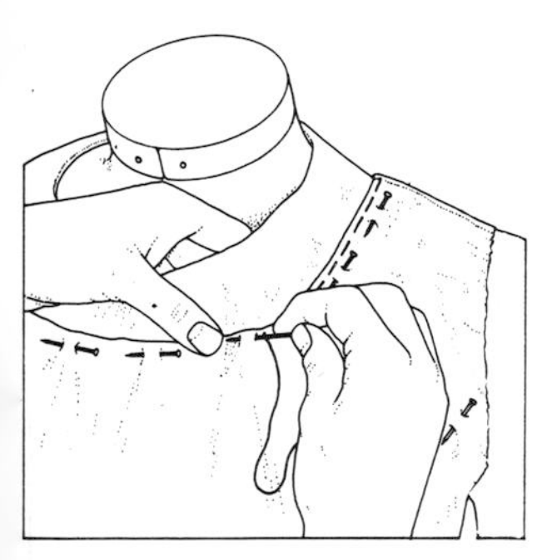

2 Cut back the lining at the neckline so that it only overlaps the edge of the neck facing by ¾in. (2cm). Fold the neck edge of the lining to the inside and tack it to the neck facing (fig. 2). Follow the same procedure at the armholes. If the garment has sleeves do not turn under the raw edges at the armholes.

Skirt lining and zip

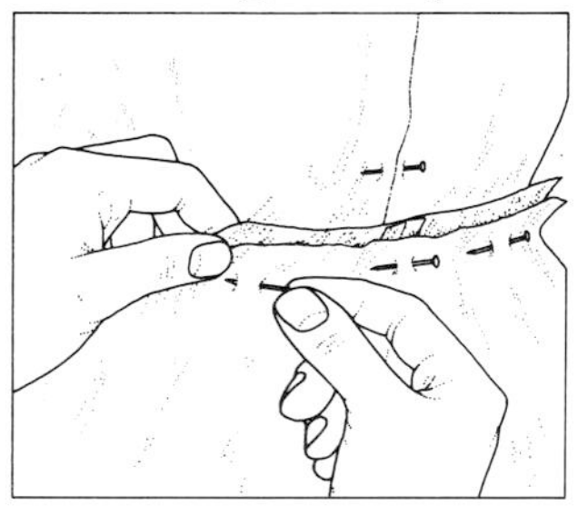

1 Pin the skirt lining to the waistline just above the stitching line. Leave 1½in. (4cm) at either side of the zip fastener for the seam turning. Fold the bodice lining over the skirt lining at the waist seam line. Pin and then slip stitch into place. If you are lining a skirt only, stitch the lining on before attaching the waistband.

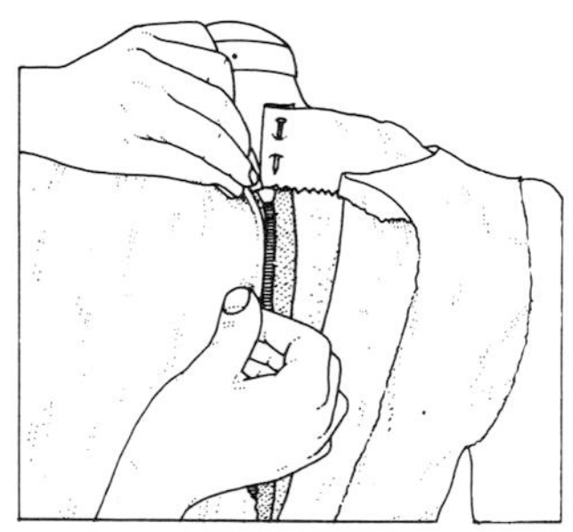

2 Fold back the seam allowance at either side of the zip fastener, then hem stitch to the zip tapes. Press and remove all tacking stitches. Trim off any excess fabric and then finish hem lining as shown on the left.

Lining a short sleeve

Make up the sleeve lining in the same way as the garment sleeve. Leave the edges unfinished. Turn the garment to the right side. Place lining over the garment sleeve. With right sides facing stitch around sleeve hem edge.

Press; pull lining to the inside of the sleeve. Roll the sleeve hemline slightly to the inside, then tack into position and press. Turn inside out and then pin and tack the lining to the sleeve crown, starting at the underarm (fig. 1). Match all balance marks and ease excess fabric evenly, then slip stitch (fig. 2).

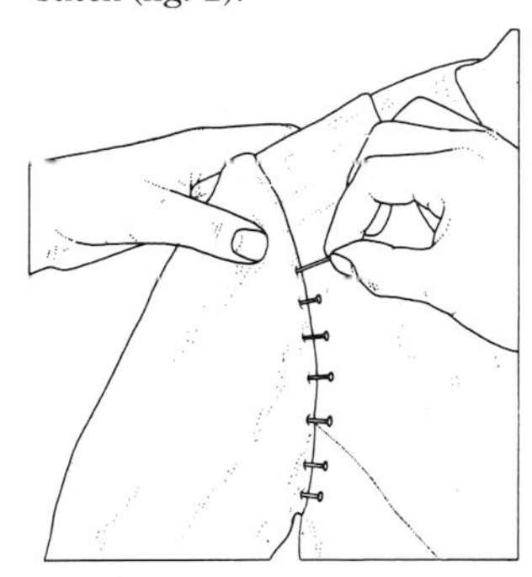

1 Pinning the crown of the sleeve lining to the bodice.

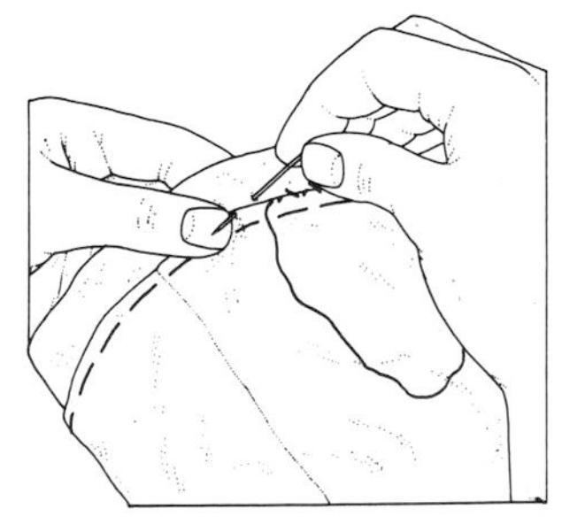

2 Pinning the bottom of the sleeve lining so that the cuff overlaps the bottom of the facing's raw edge.

Making up three different garments

Making up any garment is a simple and straightforward process if properly organized. Always tack the garment together by hand and make any fitting alterations before machine stitching. Neaten all the seams as you stitch them and press at each stage of the garment.

Blouse with button front and yoke

1 Gather the back bodice and attach to the yoke piece.
2 Gather the front bodice pieces along the yoke.
3 Attach the front bodice pieces to the yoke pieces.
4 Neaten seam edges on yoke and bodice.
5 Prepare the facings for the button and buttonhole band and attach.
6 Stitch the shoulder seams and neaten.
7 Make the collar and attach.
8 Make the sleeves and neaten seam edges.
9 Make up the cuffs and attach to sleeves.
10 Set in the sleeves.
11 Make any pockets and attach.
12 Finish the hem.
13 Make the buttonholes and sew on the buttons.

Skirt with zip, waistband and concealed pockets

1 Make the skirt front, including the front pocket pieces.
2 Make the skirt back, stitching only as far as the zip opening on the appropriate seam.
3 Attach the back pocket pieces to the garment.
4 Join the side seams, stitching around the pocket pieces to join them.
5 Make up the waistband.
6 Insert the zip.
7 Attach the waistband and complete it with a fastening.
8 Level the hem and stitch it.

Dress with centre back zip

1 Make darts in front and back bodice.
2 Join and neaten the shoulder seams.
3 Make the collar, prepare facing and join together.
4 Stitch the side seams.
5 Make the cuffs.
6 Make sleeves, neaten seams.
7 Attach cuffs to sleeves.
8 Set in the sleeves.
9 Make the front skirt.
10 Stitch together the side seams of the skirt.
11 Attach skirt to bodice.
12 Stitch the centre back seam as far as the zip opening.
13 Insert the zip.
14 Make the belt.
15 Level and stitch the hem.

Fitting garments

One of the advantages of making your own garments is that they can be made to fit your figure exactly. To achieve this, first make sure that you take accurate body measurements. Secondly, check and adjust all pattern pieces before cutting. Finally, make sure the tacked garment fits well before sewing.

Fitting adjustments

Fitting adjustments need to be made throughout the making up process, as soon as the main darts and seams have been tacked. In theory, adjustments made to one side of the body should be matched exactly on the other. Most people, however, are not exactly symmetrical and adjustments may need to be made on one side only.

The first fitting

When all the details have been checked and the garment has been tacked, you are ready for a proper fitting. Wear the underwear and shoes that you intend to wear with the garment. If adjustments have to be made, remove tacking stitches and pin corrections.

Checking for comfort

The garment should feel comfortable when you sit, move, stretch, raise an arm or bend a knee. Try on a jacket over a blouse or skirt and a coat over a dress to ensure a proper fit. For a well-fitted look there should be a reasonable amount of ease at the bust; the waistline should fit snugly but without strain and the fabric should lie smoothly over all.

Adjusting the neckline fitting

The neckline must fit well if the garment is to look professional. Bear in mind that it will be ¾in. (2cm) wider all around when stitched because of the seam allowance.

A gaping neckline can be adjusted by taking in the shoulder seams, making tucks around the neckline or taking it in at the centre back.

Gaping neckline

Re-fitted neckline

COMMON FITTING PROBLEMS

Skirt back too tight

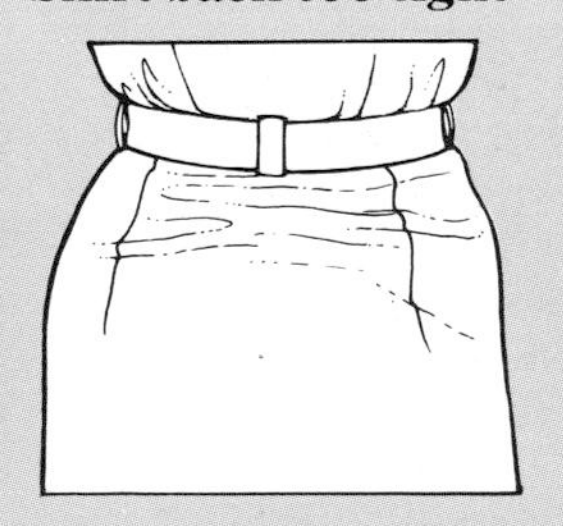

If the skirt is tight at hip level, release the centre back darts and then restitch them by curving them inwards following your own shape.

Armholes too low

Any corrections should be made at the crown of the armhole. Remove tacking stitches and re-position the armhole.

Badly positioned dart

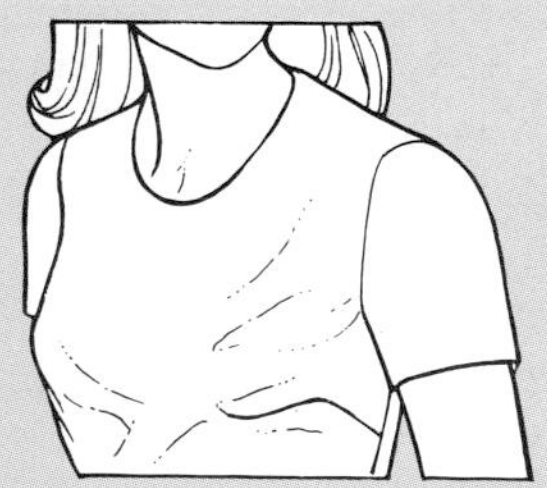

The point of the bust dart should be at the fullest part of the bust. If it is not, re-pin from the dart point.

Household sewing

There is a wide range of household items that are not difficult to sew. It is more economical to make rather than buy many articles, such as curtains, tablecloths, duvet covers, sheets and cushions and you have a wider choice of fabric.

Rounded tablecloths

Round tablecloths can be cut to any size. The cloth can just overlap the table or it can reach to the floor if a more formal effect is desired or the table base is to be concealed.

Estimating the fabric requirement

A dining table usually requires an overhang of at least 9in. to 12in. (23cm to 31cm). To calculate the fabric requirement, measure the diameter of the table and add twice the overhang measurement plus twice the allowance for a hem – generally about 1in. (2.5cm).

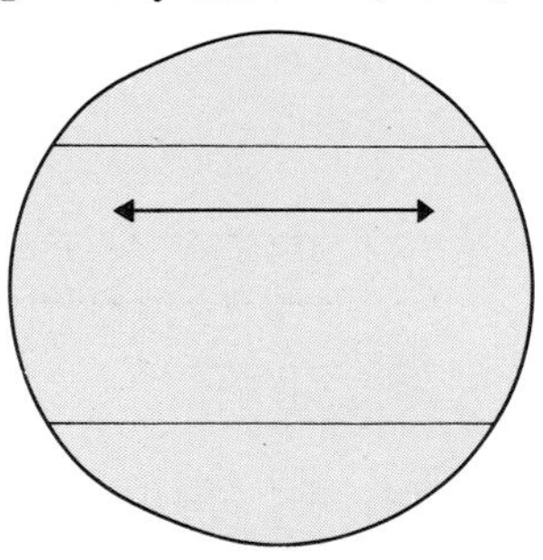

If the fabric needs to be joined in order to reach the required size follow the diagram here, joining two pieces either side of a central length so that a join does not appear in the middle of the table.

Making the cloth

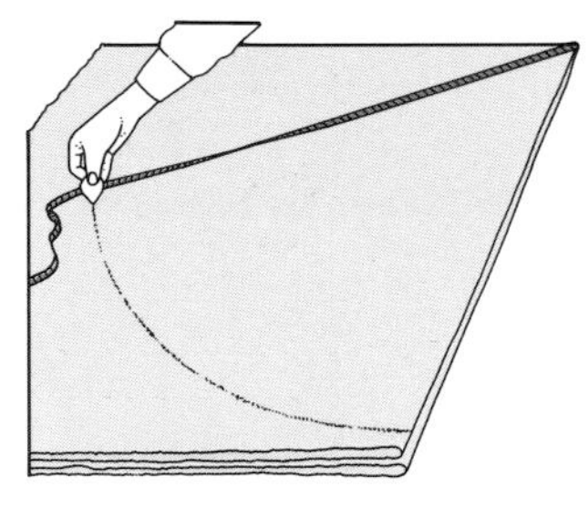

If your fabric is wide enough to cut the cloth in one piece, start by folding it into four. Draw a quarter circle directly onto the fabric with dressmaker's chalk. Cut out the cloth. Turn under the raw edge and then the hem allowance and pin.

Hemming round tablecloths

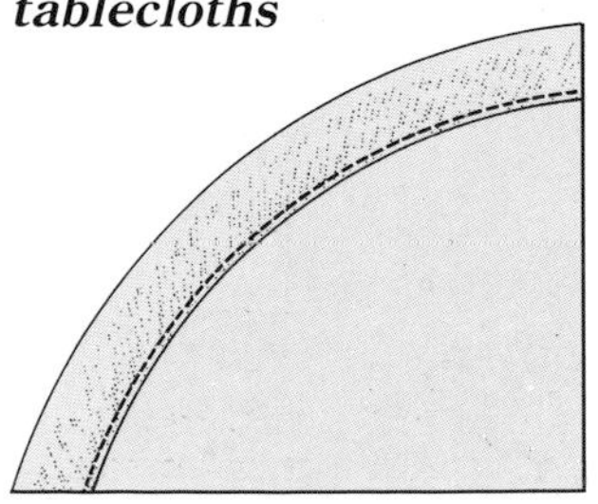

Round tablecloths can be hemmed in the normal way by turning under the fabric or they can be secured with bias binding.

Straight-sided tablecloths

Whether cut as squares or rectangles, these are the most common and useful types of tablecloth. They can be made in a variety of fabrics, cut to different lengths, and can be decorated by shaping or attaching a lace, tasselled or crocheted border.

Estimating the fabric requirement

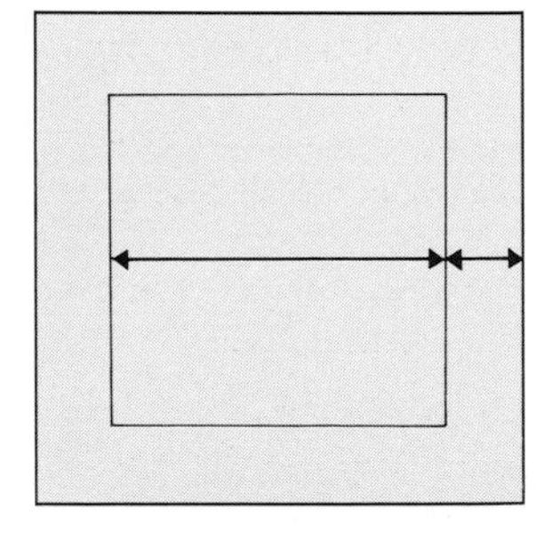

For a square cloth measure the width and add twice the overhang plus 1in. (2.5cm) for the seam allowances. For a rectangular cloth, measure both the length and width of the table. Add twice the overhang allowance plus 1in. (2.5cm). Some fabrics such as heavy linen or those which fray easily need deeper hems. In such cases add twice hem depth.

Duvet covers

If you are using a duvet, it will need a cover. The fabric can be plain or patterned but it must always be washable, lightweight and hardwearing. The duvet cover is easy to make and can be closed with a tape or zip fastener.

Estimating the fabric

Measure your duvet and add 1in. (2.5cm) to this measurement for the seam allowances. Sheeting fabric is usually the best buy because it is made in suitable sizes.

Making the cover

Using fabric of the appropriate width, cut the duvet cover to the correct measurements. With right sides facing, pin all around the case, leaving an opening large enough to insert the duvet at one end, usually about 36in. (91.5cm). Stitch all around, backstitching when you get to the opening, and clip across the corner seam allowances. Finish the seams by pinking or stitching the edges.

Closing the cover

The cover can be closed, either with a suitable length of hardwearing zip, or with Velcro or popper tape. Press the seam allowances flat and position one of the tapes on the underside of the seam opening. Pin and tack, then stitch it neatly top and bottom (fig. 1). Align the other tape on the other side of the seam opening and stitch on, as before (fig. 2).

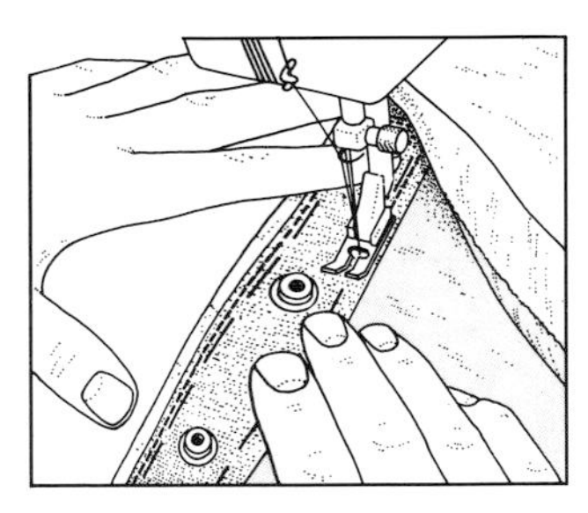

1 Stitching popper tape

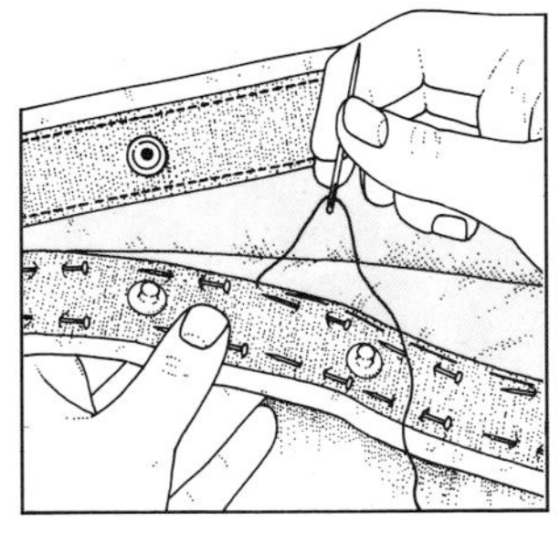

2 Stitching aligned edge

FITTED SHEETS

Estimating the fabric

Measure the length and width of the bed and add twice the depth of the mattress plus 7in. (18cm), for the tuck-in. Add 1in. (2.5cm) for hem.

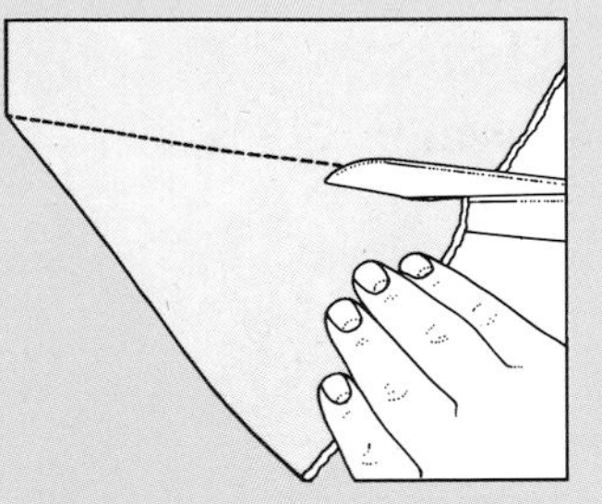

1 With the right sides facing, fold each corner across diagonally as shown, and mark a point 4½in. (11.5cm) from the corner point at one edge. Then stitch across the corner at right angles to this point. Trim the seam to within ¼in. (6mm) of the stitching line and finish the raw edges by oversewing. Repeat the same process at each corner. Fold over the raw edges by ¼in. (6mm) then ¾in. (2cm) all around, and then hem around the sheet leaving a small gap 10in. (25cm) from each corner.

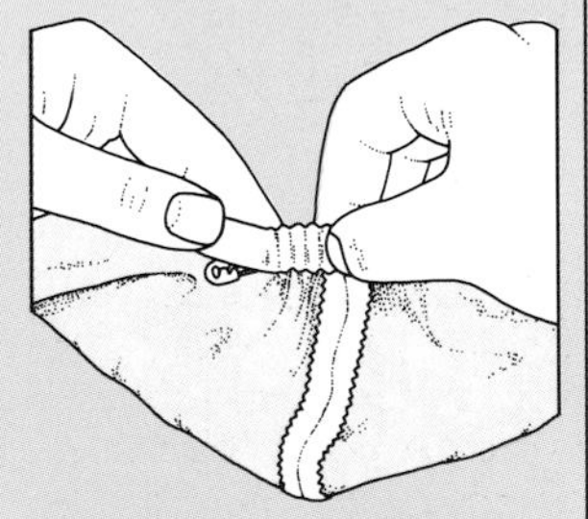

2 Cut elastic into four 10in. (25cm) strips and insert one end of each piece into each corner (see page 216 for threading instructions). Then draw the elastic along the hem edge, gathering up the corner as you do so. Fasten securely.

Scatter cushions

Scatter cushions can be made to any size or shape you want. Generally, square or round cushions are the most popular but you can make rectangles or semi-circles or any other shape, as required. They are generally used to brighten up a colour scheme and provide more padding for chairs and sofas.

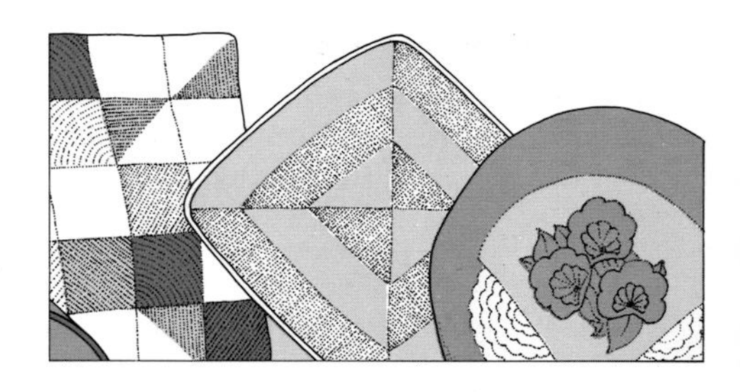

Making a square cushion
For a square cushion enough fabric for an inner and an outer cover will be needed. For a firm cushion, the inner cover should measure the same as the cushion pad, but for a softer cushion make the inner cover ½in. (1.3cm) bigger all around. Make inner cover, leaving ½in. (1.3cm) seam allowances and a 4in. to 6in. (10cm to 15cm) opening. Turn right side out, stuff with feathers or Kapok and slip stitch opening securely.

Making a round cushion
You will need enough fabric to cover the diameter of the circle plus ½in. (1.3cm) for seam allowances. You must also allow for an extra seam allowance if you intend to use a zip for fastening the cover. Make inner cover by cutting and sewing two circles, and proceed as for square cushion.

Making outer covers
The outer cover for the square cushion is made in the same way as the inner cover. For the round cushion you should cut one full circle and two semi-circles to the required measurements, with extra seam allowances for a central zip. You can finish the opening by using either of the methods shown right.

Fastening the cover with Velcro

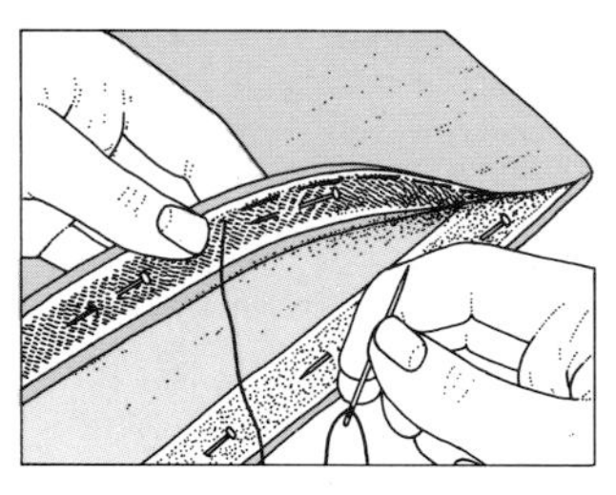

Tack and stitch a piece of Velcro tape to inside of cushion cover opening.

Fastening a round cover with a zip

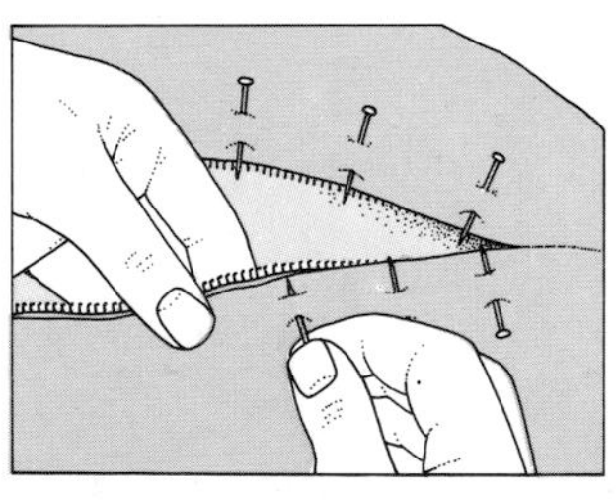

When making a circular cushion cover it will be easier to insert the zip across the underside of the cushion, for which you will need an extra seam. Attach zip onto seam allowances in usual way, then sew the two sides of the cushion together.

Making bias strips

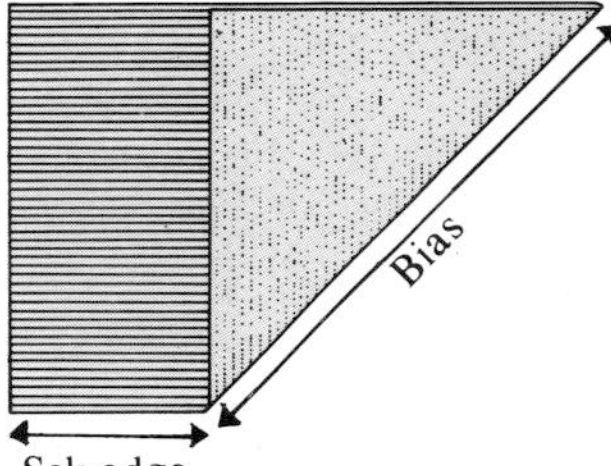

1 Lay the fabric out flat and fold it over with the straight end on the selvedge. Pin at right angles to the edge. The diagonal fold is the true bias. Rule off the width of your bias strips parallel to the bias.

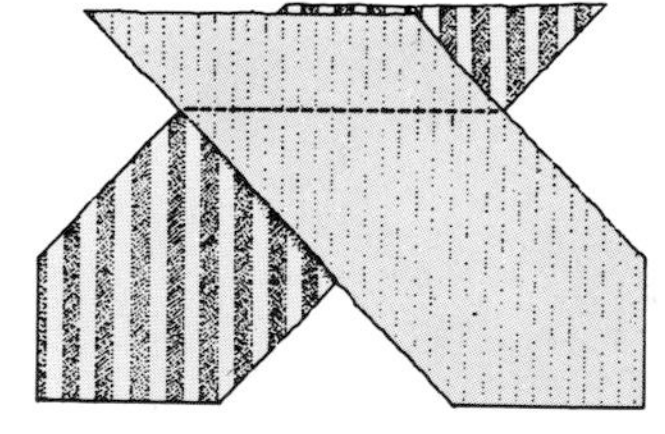

2 Cut your bias strips to four times the final width (usually 1in. to 1¼in. (2.5cm to 3cm). Pin the lengthwise ends, with right sides facing, matching pattern if necessary. Stitch ¼in. (6mm) from the edge.

Piping scatter cushions

Piped cushions can be made by stitching piping around the edges. Pipe the cushion before it is made up and then make up and close by attaching hooks and eyes or by using a zip.

Making the piping

Piping is made up of a cord cased in a bias strip of fabric as shown left.

One yard (90cm) of 48in. (120cm) wide fabric will supply about 28yds (25.20m) of bias strip 1½in. (3.8cm) wide.

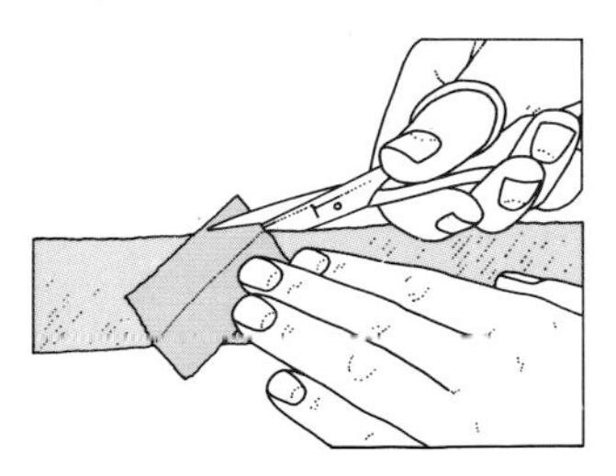

1 Sew pieces of bias strip together, clip the angle of the corners and trim as shown.

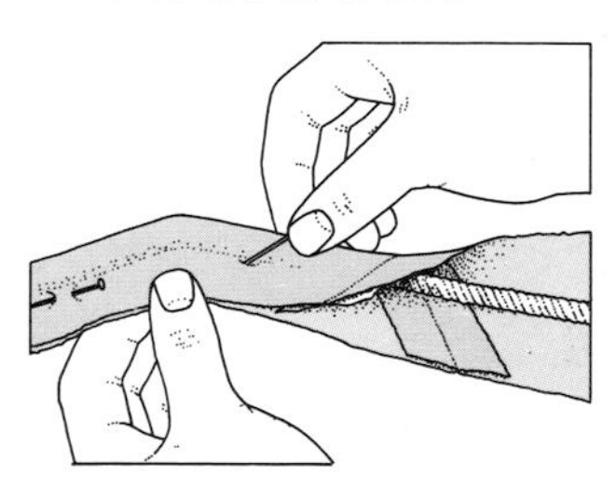

2 Place cord on wrong side of strip and fold strip in half over cord. Pin and stitch as close to cord as possible.

Estimating the fabric

To make the outer cover for a piped cushion you will need, for an 18in. (45cm) square cushion, 22in. (55cm) of 48in. (120cm) wide fabric (this allows for 2 extra strips of fabric 3in. (7.5cm) wide, for the straps); 2¼ yards (2.10m) of number 2 piping cord; press studs, hooks and eyes or a 17in. (42.5cm) zip fastener.

Making outer covers

The piping is made and attached to the edges of the cushions, and straps are then made and attached for the hooks and eyes.

Attaching the piping

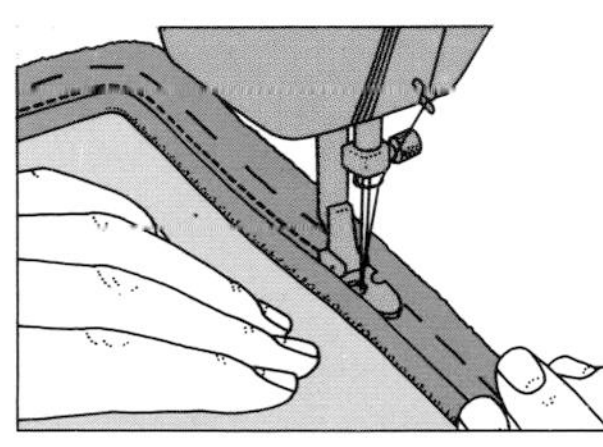

1 Trim the corners of both squares of the cover and make the piping.

Starting at the middle of the side which will eventually be left open, pin, tack and stitch the piping around the edge of the case top on the right side, with raw edges facing.

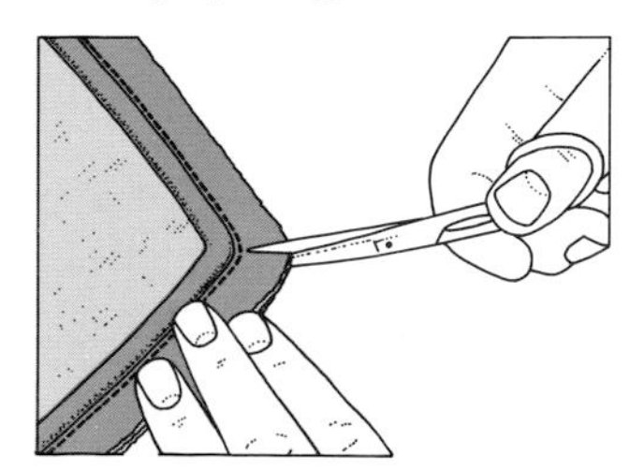

2 Clip edges of piping at corners to ease around curve.

Using straps

If the cushion is fastened with hooks and eyes, straps will be needed for a neater finish. These are made from two extra strips of fabric 3in. (7.5cm) wide. Trim these so that they are 2in. (5cm) shorter than the width of the case, and neaten all edges.

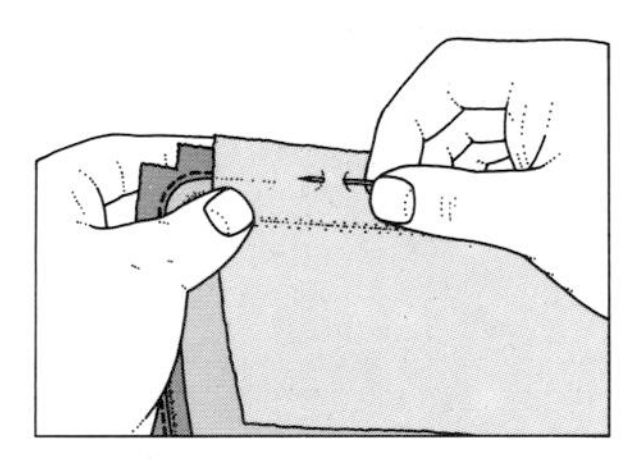

1 With right sides facing, pin, tack and stitch one strap directly to the case top on top of the stitching, holding the piping. Fold the strap over the raw edge to the wrong side of the fabric and turn in ½in. (1.3cm) of the raw edge of the strap. Hand stitch to seam line. Sew the other strap to the underside of case in same way.

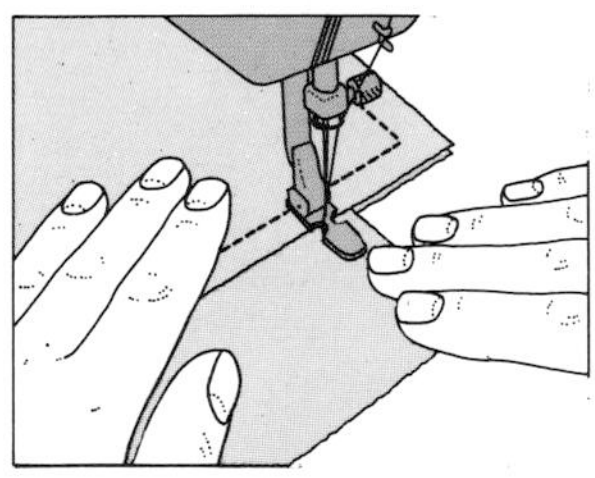

2 With right sides facing, pin both pieces of case together. Stitch on seam line around three sides and for 1½in. (3.8cm) at both ends of the fourth side.

Backstitch to secure straps and then stitch ½in. (1.3cm) in from the edge of the straps. Sew on fastenings and then turn the cushion right side out.

Curtains

When making your own curtains it is vital to get the measurements absolutely right so that you do not buy more material than you need.

First decide on the length that the curtains are to be. This should be measured from the curtain track, preferably using a steel tape or long rule because these do not bend. Sill length curtains on inset windows should hang about 1in. (2.5cm) above the sill. Apron length curtains should hang 4in. to 9in. (10cm to 22.5cm) below the sill. Floor length curtains should clear the floor by 1in. (2.5cm). For the width, measure the length of the curtain track.

Calculating the fabric requirement

Base the calculations for the width of your curtains on that of the curtain track. Allow 2in. (5cm) for each side hem and 6in. (15cm) for curtain overlaps.

If the window is to have two curtains, divide the width of your curtain track by two to calculate the finished width of each curtain. Extra allowance must also be made for matching patterns. A simple guide is to allow one repeat pattern for each width of fabric. If two fabric widths are used for each of your two curtains, then four extra pattern repeats should be allowed for.

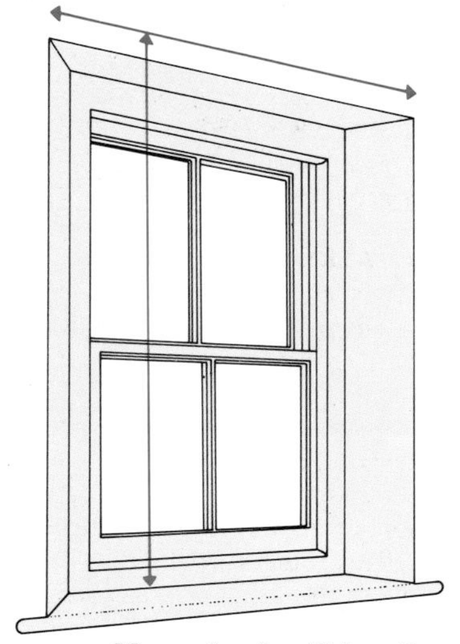

Measuring for sill length curtains

TYPES OF CURTAIN

Curtains can be of several different lengths usually sill length, apron length (hanging just below the sill) or floor length. Alternatively, the curtains can hang from a point halfway up the window. These are known as café curtains. The choice of fabric, type of heading and length of curtains depends on the shape of the window and fabric washability and durability.

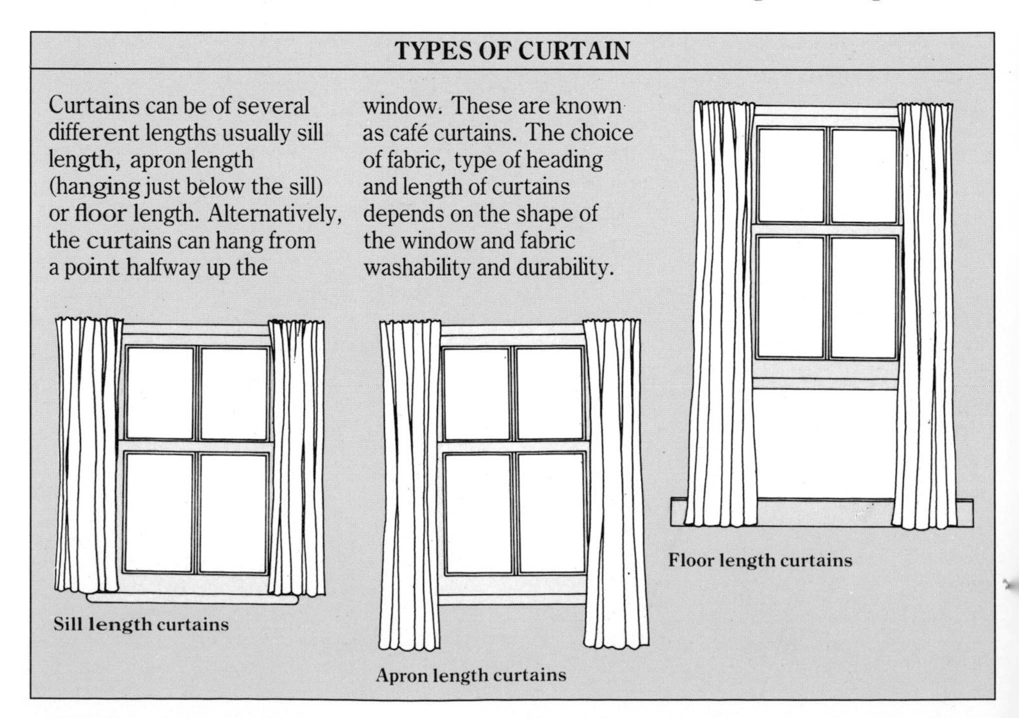

Floor length curtains

Sill length curtains

Apron length curtains

Fabric
Whatever fabric you choose for your curtains, whether it is a heavy velvet or a thin cotton print, there are certain points to bear in mind before buying. Take into consideration how much and what type of wear they are liable to get. Decide on the type of heading that the curtains will have before you buy the fabric because the type of heading will affect how much fabric you buy (the type and amount of pleating involved will dictate the amount of fabric required).

Curtain tracks
The curtain track is the rail which supports the curtains. It can be made of metal or plastic and comes in a variety of lengths. The tracks hold a series of runners to which the curtain is attached by hooks, suspended from a length of tape stitched to the head of the curtain. It is best to use metal tracks for heavy curtains and plastic tracks where a pliable rail is needed, for example fitting around a tight bay window.

Curtains can also be hung from decorative poles or rods. They can be made either of brass or wood.

Heading tapes
These tapes not only attach the curtain to the track by means of hooks, but also shape the top of the curtain. They consist of a length of tape, threaded top and bottom with cord. The tape is attached to the curtain and then gathered up, producing the pleats and also the pockets for the curtain hooks. The standard tape is available in a variety of widths and colours and can be used on all weights of curtain fabric. Pencil-pleat tape, which draws the fabric up into tightly rolled pleats, can be used on both lightweight and normal curtain fabric. It is unsuitable for use on heavy fabrics because of the tightness of the pleats.

Pelmets and valances
The curtain track, although usually hidden by the pleated heading of the curtain, can be covered by a *pelmet* or a *valance*. A pelmet is a wooden box which, when attached to the wall, surrounds and covers the track and top of the curtains. A valance serves the same purpose as a pelmet, but is made of fabric.

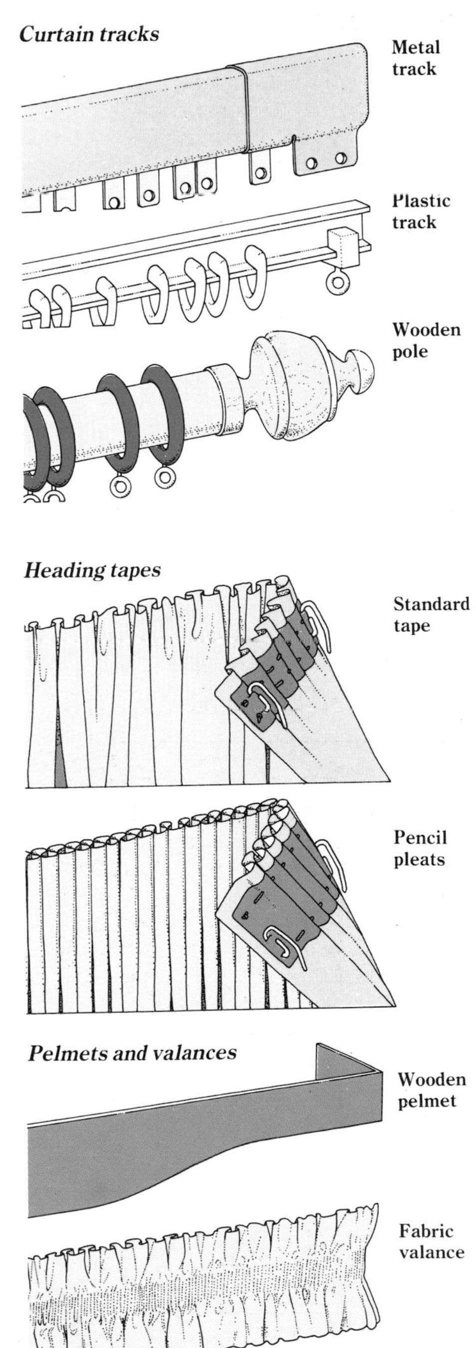

Unlined curtains

Curtains can be lined or unlined, depending on their purpose. Unlined curtains made in sheer fabric are particularly suitable for rooms where much light is needed, but lined curtains last longer, protect the curtain fabric and provide extra warmth.

Making the curtains

Having measured the window and calculated the amount of fabric required, you can now cut the fabric into the appropriate lengths.

Joining the fabric lengths

Make sure that any part-widths of fabric are on the outside edge. Use a plain flat seam to join the selvedges.

Aligning part-widths of fabric

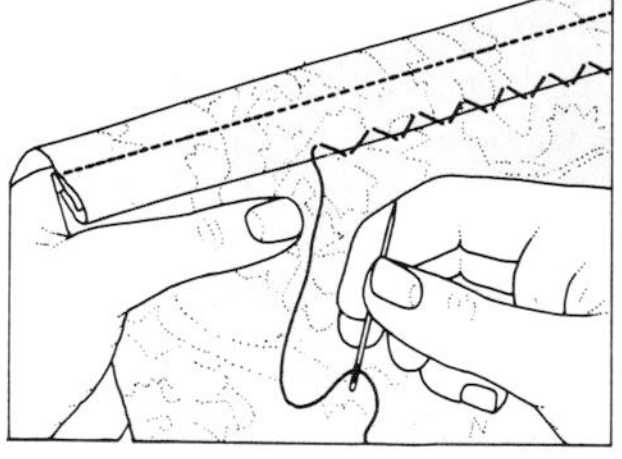

Slip stitching seam in place

Attaching standard tape

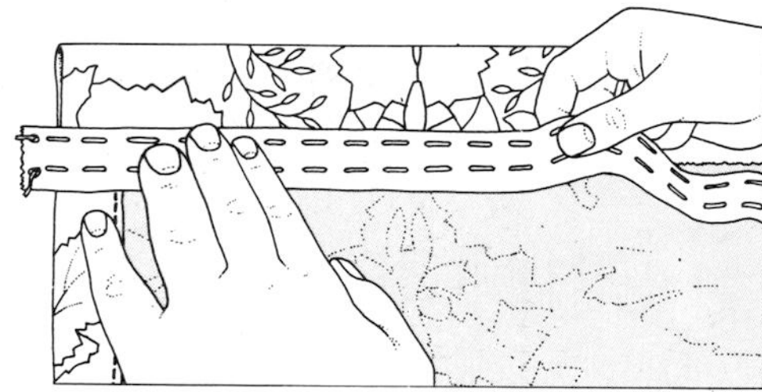

1 Cut the tape to the width of the curtain, leaving an allowance of 1in. (2.5cm) at either end. Knot one end of the tape. Turn the top edge of the curtain under by 2in. (5cm) and tack into place. Position the tape on the curtain about 1in. (2.5cm) from the top. Turn under each end of the tape and pin into position so that the knot at one end is enclosed and the cords at the other are free.

2 Machine tape into place, draw up the cord until the required gathers are achieved, then fasten the surplus cord. Insert hooks.

Hemming the curtains

1 Hang the curtains up for a couple of days before turning up the bottom hem as some fabrics stretch when hung.

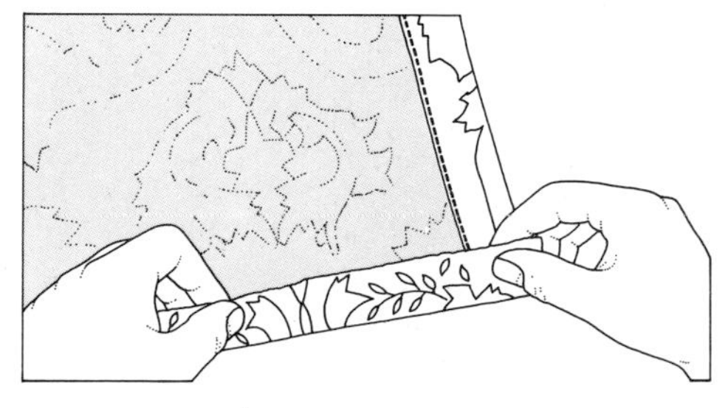

2 Turn the raw edges to the wrong side of the fabric by half the final depth. Press and then turn under the same amount again to make a double hem. Stitch into place.

Lined curtains

Measure, cut out and join the fabric as for unlined curtains. Make the lining up in the same way but use only plain flat seams to join the fabric lengths. Make the side hems on the curtains as for the unlined ones, using loose cross stitch and ending 8in. (20cm) above the bottom edge of the curtain. This allows for the hem to be mitred later on.

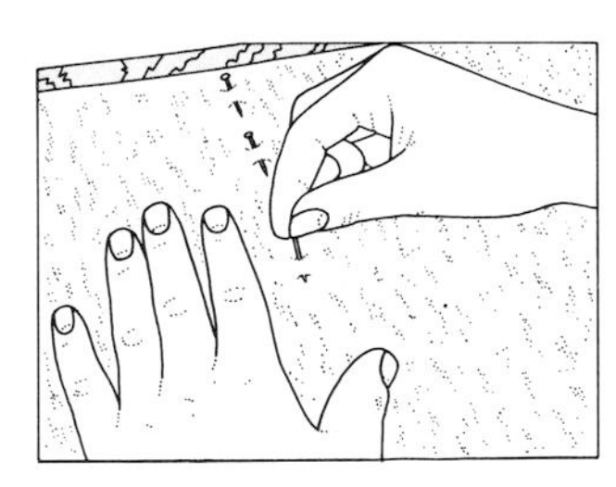

1 With wrong sides facing, place the lining on top of the curtain. Spread pieces out flat. Pin the two together down the centre line, then turn back one half of the lining.

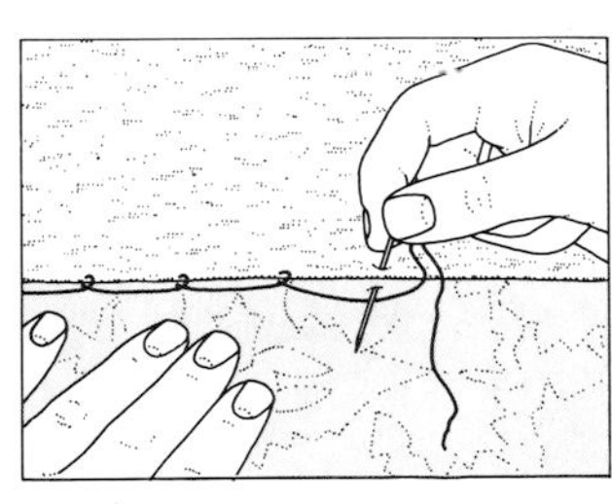

2 Lock stitch the lining to the curtain, starting 9in. (22.5cm) from the lower edge, working from left to right. Pick up one or two threads of the curtain and the lining with the needle, draw the thread around it and pull the needle through. Leave the thread fairly slack. Make stitches 2in. to 3in. (5cm to 7.5cm) apart. Repeat at wide intervals.

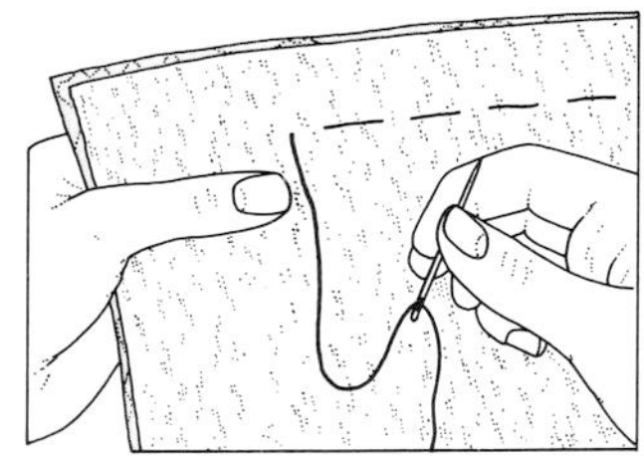

3 Tack the raw edge of the curtain and lining across the top of the curtain to within 3in. (7.5cm) of outer edges.

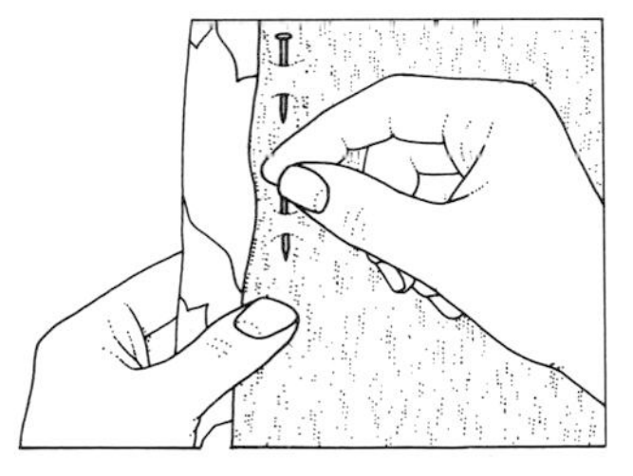

4 Trim away the lining at the sides so that it is 1/4in. (6mm) short of the curtain edge. Turn the sides of the lining under 1/2in. (1.3cm). Pin and tack to the curtain so that there is a 3/4in. (1.8cm) edge of curtain fabric. Slip stitch to within 8in. (20.5cm) of the bottom. Treat the curtain and lining as one and attach the heading tape.

MITERED CORNERS ON DOUBLE FOLDED HEM

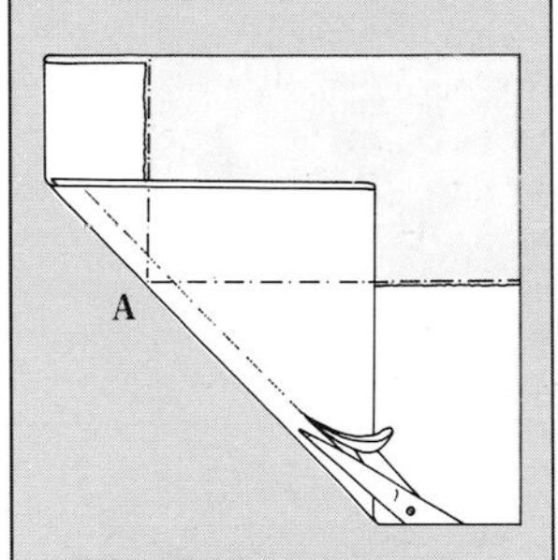

1 Hem the side of the curtains in the usual way but leave about 8in. (20.5cm) unhemmed at the bottom. Turn under the raw edge of this part of the curtain by 1in. (2.5cm). Turn up the bottom hem by half the final depth. Fold in the corner to the wrong side of the curtain so that a diagonal line cuts through point A. Press so that a crease is formed. Cut along this crease line.

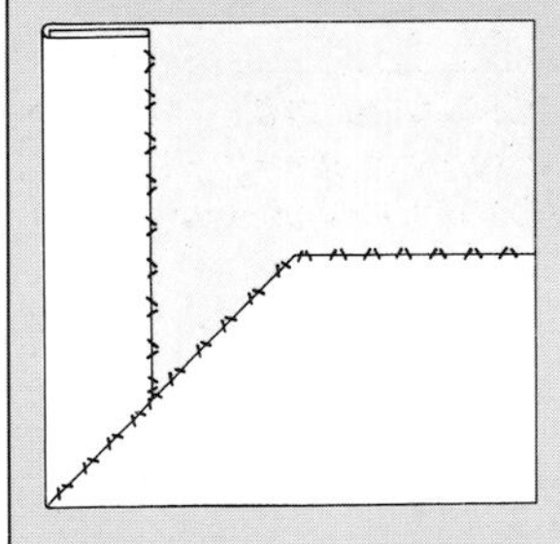

2 Fold the side hem to the wrong side by a further 1in. (2.5cm) and stitch in place. Fold up the bottom hem by its full depth and stitch in the appropriate way for the fabric. Slip stitch the mitred corner and hem together.

Index

For easy reference this index has been divided into subject sections that correspond to the chapter titles of this book. Entries are ordered alphabetically inside each section.

APPLIQUE 118–125

BASIC SEWING 192–235

KNITTING 128–161

NEEDLEPOINT 56–87

PATCHWORK 90–109

QUILTING 110–117

Acknowledgments

Designer: Nicholas Maddren
Editor: Maureen Maddren
Studio: Del & Co
Typesetters: Maron Graphics,
London and Bournetype, Bournemouth
Reproduction: Colourscan, Singapore

Photographic credits

Title page Pictures Colour Library; 6 Camera Press; 10 Camera Press; 54 Robert Harding Picture Library; 88 Camera Press; 126 Syndication International; 146 Syndication International; 162 Camera Press; 190 Syndication International.